Contemporary Doctrine Classics

Related titles from the Doctrine Commission:

Being Human
A Christian understanding of personhood illustrated with reference to power, money, sex and time

Contemporary Doctrine Classics

We Believe in God

We Believe in the Holy Spirit

The Mystery of Salvation

*The Combined Reports by
the Doctrine Commission
of the General Synod
of the Church of England*

CHURCH HOUSE
PUBLISHING

Church House Publishing
Church House
Great Smith Street
London SW1P 3NZ
Tel: 020 7898 1451
Fax: 020 7898 1449

ISBN 0 7151 4045 0

First published separately as *We Believe in God*, 1987, *We Believe in the Holy Spirit*, 1991 and *The Mystery of Salvation*, 1995, for the General Synod of the Church of England by Church House Publishing.

This combined edition published 2005 by Church House Publishing.

Typeset by RefineCatch Limited, Bungay, Suffolk
Printed by William Clowes Ltd, Beccles, Suffolk

Contents

Contents

Acknowledgements

The Doctrine Commission and publisher gratefully acknowledge permission to reproduce copyright material in this book. Every effort has been made to trace and contact copyright holders. If there are any inadvertent omissions we apologize to those concerned; please send any information to the publishers who will make a full acknowledgement in future editions.

The Commission is indebted for much of the material in chapter 2 of *We Believe in God* to *Licensed Insanities: Religions and Belief in God in the Contemporary World* by John Bowker, copyright © 1987 Darton, Longman & Todd Ltd, and reproduced with permission.

Extracts in from Samuel Beckett, *Waiting for Godot* (Faber and Faber); John Betjeman, *The Conversion of St Paul* (John Murray Ltd); Gavin D'Costa, *Christian Uniqueness Reconsidered* (Orbis Books 1990) and Stanley Samartha, *One Christ, Many Religions* (Orbis Books 1991) are reproduced with thanks.

Extracts from the *Book of Common Prayer*, the rights of which are vested in the Crown, are reproduced by permission of the Crown's Patentee, Cambridge University Press.

Members of the Doctrine Commission

We Believe in God: 1981–1985

CHAIRMAN
The Right Revd John V. Taylor
Bishop of Winchester until 1985

MEMBERS
The Right Revd John A. Baker
Bishop of Salisbury; previously Canon of Westminster

The Revd Dr John Barton
Chaplain and Lecturer, St Cross College, Oxford

The Revd Dr Gareth Bennett
Fellow of New College and University Lecturer in Modern History, Oxford; Canon and Prebendary of Chichester

The Revd John Bowker
Dean of Trinity College, Cambridge; Honorary Canon of Canterbury; previously Professor of Religious Studies in the University of Lancaster

Dr Sarah Coakley
Lecturer in Religious Studies in the University of Lancaster

The Revd Dr John Halliburton
Priest-in-Charge of St Margaret's on Thames; previously Principal of Chichester Theological College; Canon and Prebendary of Chichester

The Revd Dr Anthony Harvey
Canon of Westminster; previously Chaplain of Queen's College and University Lecturer in Theology, Oxford

The Revd William Ind
Team Vicar of Basingstoke and Vice-Principal of the Aston Training Scheme; Honorary Canon of Winchester

The Revd Dr Barnabas Lindars, SSF
Rylands Professor of Biblical Criticism in the University of Manchester; Canon Theologian of Leicester

Dr Basil Mitchell, FBA
Nolloth Professor of the Philosophy of the Christian Religion and Fellow of Oriel College, Oxford

Dr Martin Rudwick
Professor of the History of Science, Princeton, USA; previously Fellow of Trinity College, Cambridge

The Very Revd Dr Stephen Smalley
Dean of Chester; previously Canon and Precentor of Coventry

The Revd Dr Anthony Thiselton
Principal of St John's College, Nottingham, and Special Lecturer in the University of Nottingham; previously Senior Lecturer in Biblical Studies in the University of Sheffield

The Revd William Vanstone
Canon Residentiary of Chester

The Revd John Goldingay, Registrar of St John's College, Nottingham, also joined the Commission but family illness compelled early withdrawal.

CONSULTANTS
The Right Revd Kenneth Cragg
formerly Assistant Bishop in Jerusalem

The Revd Dr Herbert McCabe, OP
of the Dominican Order, Blackfriars, Oxford

The Revd Dr George Newlands
Professor of Divinity in the University of Glasgow; previously Dean of Trinity Hall, Cambridge

SECRETARY
The Revd Michael Perham
Chaplain to the Bishop of Winchester

succeeded in December 1984 by
The Revd John Meacham
Chaplain and Research Assistant to the Bishop of Salisbury

We Believe in the Holy Spirit: 1986–1989

CHAIRMAN
The Right Revd John A. Baker (until 1987)
Bishop of Salisbury

The Right Revd Alec Graham (from 1987)
Bishop of Newcastle

MEMBERS
The Revd Derek Allen (until 1988)
Vicar of St Saviour and St Peter, Eastbourne; Canon and Prebendary of Chichester

The Revd Dr Paul Avis (from 1989)
Vicar of Stoke Canon, Poltimore with Huxham, and Rewe with Netherexe, Devon

The Revd Dr David Brown
*Van Mildert Professor of Divinity in the University of Durham,
and Canon of Durham; previously Fellow, Chaplain and Tutor of
Oriel College, Oxford, and Lecturer in Theology, University of
Oxford*

The Right Revd Colin Buchanan
*Honorary Assistant Bishop in the Diocese of Rochester; previously
Bishop Suffragan of Aston*

Dr Sarah Coakley
Lecturer in Religious Studies, Lancaster University

Miss Ruth Etchells
*formerly Principal of St John's College, with Cranmer Hall, Durham,
and Senior Lecturer in the University of Durham*

The Revd Dr John Polkinghorne FRS (from 1989)
*President of Queens' College, Cambridge; previously Dean of Trinity
Hall, Cambridge*

The Revd Dr Derek Stanesby
Canon of Windsor

The Revd Dr Anthony Thiselton
*Principal of St John's College, with Cranmer Hall, Durham; previously
Principal of St John's College, Nottingham, and Special Lecturer in the
University of Nottingham*

The Revd Dr Rowan Williams
*Lady Margaret Professor of Divinity in the University of Oxford, and
Canon of Christ Church*

The Revd Dr Tom Wright (from 1989)
*Fellow, Chaplain and Tutor of Worcester College, Oxford, and Lecturer
in Theology, University of Oxford*

CONSULTANTS
The Revd Dr John Polkinghorne FRS (1988–89)
then Dean of Trinity Hall, Cambridge

The Revd Dr John Rodwell (from 1988)
Research Fellow in Biological Sciences, Lancaster University

SECRETARIES
The Revd John Meacham (until 1989)
*formerly Chaplain and Research Assistant to the Bishop of
Salisbury*

The Revd Dr John Clark (from 1989)
Vicar of Longframlington, Northumberland

The Mystery of Salvation: 1989–1995

CHAIRMAN
The Right Revd Alec Graham
Bishop of Newcastle

MEMBERS
The Revd Dr Paul Avis
Vicar of Stoke Canon, Poltimore with Huxham, and Rewe with Netherexe, and Prebendary of Exeter

Dr Richard Bauckham
Professor of New Testament Studies in the University of St Andrews, previously Reader in the History of Christian Thought in the University of Manchester

Dr Christina Baxter (from 1991)
Dean of St John's College, Nottingham, and Vice-Chairman of the House of Laity of the General Synod

The Revd Dr David Brown
Van Mildert Professor of Divinity in the University of Durham, and Canon of Durham; previously Fellow of Oriel College, Oxford

The Right Revd Colin Buchanan (until 1991)
Vicar of St Mark, Gillingham, and Honorary Assistant Bishop in the Diocese of Rochester

Dr Sarah Coakley (until 1992)
Fellow of Oriel College, Oxford; subsequently Professor of Christian Theology, The Divinity School, Harvard University

Dr Ruth Etchells (until 1991)
formerly Principal of St John's College, with Cranmer Hall, Durham, and Senior Lecturer in the University of Durham

Lady (Sophie) Laws (from 1991)
formerly Lecturer in New Testament Studies at King's College, London

The Revd Dr John Muddiman (from 1990)
Fellow of Mansfield College, Oxford

The Revd Dr John Polkinghorne FRS
President of Queens' College, Cambridge, and Canon Theologian of Liverpool

The Right Revd Dr Geoffrey Rowell (from 1991)
Bishop of Basingstoke, Prebendary of Chichester and Emeritus Fellow of Keble College, Oxford

The Right Revd Dr Peter Selby (from 1991)
William Leech Professorial Fellow in Applied Christian Theology in the University of Durham; previously Bishop of Kingston-upon-Thames

The Revd Dr Derek Stanesby (until 1991)
Canon of Windsor

The Right Revd Stephen Sykes (from 1990)
Bishop of Ely

The Right Revd John B. Taylor
Bishop of St Albans

The Right Revd Dr Rowan Williams (until 1991)
Bishop of Monmouth; previously Lady Margaret Professor of Divinity in the University of Oxford

The Very Revd Dr Tom Wright
Dean of Lichfield, and Canon Theologian of Coventry; previously Fellow of Worcester College, Oxford

CONSULTANT
The Revd Andrew Wingate
Principal of the College of the Ascension, Selly Oak, and Assistant Secretary of the USPG

SECRETARY
The Revd Dr John Clark
Vicar of Chevington; previously Vicar of Longframlington with Brinkburn

Foreword

Republished in this volume is a rather remarkable segment of the modern history of the Church of England. Between the years 1987 and 1995 the Doctrine Commission of the General Synod of the Church of England (to give it its full title) produced three reports on three aspects of Christian doctrine, namely belief in God, in the Holy Spirit, and in the atoning work of Christ.[1] Nominated by the Archbishops of Canterbury and York, the quality of the membership of the three Commissions speaks for itself.[2] Each Commission contained between twelve and fifteen members; they nonetheless managed to produce unanimous reports, in itself an achievement worthy of remark. Two previous Commissions had either failed, or had not aspired to produce unanimous reports; *Christian Believing* (1976) contained a thirty-eight page report, followed by ten individual essays. *Believing in the Church* (1981), though in many respects foundational for what was to follow, consisted in a volume of commissioned and interconnected essays. The three subsequent reports were distinguished from their predecessors, furthermore, by their having been published 'under the authority of the House of Bishops'. The implications of this phrase will be considered later in this introduction.[3]

The style of the reports has often been called 'semi-popular'. This presumably means that they were intended to be read by a wider public than normally reads works of academic theology. They contained few footnotes, and tried not to presume much theological knowledge. Occasionally, it must be admitted, they forgot themselves.[4] But more importantly, they are patently written by people for whom the practice of the faith was a matter of vital concern. The spiritual life and participation in the worship of the Church are constantly used as reference points, as well as the arguments of theologians or current intellectual difficulties. These are documents with a pastoral concern, and, because of this, stand close to the Church's public teaching of the faith.

Anglicans have been notoriously resistant to the idea that there is such a thing as Anglican doctrine, or an Anglican systematic theology.[5] And it is true that the three Commissions do not present their work as any kind of synthesis or systematic whole. The first Doctrine Commission, which was appointed in 1922 and reported in 1938, presented a report on doctrine *in* the Church of England.[6] They denied that it claimed to be the doctrine *of* the Church of England. But, of course, in describing the state of play in regard to teaching the faith, they had to make judgements on a number of disputed questions. Inevitably they wrote from within the living Anglican tradition, confirming some parts and questioning others –

precisely the activity of teachers of the faith. The same is true of the three reports republished here. They are not an Anglican systematic theology, but they teach the faith from within the Church of England, attempting to discern a faithful and true pathway for the contemporary disciple.

The purpose of this introduction is threefold; first, to evoke some important aspects of the history of English theology, which set the context for the Commissions' work; secondly, to enquire into the internal coherence of the three reports; and finally, to comment on the sense in which they can be regarded as authoritative.

I

In the first place, we should observe that one very basic feature of all three reports closely reflects a movement in English theology of the two previous decades. This concerns the conscious decision to focus attention on the content, as distinct from the methods of theology. Whereas the two previous reports had concentrated on the character of believing, that is, what kind of activity believing is in itself, the Commission, with the express encouragement of Archbishop Robert Runcie, deliberately turned its direction toward the beliefs of the Christian faith. Indeed in 1987 it was plainly envisaged by the then Chairman of the Commission, Bishop John V. Taylor, that they had begun a 'new programme' which would 'continue and develop' in the years ahead. To bring these reports into one volume in a format consistent with the latest in the series, *Being Human* (2003), is, therefore, to keep faith with an original aspiration.[7]

The turn towards the content of belief is much more than a neutral movement from one subject to another. In Britain, the study of theology at universities had been massively influenced by a philosophical movement known as 'analytical' or 'ordinary language' philosophy. This had it roots partly in the empiricism of David Hume (1711–76), but also in the scientific and logical positivism of the Vienna Circle of the 1920s. The latter movement had set out to destroy the pretensions of transcendental metaphysics, on the grounds that they lacked any possibility of empirical verification, and so were meaningless. An influential member of the circle, the Oxford philosopher, A. J. Ayer, published *Language, Truth and Logic* in 1936 (2nd ed. 1946), in effect an elegant and sustained manifesto for the view that for a statement to be true requires the direct or indirect support of some observation from experience.[8]

In this hostile context theologians had to struggle to articulate convincing grounds for the kind of truth claims that any statements about God were making. Oxford was the reputed headquarters of this movement in Britain, and Professor I. T. Ramsey, Nolloth Professor of the Christian Religion (1951–66), the theologian at the eye of the storm. He was, moreover, the original Chairman of the Commission appointed in 1967, by which time he had become Bishop of Durham.[9] (His untimely and much-mourned death in 1972 at the age of 57 removed the most direct theological contributor to the debate.) Even so a chapter on 'The Nature of Religious Language' in the 1976 report contained an echo of one of his distinctive contributions, the idea that positive statements about God are like so many 'models' which 'qualify' each other, and together point in a coherent direction.[10]

Dissatisfaction both with the pretensions of so-called 'Oxford philosophy' and with the comparatively meagre results of the theological response to it, grew throughout the 1960s. These were years in which the English translations of Karl Barth's massive *Church Dogmatics* (1932–69) began to be influential in British universities.[11]

Though the number of identifiable followers of Karl Barth was initially small (and, with notable exceptions, mostly non-Anglican), aspects of his rooted hostility to the assumptions of nineteenth-century liberalism became influential.[12] One of his central contentions in particular made a profound impact specifically in the context created by logical positivism, that is, that human beings only have knowledge of God because God has made himself known. A paragraph of *We Believe in God* makes precisely this point with startling clarity.

> It should be clear by now that believing in God is different from believing in any other truth and that knowing God is not quite like knowing anything else . . . He can never for a moment be simply the object of our thought or our knowing or our believing . . . There is no understanding of God which is not by his self-revelation.[13]

One philosophical theologian reading Barth with evident respect, and imparting that respect to his students, was Professor Donald MacKinnon, who taught for 18 years in Cambridge. MacKinnon was perhaps the most influential (certainly the most unforgettable) theology teacher of his generation.[14] He was a Scots Episcopalian layman who combined convictions about the possibility and necessity of metaphysics with radical politics, a rooted objection to existentialism, and a love of the Church's liturgy. It is his influence which accounts for the fact that such Barthian themes as are detectable in the reports make their appearance in an English rather than a Continental tone of voice.[15] This is particularly evident in the way in which account is given of the authority of Scripture, as we shall see.

If the turn towards the content of Christian believing reflects a trend in British theology characteristic of the later 1970s and 1980s, it also strikingly reveals a return to the agenda of the first Doctrine Commission of 1922–1938. The events leading up to its appointment are comprehensively portrayed in Bishop Bell's magnificent biography of Randall Davidson, Archbishop of Canterbury in those turbulent years.[16] The Commission was asked

> to consider the nature and grounds of Christian doctrine with a view to demonstrating the extent of existing agreement within the Church of England and with a view to investigating how far it is possible to remove or diminish existing differences.[17]

In its 240-page report it covers the sources and authority of Christian doctrine, the doctrine of God, the Church and sacraments and eschatology. Though it claims that its subject matter has been largely determined by current controversies, rather than by an attempt to be systematic or comprehensive, its focus is precisely on the content of Christian believing. The report, moreover, deliberately set itself the task of creating a synthesis out of differing positions. This explains, the introduction admits, why it took the Commission so long to report. But the method of 'co-operative thought', looking for 'substantial agreement' behind or beyond expressions of conflicting opinion, was to have a distinguished subsequent history in bilateral and multilateral ecumenical negotiations.[18]

The 1938 report, like the three in this volume, was also presented unanimously. The Introduction personally contributed by the Chairman, Archbishop William Temple, delightfully hints at the fun and friendships which built up in the Commission over the years. In a few places the report states openly an unresolved difference of opinion; it is also admitted that different members might well have preferred a different treatment of an issue. But precisely because the Commission embraced the practical and pastoral challenge of expressing what they had in common, for the most part, they continued in frank and open dialogue with one another until a solution had been formulated. Tellingly they add:

> To admit acrimony in theological discussion is itself more fundamentally heretical than any erroneous opinions upheld or condemned in the course of the discussion.[19]

Thirdly, the three later Doctrine Commissions contributing to this volume also set out on an enterprise that had been explicitly embraced by the 1938 Commission, that of expressing themselves 'in such a way that any who have paid serious attention to the problems of religion can follow our statement and understand it'.[20] It is hardly a surprise that some chapters, or passages within chapters, make greater demands on 'serious attention' than others – the same is, after all, true of the Scriptures themselves. The aim, however, is to make the content of the Christian faith and its implications accessible, and, above all, useful to interested people.

The criterion of usefulness, specifically in the formation of a deeper understanding of the faith, suggests that this present volume could be of assistance in a number of different contexts. In formal theological education it might be a resource for those preparing for lay or ordained Christian ministry in the Church of England; and more widely in informal contexts, leaders of groups might find passages or chapters in the reports a stimulus to new ideas and activities. In preparation for preaching and teaching from the Scriptures, the very high concentration upon the contents of the Scriptures, which is a feature of all the reports, may lend itself (with skilful use of the indexes) to frequent reference. Finally, for private study or meditation, these reports could be a help in provoking reflection and insight. The texts are not an end in themselves; nor are they 'official teaching'. They can be, and are, subject to continuing argument. But their aim is to draw as many people as possible into the process in an informed and responsible way. To do that successfully requires at least a basic internal consistency, to which we now turn.

II

In this second part of the introduction, it is my intention to highlight those specific features of the reports which, taken together, offer a broadly coherent account of Christian teaching. It is important not to claim too much; indeed diligent readers will notice that certain chapters more strongly bear the imprint of their authors than others. On the one hand, there is a reasonable case to be made for the theological consistency of these reports (including, as it happens, the most recent, *Being Human*). For a Church which for centuries has taught the faith with the aid of a catechism, the existence of a core of common teaching ought to come as no surprise.[21] On the other hand the reputation of modern Anglicanism, at least in England, is that you can believe what you want to believe and that those charged with defending the faith have no confidence in the existence of boundaries to the faith. The implications of publishing these reports 'under the authority of the House of Bishops' will concern us, however, only after we have discovered whether a genuinely common mind emerges from these pages.

Trinitarian theology/belief in the Holy Trinity

The three reports in this volume, and *Being Human*, are clear that to believe in God means to believe in the Holy Trinity. A reviewer of the third of the reports spoke of 'a clear commitment to the broad incarnational and Trinitarian structure of catholic Christianity.'[22] There are several reasons why this should not be taken for granted. One of these concerns a major strand in the response to the verificationist challenge of analytic philosophy. Some theologians accepted the criterion that without the backing of an empirical observation theological or metaphysical statements were meaningless; but then argued that these statements embodied the perspective (the German noun, *Blik*, or 'viewpoint' was adopted to express this thought) of the believer. In an influential book, published in 1963, the American Paul van Buren wrote:

> Statements of faith are to be interpreted, by means of the modified verification principle, as statements which express, describe, or commend a particular way of seeing the world, other men and oneself, and the way of life appropriate to such a perspective.[23]

The implications for the doctrines of both the incarnation and the Trinity are simple and devastating. The sense in which it is meaningful to say that Jesus is the Son of God, or that God is one Person in Trinity, is contained in the believer's perspective on the world. The account of Jesus' life, death and resurrection becomes the norm for that *Blik* or way of seeing the world, and the doctrine of the Trinity is the reassurance that for the believer, the world is 'really' to be seen in this way.[24]

In the same year that van Buren published *The Secular Meaning of the Gospel*, John Robinson, Bishop of Woolwich, produced *Honest to God*, a work which it is no exaggeration to describe as a publishing blockbuster.[25] Both writers asserted that they were responding to the views of the courageous German theologian and martyr, Dietrich Bonhoeffer (1906–45), whose programmatic call for 'religionless Christianity' to match a 'world come of age' had excited and stimulated so many British and American theologians. Robinson's other main conversation-partner, however, was Paul Tillich (1886–1965), an influence which is absent from van Buren. Thus, for Robinson, to speak of God was not to refer to a 'supernatural being out there', but rather a way of indicating the 'depth in things'. The 'Ground of our Being' was Robinson's preferred way of giving content and meaning to God-talk, which the modern world had placed (he held) in radical question.

Further challenges to traditional trinitarianism emerged with the publication in 1977 of *The Myth of God Incarnate*, a collection of essays assembled by Professor John Hick.[26] The viewpoints of the authors were various, as were their ecclesiastical allegiances. But among them were the Anglicans, Don Cupitt, a Cambridge theologian, Dennis Nineham, the Warden of Keble College, Oxford and Maurice Wiles, the Chairman of the Doctrine Commission and Regius Professor of Divinity in the University of Oxford.[27] The theses advanced by several of the contributors included the ideas that 'incarnation' as traditionally taught was no longer credible, that it was a late exaggeration and distortion of Jesus' own self-understanding, that it was an obstacle to inter-faith dialogue, and that the cultural gap between ourselves and the early centuries of the Church was enormous.

Likewise published in 1977 was another work calling for a revision of traditional doctrine, *God as Spirit*. The author, Geoffrey Lampe, was a noted Anglican patristic scholar, of evangelical background, at the time Regius Professor of Divinity in the University of Cambridge. A subtle work with a strong biblical base, it argued that what lies at the heart of Christian faith is not a set of propositions about God, but the response to God's love as exemplified in Jesus Christ. The idea of the incarnation of the Second Person of the Trinity leads to the impossible thought of one who was fully divine and fully human at the same time. Preferable, in his view, was the concept of the Divine Spirit inspiring, motivating and indwelling the human Jesus.[28]

As if these were not enough, the 1980s witnessed a very public taking leave of God by a Cambridge theologian, Don Cupitt, an Anglican priest, former Vice-Principal of Westcott House, at the time Dean of Emmanuel College, and University Lecturer. Though Cupitt did not refer to Bonhoeffer, he sympathised with, and made more radical, Robinson's objections to 'the old supernaturalist interpretation of Christian claims'.[29] For Cupitt, the history of 'objective theism', the doctrine that God is a reality external to ourselves, has run its course. On the contrary; for contemporary humanity 'God is a symbol that represents to us everything that spirituality requires of us and promises to us'.[30] The modern world has generated a new age of the spirit, which he labels 'Christian Buddhism' ('Buddhist in form, Christian in content').[31] This radical re-interpretation of Christianity was embodied in a remarkable BBC documentary television series entitled, *The Sea of Faith* (1984), supported by a publication of the same name. Its conclusions Cupitt expressed in the following words:

> The way we construct our world, and even the way we constitute
> our own selves, depends on the set of values to which we commit

ourselves . . . ethics comes first; and religion is our way of representing to ourselves, and renewing our commitment to, the complex of moral and spiritual values through which we shape our world, constitute ourselves, gain our identity and give worth to our lives. God (and this is a definition) is the sum of our values, representing to us their ideal unity, their claims upon us and their creative power.[32]

In a cascade of publications Cupitt has continued to argue for and to refine this basic position.

Critics, of course, among them philosophers as well as theologians and ecclesiastics, accused Cupitt of thinly-disguised atheism. There were academics who were riled by the density of generalisation in his works; they asked, who is the 'we' in sentences such as 'we have come to see that there can be for us nothing but the worlds constituted for us by our own languages and activities'?[33] Robust defences of the 'reality' of God's objective being, and of a non-reductive account of Christian faith, were offered in reply.[34] Nor were defenders of orthodoxy the only ones to find Cupitt's 'evangelistic tract' hard to take, or his constant dichotomies misleading, or his extreme Kantianism and thoroughgoing individualism questionable.[35] It is striking, however, bearing in mind the public profile given his views, that Cupitt's name figures only once in a Doctrine Commission publication, in an individual essay by John Austin Baker, contributed to *Believing in the Church* (1981).[36] From 1981 onwards the Commission's stance in relation to the doctrine of God, and thus to the doctrine of the Trinity, might be described as one of 'critical realism'. The word 'God' is not regarded as a way of speaking of something else ('depth' or interpersonal relations); God is real even though our language fails to describe him completely.[37]

Each of the three reports contains one or more aspects of the common Trinitarian faith which informs them all. In *We Believe in God*, a chapter is devoted to the approach to the doctrine of the Trinity through prayer (chapter 7). To pray, the report argues, with reference to Romans 8, is to have the experience of being 'prayed in' – the 'Spirit himself bearing witness with our Spirit' (Rom. 8.16). It is 'to allow oneself to be shaped by the mutual interaction of Father and Spirit' and so to grow in the likeness of the Son. This makes Trinitarian theology anything but an abstract or propositional exercise.

The flow of Trinitarian life is seen as extending to every aspect of our being, personal and social, and beyond that to the bounds of creation.[38]

The theme is developed in chapter 4 ('The Spirit of Jesus') of *We Believe in the Holy Spirit*, which is, it has to be said, one of the most demanding sections of any of the reports. Here the focus is upon 'the new world of the Christian community' (p. 177), in which the Spirit 'forms the corporate and individual likeness of Christ in us' (p. 176). To take on our lips Jesus' term for God, Abba, represents to us the gift of freedom and authority, not of effortless mastery, but of the strength to do God's will, 'a power that achieves its ends by sacrifice' (p. 178).

The same theme is approached from another direction in chapter 2 of *The Mystery of Salvation* ('The giver and the gift'), where the association of love and gift-giving is explored. The Christian faith teaches that God gives himself to us in self-giving love. Thus:

> In the incarnation and death of Jesus the Son, God *gave* himself *for us* in the once-for-all historical event which constitutes our salvation, and as the indwelling presence of the Spirit in our lives God continually *gives* himself *to us* in our present experience of salvation.[39]

These gifts of Son and Spirit are nothing less than truly God; otherwise our salvation would be put in jeopardy. The doctrine of the Trinity, as the Church came to formulate it in the fourth century, is a summary in abbreviated narrative form of the much more extended narratives of the Gospels and Book of Acts. It does not replace these narratives, but it safeguards their reality as the story of God's self-giving love.

The practical, non-speculative nature of Trinitarian theology is further illustrated in the same report by the close connection which exists in the biblical tradition between life and love. God is eternal livingness; 'only God has life inalienably as his nature'.[40] To be alive means to have received life as a gift of God. Because this gift is God's own self, it is also the common life of the Holy Trinity. Citing the Gospel of John (5.21, 26), it is clear that the divine Son may give life to other human beings. But this life is a life which has overcome death and broken its power. 'To have eternal life is to know God as Trinity'.[41] Thus the word 'life' has a range of meanings, from the biological to the theological; so also does 'love'. For human beings life and love are inseparable in the development of personhood. But the human condition of reciprocal giving and receiving is grounded in nothing less than God's own being, the loving communion of the Trinity. 'Drawn out of lovelessness by God's love, we experience the Spirit as our own power to love God and others'.[42] For a second time the Doctrine Commission comments on the theological significance of the term 'Abba' (Gal.4.6). The gift of the Spirit, who helps us to use that term, is God's openness to sharing with us the reciprocity of the Father and the Son. And it is a possibility actually mediated in history by

Jesus of Nazareth. We find ourselves 'within the open circle of the divine love, inside the story of salvation, and thus within the love that God eternally is.[43]

At this point the Commission briefly addresses the feminist criticism of masculine language we have already noted. It notes the various mitigations which have been adopted, for example alternating 'He' and 'She' as third person singular pronouns for the term 'God', or repeating 'God' or 'Godself'. The report avoids the masculine pronoun wherever possible, except where the alternative is stylistically awkward. But it rejects, on essentially biblical grounds, the use of Creator, Redeemer and Sanctifier as substitutes for Father, Son and Holy Spirit, or of Parent and Child for Father and Son. Patriarchal conclusions should not be drawn from this language, and the story of salvation does not exclude or subordinate those disciples whom Jesus calls his 'sisters' and his 'mothers' (Mark 3.35). The fact that gender is not ascribed to God should be brought out by the use of other traditional terms, such as mother and child, lover and beloved, friend and friend, and by 'appropriate new ones'. The Commission's judgement is, however, that 'the terms Father and Son remain theologically normative in Christian Trinitarian discourse'.[44]

Should this emphatic endorsement of Trinitarian theology cause surprise? As we have seen, it follows hard on the heels of a period of English Anglicanism in which the possibilities of a non-Trinitarian approach to theology had been opened up by several prominent Anglican theologians. On the other hand there were contrary indications. The reception of the work of Karl Barth has already been noted. There were other ecumenical contributors, notably Vladimir Lossky, whose *Mystical Theology of the Eastern Church* (1944, translated in 1957) revived the long tradition of Orthodox criticism of Western trinitarianism; and Karl Rahner's *The Trinity* (in German, 1967, translated 1970) also overtly critical of the marginalising of Trinitarian thought within Catholic theology. The charismatic movement likewise required serious thought about the place of the Holy Spirit in Christian theology, and redressed the lack of interest in, or even antipathy toward, trinitarian theology characteristic of theologies emphasising religious experience.

This recovery of a sense of the vitality of Trinitarian theology could well be regarded as one of the fruits of ecumenism, given such an impetus by the Second Vatican Council (1962–5). The extent to which Anglican theology received a strengthened trinitarianism can be measured by contrasting the 1976 Report, *Christian Believing* with Professor David Ford's 1999 work, *Theology: a very short introduction*. The 42 pages containing the painfully acquired common statement of the 1976

Commission laboured to justify the retention of the trinitarian creeds 'in the bloodstream' of the Church; whilst at the same time acknowledging that debate about them (including, no doubt, disbelief and dissent from them) would not be regarded as disloyalty to the faith. Twenty years later David Ford feels able to refer to 'remarkable agreement' in the 'new explosion of theologies of the Trinity', and baldly states that 'it has become basic Christian wisdom that God is Trinitarian'.[45] The trinitarianism of the Reports of the Doctrine Commission from 1987 signify the Church of England's wholehearted participation in this ecumenical movement.

The praise of the triune God is moreover a traditional feature of the liturgy and hymns current in Anglican worship.[46] The preparation of the *Alternative Service Book* was preoccupying liturgists through the 1970s. It is somewhat ironic to reflect that in the midst of the furore surrounding the publication of the *Myth of God Incarnate* liturgical scholars were newly installing 'O gladsome light, O grace, Of God the Father's face', a patristic hymn of high christological content, into the revised office of Evening Prayer. Controversies about radical proposals are not necessarily a reliable indicator of how theology is developing in any era, and the doctrine of a necessary development in the direction of greater theological liberalism simply seems untrue.

One interesting sign of this is Commission's recurrent concern for relations with adherents of other faiths.[47] Rather than being embarrassed at the uniqueness of a Trinitarian understanding of God, the Commission insists on its centrality to any inter-faith reflection. Responding to the conventional categorisation of responses to other faiths (exclusivism, inclusivism and pluralism), the Commission recommends movement beyond the ambiguities of the three positions with the help of the doctrine of the Trinity.[48]

The suffering of God

Responding to what is said to be a 'radical shift' in the modern Christian understanding of God, the Commission endorsed in all three Reports the idea of a 'Suffering God'. Necessarily this involved, as the Chairman's Preface to *We Believe in God* indicated, discarding belief in the impassibility of God. Remarkably enough that doctrine had given rise to full-length treatment of the subject by a member of the 1938 Commission, J. K. Mozley.[49]

The furthest that the 1938 Commission had felt able to go in its brief discussion of the problem of impassibility was to assert that 'the revelation in Christ discloses God as taking on himself in the Person of

His Son the suffering involved in the Incarnation'.[50] This, it asserted, is a loftier conception of the deity than one which would deny that suffering can enter at all into the experience of God.

The Doctrine Commission team for 1981–5 contained one member, Canon William Vanstone, who went on to write passionately on this subject in *Love's Endeavour, Love's Expense*. In *The Mystery of Salvation*, the section entitled 'Salvation and a Suffering God' quoted three stanzas of a hymn by Vanstone, closing with the lines:

> Thou art God, Whose arms of love
> Aching, spent, the world sustain.[51]

If we ask about the origins of this conviction, the answers are various. The Commission itself points to a 'widespread collapse' of the doctrine of impassibility in the face of the depth and scale of human suffering in the world wars. It refers to challenges to the traditional doctrine from post-second world war theologians, both Roman Catholic and Protestant. Oddly it does not mention one Anglican theologian to raise the question before the first world war, on the basis of implications of Darwinism. C. E. Rolt's, *The World's Redemption* (1913), explicitly called into question the traditional idea of omnipotence; a similar contention emerged at much the same time from B. H. Streeter, a notable Anglican biblical critic and philosopher.[52] During the first world war the theme of God's suffering with his creation was given prophetic and popular expression by G. A. Studdert Kennedy, a slum priest and Army Chaplain.[53]

Though the three reports do not offer an extended discussion of the implications of Darwinian evolution for the doctrine of God, in another respect one aspect of this background is strongly confirmed. That is, in the constant return to, and treatment of, the theme of the sacrifice of Christ upon the cross.[54] God's personal encounter with, and discovery of the power of suffering transforms the Christian's whole attitude to experience. The presence of our creator at the very heart of our pain and sorrow, by an act which is both an expression and a limiting of his being, assures us that God's power is indeed the power to show mercy and pity.[55] At the same time the very doctrine of a God who saves by sacrifice has been criticised in feminist writing as 'an attempt to exalt an alleged virtue which women have been obliged to practise in order to show that they knew their place'.[56] The Commission's brief response to that charge is to emphasise the *active* character of our participation in Christ's sacrifice; the phrase employed by the 1982 ARCIC Final Report, being 'drawn into the movement of Christ's self-offering', is explicitly endorsed.[57]

We Believe in God contains one further example of the fruitful treatment of the theme of the suffering of God, that is in relation to prayer. The agony in the garden and the cry from the cross are an indication that experience of anxiety and desolation are compatible with the active presence of God.[58] It is precisely the doctrine of the triune God which enables us to embrace both creative power and patient weakness, the Lord who is at once the 'giver of life' and who cries 'Abba, Father' in doubt and darkness. The same theme is explored in *We Believe in the Holy Spirit* in relation to the charismatic movement's treatment of failure in prayer, aridity and depression.[59] With a reference to the 'sharing of Christ's sufferings' (Rom.8.11,17), the Commission asks whether the experience of the Holy Spirit, is only thinkable as a positive, joyful state of being. With a quotation from William Temple it reminds us that loneliness, desertion by friends and apparent desertion by God was 'the way Christ went to the Father' (p. 32). With a reference to modern Catholic theologians writing on Holy Saturday, it even suggests that the Holy Spirit 'spans the unimaginable gulf between despair and victory'.[60]

The use and authority of scripture

The reports reprinted in this volume also exemplify a consistent attitude to, and employment of the Bible in the formulation of Christian doctrine. As for all the world confessional families, the turning point for the account given of this matter was the development from the seventeenth century of scientific methods in the interpretation of ancient documents. Whether such methods were illegitimate for the Christian reading of Scripture was, and still is, hotly controverted. Radical criticism became a feature of nineteenth-century European Protestantism, and by contrast the Roman Catholic authorities were hostile or cautious. In this context it is hardly surprising that Anglicans pursued a middle course. Thus, in the 1938 Report, the traditional idea of the inerrancy of the Bible was said to be inconsistent with contemporary knowledge; but, at the same time, the Bible as a whole was claimed to be 'the inspired record of a unique revelation'.[61] To use it as an authoritative source of teaching does not preclude historical-critical study, or critical judgement about ancient thought-forms, or discrimination concerning the relative spiritual value of different portions of the Bible. The culmination of God's progressive revelation is in Christ, and the 'Mind of Christ', faithfully conveyed in the religious and moral teaching of the Gospels, is 'the standard by which to judge the claim of subsequent developments to be true to the authentic spirit of the Christian Gospel'.[62]

The explosion of methods of biblical study in the mid-years of the twentieth century led the 1976 Commission to a sharper assertion of the plurality and diversity of viewpoints in the Scriptures.

> There is nothing, therefore, to be done about the Bible and its heterogeneous, dynamic character. We are stuck with it . . . Instead of deploring this character and trying to correct it, we might ask ourselves whether it may not be we who are wrong.[63]

Instead of trying to produce a coherent doctrinal synthesis out of the 'jostling biblical data', perhaps we ought to accept that it has the creative power to go on stimulating new developments 'in keeping with the Spirit of the Bible'.[64] The 1975 Report was no more explicit about the phrase, 'the Spirit of the Bible', than was the earlier report about 'the Mind of Christ'. But the discovery by biblical scholars that one must take the internal variety of the Scripture seriously, highlights the importance of the judgement to be made in interpreting its 'mind' or 'spirit'.[65]

The Commission's response to this requirement is to emphasise not so much the judgement of an individual, as the perspective on the Scriptures of a worshipping community. This had been articulated in the 1981 volume of essays, *Believing the Church*. As one contributor put it, the main burden is the story of our salvation, and in worship we seek to bring the story of our lives into conformity with that greater story.[66] Personal belief is set in the context of corporate belief, and that belief is a shared possession.

This became the conscious starting point for *We Believe in God*. The search for an answer to the question, What is God like?, begins with a common inheritance handed down through many generations. It may involve a lonely and highly personal journey.

> But it also enlists the believer in a common enterprise, in the shared receiving of a gift, in a corporate experience of worship and a joint endeavour of service in a community.[67]

The Commission does not, however, draw the conclusion that there can only be one consolidated interpretation of Scripture. 'The Bible is not the kind of book which can easily be made to yield a single and consistent doctrine'.[68] Its divergences have, notoriously, given rise to separations; others (for example, the disagreement about bearing arms) have been contained within a single communion. Both the formation and the interpretation of Scripture inevitably involve human judgements of differing kinds. It is the Anglican experience of corporate worship which contextualises the divergences.

> Scripture is . . . perhaps chiefly, the distillation of those perceptions of the reality of God which came to a worshipping community . . . God is known, primarily and characteristically, in the shared

worship, experience and reflection of men and women who meet in his name and serve him in the world.[69]

The 1981 Report, *Believing in the Church*, also laid great stress on the formative significance of story or narrative in the Bible, and on the Church as story-telling community. This emphasis came about partly in response to a substantial international movement in biblical hermeneutics associated with the names of Hans Frei (in the USA), and Dietrich Ritschl (in Germany);[70] and partly in response to the use of 'myth' in publications we have already noted. It is characteristic that the report developed this movement with a substantial contribution devoted to Story and Liturgy; by continually reciting the story which the Scriptures tell, 'the Church at worship engages in dialogue with God', going over its formative years 'to proclaim in his presence the salvation it has experienced'.[71] This is a use of scriptural narration which makes the text of sacramental significance.

Both *We Believe in God* and *The Mystery of Salvation* make much of the Bible as narrative. It is the overall shape of a single story which bestows upon the biblical books their coherence and purposefulness. 'To read in worship any portion of the biblical story – however truncated or broken it may seem alone – is to set our own lives in the context of the whole narrative framework which the Bible contains.'[72] The characterisation of God in the narrative contains aspects which are in tension with each other – mercy and wrath, for example, are not easily combined. Yet their clear attestation in Scripture is a constant challenge to us to enlarge on our understanding of God.

The Mystery of Salvation explicitly extends discussions of two further themes begun in *We Believe in God*, the consideration of historical truth in relation to biblical narrative and questions surrounding eschatology ('The End of the Story').[73] The narrative of human salvation has sometimes been told as a process *within* history; at other times, and by other writers, as an act of rescue *from* history. Or again, and this is the version of the narrative preferred in the Report, salvation may be seen as a transformation and completion *of* history. There is a striking similarity in these categories to the well-known distinctions formulated by H. R. Niebuhr in his classic work, *Christ and Culture*.[74] One might speak of these as versions of the story of salvation with characteristically different emphases. Further, within these versions and at their heart is the narrative (or rather narratives) of the passion, told with somewhat different intentions by each of the four evangelists. Finally, in the light of the resurrection, the victory of the death of Christ is illuminated by a series of images which convey a way of understanding God's act of atonement for human sin (sacrifice, ransom, justification or acquittal, or reconciliation).

A whole chapter of the report is devoted to modern 're-tellings' of the story of the cross vividly illustrating the rich narrative potential embodied within a doctrine of the atonement. In each of these ways the category of narrative or story illustrates how the diversity of Scripture carries interpretative possibilities.

Scripture, narrative and the worshipping community are brought together in the sacraments of baptism and eucharist, especially in *We Believe in the Holy Spirit* and *The Mystery of Salvation*. The role of the Holy Spirit is to create a new kind of relatedness of persons to one another. The Spirit

> is to be understood as an agency making for a unified pattern of life, unified by the way believers reflect God's gift in Christ in their self-gift to one another.[75]

Baptism is the entrance to this community, the signing, as it were, of the legal documents marking the beginning of a new story.

> Baptism marks the decisive point from which a particular story of the work of the indwelling Spirit can be told, of growth into the death and resurrection of Christ.[76]

It commits us to the ecumenical enterprise of those who belong together 'in Christ', and projects us into the ministry of reconciliation.

The eucharist continues the task of the Holy Spirit in making us children of God. This continuation of the story is obviously not a simple matter of growth and development, in an ever upward direction. Nor is it a matter wholly under the control of our conscious minds. The work of the Holy Spirit cannot be confined to language and meaning, but may employ many non-verbal triggers to bring us into renewed relationship with Christ.

It is a feature of the reports that they combine this devotional and pastoral material with an unhesitating acceptance of the necessity of scholarly critical procedures. The chapter entitled 'The God of Jesus' in *We Believe in God* (chapter 5) attempted to summarise a vast array of biblical scholarship relating to the Old Testament, the inter-testamental literature, and the four Gospels. Its reconstruction of the teaching of Jesus, the Report holds, presents 'certain points . . . which command agreement even among the most cautious scholars'.[77] Even so, such a consensus can be no more than 'a tentative reconstruction which takes account of the present state of scholarship'. In dealing with the passion narratives, the *Mystery of Salvation* acknowledges the existence of a number of discrepancies, which scholars have attempted to interpret by means of various critical procedures (notably, form criticism, redaction criticism and narrative criticism). In commenting on these methods, the Commission accepts the necessity of addressing questions of history and tradition, but also commends narrative criticism for its alertness to the sympathetic imagination of the hearer or listener.[78]

It has long been a characteristic of British biblical scholarship, not at all confined to Anglicans, to accept the risks implicit in historical enquiry. On principle, to assert that the incarnation took place at a certain moment in human history seems to imply that any justified historical technique for establishing the truth of what happened, could be used. Accounts of what happened are likewise capable of being corrected. The problems for the authority of Scripture are whether the corrigibility of historical criticism is compatible with the doctrine of Scriptural inspiration.

There is only a very brief treatment of the question in these reports. In the first place it is asserted that the language of Scripture does not present us with a complete, final and exhaustive description of what God is. God's self-revelation has come about in the languages, pictures and imaginings of individuals and groups and have been subject to testing, sharing, correcting, extending and enhancing.[79] The models employed in this process are indispensable to theology, as they are to science; both are corrigible. In a chapter devoted to 'God and our ways of knowing', the Commission quotes Einstein's famous letter to Newton, paying tribute to the concepts the latter had developed which still dominate the way we think in physics. It continues:

> Christians too have their own comparable conversation with the past. We live in the Body of Christ and therefore in the communion of saints. We too can recognise that others have left a mark upon us . . . This is to recognise a truth and an experience which we can trust, and on which we are entitled to rely – not uncritically, not as though it foreclosed every argument and solved every problem, but as a great foundation on which to live now for our time and in our day (p. 28).

The idea of 'conversation with Scripture' is given notable emphasis in the later report, *Being Human* (2003). Throughout Christian history, Christian teaching has involved an 'intensive listening to and conversation around the Bible and around the issues of life'. It has involved, also, prayer, worship and attention to others, both past and present. The actual process, and the intensity of it, is integral to the growth of wisdom in the believer and in the Church. The Scriptures are uniquely authoritative for the Church in so far as they are used in this way.[80] This is the process to which it is the aim of the reports to contribute.

It remains, finally, to consider the authority of the reports.

III

In a characteristically perceptive and generous review of *We Believe in God*, Professor Maurice Wiles, who had been Chairman of the Doctrine Commission which produced *Christian Believing*, asked:

> Is the concept of an 'agreed report' appropriate to the kind of exercise that has in fact been carried out?

He claimed that there were obvious features of the report which showed that many different hands had been at work at it. If the point of the report was to promote good thinking and publishing about the content of Christian doctrine, would not a series of books by appropriate individuals have been a better way of achieving that goal than the product of a committee? Wiles claimed that the corporate dimension integral to the idea of church doctrine could be secured 'by the fact that such a work was designed for further discussion and reflection in the whole body of the Church'.[81]

Wiles does not comment on the fact that this report, unlike its predecessors, had been welcomed by the House of Bishops, commended to the Church and published 'under its authority'.[82] But what precisely does the authority of the House add to the collective views of the members of the Doctrine Commission? Appropriately enough the reports themselves do not offer an answer to this question, which arises in the context of the doctrine of the Church – not one of the subjects considered by the Commissions. It is also the case that a full answer is beyond the remit of this introduction.

But it cannot be thought that the words 'under the authority of the House of Bishops' have no meaning. The Church of England claims to have the authority to settle doctrinal disputes; and bishops in the Church of England are, according to the Ordinal of the *Book of Common Prayer*, expected to be in the thick of controversy, teaching and exhorting wholesome doctrine and convincing gainsayers.[83] Their commendation of the reports must mean, at least, that they find in them nothing which is seriously misleading for any member of the Church. On one occasion the House required some rewriting of part of a report. At the same time, to commend them 'for study' is to suggest the continuation of a process of reflection, rather than the issuing of a question-stopping edict. There is a distinction between a report *of* the House of Bishops, and one commended *by* the House of Bishops (as the Doctrine Commission reports have been). In 1986 the House of Bishops issued a report entitled *The Nature of Christian Belief*, partly in response to public controversies concerning the Virgin Birth and the Resurrection.

A further feature of the reports is their submission by the House of Bishops, for study and debate in the General Synod. Although that body is not expert in theology, testing the reception of the reports in that forum is one way in which the prior judgement of the House of Bishops is exposed for debate by the Church at large. The next stage of that process is embodied in such study and use of the Reports as parish groups or theological courses may make of them. Both of these stages constitute the reception of the teaching contained in the report, and their reception likewise becomes part of their authority.

It turns out that to answer the question, 'What is the authority of the Reports?', is not a simple matter. They are given a measure of authority by the House of Bishops, who have their distinctive God-given responsibilities. This authority is not unchallengeable, but part of a process of reception. The process continues with their use (or, conceivably, ends with their disuse). The reports themselves anticipate such a process. *We Believe in God* states at an early stage that it distinguishes areas where debate and uncertainty are legitimate, from those where something fundamental is at stake. Here it proposes 'to use such authority as it possesses' to support those whose life, worship and testimony affirm that the Church's tradition can be 'confidently believed and proclaimed today'.[84] The same distinction was made, interestingly enough, by the Chairman of the 1937 Report, Archbishop William Temple.

The present author served, briefly, on the Commission which produced *The Mystery of Salvation*, before becoming Chairman of the following Commission, whose report *Being Human* appeared in 2002. His experience has led him to believe that the sometimes arduous activity of formulating a view on a central matter of Christian doctrine under the searching scrutiny of a dozen highly intelligent theological colleagues adds something substantial to the corporate character of church doctrine. One has to be ready to sacrifice favourite theses and idiosyncrasies to achieve an agreed outcome. Technical terms and jargon are dissected for hidden unclarities. Matters one had not considered, or if considered, dismissed, have to be appraised and reappraised. And, as always in the Church, it becomes swiftly apparent that nothing works without love. And the Commissions would not have worked if their members had not themselves been teachable. It is of course true that the outcome of the Commissions' work is flawed, and in need of correction. But it remains an achievement for a Church with a justified reputation for wide diversity of view to have formulated, with the aid of distinguished scholars, the works represented here for publication.

Stephen Sykes
November 2004

We Believe in God

In June 1986 the House of Bishops endorsed the recommendation of the Chairman of the Doctrine Commission that its reports should in future come before the House with a view to their publication under its authority.

This report is the first to be published since that date. The House welcomes the report and commends it to the Church.

On behalf of the House of Bishops
+ROBERT CANTUAR:
Chairman

Chairman's preface

The report *Believing in the Church*, which appeared in 1981, marked the completion of a stage in which the Doctrine Commission had concentrated on questions of what it means for Christians, individually and corporately, to believe rather than on the content of belief. The lessons of that report, and of its predecessor *Christian Believing* (1976), still need to be much more widely studied and absorbed in the Church of England. The Commission, however, considered that the time had come to start work on what Christians believe, and the present volume is the first fruits of this new programme.

My own position as Chairman in relation to this latest report, *We Believe in God*, is an unusual one in that I have taken only a very minor part in the work. After the publication of *Believing in the Church* I resigned from the Commission, on preparing to move to my present post. Apart from one advisory contribution as a visiting consultant in 1983, and the actual editing of the Report for publication, I have not had the privilege of sharing in the project. All the creative work has been done by those whose names appear in the list on pages ix and x.

This, however, has the happy result of freeing me to thank and to congratulate all concerned for a very positive report which many readers, I am sure, will find illuminating and enriching. It is not, and does not claim to be, a comprehensive survey either of all aspects of the Christian doctrine of God or of its complex history. Instead it focuses on particular aspects which the panel believed to be important both for churchpeople and for interested enquirers at the present time.

Chapter 1 begins from the point that belief in God continues to be a potent and widespread feature of human life today, which should challenge everyone to serious and open reflection. What does this belief entail? In Anglicanism the answer is traditionally sought through Scripture, Reason and the cumulative experience of Christians.

The report is in some sense a bridge between the earlier publications already mentioned, which concentrated on the nature of believing, and the new programme of expounding the content of belief. Hence Chapters 2, 3 and 4, though containing a good deal of the substance of the doctrine of God, also illuminate it by comparing it with the scientific enterprise, by examining the language in which it is expressed, and by surveying the way in which the Bible as a whole speaks to us about God.

Chapters 5 and 6 attempt to give a summary and synthesis of the major insights into the nature of God which are to be found in Scripture, while taking care also to bring out the distinctiveness of the various sources. The key to the Christian biblical understanding of God is Jesus Christ as believed in and proclaimed by the New Testament witnesses, who see him both as the fulfilment of past history and the determinant of the future.

So the argument passes on naturally to another characteristic element in Christian belief about God, the doctrine of the Trinity. In Chapter 7, however, this is approached in an unusual way through the experience of Christian prayer; and the insights thus derived are traced further in the teaching of some of the Fathers. The question of gender in speaking of God is also brought out in this context.

Chapter 8 then earths what has been said so far in experiences of life and worship. It is a mark of the Christian God that he can be known only from within a response of loving obedience to his call. Various forms of such obedience – in daily life, prayer, worship, personal relationships – are examined, culminating in reflection on the Eucharist and its relation to our service of God's world.

The final chapter seeks to face the ultimate question: can we believe in God as controller of that world and, as such, worthy of our trust? After examining various biblical models, the issue of the suffering of God is confronted, and belief in an impassible God discarded. The fulfilment of God's purpose for good in an eternal order is achieved only along the way of Cross and Resurrection which God himself has walked.

It is important to emphasise that the report is unanimous, and that no part of the book carries the name of an individual author. *Believing in the Church* also had the unanimous support of the whole Commission, but final decisions as to the wording of each essay, after it had been carefully reviewed by all the members collectively, rested with the individual author. The entire text, however, of *We Believe in God* has been agreed by the whole panel. This does not mean that individual members would not, left to themselves, have worded this or that differently, but that all are prepared to stand behind every sentence of the text as printed.

This is a very considerable achievement on the part of all concerned, but especially of the Chairman who initiated the project and guided it to completion, John Taylor, till 1985 Bishop of Winchester. To him all of us would wish to pay the most heartfelt tribute of gratitude and admiration. In theological thinking inexhaustibly creative, in love and devotion an inspiring friend and colleague, his leadership has been of decisive significance for the Commission's work. *Believing in the Church* has been widely recognised as a major contribution to the Church of England's task of intellectual discipleship. We hope that *We Believe in God* will also be recognised as a worthy memorial of his dedicated service as head of the Commission.

With *Believing in the Church* the Doctrine Commission regained recognition as an advisory body to which the House of Bishops of the General Synod could refer questions with clearly theological implications. Now this latest report, having been submitted to the House of Bishops for their approval, has been officially commended by them to the Church for study. It is the hope of all those who work with the Commission in any capacity that in the years ahead it may continue and develop this kind of service to the Church at large.

The writings of the Doctrine Commission cannot be 'popular' in every sense of that overworked word. We hope however that *We Believe in God* will be accessible to a large number of interested readers. We hope also that, where appropriate, it will be possible for the Commission's ideas to be communicated to a still wider readership through simplified versions, study guides and so forth, prepared by qualified people.

Finally, on behalf of the Commission, may I express our warmest thanks to those who have helped in various invaluable ways in the creation of this report, but who are not in any sense to be burdened with responsibility for its defects. First, to our Consultants, who made an important ecumenical as well as scholarly contribution; then to our two Secretaries, the Reverend Michael Perham, who served for most of the work, and his successor, the Reverend John Meacham; to Miss Keri Lewis of the General Synod Office, for her most generous assistance at all times; and to Mrs Pauline Wood, for secretarial support at our residential meetings.

+JOHN SARUM

Chapter 1
Towards a doctrine of God

'I believe in God.' Throughout this country there are individuals and communities who gather together day by day, or week by week, to praise and worship God, to pray to him and learn about him, and to be renewed in human goodness. Many are Christians; many who affirm belief in God are adherents of other faiths. Alongside these again are countless others who are only distantly or precariously attached to the forms and institutions of existing religions but who acknowledge a sense of the reality of God. Outward observances may have changed, church attendance may have declined. But religious belief and practice are still among the facts which need to be accounted for in the world of today. Nowhere has God left himself without a witness. Everywhere there are people who believe in him.

But how does one go on from there? What is this God like in whom so many people believe? What can I say about him which will give sharper definition to my belief without leading me into the error of supposing that I can reduce him to what can be caught in the net of human language? Am I still justified in believing in him despite all those apparent obstacles to belief which the modern world insistently thrusts upon my attention? In the face of the atrocities as well as the human achievements of this century, can I go on thinking of him as all-powerful, all-knowing, perfectly good? On what grounds do I prefer the Christian account of God to those of other faiths? And is that Christian account with, for example, the one-sided masculinity of its picture of God still one I can properly accept? In short, what is my doctrine of God?

These are some of the questions to which this book will be addressed. But it is important to ask at the outset what kind of answer it is reasonable to expect. The previous report of the Doctrine Commission, *Believing in the Church*, argued that it is a mistake to think of anyone's religious belief as if it were a piece of private property. Belief is a shared possession. It cannot be acquired simply from private meditation and reflection; it cannot be parcelled up in a book and handed to people to take as much or as little of it as they will. It starts from an inheritance which is the common property of countless men and women to whom it has been handed down through many generations. It is the fruit of the faithful response and search of communities as much as of the internal illumination and wrestling of individuals. It is again and again found to be not just the conclusion of an argument, but also the basis of a whole set of values, a whole way of looking at things. It may involve each person in a lone quest of conscience, a sustained venture of prayer, a private journey not only of seeking but of being sought and found. But it also enlists the believer in a common enterprise, in the shared receiving of a gift, in a corporate experience of worship and a joint endeavour of service in a community. Again and again it will be more appropriate to say (as the Church has today learned afresh to do), not 'I believe' but 'We believe'.

It follows that it will not be sufficient, when presenting a doctrine of God, merely to offer a set of beliefs which it would be reasonable for someone to adopt in the light of the Christian revelation and of the present state of human knowledge. The starting-point is not the possibility of believing in God but the fact of it. Many millions of people believe in a God of some kind; particular beliefs about God are held by Christians; and specific forms of these beliefs may be held by members of the Church of England. But it is no simple matter to identify these, or to set them out in a coherent statement. Even an exhaustive enquiry of every church member, to find out what they believed, would still not be able to answer the question 'what the Church believes'. Nor can one read off the answer from the Scriptures and the official formularies of the Church. It is true that there are statements about God which are frequently repeated and are generally accepted by church members: for example, that he is creator of heaven and earth, that he is one to whom all hearts are open, all desires known, that he is the Father of our Lord Jesus Christ. But the mere recital of these phrases will not answer all the questions nor yield a 'doctrine of God'. For that it is necessary to know how they are interpreted by believers today, in what order of priority they stand, and how far the language in which they are expressed is used in a way compatible with modern understanding. Only then will they supply material for answering the question, 'What is the Christian doctrine of God?'

The use of scripture

How, then, does one begin to identify that doctrine? Why not start with that which seems to give the most specific and authoritative information about God – Holy Scripture itself? Part of what it means to be a Christian is the acceptance of the Bible as a unique revelation of the nature and activity of God. It should be possible, therefore, at least in theory, to read off a doctrine of God from its pages.

This has, of course, often been attempted. But such attempts do not result in a doctrine of God which then becomes accepted, without further discussion, by the community of believers. The Bible is not the kind of book which can easily be made to yield a single and consistent doctrine. It consists of a large number of attempts to speak about God and to 'read' the world and human existence in the light of a belief in God, arising from various situations in the history and experience, first of the people of Israel, and then of the Christian Church. Certain fundamental beliefs, such as that God is one, and that he is the creator of all that is, run right through it. But the more carefully one studies the Bible, the more one becomes aware of ideas of God and responses to him which seem actually to conflict with one another. Thus, God is a righteous judge, who does not protect his creatures from the consequences of their sins, but God is also a loving Father, who will not abandon his people even when they rebel against him. God is awesome and holy, infinitely removed from the sphere of his sinful creatures, yet God is also known with great directness and intimacy by those who approach him with penitence and love. God is a God of peace and non-violence: but acts of great severity, even of brutality, are attributed to him.

In the face of these apparent contradictions, the sceptic may well doubt whether Scripture can be relied on to give authoritative guidance at all. But the believer who finds in the Bible a convincing experience of God and an authentic inspiration is not disposed to withdraw confidence from it so easily. The Bible's own positive qualities are so strong that it is reasonable to look for explanations of its apparent inconsistencies. It has often been argued, for example, that the Bible is a record of a developing faith, so that the more 'primitive' may be discarded in favour of the more 'advanced', or that apparent contradictions are no more than exaggerations of emphasis, ensuring that essential aspects of the nature of God are not overlooked, the resolution of these inevitable tensions being part of the ultimate mystery of God himself. But whatever response is adopted, the consequence is likely to be different nuances of understanding and different stances on matters of faith and conduct among church members.

Sometimes these differences can be contained within one community of believers. The Church has, for example, very largely been able to embrace those who think that a Christian may legitimately take up arms and those who do not. Sometimes, however, differences lead to the formation of sects and denominations, which become separated in a way that causes grief and offence to Christians and evokes derision from outsiders. It simply is not possible to go 'back to the Scriptures' to re-establish a faith that is 'true' in every particular – attempts to do so usually result in the formation of yet another sect, proclaiming the correctness of its interpretation against all comers. Doctrine can be successfully formulated only from within a community which already shares certain options out of the range of possible interpretations, and has entrenched this 'tradition' in its style of worship, thought and conduct. On many matters there is general agreement among all the main Christian Churches; in these cases appeal can be made to the historic tradition of the Church. But on others – and by no means always significant ones – different convictions are held both between and within denominations. It is in this sense that one may talk not just of the Christian but of, for example, the Anglican – or even the Church of England – 'doctrine of God'.

There is no reason to think that it must be some defect in Christian revelation which results in such divergences. Any 'scripture' is by definition something written at a particular period in a particular language and cultural setting. Even at the level of translation, it may be impossible to replace a word in one language with another from a different language-system without involving some change of meaning. Distance in historical time or in cultural context makes this problem more acute. Hence a message or event in the course of time is bound to become subject to divergent interpretations even if this was not so at the beginning. All religions with sacred writings tend to have the same problem. It is instructive, for instance, to consider the situation in Islam. There scripture is in principle considerably more unified and homogeneous than the Bible, and is expected to regulate belief and conduct with an undisputed inerrancy. Yet several sects have issued from it, each claiming to have the 'true' interpretation, and often bitterly opposed to the others, sometimes even to the point of armed conflict.

If Christianity, along with other great religions, believes that God has revealed himself through the medium of human speech and recorded words, then it cannot look for fixed, normative and universally agreed doctrine. Christians may continue to honour the fundamental role of Scripture in their access to knowledge of God. But they need also to recognise (and this is an important part of the Anglican tradition) the part played by human judgement and experience in the work of formulating the beliefs derived from it. Indeed, one of the fruits of modern critical study of the Bible has been to reveal the extent to which these factors were already present in the formation of Scripture itself.

The role of reason

What resources do Christians bring to this constant engagement with revealed truth? First, and most obviously, their powers of reason. In Western culture all are to some extent children of Plato and Aristotle. It is taken for granted that all authentic knowledge of anything in the universe should be capable of being expressed in some logically coherent system. Believers, therefore, naturally assume that the same will be true of knowledge of God. God will not violate human categories of thought. This is a significant assumption to make about one who, by definition, transcends them. Not all the world's religions make this assumption. Mystics, even in the Christian tradition, seem sometimes to call it into question when they resort to paradox in an attempt to communicate their experience – though it should be remembered that paradox is not the same as the non-sense of self-contradiction. Nevertheless, whatever other options are theoretically possible, this is the assumption on which Christian theology is traditionally based; and that is why the logically trained mind continues to have an important part to play in constructing the Christian doctrine of God.

There is a long history of Christian debate over the precise function of human reason in this process. Some have thought of it as a kind of arbiter, with the task only of ensuring that any formulation of revealed truth should be compatible with the demands of reason; others have given reason a more creative role, believing that by observation of the universe it can actually supplement the knowledge of God that is available from revelation. But whichever side is taken, there can be no doubt about the importance of reason itself. Indeed, from the beginning, questions about the doctrine of God have engaged the most brilliant minds in the Church.

Yet it is here that belief in God may seem most vulnerable today. Reason does not demand merely that a doctrine of God should be logically coherent in itself. It demands also that the truths it asserts should be compatible with other truths, derived from observation. This is the point at which believers can find themselves most strongly challenged by developments (or seeming developments) in many fields of human knowledge. Thus, there was a time a few years ago when philosophy appeared to have called in question the very possibility of making meaningful statements about anything which could not be empirically verified. The sociology of knowledge seems often to imply that all knowledge of anything is decisively conditioned by upbringing, culture and environment. There is a dramatically enlarging body of valid scientific knowledge, with a correspondingly increased potential for ever more precise prediction, and an explosive expansion in technologies of every kind, which both threaten to dominate human life and at the same time seem almost to promise a solution to all human problems. From all this has sprung a radical questioning of such ideas as providence, moral freedom and responsibility, or the possibility of change under the influence of God. To many, belief in God seems bound to retreat before these attacks. The attempts made by believers to consolidate their position, or to pick off their assailants one by one, seem to them little more than a postponement of the inevitable collapse.

But believers cannot see it like this. Their belief in God enables them to make sense of far more of their experience than science or philosophy ever could. Indeed they find they have allies within those disciplines themselves. The fact that scientists or philosophers may be Christian does not mean that they are either myopic or naive. Knowing their subjects from the inside, they see better than most, not only their own limitations, but also the significant analogies which exist between their own field of enquiry and that of religious thought and practice. Of course, the believer must be careful not to make too much of this. The fact that a scientist may be a Christian does not in itself tilt the balance of the argument between science and Christianity. The scientist may simply have failed (or not been willing) to use the same powers of analysis on religion as he or she would bring to observation of the natural world. Nevertheless, the believing scientist may provide valuable help by showing that belief and science need not be at war at all, if the proper scope and methods of each are understood. Believer and scientist each stand before immense mysteries. As each discerns better the magnitude of their field of enquiry, they become less of a threat to each other, and may even discover areas of fruitful collaboration. We shall argue that in the last resort a comparable act of faith is demanded of each. That both still find it possible to make this act of faith suggests that it should be no more difficult now than it was before for reason to accept the existence of the realities in which each believes – the reality of God, and the reality of a universe accessible to human understanding.

The appeal to experience

But reason is not the only resource which the community of believers brings to bear on its inheritance of revealed truth. Those who believe in God seldom rely on rational thought alone. They testify to a variety of 'religious experiences', from a general sense of the holy or numinous on the one hand to a sensation of being directly addressed by a transcendent being on the other. Such experiences are notoriously hard to evaluate. To some they seem an irrefutable authentication of belief in God; to others they appear dangerously subjective, to be regarded at most as provisional confirmation of belief held on other grounds. Indeed, as with reason, so with religious experience: some regard it as making a significant contribution to our knowledge of God, others as offering only certain marginal considerations of which belief in God must take some account. Moreover, not only is such experience open to the charge of being subjective, it also appears to be unequal, if not haphazard, in its distribution. Many profound believers claim to be ignorant of it; many powerful experiences fail to result in a solid faith. Nevertheless, the fact remains that in twentieth-century England many thousands of people continue to pray and to worship in the conviction that in doing so they have personal experience of God, while many others believe themselves to be addressed, guided or protected by some supernatural power. Such experience is often ambiguous, and cannot stand on its own as an argument for the existence of God. But it is right to take account of it as one of the factors which cause people to return to the sources of their religious tradition, and which give them confidence in the truth of what they have received; and later chapters will return to it in more detail.

The search for meaning

Believing in the Church was an attempt to study the interaction of these three factors – revelation, reason and experience – in the life of the Church, and the influence of this perpetual conversation on the formulation of doctrine. To use this approach in trying to determine what is believed – or ought to be believed – about God, is a difficult and complex task, and one that can yield only a provisional result, since the conversation is still going on and will continue to do so far as long as the Church exists. If it were to die down, and positions once established came to be regarded as no longer open to question, the task of a Doctrine Commission would be very much easier, and many people would doubtless feel more secure in their faith. But such definition and stability could be purchased only at the cost of severely reduced vitality in the Church. The Church's life is nourished by the interplay between that which it has received from the past and that which it experiences and reflects on in the present. This interplay is like a conversation between, on the one hand, the relatively fixed historic revelation received and passed down by the Church, and, on the other, all the constantly changing observations and thoughts which need to be related to that revelation, together with the immense variety of religious experience.

It is important not to oversimplify. Revelation may be less of a fixed point than it appears; and one of the reasons why critical scholarship has so often seemed threatening to faith is that it seems to open up so many possible interpretations of the Church's foundation documents. Equally, both reason and religious experience display continuities with the past as well as innovations. Yet a degree of polarisation certainly exists and can be observed in most churches today. In the face of contemporary challenges, some believers instinctively seek to consolidate their base of revealed truths and to stay close to traditional formulations. Others take the contest further afield than has ever been ventured before, and allow contemporary thought-forms and experiences to impose such drastically new interpretations on traditional formulations that their surprised fellow-Christians may feel justified in asking whether they still believe in God at all. This kind of tension is, in our view, a sign of vitality in the Church. It is a sign that belief in God, far from being gradually excluded by the modern world, is still robust enough both to challenge and to respond to the thinking of that world, and thus to testify to the reality of the God whom Christians proclaim.

But not only Christians. If the construction of a doctrine of God were merely a process of inference from the data of Christian Scripture and tradition, it would be an exclusive, almost domestic, matter, to be discussed only by those who already have a Christian commitment. But if, as has been argued, both reason and experience have an essential part to play, the field becomes much wider. It is part of the history of the Church of England that, as a national Church, it has maintained some kind of contact (sometimes uneasy, sometimes fruitful) with a large number of people who, though they might well not call themselves Christians, nevertheless continue to 'read' the universe in a way that postulates the existence of God. They may find that the arguments for the Christian religion, or for any religion, fail to persuade them. They may have had no experience which they would recognise as 'religious'. But they persist in searching for some meaning in human life and history, in the natural world and in personal relationships, which cannot be provided by any purely human or scientific analysis.

This search for meaning takes many different forms, and no single phenomenon in our human environment can be relied on to satisfy it. Some find that beauty, such as that of a sunrise, or the song of a skylark or a butterfly's wing discloses to them the meaning of things. Some go further, and describe the experience as a kind of personal communication which took them by surprise: they did not initiate it, it was as if they were being addressed by someone or something outside themselves. Yet at other times similar phenomena can have the opposite effect. Nature is seen as 'red in tooth and claw' – and the more vividly since the arrival of new photographic techniques. With their help brilliant TV programmes bring home to us aspects of nature we usually prefer to ignore: the way one species feeds on another, or the insignificance of the individual creature in the struggle for survival – the kind of thing which (as Charles Gore said of a visit to the zoo) should 'make one an atheist in twenty minutes'. But still the search for meaning goes on, and will not easily be either repelled or satisfied.

It is true that in the West today there is an unprecedented number of people who seem to be willing, consciously or unconsciously, to embrace a materialist view of the world. They gratefully enjoy the advantages offered by technology, and the relative security provided by insurance schemes. They accept the palliatives, tranquillisers and diversions offered by modern society to help them in times of adversity, and regard any search for meaning beyond this as irrelevant and illusory. For many, especially perhaps if for the first time they are experiencing comparative prosperity and freedom from imposed authority, this appears to be a satisfying option; and those who try to awaken in them the life of the spirit find themselves daunted and mystified by the apparent absence of any sense of need or questioning. Personal calamities can of course profoundly affect this sense of satisfaction, and reveal an inner vulnerability and a desperate need for less materialist values. But it would be wrong to deny that a marked indifference to humanity's historic search for meaning has become characteristic of industrially developed societies in many parts of the world.

Yet there remain at least as many people who will not or cannot rid themselves of the thirst for meaning. Experiencing an overwhelming sense of dislocation in the world in which they live, they seek to cope with this in various ways. Some look back to the recent, or even distant, past, and hold on to the meaning and values they remember – or imagine – as obtaining then. Others become passionately concerned with particular issues and causes that give them a reason for living which is greater than themselves. Others adopt alternative life-styles, private or communal, deliberately isolated from the utilitarian and materialist principles which seem to them to govern social and public affairs. Others again may become persuaded that their thirst for meaning can never be satisfied, and be oppressed by that desolating sense of futility to which so much modern art bears eloquent witness.

This refusal to be reconciled to meaninglessness is both widespread and pervasive. At the popular level, sociological surveys of 'implicit' or 'residual' religion reveal the tenacity with which traditional ways of 'reading' the world are held. Among intellectuals, literature and drama continue to express the condition beautifully expressed in Salman Rushdie's novel *Midnight's Children*, where it is said of a Muslim doctor that 'he was knocked forever into that middle place, unable to worship a God in whose existence he could not wholly disbelieve'. It is tempting to use such a prevalent phenomenon as an argument, even if a negative one, for the reality of the God whose 'death' is mourned so inconsolably. If there were indeed no God, then this ought to be a passing phase consequent upon the breakdown of a dominant religious culture, a temporary nostalgia destined to be grown out of. Yet in fact, even in Marxist and 'post-Christian' cultures, it seems to be intensifying rather than declining. At the very least, this thirst for meaning is a factor which must be taken account of in any serious presentation of a doctrine of God. The evidence points to there being still many people whose sense of need is exactly that of St Augustine: 'our heart is restless till it rests in thee'.

The impact of other faiths

In England today, more often than ever before, Christians find that they have neighbours who pray and worship in ways and in language not unlike their own, but who profess a different religion and whose doctrine of God is very different. Again, it is important not to claim too much for the existence of these adherents of other faiths as evidence in the battle against unbelief. Adding to the number of those who profess belief does not alter the balance of the argument about God. It is logically possible that all are equally deluded in thinking that alleged experience or inherited religious teachings and practices point to the existence of a Reality outside ourselves. But it is certainly right to think of them as allies, in the sense that they are engaged on the same enterprise. They too are attempting to 'read' the universe, and to evaluate their own experience, in the light of an inherited revelation. We believe that the Christian revelation is true in many respects in which theirs is false. But there is also much in Christian and other traditions which overlaps – enough to suggest that all are in touch in some degree with a single reality which, in these different idioms, is acknowledged and worshipped as God. They can become part of the resources of reason and experience which help to make explicit the doctrine of God implied in our own Scripture and tradition; and this should lead us to show openness and reverence towards the beliefs and practices of others. We may conclude (as is the case in much missionary thinking today) that the appropriate Christian stance towards them is to listen, and to engage in dialogue on equal terms. Such an attitude need not imply indifference to the question of the truth and the uniqueness of the Christian revelation, but it can greatly widen our view of the resources available to interpret and explore that revelation, and of the human potential which that revelation may be able to release.

Contemporary challenges and constraints

Many factors in the world today are pressing Christians to speak in new ways about God. Every theology involves a decision about priorities. The historic creeds sum up the mind of the Church on what it seemed most important to say about God at the time; and these priorities, focused in creation, salvation and judgement, remained unquestioned until the end of the Middle Ages, and have continued to provide a fixed point of reference for Christian belief to the present day. The Reformation introduced new concerns: the necessity of personal repentance, the supremacy of grace, and justification by faith alone. These became matters of supreme importance, and were duly incorporated in confessional formulations of belief which were used in addition to the creeds. In modern times yet other priorities have emerged. The threat of a totalitarian regime in Germany was answered by a new emphasis on the autonomous authority of the Christian revelation, given classic expression in the Barmen Declaration of 1934; and the flagrant economic and social injustices of the modern world have now evoked a doctrine of God's 'preferential option for the poor'.

Meanwhile yet other historical developments are calling into question ways of speaking about God which have been taken for granted for centuries. Was it a mandominated culture which led to neglect of those feminine aspects of God which are alluded to in the Bible itself? Are traditional Christian approaches to suffering and evil adequate in the face of the horrors of the holocaust and the threat of nuclear annihilation?

None of this means, of course, that the Church is free to formulate its doctrine of God in any way that meets the exigent demands of the modern world. Christians are concerned ultimately not with a doctrine of God but with God himself, who has made himself known in the unique revelation of his Son, and continues to be present in a great variety of ways to those who pray and worship and who seek to serve and understand him. We are concerned, that is to say, with an ultimate Reality which we believe to exist, and to which we claim to have privileged access through the Scriptures and tradition preserved for us by the Church. But in seeking to go beyond the mere statement that 'We believe in God', and to be more precise about what kind of a God he is, we join a conversation which has been in progress since the beginning of the Christian religion, and which in various forms must be conducted within any 'revealed religion' if that religion is to remain alive.

As was argued in *Believing in the Church*, it cannot be the task of a Doctrine Commission to capture this process in a still shot, and to say 'This you may (or must) believe.' The Commission's work is part of the process itself, and its claim on the attention of church members is not that it has been given special authority to define doctrine, but rather that it has been asked to report and comment on the present state of our Church's wrestling with the tradition we have received, and to do so in the light of recent developments in theology and of the insights and challenges offered by the world today. The Commission can try to indicate legitimate areas of debate and uncertainty; but it can also use such authority as it possesses to support all those whose life, worship and testimony affirm that the fundamental doctrines which the Church has received from the past can be confidently believed and proclaimed today. It is for these reasons that a substantial part of this report has deliberately been devoted to matters which might seem to have more to do with the contribution of religious experience than of speculative thought.

This is not to say that religious phenomena should always be judged positively. Religious zeal can become fanaticism, and result, as so often today, in strife and bloodshed. Religious conviction can degenerate into bigotry, and breed intolerance and bitterness. A passion for religious truth can produce a jealous sectarianism which is yet another cause of division in today's tragically divided world. But the fact that the debate about God can degenerate into such tragic consequences does not mean that it must do so. Indeed, part of the purpose of this book is to help to resolve within the Church of England the kind of antagonisms which arise in any Church from powerful religious experiences, as well as to offer secure grounds for the faith of those who claim to have had little or no such experience at all. Nevertheless, experience is an important element in the constant dialogue which the Church maintains with the data it has inherited from Scripture and tradition. The continuance and vitality of this dialogue make it reasonable to say that those who engage in it must be arguing about something and not nothing. In the same way, the persistence of worship, prayer and lives of service and dedication in so many communities of faith, despite the powerful pressures and ideologies ranged against them, makes the debate about God still the most important question confronting humankind today.

Chapter 2
God and our ways of knowing

Challenges to believing in God

The opening chapter drew attention to the fact – since it is a fact – that
individuals and communities, in all parts of the world and in great
numbers, gather together for the worship of God, and for the renewing
of their lives according to his will. This is something that is happening
now, day by day, week by week, in all parts of the world, despite many
claims that belief in God is a fading shadow at the end of the ages of
faith. Such claims are manifestly false.

What certainly is true is that the activity of believing in God goes on in
the context of a world which is often, and in different ways, hostile to it.
An extreme example of one way is the explicit attack of Marxist regimes
on the practice of religion outside the boundaries of what they define as
'freedom of religion'. A very different form of attack is the way in which
believing in God is still called in question, as it always has been, by the
facts of pain, evil and suffering. 'How are atheists produced?', asked
Bernard Shaw. 'In probably nine cases out of ten, what happens is
something like this. A beloved wife or husband or child or sweetheart is
gnawed to death by cancer, stultified by epilepsy, struck dumb and
helpless by apoplexy, or strangled by croup or diphtheria; and the looker-
on, after praying vainly to God to refrain from such horrible and wanton
cruelty, indignantly repudiates faith in the divine monster, and becomes
not merely indifferent and sceptical, but fiercely and actively hostile to
religion.'

That hostility may then be very powerfully reinforced by the
accumulating history of wicked and evil deeds which have been done
specifically in the name of God, and often with an appeal for his blessing
on them. 'There is no social evil, no form of injustice, whether of the
feudal or the capitalist order, which has not been sanctified in some way
or another by religious sentiment and thereby rendered more impervious
to change.' Those words were written, not by a paid-up member of an
anti-God union, but by a Christian philosopher much concerned with the
social implications of Christianity, Reinhold Niebuhr.

As if all that were not enough to call in question the sanity of believing in
God, what of all the many doubts raised by the explorations and
achievements of human intelligence? How can traditional beliefs survive

when they are called in question in so many different ways? How, for example, is it possible to believe that God can intervene or answer prayer in a universe such as contemporary physics and cosmology imagine it to be? Where, in the process of evolution, does the animal become human in such a way that there can be attributed to it a soul? What is the soul, anyway? What now can we possibly imagine will survive the death and decay of this particular body? Does a belief in incarnation imply that God is a visitor, not from outer space, but from outside the time-space continuum of this particular universe altogether? If so, how can such a belief be intelligible?

It would be easy to add to such a list of questions. What we sometimes overlook is that none of them is new. They are asked with new content and therefore with a different cutting edge. But the fact remains that it was always hard to see how God could be a participant in the events culminating in the fifth century in the sack of Rome, the disaster which motivated Augustine to write *The City of God*; or again, what part he could play in the highly mechanistic universe of Newtonian physics. Then there are other questions: how do human beings, who change so much from birth to death, nevertheless retain their individual identity through time? How are body, brain and mind related? What is the nature of the self and the soul? All these are issues with which thinking people have been concerned for thousands of years in both the Eastern and the Western worlds. And the conclusions to which they have come have, of course, been very diverse.

Does this then mean that we are in such a muddle about everything that we cannot know much about anything? No, but it does mean that our knowledge is a great deal more limited and incomplete than we usually suppose as space shuttles take off and land, as kidneys are transplanted, or our teeth are attended to with much less pain than our great-grandparents had to endure. It also means that many of the arguments and issues are still open, not only about ourselves but also about God. Despite some strong claims to the contrary, it is not true that we now know for certain that God has no reality independent of ourselves, and that to talk of 'God' is consequently no more than a way of encouraging ourselves to live more responsibly, more hopefully, more lovingly in the world.

Of course, to some people, particularly within various movements in thought and philosophy, the issues have seemed settled. Nietzsche, for example, declared the death of God as a recent event in 1887. More recently, logical positivists claimed that any statement purporting to refer to a matter of fact was meaningless, unless it could meet the demands of what they termed the verifiability criterion (roughly, that it must be tied directly or indirectly to some observation). Clearly, theology does not produce God as an object to be observed; therefore, theology was claimed to be meaningless. For A. J. Ayer, a leading advocate of logical positivism, as in a different way for Nietzsche, the debate about the reality of God was over. The issue was closed.

The challenge of logical positivism to theology, and to the claim that it does make sense to speak of the God whom we trust and to whom we pray, was immensely powerful earlier this century. Those who lived through the period with some knowledge of what was going on will certainly remember the searching questions it raised for their own faith. But time and philosophy move on. In a remarkable moment during a recent TV series ('Men of Ideas') on some creators of contemporary philosophy, Bryan Magee asked A. J. Ayer: 'It [logical positivism] must have had real defects. What do you now, in retrospect, think the main ones were?' Ayer replied: 'Well, I suppose the most important of the defects was that nearly all of it was false.'

What do we conclude from that? Certainly not that, provided we wait long enough, all these irritants will subside and disappear, and that present ways of thinking about God, or of trying to understand the demands he makes on our life and commitment, can go happily on, much as they did before. Many ways of imagining or describing or thinking about what we hold to be true, either of God or of the universe, will sooner or later turn out to be incomplete and in some respects wrong. Earth's proud empires pass away; so do its cosmologies, philosophies, anthropologies, psychologies, theologies, technologies and all the rest. But in all or most of these there can be irreversible gains, genuine and enduring achievements. Not everything is swept away. Logical positivism, in its classical form, may have been 'mostly false', but no philosopher can any longer write philosophy as he might have attempted to do before – without, that is, an enhanced sensitivity to the constraints and possibilities of language. There are irreversible gains in technology. One hundred and fifty years ago we were travelling by stage-coach, now by train, bus, bike or car; but we do not have to reinvent the wheel each time. This is not to imply that all such gains are to be equated uncritically with 'progress' in the sense of human betterment. It is simply to observe that, despite the incompleteness of human knowledge, we say and do many things with a confidence accumulated through time. And that is true also of what we say and do in relation to God.

Although our knowledge, therefore, is necessarily incomplete and in general open to correction, a great many judgements and actions are reasonably and reliably based. That is true, not just of philosophy or physics or technology, but also of theology – of what we say as a consequence of believing in God. We are entitled – and often on reflection required – to make some judgements, and to do so with confidence: that God first loved us before we loved him; that nothing can separate us from the love of God in Christ Jesus our Lord.

Such judgements do not arrive from nowhere: they arrive in the context of history and community; they arrive also, in the religious case, in the form of revelation, in words and actions and events which are revelatory of God, and not a matter merely of human invention. Consequently, those who live later in time do not have to rediscover or reinvent these things for themselves, any more than we have to rediscover the wheel.

No one can live without trusting (however critically) the communities that surround and precede them; and that remains true, no matter how often that trust is betrayed. The indispensable importance of believing, and of doing so not in detachment but in community, was explored in the report *Believing in the Church*. What is being explored in this chapter is a strange and curious paradox. Irreversible gains and highly reliable judgements are made and recognised, as much in theology or Christian living as in philosophy, technology, history, and so on. Yet they are made by those who are, to say the least, fallible, and who are limited by their time and circumstances. How can it make sense to claim that we do make reliable and trustworthy judgements, when so much of what we say or believe may be (as Ayer said of logical positivism) nearly all false?

The reliability of knowledge

It may help to pursue a little further the example of science, not least because so many people assume that it is in the sciences that knowledge is reasonably complete and certain. Yet in fact science is a prime example of a field in which genuine, irreversible gains in human understanding are combined with accounts of reality which are unquestionably incomplete, provisional, approximate and open to correction. What is more, this is not a situation which can be overcome simply by correcting our ignorance. We must now accept that in the very nature of things it will always be like that.

This is a very new situation. Only about a hundred years ago it seemed that a complete description of the universe and its workings could be given in terms of Newtonian laws and principles. The universe was regarded as a vast machine of such regularity that, if the state and position of all its components at any given moment could be known, its whole future could be predicted. We now realise that this is impossible not just in practice, but in principle. At the quantum level (describing and explaining physical phenomena below the dimensions of atoms) it is impossible, from however complete a description of the universe, fully to predict the behaviour of all its parts. We 'disturb the universe' when we observe it at this level. In making a precise measurement of momentum it becomes impossible to make the related observation of position to the same degree of precision, and vice versa. A consequence of what is in fact known as 'the uncertainty principle' (and the name itself makes the point) is that we live in a universe such that our view of it is affected by the procedures through which we attempt to observe or measure it. Knowledge at this level can never be complete.

Some philosophers of science and sociologists of knowledge have pressed the point even further. They have argued that whatever the universe may ultimately be like in itself, we can know it only through our theories, language, models and equations. None of these is able to reproduce the whole of what there really is, out there, waiting, as it were, to be described. We can only construct through our pictures or theories (whether of common sense or of science) how it seems to us. Half a century ago the physicist and cosmologist Arthur Eddington began his Gifford lectures on *The Nature of the Physical World* by asking: Is this table a comparatively permanent, coloured and substantial object, or is it a swarm of atoms which is nearly all empty space? It is, of course, both – and more than both – depending on the human context in which we encounter what we call a table, and our purposes in using or examining it. If we are sitting at it to write a letter or eat a meal, or appreciating the style of Chippendale furniture, our descriptions of the table will be quite different – but no less valid – than those we would construct in a laboratory while studying the micro-structure of mahogany or the behaviour of carbon isotopes. At the same time, the micro-structural description, arrived at by the testing of a model (see pp. 25–6 below), must explain the common sense appearance and properties of the table.

There may, therefore, be an indefinite number of accounts of a given reality, all of which are equally 'true' on their own terms. But it does not follow that any account of that reality will be as true as any other. There is some limit set over our language and our ways of imagining or thinking about the universe – a limit which is not of our own construction, but which arises from persistence and regularity in the behaviours or events which we observe (and that remains true, even when we affect the events or behaviours by our own involvement in them). That is why the worlds we live in are so reliable: you can reliably expect to fall to the ground if you step off the roof of a house; you can reliably expect to produce carbolic acid if you fuse sodium benzenesulfonate with sodium hydroxide; you can reliably expect the sun to rise tomorrow (note the conventional and strictly corrigible language), although logically you cannot be certain of it.

It follows that reliability, to be worth having, does not have to reach a degree of absolute certainty. Very different degrees and kinds of reliability are attained (and are found to be reliable) in an immense variety of different enterprises. They emerge in such things as science, history, common sense, sociology, the administration of justice, marriage, economics, orienteering, doing the pools; whereas in some enterprises (e.g. the popular, and perhaps all, forms of astrology) there is no reliability at all. Where the sciences are concerned, the constant probing and testing of reliability, generation by generation, makes them what the American psychologist, Donald Campbell, has called 'well-winnowed traditions'. To winnow is to sift the grain from the chaff; and it is by this process of sifting and testing that the sciences become well-winnowed traditions of great reliability, while still remaining provisional, corrigible and incomplete. They can never be known to give a final account of 'how the universe really is'. That may always lie beyond us. But they can give accounts which are highly reliable for particular purposes, and they can eliminate some other accounts as failing in coherence or correspondence or reference or reliability or usefulness or validity – or whatever else may be involved in truth.

That scientific knowledge is so profoundly corrigible runs counter to the popular assumption that it is the only valid way of knowing anything. The corrigibility of science can lead (and in fact has led) to massive corrections of its own past or present: the sequence from Newton's absolutes of space and time to Einstein and relativity, to Bohr and quantum mechanics, is an instructive example of this process. It also illustrates the vital point that Newton did not suddenly become 'wrong' overnight. The older theory remains valid enough (in the kind of time and space in which human beings live) for it to be highly reliable for many practical purposes. The operational success of satellites and space probes is a witness to the enduring validity of Newton's laws, even though in other ways his conception of the physical universe has long been superseded by the insights of quantum mechanics, which will no doubt themselves be eventually superseded in part by new understandings.

Nevertheless, some pictures, proposals and imaginings about the universe have been discarded completely, although for generations they seemed secure and necessary. Spissitude, phlogiston, caloric and aether were all in their time believed to have real existence. They were thought necessary, in order to explain processes such as combustion and the propagation of light. Yet all of them have had to be rejected as non-existent: the unfamiliarity of these terms today shows how completely they have been abandoned. The provisionality and incompleteness of scientific accounts might seem to imply that we can never be sure that anything is either true or false. But to recognise incompleteness does not mean that all things become possible. Some theories, like that of a flat earth, have become simply wrong. We cannot be completely right, but we can be completely wrong. Thus we live, constructively, at the end of well-winnowed and highly reliable traditions, incorporating the wisdom of the past, while at the same time transcending them. As John of Salisbury reported: 'Bernard of Chartres used to say that we, like dwarfs on the shoulders of giants, can see more and farther, not because we are keener and taller, but because of the greatness by which we are carried and exalted.'

Theology and the imagining of God

Science, then, for all its apparently massive assurance and reliability, is nevertheless corrigible and incomplete. Is theology in a similar case? Of course one cannot easily argue from one to the other. God is not an object like a universe; still less is he an object in a universe, to be explored and investigated by apparatus and experiments. Yet it is only through the mediation of our concepts that we can have any apprehension of God. This does not mean that God has no reality apart from our concepts, and that he depends for his existence or his nature on our having opinions concerning him or concepts of him. For the believer God is real, and it is his reality which sets limits to the range of language we can use about him – just as for the scientist the universe is real, and its reality is constantly testing and calling into question the concepts we use to describe it. But all concepts, pictures and imaginings about God, as about anything else, are necessarily incomplete, provisional, approximate and corrigible.

Equally, however, there is no need to conclude from this that theology has nothing to say at all. Theology inherits the long and well-winnowed experience of women and men that there is One who makes a demand upon them which is more like the demand of a person than of an impersonal object, someone to whom they respond in awe, worship, love, prayer, contemplation, adoration, and by acting in the world in ways that have that Someone as their deepest and most abiding resource. Because that demand is an objective reality, it issues in revelation, particularly in the sense that, through the effect of the divine demand on others, God speaks to us. This divine Word is mediated through the circumstances, concepts, lives and actions of God's own creation, and therefore requires interpretation. It is nevertheless identifiable as an objective divine demand upon us, not an invention of our own; and in its relation to particular circumstances and centuries it can properly be spoken of as final. It cannot be remodelled, over and over again, though its implications can certainly be made manifest in as many lives as take it seriously. Revelation enables us to speak reliably and with confidence of God, because he first 'has spoken in times past to our fathers by the prophets, and in these latter days has spoken to us by a Son'.

Yet even here – and perhaps most of all here, in relation to revelation and Scripture – we need to remember that no language, not even the language of Scripture, can supply a complete, final and exhaustive description of what God is, in his own nature. That is why all accounts of God, in all religions, end up, sooner or later, saying of God, 'not this, not this': the *via negativa* of Christianity; the *En Sof* of Judaism; the *bila kaif* of Islam; the *ik onkar* of Sikhism; the *neti, neti* of Hinduism.

In this limited sense, there is a resemblance between our response to the universe and our response to God. What we take to be the universe makes demands upon us in particular and consistent ways, to which we can respond, if we choose to, in appropriate ways. What we take to be God makes its demands upon us likewise in particular and consistent ways, to which again we can respond, if we wish to, in the ways appropriate. 'We love because he loved us first': how we discern that reality, and what we do about it, is what much of this Report is about.

So Christian languages and pictures and imaginings of God have emerged as a consequence not only of revelation, but also of the histories of innumerable individuals and social groups, in which those expressions of belief have been tested, shared, corrected, extended and enhanced. They remain, and always will remain, provisional, corrigible, incomplete and approximate. But they may also be highly reliable. Like scientific traditions, they too have been well winnowed through time, by women and men who have lived with God as one in whom they have put their trust; and they have not been confounded.

If all pictures and imaginings, even of something as relatively obvious as the observable universe, are necessarily incomplete and corrigible, there is no reason to be upset or alarmed if the same is true in theology. Since God, to be God, must be beyond complete description or precise definition, any representation of God by theology which appeared to be complete and accurate would inevitably be an idol and not God. What theologians offer are much more like scientific 'models' than literal descriptions.

Scientists work with 'models' of what they believe to be real, in order to help their understanding and exploration. But the term 'model' is not used in science in its everyday sense. In ordinary usage a model is a visible reproduction of some real object on a different scale: either smaller, like a toy train or an architect's model of a building, or larger, like the complex models of molecules in a chemistry laboratory. Such models are representations either of what can be observed or of what might be observed, given the technical capacity to do so.

Scientific 'models', however, are not visual representations – not even diagrammatic ones, like a map of the London Underground. They are procedures for enabling us to think about the unobservable. In cosmology, for example, we can imagine a form for the whole cosmos, provide it with a mathematical description, and then see how it might evolve. In theoretical science models are used to investigate hitherto unknown realities not by creating a possible representation of their form, as an ordinary model or a map might do, but by formulating a pattern of their behaviour. Models in this sense are an indispensable tool of scientific thinking.

There are here suggestive clues to the nature of theological thinking. God too is a reality that cannot be observed: 'no one has seen God at any time'. In the classic theological dictum, however, 'God is known by his acts'. As we have stressed from the start in this Report, it is from human experience that theology begins. It is through the created order, through signs or words, or through our relations to ourselves, our neighbours, and the circumstances of time and space in which we live that the presence of God is normally mediated. Theology, with its concepts and images, is not unlike science with its models, in that theology too seeks to explore the unknown and unobservable not by representations but by formulations of the divine behaviour which can then be constantly checked against experience. These theological models, whether boldly pictorial or philosophically abstract, are creative precisely because they are not literal descriptions. They are tools to enable us to think and imagine, and so to advance in our approach to truth. There is a pregnant parallel in something Clerk Maxwell once wrote about science: 'Scientific truth should be presented in different forms, and should be regarded as equally scientific whether it appears in the robust form and vivid colouring of a physical illustration, or in the tenuity and paleness of a symbolic expression.'

Faith and certainty

All this may seem remote from believing in God. But there are five important implications in what has been argued so far. First, all these questions (and all the other ones set down at the beginning of this chapter) remain vital and worth grappling with, only because that to which we give the name of 'God' makes its approach of love towards us. There is rarely any experience of God which is not at the same time experience of something else; and much of this report is about how we discern the points at which the presence of God is unmistakable. What has been emphasised in this chapter is that Christian communities in the modern world are the end-term (so far) of long and well-winnowed traditions. In ways described in our earlier report, *Believing in the Church*, the traditions protect, and make available to new generations, those points of discernment and connection with God that already anticipate, here and now, what in God's mercy will be our final condition.

Secondly, we have also tried to make clear that it is impossible to give any complete, final and exhaustive account of God, but rather that all accounts must be approximate and incomplete, even while, at the same time, being established as reliable through the winnowing process. This apparent paradox means that all theological pictures, propositions and imaginings carry with them the possibility of being found to be defective or even wrong. We should not be surprised or alarmed that this is so. Some of the pictures of God that have been imagined in the past may come to be discarded, even though, like the scientific pictures of caloric and the aether, they have long seemed to be realistic and have served many generations faithfully as ways of inter-acting with God. We no longer believe, for example, that God is correctly described as a being seated on a celestial throne who regularly consigns large numbers of human beings to a place of torment somewhere below the earth, any more than we believe that creation is correctly described as an event which began at 6 o'clock in the evening of 22 October in the year 4004 BC and took 144 hours to complete.

The ways in which particular scientific models or religious images are displaced and falsified are by no means simple in either case. It is certainly far beyond the scope of this report to explore how it happens. But what is true in both cases is that where a model is displaced and agreed to be wrong, it is still possible and necessary to ask, wrong about what? What is it that has set a limit on our language and made us realise that we cannot any longer speak in a particular way? The collapse of a particular picture of God does not mean that 'God has died' – indeed, exactly the reverse. It is precisely because we can know reliably (in the ways already alluded to and discussed much further in other parts of this report) that God is indeed making his continuing demand upon us, that we realise that some pictures *must* collapse: they are no longer adequate either to present experience or to the implications of the long and continuing traditions which represent the sifting of our knowledge of God and of his dealings with ourselves.

But, thirdly, it is important to remember the advice of Clerk Maxwell and to be generous in our use of images and pictures and symbols (within the constraints of the traditions which have enabled us to speak at all). We should not hesitate to use deeply traditional images in hymns, poetry, liturgy and art, as well as evolving new ones. But at the same time we do not suppose that the sign is identical with what it signifies. Any one of those images is limitless in what it can bring us to be and to understand and to do, as we live with it as an expression of God's relation to us, and of ours to him. Such pictures reinforce and supplement each other, and none can capture the whole reality of God.

This leads to a fourth implication. The fact that those who lived in the past may have held to certain pictures or imaginations which we now know to be defective or even wrong does not mean that they were therefore wholly wrong about everything, nor that they have nothing of value, or of judgement on us, to offer. Newton was not wholly discarded by Einstein. Indeed, Einstein addressed a famous letter to Newton (in his *Autobiographical Notes*) in which, having pointed out why Newton's physics would no longer work for all phenomena, he suddenly pulled himself up and wrote:

> Enough of this. Newton, forgive me. You found the only way that, in your day, was at all possible for a man of the highest powers of intellect and creativity. The concepts that you created still dominate the way we think in physics, although we now know that they must be replaced by others farther removed from the sphere of immediate experience if we want to try for a more profound understanding of the way things are interrelated.

Christians too have their own comparable conversation with the past. We live in the Body of Christ and therefore in the communion of saints. We too can recognise that others have left a mark upon us by the prayers they have prayed, by the love they have expressed in life, by the failures for which they have needed forgiveness and have found it. This is to recognise a truth and an experience which we can trust, and on which we are entitled to rely – not uncritically, not as though it foreclosed every argument and solved every problem, but as a great foundation on which to live now for our time and in our day. It is an accumulation, to revert to the earlier language, of irreversible gains.

Finally, it is an implication of all that has been argued here that we should learn to live with the approximate, incomplete and corrigible nature of our languages, not as a defect, but as an asset. It means that where we make judgements (as we must, since traditions of human wisdoms are winnowed, and we have our part to play in that winnowing) we must make them with immense sensitivity, extending even further Chesterton's definition of charity as a reverent agnosticism about the complexity of the human soul. It is also imperative (an imperative derived from the approximate nature of languages) that we do not speak or act towards others as though only our way of speaking, our way of imagining, is valid, to the exclusion of any other.

It follows that although there are judgements of truth and propriety to be made between and within churches (and the report *Believing in the Church* explored how and why these have to be made), we must nevertheless expect that there will be many different ways of living as Christians, both as individuals and as parts of the Church. But in this context, of the provisional and approximate nature of our languages (in which there is immense reliability but no absolute and complete account to the exclusion of all others), we can see that we need these differences to complement and reinforce each other – to realise, in fact, the Pauline picture of the body of Christ, which requires the difference of its members in order to be a body.

Where, then, is the unity? If the Church (as opposed to the churches) is to become fully itself, it will not do so by attempting to achieve a doctrinal definition to which all can assent, for some would always be unable to assent and would then risk being 'unchurched'. It can do so only by realising that our approximate languages (including those of doctrine) are approximate in relation to God, in whom, and in relation to whom, our unity already exists. If all our languages about God are incomplete, then we need each other, precisely in our diversity, to make those languages somewhat less incomplete – or to put it more positively, to enrich and strengthen the ways in which we give glory to God and service to our fellow human beings. That we then have far to go in making practical our connection with each other is obvious. But the ecumenical quest is clearly helped, not hindered, when we recognise that, as a consequence of the incompleteness of our languages, there are bound to be different ways and different styles of being Christian; and that being a Christian in one style is not necessarily betraying, or letting down, Christians who live in another.

What does betray us all is when the impression is given or asserted that all human judgements are so provisional and uncertain that we cannot rely on anything. That is a perversion of the truth. It is certainly the case, to take an example, that historical judgements are incomplete and provisional; and it is therefore legitimate to raise questions about the historicity of the Bible, or of the accounts which are offered there of Jesus. But it is quite illegitimate to draw the conclusion that it offers no basis for historical knowledge at all. That Jesus lived in Galilee and was crucified under Pontius Pilate (to take only two obvious examples) are facts at least as well attested as any others in the history of the ancient world. Of course it is true that historical judgements are provisional, incomplete and corrigible; but it does not follow that they cannot attain a high degree of reliability. Like all historical documents, the New Testament writings may not provide absolute certainty on any particular point; but it would be absurd to suppose that the historical credentials of Christianity are for that reason unreliable.

The distinction is clear: 'God' is not a word or set of images which we use as part of our approximate attempts to describe something else – some way of experiencing the universe or the depth of our relations with each other. Rather, what God truly is, is what constrains and sets a limit on our approximate language about him – just as what is, in the case of the universe, constrains and sets a limit on our approximate (and quite different) language about that. In neither case can those languages be descriptively complete. But the life and experience of people, on which theology depends, make it clear that although in our present condition we see through a glass darkly, we do at least begin to see; and it establishes reliably the belief that what shall be in the end will not end, but will make complete what is here known only in part.

Chapter 3
God, language and personality

Thomas Traherne remarks of a saintly friend that 'he was as familiar with the ways of God in all ages as with his walk and table'. The existence of lives devoted to God cannot be denied, and seems sometimes to speak so powerfully that nothing further needs to be said. But, as already mentioned, there are ways of understanding the world and man's place in it which seem to call in question the assumptions which underlie that devotion. To understand what is implied by belief in God as Creator and Redeemer, and to live that belief effectively, means relating it as fully as possible to what human beings have been able to learn about the world and about themselves – or, since so many of these things are controversial, what they believe themselves to have learnt. Traherne's friend thought similarly for, as Traherne reports, he urged the mature Christian to study philosophy, which in the seventeenth century would have included science.

The attention given to science in the previous chapter is due, chiefly, to the impact science has had upon all aspects of modern life. It has affected the entire context of modern thought in such a way as to influence those who deliberately resist it as well as those who unreservedly welcome it. Once the influence has been recognised it is necessary to respond to it critically and creatively, otherwise there is a risk of being affected more by scientific myths than by scientific facts.

Misleading assumptions about language

The effects of science have been felt not least in the realm of language. It has become common to assume that there are only two ways of using language. One is a literal, fact-stating use, which alone 'conveys information' about the way things are. This is the language of science and of common sense (thought of as rudimentary science). The other is mood-expressing, attitude-evoking language which is the domain of metaphor and myth and is not designed to carry truth: it is the language of poetry and as such 'subjective', while the other, the language of science, is 'objective'. The assumption is now deeply embedded in our culture that what is scientifically testable is the sole criterion of what is real. Hence the claims of religion are often either rejected altogether as failing the scientific test, or regarded as imaginative constructions which can have value only so long as they do not pretend to truth. Atheists generally take the former view, sympathetic humanists the latter. There are, indeed, some theologians of a radical temper who accept the humanists' analysis and differ from them only in their assessment of the importance of religion, so understood. They are convinced that the attitude to life which, in their view, it is the function of Christian tradition to express is of unique significance and can best be preserved for future generations through the institution of the Church, if only it can be freed from the obsolete metaphysics of traditional theism.

By way of reaction to such tendencies, and subtly affected by them, is a strongly conservative movement which is, for the most part, resolutely anti-critical and prepared, if need be, to maintain the literal truth of the Bible against the claims of modern science. Rightly unwilling to relinquish the conviction that religion deals with matters of fact, and deeply influenced by popular scientific culture in its conception of what facts must be like, it tends to give doctrine a quasi-scientific status and to interpret the biblical writings, wherever possible, as conveying a straightforward record of historical events.

Associated with this dichotomy between factual and expressive language is another – that between public and private domains. It is tempting, in the intellectual climate just described, to draw a distinction between an area of public truth, determined by objective methods of a broadly scientific kind, and a sphere of private preference, where the only sort of truth that obtains is what is 'true for me' or 'true for you'. Religion, it is widely felt, belongs to the latter realm. It is an essentially private matter to do with individuals and their personal feelings. This notion reinforces the conviction many people have that religion has no part to play in the corporate life of a society. Thus the age-old debate about the proper relationship between the sacred and the secular, which has nothing essentially to do with this distinction, is, in contemporary discussion, often infected by it.

The language of science

Such is the distorting effect of this assumption about the use of language upon the general understanding of religious truth that it is vital to examine its credentials. Do scientists deal in bare descriptive statements? Have poets no concern with truth? It has already been shown (chapter 2) that the nature of scientific knowledge is very much more complex than such simple contrasts would suggest. People who are alarmed at what they see as the iconoclastic tendencies of some contemporary theologians might be surprised at some recent discussions among philosophers and sociologists of science. There are, for example, those who maintain that the theories, models and equations of scientists are nothing but 'social constructions of reality', and give us no access to what that reality is like independently of ourselves. Far from providing the paradigm case of publicly accessible objective knowledge, science is regarded by these thinkers as a cultural creation of vast imaginative power which reflects human concerns rather than the structure of the universe.

Such views, like their theological counterparts, may be exaggerated. But they do serve to correct the naive assumption that science provides us with an unproblematically factual description of the universe which, once achieved, remains for ever beyond question. It is now widely accepted that that naive view requires correction in two important ways. One is that, rather than just observing what is there, scientists devise provisional models of the reality they are trying to understand, and test these models by drawing out their implications and discovering by experiment in what respects they hold and in what respects they do not. The capacity to find appropriate models is an essential element in the make-up of creative scientists, and has much in common with other uses of the imagination. It has in the past been one of the failures of the educational system that the teaching of science has rarely communicated any appreciation of the scientist's creative and exploratory role, and has too often been content to hand on the findings of science as so much cut and dried information.

The other way in which the naive view of science has to be modified is in the recognition that, as the models employed in a particular science are repeatedly qualified and reshaped, the resulting body of theory becomes an increasingly reliable set of 'representations' of reality. Thus, as was argued in the last chapter, the sciences become 'well-winnowed' traditions of great reliability, although they always remain provisional, corrigible and incomplete.

The language of poetry

If the dichotomy between the objective fact-stating and the subjective mood-expressing uses of language is misleading about science, it is equally misleading about poetry. Poetry does, of course, express emotion, but to suggest that this is all it does is to suppose that emotions are bare feelings, directed upon the environment quite independently of one's beliefs about it. There are, doubtless, moods which colour for the time being one's perception of the world, so that the poet who describes the world as seen in this mood is felt to be conveying the mood rather than some truth about the world as it 'really is'.

Out, out, brief candle!
Life's but a walking shadow, a poor player,
That struts and frets his hour upon the stage,
And then is heard no more; it is a tale
Told by an idiot . . .

But even in such a case Macbeth, in his despair, gives expression to a vision of life which challenges us as to its truth: is this how things really are? It would be a shallow interpretation of Macbeth's utterance to regard it simply as a memorable expression of a certain mood that a man might have, that was understandable in the circumstances, etc. The mood itself is similar in

As flies to wanton boys, are we to the gods;
They kill us for their sport

but a different, more explicitly pessimistic philosophy is conveyed, recognisably the same as that expressed in Thomas Hardy's final word on Tess of the d'Urbervilles:

The President of the Immortals (in Aeschylean phrase) had ended his sport with Tess.

It is not to be supposed that poets always claim truth, or at any rate ultimate truth, for what they write, especially when it is put into the mouth of a dramatic character. The dramatist presents a vision of the world as it seems to a given character in a given situation. To that extent he himself is, as it were, at two removes from reality. Yet the drama would not move us if the characters did not engage with the common world and try to make sense of it as we do. So through them he offers us something which might be true, which is, so to speak, a candidate for truth; and as such engages our emotions and solicits our commitment. We can scarcely be indifferent to it. Sometimes there is no doubt that the poet in his own person shares the commitment to which he gives expression, sometimes there may be reason to think he does not. To the literary critic in either case it may not matter. But the world could be as the poet represents it, and if it were, certain feelings would be appropriate, certain decisions justified. The relationship between the poet as uncommitted and the poet as committed (or anyone else who uses the poet's words to express his own commitment) is something like that between a mathematician and a physicist in relation to mathematical models. The mathematician devises models which could, in principle, apply to some physical reality, without himself trying to decide whether they do or not. The physicist is primarily concerned with just this question.

Hence, when Shakespeare defines the character of love, it is recognisably the Christian *agape* that he has in mind:

> . . . Love is not love
> Which alters when it alteration finds,
> Or bends with the remover to remove:
> O, no! it is an ever-fixed mark,
> That looks on tempests and is never shaken;
> It is the star to every wandering bark,
> Whose worth's unknown, although his height be taken.
> Love's not Time's fool . . .

The reader is invited, no doubt, to share the poet's admiration of the quality he sets forth, but the purpose of his cumulation of images is to make precise what it is that we are to admire: a love that offers us safety in a storm, serenely guides us, is not at the mercy of Time. The strength of the poet's own commitment is evinced by the final couplet:

> If this be error, and upon me prov'd,
> I never writ, nor no man ever lov'd.

It is upon the truth of his utterances that he stakes himself.

The notion that the poet, by contrast with the scientist, is concerned only to express emotion, in such a way that no question of truth arises, will not stand examination. Unlike the scientist he is not, as a rule, concerned to generalise and analyse, but rather to describe what is individual and unique, whether it be an abstract idea or a particular thing. In either case the use of comparisons both extends the scope of possible understanding and brings what is described into clearer focus. The reader's imagination is led on to analogies not yet thought of, while at the same time being constrained by the variety of the images to conceive of the subject with greater precision, in a way that is consistent with them all. Hence Austin Farrer writes:

> The poet is a man who has a gift for grasping fresh and profound resemblances, and that is why he works with metaphor, and why his metaphors illuminate the nature of things. This gift can only work by inspiration. (*Reflective Faith*, p. 32)

The purpose of this discussion of scientific and poetic discourse has been to dispel a pervasive assumption which makes it impossible for some people today to entertain the thought of God at all except as an aspect of human subjectivity, and which encourages others, by an understandable reaction, to construe religious doctrines with unqualified literalness. Neither scientific nor poetic language conforms to the required stereotype. It seems, instead, to be a basic propensity of the human mind to extend its knowledge by the use of the imagination, endeavouring to form images or models of the way things might be, and then testing the hypothesis in the appropriate manner. The reason why metaphor plays the part it does in scientific discourse is precisely because it is the equivalent in language of thinking with models.

The language of devotion

The language of devotion is, in most respects, closer to the language of poetry than to the language of science. Indeed it often is poetical language put to a religious use. But, as already argued, this does not in the least imply that it makes no claim to truth, or that it cannot achieve precise statement, or that what it claims cannot be tested.

The overlap between devotion and poetry is most familiar to us in hymns, and it is through hymns that most people become familiar with the doctrines of the Church. When John Newton piles image upon image in

> Jesus, my Shepherd, Husband, Friend,
> My Prophet, Priest and King,
> My Lord, my Life, my Way, my End,
> Accept the praise I bring

he is employing metaphors well known to him from the Bible where, as George Caird remarks,

> The five metaphors in most common use to express God's relationship with his worshippers are King/subject, judge/litigant, husband/wife, father/child, master/servant. (*The Language and Imagery of the Bible*, p. 177)

The metaphors used are, in these instances, all anthropomorphic and it is obvious that there are dangers attaching to this. To many of these dangers the biblical writers were, as Caird points out, alert:

> God is not, like mankind, subject to vacillation and weakness (1 Sam. 15:29; Isa. 55:8; Hos. 11:9; Mal. 3:6). Human judges may be corruptible (1 Sam. 8:3), but it is axiomatic that the judge of all the earth shall do right (Gen. 18:25). Human parents may falter in love for their children, but God's love does not fail (Isa. 49:15). Israel's loyalty disperses like a morning mist (Hos. 6:4), but God's loyalty is everlasting (Ps. 100:5). (*Language and Imagery*, pp. 175–6)

To some extent the dangers are lessened by the use, as a counterweight, of impersonal metaphors which there is little or no temptation to take literally. God is a sun, a rock, a tower, a devouring fire. Not only do these qualify the personal metaphors, and reduce the risk of misreading them, but they are more effective in conveying God's eternity, independence and awfulness.

But even when allowance has been made for the extent to which the various metaphors modify one another, there remains the question how to know which features of all of them are to be disallowed – as some must be when one is speaking of God. When the poet says of a girl,

> O, my love's like a red, red rose
> That's newly sprung in June.
> O, my love's like the melodic
> That's sweetly played in tune

we know enough about girls from common observation to tell that the poet is not taking her to be some sort of plant. We know, similarly, that if a preacher refers to 'the hand of the Lord', or if a hand pointing down from heaven appears in a medieval carving, God is not being presented as actually having a hand. God is not, in any ordinary sense, embodied. The biblical writers, when they stressed the limitations of the metaphors they used of God, relied upon some knowledge of him which was not derived from these metaphors alone and which was able to some extent to control their use. This creates a problem which is sometimes presented as a dilemma: either it is possible to make straightforwardly literal statements about God or all language about him is symbolic. In the latter case we seem, as it were, to be trapped in a circle of images, from which there is no escape. Unable to observe God directly (as we can the girl), we have no means of knowing whether, as it were, our images catch his likeness. But the former alternative is equally impossible. If God is, as he must be, transcendent, how can one say things about him that are literally true, using language in just the same sense as it is used about human beings?

This, however, is not a genuine dilemma. When models are used in science (as mentioned in chapter 2), the appropriateness of the model as a source of information about the real world is demonstrated not by direct observation of the electron itself, the results of which are then compared with the model, but by working out of the implications of the model and testing them by experiment. Again, for it to be possible to use some words literally about God, it is not necessary that they should be used in just the same sense as when used about human beings. Personal language can be used about God without its carrying all the implications that such language has when used of ourselves.

People often fail to see this because they tend to regard as figurative any language which is not employed in precisely the same sense as it is when talking about the ordinary world of things and people. So not only is 'the hand of the Lord' treated as metaphorical, or 'The Lord is my shepherd', but also any talk of God as all-knowing, faithful or loving. All such language is then liable to be dismissed as 'mere metaphor'.

But when Charles Wesley writes of 'love divine all loves excelling' he is not using human love as a 'metaphor' for divine love, but stretching the use of 'love' in its human context to represent the perfect love of God, to which love as we know it is only an approximation. Hence Bishop Berkeley distinguished between 'metaphorical' and 'proper' analogy:

> By metaphorical analogy God is represented as having a finger or an eye, as angry or grieved: by proper analogy we must understand all those properties to belong to the deity which, in themselves, simply and as such denote perfection.

Thus, he says, 'It is a mistake to say we can never have any direct or proper notion of knowledge or wisdom as they are in the deity.' Knowledge and wisdom are, indeed, personal attributes, as are love, mercy, forgiveness, faithfulness. All of these are normally encountered in human beings, but all of them can also be conceived of as freed from the limitations of their expression in human lives. Perhaps also, in spite of what Berkeley says, divine anger and divine grief may also be so conceived. (This will be one of the questions discussed in chapter 9.)

The language of devotion and the language of metaphysics

In the light of this discussion it will be seen that the use of metaphors in thinking about God is controlled, not only by the interaction between the metaphors themselves, but also by theism as a metaphysical theory. There is here some analogy to the way in which a physicist may use the apparatus of theory to control his use of models. The metaphors or 'models' used in thinking about God operate within the overall structure of a rational theory that the universe was created by a God who, as William Temple used to put it, is 'at least personal', and whose purposes may be learned in some degree through his creation and through his revelation of himself.

Some people find the whole notion of theory unpalatable in relation to religion because it suggests to them an attitude totally remote from that of worship – as if it implied that the Creator could be known in some quasi-scientific and uncommitted way. The God of the philosophers, they claim with Pascal, has nothing to do with the God of Abraham, Isaac and Jacob. True devotion does not argue to God as personal, but assumes, by the very form of worship, that God is personal. Nor is the worshipper concerned to define God's attributes or to pay him 'metaphysical compliments'.

But, once again, it looks as if this is a case of posing false alternatives. It is true that a philosopher who seeks to develop a rational case for the existence of God is not, in the act of doing so, engaged in worship; but his case, if it is sound, points to a God who must transcend human understanding and is the proper object of worship. And the language of devotion itself often gives poetical expression to metaphysical concepts:

> O Lord, thou hast searched me out and known me: thou knowest my down-sitting and mine up-rising, thou understandest my thoughts long before . . .
> Whither shall I go then from thy Spirit: or whither shall I go then from thy presence?
> If I climb up into heaven, thou art there: if I go down to hell, thou art there also.
> If I take the wings of the morning: and remain in the uttermost parts of the sea;
> Even there also shall thy hand lead me: and thy right hand shall hold me. (Ps. 139.1, 6–9)

Here are many of the 'metaphysical' attributes of God, his transcendence and his omnipresence, his omniscience and his providence. Yet the psalmist is not composing a philosophical argument, but addressing a hymn of thanksgiving: 'I will give thanks unto thee, for I am fearfully and wonderfully made.'

This should not be surprising, for the psalmist is writing superb poetry, and it is, as we have seen, one of the properties of poetry to be able to give memorable expression to a vision of the world by describing through metaphors (and through stretching the ordinary use of language) what in its essential nature can never fully be grasped. It is not the function of the poet, as poet, to assert the truth of what is thus conveyed, nor is it the function of the devotional writer to argue that truth or to analyse it. But it does, nevertheless, need to be argued, and also to be analysed, if its coherence and truth is to be vindicated against its critics.

Poets can give poetical expression to a world-view without declaring their own position. In the same way, philosophers can analyse such a view, develop its implications and examine the arguments for and against it, without declaring theirs. But everyone, whether poet or philosopher or anything else, must choose (or live as if they have chosen) how they are to view the world. This universal human predicament provides the context in which the philosopher and the poet are able to pursue their callings. It is because everyone has come to terms in some way with the limitations of human existence that rival philosophical and religious traditions develop, and it is these traditions which provide the terrain for the intellectual and imaginative explorations of the philosopher and the poet.

So the philosopher who reasons to the existence of a creator who is 'at least personal' and the poet who celebrates the presence of God in creation, whatever their individual stances, depend upon a community in which this belief is lived. The characteristic elements in worship – praise, thanksgiving, intercession, sacrament – in their nature presuppose some kind of personal relationship with God (though the meaning of the word 'personal' is very evidently stretched beyond its everyday uses). If, however, God is rightly thought of as personal, there will be significant analogies between our relationship with God and one with our fellow human beings. Thus, our ordinary dealings with other people not only enable us to stay alive and to realise our own particular purposes, but are essential to our fulfilment as persons, indeed to our becoming persons at all. These purposes depend upon a degree of mutual love and trust; and this means being open and receptive to other people, their hopes and aspirations, intentions and purposes. It follows that awareness of God can no more be purely theoretical than can our awareness of people, but must involve seeking to know and respond to his will. There is need of a continuous devotional experiment, in which those who seek to do the will learn of the doctrine.

God and the nature of persons

That the religious life has this form of personal interaction is easily recognised, though it manifests itself very differently in different communities and, indeed, in different individuals at different periods of their lives. Traherne's joyful and triumphant celebration in childhood of the presence of God in creation came to him more rarely in later life, and to many others it does not come at all, though they seek to carry out the will of God obediently. But whether marked by experiences of ecstasy or of alienation, of enthusiastic response or of sober dedication, the pattern of such a life presupposes God as its focus. It is for this reason that for many people the most convincing witness to the reality of God is that of those in whose lives his grace is apparent.

But it does not follow that the theory of the matter is unimportant, any more than it is in the case of persons. It is true that the sheer existence of persons is something which it is impossible, while sane, to doubt, since the very language needed to frame such a doubt is, and could only be, the product of a community of persons. By contrast, it is possible to doubt the existence of God. But how we conceive of persons, what we take them to be, affects profoundly the way we are able to understand them and relate to them, and the same must be true of God. For instance, to think of other people exhaustively in terms drawn from our experience of computer-based 'artificial intelligence', is to do away with any sense of their mysteriousness, of creative possibilities which transcend our present horizons; and having left no room for these in our thinking, we render ourselves unable to elicit them or respond to them in practice. If persons are thought of merely as bundles of perceptions linked together by psychological laws, there can be no awareness of their continuous identity through time, of their shaping and being shaped by their experiences, of their role as moral agents responsible for what they have done yesterday and will do tomorrow. Mr Gradgrind in Dickens's *Hard Times* is a caricature, but a salutary one, of what such an attitude can mean in practice. When confronted with this kind of analysis of what it is to be a human being, we feel bound to protest that there is more to people than just this. But protest alone is not enough; it is necessary to argue the case.

The tendency to substitute protest for argument is itself an illustration of the dichotomy from which this chapter started. There is a strong tendency for each of the two sides in the dispute just mentioned to suppose that they need take no notice of what the other says about human personality. Those on the one side claim that the model of artificial intelligence explains the physical and mental phenomena so fully that it can be regarded as having scientific warrant. No doubt a lot more detail needs to be filled in, but that is only a matter of time. If others feel that this leaves only a rather attenuated notion of what it is to be a human being, that is simply evidence of the degree of superstition and ignorance that the traditional idea has carried with it. The depths that have allegedly been left out are depths of illusion merely. Those on the other side 'know' that there is more to people than this model allows and are not to be persuaded otherwise. Like Dr Johnson on a related topic they 'know our will is free and there's an end on't'.

The current debate about the nature of human personality illustrates a further feature of talk about God in personal terms. How we think of people affects and is affected by how we think of God. Only if human beings are themselves thought of as possessing a genuine mystery and

41

creativity can they be taken as images of the divine; and their being so taken helps us to think of them in this way. At first it may seem as if the attributes of God are simply read off from ordinary human understanding of kings, judges, husbands, fathers, and so forth. In the words of the old jest, 'God made man in his own image, and man returned the compliment'. But if the king or the judge is to be the clue to the majesty and justice of God, only the disinterested king and the impartial judge will serve that purpose. Moreover the divine king or judge is also the divine parent who has all human beings as his children, so that the human ruler or judge, who follows that pattern, may not consider only their own subjects or their own fellow countrymen. Similarly Hosea's vision of God's love for Israel as being like a husband's continuing love for an unfaithful wife illuminates both sides of the comparison. Within the whole framework of belief in God the use of personal imagery for God is not to be seen as just a matter of there happening to be resemblances at hand for the religious thinker to use. The resemblances are built by God into the human situation itself:

> What is man, that thou art mindful of him: and the son of man, that thou visitest him?
> Thou madest him lower than the angels: to crown him with glory and worship. (Ps. 8.3–8)

Some implications of belief in God

It follows that belief in God makes a difference to the way we think about everything else. Nothing of importance is wholly unaffected by it. Thus, men and women have a dignity which comes of their being made in the image of God, so that they cannot be regarded merely as elaborate machines; but neither has humankind the sort of sovereign independence and autonomy which would be needed to make human preferences the final arbiter of morality. Human beings are not free to choose what shall count as human goodness, for this depends upon the purposes of God in creation; nevertheless they are themselves in a genuine, though dependent, way creative and free to decide how they will develop their gifts. Living as rational creatures in a created universe, they have reason to believe that its structure will be in some way congruous with their intellectual powers and that, if they use these rightly, they will come to know it better. They will, therefore, be prepared to trust scientific enquiry as providing a genuine, if always limited, understanding of the cosmos as it is. Fearing idolatry, they will not be willing to accord to anything less than God the devotion owed to God alone, but they will also be aware that God's kingdom cannot be confined to a purely private sphere.

Hence, while not investing all their hopes in political programmes, they will seek to maintain and promote the conditions of a free and just society.

If belief in God has such implications as these, a civilisation which has been founded upon it, however incompletely, is bound to suffer severe strains to the extent that this belief is withdrawn. There is much in our situation to suggest that faith in God has, so to speak, been 'drying out' and that we are now experiencing some of the effects of shrinkage. It might be argued that a 'scientific world-view' implies that the only valid mode of reasoning is scientific reasoning, that a scientific account of the universe and of humankind exhausts all that can be known, and that language used in a purely analytical and descriptive manner can say all that can intelligibly be said. But would not such a position, if it were held, end up, after denaturing nature and dehumanising humanity, by destroying its own credentials? For there would be no room left for rationality as a guide to truth. The only means of escape then left is a desperate attempt to rescue humanness by retreating to the only place that science cannot reach, the inner recesses of the individual mind, where all is subjectivity. Here poetry and the other arts, and even religion itself, are constrained to take refuge and, as Iris Murdoch puts it, 'the agent, thin as a needle, appears in the quick flash of the choosing will'. There is no longer any sense of an overarching purpose which gives meaning and coherence to human existence.

There are still many people who would prefer to evade these fundamental issues. Suspicious of intellectual debate, they remain confident that a humane commonsense will continue to take care of moral and political values and of the conception of humanity upon which they have habitually been based, while explicit belief in God can be regarded as an optional extra, privately available. No doubt this unreflective maintenance of generally good habits has its proper place, but the present age is one in which such habits are increasingly hard to sustain in the absence of deliberate decision. Explicit challenges increasingly demand explicit choices.

The starting-point of our argument was the existence, as an acknowledged fact, of religious devotion in its many manifestations, individual and corporate. This led to a consideration of the way in which belief in God is expressed in language and given an intellectual structure; how it is related to our understanding of the world and of humankind, as derived from the sciences, the humanities and the arts; how it unifies the emotions and directs the wills of those who accept it, or have been influenced by it, whether they consciously accept it or not.

The question remains, is it true? And how are we to tell if it is true? It is reasonable to believe that something is true if it sorts better with our individual and corporate experience of life than do the alternatives to it; if to deny it would compel us to reject along with it too much of what we otherwise have reason to believe; if to do so would force us to repudiate our deepest intuitions when they have been critically considered; if it turns out that, when we try to live by it, we find our path illuminated, not completely, but enough to take us forward step by step; if our faith is reinforced by that of others, when we have exerted our imaginations to appropriate it.

Such a test is possible. But to make it we need more than just our own individual resources of thought and experience. As described in the preceding chapter, we depend upon developed traditions which nevertheless, if they are to remain alive, require that we respond to them openly, critically and creatively. The next section, therefore, turns to look at the Church's traditions in this matter by tracing the history of the Christian understanding of God.

Chapter 4
The God of the Bible

We referred at the outset to three factors in the search for a doctrine of God: revelation, reason and experience. It is time to return to the first of these – the truth that is revealed to us in Holy Scripture. Even if, as was said earlier, Scripture is not such that an agreed doctrine of God can be deduced from it, does it not provide the indispensable data on which reason can get to work and by which all subsequent experience of God must be assessed?

For reasons which were discussed at some length in *Believing in the Church*,[1] Scripture does occupy a uniquely authoritative position among the available sources of belief. But it can be misleading to talk as if this necessarily sets Scripture over against reason and experience. Reason can indeed get to work on Scripture, but is it not already at work in Scripture? Subsequent experience may be subject to the control of Scripture, but did not a wide range of experience contribute to its formation?

The origins of scripture

We may start from the most obvious point about Scripture: that (as its name implies) it is written. Moreover it is written for the most part in forms which are recognisably literary: poetry, narrative, letters and so forth. These forms seem to presuppose in each case an individual author; and it should therefore be possible to ask how these authors were enabled to write in such a way that their work continues to carry authority among believers. How did they get their information about and their insight into God's character and workings and their ability to communicate these to so many generations and in infinitely varied cultures? This is the question to which the Church has tried to respond with its doctrine of Inspiration. In *Believing in the Church*[2] some account was given of the difficulties involved in this enterprise. Explanations have ranged from direct divine dictation given to the writer to a general control exerted by divine providence over the events and circumstances leading up to the writing. It is probably true to say that none of the traditional answers proposed to the question of inspiration has proved entirely satisfactory; and one of the reasons for this may be that each of them has worked with the presupposition of an individual author responsible for each book of the Bible. The question has consequently tended to present itself in personal, even psychological, terms: what were the circumstances, and what was the mental state, in which it was possible for the writer to have such privileged access to divine truth?

It is true, of course, that certain books of the Bible are undoubtedly the work of individual authors, some of whom are known by name. Even if subsequent editors have introduced alterations or additions to the text soon after it was composed, there can be no doubt that most of the letters attributed to St Paul are the authentic work of the writer himself. In the Old Testament a book like Ecclesiastes bears the unmistakable stamp (apart, again, from certain additions) of the mind of an individual author. But, taking the Bible as a whole, these instances are the exception rather than the rule. It is not just that we do not happen to know for certain who wrote the book of Genesis or the histories of Samuel and the Kings or the Fourth Gospel; it is rather that the question itself does not seem altogether pertinent. Many books of the Bible seem deliberately anonymous. The consensus of mainstream scholarship has long since ceased to be that Moses was the single author of the first five books of the Bible or that all the Psalms were composed by King David; and from earliest times Christians have been in doubt about the identity of the writers of some, if not all, of the Gospels. Moreover there can be no doubt that in the case of the Gospels (as a number of Old Testament books) a period of 'oral tradition' must have preceded the actual moment of writing. Sayings of Jesus, and episodes of his life story, were preserved and communicated by word of mouth, just as local stories and traditions are still preserved in 'folk memory', though there was probably a greater capacity for accurate memory in the time of Jesus than is normally possessed by people today. Clearly the authority of many, if not most, biblical writings does not depend on the authority of any individual writer; and to discuss how the presumed writer came to write as he did may be to misconceive the nature of the writing itself.

One of the most significant contributions of modern critical scholarship has been to develop this simple observation and to reconstruct the processes by which this unique literature came into being. Behind all the scholarly discussions of sources, oral tradition and literary forms lies the recognition, confirmed again and again by study of the text, that these writings are the product, not simply of individual authors, but also of communities. Even the highly individual utterances of an Isaiah or a Jeremiah have come down to us in a form heavily worked over by a 'school' of prophetic writers. The legal and historical material of the Old Testament was shaped by centuries of community experience and reflection. A collection of liturgical poetry such as the Psalter is an anthology of poems (even if originally by individual authors) used and adapted by a people in their worship. The Gospels themselves are the end-product of a period of several decades, during which information about Jesus was recalled, shared and preserved by the growing Christian churches. It can never have been true to the nature of Scripture to regard it solely as the medium through which a succession of uniquely inspired writers has conveyed the truth about God to later generations, even though such writers, named or unnamed, must have played a crucial part. Scripture is also, and perhaps chiefly, the distillation of those perceptions of the reality of God which came to a worshipping community under the impact of particular historical events, of the genius of legislators, prophets and thinkers, and finally of the encounter with Jesus himself. This in turn tells us something of immense importance about God: that God is known, primarily and characteristically, in the shared worship, experience and reflection of men and women who meet in his name and serve him in the world. What we have observed in the human apprehension of God in our own time is also reflected in Scripture itself, and is authenticated by it.

The Bible as narrative

There is another general feature which is characteristic of a great deal of the Bible and which may suggest something quite specific about God. This feature often seems to present something of a problem. If the Bible is read in order to discover what God is like, it is reasonable to look for statements describing his nature and attributes. But in fact the characteristic way in which the Bible communicates its ideas is not by doctrinal statements, nor by creeds or catechisms or summaries of the faith, but by narratives or stories. More than half of both Testaments consists of lengthy accounts of 'what happened', either in the ancient history of Israel or in the life of Jesus and of the early church. Anyone who attends a service where there are readings from the Bible is practically certain to hear some part of this narrative read; and such a person may well wonder therefore how Christians move from the Bible, with its great emphasis on 'telling the story', to doctrine, in the sense of an ordered body of beliefs about God and the world.

It is true that in many of these stories God himself is said to be acting or speaking; and conclusions can therefore be drawn from them about the nature and purposes of God. But in others the implied doctrine is less easy to discern. Sometimes the story read seems positively unedifying (for example, some of the stories in the book of Judges); but even where there is nothing at all offensive in the story, it may be difficult to see in what sense it can be the basis for doctrine. Stories are stories, not doctrinal formularies. Even if we believe that every story in the Bible is literally true, something more is needed to help us move from reading the stories to formulating doctrine about God.

In one sense it is true that a story conveys less about God than does a statement of doctrine. It does not define what God is like; it may not be completely clear with which of the actors in the story God aligns himself. Indeed stories are often morally ambiguous, and yield differing impressions of each character which are not always fully consistent with each other. Besides this, a story is always about particular incidents, not universal truths, and its 'moral', or meaning, may be impossible to express without remainder in a series of general propositions. But in another, perhaps more important, sense, stories can reveal more than doctrines. The very fact that a story is always particular means that it is prevented from degenerating into a mere idea or set of platitudes. The biblical stories in particular are very concrete, and present human experiences that we can set alongside our own. We are not simply told that God is loving, or merciful, or just, or demanding: we are shown these things in action.

To say that God is revealed in story in the Bible is to say something, not just about the Bible, but about God himself. It is a clue to the power of God to influence the human heart. Few people are led to belief in God or to an understanding of his ways by reading books of speculative theology, but many owe their faith in good measure to stories – not only the stories of the Bible, but the stories told by novelists and poets and perhaps above all the stories told by their friends. What is the 'testimony' which to many Christians is so significant if not one person's story of his or her own life, interpreted in the light of faith, and challenging the hearer, 'This happened to me; it can also happen to you'?

The God, then, in whom we believe is one about whom it is appropriate to speak by means of narrative. To this extent at least, God is personal. In Pascal's phrase, he is not the God of the philosophers, but the God of Abraham, Isaac and Jacob. He is a God who, like other persons, is often best described by presenting him within a narrative of events. But not any narrative. Certain things must be the case about the narrative if it is to speak of God. It must, in the first place, have a certain shape. The stories in the Bible, and the overall single story to which they all contribute, is a coherent and purposeful story. The biblical story is not vague, or rambling, or inconsequential; it is sharply focused and it makes overall sense. Indeed, if we are uncomfortable with the Bible it is probably in part because its strongly unitary thrust tends to threaten us with a view of human history that is too tightly organised, too coherent, to fit the ambiguities of the world as we in modern times perceive them. For the modern reader, the problem of the Bible is not that it does not hang together but rather that it seems to hang together almost too well, to make sense of chains of events that strike us as much more aimless than the biblical writers let them be. It is difficult to recognise our world in the schematised history of the books of Kings, where the kings of Israel and Judah are simply 'good' and 'bad', or in the church as described in Acts, where people are either saints or renegades. But it is important to set this feeling in context, and to realise that the biblical stories are a monument to a faith which tried to see a coherent divine purpose in events which many contemporaries would have regarded as quite random and meaningless. For both Jewish and Christian tradition faith in God is faith that his people's history does have a proper story-line, that it is not merely a succession of unrelated and futile incidents. To read in worship any portion of the biblical story – however truncated or broken it may seem taken alone – is to set our own lives in the context of the whole narrative framework which the Bible contains. Over and above the particular truths about God that some of the stories may contain, their existence as parts of one long and complete story carries a great additional weight of meaning; for it affirms that human existence is seen as standing under the purposes of God.

A second thing that may reasonably be asked of any narrative or series of narratives, and all the more in the case of narratives about God, is that the principal character should speak and act consistently and comprehensibly. A story in which the characters appear to behave in a random and unpredictable way can tell us little. If the biblical narrative is to tell us about God it must show him to have reasonably consistent intentions and attitudes. It is here, as we said at the outset, that we run into difficulties. The God of the Bible is described in many ways. Sometimes he is a severe judge who is ready to sentence some of his creatures to eternal punishment, sometimes a loving Father who wills everyone to be saved. The problem is perhaps less acute in the Old Testament, when it can be argued that a particular episode (such as God's command to slaughter the Amalekites) represents a 'primitive' stage in the people's experience. But in the New Testament, where such a solution is not readily available, there is also considerable tension between apparent opposites – between God's implacable wrath on the one hand and his infinite mercy on the other. Christians have tended to react to this tension by emphasising different aspects at different times. Present-day New Testament scholars, for example, tend to stress the evidence which points to an explicit and remarkably intimate father-son relationship with God on the part of Jesus, a relationship subsequently extended into the experience of his followers. The perception of God as devouring fire (Heb. 12.29) and awesome judge is one to which today not only scholars but most Christian people tend to pay less attention. Nor are these isolated instances, which could perhaps be dismissed as the quirks of particular authors. Both perceptions (along with many others) are well represented in the New Testament. At any particular time Christians may feel justified in emphasising one and virtually ignoring the other, but the fact they are both there forbids us from permanently discarding either. Scripture claims that the 'character' of God (if we may speak in this way) is sufficiently consistent for him to be the subject of the narrative or series of narratives it contains; but it also constantly challenges us to enlarge our understanding of that character by postulating a range of attributes that could hardly be held together in the case of a single human being.

Today's emphasis on the mercy, rather than the wrath, of God is only one example of the way in which Christian (as well as Jewish) reflection on the Scriptures tends to stress those aspects which seem most acceptable to a contemporary understanding of God and to neglect others which, though equally clearly attested in Scripture, seem to present too great a challenge to our imagining. Another example is the traditional portrayal of God by means of models or attributes derived from the activities and attitudes of men rather than women. In cultures in which power, authority and education are typically in the hands of men it is inevitable that God should be pictured with predominantly masculine characteristics. Yet here again the Bible offers a wider range of attributes. God is occasionally described in terms of tenderness and long-suffering vigilance usually thought more appropriate to motherhood than fatherhood. Jesus, too, uses imagery of himself (that of a hen gathering her chicks) which points in the same direction. Our own generation, with its concern for the equality and complementarity of the sexes, invites fresh attention to this aspect of the biblical tradition, so that the richness of Scripture's perception of God may enlarge our imagining to press beyond our own restricted models and categories of gender towards the ultimate mystery of God.[3]

A further question raised by the predominantly narrative character of biblical material about God is that of its historical truth. In recent years theologians have used the word 'myth' in connection with biblical narratives, to indicate that the meaning of the stories in the Bible goes far deeper than the significance of their historical content. They are stories expressing profound insight into the relationship of God, humankind and world. But in ordinary usage the word myth suggests a story that is not true. The myths of Greek gods and heroes, for example, are not for the most part taken as accounts of events that can be located in history. Is it now being suggested that the biblical narrative is equally 'mythical'? The reaction of many has been, once again, to stress the historical character of the biblical revelation. The Christian story, it is urged, is in the strict factual sense 'true'.

It may be that the 'myth' approach was exaggerated; it was certainly widely misunderstood. But the reaction too has sometimes been over-simple. The relationship of the biblical narrative to historical events is a complex one. In the book of Genesis, for example, the narrative moves from legendary and 'mythical' material (the creation of the world in six days, the Flood, the Tower of Babel, etc.), through episodes of 'patriarchal' history which have a real but distant relationship with known movements of tribes and peoples, into the sequence of Joseph-stories, which can be fairly precisely related to known Egyptian background – all without any perceptible change of style or intention. Similarly, two consecutive verses of Mark's gospel (15.37–38) contain the statements that Jesus expired and that the curtain of the Temple was split from top to bottom. The first of these is plainly what we would call a statement of fact. There are good grounds, however, for thinking that the second is not a description of a supernatural or freakish phenomenon but is intended by the evangelist to be a symbolic statement of the significance of Jesus's death. In that case, the two statements stand in totally different relationships to historical truth but once again the biblical text gives us no inkling that it is 'changing gear' at this point.

Although, therefore, there is good reason to believe that the story of God's involvement in the affairs of his people and of the world is firmly rooted in historical fact, we have to recognise that the actual telling of the story, if it is to bring out the significance and implications of this involvement, may depart at times from the strictly factual reporting expected of scientific historians. This again tells us something of importance about God. If he can legitimately be represented as an actor in and influence upon the course of history, the nature of this action and influence is too subtle and varied always to be adequately expressed in objective historical statement. The contribution that is increasingly being made by literary critics to biblical studies, with its emphasis on the different modes of composition and expression found in different parts of the Bible or even of a single text, has helped to illuminate not just Scripture but by implication also the nature of God himself.

Biblical history and other history

This complex relationship of the biblical narrative to history raises the further question: history of whom and of what? If any meaning is to be found in the proposition that the activity and influence of God are to be discerned in historical events, there must be some events in which this is so and some in which it is not. But how are we to distinguish between them? The status of Scripture as the primary source of knowledge about God might seem to settle the question: those events which are recounted in the Bible reveal the intentions and activity of God, others do not – or at least not to the same degree. But as soon as we begin to take seriously the character of these events as real history, it becomes necessary to bring the normal methods of historical study to bear on them. They must be closely related to other events and circumstances not reported in the Bible, and a greater knowledge of these (when it is available) can be expected to increase understanding of the biblical narrative itself. It is this conviction which in modern times has intensified research by biblical scholars into the Mari tablets, the Tel el-Amarna Letters, the 'inter-testamental' writings, the Dead Sea Scrolls and many other pieces of evidence bearing upon the environment in which the biblical history is set. But this research, entirely justifiable for the purpose of historical understanding, raises in a sharp form the whole question of historical revelation. We began by referring to Scripture as the primary source for our knowledge of God. But if Scripture cannot be fully understood without drawing upon other sources of information, does this mean that these other sources are also 'revealed'? Should we expect to find significant intimations of God's nature in the psalms of the Dead Sea Sect which are not present in the Psalms of David? May there be further 'revealed truth' about God still awaiting the archaeologist's spade?

It may have been in reaction to these paradoxical implications of the historical approach to Scripture that there has recently appeared, in the form of 'Canon Criticism', a new emphasis on the 'givenness' of the biblical material as such. A certain priority must always be given to certain events and certain historical developments by virtue of the fact that they are the subject of Scripture, and must therefore be expected to contribute, one way or another, to our knowledge of God. The importance accorded to extra-biblical sources may vary from time to time: it is in principle impossible to define exactly where sacred history ends and secular history begins. But this again is a significant pointer to the nature of God himself. If we are to be so bold as to say (as Scripture authorises us to do) that God is involved in a particular strand of human history, it would clearly be pushing this way of speaking too far to claim that we always know exactly where God's involvement begins and where it ends.

The end of the story

There is one further feature of narrative which is prominent in the Bible and which has caused a good deal of trouble to interpreters. A story, if it is to have power and meaning, needs not only to have shape and consistency; it needs also to have an ending. Indeed in some ways, as some literary critics in recent years have emphasised, the end is the most important part of the story. Stories are ambiguous and enigmatic until we know the ending or denouement, and this is as true of the story that the Bible tells as it is of any other. If we are to take seriously the notion that God is such that his relationship with human beings can be spelt out in narrative form, then the narrative, if it is to convey the truth and meaning, must have an ending. This is true of the Old Testament, where the history of Israel is consistently told in the expectation of the fulfilment of God's promises – or of the severity of his judgement – in the future. It is true also of the New Testament; but here it presents a problem. For now the conviction that the narrative of God's dealings with his people must have an end takes the form of an actual proclamation by Jesus and (for a time, at least) by his followers that the end of the story is not merely inevitable but imminent.

For centuries this disturbing aspect of Jesus's message was quietly ignored or interpreted away. But since Albert Schweitzer brought it once again into the foreground of New Testament study in the early years of this century, scholars have wrestled with the apparent non-fulfilment of Jesus's predictions after two thousand years of continuing history. There is, they have suggested, an inevitable tension in the gospel between an 'already' and a 'not yet'. Jesus brought into the world totally new possibilities for human living in relation to God; the essential conditions for the fulfilment of God's promises are already here. But the realities of judgement and ultimate salvation – the necessary 'ending' of the story – remain in the future; and if these realities are to influence conduct they must be imagined to be about to break upon humanity now, 'in this generation'. Taken as a chronological prediction, Jesus's reading of the future seems to convict him of error. Emptied of any reference to historical prediction, it ceases to exert influence on the thinking and conduct of his followers.

There seems to be no universally accepted escape from this dilemma, though in fairness it should be acknowledged that a number of respected scholars have offered other interpretations of what Jesus expected for his own 'generation'. Some see an anticipation of 'end' judgement in the destruction of Jerusalem by the Romans in AD 70; some argue that Jesus was referring at least in part to the events of the Resurrection and Pentecost. No single solution, however, commands universal assent. It may be better, once again, to accept it as a necessary consequence of the biblical perception that God may be made the subject of a narrative. A story takes place in time, and must have an ending. If God is such that he can be the subject of our story, then he can validly be conceived as working within time towards a final denouement. But to press this way of speaking to the point of asking exactly when the end is to take place is to force God into a human mould. It is clearly not true either that God wills an eternal and unchanging order on earth or that he intended an intervention such as was expected by Jesus's first followers, if not by Jesus himself. A 'doctrine of God' cannot be constructed out of either proposition. The revelation of God in Scripture serves rather to validate the idea of a God who is involved in the temporal flow of history and is the subject of a narrative that must necessarily (if it is to be understood) move towards an ending. But the contradictions which arise from pursuing this way of speaking too far warn us of its limitations, and encourage us continually to sift and enlarge our imagining of the reality to which such language points.

Inconsistencies and corrections

By way of introduction to Scripture as the primary source of the knowledge by which we are to interpret and control our experience of God, we have drawn attention to two particular features of it: its origins in community and its narrative content. These two especially are crucial for understanding the way in which an ancient written testimony may give authentic intimations of the truth about God. Other features could doubtless be added which made the same point – the prominence of poetical forms of expression, for example – but it happens that the two chosen are of particular concern to modern biblical scholarship. They are, moreover, sufficient to illustrate the point that if any written documents can claim to be a revelation of the truth about God, they must presuppose both that God is such that the literary forms used can say something meaningful about him, and also that he must necessarily transcend the models which Scripture offers for understanding him. Like the hypotheses used by scientists to describe the physical universe, the models used in the Bible to describe God are valid up to a certain point of experience and understanding, but (in theory, at least) they are corrigible in the light of new challenges to faith and further moments of revelation. But, as in science, the correction does not necessarily invalidate the existing model. It can continue in use as a guide for thought and conduct, until good reason has been shown for discarding it.

This process of correction of one model by another (which nevertheless allows a certain validity to the corrected model) can be seen both in the study of the Bible and in the Bible itself. Reference was made earlier to the problem created for all interpreters and theologians by the fact that statements can be found in the Bible about God (and about many other things) which appear to contradict one another. For many centuries this caused no difficulty to believers; indeed such instances were taken to indicate that the true meaning was to be found below the surface of the text. By various methods of interpretation (all nowadays customarily but loosely labelled 'allegorical') the subject of the passage and many of its details were taken to stand for other realities, perhaps in the sacred history, perhaps in the life of the Christian. These methods have now been generally discarded as a method of critical study; but once their limitations are recognised, they can still be used – and in fact regularly are used in particular situations – for devotional purposes.

A more 'scientific' strategy for dealing with inconsistencies was the consequence of a Darwinian 'evolutionary' approach being combined with a literary analysis of the Old Testament. According to this, a 'development' can be traced from the 'primitive' ideas of earlier strands to the more 'advanced' ideas of the later. Apparent contradictions can then be accounted for as representing different stages in this development. Subsequent scholarship has found great difficulty with this theory. For one thing, the literary sources of the Old Testament are extremely difficult to date objectively, and the argument can be dangerously circular: a certain conception of God is 'primitive' because it occurs in an early text, but we judge that the text is early only because the conception is primitive. In fact it seems impossible to trace an orderly evolution of religious ideas in the Old Testament; yet the evolutionary approach, once again, retains a certain validity as an explanation of some of the apparent changes and inconsistencies in Old Testament thought, as indeed it does as a tool in the study of all the great religions.

Other strategies have been attempted. For a time, a 'Biblical Theology' seemed possible. Under an over-arching concept, such as 'Covenant' or 'Kingdom', it was hoped that apparently competing ideas about God could be brought into harmony and a single set of theological propositions distilled from the Bible as a whole. This enterprise has in its turn been generally abandoned, and has given place to a recognition that different tendencies and schools coexisted within the one religion of Israel, and were never fully reconciled with one another. These frequent shifts of approach have often caused members of the Church to be sceptical or distrustful of the whole scholarly enterprise. Surely Scripture can be allowed to speak for itself without the help of whatever learned hypothesis happens to be fashionable at the moment? Such scepticism and distrust may sometimes be deserved. Theologians, like all academics, are capable of advancing views and hypotheses so extreme or so implausible that common sense rightly refuses to be led by them. But for the most part the suggested comparison with the necessary corrigibility of scientific hypotheses encourages a more respectful attitude. New hypotheses may improve on the old, but they do not altogether supersede them; and the continuing process testifies to the reality of that which the hypotheses seek to illumine: God himself.

Christians in fact are familiar with this process of self-correction even within the Bible. It is present in a sharp form in the relationship between the Old and New Testaments. Why do Christians still read the Old Testament? To a large extent the 'new covenant' of Jesus Christ is clearly a 'correction' of the old. Yet the Church continues to reverence the Old Testament, not just as an aid to understanding the New (which it is), but as a source of revelation about God. It too is 'the Word of the Lord'. The fact that so much has been corrected by the teaching of Jesus does not invalidate the Old Testament, any more than Einstein has invalidated Newton. It is rather that the perspectives introduced by Jesus (as by Einstein) have immensely widened the field of understanding and made previously accepted ways of 'reading' the universe inadequate.

The finality of Jesus

Here, at last, we come to the heart of the matter. In the faith of Christians, Jesus Christ himself represents the most radical 'correction' of ideas about God that the world has ever known. In him there is a finality and authority such that no comparable correction is to be expected again within human history. He does not necessarily invalidate all that is said about God in the Old Testament, or even in other world religions. But by his suffering, death and resurrection he significantly enlarges the range of human experience which can be 'read' as a testimony to the love and the power of God; and in his teaching he offers new 'models' of understanding which go far beyond what was available before. How does Jesus possess this exceptional authority to reveal the nature of God? Some would say that it was the unique event of the Resurrection which confirmed the truth of the revelation he offered; and an influential school of New Testament scholars would argue that this can be documented by historical study. But Jesus's authority depends also on a uniquely intimate relationship between himself and God, such that the models proposed by him for speaking about God have an authority that comes from an exceptional degree of personal knowledge. Does this mean that Christ was God-like, or even (as the Church affirms) God? The question is raised already in the New Testament, and the debate continues to this day. That different views are possible, both about the evidence of the New Testament itself, and about its implications for a Christian doctrine of God and of Christ, is a reminder of the inevitable imperfection and corrigibility of the models which we use for our understanding of God. But the continuance of the enquiry, and the vitality of the faith which sustains it, testifies to the reality of the God with whom we have to do, and to the ultimate authority of Jesus as the prime source of our knowledge and experience of him.

When we come, then, to ask in detail what Scripture says about the nature of God, there will always be a certain provisionality about any answer we can give. The very nature of the Bible's witness to God – its basis in the experience of a community, its emphasis on speaking about him in historical narrative, and so forth – allows us to form certain conclusions about God, and also to expect a certain consistency in the descriptions of his character. But the inadequacy of any language to encompass so great a reality must prevent us from achieving a perfectly systematic account of biblical theology, and warn us that any one account of the biblical evidence is likely to need correction (without thereby becoming obsolete) in the light of new perceptions and methods. What follows in the next two chapters claims to be no more than a survey of present scholarly opinion. drawing together those strands of the biblical witness which are most relevant to our enquiry. As such they describe a part – indeed a very important part – of the total resources available in the search for a doctrine of God. In a few decades' time such an analysis will, no doubt, look very different, just as it looked different a few decades ago. But, if we truly understand the nature of the biblical witness, this ought to strengthen, not shake, our Christian confidence in the reality of the God to whom this testimony points and in the primacy of Scripture as the path to our discovery of him.

Chapter 5
The God of Jesus

The Christian understanding of God begins from the Scriptures, and this means the whole Bible, not just the New Testament. The Bible is the record of one people's experience of God, which reached a climax of unique importance in the person of Jesus Christ. Christ marks a turning point, because one of the effects of the movement which he began – the Christian Church – was to make the religious heritage of Israel available to all people. At the same time the estrangement of church and synagogue, coinciding with the shattering effect of the Jewish War and the fall of Jerusalem, led to a parting of the ways between Jews and Christians, and to the emergence of Rabbinic Judaism in separation from Christianity. But the religion of the Old Testament is the common property of both Christians and Jews, and the Christian doctrine of God cannot be understood except on this basis.

As argued in the preceding chapter, the Bible is not a treatise about God, but a collection of writings which together convey glimpses of the story of Israel, and of individuals within Israel, in relation to God through many centuries. The books of the Old Testament have themselves had a complex literary history. Almost all of them have been edited and re-edited, or expanded with fresh material, before reaching their final form in the Bible as we know it. Thus the very first chapters of Genesis contain ideas of God which in all probability came from different periods and backgrounds. People in the time of Jesus, however, had little sense of this kind of historical development, so that it is the overall impression of the final form of the text, read in a context of worship, which shaped their understanding of God. Thus the presuppositions about God which were shared by Jesus and the Jews of his time include ideas which can be traced far back into primitive Israelite thought, and also insights gained through later experiences. These belong within a concept of God which underlies not only Judaism and Christianity but also Islam.

The story of Israel can thus be seen as a voyage of discovery. The knowledge of God is acquired gradually through the vicissitudes of many centuries by a nation which regarded itself as God's special people. But this is to look at it from a purely human point of view. It is also possible to see it as a story of the activity of God. Through the history of his people, God has been working out his purpose of creating a people capable of responding to his gracious will, and this is not for the sole benefit of Israel alone, but for all the peoples on earth. It is only when both ways of looking at the Bible's story are given full value that an authentic religious experience results. For religion is the bond between God and humankind. This bond is sometimes referred to in the Bible as the covenant between God and his people.

The Old Testament, which contains this story of God's creation of his people and of that people's growth in knowledge of God, is a collection of those books which were most highly valued as sacred writings by the Jews in the time of Christ. Most of these books were completed by 300 BC, though Daniel and Esther, at least, are most probably later. In addition there are other venerated writings from the last three centuries before Christ which were not in the end received by Judaism into its canon of sacred Scripture, and about which Christians have differed, some including them in the Canon, others, like the Church of England, placing them in the secondary category of Apocrypha. In modern times the extant Jewish religious literature of this period has been enlarged by the discovery of the Dead Sea Scrolls, which have added greatly to our knowledge of the life and thought of Judaism in the time of Christ. Thus, when we try to assess the understanding of God shared by Jesus and his contemporaries, we need to take into account the information provided by all these writings. To confine attention to the Old Testament alone would be misleading for understanding the rise both of Christianity and of Rabbinic Judaism.

The beginnings of Christianity are documented by the books of the New Testament. In this case the collection of writings is not the fruit of centuries of literary evolution. Nevertheless, behind the Gospels in particular there is still a complex process in which, for example, oral traditions, popular memories of Jesus, missionary preaching and written material have all played their part. Moreover, the Gospels are not modern critical biographies, aiming at impartiality, but the work of writers who were deeply committed to the gospel message. There are areas of literary overlap between Matthew, Mark and Luke, but these reveal some of the ways in which the evangelists felt free to alter or expand or abbreviate their sources. The influence of a doctrinal interest, too, must be allowed for in all four Gospels. The Gospel of John raises particular questions from this point of view, and scholars are divided on the question of its value as historical record, while recognising its great importance as a presentation of the meaning of Jesus for faith.

These factors must be taken into account when we attempt to discover the central teaching of Jesus, and to see how the Church's faith in Jesus affected the Christian concept of God. The books of the New Testament belong to the time when Christian faith was in the process of being hammered out. Thus we shall need to look at the evidence of the New

Testament for two different purposes. In the present chapter we shall be concerned with the understanding of God in ancient Israel, in Judaism between the Old and New Testament periods, and in the teaching of Jesus himself, and we shall be especially interested in the features which characterise, and may be held to differentiate, his concept of God. In the next chapter we shall try to see how the Church's faith in Jesus has brought about a distinctively Christian doctrine of God without denying the Old Testament inheritance.

The God of the Old Testament

The sheer variety of the literature of the Old Testament, and the length of time which went into its making, counsel caution in embarking on a composite description of its witness to Israel's understanding of God. There are, however, certain constants of fundamental importance. Moreover, though it is possible to perceive primitive ideas which are eventually discarded, the process is not a matter of deliberate change, but of a gradual enlarging of perspective, which eventually effects radical correction without denial of the past. The stability of Israel's concept of God is in fact one of the most striking features of Old Testament religion. In what follows, four leading ideas will be taken in order to focus the main themes.

(a) The God of the Old Testament is always and everywhere conceived as a *personal* being. From the ancient stories of the patriarchs in Genesis to the latest retelling of Israel's history in the books of Chronicles, the God whom we meet is one who makes plans and implements them, enjoys successes and experiences frustration when human beings resist his will, changes his mind and formulates revised plans for reaching his ultimate goals. He maintains personal relations with his people through speech. Those who are close to him, like Abraham, may have conversations with him. He addresses the people as a whole through prophets. When a prophet says 'These are the words of Yahweh' he speaks in the manner of a state messenger who says 'These are the words of King So-and-so'; they are uttered by the agent, but they come from the master. Sometimes, it seems, the prophets believed that they heard with their own ears words which God himself made audible; sometimes, perhaps, they saw themselves as putting into their own words convictions felt within, which they believed came from God. The laws of Israel similarly are expressed as words of Yahweh rather than the enactments of a king or a religious teacher.

The actual content of Yahweh's speech also reflects his personhood. He gives vent to the feelings of a person, not only love, joy and compassion, but also regret, jealousy and anger. Though he can be likened to a lion or a rock, most characteristically people think of him in human terms. So we find him compared to a king or a shepherd, to a father, mother, husband or potter. He is the dynamic, living God. The ban on images of God in the Law actually reinforces this. For the lively, energetic, moving, acting and speaking God of Israel can never be captured in a static image.

Being personal involves relationships on both sides. God is not only one who speaks, but also one who is addressed. The Psalms exhibit astonishing freedom in addressing God. Besides expressions of love and gratitude and trust, there are uninhibited grief and rage and doubt. The people of Israel always assumed that God is real enough and personal enough to appreciate the sharing of their hopes and fears; that he has not only ears to hear but feelings to be aroused and energy to be activated. The God of Israel is one who invites his children to the shared speech of conversation, and thus to shared involvement in his world.

(b) For, secondly, the God of the Old Testament is himself involved in the world. At first, perhaps, conceived as a clan God, concerned for his own people, in the classic period of Old Testament religion he is perceived as the sole creator of the world. Though he is in himself independent of the world, and far too great to be in any way confined to it or captured in it, he is its creator and directs its story. He looks after the destiny of his people. It can even be said that he has a covenant with them to be their God, that he has chosen one people out of all the nations as his own. By the sixth century BC the covenant concept has been extended to creation, and the bow in the cloud in the story of the flood is the sign that Yahweh will never again destroy human-kind. Moreover God's purpose is the ultimate good of his people, and even disasters are intended for their correction. The prophets again and again upbraid the people for their failures to keep the covenant, and threaten dire punishment. But if Israel will only learn the lesson of its disobedience, there is always hope for the future.

God's involvement with the world is not confined to national and international affairs, set in the great sweep of history from first Beginning to final End. He is also the source of the world's stability and life. He provides breath for all living creatures, and rain that the plants may grow. He is involved in human life as provider, healer and friend. Sometimes, as in Proverbs, it is too easily assumed that his providence is certain to issue in prosperity for the righteous and misfortune for the wicked. But as this does not accord with experience, it is not surprising to find Ecclesiastes putting forward a counter-interpretation of life, uncharacteristic of Israel's general understanding of God; and at times deeply cynical and pessimistic. This problem, inherent in all theistic religion, is faced at a deeper level in the agonising of Job and in the prophecy of the Suffering Servant in Isaiah 53.

(c) Thirdly, for all his personal qualities and involvement with the world, Yahweh is not just a human person writ large. The Old Testament's way of referring to his distinctiveness is by speaking of him as the *Holy One*. Holiness denotes the mysterious otherness of God, belonging to the heavenly realm, demanding the response of awed worship on the part of humankind, terrifying his people with thunder and portents when he gives the Law on Mount Sinai. God's holiness is inseparable from his righteousness and love. He is both merciful and just, and both these qualities inspire awe. Isaiah, who in his vision heard the seraphim cry 'Holy, holy, holy' (6.3), asserts that 'The Lord of Hosts is exalted in justice, and the holy God shows himself holy in righteousness' (5.16). Thus the concept of holiness, which is not necessarily an ethical idea in itself, is in Israel's religious consciousness inseparably bound up with ethical qualities. Those characteristics, mentioned earlier, which make it possible to speak of Yahweh as personal, are not in conflict with his holiness.

The link between God's holiness and his love is captured in a phrase from Isaiah's northern contemporary Hosea, whose perception of Yahweh breaks through the stereotypes of power and authority to the tenderness of God. Hosea's understanding of God's involvement with Israel is expressed in terms of a parent with a wayward child, whose love will not let him go, however far he strays. 'I will not exercise my fierce anger . . . for I am God and not man, the Holy One in your midst' (Hos. 11.9). Such is the steadfast love of Yahweh that, even at the moment of wrath, one can plead with him to remember mercy (Exod. 32.11; Hab. 3.2).

Justice and love also come to be expressed in the Law of Moses, which is the basis of the covenant between Yahweh and his people. In Deuteronomy the Law is presented to the people as the expression of God's love and his gift for their good; and they in their turn must respond with obedience and with love for God. Similarly, in the Priestly strand of the legal codes of the Old Testament the people themselves are to be holy in order to maintain fellowship with the holy God. Rites of purification are provided and sacrifices are prescribed to maintain the holiness of the people.

(d) Fourthly, the love and justice of God are held together as two sides of one coin by the insistence of the Old Testament that God is *one*. Though he may be pictured as holding court surrounded by angels, he is never the centre of a mythology of squabbling and intriguing gods, like the gods of Canaan and Babylon. The attributes and functions of God are not split up among a multiplicity of divinities. The temptation to do this, which recurs over a long period of Israel's religious history, is considered to be apostasy from Yahweh, a choosing to 'go after other gods'. Nor is there anything in the Old Testament to suggest an ultimate dualism, whereby the principles of love and justice are ascribed to different gods. The Law makes the solemn affirmation 'Yahweh our God, Yahweh one' (Deut. 6.4) and the great anonymous prophet of the sixth century BC has Yahweh say, 'Maker of light and creator of darkness, maker of peace and creator of evil, I Yahweh do all these things' (Isa. 45.7).

Nevertheless we have to beware of oversimplification. From the earliest time the Spirit of Yahweh was spoken of in a way that almost separates it from Yahweh himself. The Spirit comes mightily upon Jephthah (Judg. 11.29) and Saul (1 Sam. 10.6) and speaks through the prophets (1 Kgs 22.24). But this does not mean that the Spirit is thought of as a separate god. It is a faculty or attribute of God himself, objectified in order to speak of God's power within persons without compromising his essential otherness from humankind. In later times the Wisdom of God (sometimes personified as a woman) is treated in the same way.

Furthermore the Old Testament embraces the idea of angelic spirits, both good and bad, who are subordinate to Yahweh and influence the thoughts and actions of humankind. This idea becomes much more prominent in the later period, particularly in Daniel, the Apocrypha and the Dead Sea Scrolls, probably as a result of Persian influence. One such spirit is the Adversary (the 'Satan'), who is used by God to put people to the test. From the fourth century BC onwards he becomes more prominent as the author of evil, and this shows how the Jews at this later time were reluctant to attribute evil to the direct action of God. Nevertheless God always remains in ultimate control. If the course of human history is interpreted in terms of the conflict between cosmic powers of good and evil, the defeat of evil is certain, because God will triumph in the end.

Finally, if God is in control of human history, it follows that his goodness can be fully displayed only in the salvation of his people. The vicissitudes of Israel's history are always seen in relation to the unfolding of the will of God. The suffering of the Babylonian exile is his punishment for the nation's sins. At the same time there is always hope of restoration and a glorious future. The Messianic hope began as simply hope for the restoration of the Davidic monarchy after the exile was over. Only when that proved to be impossible did Messianism take more varied forms.

But the oneness of God also led some prophetic souls towards universalism. The one God of all the earth could not be indifferent to the fate of the other nations. This was perceived, for example, by the author of Isaiah 40–55, the anonymous prophet already mentioned, who spoke of Israel's vocation to be 'a light to the nations, that my salvation may reach to the end of the earth' (Isa. 49.6). But such glimpses of universalism are rare in the Old Testament.

Between the Old and New Testaments

The Old Testament closes with the story unfinished, and the scene is still not set for the entry of Jesus on the stage. The restoration which followed the Exile, late in the sixth century BC, did not fulfil the expectations voiced by the prophets. Israel now became a province in the empire of a foreign overlord. After the conquests of Alexander the Great a popular idealisation of Greek culture threatened the distinctive understandings of other faiths. Local religious practices everywhere were assimilated to the Greek pattern, and the worship of the universal God of Heaven was widely absorbed into the worship of Zeus. Inevitably there were Jews who wished to bring their culture and religion into line with these tendencies, and they had the favour of the imperial power. The Maccabean Revolt of 167 BC was not just a struggle against foreign domination. It was primarily a life and death stand for the traditions of Israel's faith, focused on the right to live and to worship God according to the Law. Thus the biblical understanding of God was central to the issue. Men and women gave their lives on behalf of God's Law. The memory of the Maccabean martyrs dominates the religion of Judaism in New Testament times. It also explains the tenacity with which the Law was held and promoted in the Jewish communities throughout the Greco-Roman world.

The success of the revolt, however, did not produce the fulfilment of Israel's ideals. The new rulers, successors to the Maccabees, held on to their precarious independence by wars and diplomacy among the superpowers, and themselves became corrupted in the process. It was the period of the emergence of sects and parties. An open attitude towards the faith of others was maintained by the Sadducees, who combined religious conservatism with a lofty philosophical outlook. Drawn chiefly from the aristocratic and high-priestly families, their first concern was for the safety of the state. The spirit which animated the revolt lived on in the Pharisees, the Essenes and the Zealots. The Pharisees were concerned to promote the religion of the people, and encouraged exact keeping of the Law to this end. The Dead Sea Scrolls have revealed a sect (probably the Essenes) which had opted for complete separation from temple and state, which were regarded by them as hopelessly corrupt. The sect was devoted to study of the Law, and regarded itself as the sole heir to the destiny of Israel in the plan of God. 'Zealots' is a term loosely employed to cover all those who looked to a holy war of the Maccabean type to bring about the salvation of Israel. To others, however, the times were too troubled for them to discern any divine plan of salvation. Nevertheless despair leads to hope against hope, and many believed that the intervention of God would not be long delayed.

The Judaism into which Jesus was born was thus different from the world of the Old Testament. Brought up in this setting, his understanding of God and his teaching about God naturally take some of their colour from the characteristic emphases of Judaism in his time, as these had been formed in response to the pressure and experiences of the Maccabean age. Four features in particular need to be borne in mind.

(a) First, the centrality of the Law in Jewish religion had been greatly enhanced by the struggle. At a time when God's power and otherness were dramatically magnified by the experience of life in the enlarged perspectives of the Greco-Roman world, there was a danger that his greatness and purity might place him altogether beyond the reach of human littleness and sinfulness. But because the transcendent God was immanent in the Law, love for God could be expressed in love for the Law, and attention to its detailed demands could ensure that a person was in right relationship with God. The Law was not only central to worship, but touched people at every point in their daily lives. The natural description of devout people was that they walked according to the Law blamelessly (cf. Luke 1.6). Conversely less devout Jews tended to care less about the niceties of the Law, especially on matters that appeared irksome and pointless.

(b) Secondly, the troubled times leading to the Maccabean Revolt had led many devout people to seek for visionary experiences which would reveal God's will for his people, and so bring reassurance. They hoped to penetrate the secrets of Heaven and to determine the divine plan for the future. The apocalyptic literature comes from this circle, Daniel 7–12 and Revelation (a Christian work) being the best known examples. It is important to realise that real and profound religious experiences lay behind the production of this kind of literature, which continued throughout the New Testament period. Such experiences implied a direct knowledge of God and his will, comparable to the inspiration of the Old Testament prophets. This carried with it the danger of conflict with those who held that the Law was the sole repository of the revealed knowledge of God (cf. Ecclus 34.1–8).

(c) A third feature of the times is the expectation of a Messiah. It has already been observed that many were convinced that God would soon intervene in history to establish his own rule everlastingly.

Disenchantment with the successors to the Maccabees led many to long for the restoration of the house of David, a king who would bring freedom and justice to the land. This was only one of the forms which the Messianic hope took in this period, but all were agreed that the era of justice and freedom would come only by the act of God in fulfilment of his age-long promises. But how would that act be mediated? Would it be by the political activism of the Zealots, who saw themselves as under solemn obligation to free the land from foreign rule, and eventually precipitated the Jewish War of AD 66–70? Or were the devout called not to act themselves, but only to 'look for the consolation of Israel' (Luke 2.25)? The Pharisees, who were opposed to political activism but shared the hope of the Messiah, encouraged patient waiting for God to intervene in his own good time. The visionary literature in general saw God's action in cosmic rather than political terms, though it implied that this action would not be long delayed. It sometimes portrayed a specific programme of events: cosmic disturbances terminating the present world order, the resurrection of the dead, the judgement of the nations, and the fulfilment of God's purpose of endless blessing for the righteous.

(d) This notion of the resurrection of the dead constituted a fourth point of importance in the faith of Judaism in the time of Jesus. In the Old Testament the state of the dead is virtually non-existence, cut off from the joy of the presence of Yahweh. By New Testament times, however, most Jews had come to believe in a future state in which the injustices of earthly life are done away. Here again the Maccabean experience had been crucial. Between the individual's death and the general resurrection the soul, separated from the body, would go to a place of waiting, where the reversal of destiny for the successful oppressor and the undeserving sufferer could already begin. Especially in the teaching of the Pharisees, rewards and punishments after death became the sanctions of moral teaching. God was seen as the judge who weighs the life of the individual to see how far he has met the demands of the Law. Thus Judaism affirms that God's sovereignty extends to the dead as well as to the living, so that the righteous of every generation are destined to have their share in the everlasting kingdom.

Jesus and God

For reasons that have already been explained it is not easy to make a synthesis of the teaching of Jesus out of the Gospels. But certain points stand out which command agreement even among the most cautious scholars.

We can begin from the first of the four features just mentioned, the place accorded to the Law in contemporary Jewish spirituality. The transcendent God was thought of as immanent in the Law, and this meant a shift of the emotional centre to the Law itself. A similar tendency can also be seen in the exaggerated use of reverential language, whereby mention of God was avoided or alternatively expanded with epithets of majesty. It is well known that by this time the name of God was never normally spoken, even when reading the scriptures.

But the most notable feature of Jesus's spirituality was that, without in any way denying the Law, he did not relate to God through the Law but directly as 'Father', and invited his hearers to share in the same relationship. Though God was indeed known and addressed as 'Father' in Judaism, the image was not a prevalent one, and as far as we know the Aramaic word 'Abba' was not used to address God in prayer in contemporary Judaism. It was the family word, implying both affection and respect, used not only by children, but also by the disciples of a rabbi. It thus suggests an attitude of humility, obedience and reverence, as well as one of dependence, security and confidence.

There is thus a new richness of content in Jesus's concept of God. Fatherly attributes come to the fore in his teaching. God is one who loves, cares, gives, listens, welcomes, seeks, accepts, forgives, provides. The concept is positive, and there is little hint of the darker father-image associated with the idea of the angry God. The fatherly love of God extends also to expectations and demands. It is particularly striking that in his anguished prayer in Gethsemane Jesus prays, 'Abba, Father, all things are possible for you. Take this cup from me. Yet not what I want but what you want' (Mark 14.36). God is the Father who loves him, and therefore Jesus can bring to him his longing for relief. God is also the Father who has expectations of him and therefore Jesus accepts that ultimately his will is what counts.

Whatever the sense in which Jesus saw his own sonship as special, he emphasised that God behaves like a father to all, and all are invited to relate to him as his children. He encourages his disciples to pray 'Father . . .', as he himself does. The Lord's Prayer parallels the Gethsemane prayer in working out the implications of God's fatherhood in terms of both authority and caring. For the disciples too, praying to the Father involves the desire for his name to be hallowed and his reign to come, before they can expect him to concern himself with their basic needs for food, forgiveness and protection from evil. He is, as Matthew emphasises, a heavenly Father, one who commands all heaven's resources for the fulfilling of his people's needs, but also one who must be reverenced as the Lord of heaven.

Jesus's conflict with the Pharisees arose from this teaching, because he sought to promote a more direct approach to God, to which the minutiae of the Law were a hindrance rather than a help. The Pharisees, like Jesus himself, were genuinely concerned to raise the standard of religion among the people, but their methods were diametrically opposed to his, because they sought to achieve this aim by stressing exact observance of the details of the Law. But the intensity of the conflict is to be explained by the second of our four points, namely that Jesus belonged with the visionaries of his time and claimed direct authority for his teaching from God. It is clear that he was popularly regarded as a prophet. Not being an ordained rabbi, he had no teaching authority other than his personal claim to divine inspiration. So the conflict concerned not only the substance of his teaching but also his personal authority as a teacher.

The God whom Jesus proclaimed was a God whose intervention in history was imminent: 'The time is fulfilled, and the kingdom of God is at hand; repent and believe in the gospel' (Mark 1.15). This corresponds with the third feature of the intertestamental period. Jesus's teaching, as we should expect, had more in common with the apocalyptic notion of direct action by God than with the political expectation of the Davidic Messiah. In accordance with the Jewish tendency to avoid expressions suggesting that God might be visible, Jesus spoke of the coming of the kingdom of God as a circumlocution for the coming of God himself. And this is the gospel – the good news – because the God who is coming is the God who is already known as Father, and his kingdom will mean blessing for the poor and the sad and the outcast. They will be rich and be glad and have a great reward (Luke 6.20–23).

Jesus preached with a great sense of urgency, because he believed that the time was short (Mark 9.1). But the content of his message referred to the present as well as the future, because his own words, with their impact on his hearers, made God present already through their concentration on the God who was coming. Even as he speaks the reign of God dawns. Already in Jesus's ministry the blind receive their sight, the lame walk, and the poor have the good news preached to them (Matt. 11.4–5).

The implementation of God's kingship turns upside down the expectations of the world and conventional religious tradition. The blessings of God's reign are given, not earned, so that they come to all, no matter how long they have worked for them. The prodigal son finds an unexpected welcome from a prodigally loving father. The child is the model for the receptivity that embraces God's reign, and God's heart fills with joy when one sinner repents (Matt. 20.1–16; Mark 10.15; Luke 15.11–32, 18.9–14).

There is thus no suggestion that there is no need of repentance. Jesus announces an imminent confrontation with God in all his holiness, purity, goodness, mercy and love. It is not enough to point to one's religious status or religious observances, for God's demands extend far beyond the outward righteousness for which these commonly stand. Where the law prohibits murder and adultery, Jesus on behalf of God forbids hatred and lust within the heart. We cannot expect God's forgiveness at the judgement, if we are not willing to forgive others ourselves. And just as the coming day of salvation was already dawning in the ministry of Jesus, so the response to his message from God already anticipates the judgement (Matt. 12.32). To reject his message is to repudiate the Spirit of God himself (12.31).

Jesus is aware that his teaching makes great demands. The reign of God is like a pearl of immense value, which a merchant might sacrifice all his assets to obtain (Matt. 13.46). For the disciple who wants the life of the coming age it is not enough to keep the commandments; he must sell all and give to the poor (Mark 10.21). Response to God's love allows no compromise. The opposition to Jesus will inevitably be reflected in persecution of the disciples. They too must take up their cross and be ready to lose their life in order to save it (Mark 8.34–36).

Jesus did indeed pay with his own life for his fidelity to his mission from God. He was crucified as the Messiah, the king of the Jews, and this implies that, however much he distanced himself from popular political expectations of the Messiah, he saw his role as in some sense having a Messianic character. If the coming day of salvation is already partly fulfilled in his ministry, and if the judgement is anticipated in his words, then he is the agent of God's kingdom which is imminently expected. It is important to realise that his sense of urgency was simply the catalyst of his message from God. The failure of the expectation of the coming of God does not render it invalid. As we shall see in the next chapter, the Church after the resurrection soon began to realise that the mission of Jesus, culminating in his death, was part of the final intervention of God, so that never again could it be claimed that God's decisive act on behalf of the world lay wholly in the future, without regard to what God had already done in Jesus.

Jesus taught that from those to whom much is given, much is expected, and the cross is the ultimate test of his commitment to that message. At the outset of his ministry, it appears, he was tempted to put God's fatherly love to the proof (Matt. 4.1–11). Before his arrest at Gethsemane he was tempted again to seek a way out of the ordeal. But this human shrinking must be set against both his repeated conviction that the danger to his life could not be avoided and his determination to make of his life a sacrifice to God. 'For the Son of man also came not to be served but to serve, and to give his life as a ransom for many' (Mark 10.45). By making of his death a sacrifice, Jesus affirmed his teaching about God, whose power extends beyond the grave (our fourth feature of the intertestamental period), who 'sends rain on the just and on the unjust alike' (Matt. 5.45), and whose will for the salvation of humankind cannot ultimately be thwarted (Luke 12.32). The cross is not something external to Jesus's mission and message, an end imposed upon them by others, but the heart and crown of his life and teaching.

Conclusion

The God of Jesus is the God of the Old Testament, personally involved in his creation, holy and one. In him justice and love are held together. His ultimate triumph over evil is sure. Through his Spirit he is the author of all zeal for goodness in humankind. His ears are open to the prayers of his servants, who can speak to him in their hearts.

Jesus must have appeared to his contemporaries as a visionary, a charismatic prophet concerned with the renewal of religion at a time of great perplexity. Working under a great sense of urgency, he declared that the triumph of God's love was imminent, and that this would be primarily a time of blessing for the oppressed. Renewal is a matter of the heart and the springs of action. It requires a vital relationship with God, whom Jesus teaches his followers to address as 'Father'. Suffering is the test of this relationship, but it cannot destroy the assurance of the ultimate providence of God.

The message of Jesus was addressed to his fellow Jews, and he never questions the validity of the Law. But it is evident that his teaching operates at a deeper level than observance of the Law, and is easily translated into other situations. Thus, though examples are rare in the teaching of Jesus, there are times when he is shown as looking beyond Israel (cf. Matt. 8.10–12). Through Jesus the way is opened for the religious inheritance of Israel to be made available to every people, and the God of Israel can be known as the God and Father of Jesus Christ, Lord and brother of every human being.

Chapter 6
The God of the disciples

The history of earliest Christianity shows a very remarkable development in the understanding of God, which eventually found expression in the doctrine of the Trinity, Father, Son and Holy Spirit, three Persons in one God. This formulation was not reached until after New Testament times. But it depends upon the evidence of the New Testament, and so has its origin and justification in the experiences of the first two generations of Christians whose thoughts are reflected in those writings. This chapter will try to enter into the minds of these early followers of Jesus, in order to see how the Christian understanding of God developed in the ways that it did. It will be necessary to pay particular attention to the ways in which they thought of the relationship between Jesus and God, because it is their account of this relationship which is the essential basis of the Trinitarian doctrine.

The aim of the last chapter was to pierce through the work of the evangelists to Jesus himself, to recover, as far as may be, Jesus' own understanding of God. This required a critical handling of the Gospels, whose writers shared a well-developed Christian belief. Scholarly critical procedures are still necessary in any attempt to assess the witness of the New Testament to the earliest expressions of that Christian faith and to its subsequent development within the New Testament period. As before, it will be impossible to do more than provide a tentative reconstruction which takes account of the present state of scholarship.

The starting point must be the common ground in the understanding of God which the disciples, particularly Peter and the other apostles, shared with Jesus himself. They had grown up with the same Jewish inheritance, and were drawn to him because he spoke to their condition in those perplexing times. They shared the contemporary longing for divine intervention. His teaching had given them grounds for hope, and they had committed themselves whole-heartedly to his mission. Jesus's teaching about God, and his use of the simple address 'Father' in prayer (attested by Paul in Gal. 4.6 and Rom. 8.15, which show that even among Greek-speaking converts the Aramaic form 'Abba' was used) had profoundly affected their convictions as to who Jesus was. They saw him as uniquely the agent and spokesman of God's kingdom, as traditions such as that of Peter's confession at Caesarea Philippi (Mark 8.29), declaring him the Messiah, make plain. In retrospect, too, their beliefs about Jesus were deeply affected by the events leading up to the crucifixion, and especially by his attitude to his own death. Recalling that Jesus had proclaimed the forgiveness of sins in his message of the grace of God's kingdom, they now came to see his laying down of his life as securing that forgiveness.

Any hope that Jesus was the Messiah might have seemed to be irrevocably shattered by his death. The Easter proclamation proves that this was not so. The resurrection of Jesus was immediately cited as the grounds for asserting that Jesus was the Lord's Christ. This vindicated the claim of Jesus to be the spokesman and agent of God's kingdom. As the last chapter showed, the message of Jesus could not be separated from his personal relationship with God. If his disciples were to renew his mission after his death, this would depend on the vindication of his status as one chosen, sent or empowered as God's representative. Hence the first step in the process by which Jesus was given a unique place in relation to God was inextricably bound up with the events which led to the renewal of his Gospel message.

Jesus the Christ

The oldest record of the resurrection of Jesus is the tradition, evidently derived from the Jerusalem church, which Paul quotes in 1 Cor. 15.1–11. This includes what may be regarded as the official list of appearances of the risen Christ, beginning with Peter. Paul adds his own conversion experience on the Damascus road to round off the list. The importance of this passage for our present purpose is that it is not the work of Paul himself, but an authoritative formulation which he is at pains to quote carefully and accurately. It thus provides the oldest evidence we possess for the preaching of the first Christian church.

The statement begins by asserting that 'Christ died for our sins in accordance with the Scriptures' (verse 3). Not only does this take for granted that the death of Jesus was a sacrifice for sins, it also retains the title 'Christ', which means that his death, so far from disproving his Messiahship, is actually seen to be a Messianic act and to accord with the plan of God revealed in scripture. (It is very likely that the Old Testament background chiefly in mind here is the Suffering Servant poem of Isa. 53.)

Secondly, the tradition affirms of Jesus 'that he was buried, and that he was raised on the third day in accordance with the Scriptures' (verse 4). (This may be a reference to Hos. 6.2, taken as speaking metaphorically of resurrection after three days, but this is not certain.) This ancient summary of faith thus includes in God's plan not only the suffering of the Messiah but also his resurrection. The carefully listed appearances attest his present position as the Messiah in heaven. He is risen, and therefore he is the 'first fruits' (1 Cor. 15.23) of the general resurrection. Unlike the rest of humankind who, as we saw, were believed by many in Judaism to go after death to a place of waiting until the general resurrection and the judgement, Jesus has been raised by God to the throne of honour at his right hand. That this has happened precisely because he is the Messiah is a belief supported from the earliest times by reference to Ps. 110.1, 'The Lord said to my lord, Sit at my right hand, until I make your enemies your footstool', which is quoted or alluded to a number of times in the New Testament. It follows that Jesus still has his Messianic task to perform, and that is to be God's 'right hand man' in the coming divine intervention, when death, the 'last enemy' (1 Cor. 15.26), is destroyed at the general resurrection, and God's plan for humanity is accomplished.

Thus, in renewing the gospel of Jesus, the apostles can assert that the loving forgiveness of God has already been demonstrated in the death of Jesus, and the promised blessings of the kingdom are assured because Jesus's own resurrection indicates that he is already waiting at God's right hand to confer them at the general resurrection and the judgement. The concept of Jesus's Messiahship has been filled out with an original and creative use of scriptural texts to interpret the events of Good Friday and Easter. The present position of Jesus as Messiah and Lord is thus reinforced, and becomes the guarantee of the certainty of the message which Jesus gave, and which is now passed on by his disciples. At the same time, though this moves the person of Jesus to the centre of the proclamation, it in no way reduces Jesus's concept of God. The fact that the early Christians arrived at this fresh understanding of Jesus, and saw him not only as a triumphant but also as a suffering Messiah, makes it absolutely plain that the initiative rests with God, whose love for his human children extends even to involvement in suffering. In the unforgettable words of John 3.16, 'God so loved the world, that he gave his only Son, so that every one who believes in him should not perish but should have eternal life.'

Two more things need to be said before moving on to further developments. First, it is a mistake to suppose that the earliest Christians were puzzled about the identity of Jesus, and by dint of casting in their minds around various options eventually came up with the idea that he must be the Son of God. In the light of the resurrection they had no doubt that Jesus was the Messiah; and it is this affirmation which underlies the central New Testament confession, 'Jesus is Lord'. The various developments in Christology were the result of drawing out the theological implications of this basic confession.

Secondly, the role assigned to the risen Christ as God's agent at the judgement presupposes that this divine intervention was eagerly awaited, as is clear, for example in 1 Thess. 1.9–10. The disciples had this expectation, because they were already hoping for such an action of God when they came to Jesus, and this was the context in which they listened to his preaching. Though much of Jesus's teaching is timeless, it is not convincing to eliminate this expectation altogether from that teaching. Were the disciples, and presumably Jesus himself, simply wrong about this? There is no easy answer to this question; but it can be said without hesitation that both the teaching of Jesus and the proclamation of the disciples contain features which could, and in the long run did, provide a way through. For Jesus the expectation of the coming of God in person, already preached by John the Baptist, was the catalyst of his own teaching on the encounter with the kingdom of God. The coming of this kingdom was, as we have seen, to some extent already present in his own ministry, so that he could perceive authentic signs of the kingdom in the response to his message. For the disciples the sacrificial death of Jesus and his exaltation to the right hand of God were the first stage in the actual intervention of God, so that life under the lordship of Christ again anticipated the future kingdom; and this remains true, however long the final act of the coming of Christ is delayed. The Easter proclamation binds together past, present and future. This is splendidly expressed in Paul's statement concerning the meaning of the eucharist in 1 Cor. 11.26: 'For as often as you eat this bread and drink this cup, you proclaim the Lord's death until he comes.'

Jesus the son of God

The idea of Jesus as the exalted Messiah at the right hand of God does not necessarily introduce a change or development into the understanding of God himself. Jesus's understanding of God is taken over by the disciples. His sacrificial death, being seen as God's act of reconciliation with humanity, does of course enlarge their understanding of God's involvement in the suffering of his children. But there is no crossing of the boundary between the man Jesus and God. This might, however, seem to have happened when the title 'Son of God' is used. Several points have to be taken into consideration.

(a) 'Son of God' can have a variety of senses. We are all 'children of God' inasmuch as we are part of his creation, and he is our Father in heaven, as Jesus himself taught. We are specially his children when we do what is pleasing to him (Matt. 5.45). Jesus himself is obviously a son of God in this sense.

(b) More specialised usages can be seen in such passages as Job 38.7, describing the creation, 'when the morning stars sang together, and all the sons of God shouted for joy'. Here it is the angels who are referred to as 'sons of God'. This possibility is faced and rejected with regard to Jesus in Hebrews 1, where Jesus as *the* Son of God is explicitly differentiated from the angels.

(c) The phrase can also be used for the Messiah, as in Ps. 2.7, which may be the passage referred to by Paul in Rom. 1.4. Jesus, who is in any case 'descended from David according to the flesh' (verse 3), has by his resurrection been designated Son of God in power. The phrase denotes his status in relation to God, and there is no sense of divine begetting involved. But Jesus the Messiah in his heavenly and exalted state, exalted indeed above the ranks of the angels, clearly has a unique position very close to God. Indeed, the New Testament church's use of Ps. 110.1 ('Sit at my right hand') suggests at the very least a share in God's government of the universe. This is certainly picture language, but picture language has to be used when speaking of the invisible things of heaven.

(d) This sense of the closeness of Jesus to God was enhanced further by his own spirituality, with its characteristic feature of the address to God as 'Abba'. From the beginning this made a profound impression on the disciples, and it soon led them to assume a special relationship between Jesus and God. From this point of view 'son of God' denotes not only status (the exalted Messiah) but also a relationship to God as Father in something more than the sense in which all of us can be children of God. Jesus is the Son of the Father in an exclusive sense. Paul shows the distinction in Rom.8 by describing Christians as 'adopted' children. The Father and Son relationship is expressed in words attributed to Jesus in Matt. 11.27, and is also an omnipresent theme in the Gospel of John. For John the relationship implied by the 'Abba' form of address has become reciprocal. 'The Father loves the Son' (John 5.20), and Jesus can even say, 'I and the Father are one' (10.30). Jesus in John's Gospel can often appear to be a forbidding figure, but not in his relationship with God, which shows a striking tenderness. Moreover, the disciples themselves can enter into this loving relationship through their relationship with Jesus (14.23). The disciples' experience of union with the risen Christ takes them into the unity which exists between him and the Father (17.20–21). Thus, as Paul saw, Jesus is the focal point for all people of the experience of being a child of God, for all, that is, who can pray to God as 'Abba', in the spirit of Jesus himself.

(e) The sonship of Jesus is thus a matter of relationship. John's word *monogenés* (John 1.18) was wrongly taken in the history of doctrine to denote 'only-begotten' (so AV), but actually means 'unique' (RSV only).

It does not carry with it the notion of a divine begetting, nor does it necessarily imply pre-existence. For this idea we must turn to other aspects of the New Testament's witness to the disciples' understanding of Jesus and God.

Jesus the word and wisdom of God

The proclamation that Jesus is the Christ opened up a new depth of understanding of personal relationship with God, which is focused in Jesus, but is available to all. The proclamation has, however, other consequences also, because the claim that Jesus is the Messiah is not a timeless statement, but relates to God's purpose and plan. If the general resurrection has been anticipated in Jesus, it means that part of God's plan has been accomplished in him by anticipation. The thought that God has a plan of redemption belongs to the determinism which is characteristic of Judaism in New Testament times. The visionaries of the intertestamental period sought to discover God's plan for the future in the certainty that it was already available in the secrets of heaven, if only these could be unlocked. As we have seen, the disciples interpreted the death and resurrection of Jesus in the light of the Scriptures, in which the events of redemption were revealed in advance, and had now come to pass in his person.

This sense of the divine plan can be seen in Paul's statement that 'When the time had fully come, God sent forth his Son' (Gal. 4.4). This implies that the proper time according to God's plan has been reached. It does not yet amount to a statement of the pre-existence of Jesus himself.

However, when Paul describes Jesus in 1 Cor 1.24 as the true 'Wisdom' of God, his representative through whom alone righteousness, sanctification and redemption from sin are possible (1.30), the discussion is taken further. The equation between Jesus and 'Wisdom' is not developed in this passage. Yet here we have the beginnings of a new understanding of Jesus's person, in which he is regarded as the present expression of a divine Wisdom which existed before time began. Behind this language there is the figure of Wisdom in the Old Testament and intertestamental period, an attribute of God which is personified almost as something separate from him, in much the same way as happens with the Spirit of the Lord. Notable passages for the personification of Wisdom are Proverbs 8, Wisdom of Solomon 6–10 and Ecclesiasticus 24. The same background explains Paul's description of Jesus in 1 Cor. 8.6 as the Lord 'through whom are all things and through whom we exist'. For in these passages Wisdom shares in God's creation and dwells protectively among his people.

Similar ideas occur in Col. 1.15–20, where Jesus is called the 'image' of God who 'exists before everything' (verses 15 and 17). As in the Corinthians passages, Jesus becomes the one who reflects God's nature on earth, having participated before time in his creative activity (verse 16). But in two respects new ground is broken in this passage; and in both cases the writer emphasises the intimate relationship which exists between the Father and the Son. First, the statement in verse 19 that 'in him (the Son) the complete being of God came to dwell' implies that the final self-disclosure which takes place in Jesus, the Messiah, connects once and for all the spheres of natural and revealed religion. Here are the real beginnings of what was later to flower as 'incarnational theology'. Secondly, Jesus is identified as the goal, and not merely the origin, of creation: 'the whole universe has been created through him and for him' (verse 16). Clearly the understanding of God which allows such a place for his creative and recreative agent, who, having shed his blood to reconcile the universe to himself, can now be regarded as 'in all things supreme' (verse 18), marks a step forward of momentous significance.

Outside the Pauline writings a very similar idea is expressed in terms of 'Word' rather than 'Wisdom', using a term which would be familiar to Greeks (from the Stoic philosophers, for example) as well as Jews (e.g. Genesis 1, 'God said . . .'; cf. Ps. 33.6, Wisd. 18.15). The key passages are Heb. 1.1–4 and John 1.1–18. Both echo ideas about Jesus already noted in Corinthians and Colossians. Hebrews 1 declares that the God who 'spoke' in creation and in history through the prophets has now finally and fully spoken to us in his Son for the purposes of a new creation. These verses draw on the poem on Wisdom in the Wisdom of Solomon (7.2–8.1).

In the prologue of John, however, the Word is personified in the manner of the Old Testament Wisdom poems, especially Ecclesiasticus 24. John's choice of 'Word' rather than 'Wisdom' may be due to the need to avoid the personification of Wisdom as a woman, which is found in this and other poetic models ('Wisdom' is a feminine word in both Hebrew and Greek.) For here the Word is not only God's partner in the creation and the light that illumines every human being, but is incarnate in Jesus himself. In him the Word becomes flesh (John 1.14). Thus he is not merely, like the prophets, a person through whom God speaks, but the actual embodiment of the Word of God. Just as the Law, so dear to the Jewish people, was held to be the embodiment of the pre-existent Wisdom (Ecclus. 24.23), so Jesus is the incarnation of the pre-existent Word. Just as the Law, like the manna in the wilderness, was held to be the nourishment of the soul, so Jesus is the true bread from heaven which gives life to the world (John 6.32–33). Just as Hebrews describes him as the 'radiance of God's glory' (Heb. 1.3), so John tells how 'we saw his glory, glory as of a father's only son' (John 1.14). Jesus is the human face of God, and to see him is to see the Father (14.9). He is the incarnate Son; and just as the Wisdom of God at the creation 'was at his side each day, his darling and delight' (Prov. 8.30 NEB), so the Word of God can be called his Son from the beginning. The mutual relation of Father and Son, which is central to the spirituality of Jesus, and which characterises his relationship to God as the exalted Messiah, applies too to the Word of God, of which Jesus is the incarnation. Thus the prayer of Jesus in John 17 includes the thought of the 'glory which I had with thee before the world was made' (verse 5).

It should now be clear that the New Testament precludes the impression that Jesus is a man raised to divinity alongside God to form a second God. It is not, then, a case of the deification of a human being. As the exalted Messiah he is 'the first-born among many brethren' (Rom. 8.29), bringing all humankind into union with God; but as the incarnation of the Word of God he partakes of the nature of God himself, making God accessible to our race in his human life. It is the preaching, healing, loving, suffering Jesus who, as the Word made flesh, has made God known (John 1.18).

The God who is made known

The passages discussed all claim, in their own way, that with the coming of Jesus Christ the Creator is made specially accessible to his creatures. But they also reflect a new and developing appreciation of the *kind* of God who has come in the Son. For example, John's portrait of Jesus as the enfleshed Word of God, who came from the Father (John 10.30, 16.28) and lived among us (1.14), represents a profound understanding of incarnation, and one which was to have a far-reaching effect on subsequent Christian doctrine. But it also contains implications for the Christian view of God himself, whose sovereign purpose 'that the world might be saved' (3.17) was brought about, John shows us, by means of a total self-giving love. The exact quality of that love was manifested in his only Son, crucified and glorified (3.13–17).

The significance which the New Testament gives to the death and resurrection of Jesus offers us a further important insight into the early Christian understanding of God. For in the crucifixion and exaltation of Jesus God enters into human suffering, and is intimately related to his people. He is revealed not only as the providential Father of humankind, who was specially present and active in the life of Christ, but also as the Father of a crucified Son. God's involvement in the ministry and message of Jesus, which constitutes the divine initiative in salvation, extends to his death and resurrection as well.

The passion of Jesus appears from the perspective of history to be utter tragedy. But seen from the divine viewpoint it is the climax of Jesus's declaration of God's love. The sacrificial value of the death of Jesus as an atonement for sin is already declared in the earliest preaching of the disciples (1 Cor. 15.3). The same idea is taken up and expounded in other parts of the New Testament. Thus the writer of 1 Peter holds up before his readers, as an example for them to follow, the way in which on our behalf Jesus shared, but also transformed, the tragedy of human suffering (1 Pet. 2.20–25).

Among the New Testament witnesses Paul and John, in particular, highlight the significance of the cross for the understanding of God. Paul indicates, first of all, that God entered into the suffering which Christ's passion involved. 'He who did not spare his own Son', he says, 'but delivered him up on behalf of us all, how shall he not also with him freely give us all things?' (Rom. 8.32). Here the fact that it is the Father who has delivered up his Son preserves the divine initiative, so that the human tragedy can be seen to have its providential side. But because it is God himself who 'does not spare' Jesus, in that gift to us he is deeply involved in the total act of redemptive suffering.

The same thought is reflected in John, who goes further than Paul in his delineation of the nature of God's gift by stressing the filial obedience of Jesus to the Father, and by relating that to the cross as its culminating point. Jesus, according to John, accepted death as the fullest expression of his sonship. The proof that he is 'from above' is seen in the fact that 'the Son of man *must* be lifted up' in death (John 3.14). But the cross itself provides the ultimate demonstration of the moral unity between Jesus and the Father (cf. John 8.28), and in this way not only reveals the obedience of the Son in completing the work which the Father gave him to do (17.4), but also characterises the nature of the God who initiated the work of salvation in the first place. By 'giving' his Son to the world which he loved, the Father, in John's view, entered fully into the suffering which that entailed.

John's account of the death of Jesus as 'glorification' brings out another insight in the early Christian understanding of God. For the death and resurrection of Jesus not only made the first believers aware of God's involvement in his suffering world, they also spoke of the new and permanent relationship with the Father which is possible through the Son. When John describes the approaching death of Jesus, or his actual crucifixion, as a 'glorification' (e.g. John 7.39, 12.23), this implies that in the very moment of 'lifting up' in agony it is possible to see the exaltation of Jesus to his designated place 'at the right hand of God' (Heb. 10.12, cf. Ps. 110.1), with its promise of final blessedness for all who believe. Similarly, what began in the incarnation was completed by the cross. Just as during the earthly ministry of Jesus the life-giving presence of God was brought to humankind, so in a final act of self-giving on the cross, through which Jesus returns to the Father (John 13.3), the eternal life or 'glory' of God becomes available to every believer for all time.

The spiritual implications of such a 'glorification' are very rich indeed. Because the Word of God has dwelt among us (John 1.14), it is possible not only to see God but also to abide in him through Christ (17.21). Such an intimate indwelling, furthermore, is complemented by the fact that God abides in the believers through the risen Jesus (14.23). Paul uses different language to make the same vital point. The life and death and resurrection of Jesus together are the basis for a mutual indwelling: God in us (1 Cor. 6.20) and we in God (Col. 3.3). The church has peace with God through Jesus Christ (Rom. 5.1); and its spiritual inheritance is such that its members can be described as 'God's heirs and Christ's fellow-heirs' (8.17). The vision is completed by the author of Revelation, who glimpses a 'new heaven and a new earth' in which God dwells at last among his people. 'He will dwell among them and they shall be his people, and God himself will be with them' (Rev. 21.1–3).

The holy spirit

How is this new quality of divine life, to which the New Testament in varying ways bears witness, to be sustained on earth? The answer to that question takes up the Old Testament teaching on the spirit of Yahweh, generally referred to in New Testament times as the Holy Spirit. From the first Jesus claimed that his prophetic ministry was inspired by the Holy Spirit (Matt. 12.28), and indeed his baptism by John was interpreted as his Messianic anointing by the Spirit (Mark 1.10–11). According to prophecy the coming age would be marked with a general outpouring of the spirit (Joel 2.28, cf. Acts 2.17), and this could already be seen in the charismatic gifts in the church (1 Cor. 12).

In the writings of Paul, however, there is an explicitly Christian development in the understanding of the Holy Spirit. In Paul's thought the Spirit indwells both the church and the believer; and the meeting-place of the spirit of God and our spirit is the believing community, and that community alone (cf. 1 Cor. 3.16–17, 6.19). Moreover the Spirit's help is a necessary precondition of Christian faith (1 Cor. 12.3). From such starting points arises Paul's further insight that only when the Spirit indwells the church can its continuing life be sustained, and the gifts of God regularly manifested (12.4–10).

John develops in a highly significant manner the understanding of the Spirit noted elsewhere in the New Testament. To some extent John shares with the other Gospel writers an 'endowment' view of the Spirit. In his account of Christ's baptism too the Spirit descends on Jesus 'as a dove from heaven' (John 1.32a), and after the resurrection Jesus is said to give the Holy Spirit to his disciples to equip them for their mission (20.22–23). But unlike the other three Gospel writers, John stresses that the Spirit *remains* with Jesus from the moment of his baptism onwards and throughout his ministry (1.32b, cf. 7.39); and the Spirit who remains with Jesus during his earthly work also dwells in the church after his glorification (14.16–17). The concept of an indwelling Spirit, creating as well as demanding a mutual indwelling between God and the believers, is thus one which John shares with Paul.

The further and particular contribution which John makes to the Christian apprehension of the Spirit's nature, however, lies in his description of the Spirit in personal terms. In the 'farewell discourse' (John 14–16) the Spirit is spoken of as the Paraclete. There is good reason to argue that this word is used to present the Spirit in personal terms as the *alter ego* of Jesus himself. Thus after the resurrection the nature and activity of the Paraclete are similar to those of Jesus before his glorification. But while in these chapters the Paraclete is *like* Jesus, acting for him in the early Christian community, he is also *distinguished* from Jesus. He is sent by Jesus to the disciples from the Father. Indeed he is explicitly identified as the Holy Spirit (14.26), who after the exaltation of Christ helps his followers. By thus personalising the Spirit, and also seeing him as the distinct *alter ego* of the divine Son of God, John goes much further than other New Testament writers, including Paul, and moves the Christian understanding of the Holy Spirit in a direction which eventually produces the trinitarian formula of God.

The New Testament views of the Spirit, we may conclude, build on Old Testament teaching and develop it. In so doing the Christian perception of the Spirit adds significantly to the understanding of God himself which was developing in the early church. In the light of the incarnation and glorification of Jesus Christ the Spirit of God is thought of not only as the outgoing power and presence of God, but also as personal in a manner which distinguishes him from both Jesus and God. This thinking moves beyond the Old Testament view of the Spirit as the transcendent God intervening from time to time in his creation to an understanding of the Spirit as abiding in the life of the Christian community and of the

individual believer, inspiring both, and transforming them into the
likeness of Christ.

Conclusion

We can now draw together the threads of this chapter, in which we
have been thinking of the effects of the coming of Jesus on the disciples'
understanding of God. This coming brought a new realisation of
God's accessibility, a recognition of his entrance into human suffering
and of his relationship to his people, and at the same time a new
estimate of the persons of Christ and of the Spirit in relation to God
himself.

The Christian story is a story of grace, the grace of God's kingdom
preached by Jesus and demonstrated in his sacrificial death. From the
very first the disciples proclaimed that he was risen and exalted as the
Messiah and Son of God. Thus the cross was seen to be the act of God's
love, assuring a final outcome in the salvation of all who believed. In
making this proclamation, they set Jesus so high, far above the ranks
of angels, at the right hand of God himself, that there was a well-nigh
irresistible pressure to 'make him equal with God', as the opponents of
the Christian message were not slow to point out (John 5.18, 10.33). Yet
this pressure could never lead to the conclusion that Jesus was a second
god, because it was the love of God himself that had been demonstrated
in him, and which had become accessible through him.

In fact the way to a resolution of the difficulty had been prepared by the
personification of the attributes of God within the Jewish religious
tradition. The Christian idea of the Holy Spirit in the New Testament,
for example, is not fundamentally different from that of the Spirit of
Yahweh in the Old Testament, although, as we have seen, it has been
greatly enriched as a result of experience. Similarly the Wisdom or Word
of Yahweh was available to express God in relation to his creation,
especially in salvation history and in the Law considered as God's gift. By
seeing Jesus first as the expression of God's Wisdom (Paul) and then as
the actual embodiment of his Word (John), the unique role of Jesus in the
history of salvation could be given a theological explanation by those
who were aware that through him they were incorporated into God's
kingdom as his children, and already shared in the gifts of the Spirit
which belong to the kingdom. Thus God, the God of Israel, is also
known as the Father of his crucified and redeeming Son, and in the
distinguishable person of his sanctifying Spirit. But precisely because
these are, theologically speaking, also functions or attributes of the one
God, the unity of God is not impaired.

The beginnings of Christian doctrine in the New Testament are varied and tentative, and it remained for the Church Fathers to work out the implications of them. But the Christian doctrine of God is not a speculative theory. It is an attempt at understanding a profound religious experience, centred in the life and teaching of Jesus. It is an experience which is superbly captured in the words of Paul's greeting at the close of 2 Corinthians (13.14): 'The grace of the Lord Jesus Christ and the love of God and the fellowship of the Holy Spirit be with you all.'

Chapter 7
God as Trinity: an approach through prayer

1. Why the neglect of the doctrine of the trinity today?

Christians confronted with the claims of other religions may be aware that their faith can be distinguished from other brands of theism by its particular kind of trinitarian structure. It is neither bald, undifferentiated monotheism, nor is it polytheism. Yet the majority of Christians in the West today, it must be admitted, would be hard pressed even to give an account, let alone a defence, of the developed doctrine of the Trinity as expressed in Christianity's historic creeds and the documents of its Councils. Most professing Christians know how to use the language of Father, Son and Spirit in the varied and unsystematic way that we find in the New Testament. There are 'rules' for this language that are generally acknowledged in the Church. Christians know that there is something wholly inappropriate, for instance, in saying that 'God the Father died on the cross', even if they cannot give a coherent explanation of the reason. The way Luke unfolds the story of God's salvation is the dominant influence here in controlling our use of the language of Father, Son and Spirit: at the historical level there was first the Father God of the Old Testament, then the Son, then, at the Son's 'departure', the Spirit.

What many perhaps do not realise is that efficiency in operating the 'rules' of this New Testament language is still a very far cry from acknowledgement of God as Trinity. Even Paul's familiar grace in 2 Cor. 13.14 is not trinitarian in this stricter sense: 'the grace of the Lord Jesus Christ and the love of God and the fellowship of the Holy Spirit' clearly indicates that 'God' here means the Father alone, despite the close (but theologically unclarified) juxtaposition of Son and Spirit.

The developed doctrine of the Trinity, then, is another matter. This was enunciated by the end of the fourth century, and is implied by the Nicene creed, the creed used today in most celebrations of the eucharist. Here God is seen as eternally triune, which means that in the Godhead there are united three 'persons' ('hypostases'), who are distinguishable only by number and relation to one another, and inseparable in their activity. It is this latter understanding of the doctrine of the Trinity with which this chapter is concerned; and it is this that seems to have lost its allure for the majority of contemporary Western Christians, so that Karl Rahner has justly remarked that 'Christians, for all their orthodox profession of faith in the Trinity, are virtually just "monotheist" in their actual religious existence' (*Theological Investigations* IV. 79). Many, that is, if asked to describe 'God', would give a description of the Father only.

Why is this? Many factors have contributed to this quiet anti-trinitarian tendency in Western Christianity, and cumulatively they are certainly powerful. As far back as the medieval period, scholastic theology made philosophical discussion of God as *one* a prior and preliminary task to discussion of his revelation as three-in-one; and this in itself, it has been argued, implicitly promoted an undifferentiated monotheism at the expense of trinitarianism. But even more significantly, people today are now heirs of the Enlightenment. They are not afraid of a critical approach. Many are less prone to believe a doctrine simply because it is taught or because it is part of our tradition. 'The wise man apportions his belief to the evidence', wrote David Hume. Free enquiry must take place, and if it does not lead to orthodoxy, then this is part of the liberty that must be granted to the human mind. 'Whosoever will be saved . . . (must) . . . worship one God in Trinity' is not the kind of constraint which Christians of this generation are likely to heed.

In modern theology, too, there is a good deal to militate against belief in the doctrine of an eternally triune God. As we have seen, it appears at first sight to have been built up from the inherited belief in the Father God of Israel as the one supreme God, through the growing awareness of Christ as God, and of the Holy Spirit as co-equal with the Father and the Son in his divinity. To explain how all three could be God and yet affirm belief in the one God without 'confounding the persons' or 'dividing the substance' was the task of the leaders of the early Church. But today it is nothing like so clear that the evidence provided by the New Testament and related sources demands this belief in the divinity of Christ and the distinctness and divinity of the Holy Spirit in the way it was understood in the early Church. Historical-critical study of the New Testament has here been the major force for criticism and change; and the portrait of Jesus of Nazareth which emerges from nearly two centuries of enquiry has for many become far more alluring than the seemingly alien formulas of fifth-century Chalcedonian orthodoxy.

Furthermore (in the Western Church in particular) the doctrine of the Holy Spirit has received limited attention. For centuries orthodox trinitarianism led to the inclusion of the Holy Spirit with the Father and the Son in doxologies, prayers, ascriptions and most artistic representations. But in speaking of the Spirit of God at work in the cosmos, were Christians perhaps really just meaning God the Father at work in a particular way? Is there any need to apportion a separate 'hypostasis' to the Holy Spirit? Is this not basically a question of imagery and language? Even in the most charismatic circles today the experience of the Spirit is the experience of God with us. Do we then really need 'another Paraclete?' Or is John making this distinction simply to account for the difference between the historical experience of Jesus among his disciples and the continuing presence of the risen Christ in the church?

There is therefore a good deal in modern Western theology to dispose people towards the undifferentiated monotheism which has been detected in twentieth-century Christians. Some would argue that the experience of dialogue with other faiths makes abandonment of traditional trinitarianism an even more compelling possibility. A further consideration, highly significant for an age intent on authentication by direct experience, was put classically by Schleiermacher (*The Christian Faith* II 738): 'The Trinity is not an immediate utterance concerning the Christian self-consciousness.' That is, or so Schleiermacher claimed, the doctrine of the Trinity is not apparently verifiable through religious experience. But this is an assertion which calls for careful enquiry.

2. Rediscovery of the triune God: an approach through prayer

Most Christians would probably say that their experience of God is not obviously or immediately perceived as trinitarian in structure. But does a deepening relationship to God in prayer, especially prayer of a relatively non-discursive or wordless kind, allow one to remain satisfied with a simple undifferentiated monotheism? Naturally there are all sorts of tricky philosophical difficulties about this line of approach. The phenomenon of prayer is varied, and certainly not easy to describe with exactitude. Further, its interpretation is inevitably affected by certain cherished concepts (e.g., biblical ideas, tradition and liturgy), so that there is some circularity in the attempt to capture in terms of doctrine what may be happening. Moreover, competing interpretations abound for so-called 'contemplative' experiences (including the Buddhist way of eliminating the concept of God altogether). But this does not mean that it is impossible to find in the activity of Christian prayer some telling experiential basis for trinitarian reflection.

What is it that Christians who attend silently to God discover? We are not talking of some 'contemplative' elite, but of anyone who regularly spends even a very short time in a quiet waiting upon God. Often, it must be admitted, what will be encountered is darkness, obscurity and distraction. It is no wonder that the experience has such a strange lack of obvious content, for the relationship is one unlike any other, one that relates those who pray to that without which they would not be in being at all. It is (and here Schleiermacher was surely right) a relationship of 'absolute dependence'. Yet perhaps, amid the obscurity, a little more may be said. Usually it dawns bit by bit on the person praying that this activity, which at first seems all one's own doing, is actually the activity of another. It is the experience of being 'prayed in', the discovery that 'we do not know how to pray as we ought' (Rom. 8.26), but are graciously caught up in a divine conversation, passing back and forth in and through the one who prays, 'the Spirit himself bearing witness with our spirit' (Rom. 8.16). We come to prayer empty-handed, aware of weakness, inarticulacy and even of a certain hollow 'fear and trembling', yet it is precisely in these conditions (cf 1 Cor. 2.3–4) that divine dialogue flows. Here then is a way of beginning to understand what it might be to talk of the distinctiveness of the Spirit. It is not that the Spirit is being construed as a divine centre of consciousness entirely separate from the Father, as if two quite different people were having a conversation. Nor, again, is the Spirit conceived as the relationship between two entities that one can assume to be fixed (the Father and the person praying), a relationship which is then perhaps somewhat arbitrarily personified. Rather, and more mysteriously, the Spirit is here seen as that current of divine response to divine self-gift in which the one who prays is caught up and thereby transformed (see again Rom. 8.9–27, 1 Cor. 2.9–16).

Now if this is so, then, logically speaking, what the one who prays comes first to apprehend is the Spirit in its distinctive identity, and only from there do they move on to appreciate the true mystery and *richesse* of the Son. This too is of course a Pauline insight (1 Cor. 12.3: 'No one can say Jesus is Lord except by the Holy Spirit'), but needs spelling out further. For the apprehensions to be made in the light of prayer about the second person of the Trinity are varied, and only indirectly lead one back to the human career of Jesus of Nazareth, although they do indeed lead there.

First, and most fundamentally, when Christians pray like this, their experience of participation in a divine dialogue is an experience of a God who actively and always wills to be amongst us, God Emmanuel. This being so the very structure of prayer is already 'incarnational' (in one sense of that admittedly ambiguous word), and thus immediately focuses attention on the second person in the Godhead.

But second, and more specifically, in allowing the divine activity of prayer to happen, the one who prays begins to glimpse what it might be to be 'in Christ' or to 'have the mind of Christ' (1 Cor. 2.16), or to be 'fellow heirs with Christ' (Rom. 8.18). It is to allow oneself to be shaped by the mutual interaction of Father and Spirit; and in praying the prayer of Christ, in letting the Spirit cry 'Abba, Father' (Rom. 8.15, Gal. 4.6) to make the transition from regarding Christ merely as an external model for imitation to entering into his divine life itself. Paul does not idly say, 'It is no longer I who live, but Christ who lives in me' (Gal. 2.20). To discover this posture of prayer is to be remodelled by the activity of God in the redeemed life of 'sonship' (Rom. 8.15). It is to become nothing less than 'other Christs' in the particularity of our lives, not by any active merit of our own, but simply by willing that which already holds us in existence to reshape us in the likeness of his Son.

But thirdly (and here the reference to the historical life of Jesus of Nazareth again becomes vital), the God whom Christians meet in this prayer is also one who appears, sometimes for very long periods, to desert us; or worse still (as in St John of the Cross's 'Night of the Spirit') to press upon us with apparently negative pressure, causing disturbance, deep uneasiness, the highlighting of sin and even the fear of insanity. Such are the death-throes of the domineering ego. But only in the light thrown on the activity of the Trinity by the story of Christ is this endurable. If we are being 'conformed to the image of (the) Son' (Rom. 8.29), it is precisely aridity and disturbance that we should expect. Only through suffering comes glorification (Rom. 8.17). If we take our cue from the agony in the garden, or from the dereliction of the cross, then the authentic cry of 'Abba' (Mark 14.33–6) indicates that the most powerful and active presence of God is mysteriously compatible with the all too human experiences of anxiety and desolation. Only afterwards do we come to see that what we had thought to be divine absence was in actuality the grace of divine hiddenness. Fidelity to prayer in times such as these, though not always perhaps very consciously Christ-centred, is the measure of our Christ-shaped love.

Fourth, and equally significant in its 'incarnational' implications, is the disconcerting discovery in this kind of prayer that the God who acts thus in us wants us whole, conscious and unconscious, soul and body. 'We await the redemption of our mortal bodies' (Rom. 8.11, 23), for the test of the authentic activity of the Spirit is the apprehension that Jesus Christ has 'come in the flesh' (1 John 4.2). Though Christian tradition is notoriously littered with those who have evaded these implications, it is truly an effect of this prayer that we are gradually forced to accept and integrate those dark and repressed strands of the unconscious that we would rather not acknowledge, and along with these, all aspects of our sexuality, both bodily and emotional.

But it is also true, fifthly, that to find ourselves 'in Christ' is gradually to break through the limitations of the individualism and introspection that often characterise prayer in its earliest stages. The Pauline language about being 'in Christ' describes a mode of being or a status rather than an experience. But because it is corporately shared, it calls in question the supposed absoluteness of the self as an individual or self-contained entity. For all prayer has its corporate dimension; and to pray 'in Christ' is to intuit the mysterious interpenetration of individuals one with another, and thus to question our usual assumptions about the boundaries of the self. It is to discover that central aspect of Pauline christology, the notion of the mutual interdependence of the members of the 'body of Christ' (1 Cor. 12); it is to perceive the flow of trinitarian love coursing out to encompass the whole of humanity.

Sixthly and lastly, the whole creation, inanimate as well as animate, is taken up in this trinitarian flow. To make such a claim could be reckless. Yet it has often been the perception of the mystics to see creation anticipatorily in the light of its true glory, even while it is yet in 'bondage to decay' and 'groaning in travail' (Rom. 8.21–22). Although concern with prayer experience may at first sight reflect a peculiarly modern obsession with direct personal authentication (and indeed carry with it dangers of a kind of narcissistic introversion), nonetheless sustained prayer leads rather to the building up of community than to its dissolution, to intensification rather than atrophy of concern for the life of the world.

The attempt has been to indicate an experience of prayer from which pressure towards trinitarian thinking might arise. As such it is simply a starting point, and no more. But it is clear that we do not here begin with two perfect and supposedly fixed points, Father and Son, external to ourselves and wholly transcendent, with the Spirit then perhaps (rather unconvincingly) characterised as that which relates them. (That, of course, is a caricature of the 'Western' doctrine of the Trinity, but it is a prevalent one.) Rather, we start with the recognition of a vital, though mysterious, divine dialogue within us, through which the meaning and implications of being 'in Christ' become gradually more vivid and extensive. Thus the Trinity ceases to appear as something abstract or merely propositional. It is not solely to do with the internal life of God, but has also to do with us. The flow of trinitarian life is seen as extending into every aspect of our being, personal and social, and beyond that to the bounds of creation.

This approach has strong roots in the thought of Paul. Despite this fact, reflection on prayer is often thought not to have constituted a significant resource for trinitarian discussion during the tortured years of controversy which led to a normative statement of the doctrine at the end of the fourth century. But was this really so? To this question we now turn.

3. Roots in the tradition

Many accounts of the development of the doctrine of the Trinity pay limited attention to the personal encounter with God through prayer. A good deal of the material available for a study of this development was provoked by challenge and controversy, and it is understandable that historians of the doctrine should focus their attention on the proceedings of Church Councils and the writings of theologians attacking or defending particular positions, as well as emphasising the political considerations that often became entangled in the debates.

Yet the resulting account of how the church came to profess first the faith of Nicaea in 325, when the Son was declared to be 'of one substance' with the Father, and then that of Constantinople in 381, by which time the doctrine of the Trinity was given normative expression, is sometimes tidier than it deserves to be. The New Testament, after all, presents varied traditions of early Christian belief about the person of Christ and of the Holy Spirit. It is all too easy to take, for example, the Luke-Acts sequence of the revelation of the God of Israel through the story of Jesus to the day of Pentecost, and to see the pre-Nicene church first establishing Christ's identity with, yet distinction from, God the Father, and then in the wake of Nicaea doing the same for the Holy Spirit. Considerations as to whether the Spirit is in fact regarded by the New Testament authors as a separate Person tend to be brushed over in the light of the strong emphasis on his full acceptance as such in the late fourth century. The tendencies of the second-century defenders of Christianity to think in terms of only two divine Persons, the Father and the Son, are seen as a fumbling after truth. Whatever happened *en route*, the faith of Nicaea is assumed to be at least embryonic in the earliest traditions of the primitive church.

The study of controversy, however, is not without its purpose. Councils concerned with faith in the Trinity were not periodic bureaucratic reviews of a continuing theoretical problem, but were urgently called to meet passionate demands. What was the source of this passion? Why did it manifest itself only rarely in academic circles but all too frequently at congregational level, in the gossip of the court, or in banter over the shop counter? Were all the Lord's people theologians? Or was their argument about their own experience of God as Trinity, and the variety of the interpretations of this experience?

It is important in the first place not to underestimate the degree to which Christians of the first three centuries at least were committed to the regular practice of prayer and worship. People in the ancient world would never have called themselves Christian simply because they believed themselves to be clean-living citizens who dropped into church on family or civic occasions. Baptism marked a clean break with the past. Preparation for baptism lasted two and sometimes three years, and a strict watch was kept over the candidates by their sponsors. The end of the course demanded daily attendance at church; and throughout they were directed to pray at least twice a day (morning and evening, and in some places also at the third, sixth, and ninth hours of the day), and were urged to attend the assemblies of the church in the mornings (Hippolytus), where they would be assured that angels and saints prayed with them (Origen). In other words Christians of this period tended to spend a good deal longer in prayer and reflection than many of their twentieth-century counterparts, and the idea of 'the spiritual life' as something only seriously practised by a special group of professionals was wholly alien to the outlook of the period.

Second, the public prayer of the church allowed considerable opportunity to the congregation for being receptive, for listening and for being 'prayed in'. Congregations at the liturgy for the first four centuries were for the most part silent. There were some responses, but very few. Responsorial psalms were introduced, hymns were composed, but the tendency to leave all the music to the choir increased as the years went by; and, with the increasing gap between the language of the liturgy and the vernacular, people no longer 'followed the service' in detail but simply allowed themselves to be caught up in the flow of the eucharistic action, which was felt by them to unite heaven and earth and to bring them through Christ by the Holy Spirit to the Father.

If we were to say then that the understanding of God as Trinity grew in the early centuries through the Christian's experience of God in prayer, then the opportunity for this was not inconsiderable, and we must now look at this experience in more detail.

(1) *The public prayer of the church.* Two examples may be given to illustrate the intrinsic connection between eucharistic prayer and trinitarian reflection, and thus to indicate how liturgical usage was operative in fostering and guarding some sort of trinitarian notion of God.

(a) The introductory dialogue to the eucharistic prayer in the Western liturgy begins with the words 'The Lord be with you'. Recent scholarship has suggested that this phrase is either a statement or a prayer, meaning probably 'The Spirit of the Lord is with you' or 'May the Spirit of the Lord be with you'. The reply from the congregation is 'And with thy spirit' ('and also with you'), praying that the celebrant may be given the Spirit of God in order that he may properly celebrate the eucharist. For a long period the eucharistic prayer was prayed extempore (Justin, *I Apol.* 65 ff), and presidents of the eucharist were chosen (among other reasons) for their recognised gift of offering prayer of this kind. Hence the importance of invoking the Spirit of God, since 'we know not how to pray as we ought' (Rom. 8.26). In another example, this time from the Byzantine liturgy, before the eucharistic prayer begins there is a dialogue between priest and deacon in the course of which the priest prays, 'May the Holy Spirit come upon you and the Power of the Most High overshadow you' (as at the Annunciation), to which the deacon replies, 'May the same Holy Spirit celebrate with us all the days of our lives'. This echoes the same theology, even though by this time the central prayer of the eucharist is no longer extemporised. The experience attested by St Paul therefore (1 Cor. 2, Rom. 8) is here highlighted in the liturgy. We do not presume to come to the Lord's table by our own efforts. We are brought to the presence of God through Christ by the Holy Spirit.

(b) It would of course be equally true to say not only that the celebrant of the eucharist is conscious of being prayed in by the Holy Spirit, but that the prayer which he offers is not his but the prayer of Christ – in other words, Christ prays in him. This, however, needs to be understood carefully. We could say that the celebrant of the eucharist in Justin Martyr's time was conscious that the eucharistic gift of the body and blood of Christ was given in virtue of 'the prayer of the Word who is from him' [*sc.* God the Father] (*I Apol.* 66.3) (and not by any mystical incantation of the celebrant as the emperor might have heard about the mysteries of Mithras). In this case the response is to the prayer of Christ who prays through his mystical body, the church. In this connection, Origen also notes that this too is the experience of Christians who prepare themselves by obedience and devotion for prayer, who will then 'participate in the prayer of the Word of God who stands in the midst even of those who know him not, and never fails the prayer of anyone, but prays to the Father along with him whose mediator he is' (*De Oratione* 10.2). Thus Christ himself in this instance does the praying, and Christians who pray (cf. *De Orat.* 22.4) become like Christ through their prayer: like him they are sons, like him they cry 'Abba, Father', and all this by the indwelling of the Holy Spirit. So that Christians being 'the image of an image', i.e. being like Christ, who is the 'image' of God (*De Orat.* 22.4), pray *as* Christ and pray Christ's prayer. 'Now you became Christs', writes Cyril of Jerusalem, 'by receiving the . . . Holy Spirit; everything has been wrought in you because you are the likenesses (i.e. images) of Christ.'

(2) *Prayer in general.* If in liturgical prayer it is possible to discern the pattern of a trinitarian experience of God, of being brought to the Father

through incorporation into the Son by the power of the Holy Spirit, then we should expect the same to be true of accounts of prayer in general. This is certainly the case in some authors. Origen's treatise on prayer belongs to the latter part of his life and was written at Caesarea. We have already given some indication of his understanding of the dynamic of prayer, and it is significant that the introductory chapter is given to an exploration of the themes of 1 Cor. 1.30–2.11 and Rom. 8.26 ff. It has already become clear that, for Origen, it is the Spirit who initiates prayer, who makes us Christ-like, and so brings us to the Father. Origen is also insistent that 'we may never pray to anything generated – not even to Christ – but only to God and the Father of all, to whom even Our Saviour himself prayed as we have already said, and teaches us to pray.' Christ for Origen is always High Priest, always Intercessor, always Son as we become sons, so we never pray to him but only through him. Origen's teaching on prayer here is clearly linked with his trinitarian theology, in which the Son is not truly co-equal with the Father, and for which he was later censured. It cannot therefore be claimed that those who pray aright end up inexorably in trinitarian orthodoxy. But it can at least be said that any genuine experience of Christian prayer involves an encounter with God perceived as in some sense triune.

Basil the Great's treatise *On the Holy Spirit*, on the other hand, recounts a similar experience with a modified conclusion in the direction of a more traditional orthodoxy. On first reading it is a keenly dogmatic work written in the heat of controversy, with a good deal of invective against the poor logic of the heretics. Well known (and often greatly disliked) for his defence of Nicene orthodoxy, Basil appears here as a staunch defender of tradition, not least of the baptismal formulas of the church, with the result that one could read him as a person with 'party' interests and a merely intellectual grasp of the position he feels bound to defend. From what we know of his life, this is clearly to underestimate him. Given to the monastic life from an early period, and never as archbishop abandoning his ascetic practices of prayer and self-discipline, it is not surprising that something of personal experience emerges in the course of his defence. The following passage reflects his personal discipline as well as his vision of truth:

> The Spirit comes to us when we withdraw ourselves from evil passions, which have crept into the soul through its friendship with the flesh, alienating us from a close relationship with God . . . Then, like the sun, he will show you in himself the image of the invisible [sc. the Son], and with purified eyes you will see in this blessed image the unspeakable beauty of its prototype [sc. the Father] . . . From this comes knowledge of the future, understanding of mysteries . . . a place in the choir of angels, endless joy in the

presence of God, becoming like God, and, the highest of all desires, becoming God. (*On The Holy Spirit*, 9.23)

The significant feature here is that through this direct encounter of the individual's spirit (or soul) with the Spirit of God (cf. 1 Cor. 2, the spiritual with the Spiritual) we are enabled first to see Christ and through this perfect Image to behold the Father, and secondly, as a consequence of our inner illumination, to become spiritual ourselves through God's gracious act of deification. The entire experience, in other words, is trinitarian; and Basil here is setting out a distinct logic and progression in the roles of each divine 'person' in assimilating the Christian to God. Hence, although all three 'persons' do indeed act together, it is important to note that Spirit and Son cannot be seen as mere alternatives.

4. Conclusions

What then, may be concluded from the analysis of these Pauline passages and their spiritual and trinitarian significance for the early Greek fathers? We have seen that the development of the doctrine of the Trinity in the early church, though so often and necessarily described in terms of theological controversy and the activity of Councils, has its roots firmly in Christian experiences of God through liturgy and personal prayer. The technical trinitarian formularies that were eventually agreed in the fourth and fifth centuries grew in part out of that experience. Nevertheless they were primarily intended as defences against theological alternatives that were deemed misleading, and in themselves rarely conveyed much to inspire and reveal the true nature of the Godhead. Nor indeed did their original exponents propose them as descriptions of their trinitarian God. Rather, they provided the best available means of protecting from erroneous interpretation something that was to a large degree intellectually overwhelming. Only two centuries after the Council of Constantinople, Maximus the Confessor could express his profound dissatisfaction with the use of the term *ousia* ('substance') about the Godhead at all. His objection was spiritually motivated: the reality of God must of necessity transcend all attempts to capture it, even in these hallowed conceptual terms.

If then it is the experience of prayer, both personal and corporate, which is our primary access to God as Trinity, several important conclusions accrue for today. First, we become aware that prayer must have priority, and that no amount of sheer intellectual effort on the one hand, or authoritarian bludgeoning on the other, will effect a lively belief in a trinitarian God. One may undergo the regular discipline of reciting the Athanasian creed; but to no avail if 'the one thing needful' is lacking.

Secondly, the experience of being mysteriously caught up by divine dialogue into the likeness of Christ, while indicating the necessity for thinking in some sort of trinitarian terms, will never in itself yield hard-edged conceptual certainty. The actual business of prayer is itself so varied that the fact that there are differences between various conceptual models for the Trinity should not so greatly surprise us, nor should the constant impression, especially when examining the mystics of the church, that their experience continually chafes at the limits of the traditional and authoritative formularies. This is not to say that it is impossible to establish workable and agreed criteria for distinguishing good from bad doctrinal accounts, or even for effecting some rapprochement between Eastern and Western traditions. But it does mean that any desire for crude and absolute certainty is likely to go disappointed.

If this is so, then, thirdly, light may also be thrown on the pressing contemporary issue from which this chapter started: that of Christianity's relation to other world religions. For here we confront a paradox. On the one hand, the approach to the Trinity through prayer does indeed point up differences between Christianity and other forms of faith. Not only does the Christian who prays, if the account given here is sound, come to discover some felt need for a particular sort of threefold differentiation in the Godhead, a feature unique to Christian theism; but there are also the further ramifications of the 'incarnational' characteristics of prayer – the positive attitude to the body and to the material world on the one hand, and, even more significantly, the haunting image of a God exposed in Christ crucified, of divine presence mediated precisely through weakness and dereliction. These, surely, are the central distinguishing features of Christian theism. Yet from the same experience of prayer emerges the other side of the paradox. For the obscurity, the darkness, the sheer defencelessness of wordless prayer usually lead rather to a greater openness to other traditions than to an assured sense of superiority; and the experience of God thus dimly perceived brings about a curious intuitional recognition of the activity of 'contemplation' in others, whether or not the concept of God to which they adhere is congruous with the Christian one. This latter factor we can surely ill afford to ignore, however difficult it is to incorporate it into a convincing intellectual solution to the problem of vying religious truth claims.

Fourthly, an approach to the Trinity through prayer has implications for the currently vexed issue of masculine and feminine language as applied to God. This is neither a digression, nor a purely contemporary fad, as any comprehensive survey of trinitarian thought would quickly make plain. It has again and again been the insight of those given to prayer that description of the triune God which is not fatally inadequate must somehow encompass, as a matter of balance, what we are conditioned to call feminine characteristics – patience, compassion, endurance, forgiveness, warmth, sustenance and so on – no less than the strength, power, activity, initiative, wrath and suchlike that our society has tended to regard as peculiarly masculine. Sometimes in the Christian tradition this insight has led to a somewhat curious compensating for the assumed masculine stereotyping of the Father by the use of feminine language to refer to one of the other Persons – Spirit or Son. (In the early Syriac theology and in the pseudo-Macarian homilies, for instance, the Spirit is feminine and motherly; in Julian of Norwich, as is better known, Christ is described as 'Our Mother'.) At other times, and perhaps more convincingly, there has been a primary insistence on the ultimate unknowability of God, transcending all categories of gender, combined with a secondary realisation that prayer also forces us to recognise, at the level of anthropomorphic description, the need for a balance of so-called masculine and feminine characteristics in the undivided activity of all three 'Persons'. (Gregory of Nyssa at times approaches this position.)

Just as it is a not uncommon experience among those who give themselves seriously to the practice of prayer that sooner or later they have to face their own need of an integrated sexuality, and of an inward personal balance between activity and receptivity, initiative and response, so too prayer may bring us to a deeper, more comprehensive and more satisfying doctrine of the triune God. Through prayer God can be recognised both as the creative power on whom all depend for their existence, and also as the one who in the dereliction of Christ's cross is disclosed as enduring in patient weakness, and coming perilously close to defeat. The Spirit who prays in us and is known in prayer is indeed Lord and Lifegiver, but also one who cries 'Abba, Father' with us in doubt and darkness and in the sharing of Christ's sufferings. Both man and woman are 'in the image of God', and God is the fullness of the Trinity. The 'masculine' and 'feminine' qualities (as we call them) which we all share in varying admixture are both of them for us clues and glimpses of the wholeness of divine life and love.

Chapter 8
God known through encounter and response

It should be clear by now that believing in God is different from believing in any other truth and that knowing God is not quite like knowing anything else. There are several reasons why this must be so, and one of them is that God is essentially and forever the Initiator and Animator. He can never for a moment be simply the object of our thought or our knowing or our believing. In some way he is always the prompter of our search for him, the director of our speculation about him, the giver of our faith in him. There is no understanding of God which is not by his self-revelation.

Call and obedience

Yet he brings this about without infringing the freedom of our relationship with him or emasculating the part we play in it; and one method by which he achieves this is that of call and response, a theme which runs through the whole Bible. People, both individually and corporately, experience God as the One who calls at a particular time and with a specific demand. Individually or corporately they are free to respond or to refuse. If they obey, they learn through the exigencies and the rewards of their fidelity more than they knew before about the God who issued the summons and was with them in the enterprise. Thus, the God who reveals himself to Moses as 'I AM' also says, 'Come now, I will send you to Pharaoh', and it is through Moses' eventual (and rather unwilling) response to this edict that he comes to that profounder knowledge of God which makes him the greatest of all the leaders of God's people Israel. We are indeed as free to accept or dissent from statements about God as to obey or resist his commands. But it is in the process of obedience that a learning takes place far deeper and more personal than the mental acceptance of propositions, because it is not just a learning but a loving. In the words of the ancient tag, *Quantum Deus diligitur tantum cognoscitur*: 'God is known in proportion as he is loved.' This nexus of knowing, loving and doing appears especially strongly in the Epistles and Gospel of John. 'He who loves is born of God and knows God. He who does not love does not know God.' 'This is the love of God, that we keep his commandments.' 'If any man's will is to do his will, he shall know the teaching, whether it is from God or whether I am speaking on my own authority' (1 John 4.7–8; 5.3; John 7.17).

This 'willing to do the will' which is the means by which we come to know God speaks of an obedience and commitment that is neither slavish nor coerced, but spontaneous. The divine call does indeed, for those who respond to it, have something irresistible about it, but their response is like that of a poet to the Muse, or of a lover to the beloved, or of a free people to the call to withstand tyranny. In our response to God's call there is a strong element of 'We can do no other'. In the Johannine writings just referred to, the supreme example of this is Jesus himself. His own unique knowledge of God his Father is bound up with obedience to his Father's will. 'My food is to do the will of him who sent me and to accomplish his work.' 'Truly, truly, I say to you, the Son can do nothing of his own accord, but only what he sees the Father doing.' 'You have not known him; I know him. If I said, I do not know him, I should be a liar like you; but I do know him and I keep his word' (John 4.35, 5.19, 8.55).

It is, of course, a religious commonplace that good people are the ones who know God best. Then why is it that those through whom humanity has learnt most about God have consistently come into conflict with the guardians of conventional piety? There are many reasons that could be given, but one of them is a certain inertia of the imagination. Every one of us is capable of seeing things in a fresh way and expressing them with originality, yet most of us for most of the time settle for some familiar generalisation. Consider how people communicate their response to natural beauty or their appreciation of one another. The view was 'lovely', and they were 'nice', the moon is 'silvery' and babies are 'sweet'; and how refreshing it is when someone's response, probably a child's, generates the sparkle of a more unusual word! So it is with our obedience to God. For long stretches of time we reduce this to a taken-for-granted convention of goodness, and how startling it is when some individual or some community feels impelled to go beyond that in obedience to a more spontaneous, more exacting vocation!

Having the will to do God's will means something more specific than 'I will be good'. Even if it is only crossing the road, like the Good Samaritan, to take responsibility for someone else's need, it involves a change of direction, and perseverance in some venture of which the limits are not yet defined. This is how 'willing to do the will' becomes a discovery of God. Simone Weil was a young teacher of philosophy with an exceptional purity of intellect that would allow no sentiment or inclination to distort the honesty of her pursuit of truth. She became convinced that this pursuit is not only defined by a code of morals common to all, but that for each one it consists of a succession of acts and events which are strictly personal to him, and so essential that he who leaves them on one side never reaches the goal . . . and not to follow such an impulse when it made itself felt, even if it demanded impossibilities, seemed to me the greatest of all ills. Hence my conception of obedience; and I put this conception to the test when I entered the factory and stayed on there.

Her experience as a factory worker branded her with a profound sense of affliction, her own and that of others. It was in the midst of this affliction, the fruit of her obedience to that specific vocation, that, as she was reciting a poem for her comfort, Christ himself came down and took possession of her. Of that moment of revelation she wrote: 'In my arguments about the insolubility of the problem of God I had never foreseen the possibility of that, of a real contact person to person, here below, between a human being and God.'

The 'willing to do the will' by which we come to the knowledge of God need not involve anything so dramatic or devastating as this. But however small-scale and mundane the divine demands may be, our response will involve us in some kind of break-out from a routine. Sometimes the first steps are so imperceptible that we do not realise how deeply we have committed ourselves until it is too late to turn back without breaking faith. This happens especially when those first steps in obedience have brought us into fellowship with others who are already more consciously committed. Those whose personal experience has led them, for example, to be concerned for sufferers from a particular illness, or for victims of some social problem, will recognise this process of being drawn imperceptibly into a deeper and deeper involvement. It seems to have been like this for many of the first disciples of Jesus Christ.

So response to God's call is the way to the knowledge of God's nature. It is the real embodiment of that faith by which alone we may enter a relationship with God. The Epistle to the Hebrews, and the Acts of the Apostles in its account of Stephen's address to the Council, both emphasise this aspect of the faith of Abraham which St Paul had already taken as the archetype of Christian faith. The crux of Abraham's response is shifted from his trust in God's promise of an heir to his boldness in setting forth into the unknown to find a promised land. In the Epistle of James the crux of Abraham's faith is found in his readiness to sacrifice Isaac, but the point he draws from this is the same, namely that faith is embodied and brought to completion through action. Despite Luther's scornful dismissal of James, the same boldness in obedience is the essentially Lutheran concept of saving faith. A quotation from a

Lutheran of this century provides a perfect commentary on the 'willing to do the will' which brings us to the knowledge of God. In *The Nature of Faith* in 1959 Gerhard Ebeling wrote:

> We know that faith is hindered both by a lack of understanding and by a lack of daring, or, more strictly, by a lack of willing. . . . For as not understanding can be the cause of not willing, so also not willing can be the cause of not understanding. In fact, in the last analysis both come from the same root, and only thus can they be properly grasped.

The obedience of prayer

So let us consider some forms of Christian activity which, beginning in simple obedience, tend to draw one into a more complex involvement and a deeper understanding. The first is the activity of prayer. Most people who pray begin to do so in simple obedience. They are called or taught to pray – whether in their childhood home, or at the time of confirmation or conversion, or through a personal experience of challenge, bewilderment or need. Few people begin to pray in a coolly enquiring or experimental spirit; few turn to prayer as simply an option or resource. Even when it is personal need which first evokes prayer, prayer does not present itself as merely one option among others, to be discarded if and when the need has passed. The fact is rather that need reinforces a calling or obligation to pray which was previously neglected or disregarded.

Prayer begins in obedience – as something owed to God or called for by God. If we follow the road of obedience we find ourselves at a quite early stage 'taking in' certain truths about God – taking them in so naturally that we scarcely notice that we are doing so. We take in that God is approachable; that he is not a volatile and potentially explosive power-source which may destroy those who approach too near. When we pray we do not find ourselves afraid of 'touching the Ark of the Covenant' and being struck dead. We also take in that God understands our prayer. We do not find ourselves anxious lest a lack of expertise on our part may prevent our prayer from reaching God or may somehow mislead him when it reaches him. Again, we take in along the road of obedience that God is One – the God of 'all things in heaven and earth'. The practice of prayer does not give rise to anxiety lest we might unknowingly be addressing a particular prayer to 'the wrong god', or lest the matter over which we pray may fall outside the competence or concern of the God to whom we pray. The practice of prayer leads rather to increasing breadth and comprehensiveness in the range of prayer, to a growing sense that every facet of ourselves may and should be exposed to God in prayer and every aspect of the world's life laid before him.

No doubt many people have been 'told' these truths about God before ever they begin to pray. For them the effect of the practice of prayer is to change merely theoretical truths into strong and telling motives for gratitude, trust and a widening sense of responsibility. Through prayer mere assent to truth becomes involvement in, and subjection to, the existential pressure of truth.

But the truth of God which is taken in through the obedience of prayer is not always taken in easily. There is often struggle and difficulty to be met on the road through obedience to understanding. Difficulty arises for some people as they try to pray comprehensively, bringing before God every facet of themselves and everything they know of the needs and distresses of others. If they learned to pray in childhood they were probably taught to aim for such comprehensiveness by praying in an ordered sequence – under successive headings of confession, thanks-giving, petition, intercession and so on. Probably they were taught also to think out, and to identify rather precisely, particular sins to be confessed on a particular occasion or particular requests to be made on behalf of their family or neighbours. In the years of childhood this kind of systematic prayer often 'works well': and so it does for some people throughout their life. But others find it increasingly difficult as their understanding both of themselves and of the world around them becomes more complex and sophisticated. They find that the separate categories of prayer tend to merge and coalesce: the confession of sin merges into gratitude for the gift of forgiveness, intercession for others into penitence for one's general insensitivity to their needs. They find that, instead of saying to God first 'sorry' and then 'thank you' and then 'please', as they were taught to in childhood, they need to say all three things at the very same time, so that the precise content of their prayer cannot be expressed in words or even identified in thought. Thus they find themselves reduced to an inarticulate silence. Similarly, in the complexity of adult life it is often extremely difficult to know exactly what it is that one should be bringing before God or asking of him. A person whose marriage is breaking apart will simply not know wherein his or her sin precisely consists, and a parent whose wayward son has been brought before the courts will simply not know precisely what should be asked for on the son's behalf. So again the aspiration to pray thoughtfully and comprehensively passes into confusion and ultimately into a kind of pleading silence.

When prayer passes into silence it may seem to fail and to be of no avail. But, wrestling with this apparent failure, some people find in it a deeper understanding. For when they themselves have fallen inwardly silent and, in the ordinary sense of the term, have ceased to pray, they have a strong sense that prayer is continuing in or through them, that when one has ceased to be the agent of prayer one may still be the place of prayer. So they begin to understand for themselves the truth of St Paul's teaching about the prayer of the indwelling Spirit, about that divine dialogue between the Spirit and the Father which belongs, as we were reflecting in the preceding chapter, to the inner life of the Trinity. In the silence which is the apparent failure of one's obedient prayer one may come to understand that it is not only or primarily by our human prayer that the world is 'bound with gold chains about the feet of God'. The strong and unbreakable 'chain' is the mutual communication of the Spirit who indwells the world and the eternal Father: and through the obedience of prayer we may come to recognise this chain as passing through ourselves.

Another difficulty with which some have to wrestle on the road of obedient prayer – and especially, it seems, those who follow the road most faithfully and furthest – is the experience in prayer of distress, darkness, pain. It is not everybody who meets this difficulty. Some find experience of prayer a steadily peaceful and joyful experience. For them the yoke of obedience is easy, and the burden light. But for others the yoke can be painful and the burden crushing. The total exposure of oneself in prayer can be almost a breaking apart of oneself: prayer for a suffering world may leave one appalled by that suffering; the 'approachable' God to whom one began to pray may seem to withdraw himself and leave one disregarded and abandoned. No one, at the beginning, expects prayer to be so costly, and those who find it so have by then gone so far along the road of obedience that they continue on it almost of necessity. Some, in so doing, come to an understanding of God which previously was beyond them. The darkness and pain which they experience is recognised as a sign not of the absence of God but of the nearness of the God who is revealed in Christ: the God to whom they have come near is the God who has disclosed himself in the suffering figure upon the Cross. Those who are led along the road of obedience into pain and darkness may find themselves discovering, so to speak, 'what it is like' to be the God who is revealed in Christ crucified and come to understand a dimension of the being of God which previously was hidden from them.

A third difficulty met in prayer – and met at some time by almost all who pray – is the difficulty caused by 'unanswered' prayer. This also may lead in a quite simple and direct way to a larger or deeper understanding of God. One prays for something with a good conscience, confident that what one asks for is good and right and must be in accordance with God's will; but what one asks for is not given or does not happen. After a number of such disappointments the temptation arises to abandon prayer, but many resist it and, out of sheer obedience, continue to pray. Along the road of obedience which continues beyond disappointment one begins to be aware of certain resonances between what one prays for and what actually comes to pass. These resonances are too inexact to be called direct answers to prayer. Rather they suggest an ordering of things with which one's own prayer is not wholly discordant. To put the matter crudely: one prays for the particular and, although the particular does not come to pass, something does come to pass which shows that particular in a different light and alters one's attitude to it. Many people have prayed that a sick child may live, and yet, when the child has died, have been able to see in the death and in many human details associated with it, a deeper dimension of that loving will for the child which animated their own prayer. Having prayed with a loving purpose of their own, they have become aware of a larger purpose which is not opposed or indifferent to their own but which is wiser and more comprehensive.

Resonances of this kind, discerned along the road of obedience, tend to enlarge and refine one's understanding of God's will and purpose. The simplistic confidence that, because such-and-such seems good to us, it must be the will of God, tends to become awareness of a divine will and purpose which, though beyond our comprehension, is yet to be trusted in all things. So the practice of prayer moves away from any aspiration to influence the will of God into conformity with our own, and towards the aspiration to align our own will more closely with whatever may be the will of God.

'Thy will be done' is not a word of acquiescence said with a gesture of helplessness nor a comment on the unavoidable. It does not mean 'May thy will happen', nor 'May thy will be passively suffered'. It means 'May thy will be accomplished, wrought out'. God's will is to be done on earth in the same manner in which it is done in heaven.

The obedience of service

John 5.17 gives an arresting comment of Jesus that there are no sabbaths in divine grace. 'My Father works all the time, and so do I.' Jesus had been attacked for healing on the Sabbath, the holy day commemorating God's rest after completing and laying aside the work of creation. But the glad benediction of Sabbaths was meant for human well-being, and that well-being is not to be overridden or suspended by a ritual duty. Such a duty, for all its value, must not impede the compassion which is always compelling, and which is the secret of the divine activity itself.

To the average person the embodiment of 'real Christianity' is the Good Samaritan. Here is one who devotes himself to the service of human need – without regard to the origin, race, class or character of the wounded man or to anything else except the fact that he is a 'neighbour' (i.e. that he is 'near by') and that he is in need: and here is one whom Jesus used as a direct and pointed example to his followers: 'Go and do likewise.'

The traditional manner of Christian obedience has been direct and personal action on behalf of someone so physically 'near' that he or she can immediately receive the benefit. Through such obedience there may come about a genuine 'meeting' between person and person – a meeting marked, at its best, by pity, understanding and love on the one side, and on the other side by a gratitude which is moved not only by the gift or service itself but also by the tenderness and love which have motivated it. Where there is such a meeting, where love in giving meets graciousness in receiving, both sides seem to be blessed: and one might say that obedience to Christ's command has, for a moment, 'brought in the kingdom of God'. Where need meets love, something happens which cannot easily be described in utilitarian terms; the occasion has a dimension of depth which can only be interpreted in the language of theology.

Therefore it is not surprising that the Church has traditionally emphasised that manner of obedience which consists in the direct and personal service of need: and the manner has not become irrelevant at the present day. Indeed it is often recognised even in the secular world that in the great cities of our day the most widespread of all needs is one which can be met only through direct and personal 'meetings' – the need of the lonely, the frightened and insecure, the individual 'lost in the crowd'. It would be ironic if the traditional manner of Christian obedience should be discarded by the Church at the very time when the value of it is so widely recognised in the secular world.

But in this world there are many people in need who are 'near by' in the sense that we know about their need and could do something to alleviate it but not 'near by' in the sense that their need can be met by direct and personal service. The need of the world's poor and oppressed is not to be met by fund-raising for relief organisations, by VSO, or by writing letters on behalf of the victims of injustice. Of course there are countless situations in which such direct help is all that can be given: and no Christian would depreciate its importance. But there is another manner of Christian obedience which is essential if the situation of the poor and oppressed is to be radically transformed in the long term – the indirect manner of pressing and working for political, economic and social reform.

Those who advocate this manner of obedience would not deny the importance of the traditional manner in certain circumstances. They would not suggest that the Good Samaritan should have left the traveller to die, and set off to campaign for better policing of the roads. But they would suggest that the very good possibilities that are present in direct and personal service may also become a source of self-indulgence and illusion. The 'good feeling' that attends a loving action which is directly received may become the actual motive for doing it – a self-indulgent motive: and preoccupation with a need that can be directly met (perhaps for a good meal) may blind us to the real need which cannot be directly met – the need for justice, a fair wage or equality of opportunity. In the seats of power, personal kindness may actually diminish awareness of the oppressiveness and even cruelty of one's lifestyle and social role.

To this, of course, the 'traditionalist' may reply that the more indirect and political manner of obedience also contains moral ambiguities and dangers. The acquisition of power, which is the immediate goal of political activity, all too often compromises devotion to what must be, for a Christian, its ultimate goal – 'the good of one's neighbour'. It must also be recognised that the political manner of obedience, even when it keeps the ultimate goal in sight, tends to become so indirect and professional in its methods that it may make its followers unperceptive of need which is close to them and might be directly and personally met. (Both the Priest and the Levite who passed by on the other side were professionally concerned for 'the good of society': perhaps it was because they were so preoccupied with it that they passed by.)

One might say that the varieties of human need can be gathered into two broad categories – the need for love which can best be met by direct and personal action and the need for justice which can best be met by indirect and political action. What is essential is the recognition that both the traditional manner of response to human need and the political manner are manners or methods of obedience. Both contain moral dangers and ambiguities; but both at their best can be honest and obedient responses to Christ's command, 'Go and do likewise'.

In Judaism there is a famous saying put into the mouth of God: 'Would that they forgot me and kept my Law!' To be sure, deep and sublime concepts do lie behind Judaic faith. One cannot enjoin divine will and be unrelated to the divine nature. But the emphasis throughout is on doing rather than conceiving, on obeying rather than subtly credalising. 'Hear, O Israel, the Lord our God, the Lord, is One: and thou shalt love . . .' 'Hearken and do . . .' That 'indicative' of the divine unity, terse and sublime, is in no way a proposition about bare number, 'for number cannot reach him'. It has to do with an unrivalledness, where only God reigns over the entire loyalty of an undivided will. It demands not merely a single worship and an anathema on idolatry, but an inclusive fidelity to God's moral purpose.

It is this categorical imperative, the claim of God without an 'if', which underlies the whole prophetic tradition and condemns all rites and forms which substitute acts of devotion for attitudes of righteousness. 'Bring no more vain oblations, cease to do evil . . .' Honour from the lips may hide the dishonouring heart, people using God to evade God, that is, taking his name in vain. A biblically nourished theology is bound over to this mandatory awareness of the divine imperative and, what is equally important ethically, of the imperative as divine.

It is worth recalling how strongly this dimension, in a distinctive idiom, informs Islam. The *Amr*, which 'descends' at creation with the divine mandate 'Let there be . . .', comes down also as the celestial command directing the created universe and mandating the prophets. Indeed, for the whole Quranic faith the divine relationship to man and history is essentially didactic, hortatory, directional. There is nothing more than prophecy. Revelation is guidance: response is in its 'straight path'. The whole of humanity is understood to have been confronted, in cosmic encounter in primeval time, with the question from God, 'Am I not your Lord?' And in the womb of being which enfolded all generations all have replied '*Bala*, yes! we so acknowledge' (Surah 7.172). The task, then, of *dhikr* (one of the titles of the Qur'ān, as well as the term denoting mystic discipline) is the steady recall of this pledgedness to God which human forgetfulness – a Quranic clue to evil – is all too liable to nullify.

'Hold God in awe' might be said to be the central urge of all Semitic theism and it is one in which Christian faith is partner. We are right to see it tempered and controlled by the distinctively Christian sense of the divine indicative. But this distinctively Christian theology of the Incarnation and of grace in no way excludes the meaning of the divine imperative, which certain contemporary theologians, especially in the Third World, have passionately renewed. Rather it is well to see the vital interfusion of will and nature in our understanding of God, and of will and wonder in our presence in him through worship and prayer.

For, as we saw earlier in this chapter, God's command is never compulsive or arbitrary. Were it so, it would not admit of a truly human relationship. The very creaturehood which is duly commanded by the Creator is a responsive personhood only on condition of being moved not by mere order but by consent of will. This, of course, is the perennial problem of grace. Unless we see and will it of ourselves, the 'ought' – albeit from God – is not morally discerned. The divine strategy (if we may so speak) has to do with the sort of imperative which can be willed within our will. No mere power ever established personal relationship. As John Oman finely said, 'God is willing to fail until He can have the only success love would value.' Hence the deep paradox of the command 'Thou shalt love . . .', whether it be love of God or of neighbour. Love is indeed obligatory, but becomes impossible in the presence of sheer omnipotence. If God's relations with us were those of that sort of almightiness, our wrongness before God would be the easiest situation to correct or the most incredible one ever to have arisen. So to take sin seriously – which is the other side of holding God and his commands in awe – is to know how loving is the sovereignty in God which at once makes us for love, and makes us know we are so made, yet also in his patience waits upon our making of ourselves according to this love. The divine imperative is the more awesome in becoming also the human responsibility.

Coming at it from this angle, we can perceive in a fresh way the wonder of the Incarnation. A 'substance' Christology – 'One in being with the Father' – has had a long and perhaps necessary primacy in Christian thought. But a 'will' Christology, complementarily, would say: 'One in doing with the Father . . .', 'in the beginning was the deed . . .', and 'the deed was among us like a tent pitched . . . and we saw the glory'. Jesus saw all that he did as response to God's will, his life and teaching mediating God's will to others. 'What the Father does the Son does . . .' The first Christian believers saw in the love that suffered on the Cross the definitive reading of the divine mind. Within the evil situation they perceived the fulfilling, and defining, of the divine nature. In a setting which epitomised the wrongness of human wills confronted by the divine will present in Jesus, Christians have found the perfect analogy of God. Faith designated that event to be the supreme expression of how God is God. We know God, so to speak, within the 'doing' of Jesus, and that knowledge requires of us a doing of God's will by the same pattern. Thus to know is to do, and to do is to know. Theologically what is indicative of God happened within the imperative in Jesus. Where we learn what manner of persons we are commanded to be is where we know what manner of love the Father has bestowed on us. But the knowledge of that other is only truly possessed in a will to be conformed to the same obedience. As Jesus had it, 'I in them and thou in me'.

Obedience to the holy

A third type of encounter and response through which God is known to many is that of going to church; and church in this context means an actual building in a neighbourhood, be it in a city, town or village.

Architecturally it may be very ordinary and have little to commend it, but it is itself a bearer of meaning in the community. It is often the focus of all kinds of expectations, not just among those who go to it regularly but also for those who go only occasionally. The building is far more than just a meeting place for a 'religious' minority who use it Sunday by Sunday.

It is seen as a source of well-being in a place, and it has often been noted that if it is in danger of falling down or of falling into disuse money is given by all sorts of people who seem to have little to do with what goes on inside it. This is true not just in picturesque villages and anonymous suburbs but in run-down inner city areas. A church building is seen as hallowing a place and if it is taken away or has its use changed then the feeling is that the place itself has been devalued.

The symbolic value of the building may be regarded by some as little more than superstition or at best 'folk religion', because 'church' should mean much more than just a building. But it remains a phenomenon that needs to be taken into account. There is relatively rarely as much fuss when a secular building which has been in long public use is demolished. It may be the regular worshippers who pay for the upkeep of the building and struggle to keep it in good repair, but nevertheless it is seen by the community as belonging to everyone.

In addition it has often been noted that those who go to church regularly are seen by others who do not go as their representatives. Through them they are kept in touch with 'their church', even if it is in a way that is one removed from commitment. At certain times of the year, Midnight at Christmas, Mothering Sunday, Harvest Festival and perhaps Remembrance Sunday, they will themselves go to church, and on the strength of this will see themselves as belonging, as 'keeping in touch with base'. There is a feeling that everyone has to have a religion even though it may not be clear what function that religion has. In addition, even in new areas there seems in many places to be an expectation that there will be a person who will be 'their vicar'. Upon him, too, various expectations are placed, and he is judged by the way he lives up to them. Often the idea of what a vicar is and does may be very inadequate, but it is always assumed that there is a relatedness which is not dependent even upon knowing the vicar's name.

Inevitably the church building is the place for important and well-remembered events. Family baptisms, weddings and funerals and the jumble of memories that go with them are all held together by the building. To a casual observer they seem to be quite different events, long separated in time, but for the family involved they are episodes which hang together.

... because it held unspilt
So long and equably what since is found
Only in separation – marriage and birth,
And Death, and thoughts of these – round which was built
This special shell?
(Philip Larkin, 'Church Going', *The Less Deceived*, Marvell Press,
p. 29)

This inter-relatedness between people and places finds expression in other ways. Some places are remembered because events of significance happened in them to individuals, groups or nations. They are visited by people who are too easily dismissed simply as tourists, who go in fact for some deeper reason than they are themselves aware of; and they find that in some strange way the place engages them in a way they cannot account for or describe.

In the case of the Holy Place, however, there is another dimension. God is found there, and is experienced in a direct and particular way which does not happen elsewhere. It is easy to dismiss this experience as purely subjective; yet there is evidence that, for some people anyway, their lives have been changed by their visit. They say that it was the place itself that spoke to them. It could be the Holy Places in Jerusalem, Lourdes, Iona, Glastonbury or Lindisfarne, or a host of others, but these centres of pilgrimage have a significance which shapes their lives and in memory is cherished and visited time and time again.

This sense of the holy in a place is not an experience shared by everyone, but it does extend to other areas of experience. A hymn sung to a particular tune, a version of the Bible, can carry a sense of the holy which to a person who does not feel in the same way is no more than sentiment or superstition. The strength of feeling which is thus called out is often surprisingly deep. The fact that Christians of different traditions revere different places, books, etc. is secondary, as is the fact that these feelings are not limited to those who expressly believe the Christian faith. What they have in common is the idea that it is right to defend certain things passionately and often sacrificially not for utilitarian reasons but because that is the response that seems to be demanded by the person, thing or place in question. It is holy. God is to be found within it.

The encounter with the holy is not to be found only in places which can have a 'religious' label put upon them. Indeed, as Alister Hardy points out, 'Contrary to the premise on which most Christian evangelism is planned the awareness of God's presence has little to do with preaching or teaching. It is most often found in solitude and is triggered by natural beauty, music or literature, or by illness, depression or despair.' Some people who have this kind of experience carry on in much the same way as they did before the experience, but a significant number of people feel driven to church because in the church they expect to have these experiences validated and given a context within which their life can take on a new meaning and purpose. For them the meaning of the experience is that they have been addressed by God and it is self-authenticating.

The experiences are all different but what they have in common is that they were unexpected and unearned. This unpredictability can be experienced on the one hand as a kind of overflowing, something that crowns or seals a deep experience, or conversely it seems to be felt when people have come to the end of their own resources and find themselves facing an abyss. Then the experience is of someone who comes unexpectedly and fills an emptiness.

These experiences are difficult to systematise but there are enough similarities in them to form a cluster of meaning which is part of the data to be considered.

Pascal talked of *Deus Absconditus* to describe the sense of the universe being called forth by God and then ignored by him, and certainly this is an experience which many Christians would say they shared, not least in a post-Holocaust world. But, as we have indicated, the experience for some is exactly the opposite, that is of God suddenly making himself known even though until that time he had remained unknown and of no account.

> I don't know Who – or what – put the question, I don't know when it was put. I don't even remember answering. But at some moment I did answer Yes to Someone – or Something – and from that hour I was certain that existence is meaningful and that, therefore, my life, in self-surrender, had a goal.
> (Dag Hammarskjöld, *Markings*, Faber paperback, p. 169)

A Christian interpretation of this phenomenon is to say that such things happen because that is the way that all that is made has been made. Every created thing is capable of bearing the weight of glory. It is possible to turn but a stone and start a wing, or to say with Blake that everything that lives is holy. One of the features of contemporary life is an interest in conservation and related issues, and with this a new awareness of place in the natural order and the crucial role that this has within it. There does seem to be a need for what Charles Williams called 'the way of affirmation of images' to be laid alongside the *via negativa*, which can help to explore creatively the way that so many people find meaning in the created order.

This sense finds specific Christian expression in the Sacraments which have a central part in the life of the Church. Characteristically the way they are defined within different elements of the Christian tradition is wide and varied. On the one hand their importance is made clear by the fact that they are closely circumscribed and safeguarded, and the way they are celebrated and received is laid down by canon and regulation. On the other hand there are wide divergences in attempts to formulate their precise meaning. This wide divergence is seen clearly in the different ways in which churches, while agreeing on the centrality of the Sacraments, go about the business of administering them. One tradition will say, for example, that the Eucharist is so important and holy that it should be celebrated only rarely and then with a good deal of preparation, while another tradition will say that the Eucharist is so important and holy that it should be celebrated every day.

To some the Sacraments are tied very closely to the life and redemptive death of Christ. They gain their meaning and authority from commands like 'Go and make disciples of all nations, baptising them in the name of the Father and of the Son and of the Holy Spirit' and 'Do this in remembrance of me'. They are the distinctive way in which the Church remembers Jesus and is faithful to him; the Church continues to do what he did.

By others they are given a more extended significance. At the end of his novel about a French curé, *The Diary of a Country Priest*, Georges Bernanos paints a haunting picture of the death of the priest. The tubercular figure who had ministered with such love and devotion to his flock is now dying without the comfort of the Church which he himself had given to so many. There is no priest on hand to give him the last rites. The friend who is with him says how sorry he is that he has to die like this, but the priest whispers to him, 'Does it matter? Grace is . . . everywhere', and then dies.

For him clearly the grace that came through the sacraments could not be separated from the grace which was present and apparent through all creation. The world was 'charged with the grandeur of God'. Seen in this way the whole sacramental life of the Church is a sign to the whole world, pointing it again towards its own life so that it can find within it the presence of God.

The very earthiness of the raw material of the sacraments, water, bread, wine, human love, being sorry and receiving forgiveness, knowing the touch of human hands, all these things are not there to be taken for granted and made into narrowly ecclesiastical things, but are to be seen as some of the ways by which God makes himself known in the world.

They remind people that God can be met in the everyday, in creation as well as in redemption.

They are capable of being understood at a highly sophisticated level and yet at the same time their meaning is grasped profoundly by 'simple people' who come week by week to receive them. The very regularity of their coming speaks of their understanding. For them the weekly receiving of the Sacrament of Holy Communion is the event that shapes the week and that holds all things together. It is commonly said, 'I do not know what I would do without it' or 'My week does not seem complete without it'.

This coming to the Sacrament has two elements, the first being one of offering, of bringing in their world and their concerns, but more important is the element of receptivity, of being given something, the Body and the Blood of Christ. And, of course, people themselves are often sacraments. A meeting with a person who is holy, or a holy community, is often a profound experience. We cannot define what their holiness is, but somehow we are aware of some extra dimension, of an openness and an availability which speaks to us and makes us feel on the one hand inadequate and on the other enriched just by being with them. There is a sense of having met with God.

This sense of meeting with God, of depending upon him and being receptive and open, which is characteristic of the language used to describe both prayer and sacraments, is also used by many to describe their experience of reading the Bible or indeed having it expounded. It is the Word of God and the Word from God addressed specifically to them. They describe how they have been nourished in their lives by particular texts or verses. The Gideon Bibles put in hospital lockers or left in hotel bedrooms are not always dust-gathering ornaments. It was not just St Augustine who found his life changed by reading a particular section of Scripture at a time of great turmoil in his life.

Holy places, sacred words, sacraments – all not only give to us but, in a strange and often at least dimly recognised way, lay claim upon us. It has often been observed how Latin-speaking Christianity gave to the central acts of Christian worship the name *sacramentum*, borrowed from the soldier's oath of allegiance to the Emperor, just as *Christianoi* was a term about loyalty not about a school of thought. Both Baptism and the Eucharist have to do with dedication to Christ, and identification with Christ. The one is a pledge given in grateful recognition of redemption; the other is the steady remembering and re-enacting of its meaning and claim. 'It is the mystery of yourselves', said Augustine, 'which is laid upon the holy table: it is the mystery of yourselves that you receive.'

My life must be Christ's broken bread,
My love His outpoured wine,
A cup o'erfilled, a table spread,
Beneath His Name and sign,
That other souls, refreshed and fed,
May share His life through mine.

It was not by self-reservation or remote control that the incarnate love redeemed the world, but by presence and participation. There is no authentic relation to God which is not realised through relation to people. 'When you bring your gift to the altar,' said Jesus, 'and there remember . . . first be reconciled.' Why 'and *there* remember' unless the place of divine presence is also the thrust – the nudge, could we say – of human community? In the grace of the Incarnation and in the calling of the Church the divine engages with the human and the engagement is by action. Worship means the recruitment of the will for the active translation of the meaning of that worship in the real world.

Here, as Thomas Merton remarked in his *Conjectures*, 'too simple a notion of the will of God may short-circuit all religious integrity'. Here, therefore, many difficult decisions must be made, which we may not always rightly judge, about what integrity requires of us, as persons, citizens and believers. It must always be a dynamic and a risky engagement with human situations if we are really to know 'God working in us to will and to do' what is after his mind. Certainly it will never mean a mere avoidance of offence, or the supine self-exoneration which protests 'I never did any one any harm'. That indicates a severely private and obtuse world. Instead one of the evident duties of the will that knows God in Christ is – put paradoxically – an appreciation of evil. Early this century R. C. Moberly, in *Atonement and Personality*, wrote the theme of 'vicarious penitence' into the thought of his day. He may not have resolved all the issues it raises. But he set squarely within the will to know God a lively sense of the perversity in human nature. It is urgent that some at least among us should be constrained, as it were, to apologise to God, to be able still to identify blasphemy for what it is, to register the tawdry, the sordid, the devious, for what they are, and expressly resist and refute their unhallowing and distorting of the world and of humanity. To do so is to feel about what is and ought not so to be, what ought to be and is not. 'With everyone sold on the good', asks a character in Saul Bellow's *Humboldt's Gift*, 'how does all the evil get done?' 'Could it have come from us?' asks Edwin Muir in his poem 'The Good Town':

. . . That old life was easy
And kind, and comfortable: but evil is restless . . .

How could our town grow wicked . . .
and we, poor, ordinary neutral stuff,
Not good, nor bad . . . we have seen
Good men made evil wrangling with the evil,
Straight minds grown crooked fighting crooked minds.
Our peace betrayed us: we betrayed our peace.
Look at it well. This was 'the good town' once.

Is it not in such a lively sense, not simply of *mea culpa*, my fault, but of *nostra culpa*, our fault, that we learn a true corporate penitence? This means a will to honesty about the world, its liability to blight and deface its most precious blessings in a rape of nature, or a travesty of sex, or a jungle of politics, or a treachery of religion.

Such contrition, such refusal of self-justification, moves into doing. Liberation Theology in recent decades has certainly focused, if it has not resolved, the relation of faith and society. Some western Christian reactions to it have sounded like pleas for non-disturbance and the *status quo*. But Liberation Theology recognises that there are situations of injustice, poverty, oppression, deprivation, where there can be no honest neutrality. For to be neutral is to connive.

The God of the Bible cannot be grasped as a neuter Theme: he stops being God the moment his injunction ceases. And man has many resources at his disposal to cause this command to come to an end. He need only objectify God in some way. At that moment God is no longer God. Man has made him into an idol. God no longer commands man . . . The question is not whether someone is seeking God or not, but whether he is seeking him where God himself said that he is.
(José P. Miranda, *Marx and the Bible*, SCM Press 1977, pp. 40, 57).

'Where', for the liberationists, is with the poor and the oppressed. Justice has a prior claim over worship and ecclesiastical organisation. Contemplation can never displace command. The passionate urgency of Liberation Theology finds all the meaning of divine transcendence in the moral imperative. Taken at its face value, such a position is intellectually unacceptable because self-negating; but the urgency and passion which inspire it must surely be ours. We must take its prophetic call to heart while at the same time being no less urgent to adore, for the sake of that very same passion and urgency, the God of the infinite spaces and the unfailing stars, of poetry and wonder and ever glad surprise. 'Love of neighbour' is inseparable from 'love of God'. If they are to be distinguished, for the sake of the commandments themselves and our own limited perceptions, must there not be nevertheless a knowledge and love within our will which, because they are for him alone, are thereby ever alerted to his human ones 'where he has said that he is, in the midst of life'? If, in Micah's words, we are 'to do justly and to love mercy', we must surely also 'walk humbly with our God'.

The meaning of the great Vision of Judgement in Matt. 25.31–46 has gone deep into Christian poetry and imagery. 'The poor of the world are my body, said he.' Christ incognito is ever at hand, serving and to be served. 'Inasmuch as you did it to one of the least of these my brothers, you did it to me.' Is not all such compassion, in Paul's phrase, a 'discerning of the body', that body of humanity into which by birth came the Son of Man, thereby made like to his brethren? For the purpose of the parable, the knowing was in the doing even if awareness was first wanting. 'Lord, when did we see *you* sick?' Within the answered imperative of compassion was the secret of the divine presence.

If we would know God in the authentic Christian tradition of his knowability in Christ, we must learn a will to be conformed to the image of his Son. The Eucharist as the apex of our praying discloses the self-giving of Christ, incorporates us into his ministering Body, and engages us imperatively with the body of humankind, there to belong and to act 'in the knowledge and love of God'.

Chapter 9
The God in whom we trust

Few people are more widely admired than those who pass through extremes of personal suffering or public calamity without bitterness or hysteria and with a quiet and hopeful confidence; and if such people attribute their confidence to faith in God their 'witness' or 'testimony' is very important. It may well persuade a doubter or unbeliever to enquire more seriously into the nature and content of this faith, a faith which can have such admirable consequences in times of distress.

In reply to an enquiry of this sort it is not enough for Christians to assert, as the content of their faith, simply that 'God exists' and 'God is good'. The enquirer will see here no adequate grounds for hope and confidence, unless it is also made explicit that it is this good God who is actually 'in control' of the world, that it is by his good hands that all things are ordered and that, therefore, despite appearances all things that happen are included within his good purpose and lead to ultimate good.

The enquirer will recognise that such faith in God's control must be a source of hope and confidence in all circumstances, but will also almost certainly question its credibility. Can it really be by the control of God's good hands that the disaster at Aberfan came about, or some devastating flood or drought or, indeed, the Holocaust? At the very least Christians will have to give some further explanation of their faith that, when these things happened, God was 'in control'. What kind of illustration or analogy or 'model' will help us to understand this alleged control? Is it like the tight control of a computer programme over the operation of a machine? Is it more like the occasional intervention by which a teacher keeps a class 'under control'? Is it perhaps like the distant control of a military commander over an army numbered in millions?

Christians can hardly avoid responding in some way, positively or negatively, to such models. They realise that no model drawn from within the world can adequately express the relationship between the world as a whole and the God who is the source and ground of its being, and that no model therefore should be pushed too far or claimed to explain everything. But they will also recognise that one model may be more, or less misleading than another, and, in particular, that an enquirer's difficulties may arise precisely because one particular model is pressed too far. Even if the Christian understanding of God transcends the need or possibility of models or analogies, the enquirer's probings do not. For the enquirer's sake, therefore, if for no other reason, Christians must be open to discuss in terms of possible models that divine control or ordering of the world which is the ground of Christian confidence in times of distress and apparent catastrophe.

Images of divine control

Many Christians would hold that the authentic and authoritative model of divine control is given to us in the biblical image of the Sovereignty or Kingship of God. Certainly this image pervades the Bible. But its force may be lost on the modern enquirer simply because the power of kings is so much diminished and their role so greatly changed in the modern world. What we expect of kings is not what the biblical writers expected. In us their image evokes respect but may inspire little awe. Furthermore the biblical expectation, though greater than our own, is not entirely consistent or homogeneous. Two rather different images of kingship, two rather different 'pictures' of what a good king is and does, appear in the Bible.

One such image appears in the Wisdom of Solomon, and is quite close to Plato's image or concept of the 'philosopher-king'. Here kingship is 'the upholding of the people' (6.24). The King will 'set the people in order' (8.14) and 'order the world according to equity and righteousness' (9.3). He knows 'all things that are either secret or manifest' (7.21). The wisdom which teaches him what is right also enables him to achieve it in his kingdom – for that wisdom is 'the worker of all things', 'cannot be obstructed', 'oversees all things' (7.22–3) and, 'reaching from one end to the other, sweetly orders all things' (8.1). The image is of someone by whose wisdom and power everything is so controlled that nothing can be present in the kingdom which is alien to his will, nothing can happen in it save by his 'ordering'.

In Psalm 72 a distinctly different image of kingship appears, which may be called the image of the 'saviour-king'. In the realm of the saviour-king certain things appear which are quite definitely not in accordance with the royal will; and the greatness of the king lies in the readiness and effectiveness with which he redeems or redresses these things. The king will 'defend the poor . . . defend the children of the poor and punish the wrongdoer' (verses 2 and 4). He will 'deliver the poor when he crieth; the needy also and him that hath no helper' (verse 12), and in his sight the blood of the poor will be 'dear' (verse 14). Clearly it is not by the will of the king that poverty and oppression exist in his kingdom. His role as a good king is to respond to them with remedy and redress, to act as King David is prepared to act when Nathan tells him of the poor man deprived of his 'one ewe lamb'. Unlike the philosopher-king, in whose kingdom nothing can occur which is alien to the royal will, the saviour-king is constantly meeting, redressing and redeeming that which is alien to his will.

So the biblical image of kingship has at least two facets, and both these facets appear when human kingship is used as a model of divine sovereignty. Sometimes biblical writers insist that a certain event, disastrous as it appeared to human eyes, was in fact willed by God for his own purposes. So it was that Pharaoh's heart was hardened and that Nineveh repented when Jonah preached. In these cases God is represented, so to speak, as the philosopher-king in whose realm, despite all appearances, everything happens precisely as he wills and ordains it. But in many other cases it is as the saviour-king that God appears – responding to actions and situations which are alien to his will, hearing and punishing when the blood of Abel cries to him from the ground, turning to good the evil which Joseph's brothers do to him, avenging the death of Uriah the Hittite by the death of Bathsheba's child, punishing the sin of his people or remitting punishment in response to Moses' intercession, pleading with his people through the prophets, stirred to action when they are enslaved in Egypt or oppressed by foreign invaders. In such situations it is very clear that God is responding to what he has not willed, that he is the saviour-king, acting to set right what is wrong, to redress, redeem and deliver.

In the kingdom of the philosopher-king all is, so to speak, 'programmed' by and in conformity with the sovereign's will. In the kingdom of the saviour-king many things must be won into conformity with the sovereign's will. Both these images of divine control are present in the Bible, but it is undoubtedly the second which predominates; and this image, in contrast to that of the philosopher-king, suggests a God who is not only attentive to his people but also close to them, involved with them. The philosopher-king is raised above any involvement in such distresses as his people may experience, because those distresses are actually willed by him for his own good purposes. But the saviour-king is so close to his people that he can be roused to anger by the appearance among them of things alien to his will, and be vulnerable to the grief which cries, 'What have I done to you, O my people, and wherein have I wearied you?' God the saviour-king shepherds his people, leads them, pioneers the way for them out of slavery and the shadow of death. He is acquainted with his people's distresses from the inside. He bears their griefs and carries their sorrows; he shares what his people endure. He travels with his people through the wilderness – even 'dwelling in tents' as they do – and, as their leader, is not exempt from the perseverance and faithfulness which that journey must entail. The important biblical concept of the faithfulness of God suggests very powerfully his involvement in the labours and struggles of his people.

It has already been remarked that kingship in the modern world is not what it was: a modern king dignifies rather than controls the nation's life. Therefore it will not be much help to a modern enquirer if we explain our understanding of God's control of the world in terms of the model of the saviour-king. Can this model be translated or updated? One possible and promising translation is into the language of artistic creation, an activity much analysed and discussed today.

The artist in any field gives being to a work of art. It is he or she who makes it what it is. Admittedly, pre-existent materials are used; but of the work of art as such the artist alone is the creator – it is out of the artist's spontaneity that the work of art comes into being. But that spontaneity must be expressed within some kind of form – a canvas of a particular size, a certain verse convention. The artist chooses the form; but the form once chosen exercises a degree of constraint or discipline on his or her spontaneity. Spontaneity does not simply flow, nor is art simply 'doodling' with a pencil or strumming as one pleases upon a stringed instrument. In artistic creativity a certain struggle or adventure is involved – the endeavour to contain and express spontaneity within form. In this endeavour there is no programme or blueprint to follow. The artist is reaching out towards a vision or possibility which is not yet fully formulated even in 'the inward eye', and which appears with increasing clarity only as the work proceeds.

If we now apply this model to God, we may find that it helps us to approach some aspects of the age-old problem of evil. Having freely chosen to create something in a particular 'medium', God may no longer be free to escape the constraints which that medium imposes. The question why God 'allows' an earthquake, a volcanic eruption, a flood or a drought – things which may take a heavy toll of innocent human life – needs to be set in the context of the fact that the creation of any environment suitable for living beings (which in any case depends upon an extraordinarily fine balance in the chemistry of the atmosphere) entails accepting a variable climate with all those instabilities which lead (from a human point of view) to disasters.

There is, however, a further aspect of the artist model which may take us somewhat nearer to the heart of evil and suffering. At this point it may be helpful to think of a sculptor rather than a painter. Once the medium (a block of stone or wood) is chosen, then, as we have said, it imposes its own constraints. In the artist's mind is a clear idea of the intended shape; but certain unforeseen factors may intervene. The material used may have a grain, a knot or an imperfection which resists the creative intention; or a cut may be made which is actually 'wrong', in the sense of not being exactly what was intended. It is here that the greatness of the artist appears in the skill and patience needed to 'win back' that which is 'wrong'. The wrong is not simply left as it is, as it might be by an inferior artist, nor is it simply eliminated or cast aside – for it is an authentic element in the artist's spontaneity. Still less, of course, is the whole work abandoned. The great artist wins back that which is wrong, works with peculiar intensity to find a way by which that imperfection or error may be made to contribute to the total vision rather than detract from it, to enrich it rather than impoverish it. This struggle to win back, and the capacity to do so, is mysterious and difficult to analyse, but anyone who has ever created anything will be well aware of it. It is the exercise of a special and unique kind of 'control' – a control which redeems rather than prevents the wrong, which draws into the overall purpose that which obstructs that purpose. The control of the artist is a 'saving' rather than a 'programming' form of control. 'Creation' is also a continuing 'redemption'.

The nature of artistic creativity is of so much interest at the present time that, if it were offered as a model of God's control or ordering of the world, it might well prove thought-provoking and suggestive to enquirers. It is not strictly a biblical model, but there are strong and clear resonances between what it suggests and what is suggested by the dominant biblical image of God as saviour-king. The model suggests that, while the world and everything which it contains is God's work, some of the things and events within the world are 'not what God wants' and are in need of winning back or redeeming into the ambit of his good purpose. To some people this will be a feature of the model which enhances its credibility. It will also be more credible to some, because it suggests a God who, so far from presiding in distant serenity over a fallen and anguished world, is constantly involved in the close encounter of redemption.

The artist-model is not, of course, of use only to throw light on the problem of evil. It is also a way of picturing the creation itself. In this respect it is certainly more adequate than the 'clockmaker' model, which has been popular ever since the eighteenth century, and which still affects the thinking of many religious people today. According to this model, the Creator is imagined as setting up an immensely complex piece of machinery and then letting it run according to its own laws and mechanisms. Everything that happens is the result of something that happened previously, and this long interconnected series of happenings can in theory be traced back to the original devising of the Creator. It was a model which was always felt to be seriously inadequate as soon as human beings were brought into the picture, because it presupposed that the Creator had planned to its last detail the great history of life on this earth, and that, having set it in motion, he was now allowing it to run its predetermined course. Such total determinism, even apart from the philosophical difficulties it raises, has never been felt to be compatible with the experience of what it is to be a free human being; and even as a way of understanding the world of nature, the 'clockmaker' model is quite out of touch with contemporary science. Modern genetic and evolutionary theory cannot possibly be reconciled with such a crudely mechanistic interpretation of the universe.

But the artist-model in turn becomes less appropriate as soon as it becomes necessary to offer an interpretation of the phenomenon of human life. Even if the materials an artist uses bring with them some constraints, it is still the artist who is in control. The materials are inanimate. They can be selected or rejected at will. They have no place in the artefact unless the artist makes use of them. The moment that among the materials the creator uses are found living beings – and still more if those living beings have free will – the artist model is inadequate. This is the meaning of the story of Pygmalion. If the statue comes alive, its relationship with the sculptor is totally changed.

To complete our account of the relationship between the creator and his creation – or between God and human beings – we must therefore explore a further 'model'. The one that lies to hand is one which occurs in many religions and is of great importance in both Judaism and Christianity. This is the model of parent and child. The parents are (in a sense) the 'creator' of their child; but the child is endowed with its own independence, its own free will, and the relationship of the parents to the child may become the arena for a prolonged tussle of wills. Parents consider they know what is best for the child, and seek to direct it in the right paths. The child believes it knows better, and may disregard or disobey the admonitions of its parents. In the early stages the parents may have to use force or material sanctions to impose their will on the child. But as the child grows into adulthood it becomes physically independent of them. They experience the joy and the risk of letting the child be itself, though they may also from time to time use persuasion, accompanied perhaps by threats of disinheritance or other material disadvantages, to influence the child's free and adult decisions.

It is this later phase in the relationship which has provided the most familiar model for the relationship between creator and creature, namely that of a father and son. In the Judaeo-Christian tradition it is clearly taught that, in order to persuade his human child to live in the right way, it is essential that God, like a father, should make clear to the child what kind of conduct is demanded. The father 'legislates'; he provides a law or moral standard by which his offspring shall live.

But suppose the child disobeys the father, what then? The model of father and child suggests that, having created beings endowed with free will, God may well decide to accept the constraint involved, not reducing them to automata or treating them as infants after they have grown up. He then does not manifest his power unambiguously and irresistibly, but influences them by persuasion, not by force – and indeed shows great resourcefulness in doing so. He inspires some to expound and elaborate his law. He sends others as prophets, messengers and saints to exhort and influence his erring creatures. He allows men and women to glimpse the rewards which follow right behaviour and the disastrous consequences of sin and error. He is patient with their rebelliousness and lovingly waits for their return. From this point of view the Old and the New Testaments have much common ground. They are both examples of the richly varied appeals made by the creator to his creatures to direct their lives according to the creator's will and purpose.

Yet what happens? The children still disobey, the creatures disregard the will of the creator, sin and error abound, the law is disregarded. At this point the model of the father and child can be used in different ways. How does the father react? He may simply be angry and redouble his threats. If his children disobey, they know what is coming to them; if they continue in their wickedness, they will lose their inheritance. There is nothing more the father can do. Everything that can be said has been said, every appeal has been tried, the consequences of rebellion are as clear now as they have ever been. Being patient and merciful, the father keeps the options open a little longer. He may punish, but he withholds ultimate retribution. But who knows whether he will not eventually lose patience and disown his children altogether?

But the significant feature of the use of this model in Judaism and Christianity lies in the great emphasis which these two religions place on a further application of it: the relationship is one of love. In the Old Testament this is expressed in terms of the father's continued faithfulness and long-suffering. Again and again, the children turn away from the right path and deserve all the penalties which the father has the right to inflict; again and again, he relents and gives his children another chance. Indeed he has let it be known that he never will altogether abandon them to their fate. Their promised inheritance may be indefinitely delayed by their wrong-doing; but such is their father's love towards them that he will never despair of them. He will keep the options open. In the New Testament, the very point of the contrast in Hebrews 12 between God's discipline and that of earthly parents is that, while human parents often act out of mixed motives, God's discipline is prompted purely and exclusively by love.

Christianity uses the same model, but gives it a radical extension.

On the one hand it proclaims that God's children now have new resources and opportunities for conforming to their father's will. It is God's gracious gift, and not our own capacity for self-improvement, which makes it possible for us to fulfil his purposes for us beyond anything we could achieve by our own abilities. On the other hand, it dares to ask: if the children continue to disobey their father, to spurn his gifts and promises, and to prefer their own independence, is the father not hurt? If the model of father and children allows us to talk of the father's love, surely we can press the analogy and say that the father suffers from the disobedience of his children, that the creator, by loving his creation, makes himself vulnerable to being spurned and abused by them?

The suffering of God

The idea that God loves his creatures as a father loves his children and consequently suffers when his creatures fail to respond to that love is at the heart of the Christian understanding of God. It was 'through Christ' that God reconciled the world to himself – and Christ suffered and died upon the Cross, as a result of the failure of the world to acknowledge and respond to God's love. So, it would appear, God suffered; and if so, our model suggests that he may continue to suffer whenever his creatures reject his purposes for them, somewhat as a human father suffers when his children reject his loving care for them.

Moreover, this way of understanding God's relationship with his creatures enables believers to confront the problem of evil with a new confidence. Again and again, human beings are subjected to suffering, sometimes in consequence of their own sinfulness, sometimes as victims of totally (as it seems) unmerited and inexplicable calamities. Why, they cry, does God allow this to happen? The beginning of an answer may be found, as we have seen, in the notion of constraints inherent in any act of creation: given that God used his freedom to create a world that would be an appropriate environment for free, adventurous and potentially loving human beings, he accepted the constraints imposed upon him by that creative activity, and is therefore not free to obviate all the consequences which cause us to suffer (though, in answer to prayer, he may obviate some). But the father-model is also capable of suggesting a more profound and ultimately far more sustaining answer. Just as a human father suffers if the circumstances in which he has deliberately placed his children for their good turn out to cause them suffering, so we may say that God suffers because of the sufferings of his creatures. We may even say that God is so 'involved' in their suffering that he is actually 'in' the suffering itself. Many Christians would say that it was precisely by coming to grasp and experience this presence of God within human suffering that they have been enabled to bear it and accept it themselves.

But at this point serious misgivings arise. Have we pushed the use of our model too far? Certain things, we believe, must be true of God; otherwise he ceases to be God at all. If we are to attribute suffering to God, must he not cease to be permanent and unchangeable? Does not the believer, struggling against evil and sorrow, require a God who is strong, trustworthy and constant?

There is a technical name in theology for the doctrine which meets this requirement: the impassibility of God. According to this, God by his very nature cannot suffer; and if our father–son model has led us to say something which traditional doctrine explicitly excludes from consideration we must be prepared to abandon it. But in fact this doctrine requires closer examination. If it is to be taken to mean that God does not suffer as we suffer, what becomes of the person of the incarnate Christ? Are we to say that his human nature obviously suffered mental and physical agony, but that the divine nature (i.e. the Word united to the human nature) was somehow anaesthetised by virtue of the simple fact that divinity cannot suffer? But this is to make a nonsense of what the Christian tradition is saying about the person of Christ. Certainly the classical position (as enunciated, for example, at the Council of Chalcedon) is that the two natures in Christ – human and divine – are distinct. But it also states that the two natures are united in one single person and that therefore if Christ suffered then the whole Christ suffered.

It could of course be said (as in the Theopaschite controversy of the sixth century) that this was God temporarily dipping his toes in the waters of human anguish. 'One of the Trinity suffered', but not for long, while the Father and the Spirit remained as aloof as before. But to say this is to distort the doctrine of the Trinity, to fly in the face of the truth that the three Persons are as inseparable in their nature as they are in their creative and redemptive activity. If one suffers, then all suffer, or better, if God is in Christ suffering for our redemption, then this is the sign and guarantee of the Triune God's eternal involvement in human suffering and human destiny. For authentically Christian speech about God is always speech about the Holy Trinity. To think about God's relation to suffering simply in terms of the Father and the Son as separate Beings with different 'histories' (and to leave out the Spirit altogether) is not thinking about the Christian God at all.

Equally false to a Trinitarian vision of God, however, is any treatment of the Persons of the Trinity as if they were replicas of one another, so that whatever we say about the Incarnate Son can be said in the same terms about the Father. The Letter to the Hebrews, for example, says that the Son 'learned obedience through the things that he suffered' (5.8). Any doctrine of genuine Incarnation must say something of this sort. But Christians, at least in the mainstream traditions, do not say that God as God has to go through suffering in order to learn, develop or mature. In God, the wholeness of divine perfection has always been there, and is being brought to bear upon the cosmic drama of pain and evil. It is of the Incarnate Son, sharing in human existence within Space-Time, that we can properly say that he experienced the authentic process of growth into human wholeness, albeit with the appropriate perfection at each stage.

That incarnate experience, with its intense joy as well as its depth of suffering, is our supreme clue to the mystery of God's relation to suffering as God, but it is not a direct picture of that relation. It offers us a creative and decisive insight but it also poses further questions for theological reflection. One of the most important and toughest of these questions is that which lies at the heart of the argument about impassibility and immutability – can God be affected by his creation, and does God change?

The most venerable theological position is that we cannot admit the possibility of change of any kind in God, since he is perfect and, therefore, any change must be for the worse. Consequently we may not say that God suffers, since suffering by definition implies being affected, one way or another, and so changed. On the other hand we meet in the Old Testament an insistence that 'the Living God' is to be recognised by his capacity to react and respond and adapt his actions to changing circumstances, and to find a way round each new frustration. Such a God, by virtue of creating in Space and Time a universe with some degree of inbuilt freedom, exposes himself to being acted upon and, in that sense, being compelled to change.

The victory of God

Nevertheless, when we come to talk about suffering, we are speaking of change which, in our human experience, is diminishing, damaging, even destructive. Suffering may leave permanent scars or disabilities, even in those who endure it most bravely and lovingly. Many of these human concomitants of suffering may not be very illuminating clues to suffering in God. But one human phenomenon is of crucial importance, and this is what we may call consistency, faithfulness, reliability. Whatever changes some sufferers undergo, they come through with their integrity unimpaired, their loyalty to those they love or to what they believe in still strong and true. In that sense we feel that they, essentially, have not been changed. Within the context of our human incompleteness that degree of mature strength is usually attained only through many knocks and agonies, for we are again talking about the kind of wholeness we discern at the close of the great tragic dramas. But if something corresponding to that hard-won wholeness has been an attribute of God eternally, then we may see how he remains ever the same even though he takes upon himself the suffering of the world. But the Christian faith is not just that, in Christ, the burden of suffering and evil in the world is shared by the Triune God in his love and compassion. In the Resurrection, it has been decisively overcome. Cross and Resurrection are both of them parts of the one integrated self-revelation of God, and the faith of the Christian is focused upon this double but indivisible action of God in Christ. Cross-and-Resurrection proclaims that divine victory comes, but also that it always comes through bitter conflicts; deliverance from evil comes, but always comes by absorbing the evil in patient forgiveness; new life is given, but has always to be given through dying. This is the significance of Christian baptism. We are baptised, according to St Paul, into the death of Jesus and into his burial, in order that we may enter into his resurrection life and become, together, his Body, alive in this world with a life which is already 'hidden with Christ in God', and will there endure eternally.

It is, therefore, precisely because they are Christ's Body in this world, baptised into the pattern of his death and resurrection, that Christians are those who enter into the long-suffering patience of God, sharing his victory over evil by absorbing it in inexhaustible forgiveness, and waiting with him in sure and certain hope of the ultimate triumph of love. The nature of this triumph is revealed unmistakably in the Gospel stories of the first Easter Day. Jesus returns to his friends in a new and transcendent life and power; but the love and forgiveness that marked his earthly existence are unchanged, and the Risen Body still bears the scars and wounds of the Crucified. To pick up our earlier analogy, in the hands of the divine artist what went 'wrong' has become the central and distinctive feature of an even greater work: 'See my hands and my feet, that it is I, myself.'

The Resurrection does not cancel or merely redress the truth that shines from the cross; it confirms it. This is the eternal nature of divine power and victory, insofar as our human minds are capable of grasping it.

This God does not promise that we shall be protected from the accidents and ills of this life, but that those who open themselves to him will be empowered with the human resources of endurance, insight and selflessness that can turn misfortune to good account. The well-known words of Phil. 4.13 in the older versions, 'I can do all things through Christ who strengthens me', are in fact a misleading rendering. The truer sense, which is also more appropriate in the context, is, 'I have strength to cope with anything'.

That in which we put our trust is essentially the constancy and reliability of God; and this is, in fact, all the more solidly established through this understanding of his nature and his purpose. His faithfulness consists in his unbreakable commitment to his people and, as the scriptures also indicate, to his whole Creation. He will never turn back from the love which binds him to the world and which remains his way with the world to the end of time. It is a way that embraces the 'changes and chances', in all their arbitrary freedom, within the 'eternal changelessness' of a love that bears, believes, hopes, endures all things. By its very nature that love is at once the source of the grace we need in this life, and our hope of glory in the life to come.

We Believe in the Holy Spirit

Chairman's preface

On behalf of the Commission I wish to place on record our gratitude to several people who have given us invaluable help in the preparation of this report:

> to the Bishop of Salisbury, formerly Chairman of the Commission whose creative and generous mind we have greatly missed;
>
> to two members of the last Doctrine Commission, the Revd Dr John Barton and the Revd Dr Anthony Harvey, who have both produced preparatory papers on which we have drawn;
>
> to the Revd Canon Michael Green and the Revd Tom Smail, who have both written notes for us in which they have drawn on their close knowledge of the charismatic movement;
>
> to our two consultants, both of whom attended some of our meetings: the Revd Dr John Polkinghorne FRS, who, during our work on this report, became a member of the Commission; and the Revd Dr John Rodwell, to whom we are particularly indebted for much intellectual stimulus;
>
> to our ever-loyal and efficient secretary, the Revd John Meacham, who has contributed in countless ways to the work of the Commission, who has prepared the indices to this report and whose ill-health has so greatly saddened us;
>
> to the Revd Dr John Clark, who took over the duties of secretary in the final stages of the preparation of this report;
>
> and to those who have given us secretarial support at our meetings, notably Miss Keri Lewis, Mrs Pauline Druiff and Mrs Doris Kay of the General Synod Office.

This report, like the last, *We Believe in God*, comes with the approval and agreement of the entire Commission. Each chapter was drafted by one person, who in some cases drew on material supplied by others; each chapter once drafted was considered, revised and refined by the entire Commission, a process which in the case of some chapters was repeated several times; final editorial touches were made by the Chairman. Left to ourselves, some of us might well have preferred to express certain matters rather differently, but all our members have endorsed the entire report.

Also, like the last, this report is published under the authority of the House of Bishops and is commended by the House to the Church for study. It is humbly offered to the Church at large in the hope that it will enable many interested readers to believe in the Holy Spirit with deeper understanding.

+ALEC NEWCASTLE

Chapter 1
Introduction

The Holy Spirit may without exaggeration be called the heart-beat of the Christian, the life-blood of the Christian Church. In the second half of this century the words 'We believe in the Holy Spirit, the Lord, the giver of life' have acquired greater depth and meaning for Christian people in every tradition. The Holy Spirit has recovered a prominent place in Christian testimony and experience, in hymns and in prayers. In this study of this topical subject we seek to explore the meaning of these words from the Nicene Creed.

For the title of our work, however, we have drawn on the simpler, terser words of the Apostles' Creed, just as in 1987 the Doctrine Commission drew on the opening words of the Apostles' Creed for the title for its report, *We Believe in God*. Like its predecessor this report concentrates on the content of belief rather than on the nature of believing. It is offered to the Church to provide guidance in understanding the doctrine of the Holy Spirit and to stimulate thought, study and discussion. The authors of both reports have encountered the same difficulty: both reports are about God. God as Trinity we believe to be both hidden and revealed, mysterious and yet somehow manifested within the created order. The former report suggested ways in which the trinitarian nature of God may be understood and experienced, particularly in prayer and worship; some of these suggestions are developed in this report. With regard to belief in the triune God and particularly in the Holy Spirit there is in the scriptures and in the Church's tradition an astonishing variety and profusion of hint and assertion, of metaphor and image. These various claims and insights resist any attempt to fit them into a fully coherent pattern. We have not attempted to make a comprehensive survey of such a vast and untidy subject; rather, we have tried to draw on some of the principal strands to be found concerning the Holy Spirit in the scriptures and in the Christian tradition, and to develop them in such a way as to illuminate their relationship both to one another and to certain current questions and concerns. In our work we have often been reminded that the task of theology extends beyond the handling of scripture and tradition, and that it relates to wider areas of human understanding, particularly to the natural order and to the ordering of society.

Some of these problems are not new. When Paul, for instance, came to Ephesus he found there some disciples, who told him, 'We have never even heard that there is a Holy Spirit' (Acts 19.2). Since then all instructed Christian believers and certainly all theological thinkers have heard that there is a Holy Spirit, but many Christian people have not paid much attention to the Spirit in their thinking and praying. Whitsun (or Pentecost) as a festival does not attract many more worshippers than does an ordinary Sunday, and throughout the Christian centuries theologians in general, at least in the west, have devoted surprisingly little attention to the Holy Spirit. Indeed those who have treated the Holy Spirit and the work of the Spirit have tended to discuss the influence of the Spirit in the Churches, the sacraments and the Christian life rather than to engage with the primary biblical material.

The narrative of Paul's visit to Ephesus goes on to recount how he baptized the disciples, to whom we have referred, in the name of the Lord Jesus 'and when Paul had laid his hands upon them, the Holy Spirit came on them; and they spoke with tongues and prophesied' (Acts 19.6). In every century since there have been those who, in the power of the Spirit, have prophesied and spoken in tongues, and some who have claimed that these manifestations are necessary consequences and signs of the Spirit's presence and activity. Thus against a background of relative neglect of the Holy Spirit in western Christian thinking and devotion there have been vigorous and dramatic movements, from the Montanist movement of the second and third centuries to revivalist movements of the present day, which have claimed to be the sole authentic expression of the Spirit's work. Moreover, in our own day charismatic movements have deeply affected many congregations, individual worshippers, and also to some extent the entire flavour of our Church's life. These developments have been treated descriptively in two recent reports: *The Charismatic Movement in the Church of England* (1981) and *The Good Wine: Spiritual Renewal in the Church of England* by Josephine Bax (1986). Our report *We Believe in the Holy Spirit* seeks to set these particular expressions of the Spirit's work within the wider setting of the Church's life and to relate the emphases prominent in the thinking and practice of the charismatic movement to other emphases in the biblical revelation and Christian tradition.

Equally, we hope that our report will help many worshippers to appreciate and appropriate more of the riches of Christian thought and experience with regard to the Holy Spirit. Most believers have some sort of mental image of the Father and the Son, but the Spirit seems to be all the more intangible and presents greater difficulties to the imagination. Also, the self-effacing character of the Holy Spirit presents us with a particular problem, for we are told that the Holy Spirit bears witness to Christ (John 15.26). Our hope is that we enable 'ordinary churchpeople' who may or may not be caught up in the charismatic movement to think more clearly and express themselves more articulately about the very life of God in which through the Spirit they and we already share; in this connection the activity and experience of praying form a sensitive area to which we give particular attention.

It is, however, not only the ordinary, non-professional, theologically lay Christian who experiences difficulties in thinking about the Holy Spirit. These difficulties, and others too, are faced by the professional theologian. Within the last twenty years some influential figures in English theology, faced with the problem of thinking about God and with traditional trinitarian language, have reached conclusions which in effect dismantle the Trinity: language about the Holy Spirit is regarded as metaphor for divine action in the world or just as a way of referring to God, more particularly to God in relation to the world. By contrast, in common with the universal Church we maintain the appropriateness of, indeed the necessity for, traditional trinitarian belief in the Holy Spirit as a distinct mode of being or Person within the Trinity: here again it is the prayer of Jesus in Gethsemane and of Christian people through the Spirit, which is for us the area which contains the most promising and compelling insights. In the last resort 'no one comprehends the thoughts of God except the Spirit of God' (1 Cor. 2.11), but Paul is quite clear that his readers in, for instance, Galatia (Gal. 3.2) and Corinth (1 Cor. 2.12) have received the Spirit, and it is our conviction that to his language about our participation in the Spirit (2 Cor. 13.14) justice can best be done by belief in the Spirit as a distinct 'hypostasis' or Person integral to the very being of the godhead. This is discussed more fully elsewhere in this study, particularly at the end of the next chapter.

The full personhood of the Spirit within the Trinity is but one of several questions with which we are faced in thinking about the Holy Spirit. The Commission also considered the move made by some modern theologians with feminist sympathies to see the Holy Spirit as a 'feminine' principle in the Trinity. The idea has some interesting, if sporadic, support in the tradition, especially in the early Syriac patristic material, where the word for 'Spirit' is itself feminine in gender; there has also been the occasional startling, and quite spontaneous, iconographical representation of the spirit as a female figure. It was generally agreed by the Commission, however, that the *compensatory* projection of one 'female' figure into the Godhead, especially where this carried uncritical assumptions about the appropriate characteristics of 'femininity' (such as being soothing, mothering, constantly available at home, or mediating between the more prominent 'male' persons of the Trinity) was indicative more of traditional assumptions about power relations between the sexes than of a positive way forward in trinitarian theology. In other words, the far-reaching consequences of feminist challenges to traditional Christian theism could not adequately be met by changing the gender associations of one Person of the Trinity.*

Another source of difficulty consists in the common associations of the term 'spirit'. For some the word 'spirit' evokes ideas of ghosts or of beings which are said to communicate with us from beyond the grave through mediums or various forms of physical manifestation; in this sense spirit or spirits are irreducibly material. For others the word 'spirit' is linked with certain inward features of human beings, particularly with conscience, creativity, aesthetic experience and religious awareness. In other contexts the word connotes that which binds people together in a common enterprise, in a group or movement, with a shared vision and values. With regard to the dead the word 'spirit' is often used to describe their influence which is perceptible long after their life, as one might say that the spirit of Napoleon is still felt in France to-day. Christian discourse about the Holy Spirit is different from any of these common meanings and uses of the word 'spirit'. We are dealing not with the material manifestations, nor with the purely subjective, nor with an influence which comes from Jesus and is perceptible centuries after his death, nor in some vague way with the divine, nor with something which characterizes and distinguishes humanity from the rest of the created order, nor with anything which science would classify as matter or energy.

When we turn to our Bible we find in both the Old and the New Testament a wide range of meaning for the words translated 'spirit'. So far as the Old Testament is concerned, it is arguable that the use of the word 'spirit' with reference to God is borrowed from its use with reference to human beings, who are all animated by breath. If this is the case, 'spirit' is first applied to people and is then applied by extension to God, who has a divine, a holy spirit, not the feeble kind of spirit which we have and which deserts us at death. Spirit is breathed by God into human beings for their very life, for the empowering of individuals with respect to particular tasks, and for the activity of prophecy. Once, however, the term spirit has been applied to God, then spirit becomes that which God essentially is; those beings are most truly spiritual whose nature and existence are most completely like God, and determined by God's creative and saving power. We need also to mention that the religion of Israel needed to do justice to a faith in God who was believed to be both infinite, eternal, unapproachable, and also active here and now in human affairs, indeed in the hearts and minds of human beings. From

---

* The paper by Sarah Coakley originally presented to the Commission on this theme is now published in ed. M. Furlong, *Mirror to the Church*, SPCK, 1988, pp. 124–35.

the time of the exile onwards and especially in some of the latest parts of the Old Testament we find that terms such as the Spirit of God, like the Wisdom or Word or Law of God, are used with reference to the work of God in creating the universe and to the presence of God in sustaining it. We note that this terminology about the divine activity in creating and sustaining the universe is generally claimed by the New Testament writers for Christ, rather than for the Spirit. That is a major shift of emphasis between the two testaments, and it is this shift which in part explains why (as we have seen) some Christian thinkers find no need to treat the Holy Spirit as a distinct Person.

When we turn to the New Testament we discern both continuity and discontinuity with the Old. The New Testament writers develop many of the ideas and images used in the Old Testament. However, as we have seen, they do not hesitate in one major respect to use the language of the Old Testament in a quite different sense, a sense derived from their conviction about the centrality of Jesus Christ in God's providential design for the universe and more particularly about the centrality of the redemption wrought by him.

Within the New Testament itself there is both unity and diversity in the material concerning the Holy Spirit. We draw particular attention to two important features where there is unanimity among the New Testament authors who treat them. First, according to all four gospels the Spirit was closely associated with the baptism of Jesus, descending upon him then. The Spirit thus was understood to have in some sense inspired and empowered Jesus in his public ministry of preaching and teaching and in his performance of mighty works. His ministry reached its climax and fulfilment in his passion and crucifixion. Our understanding of the work of the Spirit is thus shaped and moulded by the course of Jesus' life and, more particularly, by his death. Further, the Spirit is believed to be powerfully at work in connection with Jesus' resurrection from the dead (Rom. 1.4). Christian faith is properly Christocentric and is centred on the events of Good Friday and of Easter. This framework of reference governs our understanding of the work of the Spirit whom we believe to be the Spirit of God and of Christ. Further, we note, what may be one of the few references to the Holy Spirit in the Epistle to the Hebrews bears upon the sacrificial obedience of Christ, 'who through the eternal Spirit offered himself without blemish to God' (Heb. 9.14). In our view it is particularly significant that, in Gethsemane on the night of his betrayal to death, Jesus prayed, 'Abba, Father' (Mark 14.36), and that the only other occasion on which we find this expression in the New Testament are two passages in Paul's epistles (Rom. 8.15; Gal. 4.6) both of which deal with the work of the Spirit; in the chapters which follow, particularly in 'The Spirit of Jesus', we shall return to these passages which we consider to be of crucial importance. They establish the Christological and Christocentric viewpoint which for us is one of the principal bases for understanding the Holy Spirit. The Christological or Christocentric reference also controls the discussions in the chapter entitled, 'The Spirit and Power', in which we try to evaluate within a Christological perspective the claims to the exercise of power sometimes made by those who have become vividly aware of the Spirit's powerful operation for good in their own lives and ministries.

The second respect in which we find a common mind, or the reflection of a common pattern, among the New Testament writers lies in the conviction that the Holy Spirit is shed or spread abroad as a consequence of the death and resurrection of Christ; that it is within the life and fellowship of the Christian Church that the Spirit is, as a consequence, powerfully at work; and that the Church is the particular sphere of the Spirit's operation. This conviction was expressed most provocatively in the fourth gospel; 'as yet the Spirit had not been given, because Jesus was not yet glorified' (John 7.39). His glorification was his being lifted up on the cross and to heaven; John 19. 30,34 may convey to us the conviction that at the moment of Jesus' death his Spirit was conveyed to his disciples; John 20.22 certainly conveys the conviction that, after Jesus had ascended to the Father, he breathed the Holy Spirit upon the disciples and that within their fellowship the Spirit is powerfully at work in the ways about which we read in the farewell discourses. From the Lukan writings a similar pattern emerges; after the death and resurrection of Jesus, the Spirit, who had been active in Jesus' ministry, was given to the founder members of the young Church on the day of Pentecost, and within the Christian Church the Spirit is at work. Indeed the work of the Spirit in the young Church, as it is presented in the Acts of the Apostles, provides striking parallels with the work of Jesus, as described in Luke's gospel; thus the conviction is conveyed that the Spirit which once rested upon Jesus is now to be found within the Christian Church. Paul, too, while he has scarcely anything to say about the ministry of Jesus, is quite clear that 'God has sent the Spirit of his Son into our hearts' (Gal. 4.6), and that this Spirit is to be found in Christian believers and in the Christian communities of which they are members. These various authors all write within a common viewpoint with regard to the work of the Spirit; as each is addressing a different pastoral situation, each draws attention to different elements in the Spirit's work and has his own particular emphasis.

When we turn to the elements of diversity in the treatment of the Spirit's work by the New Testament authors, the use of the term Paraclete, solely in the Johannine writings, is a very obvious example of particular usage. In our final chapter we shall draw some attention to this feature in the tradition and to the theme suggested by it, namely that the Spirit is our counsel, both prosecuting and defending.

It is not surprising that the Lukan writings have been so influential on subsequent Christian thinking about the Spirit; Luke's gospel contains many references to the Spirit in connection with the conception and birth of Jesus as well as with his ministry, and the Acts extends the period surveyed to include the first three decades of the Christian Church, with the implicit understanding that the era of the Church will continue for a long time. This presentation has governed the evolution of the Christian year; it has also influenced the phraseology of familiar prayers, of blessings, and even of the baptismal questions which might be taken to imply that God worked in successive phases as Father in creation, as Son during a brief period for our salvation, and now in the era of the Church as Spirit for our sanctification. According to this linear view of revelation the Spirit unfolds and communicates to us what has already been achieved by the Son. As we have seen, this treatment of the saving history is consistent with the view that the era of the Spirit opened with Pentecost and the Spirit's principal sphere of operation is the Christian Church.

We do not in any way deny or contest that the Holy Spirit is particularly at work in the Church by covenant and promise, and that participation in the Spirit within the Church has been a means of growth in holiness for countless Christian believers. Indeed we devote an entire chapter 'Spirit, Sacraments and Structures' to developing some of the implications of these convictions. However, we are not content with the linear model as the most satisfactory one available. It can convey a misleading impression, namely that God worked *successively* either through three different modes of revelation or through three different modes of being. Christian writers, both within the patristic period and more recently, have drawn on the wide range of biblical material, to which we have already made some reference, and tried to relate the various biblical insights and assertions with the fundamental Christian belief that God is Trinity. The linear view on which we have already touched led naturally to an understanding of the godhead closely linked with the work of God in creation and salvation, with the divine 'economy' as it has sometimes been called. However, in no sense did God *become* Trinity; God is and always has been Trinity. Once that point has become clear, it follows that in whatever one Person of the Trinity does the others always and necessarily have their part to play, and that all are fully involved in creation, redemption and sanctification. (As we have already noted, this will be treated more fully towards the end of the next chapter). We have taken this fundamental tenet of the faith with full seriousness, and it has affected our thinking in three principal respects.

First, with regard to our own experience of the Christian life we have explored the implications of Paul's thinking, particularly in Romans 8. Through the agency of the Spirit believers are caught up, as it were, into the life of the Godhead, incorporated through the activity of the Spirit into the Son, given there the firm and assured status of children of God by adoption, enabled to join in the Son's ceaseless prayer of *Abba* to the Father. This chapter in the Epistle to the Romans presents to us the being and work of God as irreducibly and necessarily threefold rather than monist or bipolar; the experience of Christian praying provides a corroboration of this insight and a foretaste of that communion or fellowship of the Holy Spirit, in whom we have fellowship with the Father and with his Son Jesus Christ. An important consequence of this understanding of the being and work of the Spirit is the seriousness and depth which it perceives in prayer and worship. Prayer, both individual and corporate, is the means whereby we through the Spirit are enabled, as it were, to share in and grow in the divine conversation of love, both initiative and response, which constitutes the relationship of Father and Son.

Second, if God be Trinity, then the Spirit works together with the Father and the Word in the work of creation. A purely biblical theology may not at first sight lead us to that conclusion, but any attempt at systematic theology which takes trinitarian faith seriously must do so, and in so doing it will pick up and develop hints in the biblical tradition. Thus a chapter entitled 'The Spirit and Creation' is an integral part of our work; in it we have sought to do justice to fundamental trinitarian insights in terms which are consistent both with the biblical tradition and with our understanding of the world. In this chapter we have drawn attention to the twin elements of order and flexibility, of structure and development, of consistency and openness, of regularity and originality, all of which physical scientists perceive to be at work in the evolving universe. We have sought to show that these elements cohere with biblical conviction that, in the work of God and therefore of the Spirit, we find both order and rationality and also innovation and surprise. In his book *The Holy Spirit* Professor C.F.D. Moule puts forward the argument that generally in the New Testament 'Spirit is confined to the Church and the new creation. Christ has cosmic functions . . . but not the Spirit' (p.20). After some further discussion he continues, 'All this is not to say that it is illegitimate to use the term "Spirit" in the broad and generalised way that is now common – provided the user knows what he is doing' (p.21). In our treatment of the work of the Spirit in creation and in the evolving universe we have avoided using the term 'Spirit' in a broad and generalised way, seeking rather to do justice to the implications of a fully trinitarian faith. Moreover, as we have already noted, we are aware what we are doing in building on and developing the explicit biblical assertions about the Spirit's work.

In the same paragraph Professor Moule continues, 'It is extremely difficult to avoid using "inspiration" (which is a "spirit" word) to describe the genius of creative artistry' (p.21). This is one of several factors which have moved us to include in our work a chapter on 'The Spirit and Creativity'. If the work of the Holy Spirit is to be discerned within God's creative activity, then the work of the artist and craftsman, of the inventor and researcher are spheres in which we should properly expect to find the Holy Spirit at work. This chapter refers especially to the work of the composer, the painter, the poet and the novelist; in the work of them all there is an element of imaginative engagement with the constraints of certain forms and means of expression, a combination not unlike that which we discerned in the way in which God is continuously active in creation. Since we are created in God's image, it is appropriate to think of human creativity as a reflection of God's own creativity.

The third important implication of our fundamental conviction about the trinitarian nature of the being of God lies in our conviction that the Spirit, though particularly at work within the Christian Church (as we have noted) by covenant and promise, is also at work outside it, in the lives and characters of people of other faiths and of no faith. We touch on this point in our chapters concerning creation and creativity. Indeed at several points in this report we note in passing that the Spirit is active outside as well as inside the Christian Church, for 'the wind blows where it wills' (John 3.8). The same Greek word means both *wind* and *spirit*. This point coheres naturally with the other two, both of which tried to do justice to the presence and activity of God (and *a fortiori* of the Holy Spirit) outside the confines of the Church. Naturally the touchstone of the quality of the Spirit's activity in the life of any person, whether Christian or not, is the evidence of a Christ-like spirit. Wherever that spirit is to be found, it must surely be attributed to the unseen, inward working of the Holy Spirit. A haunting chant often sung in our churches and popularized by the Community of Taizé contains the words, 'Ubi caritas et amor, Deus ibi est' (Where there is love and charity, there is God), and if God be there, then the Holy Spirit must be there, for the Spirit is pre-eminently the Spirit of love; more still, the Spirit is believed to be the very Spirit of love who binds together Father and Son in their reciprocal self-giving.

Our conviction that the Holy Spirit, while particularly at work within the Church, is also at work outside led us to consider carefully the possibility of our devoting more attention, in connection with this report, to the Spirit's work in relation to other faiths. We came to the conclusion that other faiths are more appropriately discussed under the heading of Salvation, itself the subject of our next report. Having merely mentioned here this important dimension of our subject, we intend to return to it for more thorough treatment in our next report.

The principle set out just now in connection with the first two consequences of taking trinitarian faith seriously, namely that rationality and inspiration are not incompatible with one another and indeed require one another, has informed our understanding of the work of the Spirit in connection with the charismatic revival. Another way of expressing this principle is to say that God is a God of order as well as of freedom, of continuity as well as of innovation, of regularity as well as of surprise. If all this is true about God, it must hold true of the Holy Spirit. That we understand to be the overriding message of 1 Cor. 12–14, an extended passage which bears directly on problems attending manifestations of the Spirit in the Corinthian church. There is no doubt that in our day the charismatic movement has brought spiritual vitality to many individuals and congregations and thus to the life of the Church as a whole. However, all religious movements, and indeed religion itself, stand under judgement; all can become subject to rigidity and formality; all types of piety can become means of self-indulgence, and all need to be set repeatedly against the touchstone of Christ-likeness, which is the only authentic mark of the Spirit's activity.

There are indeed varieties of gifts; we value the charismatic movement for all the undoubted good it has brought to the Church. We make sympathetic response to it and a theological appraisal of some of its features, particularly in our chapter 'Is this that?' Equally, we wish to affirm and support those whose experience of the Christian life, with regard both to faith and to prayer, has been rather different. For instance, within the principles on which we have worked there is room for regarding rational reflection, which seeks the coherence of all truth, to be just as much evidence of the work of the Spirit as sudden illumination or revelation, for the Spirit is the Spirit of order as well as of surprise. (This is one of the lines of thought developed in our chapter 'The Spirit of Truth'). Similarly we are convinced that not all prayer has to be charismatic prayer; ordinary, apparently pedestrian prayer (that is to say, the daily prayer of most Christians) should be understood as prayer in the Spirit just as much as more spectacular prayer. Further, liturgical prayer in the office and Eucharist, and prayer which struggles or groans in difficulty and darkness, should be valued as authentic praying in the Spirit just as much as the spontaneous, keenly and vividly experienced prayer of the new convert or of the newly charismatic congregation. Within the body of the Church in which varieties of gifts are distributed, we all need one another, and it may well be that we can all critically appreciate one another and learn from one another. Certainly our hope is that our work will help to integrate thought and feeling, the reflective and the affective, within the life of the Church as a whole and in the lives of its individual members.

People quite frequently speak of some phenomena, particularly those displayed in charismatic circles, as signs of the 'direct' activity of the Holy Spirit. Instead of being known through the indirect means of the ordinary life of the Christian community, its words and acts and structures, the Spirit is encountered with no intermediaries or interpreters. Such a view is easy to understand. From the earliest days of Christian faith, people have identified moments of transition in their lives of prayer when they feel they no longer know God at secondhand but can confirm what they have been told by others out of their own experience (cf. John 4.42). But there are problems in using the language of 'direct' and 'indirect' encounter too simply. It will not do to say that God ordinarily acts through indirect means and then for specially important occasions dispenses with them: this would make the incarnation rather hard to understand – as if God could have found a better means of communication than the truly human life and acts and death of Jesus. There is also the danger of imagining that words or insights associated with 'direct' encounter are not subject to the ordinary processes of discernment, reflection and testing in the Christian community. Even in circumstances where we are confident of having broken through some kind of barrier in our relationship with God, we are still the people we always were, our minds and imaginations working in the ways our past experience has made possible for us. God seems never to work by completely annihilating our nature and our history. So perhaps it is better to avoid the problematic language of 'direct' and 'indirect' (or 'immediate' and 'mediated', in the language of Roman Catholic controversies on this question in the 1920s and 1930s). If we need to signal the significance of the moments of breakthrough and transition, much of the literature on prayer suggests that we should talk of it as a process whereby more and deeper levels of the human personality are brought into our knowing of God, rather than as God acting more directly. It is true that as more of the personality becomes involved, many words or pictures that were once helpful will naturally fall away, and there will be less sense of *consciously* depending on things learned from others. But this should not be taken to mean that at such moments God suspends our human ways of knowing and gives us a kind of other-worldly infallibility. Thus in this book we shall speak a great deal about 'experience of the Holy Spirit', but this should not imply some kind of raw experience independent of the normal functioning of our human powers of understanding and interpretation in the light of tradition.

This introductory chapter has sought to set out some features lying in the background which have led to our choice of this subject; to draw attention to some of the more important convictions which have influenced our own thinking and which we have tried to convey; to indicate the chapters in the report in which these convictions receive fuller treatment. It will be apparent to the reader that we stand in that Anglican tradition of which Hooker is the most celebrated exponent. Thus scripture is our supreme authority; scripture is properly understood within the Church. On questions to which scripture does not address itself the Church may develop the teaching of scripture, so long as it does not contradict scripture. As we noted at the outset, we have not attempted an exhaustive survey of topics associated with the Holy Spirit. It will, however, have become clear that we are persuaded that understanding of the Spirit, knowledge of the world, and engagement in prayer and worship go hand in hand. Therefore it is fitting that the next chapter should be entitled 'Charismatic Experience: Praying "in the Spirit" '; it has been based on a number of interviews with Anglican charismatics in a particular congregation. We were asked to reflect on the charismatic movements; therefore we have gone there first and done some fieldwork, on which we have done some theological reflection.

Chapter 2
Charismatic experience: praying 'in the spirit'

> There is little to attract the unbeliever in the traditional, organized church . . . We have neglected our prayer life; we have stopped listening to God; . . . (yet people are) hungry and thirsty for God or or some form of spiritual reality.
>
> (David Watson, 1980)

> If the Holy Spirit is in you, you will comprehend well enough His action within you . . . All those who have been baptized in the Holy Spirit have put on Christ completely; they are children of light and walk in the light which has no decline.
>
> (Symeon the New Theologian, early eleventh century)

The charismatic renewal today calls as controversially as did Symeon in his very different Byzantine milieu for an intense commitment to prayer and the expectation of specific experiential effects from the invocation of the Holy Spirit. Symeon too spoke to what he regarded as a tepid generation in the Church; and for him the blasphemy against the Holy Spirit was precisely the denial that the Spirit could be vibrantly experienced now, 'divinizing' Christians (to use his eastern terminology), catching them up into the very life of the God-head, making them nothing less than 'sons of God by adoption and grace'. (See Symeon the New Theologian, *The Discourses*, esp. XXIV, 4.)

In a similar way that challenge has been laid at the door of the established churches and denominations in the last quarter century by the influx of charismatic influence. And so some hard questions, with which this chapter is concerned, are rightly pressed: *are* we truly a praying Church? What (if anything) do we expect of the activity of the Holy Spirit in prayer? Is the Holy Spirit uniformly and universally present or only sporadically available? Is indeed a failure to reflect on the Spirit any sign of the Spirit's absence (or vice versa)? Does the Holy Spirit always guarantee consoling or emotionally satisfying experiences (as the somewhat misleading translation of Paraclete as 'comforter' could suggest)? And, even more fundamentally, what *is* an 'experience' of the Holy Spirit? Is it in any clear way distinguishable from an 'experience' of the Father or the Son? And, if not, why should we wish to speak of the Spirit as a distinct Person at all?

If we are to confront these issues cogently for today, we must surely do so not just by drawing on scriptural and credal authority (although these are fundamental, as we shall see in the course of this book), but by reference precisely to some of the various and rich experiences of the charismatic constituency in the Church as we find it now. Thus this chapter is largely based on a number of in-depth interviews with Anglican charismatics from a particular church which was deemed to be representative of the development of the movement within the Church of England. The interviews were conducted with men and women of different ages, social backgrounds and education, all of whom have, however, been involved in 'renewal' for some lengthy period (between ten and twenty-five years). They can thus speak with some perspective of time on the phases of development that the movement has undergone in relation to 'prayer in the Spirit', and this at a moment when, self-confessedly, the movement within Anglicanism seems to be facing a crisis of decision and direction which is closely (and interestingly) related to attitudes to prayer. Thus, out of the evidence of contemporary *reportage* emerge theological themes of recurring significance.

The movement within denominational Christianity in general has been said to be in decline: whether this is so in numerical terms is not our concern here, but rather what shifts in understanding may be occurring in relation to our questions about the Spirit and prayer. As a means of comparison in these investigations interviews were also taped with some members of a recent split-off group from the Anglican charismatic church studied, a Fellowship loosely associated with the 'Restoration' movement and now fast making new converts of its own. The members of this group tend to be younger Christians (not necessarily younger in age); they also span an interesting range of class and educational back-grounds: there are professional people here too, and a large gathering of students, but in general the ethos is less middle class than in the Anglican congregation. Manifesting a much purer 'sect'-like form than can be achieved within the episcopal structures of Anglicanism, and also a much more rigorous biblical fundamentalism, this group's maintenance of high levels of prophecy and public tongue-speaking in its worship distinguishes it from what is now the norm in its present Anglican counterpart. Here worship had already become somewhat formalized and sedate before the split-off, and indeed for those who left this was seen as a loss of contact with the Spirit's drive and purpose. The Anglicans have in the meantime reverted to at least the outlines of the ASB's requirements.

Is this a sign of decline and lack of direction in the Anglicans' case (as the Fellowship tends to read it), or rather a new phase of deepening maturity, a distinct pressure of the Spirit towards a new synthesis with tradition (as the Anglican minister reads it)? To answer this, we need to look at the witness of those concerned, and only from there suggest a theological judgement based upon this. What is sure, however, is that we have here a fascinating correlation of sociological and theological factors, different attitudes to the Holy Spirit and prayer being *aligned* with different socially-constituted groupings. To anticipate: the purer 'sect' form, with its rejection of ordained ministry, commitment to egalitarian exercise of 'gifts' (and yet strict refusal of teaching roles to women on fundamentalist grounds), expects high feeling states as the norm in public prayer 'in the Spirit'; whereas the Anglican community, with its self-styled hybrid of 'sect' and 'church'-type organization (the episcopal structure combined with 'elders' and much lay leadership, including some cautious use of women in positions of authority), seems to be moving towards a less sporadic and emotionally dramatic understanding of the Spirit, encouraged by its minister to believe that a new phase of the renewal has been entered, the 'recovery of gifts' being succeeded by the 'recovery of disciplines'. How does this shift of emphasis affect the theological questions with which we are concerned? And what broader theological and historical perspectives may we apply to the divergence between the two groups? We shall look at a number of selected questions in turn.

1. Encountering renewal, 'experiencing' the spirit

(a) The interviews

It was in questions concerning the initial 'experience' of the Spirit, and the continuing effects of regular prayer 'in the Spirit', that we found least divergence, indeed, negligible divergence, between the two groups. The vexed question of the meaning of 'baptism in the Spirit' (addressed in detail in the next chapter) was not explicitly raised by the interviewer, and, perhaps significantly, was not an issue for polemicizing by either group. But to the general question, 'How has your prayer changed since you encountered renewal?', there were answers such as, 'There was a sense of new *excitement*', or, 'It was so delightful to find that it was acceptable to be openly *enthusiastic* about God'. 'Affective' (positive emotional) states, then, were universally acknowledged, the sense of a great release of feelings, especially positive feelings of praise and exaltation, that had previously been held back. But even more significant for our question about what characterizes the 'experience' of the Spirit, specifically, was the reiterated remark that people had in a new way found prayer to be a 'two-way relationship', not just a talking at God, but God (the Holy Spirit) already co-operating in one's prayer, energizing it from within, and no less also responding in it, alluring one again, inviting one into a continuing adventure. This was said to be 'the real thing', 'making yourself a channel for the Spirit's work', an intermingling of the human desire for God and the Spirit's interceding to the Father (cf. Rom. 8.27). With this then came the sense of prayer in the Spirit becoming a uniting thread in one's life, 'an all-encompassing relationship', so that prayer became no longer one activity (or duty) amongst others, but the wellspring of all activities. Thus Paul's injunction 'Pray constantly' (1 Thess. 5.17) took on a new meaning, as did Jesus' insistence on trust, faith, and confidence in prayer ('Ask, and it will be given you' (Matt. 7.7)), even though it was admitted that one did not always get what one expected.

(b) Commentary

The actual prayer methods of the people interviewed were enormously varied, as varied as were the people themselves. It was taken for granted that there would be a commitment (indeed an intense commitment) to the usual range of verbal prayers, expressing penitence, praise, petition and intercession; but beyond that most people also made regular and disciplined use of some sort of scriptural meditation. Moreover, it was striking how ingenious and resourceful people had been in working out structured patterns of praying suitable for their own psychological type or mode of life. One husband and wife were somewhat startled to have the interviewer comment that their preferred methods of prayer were almost indistinguishable from (respectively) Luther's 'Simple way to pray' (using each phrase of the Lord's Prayer meditatively in turn), and Ignatius Loyola's 'composition of place' in *The Spiritual Exercises* (thinking one's way imaginatively into a gospel scene). Being of a fundamentalist bent they preferred not to rely on 'tradition', but had painstakingly evolved their own ways.

Likewise, it is worthy of comment that the expected reference to Romans 8.14–27 (in relation to the crucial experience of the Spirit praying in one) did not in general lead to any clear reflection on the importance of this in *trinitarian* terms. The interviewees assumed without question that the Spirit was in some almost inexplicable way experientially distinct from the Son (despite the confusing shifts in Paul's language in Rom. 8.9f.). But the possibility that this experiential starting point might provide some sort of response to those theologians currently challenging the Spirit's distinct personal existence, or otherwise dismantling the doctrine of the Trinity, was far from their minds. In general these controversies had not impinged on them at all (as indeed would be true in most parish contexts). Distant too was any thought that ontological trinitarian reflection might be 'earthed' here, leading perhaps to a reassimilation of the eastern patristic model of 'deification' with which Symeon was familiar – the Spirit *incorporating* one into the life of sonship and so bringing one to the Father.* Such categories sounded alien to those of fundamentalist background, although there was a marked, and perhaps unexpected, willingness to consider the possibilities. In short, and doubtless unsurprisingly, there was little knowledge shown of trinitarian controversies in Christian tradition at all, or of where in the history of east/west divergence on this issue the charismatic approach would find its natural allies, if any.

That this is unsurprising, moreover, is a matter in part of our western religious heritage, with its much bemoaned bifurcation of thought and feeling, scholastic theology and piety; and this historical background is worthy of brief (if inevitably over-simplistic) reflection, especially in view of charismatics' much-vaunted claims to a recovery of spiritual 'wholeness'. For not long after Symeon was controversially reasserting the significance of the felt apprehension of the Spirit in the east, the west too, though in very different cultural and political circumstances was engaged in an extraordinary shift of consciousness which also evidenced a fresh discovery of 'feeling'. The twelfth century, it has been argued, produced the 'discovery of the individual'; it also witnessed the rise of the age of chivalry, and the complex rituals of courtly love. In the Church's musical life of late twelfth-century France, too, were unleashed strikingly passionate ululations, elongated melismas wound over the traditional plainsong chants. The theological counterpart of all this, one might argue, was Bernard of Clairvaux's fresh assimilation of affective strands in Augustine, which resulted in a new turn to 'feeling' as an indispensable component in spiritual growth. 'Instruction makes us learned', says Bernard, 'but feeling makes us wise'. Moreover he could go on to make startling use of erotic imagery in his construal of the soul's desire for God. He was, after all, addressing young monks in the Cistercian reform who had not been shielded from an adolescence in the world by growing up as child oblates.

Yet if writers in the twelfth century moved to incorporate feeling and body metaphors as positive features in spiritual development, by the fourteenth century there was a discernible, and tragic, disjunction occurring between intellectual, scholastic approaches to God on the one hand, and pietistic feeling-and-body-oriented approaches on the other. This was carried over in a different way into theories of prayer, so that, for instance, 'contemplation' could be construed either as the pure 'intellect' communing with God or, quite differently, as a

---

* This approach was pursued systematically in *We Believe in God*, chapter 7.

deliberate shutting down of the mind in favour of the will or 'affectivity'. In a variety of ways piety and theology were being rent apart in the west.

Thus it is a striking irony that, in the fourteenth century, just as Gregory Palamas' defence of 'hesychast' practices was defending the use of the body in prayer and effecting in the east an extraordinary and unexpected *synthesis* of 'affective' and 'intellectual' traditions of prayer in that context, the west was busy driving a wedge between them.

Moreover, we are still in thrall to these disjunctions, as the history of western Christian sectarianism since the late medieval period witnesses. For here it has tended to be the sectarians *in revolt* who have highlighted, sometimes in extreme forms, the significance of 'affective' or 'enthusiastic' prayer-states, and simultaneously claimed the (neglected) Holy Spirit as their own. In this western historical perspective, then, the contemporary charismatic movement calls forth a certain feeling of *déjà vu*: the pietistic emphasis on feeling and bodily response, the sectarian ethos, the claims to direct experience of the Spirit, and an undercurrent of strong anti-intellectualism – all these might be expected to hang together in the western context just described. Even if such western movements are not demonstrably a manifestation of social or economic 'deprivation', then, they may bespeak a more subtle form of 'affective' deprivation in 'church' type western Christianity, a deprivation which goes back to the same divide between 'affectivity' and intellect, spiritual experience and reflective tradition, to which we have just drawn attention and which may be characteristic of western (or at least of North Atlantic) culture as a whole.

What is new in contemporary 'renewal', however, and so vital for our present concern of prayer and the Spirit, is the incorporation of this 'sectarian' constellation of themes *within* established 'church' frameworks, including Anglicanism. Could this in fact provide the possibility of a new *rapproachement* between the disjunct traditions which we have been considering: affective piety on the one hand, and informed reflective theology on the other (the latter rooted as much in an intellectual assessment of *tradition* as of the Bible)? That this tension might be ridden is self-confessedly not the aim of the purer 'sectarian' house-churches currently fast gaining adherents. But that it may be the task implicitly confronting intra-Anglican charismatics, in a new phase of their development, is borne out further by reflection on the specific theme of 'tongues'.

2. The spirit and 'tongues'

(a) Interviews

Here we can indeed chart a distinct difference of emphasis between the two groups studied. For whereas the Anglican charismatics in the church have now almost ceased to use tongues in public worship (the exception being the occasional, unplanned, and indeed eerily beautiful use of corporate 'singing in tongues'), the Fellowship group deliberately encourages corporate praise in tongues, especially in the often jubilant and noisy introduction to their services, and claims a much greater 'cutting-edge' and 'specificity', too, to their public prophecies. The divergence may partly result from the departure of some of the more 'activist' worshippers from the one group to the other. But there is also, implicitly, a different reading of 1 Cor.14 in play in the two groups. The Anglicans, curbed in public tongue-speaking to some extent by their minister, after some episodes which were thought to be excessive and unedifying, are now preferring in the main to keep their tongue-speaking as a private 'love-language' *to* God (see v.2), having found a plethora of tongues and interpretation somewhat repetitive or trite (see v.19). In contrast the Fellowship is much more anxious to exhibit the 'gifts' in their full range (especially tongues and prophecy, understood as sent *from* God), and to witness to 'unbelievers' and potential converts (vv.21ff.). Here, then, is a noticeable difference in opinion over whether the Spirit's presence always is, or should be, publicly or dramatically manifest.

But in fact it is in the private use of tongues that the most interesting material emerged in discussion with the Anglicans. For it was striking, again, how in certain ways their (very diverse) use of tongues converged spontaneously on certain themes from the contemplative traditions of the Church, traditions with which most of them were not in any direct way familiar, and indeed against which their fundamentalist convictions would naturally prejudice them. Thus, whereas the dominical warning against 'vain repetitions' (Matt. 6.7 AV) made them wary of repetitive or mantric prayer, even of the 'Jesus prayer', they were ready to acknowledge that their 'tongues' often had a repetitive and formalized sound, and could be serving a similar function. Some, indeed, used 'tongues' as a regular discipline of prayer. A memorable example was a charismatic plumber, who often prayed in tongues as he worked alone. ('There are some very prayerfully laid pipes in this area', he remarked.)

Similarly, whereas some saw silence in prayer as mainly an absence of thought, or a sign of perplexity, and wished to *fill* such silence with tongues, others could voice the thought that silence could actually be the 'point' or 'end' of tongues, that to which tongues naturally led.

(Certainly this could sometimes be witnessed communally in a very sensitive and quiet use of 'singing in tongues' at the evening service, ebbing away into intense stillness and corporate awareness.) Thus, when faced with the charge of the Fellowship group that the Anglicans were losing their 'cutting-edge' in playing down their public use of tongues and prophecy, the minister's response was, 'God is trying to speak to us: *that* should be the feeling.' Others said there had been a certain 'hardness' in some of the more strident public tongues, which had simply 'felt wrong'.

It was the diversity of the application and theological interpretations of private tongues that was most remarkable, however. It was said to be a 'short cut' to God, a direct release of joy or feeling, a way of 'getting out of the way' so that the Spirit could act directly, a prayer for when 'words failed', whether through loss, perplexity or grief, a means of becoming 'like a child' (see Matt. 18.3), or, used authoritatively, a prayer for warding off danger. While only a few interviewees were familiar with, or happy with, the psychological language of 'releasing the unconscious', or 'exposing one's inner life' to God, all stressed the healing qualities of this prayer, its directness, and its short-circuiting of normal checks and defences. Above all the theme of 'ceding to the Spirit' was stressed, the way in which tongues averted one's normal and natural tendency to 'set the agenda', especially in the areas of counselling and illness. Tongues were found to reach directly to the root of a problem, so that 'if one did not know what to pray for before, one does afterwards' (see Rom. 8.26). In sum, it was found in the Anglican community that tongues were continuing to be used in diverse and rich ways, in private prayer, in small house groups, and in the semi-private counselling or healing sessions which attended evening communion. But more overt or spectacular usages of tongues in public contexts had become the prerogative of the Fellowship group.

(b) Commentary

The Anglicans, with almost no exception, were emphatic that tongues were 'not the be all and end all', although they admitted they might not have said that a decade ago. They felt that this gift had 'fallen into place', and it was not necessarily for everyone; whereas in the Fellowship it was expected as 'normal' for all 'real Christians', and seemed to be being used in a much more overt and self-conscious way as an (effective) instrument of conversion alongside the other 'gifts'. Only a few interviewees, however, knew anything of the instances of 'tongue-speaking' found in spiritual writers dotted through the tradition. Interestingly here, in writers as contextually diverse as the Desert Fathers and St Teresa, what is noteworthy is how little is made of it: it is simply a natural outflowing of expressiveness in one already deeply committed to prayer. It is recorded of abba Ephraim, for instance, that his prayer was sometimes like 'a well bubbling out of his mouth' (*Apophthegmata Patrum*, Ephraim 2). Over a thousand years later Teresa's autobiography quite passingly refers to a type of prayer in which 'The soul longs to pour out words of praise . . . Many words are then spoken . . . But they are disorderly' (*Life*, ch. 16). And there are many other such scattered examples from the tradition, giving the lie to the suspicion that this gift has been totally dormant since the apostolic age. 'Singing in jubilation', likewise, is seen by Augustine and others as a wholly natural way of letting the Spirit pray in one: for 'this kind of singing (*jubilum*) is a sound which means that the heart is giving birth to something it cannot speak of' (*Sermons on the Psalms*, 32.8).

But again, as we have already intimated, only a few interviewees were beginning to take note of the parallelism in charismatic and contemplative traditions, or to explore the burgeoning popular literature on this theme of the 'recovery of disciplines' from such traditions, although this was clearly being encouraged by the Anglican minister. Once again one felt that the church was at a point of decision: whether to modify its exclusive biblicism, accept a quieter form of worship, and turn to a broader and more intellectual assimilation of tradition; or whether to reassert the more overtly 'enthusiastic' worship of some years previously, and engage consciously in 'power evangelism'. A small minority wanted much more public tongue-speaking to re-emerge (and it is significant that a few of these people left the church during the period of this research); others saw its dangers as 'an excuse not to think' (see 1 Cor. 14.19). Exactly, however, at the axis of this decision also lie the issues in our last set of themes.

3. Prayer and failure, prayer and aridity, prayer and depression

(a) Interviews

It was in these areas that the greatest ambivalence was found in the interviews, and the ambivalence cut across the two groups. Does 'failure' in prayer, or the common states of dryness ('aridity') and depression when afflicting those who pray, indicate that the Spirit is necessarily inactive or impeded here? Is the Spirit's work in any sense compatible with human failure and weakness?

'Failure' in prayer was confronted movingly in one interview with an Anglican 'elder', a man who for long years had wanted to 'come into tongues'. Repeatedly his friends had prayed for this, but to no avail. The same man's wife was also virtually crippled by back pain; again, repeated prayer had brought little relief. It was poignant to have to ask how he could explain this. His response was that he could only finally 'bow to God's sovereignty'; and in relation to tongues, after great disappointment, he had come to accept, 'I've just got to be me, and that's the Lord's job'. When the interviewer enquired whether such evident humility could not itself be a work of the Spirit, he assented, though there was a sense that this was a new idea. One might juxtapose the thoughts recorded by John Cassian here: 'Wonders and powers are not always necessary, for some are harmful and are not granted to everyone . . . Humility is the queen of all the virtues' (*Conferences*, 15.7).

Attitudes to aridity in prayer were mixed, too. Many of those interviewed felt that joyousness should be the norm (and in the case of one member of the Fellowship group, this was particularly emphatically expressed); but all when pressed admitted to phases of dryness themselves, most explaining them as correlated to stress or other passing human factors. Only one person, interestingly, surmised that dryness might actually be in some circumstances a sign of progress, of the Spirit 'driving one into the desert' to 'sharpen one's thirst' (see Mark 1.12f.). But no sustained explanation of this was made; there was no reference, for instance, to St John of the Cross' detailed explication of this as the prayer of 'the night of sense', moving one on into 'contemplation', a form of prayer emotionally less satisfying than before, even felt as a 'failure' to pray, and yet characterized by a continuing and restless desire for God.

On depression, however, there was the widest range of response. A minority of people (in both the Fellowship and the Anglican church) felt that depression was largely self-absorption and should be dealt with rapidly and effectively by prayer and exhortation. People in both groups believed in the devil and the demonic but on the whole were not happy with the idea that individual demons caused illness or depression (a view powerfully influential in the area, however, as a result of the 'demonic deliverance' liturgies of a 'healing centre' recently established locally). This sort of particularized personification of evil had been deliberately averted by the minister within the Anglican group. In a particularly interesting interview with a psychiatrist, who is also a member of the Anglican congregation, it was admitted that being a Christian was sometimes a distinct 'risk factor' in depression, because of the possible mood swings from a high affective state into the reverse, the rigorous standards imposed upon the self, and the feelings of further guilt if prayer was not effective in relieving the condition. Often she found the best way through was to set aside theological language altogether, and insist, 'This *isn't* a sin problem; you have a health problem that can be effectively treated with drugs.' It was important, then, that religious people should feel no guilt or shame about accepting medication when needed. The same doctor was, however, wary of saying that the Spirit could in any way be working actively in and through a depression, especially severe psychotic states, although she conceded that 'less severe episodes' could sometimes lead to a 'greater dependence on God'.

In general, then, there was an agreement amongst those interviewed that Christians should not normally be depressed, and that their mood should primarily be characterized by joy. Once again there was only one commentator who strongly urged that to demand the continuous maintenance of a high feeling state was actually 'unbiblical'. 'What of Gethsemane, not to speak of the prophets and the psalms?' The same person distinguished importantly between clinical 'depression' and spiritual 'desolation'. The former he saw as a recognized 'illness', and, just as Jesus had in the gospel stories invariably responded to those who requested healing from sickness, so in this case, too, he believed, the sufferer should rightfully pray to be relieved. In the case of spiritual 'desolation', however, (and he admitted depression and desolation might be difficult to disentangle without the discernment of an experienced spiritual guide), one could be confronting the particular activity of the Spirit itself, moving one on into a painful new phase of growth, a sharing in some sense in Christ's own passion.

(b) Commentary

It was clear that here we had reached a theological crux. If the Spirit's activity was deemed in some sense incompatible with 'low' feeling states, then either a necessarily sporadic understanding of the Spirit's activity was in play, or else there was a lurking dualism (as in the questionably orthodox early fifth-century Macarian homilies, where Satan and the Spirit wage war with equal force for the overlordship of the 'heart', the Spirit being associated particularly with the 'feeling of assurance'). But what then of the possibility of genuinely Christ-like dereliction? Could it not be, as von Balthasar has so movingly expressed it in his theology of 'Holy Saturday', that the Spirit may not only on occasion drive one into a sharing of Christ's desolation, but actually be that in God which spans the unimaginable gulf between despair and victory?

Such thoughts about the Spirit are already foreshadowed in the New Testament (e.g. Rom. 8.11, 17). But they have been spelled out since then with the profoundest practical and psychological insight by spiritual writers as diverse as Diadochus of Photice in the east (fifth century) and John of the Cross in the west (sixteenth century). Diadochus, for whom 'regeneration' in the Spirit is central, speaks of God deliberately 'receding' at times 'in order to educate us', 'to humble the soul's tendency to vanity and self-glory'; through 'feeling ourselves abandoned . . . we become more humble and submit to the glory of God' (*One Hundred Texts*, 89, 69). This is somewhat akin to John of the Cross's first 'night of sense', where prayer seems to lose all its former sweetness. Much more terrible, though, is John's description of the trials and disorientations of the second 'night of spirit', in which God draws so painfully and purgatively *close* that the experience is akin to that of a log being thrown into a devouring fire (*Dark Night*, Bk. II. X). If such as this, then, is truly an implication of Paul's invitation to be compelled by the Spirit into the sharing of Christ's passion, then it has to be said that it is an implication on which so far only a few of those interviewed in our survey had reflected deeply.

Here too, then, it may be that the charismatic movement now faces a dilemma, and one with fundamentally trinitarian implications: is the Spirit only to be a 'triumphalist' Spirit, bearer of joy and positive 'feeling'? Or, if this is Christ's Spirit, breathed out of his scarred body, 'one in being' with Father and Son, must we not allow as much for the fire of purgation (T. S. Eliot's 'flames of incandescent terror') as for the refreshment of the comforting dove? William Temple's memorable words are worthy of recollection here:

> When we pray 'Come, Holy Ghost, our souls inspire', we had better know what we are about. He will not carry us to easy triumphs and gratifying successes; . . . He may take us through loneliness, desertion by friends, apparent desertion even by God; that was the way Christ went to the Father . . . He may lead us from the Mount of Transfiguration (if He ever lets us climb it) to the hill that is called the Place of a Skull . . . The soul that is filled with the Spirit must have been purged of all pride or love of ease, all self-complacence and self-reliance; but the soul has found the only real dignity, the only lasting joy. Come then, Great Spirit, come. Convict the world; and convict my timid soul.' (*Readings in St John's Gospel*, 16.8–11, pp.288f.)

Conclusion

In this chapter we have confronted recurring issues of prayer and desire, prayer and feeling, prayer and pain. The material gleaned from the interviews and participant observation cannot in itself, and without further reflection, solve the hard questions about the nature of the Spirit posed at the beginning of the chapter; but just as 'sect' and 'church' diverge in theology as well as social structure, it is clear that our Anglican community is caught in that tension, and poised in the act of decision between vying theological possibilities. And it may well be, as its minister strongly believes, that it stands on the brink of new, and deeper, perceptions of the Spirit's guidance and intent for the future of the charismatic movement as a whole.

What all the charismatics interviewed shared, however, and what they continue to challenge the Church with, is a deep and impressive commitment to the adventure of prayer, and the call to rediscover an unimpeded participation in that infinite desire of God for God which we call the Spirit, and in which we are drawn into union with Christ. That it is indeed possible to enter into this divine relationship with willing and excited co-operation is what the movement, in all its diversity, testifies to. But it is a participation that can never allow the certainty of attainment or superiority: Bernard of Clairvaux has well said, 'There is no proof of the presence of the Spirit which is more certain than a desire for ever greater grace' (*2nd Sermon on St. Andrew*, 4). Indeed, if Bernard is right, we may well reassure those harbouring anxieties about 'sinning against the Holy Spirit', that their very disposition of penitence and concern is an indication of this divine desire in them (see also below, Chapter 10, 'The Holy Spirit and the Future'). Where there *is* prayer, then, and above all that inchoate desire for 'ever greater grace' which destroys all complacency, there indeed is the Spirit already active and effective. Or, as John Chrysostom put it conversely, 'If the Holy Spirit did not exist, we believers would not [even] be able to pray to God' (*Sermons on Pentecost*, 1,4).

In this sense, then (to return to the hard questions we posed at the outset), *all* prayer is prayer 'in the Spirit';* for it is already prompted – however unconsciously in the pray-er – by that divine restlessness that ceaselessly yearns towards the Father. And in this sense, too, a failure to reflect consciously and *theologically* about the Spirit is only a failure if there is also a failure in prayer itself, a failure, that is, to court that flow of divine reciprocity within one, to invite God as Spirit (as Diadochus

---

* See again Rom. 8.9ff. for the characteristically Pauline themes of the Spirit's 'indwelling', and of prayer as precisely the prior activity of the Spirit in one. In line too with this generalized interpretation of 'prayer in the Spirit' is Eph. 6.18: 'Pray *at all times* in the Spirit, with all prayer and supplication.' With this theme of the Spirit's omnipresence should be carefully contrasted Paul's phrase in 1 Cor. 14.15: 'I will pray with the spirit', in which Paul is commending the openness to God of the *whole person*, both through the reflective mode of prayer, and through prayer as a more direct response to God ('as I am inspired to pray', NEB).

once put it with a lovely artistic metaphor) to 'paint the divine likeness on the divine image in us' with the 'luminosity of love' (*One Hundred Texts*, 89).

As for our question about the experimental *distinctiveness* of the Spirit in prayer, here is an area where the supposedly remote concerns of early Church trinitarianism are pressingly apposite, and perhaps especially for charismatics. For while charismatics run no danger at all (as others may) of neglecting or relegating the Spirit to metaphysical redundancy, there may be, as we have hinted, a danger of associating particular *sorts* of experience with the Spirit (and possibly others with the Son and Father); and this, as the debates of the fourth century highlighted, may lead either to an implicit tritheism (a belief in three different gods), or else to a sporadic, instrumentalist, and possibly impersonal, vision of the Spirit.

It was precisely to counteract such possibilities that the language of 'one in being' was applied to the Spirit alongside Father and Son. For our experience of the Spirit is an experience of *God*, no less, and whatever divine characteristics are experienced in the Spirit are also the divine characteristics of Father and Son. What then of the *distinctiveness* of the three? Fumbling to express the inexpressible, the late fourth-century Cappadocian Fathers spoke (in what seems to us forbiddingly abstract terms) of the 'internal relations' of the three Persons as being their only distinguishing feature. Their attempted explanations were often abstruse and polemical, and assumed a philosophical framework which we no longer take for granted. But fundamentally they argued from their own profound spiritual experience: if the Spirit was that in God which constantly called and provoked them (most explicitly in prayer) in yearning towards the Father, then it was the Son, in his filial dependence on the Father, with whom they were being united through this life of prayer. In other words, it could not be different *sorts* of 'experience' (in the sense of emotional tonality) that were associated with the three Persons in their one divine flow of activity, but only the particular way they were related to one another internally: Father as source of all, Spirit as divine goad in restless quest for creation's return again to the Father, Son as the divine prototype of that redeemed and transformed creation. The Spirit then was *eternally* active, ceaselessly 'indwelling' the 'saints', to use Pauline language; this was not to deny *particular* goadings of the Spirit, too, the divine freedom to direct and prompt in special or dramatic ways, as is more characteristic of the Lukan theology of the New Testament.

But why, one must probe further, did the early Fathers need to call the Spirit a *distinct* Person? In the case of the Son this was obvious: he had been incarnate, had prayed to the Father as clearly distinct from himself. But why should not the Spirit be seen merely as a metaphorical expression for the divine outreach? In the lengthy process of developing a trinitarian theology, was it simply an accident that the Spirit was declared a distinct Person, by a rather simplistic deduction from the threefold structure of the baptismal formula? If we are to understand the real logic of this process of theological evolution and to respond convincingly to the suggestion that we are here dealing only with metaphors, we must continue to explore what it is in the history, language, reflection and experience of the Christian community that has made theology resist such a reduction in the status of the Spirit. And to do this involves, as this chapter has hinted, understanding that area where the experience of charismatics and of contemplatives so significantly converges: in that profound, though often fleeting or obscure, sense of entering in prayer into a 'conversation' *already in play*, a reciprocal divine conversation between Father and Spirit which can finally be reduced neither to divine monologue nor to human self-transcendence. We are dealing here, of course with matters almost inexpressible and thus open to every kind of question about appropriate interpretation. But that there is something irreducible here, which tradition has named 'Spirit', is vividly and freshly testified by the contemporary charismatic movement.

As for the implications of our survey for the relation of the Holy Spirit to 'feelings' – whether pleasurable or painful – this is a matter too, as we have indicated, that calls for deepened trinitarian (and so Christological) reflection, an issue to which we shall return in Chapter 4. But in the meantime we need to look at some more precise exegetical concerns raised also by the charismatic movement. We shall ask whether, and to what degree, the experiences which we claim of the Spirit today can actually be identified within the experiences of the earliest Church of New Testament times.

Chapter 3
Is this that?

In this chapter we attempt to review that Christian experience which claims to stand in direct relationship to the reported experience of the first Christians in the New Testament. We do not provide a survey of the full phenomenology of Christian experience or spirituality down the centuries, but simply an evaluation of those present-day affirmations of being inwardly and sensibly moved by the Holy Spirit. Such claims, to be worthy of evaluation by the Church, must establish some relationship with the New Testament and to be the fruit of responsible exegesis of passages from it. In effect, when someone today says 'this' (contemporary experience of the Spirit) is 'that' (apostolic experience of the same Spirit), then we are to test the claim by the touchstone of scripture.

When we do this, we are perhaps treading old ground, and yet reading it for contemporary and even novel reasons. Theologians, particularly those in the reformed tradition, have generally conceived their task as one of formulating their theology through a systematic tackling of the scriptures. There have also been many in past ages (as in the present) who follow the way of spontaneity, either as the mood of a prophet has led them, or as they have felt themselves or observed others to be so moved. It has, however, taken the modern pentecostalist Christians, and especially their manifestation as charismatics in the mainline Churches, to lay a great emphasis upon inner experience, interpreting it as the workings of the Holy Spirit, whilst referring it to the scriptural revelation. This moves us to express their doctrine as 'this is that', for they use the precedent of Peter's address on the day of Pentecost (Acts 2.16), when the phenomena then evident were interpreted as the fulfilment of earlier scriptures. The formula, 'this is that', sums up a particular genre of exposition. Because it refers itself to scripture, we follow its own principles and test its exegesis.

In the New Testament there are both individual and communal models for the Spirit's operation. The individual model, which predominates in the Old Testament, persists but it is not the norm. Thus the Spirit is believed to operate within the community of faith. Nevertheless individuals can receive the Holy Spirit (e.g. Acts 19.2; Gal. 3.2), be full of the Spirit (e.g. Acts 6.3; 11.24), speak through the Spirit (e.g. Acts 2.4; 21.4). Moreover, those who received the Spirit seem to have received clear evidence in their own lives that the Spirit had come upon them; even if they were not absolutely overwhelmed by the transcendent, their experience seems to have been almost independent of their own selves or wills. They may not have felt better (that would be a hard point to investigate, though one imagines they usually did); yet they did most certainly act differently. The most notable instances of people so receiving the Spirit are in Acts 8 (the Samaritans) and Acts 10 (Cornelius' household).

In the former instance there was something so visible that Simon Magus could ask for the power to imitate the apostles who were, apparently, by their prayer with the laying on of hands bringing the Samaritans to a point of crisis. One most naturally reads the passage in the sense that the apostles passed down the row of disciples; that as they did so, they laid their hands on the disciples; and that, as if a spectacular wave or ripple followed them, the recipients were audibly or visibly affected in word or tone or deed. Why else should Simon Magus have thought there was something worth purchasing?

In the latter instance, that of Cornelius, the Gentile household was so dramatically affected that Peter saw and heard enough to make him gasp, 'Quick, get the water'. No doubt in the economy of God it had to be spectacular if it was to convince Peter he should baptize Gentiles. It had to precede the end of his sermon, and certainly to precede the baptism. We cannot but agree something outwardly notable had happened.

It looks on closer inspection as though, in various other cases of initial conversation reported in the Acts of the Apostles, the first experience of the Spirit is not always so dramatic. Indeed the two instances cited above belong to those dramatic events which mark the crossing of well-signalled boundaries: into the age of the Spirit at the beginning of Acts 2; into Samaria in Acts 8; and to the Gentiles in Acts 10. We gather that the converts in the latter part of Acts 2 are promised the gift of the Spirit (2.38) following repentance and baptism; we also see the beginning of a pattern of joyful, loving and unself-protecting community life. The question at issue is the experience of the Spirit. What then were the disciples experiencing? We may well have a further question: how far may the Church today expect or hope that the conditions of the Spirit's operation in the first generation will be reproduced amongst us? The answer to these questions depends on our establishing what is being reported from the first generation.

Here three notes of caution about the interpretation of scripture need to be made. In the first instance, it is arguable that the Acts and the gospels have been written with a view to establishing some particular patterns of Church life, and particularly that they have been so written for the sake of making some impact on second and third generations of Christians.

The case is wide open and in scholarly terms inconclusive. On the other hand, the main Pauline corpus sits immovably in the reigns of Claudius and Nero, and witnesses (however allusively and sometimes infuriatingly) to conditions among Christians of the first generation. But, although Acts portrays Luke as Paul's fellow-traveller, we cannot immediately harmonize passages in the Acts with those in Paul, as if they were all part of one homogeneous literary whole (and perhaps we ought not to want to do so).

Secondly, we recognize that the present Christian experience of the reader may impose a pattern of understanding upon the New Testament text. Just as Peter on the day of Pentecost said, 'This is that which was prophesied by Joel', so later generations have always been ready to say, 'This is that which was experienced in the New Testament Church'. The apparent force and reality of current Christian experience attaches itself to some part of the New Testament evidence, which becomes to those with the particular experience its non-negotiable point of reference. The pastor and the interpreter of scripture then have the task of affirming, where possible, the integrity and validity of the particular Christian experience, and also of inserting the knife-edge of honest enquiry between that experience and its alleged biblical precedent, archetype or warrant. This is a pastoral task, because such enquiry may well be felt by others as an assault upon their Christian integrity (and indeed on their knowledge of God). Further, to persuade others that this task is proper and Christian, and not ultimately destructive, can liberate the mind in its approach to scripture and also liberate the interior life in the Spirit.

Closely related to this point is the fact that lack of a particular experience among Christian leaders or thinkers at a particular time may also well affect, and indeed govern, their understanding of the New Testament. It can well be argued that because the sixteenth-century Reformers of the Church generally were not experiencing dramatic visitations by the Holy Spirit, they were the more impelled to say 'This is not that', and further (by a kind of spiritual logic), 'We must not expect it to be'. To put this another way: that which was not experienced came to be expounded as unnecessary, or even, in the economy of God, wholly withdrawn or forbidden. Thus there arose in the Reformation period the doctrine that the dramatic visitations of the apostolic age were God's bridging device to bring the Church safely to the period when the whole New Testament would have been written, and at that stage (and only then) 'normal' Church life could proceed. The Reformers were passionately engaged in a battle of ideas and in a struggle for a new approach to the Bible. Those who most prized dramatic Christian experience (the Anabaptists) were observed to be often the most destructive of the existing order. Thus the sixteenth-century Reformers, who wanted everything done 'decently and in order', almost by definition treated the apparent subjectivism of a radical Christian experientialism as incompatible with the goals of the Reformation. The so-called 'phantasizing' of the Anabaptists was strictly beyond the pale, for the Spirit is the Spirit not of chaos, but of order.

With those cautions noted, it is possible to return to the New Testament. What then did the first-generation Christians from Pentecost onwards experience? Is it accessible to us? Can it, indeed, be reduced to writing? Does it include outward 'miracle' as well as inward joy and even ecstasy? Further, what status does it have for Christians living today? We may even ask: how far is direct or unmediated experience of Almighty God possible on this earth? In asking this last question we recognize the difficulty of defining what would count as 'direct' and 'indirect'. In our introductory chapter we have already referred to this difficulty, and we note that some at least of the experiences recorded in the New Testament (and it is the New Testament as much as today which is here under investigation) have an immediacy of force about them such as to keep the question before us.

Certain features of the Church's life in the first generation provide a framework for this investigation. The Church was undoubtedly Christocentric. (This Christocentric note occurs repeatedly in this study.) The Lord has risen from the dead, departed from the sight of the first disciples and sent his Spirit. Nevertheless, he was 'with' them always (e.g. Matt. 28.20; John 14 *passim*; Acts 4.29f.). Their faith was directed towards this reigning Jesus, and their service and actions were done in his presence, in his 'Name' (a key concept), and certainly for his sake. Such redirecting of the thrust and goals of human life inevitably affected the feelings, emotions, and moral core of the followers of Jesus, and it was constitutive of the very beginning of Christian experience. We may properly suggest that such experience should be traced to the unseen work of the Spirit, and that the case is not so much psychological as pneumatological. However, the starting point in any reflection by Christians upon their experience would surely have been their response to Jesus, as we have indicated.

Next, we have clear evidence that the Church in its earliest days was undoubtedly a loving fellowship. The free interaction of its members with one another reflected in the early chapters of Acts (and at least sought, if not found, by Paul in his letters) provided an important context for this experience. Supportive and outgoing links of friendship, caring, intimacy, and practical help would themselves be bound to affect this experience. Surely it felt different to be a Christian?

In addition, the Church at its best had a bold front towards society around (e.g. Acts 4.32f.; 1 Cor. 2.4). The necessity (a necessity of both external injunction and internal constraint) for a faithful testimony also surely affected how they felt? At times (e.g. with Stephen) this could lead to suffering. Yet suffering for them was touched with joy and with glory; it was a privilege to suffer for Christ's sake (Matt. 7.13f.; Acts 5.41; Phil. 1.29; 1 Pet. 4.12ff.; etc.), though, even then, some hesitated.

A closely related point is that at some times and places they saw the message of God, the good news, to be powerful in reshaping others' lives and in delivering them into the Christian conviction, the Christian fellowship, and the Christian readiness, if necessary, to suffer for their Lord. The experience of the Church, as it received converts, was bound to be shaped in dependence on the power of this message, power which was understood to be also the power of the Spirit. (The implications of this point are considered at length in Chapter 6.)

In association with all these features the following unexpected phenomena are reported in the Acts of the Apostles: extraordinary expressions of thought or feeling ('other tongues'), the 'shaking' of an assembly, highly benevolent providence (e.g. delivery from prison, guidance of route), dramatic healings (including expulsion of demons and raising of the dead), dreams and visions, precognition of the future, and possibly 'prophecy' (though this last may not be extraordinary, or it may be included under one or other of the previous headings). On occasion, as in the conversion of Cornelius and his household, several of these phenomena occur in close conjunction and are presented as the means whereby God's goal is achieved. There are also phenomena of judgement, whether temporary (as with Saul's blindness), or more drastic (as with Ananias and Sapphira). Most of these occurrences have parallels in the recorded ministry on earth of Jesus; thus they move the reader towards an integrated understanding of the experience of the first generation of Christians. The principal cause for hesitation arises from the question whether there is (or has to be) a 'this', a present occurrence, genuinely comparable to the 'that' of the New Testament, and, if so, how normative or prevalent such occurrences are in Christian experience. While we need to bear in mind all these features of the Church in its earliest decade, it is clear that the sharpest exegetical question today is raised by the phenomena to which we have just drawn attention. We all may puzzle at the meaning of Jesus' statement that the believer will do greater works than those of Jesus himself (John 14.12) (though this statement may refer to the worldwide ministry of the gospel of salvation and new birth in the name of Jesus); but the specific instances of the actual works of Jesus and their bearing upon the ministry first of the apostles, and second of us, have become for us a major issue in our day.

The modern charismatic movement (at least in Anglicanism) has tended to value very highly the narratives in the Acts of the Apostles, but in practice to depend for its own expectations more upon the gifts listed in various places in the Pauline letters and summarized also in 1 Peter 4.8ff. A common parlance has arisen whereby congregations are characterized as those where the gifts are exercised, and, on inspection, it proves that the common run of such expected gifts is a three-some of tongues, prophecy and healings.

With regard to these gifts, we should note that they are experiences which belong to the whole Church and are given to be shared between Christians. They may, both in theory and in practice, be more moving to the recipients than to the ministrants of the particular gift; in that respect they may be no different from, say, preaching, and but little different from the ministration of sacraments. There is, of course, a practice of speaking in tongues in private prayer, but that is a separate issue, to which we have referred in Chapter 2.

The supernatural feature which has become part of the theological currency of charismatics and does have specific internal implications for the one who has it, is baptism in the Spirit. This is a conventional term for an overwhelming or critical experience of the power and presence of God. Whilst in some circles a claim to this experience might well be interpreted by a non-charismatic as an indication of conversion *de novo*, in more evangelical circles this term is often used to describe a second and post-conversion crisis, not unlike the second blessing of the older holiness movements. It has to be recognized that it is the experience which has led to the use of the terminology. The experience, whilst not received personally by all those who have been labelled charismatics, is nevertheless fairly widespread, and sufficiently so for it to need a common terminology, and to be offered pastorally by the laying on of hands with prayer to those who express their need. It is discussed more fully below.

Scripturally, such a use of the expression 'baptism in the Holy Spirit' has a certain first-blush plausibility: a baptism is a once-for-all event; it has a God-given objectivity; the term can be used metaphorically (as by Jesus about his death); and indeed the teaching of John the Baptist almost suggests that his outward baptism by water is but a shadow of the true baptism which is inward and is the swamping or saturation by the Holy Spirit. However, we need to exercise caution; although the experience of the disciples in the upper room on the day of Pentecost is often expounded as their reception of baptism in the Holy Spirit and as fulfilment of John the Baptist's prediction, there is little other relevant scriptural evidence. There is, however, a passage in which Peter (Acts

11.15f., cf. 15.8) compares the initial experience of the first Gentile converts with the experience of the day of Pentecost. Similar phraseology is used about the phenomena (though without the term 'baptism in the Spirit') in Acts 8 and Acts 19. In the rest of Acts there is no mention of such a baptism, nor is there in the epistles. We have therefore to be careful lest we convert into a universal doctrine of the faith an instantaneous experience which marked three or four special occasions in the Acts of the Apostles, but is not otherwise portrayed as a norm of spirituality or of response to God. These passages encourage us to identify the occasions which are called a baptism as instances of the initial experience of the Holy Spirit, not as a second blessing. This experience, which is often called baptism in the Spirit, should be both welcomed and also tested. It is, however, not universal; true commitment, discipleship, and experience of the Holy Spirit can and do exist without such a crisis. Hence it should not be erected into an essential requirement of the faith, and to call such an experience the baptism in the Spirit can convey the wrong messages, as though it were a norm for every Christian. We may well need for this experience some descriptive term which sounds less like an indispensable requirement and is more in accord with scriptural usage.

If, however, charismatics for the last quarter of a century have been particularly concerned about the three gifts, to which we referred earlier, and about baptism in the Spirit, more recent developments have taken the experiential claims forward into other areas. A notable modern instance is to be found in the ministry of the Californian evangelist, John Wimber. His 'Vineyard' churches both integrate the gospel narratives with the Acts experience and see it as normative for Church life today. The 'Vineyard' exegesis, as generally understood, is typified in an exposition of Matthew 28.20 which interprets the observing of Jesus' commands as truly covering 'all that I have commanded you'. This precludes us from simply referring to it as the obedience to a moral code, as the handing on of a somewhat cerebral gospel, or as the observance of a life of prayer. Rather, the whole scheme of the Church's life, from the Ascension to the Last Judgement, is to be marked unmistakably by those distinctive features of Jesus' own ministry which have a disruptive, miraculous, and yet marvellously salvific character to them. That is how it was in the Acts of the Apostles; indeed Wimber claims that apostolic evangelism is 'power evangelism', the good news reaching people with the miraculous power of God to heal accompanying it. We do not look outside or far ahead for the kingdom; it is with us and within us and among us, and the signs of the kingdom are the clear evidence of it. Signs and wonders, to which we give further attention in our chapter, 'The Spirit and Power', have become more gripping to English charismatics (especially if they have witnessed one of John Wimber's meetings); moreover, the agenda and priorities of Wimber have started to run alongside the older charismatic concerns.

Other gifts have come into play also (particularly the 'gift of knowledge'), and a great emphasis has been placed upon Wimber's particular interpretation of the Kingdom. It should be noted that this kind of kingdom theology is the reverse of that of the liberationist, or even of the standard ecumenist; it understands the kingdom to be found within the Church, in narrower compass than the Church itself, whereas in the more usual current exegeses the kingdom lies beyond the Church and has a far wider compass than the Church. Further, in John Wimber's own ministry there has been sufficient evidence of the 'signs following' (cf. Mark 16.14ff.) for the whole message itself to be widely believed. Whilst this appears to be taking the charismatic emphasis on the 'gifts' in 1 Cor. 12.28 to its logical end, not all charismatics have felt able to follow John Wimber to that end. Indeed we have mentioned the remarkable events associated with John Wimber's ministry without necessarily endorsing their explanation. The facts are well documented; their cause or causes are open to more than one explanation, even to more than one theological explanation.

What then are the new features which are held by some to be a proper part of Christian ministry? Whilst healings are common to older charismatics and the new agenda, the insistence is now that they are the outworking of the programme of signs and wonders. Furthermore, the 'word of knowledge' (1 Cor. 12.8 AV) received a conventional and widely believed exegesis, so that it has come to mean 'divinely given insight into the presence in a room of persons with this or that (nameable) complaint, which God can (or will) heal'. Perhaps each such raising of the contemporary profile of the miraculous has to begin with assertions of the power and goodwill of God towards humanity qualified only by the requirement of faith on the part of the recipients; then, in the light of hard realism and in facing of the facts, the assertions can be subtly qualified. The charismatic movement has had a public life of twenty-five years in the Church of England and has developed sensitivity and self-criticism. John Wimber, however, ranks as a relatively new phenomenon, and he is heard (though he speaks and writes in a fully responsible manner) as reflecting the bolder claims of the earlier phase. There has to be a general readiness to look for God's continuous work (by the Spirit) in the world and in the Church, lest the extraordinary acts of God today appear purely interventionist and seem to testify to God's real absence from the world for the rest of the time, even the surrender of it to the devil.

Before any charismatic movement existed in the mainstream denominations, Lesslie Newbigin was writing in *The Household of God* (1953) that a third strand of authentic Church life was now to be found alongside what he called the institutional model (Catholicism) and the word model (Protestantism), this third strand being the pentecostalist or experiential model, the company of the Spirit. As this strand is now found so strongly within the mainstream Churches, and indeed within the Church of England, its teaching about distinctive features of Christian experience, on which we earlier touched, must inevitably come under scrutiny. We now inspect some of these in turn.

(a) Baptism in the holy spirit

We have already (pp. 165–6) treated this subject quite fully. Here in summary we note our conviction that the pattern discernible in the case of the very first disciples is not to be considered normative for those who become Christians after the outpouring of the Spirit in the upper room at Pentecost; that the arguments for regarding baptism in the Holy Spirit as inseparably linked with conversion and initiation (as set out, for instance, by J.D.G. Dunn in *Baptism in the Holy Spirit*) are compelling; that baptismal language has been inappropriately applied to a later (often dramatic) stage in the Christian life when a believer enters more fully into what he has already received. In short, we are not at all persuaded that the life-changing crisis experienced by not a few Christian people at a time subsequent to their initial conversion is appropriately called baptism in the Holy Spirit. Those who apply this term to this experience need to go to school with the Bible's own teaching on baptism in the Spirit. In the terms of the title of this chapter, we have identified a clear instance in which, in our opinion, 'this' which is experienced to-day is not identical with nor corresponds with 'that' which is alleged to match it in the New Testament.

(b) The gifts of the spirit

Three passages from the New Testament particularly claim our attention. In 1 Peter 4. 10f. the gifts may be classified as those of speech and of service to be used in discipleship and in the Christian mission. The list presumably is not exhaustive, but illustrative of a wider principle, namely that individuals with their particular gifts corporately contribute a wide range of faculties, skills and activities.

In Romans 12.6ff. we find a similar pattern, though here we note that some of the gifts appear to be spontaneous or instantaneous, whereas others clearly used conscious preparation and planning, and some are of more limited duration than others. Paul underlines the importance of love; each member of the community values the gifts of the others, sees the harmony of the community being promoted by the diversity of its members' gifts, and properly exercises his own gifts as a means of love to others.

We find the most extended treatment of this subject in 1 Corinthians 12. Here the term 'gift' is clearly interchangeable with service or working (forms of work – NEB) (vv. 4ff.). Thus there is no identifiable entity called exclusively a 'gift'. Moreover, the actual functions described in this chapter correspond with the general classification of speech and of service, which we have already discerned with regard to 1 Peter. The 'gifts of healing' (v. 9) and 'the working of miracles' (v. 10) do, however, raise some further questions about the range of Christian ministering, which we shall shortly consider. However, the principal purpose of this entire chapter in 1 Corinthians is to illustrate the diversity of the body and the divine necessity for its members to live in harmony with one another. Paul could have made his point by any illustration from the variety of functions and gifts within the body. In this chapter he is not intending to concentrate on the particular implications of the various specific activities listed.

We take an illustration from a reference in 1 Cor. 12.8: if anyone today claims, with regard to a gift which he or she is regularly exercising, that 'this' is the 'utterance of wisdom' or 'the utterance of knowledge', the burden of proof must rest with the person who makes the claim. Commentators are by no means clear about the meaning of the expressions used in this passage, and some of the more popular exegesis of this and of other passages appears to be based on an insufficiently careful handling of the text. We thus need to treat with caution any claim to exercise the gifts to which reference is made in 1 Corinthians.

(c) Tongues and prophecy

In considering these phenomena, which have received much attention in recent years, we turn particularly to 1 Corinthians 14. From time to time we hear charismatic phrases such as, 'This is a church where the gifts of the Spirit are exercised', which means that tongues and prophecy are used in public. Against this background we make the point of detail that (despite the translation in the RSV) the word 'gifts' is not used in 1 Corinthians 14, though it is in 1 Corinthians 12.31. More fundamental is the realization that Paul does not regard tongues and prophecy as the most eminent or most desirable functions. We assume that he was addressing a situation in which prophets and those who spoke with tongues competed with one another and even ceased to worry whether they communicated with one another. Thus Paul invokes the principle that there should be genuine communication between the various members of the Corinthian church, a principle which makes for the edification or building up of the Christian community.

As we consider the ways in which the title of this chapter bears upon prophecy and tongues, we are faced with a particular difficulty. With regard to tongues, are we dealing with unknown sounds which require interpretation, or with unknown sounds which require expression in intelligible speech; or are we dealing with foreign languages known to the speaker and with their translation into a language known to the hearer? It is notoriously difficult to be precisely certain either about the tongues to which reference is made in 1 Corinthians 14 or about the situation in the Corinthian church in terms of which this chapter should be understood. Therefore it is even more difficult to draw from this chapter matters for detailed application in the life of the Church today. We need to learn more about prophecy in New Testament times before we can lightly identify 'this' with 'that'. Moreover, with regard to prophecy also, caution is necessary. In the Old Testament, and in the early history of the Christian Church as well, there is evidence of both genuine and spurious prophecy. There is a need to test the Spirit and to test the application of any word of God to any particular situation.

It will have been clear from our treatment of tongues and prophecy that we do not consider them to have no proper place in the life of the Church today. Along with a number of other features of the Church's life (e.g. liturgy, prayer, depth counselling, meditation), they can be valuable helps to worship and to the practice of discipleship, but about their derivation from or their revelation in the scriptures we should not assert more than is justified by the evidence. In any case, even if we were certain what tongues and prophecy were in 1 Corinthians 14 and that they were being strongly commended to us in that form, we should need to bear in mind the principles contained in 1 Corinthians 12, that diversity is positively valued and that we are discouraged from desiring the gifts of other people or from insisting that other people should have ours.

(d) Healings

In our chapter 'The Spirit and Power' we give some attention to the healings reported in the gospels and in the Acts of the Apostles. In the epistles they have a place in lists of gifts (1 Cor. 12.9, 28ff.); they are examples of the variety and range of gifts in the Church, but nowhere in the epistles are they treated at length. There is today a great deal of literature about healings and a large corpus of healings actually recorded. Nowadays people may well have different expectations with regard to health from those which were current in New Testament times. Moreover, both then and now healing may properly include the result of the work of doctors. We do not, however, find it easy to make a quick or direct transfer from New Testament times to our own; 'this' and 'that' are not necessarily identical. The Church has certainly been given authority to combat illness, but we do not find evidence in the scriptures to support the view that the Church has been given by its Lord the certainty that the cure of mental or physical illness will always accompany the deeper healing offered.

(e) The word of knowledge

Reference to this gift is made in 1 Cor. 12.8 and nowhere else in the New Testament. This slender basis makes it very difficult for us to determine whether any particular present-day practice or ministry is a 'this' which gives expression to a New Testament 'that'. The explanation of this gift, which we noted on p. 167, may or may not be accurate: namely that it refers to trustworthy insight into the physical complaints of persons whose presence in the room may not even be known. The term is patient of several meanings, and (as with tongues and prophecy) it is exegetically unsound to assert that one meaning which corresponds with some practice in today's Church *must* be for that very reason the one given us by God. Equally, as with other gifts discussed above, any insight into or intuitive understanding of another person's ills should nevertheless be valued highly as a gift from God, even if it cannot be given the title of a scripturally revealed gift of the Holy Spirit.

This discussion of gifts has been restricted to those actually mentioned in 1 Corinthians. We shall not want to tie the notion of gift too tightly nor to limit its range to the specific functions discussed in that epistle. We have concentrated on that epistle in order to meet on their own ground people in today's Church who attribute such importance to the gifts included there. Our own agenda for discussing the experience of the Holy Spirit in today's Church might well concentrate on some rather different gifts and functions.

We conclude our discussion of the gifts claimed by some charismatics with a reference to a very widespread feature of the charismatic movement, namely the sense of joy. This joy is rooted in a keen sense of the nearness of God and in confident conviction of God's immediate engagement with Christian people. As the charismatic movement has matured, so too has this sense of joy; at earlier stages in the movement joy tended to be associated primarily with God's providential care for the individual, now rather more with an awareness of God's sovereignty over the entire world. Further, many people associated with the movement have discovered the integration of joy with suffering to be a crucial stage towards personal and corporate maturity.

Conclusion

In this chapter we have been considering and testing some of the claims made by modern charismatics that 'this' which they know at first hand in their own lives and ministries is precisely identical with 'that' which we read in the Acts and in the epistles. We have been maintaining that those who make such claims should test them more thoroughly in the light of the scriptures to which they themselves appeal. That said, 'faithful are the wounds of a friend' (Prov. 27.6). We rejoice that, at a time when there has been a move away from what may have been an excessive concentration on the rational and cerebral in society at large, new joy in the Spirit has deeply affected the life of a somewhat sober institutionalized Church, not least in acting as a counter to a certain type of cerebral and over-verbalized Anglican worship. Put succinctly, the charismatic movement has insistently kept before us certain truths which should have a prominent place in the Christian life: every member of the Church properly has an active ministry; the gospel enables people to be self-accepting, to be transparent to others and to express themselves with openness; there is a dynamic and experiential element in being a Christian; God's power is accordingly to be expected and sought in life and practice, together with a genuinely optimistic hope that God's hand will be at work in the world.

At the same time we feel bound to mention some features of the charismatic movement which have caused pastoral problems, and to make some theological comments on them. In the first place there is a subtle group pressure towards constant joy, with perhaps insufficient awareness of psychological typecasting. The confidence and outgoingness which may be natural to the extrovert (and the insensitive) should not necessarily be viewed as the certain marks of 'victorious living'. The ebullience characteristic of some charismatics may be inappropriate in many lives for internal or external reasons; it may even desert those who have it, when they are under stress, or physical pain, or clinical depression. If the dominant model of Christian daily living and spirituality which those persons encounter is one of continuous euphoria, then the actual Christian fellowship which is supposed to be supportive and therapeutic not only feels uncaring and judgemental to the sufferers, but also inevitably makes any depression worse.

Then we note great prejudice in favour of the inner impulse in the sphere of guidance. The immediacy of God's presence leads believers to expect direct, 'hot line' guidance from God in all, or at least nearly all, situations. This can take various forms: for instance, a prophecy from another which rings true to the recipient's situation, a text of scripture which leaps out and carries a contemporary directive, a dream, an inner urge, a mental picture; all these are recorded, are part of the everyday parlance of charismatics and are open to a friendly critique. However, they need to be tested theologically, both by objective standards of scripture, principles of hermeneutics, and a theology of God's guidance.

Further it is undeniable that in the charismatic movement there is a markedly pietistic strain and there has been a tendency to withdraw from the world and to look inward. The Church of England may well have needed this type of spirituality, and it may well be argued that our society needs this. However, in the last couple of decades Evangelicalism within the Church of England has been recovering a social conscience, which it has integrated with its primary sense of missionary vocation. There are those who regret the extent to which this inward looking strand in the charismatic movement has hindered these developments.

In any case, the charismatic movement sometimes exhibits a frail ecclesiology. The doctrine and the institutional life of the Church are frequently downgraded in the movement and regarded as hindrances to the gospel. Earlier in this chapter we touched on the matter of order, which in our chapter on creation we shall develop in a rather different direction. Order is not necessarily boring or trivial, nor is it to be equated with the merely seemly or decorous. Openness to change, vitality, warmth and surprise all need to be balanced by continuity, regularity, stability and rationality. In other words, structure and form are as important as the living content; both should be understood as the work of one and the same Spirit. A similar point is often made with regard to the stress laid within the charismatic movement on certain feelings and emotions as against the proper disciplines of the mind, a matter to which we give further attention in the chapter, 'The Spirit of Truth'.

Under the heading 'Is this that?' we have made an appraisal of some of the claims of the charismatic movement with regard to the present operation of the Holy Spirit. Although we have dwelt on some of the problems raised by the movement, we gladly acknowledge that these problems are mainly the side-effects of a zeal in the Spirit which we whole-heartedly welcome and in which we recognize the hand of God. In this chapter we have been pleading that the distinctive features of that zeal be brought to a more thorough testing in the light of those scriptures to which the movement itself so often appeals. We make this plea for the very reason that we are so deeply appreciative of the movement's strengths. Before we turn to further consideration of the Spirit's work in the Church, particularly in connection with its sacraments and structures, we shall try to do justice to the Christocentric element which has been implicit in our study hitherto, and at times explicit in it.

Chapter 4
The Spirit of Jesus

The early Christian communities, as we meet them especially in the Acts of the Apostles and the letters of Paul, certainly seem to have spoken of the outpouring of God's Spirit in these last days primarily in terms of tangible effects; effects perceptible in the natural order, not only in the 'inner life', healings and inspired utterance as well as a renewed sense of God. As we have already seen, the distinctiveness of being a Christian was inseparably bound to distinctive experience, and, to a degree which some modern Christians outside the charismatic movement might find somewhat alien, to 'works of power'. It is not surprising that, as Paul's Corinthian correspondence suggests, the free exercise of spiritual power, in this very concrete sense, had come to be seen in some communities as the central business of the Christian assembly. Gifts are given for use; and the gifts of the Spirit cry out for exercise and expression.

Paul's critique of such an assumption, especially in 1 Corinthians, is centred upon the question of what it is that the gifts are given for. They are for the building up of a community; not just community in general, but a specific sort of community whose identity is defined and characterized by being 'in Christ'. What this means in concrete moral terms is spelled out in 1 Corinthians 13, where love is presented as the context within which all particular spiritual gifts are exercised and by which they are tested. All must employ their gifts for the health of the Church, and that health is precisely a matter of looking to the interests of each other, sensitivity to each other's needs, material and otherwise, giving place in love to each other. There may be a pressure felt to exercise and express what the Spirit is thought to be giving, the pressure to use 'tongues' for praise in the assembly, or to correct the immature Christian practice of another in matters of dietary regulations (1 Cor.8; 10–12;14; Rom.14–15), but this must be subordinated to deeper priorities, common priorities. The shape of the Church's life must be moulded by a bearing with and attending to each other, a reverence for the other as object of Christ's costly love (Rom.14. 1–12,15; 1 Cor.8.11). What the form of Christian life together must make visible is that kind of relatedness, a condition in which rights and individual assertion are ruled out. There is no need for assertion because God has already and authoritatively affirmed the worth of human being through the divine action in Christ, which is itself an action of renunciation, giving place in love (Rom.15.1ff.; 1 Cor.10.32ff.).

So it would be possible to answer the question 'What is it that is distinctive about the Christian assembly?' in more than one way. At the surface level, there are striking and exciting phenomena to which appeal can be made; but Paul presses the question of their purpose and of the ultimate unifying form of Christian life together. God has poured out the Spirit; but that Spirit is to be understood as an agency making for a unified pattern of life, unified by the way believers reflect God's gift in Christ in their self-gift to one another. The focus of unity is thus God's primary gift of Christ; what shapes and characterizes the unity of Christians is the form, the 'likeness' of Jesus Christ, whose 'mind' the community shares (1 Cor.2.16; Phil.2.5). Thus if it is Spirit that makes the Church what it is, Spirit is what forms the corporate and individual likeness of Christ in us; and we shall not be able to use the language of Spirit without at some stage beginning to speak of Christ. For Paul, *pneuma* can no longer be a word that simply describes an agency from which flow signs and wonders; it is what sets us free to take on the likeness of Jesus. And this is shown in our being able to take on our lips the language of Jesus, calling God *Abba* (Gal.4.6; Rom.8.15), in the sure hope of a comprehensive transfiguration of the whole of our created condition, the whole of our relatedness to each other and the rest of the created material world.

This deepening of insight is not merely an individual quirk of Paul's theology. We may set beside it the way in which the tradition about Jesus itself deals with the question of miracle and power. In Mark especially, miracles are not generally performed in response to requests for manifestation and proof (8.11f., 11.27ff.); they are specific acts of compassion (1.41) or, occasionally, prophetic or warning signs (11.12ff., 20ff.). They are bound up with the whole work of showing and proclaiming the kingdom, and so with the general demand for repentance and faith. In Matthew, the healing miracles are signs of the presence of a time of crisis and fulfilment (11.2ff.), the incipient presence of the rule of God (12.28). They are a challenge and a promise, but not a simple guarantee of authority any more than they are in Mark. They are there in virtue of the kingdom, for its sake, and the essential point about the kingdom is the restoration of a people gathered, accepted and healed by God.

The gospel narratives, of course, are written by people who believe that in their life together the rule of God is being exercised through the Lordship of the risen and exalted Jesus: they believe themselves to be living in the more immediate presence of God's rule that is the result of Jesus' resurrection. The promise and preaching of Jesus in his ministry is set in the light of that sequence of events which creates the Church, the events of Easter. The Lord of the Church, in loyalty to whom we live under the victorious rule of God, so that we are delivered from the rule of sin and the death-dealing powers of this present age, is a Lord who has entered upon his kingdom through agony and death. Thus the signs that point to the kingdom in Jesus' ministry are to be interpreted ultimately out of the experience of a divine rule that is achieved through surrender, loss, powerlessness. The miracles are indeed works of power; but to understand that power in its fullness we must understand, on the one hand, how it works at its critical moment, by absorbing hatred and rejection without defence or retaliation, and what it works towards, a community of reconciliation.

The new world of the Christian community, then, in which God rules and God's Spirit is shed abroad, is a world whose forms and meanings depend on the reality of a power that 'loses' itself to bring about its purpose; and that purpose is a community of persons built up, nurtured and bound together by the same reality of self-gift in its daily transactions. What unites and shapes this community is thus continuous with what it is that shapes and defines the work of Jesus in its completeness, its paschal fulfilment. To raise, with Paul, the question of the final purpose of activity that is seen as Spirit-directed is to open up the whole issue of how God's purpose is made actual and effective in the history of flesh and blood. Once we have asked about the context of the more dramatic experiences of the Spirit that seem to have been so formative for many early communities, we are on the way to asking questions about Christology. How are we to speak of the Spirit in relation to Jesus, in whom God's purpose is supremely and creatively embodied in our flesh and blood?

The Spirit of the community is the Spirit of Jesus; so much is regularly taken for granted. At the level of works and manifestations, this can mean no more than that believers have access to the same sources of power as Jesus; their signs and healings validate their claim to be of 'one spirit' with the Lord. But if we now take seriously what has been said about the inadequacy or ambiguity of wonders in themselves, and about the context of the kingdom in which alone these wonders make sense, then the unity of 'Spirit' between Jesus and the community must involve more than simply the production of comparable miracles. Close to the heart of Paul's conception of the Spirit (indeed of his whole understanding of the life of faith) is the idea of the formation in believers of the likeness of Christ – as we have seen in the first section of this chapter. Most specifically, believers are drawn into the same relation with God as is exemplified in Jesus. Jesus called God *Abba*, and his whole identity for God and before God rests upon this assumption that the God of Israel can be confidently addressed as a loving parent. The gospels underline this in many different ways, from the repeated 'My heavenly

Father' of Matthew to the profound statements of identity in will and action between Jesus and the God of Israel in the fourth gospel. The tradition shared by Matthew and Luke preserves the prayer taught by Jesus to his disciples, the 'Our Father', which carries in it the assumption that Jesus' relation with God is something we are enabled to take on; and this receives its most far-reaching expression in the Farewell Discourses of John 13–17.

So Paul can give a very exact meaning to the notion that God gives us the 'Spirit' of Jesus who is the Son of God; and in Galatians 4 a further crucial link is made. We have the Spirit of God's Son and are authorised to call God *Abba* as did Jesus; this represents the gift to us of an inheritance of liberty and authority. To be in the relation that entitles us to call God *Abba* is to be delivered from slavery, in particular, from an anxious servitude to the forms and conventions of cultic practice. These (Paul believes) belong to a dispensation which is only provisional and which derives from spiritual powers of lesser authority, not from the true God alone, the God whose own freedom is the source of covenant and promise. Perhaps even more powerful is the cluster of images in 2 Corinthians 3. The life God promises in covenant is given by the Spirit in a relation in which all 'veils' are removed between us and God; in this directness of relationship is to be found liberty, and that liberty is the reflection of God's glory in the life of the believer.

But what is that liberty, that glory, as it appears in the life of Jesus himself? For the fourth gospel, it is the liberty to do the Father's will in laying down his life; the Son of Man is glorified in his betrayal and death. Even in Mark, it is striking that it is in Gethsemane that we find Jesus addressing God as *Abba* as if it is this and the events which follow that show the heart of his relation to his Father. In this light, the work of God's Spirit relates closely to Paul's insight about power made perfect in weakness. The humanity that is shaped by God's Spirit is defined in connection with the cross. The new humanity is, as we have seen, dependent on a power that achieves its ends by sacrifice. More specifically, we can now say that the union of believers with Jesus is also a union in vulnerability: God attains what God purposes in Jesus and in us through the full confrontation of the violence of the human world and the mortality of the human condition itself. And the paradox of belief is that freedom and authority, the 'empowering' of the Christian life, rest upon a primary act of surrender to death. Jesus is raised to share the Father's freedom and authority through holding back nothing in his obedience. To be with him in glory is to share 'a death like his' (Rom.6.5; 2 Cor.4.10f.).

To be 'like God' then, to share and manifest God's glory is to be set free from the fantasy that we can and must attain invulnerability and mastery, that we can fashion a context for ourselves without 'ragged edges' and risks. As the story of Adam and Eve hints, the human temptation to be godlike rests on the longing for an immortality that will set us free from all the constraints of the body, the world, death, other people; but God's gift of Godlikeness gives freedom within these things – the freedom of Jesus. This is a freedom for relationship, community, the freedom proper to the kingdom of God, the people of God. If 'Spirit' is what makes the Christian people distinctive, Spirit is what creates a personality free for love, mutuality, creativity, free within the bounds of life in the world, not promising some conquest or escape from it.

This is expressed in the link made between the Spirit and Christian initiation (1 Cor.12.13; Eph.4.4f.). The descent of God's Spirit is a clear and central motif in the traditions about Jesus' own baptism, and the Lukan accounts of Christian baptism confirm that it was natural to look for manifestations of the Spirit's work in connection with initiation. However, Jesus' baptism is an 'initiation' into the whole of the mission that culminates in the cross; and Paul insists that if baptism is an identification with Jesus, it is an entry into the process of cross and resurrection. Baptism and the other features of initiation represent the beginning of that life in which Christ is formed; if the Spirit of God forms Christ in us, the Spirit is what is at work in our symbolic sharing in Jesus' cross and resurrection at our initiation. Here we begin to live in the Spirit, not primarily because extraordinary gifts instantly manifest themselves, but because the liberation of our humanity for life among God's people, the liberation accomplished in Jesus' death and resurrection, becomes real for us and in us.

The liberation effected by Easter is pure gift to humanity; but since cross and resurrection are inseparable from the whole of Jesus' ministry, we are led to say that the whole of Jesus' life is likewise pure gift. He is not an exemplary wonder-worker, but neither is he simply an example of liberated or Spirit-filled humanity. We receive our liberation as a result of his gift of himself to his Father in his life and death. It is thus Jesus who creates the conditions for our re-creation. And if so, his life is not just a pattern for us to imitate: our ability to grow into his likeness depends on his initiative, not ours, his gift, not just our innate capacities. Our relation to him is always going to be asymmetrical. We receive the Spirit as a transforming power in our lives because of the work done for us in the living and dying and rising of Jesus.

If the whole of Jesus' identity is God's gift to us in this way, Jesus' relation to the Spirit cannot be exactly like ours. He is the source from which the Spirit's power flows to us; he is the definition of what life in the Spirit is like, and he is also the means whereby that life becomes liveable in the world, in us. We have to say that in one sense Jesus lives out our human vocation to be children of God, as some theologians have put it; but that in another sense he lives 'naturally' what we have to learn. To be a human child of God, without interruption, without unfaithfulness, to receive and express the purpose of God in the midst of human pain and vulnerability without turning aside, without our ordinary experience of grace as a gradual overcoming of our native fear and destructiveness – this is what is seen is Jesus. This is why the gospels, although they present the story of the baptism of Jesus as a crucial moment of decision and a point of entry into deeper awareness of the Spirit's work, do not suggest that the baptism is a moment of conversion, of entry into a new life at odds with what has gone before. They show this event rather as the uncovering of what has always been there in Jesus, since his birth or conception. Even Mark, who has no stories of Jesus' birth, treats the baptism as the event which simply inaugurates Jesus' preaching; we have already been told who he is, in the first verse of the gospel; and there is no hint of a dramatic summons and change, lifting Jesus out of the life he previously leads. He *is* the Son of God, and John's baptism merely anoints the Son for bringing his mission to fulfilment.

Jesus is already what we are called to be: already and forever ahead of us. Our human vocation now comes to us through him. We could sum this up by saying that in him God's calling to the world and the world's response to God are fused together: there is no gap between the first and the second. The human yearning of Jesus to give himself to the Father and see God's will done (e.g. Luke 12.50) is completely at one with God's own yearning to bring the world back home (to God). In Jesus, God is at work in the longing for God. It is this idea that has led Christians from the earliest days of their faith to say that Jesus of Nazareth cannot be spoken of only in terms of a human identity; he embodies or represents something about God. This is the origin of the doctrine of the incarnation, the Christian belief that in Jesus the source of his acts and indeed of his very being from moment to moment is the eternal Son or Word of God. If God acts decisively in the life of Jesus, God is a God who acts not only in giving but also in responding: God acts to heal us and to call us and to re-create us through an act of responding, through the loving self-surrender of Jesus to his Father's purpose; if we take this seriously, we must conclude that God's life is not just an act of pure giving but also somehow includes the receiving and giving back of love. Jesus is able to live out the life he does, not because he has 'invented' the kind of human life that best pleases God by his own imagination, but because his humanly free obedience and love are borne along, shaped and sustained, from the first moment of his existence, by the eternal reality of God's loving response to God's own love, God's delight in God. Jesus is the reality of God's love for God passed through the prism, we might say, of a suffering and struggling human reality.

So Jesus *is* a 'Spirit-filled' human being, one in whom God's Spirit has achieved a masterwork, a wholly consistent life of loving freedom towards God; but he is thus because what is being formed and shaped in Jesus' human life is the likeness of an already-existing perfection, God's loving answer to God's own generosity. The Spirit shapes in Jesus the life of the everlasting Word. It is this life, of course, which the Spirit seeks to shape in all of us; but before we are free to grasp it, to hear God's summons to be daughters and sons of a divine parent, we must be set free and have our eyes opened by a life that shows both the divine call and the possibility of living out a full response to it, and which takes away, by the great absolution pronounced in cross and resurrection, the fear and slavery of sin which keeps us from our true vocation. As the incarnate Word, Jesus both receives the Spirit, energizing the life of the eternal Word in this specific human body and soul, and gives the Spirit, pouring out the gift he has been given. He gives freely because he has received wholly; he has authority to give because he is himself caught up in God's own generosity. The Spirit is both the gift and promise of the Father and the gift of the risen Jesus (e.g. Luke 24.49; John 14.16, 26; 15.26). If Jesus is the supremely 'Spirit-filled' person, this does not mean that he has unrivalled capacities for miracle and mastery, or even that he is a supreme example of selfless love, but that he is the one around whom the community of God's sons and daughters is gathered, gathered by the creative power he bestows, the life of the Holy Spirit.

In recent years, some distinguished theologians, above all Geoffrey Lampe, have proposed that we should qualify our commitment to a trinitarian theology and think instead of a theology of 'God as Spirit' (as in the title of Lampe's Bampton lectures and subsequent book). 'Spirit' is simply a term for God's outreach to the world, and Jesus is the highest embodiment of that outreach. There is much insight in this; it is certainly true to say that the Bible encourages us to think of the Spirit as that which makes God's life active and accessible outside the being of God in itself. But it should be clear how what we are outlining here differs from such a view. We have insisted that when the divine life is thus given in and by the Spirit, what is given is a life that is already in movement and relationship. God is the giving life of the one Jesus calls Father; and God is also the responding life that is shown in Jesus as Son. In relation to the world, God gives the divine life by giving access to the divine response, the divine joy, that is defined in Jesus, the Word made flesh.

But there remains a problem about the Spirit's own status. It may seem as if we now have a Godhead of two identifiable terms, 'Father' and 'Son', plus a rather nebulous power flowing from them. Is this really a trinity? A lot of theological language, especially in the western tradition, has given this impression, and Eastern Orthodox theologians have often pointed out the danger of reducing the Spirit to an impersonal thing, rather than a substantive, purposive agency. It is easy to see why a writer like Augustine could describe the Spirit as *donum*, the gift which the Father and the Son give each other, and give to the world: this is imagery deeply rooted in the biblical ideas we have been exploring in this chapter. But in isolation it can indeed be misleading; and it may well be that the comparative neglect of the theology of the Spirit in a lot of western European theology until fairly recently has something to do with the notion that the Spirit is not the same sort of entity as the Father and the Son. But on what grounds, then, do we talk of the Spirit as a Person in the Trinity?

We must take care not to be misled by the word Person. 'Father' and 'Son' are words which easily lend themselves to images of personality rather like our own personal being, while 'Spirit' does not. But once we realise that we are speaking of realities that eternally constitute each other in their relationships to each other, we should be able to see that 'Father' and 'Son' are more than just magnified human-type consciousnesses; and this may help us to see also that 'Spirit' is not necessarily any less 'personal' in the sense appropriate to God than the other two terms. Certainly it is not adequate to say that the Spirit is just a function of two more vividly or concretely presented subjects. But how exactly are we to think of this distinct eternal reality we call the Holy Spirit? We can describe the Spirit's work in the process of redemption – in the life, death and resurrection of Jesus, and in the experience of believers who are being re-created in the likeness of Jesus. This is what traditional theology termed the 'mission' of the Spirit. But characterizing the eternal life of the Spirit in relation to Father and Son – the 'procession' of the Spirit in the Trinity – is far harder. We cannot, in the nature of the case, expect to arrive at a neat and final solution: trinitarian theology is not like that. But there are two sets of ideas and images that may give us some clue.

First of all, affirming the independent reality of the Spirit tells us that the perfect mutual love of Father and Son, the completeness of giving and receiving in God, is not all that should be said about the divine life. There is no hint of an exclusive mutual absorption: the life of God is also an eternal movement of self-sharing, so that the relation of Father and Son is open to a world of possible beings. God is the primary gift of the Father's love; God is the perfect responding to and mirroring of that love as Word or Son; and God is the gift, to all that lies beyond the divine life, of a share in that fullness of response. It is not that God is compelled to create, but that there is in the richness and perfection of divine life a natural and irreducible momentum towards the sharing of that life, a divine longing for the life of God to be lived in the world that God's love creates in freedom.

But this may still sound as though the Spirit is somehow subordinate, an 'extra' to the primary reality of Father and Son; so these notions must be balanced or supplemented by a second set of ideas. We encounter God the Spirit in the 'overflow' towards us of the life of Father and Son; but the relation of Father and Son already shows the divine momentum towards sharing, in the Father's pouring out of the divine life to the Son. Should we then think of the Spirit as the ground of this self-sharing by the Father? One modern Orthodox theologian (Paul Evdokimov) has said that the idea of the Spirit proceeding from the Father and the Son would be acceptable only if we could also say that the Son comes forth from the Father *and the Spirit*. This is to say that the Father's act of bringing the Son to birth is not an arbitrary movement arising out of some abyss of divine will, but is in accord with the eternal fact of the divine impulse to self-sharing, something which is not simply identical with either Father or Son, but a distinctive note or moment in the harmony of divine action. In this perspective, the Spirit is what makes the Father-Son relationship itself possible, as well as what makes this relation open to a world in which images of God's life are established.

None of this 'explains' the life of God as Trinity. It serves to open our eyes to the fact that we cannot do trinitarian theology without reflecting on the Holy Spirit as that which *completes* the coherence of the divine life – that in virtue of which God is an everlasting movement of *giving away*. The Father gives life to the Son, the Father and the Son give their life to the world, the creation gives itself in praise to the Father through the Son; and what makes this one single act of God's love is the unity of the Holy Spirit, working in both divine and created love.

The debate that divided eastern from western Christendom as to whether the Spirit proceeds from the Father (as in the original Nicene Creed) or from the Father and the Son (*filioque*, as in the later Latin versions) has some bearing here. Eastern Christians still hold that the *filioque* is symptomatic of the weaknesses of western theology, obscuring the distinctiveness of the Spirit, and making the Spirit inferior, absorbing it into the Father and the Son. As we have noted, there is some substance to this charge. But some modern defenders of the *filioque* have insisted that we must not divorce our language about the Spirit from the Father's purpose to bring creatures into the life of the Godhead by adopting them as sons and daughters in the Son. If we talk about the Spirit in abstraction from this, we are in danger of turning the Spirit into a vague principle of general religiosity. The Spirit's work is to form a Christlike humanity, not simply to spread abroad sensations of the transcendent; to create the relationships that constitute the kingdom of God, not to nurture individual religious intensity. The *filioque* may not be the best means of keeping all this in view, and no eastern theologian would quarrel with these insights; but, for all its inadequacy, the controversial formula may have helped some theologians not to lose sight of the proper connection between the Spirit, the kingdom and the work of Christ.

The trinitarian picture has as much to say about us as about God. In defining our vocation in terms of Christ and the eternal Word made flesh in him, we are told that Godlikeness is never a matter of pure independent initiative. There is in God not only perfect giving but perfect responding. Listening, receiving and depending are not contradictions of divine freedom and creativity. Thus we are not obliged to struggle for a life without dependence and receiving if we wish to be free: if God is Trinity, and if the life of Jesus embodies the life of God as response, we shall find our proper creativity and liberty not by distancing ourselves from others but by learning to receive from as well as give to others in a community of mutual interdependence. And if God is Spirit, we are reminded that our very response to God is a channel for God's giving through us to the world; our growth in the likeness of Christ is inseparable from the mission of the Holy Spirit, in whom the life of God and God's children is constantly widening out to the horizon of the whole creation. To speak in a certain way of God's nature on the grounds of God's action in revelation is to commit ourselves to a particular vision of our calling in the world; this is why the theology of the Trinity is far from being a matter of detached speculation.

What has been outlined in the preceding section clearly bears on our thinking about the Spirit in creation. A certain amount has been written about the Spirit as the agent of God's presence in the created order at large (outside the bounds of the visible Church), building on the fact that, in the Old Testament and Apocrypha, 'Word', 'Wisdom' and 'Spirit' are sometimes overlapping expressions for God's presence and agency in the orderliness and beauty of creation (e.g. Wisd. 9.1f., 9, 17; and perhaps Gen. 1.2 and Ps. 33.6), and 'Spirit' may be connected with the skill of the craftsman in making objects of beauty (Exod. 35.31). On this basis, it seems possible to develop a theology of the Spirit at work in art and science, the formation of beauty and the discovery of order, as we attempt in Chapters 8 and 9 of this study. However, for this to avoid the pitfall of once again making the Spirit only a general force for self-transcendence, it needs to be related to what we have described as the primary focus of the insights of the New Testament about the Spirit.

Spirit is the agency that communicates to creatures the possibility of calling God 'Abba', as Jesus called the God of Israel, so that we may speak of the Spirit as the 'overflowing', the outpouring into that which is not God of the divine relationship of gift and response shown to us in Jesus' relation with his Father in heaven. Spirit of God acting to draw creation towards the fullness of the trinitarian life. Thus the Spirit's presence and work should not be seen only in the transfiguration of human lives. Creation as a whole responds to God by being itself; it gives glory to God by reflecting back to God something of the divine beauty, abundance and rationality. If the orderliness, the intelligibility, of the world is its share in the reality of God as Logos, then the variety and resourcefulness of the concrete actuality, the life, of creatures has to do with the reality of God as Spirit. The life of the natural world is disfigured in all kinds of ways, and often appears to us as terrible, hostile or meaningless. But part of the good news Christians proclaim is that at the heart of things, God remains faithfully at work, drawing all things Godward; and we are never wholly robbed of the capacity to see creation as a single movement towards God, an act of cosmic 'praise'. The implications of this will be explored further in our chapter 'The Spirit and Creation'. For the present we shall note only that such a model of creation-as-praise may help us to see how the Word that is incarnate in Jesus can be called the 'beginning' or 'first principle' of all creation. The Word of God in eternity, Jesus of Nazareth in time, show what it is for God's will to share the divine life, to have 'free play', for that will wholly to realise itself. The whole of creation moves towards this realization which is already accomplished in the incarnate Word, the perfect act of praise or glorification. Paul in Romans 8.22ff. speaks of the 'labour pains' of creation waiting for the realization of God's freedom within the world of space and time; and that waiting and longing is the urging of the Spirit. For the believer, the mystery hidden from all ages, God's purpose to bring into eternal life many sons and daughters, reconciled to God, to each other, and to the whole of their environment, has now been revealed, and those whose eyes have been opened to it 'were sealed with the promised Holy Spirit' (Eph.1.13). By the 'pledge' of the Spirit (2 Cor.5.5; Eph.1.14) the created life of the present age becomes the life of God's future: it enacts and shows the goal purposed by God for all creation, because it reflects the life lived out in Jesus. The Old Testament promise to which reference is made in Acts 2.17, that God will pour out the Spirit in the last days, is fulfilled in the creation of that Christlike life that is both free of the slaveries and sins of the present age, and yet wholly committed to finding and serving God in the present moment.

We have said that there is a Christological criterion by which the 'achievements' of the human spirit' must be tested. The same is even more clearly true where Christian spirituality and Christian sanctity are concerned. We have some fairly clear standards of discernment for the 'spiritual life' if we consider how human identity is moulded by God's Spirit in that life where it has free play. To the extent that some traditional ideals of humility have produced immaturity and dependence in Christian lives, we must question whether they are truly related to the life of the Spirit. They can produce people for whom dependence means an obsessive conviction of inferiority, people who lack the capacity to take responsibility as adults for their actions. A particular sort of convent spirituality has been specially prone to this; and in the works and life of a great monastic reformer like Teresa of Avila, we can see the tension between the culturally imposed ideals of humility for women religious and the bold conviction that proper dependence on God makes one a friend, not a slave, and equips one for courageous resistance to various kinds of cultural tyranny.

But equally, the ideal of the 'moral athlete', the person struggling towards self-mastery, afraid of exposing vulnerability and admitting need, stands under the judgement of the Spirit's work in Jesus Christ. Jesus does not avoid the pain of admitting human need, as when he begs the disciples to watch with him in Gethsemane; in relation to those whom he comes to redeem, 'he is not ashamed to call them brethren' (Heb.2.11). His is not a humanity seeking perfection in isolation and independence. There is nothing here of what T. S. Eliot called 'the fear of belonging'. Those who cannot 'belong' to and with others and God may show it in various ways, for instance the dread of making human commitments, the unwillingness to share problems, even the obstinate insistence that there are no problems in one's relation to God and others that cannot be solved by will. Catholic ideals of priestly spirituality have often fostered just such a suspicion of sharing, just such isolation, fear of admitting need, and concentration on will; and this has played an important part in setting the priest at an emotional as well as a social and cultic distance from the laity. But there is also a Protestant tradition of being reluctant to admit the role of the body and its senses in worship, and nervous about raw emotion. The charismatic movement has been the vehicle of a true judgement of the Holy Spirit upon moralistic and cerebral styles of evangelical piety.

But the critique does not stop here. 'Charismatic' devotion in turn raises the problem how the believer integrates the experiences of loss or absence as well as those of nurture, support and guidance into a whole pattern of discipleship. A relentless insistence that what is normative for Christian experience is what is clear, unambiguous and positive can push the pendulum back towards another kind of dependency or infantilism. Here, in fact, we return to the starting point of this chapter. The identification of the Holy Spirit's presence with the presence of manifest works of power and total subjective clarity about the will of God must sooner or later come to terms with the tensions about this in the tradition about Jesus, above all the Gethsemane narratives. Any account of how the Spirit is to be discerned in human lives must take in the possibility (to say the least) that the Spirit works also in those circumstances where we are forced to 'take our own authority', to decide and act without a single and simple validation either from subjective certainty, a sense of guidance, or from confirmatory wonders. And it must likewise confront the possibility that this represents not a spiritual deficiency but a moment of costly breakthrough to some fuller maturity. Our reflection on the Spirit's presence and work can be informed by the spiritual tradition most often associated with St John of the Cross, which claims that greater intimacy, fuller union, with God may involve a deep and disorienting loss of the sense of God tangibly and specifically at work, or of God as a discernible 'other'. This is not a denial of the abiding centrality of the concept and experience of relation with God, not a capitulation to the mysticism of absorption or identification; it is simply a recognition that the experiential content of this relation will vary, and that being entrusted by God to decide and act without tangible assurance marks an advance in the intimacy between creator and creature, and so can be interpreted as the Spirit's work in us. It is the moment where suffering and promise may coincide, where death and 'Godlessness' are taken into the reality of being the child of God. The Spirit lives in our risks as well as our securities, our hurts as well as our triumphs; indeed, in a significant sense, the Spirit is more alive and at work in these risks and hurts, to the extent that these are signs of our growth.

All this is best elucidated not by theory, but by the lives of believers. Our own century is perhaps particularly rich in examples of a Christian holiness that speaks of the sort of freedom and 'authority' we have been discussing, a freedom growing out of committed belonging, givenness to God, and authority free from self-assertion. It may be (as in the early centuries of Christianity) a freedom shown in resistance. We might think of the Austrian peasant Franz Jägerstätter, a solidly conservative Catholic executed for his refusal to serve in Hitler's armies, despite relentless pressure to conform from his own pastors as well as the secular authorities; or of Beyers Naudé, resigning his comfortable pastorate in Pretoria with a sermon on the text, 'We must obey God rather than men', and embarking on a lonely struggle against apartheid in the name of Christ, turning his back on the bright career expectations of his Afrikaaner milieu; or of Janani Luwum's mortally costly witness to the gospel in the nightmare circumstances of Amin's Uganda; or of Dietrich Bonhoeffer, though his story raises the complex issue of how the Spirit may be discerned in action as well as passive resistance to authority.

There are countless ordinary believers, Orthodox and Protestant, who have suffered in the camps of psychiatric hospitals of the Soviet Union. Again, we may see the same freedom in the crossing of boundaries, in the often solitary witness of those whose exposure or surrender to God's Spirit has empowered them to break through the limits of their religious or secular culture for the sake of the kingdom. There is C.F. Andrews in India, or Dorothy Day in America, seeking an authentic involvement with the homeless and jobless in the days of the Depression and its aftermath; nearer home, there are great bridge-builders between classes and peoples such as George Bell and Dick Sheppard. And the mention of Bell reminds us of those whose holiness has had to be worked out by bearing the pains of belonging to an institution indifferent or unsympathetic to them, a profoundly imperfect and often complacent Christian community that regularly treats them as marginal.

But such dramatic instances do no more than bring into clearer focus the birthright of all who are in Christ. Their liberty from the constraining definitions of class and race, temperament and taste, their freedom to discover a new and creative identity in Christ, both feeds and is fed by the naked, trustful prayer of the Spirit in us, *Abba*! In countless diverse biographies, the likeness of the incarnate Word is being realised by the Spirit; the form of structure of the life of Jesus as God's dedicated child is 'translated' and vivified afresh by the Spirit's vital energy. And in all this, the glory of God's own life of gift and communication is manifest in and to creation: 'This comes from the Lord who is the Spirit.'

Chapter 5
Spirit, sacraments and structures

In the previous chapter we have already touched on the way in which the Spirit's role is the creation of a certain kind of community. It is to be a community which reflects the divine life as revealed in Jesus, one of mutual inter-relationship and interdependence. Our giving of ourselves to others is to be a truly free gift, not one which merely establishes new patterns of submissive dependence, while our receiving must be of a kind that both fully acknowledges our need of others and enables us at the same time to reach out beyond the gift to a giving in turn of our own. It is precisely this pattern of giving and receiving, and giving through receiving, that constitutes one of the most distinctive aspects of the Christian concept of liberty. True freedom is not freedom from others but freedom for others and with others in the context of a serving and caring community, and that is why the New Testament can speak dialectically of freedom and slavery being but two sides of the same coin (e.g. Rom.8.21; 1 Cor.7.22; 9.19; 1.Pet.2.16).

Both in the Bible and in the tradition of the Church the creation of such a community, the Body of Christ, has been seen as the special work of the Spirit. Later in this chapter we shall look at some of the other features of that work. It is appropriate that we should begin by looking at the sacramental actions of the Spirit because baptism has normally been taken as the point of entrance to the community. 'Truly, truly, I say to you, unless one is born of water and the Spirit, he cannot enter into the kingdom of God' (John 3.5). Yet our theology must be capable of application to the realities of the world as it is; so it is important that our discussion should reflect present baptismal practice in all its complexity.

In the ASB Baptism Service the priest thanks God the Father that 'by your Holy Spirit *this child has* been born again into new life, adopted for your own, and received into the fellowship of your Church'. Of these three phrases it is probably the last which makes clearest and most obvious sense to parents as they present their child for baptism. Certainly this notion of baptism as the sign of admission to membership of the Church finds echoes in scripture, as for example in John 3.5 (already quoted) or Colossians 2.11ff., where Paul makes a comparison with the Jewish initiatory rite of circumcision. But the first phrase too has its scriptural precedents, even in that same chapter of John and at rather more length in the related notion of dying to sin and rising with Christ in Romans 6.

Yet perhaps inevitably there is a certain embarrassment about using such language about young children who have not yet committed deliberate sin. This may well be the reason why the prayer which up to this point has followed the Prayer Book now pursues a rather different course from that followed in 1662: 'And humbly we beseech thee to grant, that *he*, being dead unto sin, and living unto righteousness, and being buried with Christ in his death, may crucify the old man . . .'.

These two contrasting elements in traditional accounts of the sacrament certainly make understandable present tensions and conflicts of approach. On the one hand there is the desire to exclude none who wish to bring their children into the presence of God, while on the other hand there seems the equally insistent demand that the notion of baptism should be linked to personal decision and a changed life-style. Yet the answer to the dilemma, and with it to the role of the Spirit in this sacrament, is ready to hand. It is there implicitly in the mediating phrase, in the idea of adoption. Paul twice (Rom.8.15; Gal.4.6) uses the image of our being given the Spirit of adoption so that we have now become fellow sons and daughters with Christ and thus enabled like him to address his Father as '*Abba*'. At one level adoption is something immediate. It comes into effect as soon as the legal process is complete. But, as all parents of adopted children realize, the reality is rather different. In terms of relationship between parent and child, gradual process rather than instantaneous act best characterizes what occurs. For, while the declarative legal act removes any possible insecurity from the relation, the subsequent bonding can take as long as several years to complete. So likewise with baptism. Our heavenly Father has, as it were, in baptism signed the necessary legal documents, but as in adoption this marks the beginning of a story, not that about which nothing further needs to be said. Baptism marks the decisive point from which a particular story of the work of the indwelling Spirit can be told, of growth into the death and resurrection of Christ, and just as some human adoptions are more successful than others (and, frankly, some even fail), so much the same can be said about these divine stories. In baptism the promise of the activity of the Spirit has been made explicit, and the Spirit is now there addressing the baptised through the community of faith, through the parents, and in numerous other ways. But sadly, as with adoption, the loving action does not always meet with a response, and the recalcitrance of the other party involved can make any further deepening of the relationship impossible.

Even with all these qualifications it needs to be acknowledged that there will be some for whom such an analogy is deeply unsatisfactory. They will hold that to insist that God always does something in baptism is to put the emphasis in the wrong place. For them what matters is the response of faith in Christ and, though the sacrament is not to be repeated, it remains an unfruitful sign until then.

As we have already seen, one source of misunderstanding about baptism is to be found in a confusion between act and process. Another is to be found in a failure to grasp the relation between individual decision and social formation. We live in a world which so stresses individualism that for many it has become problematic how parents and godparents can possibly make promises on behalf of an infant. From there it is then but a short step to the view that the only viable model must be personal conversion and individual decision in adulthood. Yet on reflection it surely must be conceded that the difference between adult and infant baptism is more a matter of degree than kind.

All of us are agreed that we are wholly responsible for all our adult decisions. It is not for us to let ourselves off the hook, but the world is not as simple a place as we should like to believe. The young adult's confession of faith is not just a product of his own reflections; it is also a matter of such apparently extraneous factors as whether or not his . girlfriend happens to be a Christian, whether or not the local priest is a powerful personality, or whether or not the worship in the local church corresponds with his particular aesthetic sense or lack of it! Similarly with the child. The very fact that this couple has chosen to bring this child to this Christian community for baptism is a contribution to the child's final decision. It suggests attitudes of the parents which are fundamentally religious, even if they hardly ever attend church again. Some argue that this can be well catered for by services of thanksgiving, but such a view does not do justice to the parents' desire also to identify the child with the Christian community *per se* and to see their child growing up in essential sympathy with that community. Sometimes there may be little more than superstition or a desire to please the grand-parents, but with the decreasing incidence of religious conformity in our society this is less and less likely to be true. In our attitudes to baptism we need to take seriously that strange paradox of English religion, namely the very high proportion of the population who say their prayers every day, including the Lord's Prayer, and yet seldom come to church. The verbalism of so much worship as well as its forms of music play a role in deterring attendance, as does the sociological dimension of the absence of 'people like me', perhaps especially for the working classes. Such factors have in the past largely been discounted or ignored within the Church, but the sociological factor is now one with which the regular churchgoer is himself regularly faced in the present variety of forms of worship within the Church of England. For what is boring and unhelpful to one individual may be profoundly moving and inspiring to another, with the result that it is all too easy to understand, if not to approve, when some lapse because the Prayer Book is no longer available locally or because all that is available is choral services which win a ready response from Radio 3 listeners but not from Radio 1! In short, there just is no escaping the sociological factors which contribute to belief; thus, in understanding this point, with regard to infant baptism we only make explicit what is implicit in all life.

Rather than use the Prayer Book language of 'incorporation', the ASB generally prefers to speak of admission to a 'fellowship' or 'family'. Both are essentially welcoming terms, and as such are themselves welcome in stressing the unconditional character of God's love. Something has also been lost. The notion that the Spirit works our incorporation into the Body of Christ suggests something mysterious, a process which is beyond our faculties quite to understand, and that is surely exactly the case with baptism. How the Holy Spirit indwelling us is able to use the various psychological and sociological factors which help to make us the people we are is beyond our capacity to understand. All we can say is that the Spirit is at work, and that work is not just a matter of who we are and what we decide; it is also a matter of the social whole and of the Spirit at work in others besides ourselves.

To change the analogy from adoption to marriage, of course the vows publicly made in both cases are important, but these must not be stressed to the exclusion of what has led up to them and what will continue thereafter. Indeed, the couple's promise to each other represents a crucial stage, but there has been a process which led up to these promises, just as the vows are made truly effective only in the continuing story which follows. The sacramental sign should thus be seen as identifying a key moment rather than the sole locus of activity. It is the key moment precisely because a sacramental act does indeed make effective what it is trying to convey. In the case of marriage, without those promises to each other the couple would remain without obvious direction. They would be drifting, they knew not where. So likewise without the promise of parents and godparents endorsing the promise of God to bring about new life in the child, the child too would remain essentially directionless, part of no particular community, part of no particular set of social influences. Instead the child has been transferred from those of the 'world' to those of God, to the workings of the Spirit who makes the Body of Christ.

As with the marriage vows, this is only the beginning of the story. The story continues at confirmation, when the young adult ratifies the promises made on his behalf when a child. But it continues well beyond this, throughout our lives. It is here that the work of the Spirit in the sacrament of Holy Communion becomes relevant. Modern liturgies, including the ASB, have rightly restored the epiclesis, the invocation of the Holy Spirit in the consecration prayer. Though retained in the east, this practice had long fallen into desuetude in western Christendom. Some may feel such restoration to be appropriate because in the Eucharist there is some degree of analogy with what happened in the Incarnation, and this is indeed reflected in some of our communion hymns. For instance one verse of 'Lord, enthroned in heavenly splendour' contains the lines 'Though the lowliest form doth veil thee/ As of old in Bethlehem'. Others find it more helpful to extend the reference and to think of the Spirit that brooded over the waters at the dawn of creation now offering back to the Father, through us, all of the material creation. This is the way in which the offertory sentences which can be used in Rite A of the ASB are sometimes interpreted: 'Blessed are you, Lord, God of all creation. /Through your goodness we have this bread to offer, /which earth has given and human hands have made. /It will become for us the bread of life.' But, however one understands the role of matter in the Eucharist all would agree that the restoration of the epiclesis is valuable in stressing the activity of the whole Godhead in our salvation. Thus the same pattern is to be observed throughout: the Holy Spirit makes us children of God along with Jesus, though with the obvious difference that he was Son of God from the beginning, whereas we are God's children through adoption and grace.

Holy Communion unlike baptism is an oft-repeated sacrament; thus there is not likely to be the same danger of misunderstanding the sense in which the sacrament is decisive, to the exclusion of the process which follows. Indeed this 'sacrament for sinners' is a constant reminder that the process of our salvation is not complete, that repeated failure and its recognition is one of the clearest marks of what it is to be a Christian. From baptism we are formally God's sons and daughters, but the Spirit's task of making us God's children is far from easy. Yet for any progress to be possible we all need to recognize our failures and our inability to do anything about them on our own. Thus it is particularly appropriate for our stretching out our hands in needful expectancy at Holy Communion to be seen as a work of the Spirit. For it is only as we increasingly recognize our lack of self-sufficiency that we can be drawn closer into union with him who is pre-eminently God's Son.

Because the Eucharist is repeated, it cannot be misunderstood in the same way as baptism is; it is, however, still subject to different sorts of misconception. Two in particular may be mentioned. First and most obviously, because we talk of the Christian pilgrimage in terms of development and growth there is the danger of thinking that the story must always proceed positively in one direction. This notion may perhaps make people think that, if they lapse from the faith, they could never have been sincere Christians in the first place. The experience both of the saints and of human life in general can be used to refute this charge. From the experience of the former we learn that sanctity, so far from bringing an awareness of progress, actually brings an increased sense of one's distance from the goal and continued need for God's aid. It is precisely this which makes humility such a characteristic feature of sanctity. Equally in ordinary life, middle-age can often bring with it a dulling of the enthusiasms of youth and a greater materialism, though prompted by the best of motives in concern for the welfare and future of one's family.

The other possible misunderstanding is the confining of the work of the Holy Spirit too narrowly to conscious response. It is all too easy to suggest that what really and alone matters is the type of attitude of penitence, attention and commitment with which we approach the service, as though God is concerned only with our rational faculties rather than with our whole selves. Here surely a major positive merit of the charismatic movement must be acknowledged, for it has unequivocally drawn attention to the way in which we are larger than our conscious selves. Phenomena such as glossolalia or demonstrable emotion in charismatic worship offer the Church a salutary reminder that holiness is a matter of the whole personality, not just of the intellect. Thus the fact that a communicant is unaware on a particular occasion of the effect of God upon him should in no way lessen his belief in God's transforming presence. When we recall how much of our personality operates at other than a totally conscious level, there ceases to be any contradiction in the notion of our responding to the work of the Spirit without our being aware of it. This realization is seen to be part of the normal pattern of things. Such talk should not be taken as implying any necessary interference with the individual's personal dignity and freedom. For, though our subconscious and unconscious are not immediately under our control, they are to a great extent mediately so. That is to say, much of our response at that level is a function of our conscious motivations and desires. We create our own hidden psychology by our conscious decisions and by the aspirations which we form. Of course we cannot be held responsible for what happens to us as children, nor should we think of people forming deliberate intentions to suppress certain aspects of themselves into the unconscious. It is not that easily under our control, but the attitude which we adopt to our existing conscious desires and feelings is under our control; it is often precisely because of our failure to deal honestly and responsibly with them that the resultant suppression into the unconscious occurs. For example, it is precisely because we refuse to face certain facts about ourselves that these eventually get buried into our unconscious and are then projected as faults onto others. An instance of this would be malicious identification of sexual sin in others. Since, however, the notion of the unconscious is so heavily connected with Freud and with the largely negative role which he assigned to it, we need also to recall the very different treatment which it receives from many other psychologists, including Jung.

Whether Jung is right in his notion of the collective unconscious need not detain us here. Of great importance is the way in which recognition of this life larger and richer than ourselves can also save us from the false alternative which is so often drawn, in respect of the sacraments, between conscious response and no response at all. Very often the communicant, despite careful preparation, may feel quite unaware of the presence of Christ. This does not mean that God is absent, or that the Spirit is not working unseen in the unconscious to bring him into closer relation and conformity to his Saviour, who is the Son *par excellence*. This explains why questions of liturgy cannot just be reduced to those of language and meaning; it also provides yet another element in the justification of the epiclesis. The Spirit will be using a whole range of triggers, non-verbal as well as verbal, to bring us into relation with the sacramental Christ, a relation of which we may or may not be aware at the time.

Furthermore, even our conscious response should not be seen as solely rational. The stress in our society on individual responsibility and rationality can be overdone, especially when it makes worshippers feel guilty because their attention regularly wanders during services. By contrast we need to insist that this wandering of attention can indeed sometimes be the work of the Spirit. The communicant for example who passes almost the entire service in a dream, who is unable to answer the question what hymns were sung, is not thereby failing to respond. Dreams too are one manner of response. In fact one suspects that liturgical scholars have not always been as astute as they might be in realizing how many minds wander during a service and how correspondingly important it becomes for the mind to have something rich in meaning and allusion on which to focus when it returns to the words. An illustration of this would be the difficulty created for some by the adoption in many modern liturgies, including the ASB (Rite A, sec.85), of the phrase 'Lord, I am not worthy to receive you' as the response to the invitation to communion. A bare statement of fact has replaced the rich allusion of the original, 'Lord, I am not worthy to have you come under my roof' (Matt.8.8), with its implicit suggestion of God's coming to dwell in the heart of the believer (cf. John 14.23). In other words, even when we are thinking only about the conscious response, we should be on our guard against too narrow a conception of the Spirit's operations. Although Christ in accordance with his own institution of the sacrament is made present through the bread and wine in a distinct, God-given way, the Spirit conveys the effects of that presence in manifold ways, ways as manifold as the depth and variety of human beings themselves.

So far we have concentrated in this chapter rather narrowly on the two sacraments of baptism and communion. This was meant in no way to suggest that the transforming power of the Spirit leading us on the path to holiness was only to be found there, only that the Spirit's role in these sacraments needed most discussion because most often misunderstood. The other obvious area of misunderstanding lies in the claim that the Spirit is operating in the Church as a whole, guiding its destiny with the same sort of care as is assigned to particular individuals. Indeed it is sometimes insisted that the word 'Church' can be written only with small letters, precisely because God's relation is with individuals and their call to repentance and commitment, not with the institution as such.

Any intention to set the Church over against its individual members is quite wrong. Equally wrong is any suggestion that we can exist as individuals without acknowledging our interdependence in what is necessarily social, namely the Body of Christ. That capital letter does not imply a claim to perfection, for the Church is (like its members) on a pilgrimage, on a pattern of growth directed by the Spirit; just as our failures do not disprove the working of the Spirit within us, neither do the failings of the institutional Church. Indeed stress on the role of the Spirit can sometimes free the institutional Church to become more aware of its imperfections. Arguably this is what happened in the change between the first draft of *Lumen Gentium*, the Second Vatican Council's Constitution on the Church, with its static image of the Church as 'the mystical Body of Christ', and the final version which sees the Church as a community on the move under the dynamic guidance of the Spirit.

Certainly interpretations of the Nicene Creed have almost always closely linked the article on the Church and that on the Holy Spirit. For example in the Middle Ages Albert the Great, the teacher of Aquinas, could write, 'I believe in the Holy Spirit not in himself alone, as the previous article states, but I believe in him also as far as his work is concerned, which is to make the Church holy'. As with the individual, so with the corporate Church, holiness is what the Church aspires to, rather than what it already has; thus when we affirm belief in 'one, holy, catholic and apostolic Church', we are affirming that towards which the Spirit is leading us rather than what we already possess, though as with baptism there is also a clear sense in which it already fully exists in the plans and intentions of God.

Among the great merits of the charismatic movement is the way in which it takes seriously the capacity of the Holy Spirit to transform our lives in the here and now. The charismatic movement itself is surely in part a protest against over-rigid ecclesiastical structures, which embody a claim that the Spirit can be 'dispensed', yet not in such a way as fundamentally to transform either the individual or the community. Nevertheless, if the call to holiness on the part of the Church is taken seriously by charismatics, they sometimes show much less awareness of what it means to affirm its unity and catholicity. In this they are by no means alone, and we have already touched on this point towards the end of Chapter 3.

One of the continuing tragedies of Christianity is the recurring temptation to assume that unity must mean uniformity. In part this may have been due to the western Church's tendency to assume that the divine unity could be guaranteed only by minimizing the distinctions between the Persons of the Trinity. The Church was then required to reflect the same kind of model; but fortunately theologians like Jürgen Moltmann are requiring us to think again, as at a more popular level is the enormous popularity of the Andrei Rublev icon with its image of the three Persons as the three angels of Mamre (cf. Genesis 18), united in a circle of love that cannot be broken. Much more insidious has been the natural human arrogance of us all in supposing that everyone is like ourselves and must therefore be expected to conform to that likeness. In fact it is harder to think of a more decisive factor in explaining the failure of so much missionary activity at home and abroad than this refusal to consider that for other cultures and other individuals very different ways of worship and practice may be appropriate. Indeed one can say for certain that if the more emotional type of charismatic experience were to be taken as the norm for all Christians, then the failure of the Church to affect large parts of humanity is guaranteed. The display of emotion is just so unnatural to some individuals that to demand such worship of them would be to ask of them a living hell. This is of course strong language, but this is intended only as one instance of a more general phenomenon. Our remarks apply equally to any vicar who supposes that choral mattins with intellectual sermon is the norm for all and that Christians in the parish who fail to attend should be blamed for failing to do so. The richness and diversity of human personalities is a divine gift and ought to be treated as such. So far as the activity of the Holy Spirit is concerned, this realization will mean that we shall envisage the Spirit as operating in diverse ways which correspond to this diversity.

It may well be objected that there can be too much diversity; otherwise there cannot be unity at all. There may be some truth in this contention, but the amount of uniformity required is frequently exaggerated, with the uniformity of a particular grouping or even of a particular parish being simply projected onto the Church at large. Yet none of this can really undermine the basic truth of the objection, that there must be something that holds the Church together. The Bible, the liturgy and the historic formularies all play their role, and among them a special position belongs to the creeds. This in no way suggests their superiority to the Bible or liturgy; indeed it would seem obvious that they are incapable of inspiring us in the same way. That does not lessen their significance in providing an agreed framework of interpretation without which the Christian community would be unable to maintain its distinctive identity.

We need to take account of the fact that there are in the Church some who challenge the traditional interpretation of the creeds. However, such challengers cannot realistically assume that their positions must be considered on a par with the common faith of the Church. Perhaps the best way of conceiving their role is to suggest that they must perceive of themselves as prophets on the margins of what is believed, and who are called to turn those margins into central perceptions of the faithful, if it is really the Spirit's will. Many such reformers are of course impatient and want change immediately, but if only they would take seriously the fact that their views are not yet those of the community, they would be much less disturbing to the sense of the Church's unity which conservative and radical alike wish to preserve. If the radicals need reassurance about the possibility of change in the Church, they need only reflect on the changing understanding of the nature of hell. No longer among Anglicans is it generally believed to entail an eternity of torment.

If the type of unity which the Spirit works to effect in the Church needs to be rethought, so does the nature of the catholicity which the Spirit is working to create. The ecumenical movement has made us all much more aware of what we have to learn from other denominations. Indeed the present charismatic movement, which seems to have had among its antecedents the Holiness Movement in American Protestantism at the turn of the century, has itself permeated what it must have regarded as the most unpromising denomination of them all, namely Roman Catholicism. Unfortunately with that open ecumenical spirit has also gone a decline in historical awareness and in a sense of the Church's catholicity stretching back over time as well as across denominational barriers. Thus within Anglicanism its classic works of previous centuries are left almost wholly unread at theological colleges and when there is added to this the very large numbers coming forward for ordination who are first generation practising Anglicans, the Church of England's current crisis of identity becomes more readily explicable. The community jumps from the twentieth century to the first without very much sense of what has gone between, or if it has such sense, no awareness that the centuries in between have also been an informed part of the Spirit's continuing work. Ironically, even that western denomination which was in the past most concerned about its continuing historical identity displays now a very different face. Even many Roman Catholic theologians write only with reference to the Bible, while the laity now have less awareness of the generations of saints who have made their church what it is.

Yet we surely have much to learn from the past. One seldom finds for example any charismatic meditating on the gift of tongues enjoyed in the congregation of Edward Irving in the London of the 1830s and in the essentially Catholic forms of worship in the Catholic Apostolic Church which derives from Irving's work. Again, uninformed contempt for the Middle Ages is sometimes heard; yet they share with the present charismatic movement a concern for prophecy. One need only think of Joachim of Fiore's prediction of the future age of the Spirit and the enormous influence exercised by that prediction, especially on radical Franciscans and also on society as a whole, even beyond the Middle Ages. The point may be put more generally: the visionary ideals of the Middle Ages as reflected in the new religious orders, or the seriousness of purpose which characterised the Reformation, cannot but offer a severe reprimand to the Church of our own day which, though less corrupt and of gentler spirit, even within the charismatic movement itself seldom displays the sheer verve and enthusiasm of such a past.

However, one difficulty in such appeals to the past is the feeling that the Spirit must be associated with progress, leading us into all truth; consequently it is felt that appeal to the past must necessarily be a retrograde step. Ironically this is an assumption which plagues even those who are prepared to appeal to the past. A recent instance would be the way in which those in favour of the ordination of women frequently refer to the move as a work of the Spirit, while seldom, if ever, do those against this development describe their action in similar terms. Presumably the difficulty lies in the use of the dynamic images of the Spirit to advocate apparently staying where you are. Irrespective of the rights or wrongs of that particular issue, the conservative needs to take seriously the fact that the re-appropriation of the past is never exactly the same on any two occasions. The particular concerns which we bring to some past document or event make us read it in new ways; thus the appeal to the past can be just as new and fresh in its insights for our own generation as appeal to current ideas or to practices elsewhere in the contemporary Church. Also we need to bear in mind that, just as the individual's path towards holiness is not uniform but may regress, so too may that of the Church. This may seem too obvious to need mention, but it is not so often noted that the past can provide the basis of a critique of the Church's present. The sixteenth-century Reformation itself was not simply an attempt to return to the purity of the New Testament. Augustine in particular, who lived long after the main lines of the New Testament canon were established, was used as the basis for a critique of contemporary sixteenth-century theology. Likewise one of the major factors in the changes of the forms of worship which have taken place in the past twenty years is an awareness of the extent to which the worship of the first millennium differed from that of the second.

Such comments as these make all the more acute an issue hitherto not explicitly raised in this chapter, namely the question of truth. How can we believe that the Spirit will guide the Church into all truth when its history has been so complicated and at times shameful? Our chapter specifically on 'The Spirit of Truth' will draw attention to the numerous ways in which the term might be meant, and the implications of its different uses. Certainly we must be aware of the way in which our own society is dominated by an empirical conception of knowledge; our fellow Christians are thus under pressure to attempt empirical 'proof' through experience of God's activity in our midst. This is not to deny the validity of such experience, only to reassure those who cannot believe it or are unable to find it in their own lives. We have to be careful not to decry the sort of confirmation which comes from the conviction that their own understanding of faith makes coherent and meaningful sense of their lives.

This is of course to concede something to subjectivism, but only in the sense that not everyone has the time or the opportunity to examine in depth the complex questions of the foundations of our knowledge. (Nor is it the task of this Doctrine Commission to look at that issue!) Instead this chapter must end with the conviction that if the Spirit's activity in the Church is to be understood in terms of guidance, then this guidance must be leading the Church into what is more than merely subjective truth. Again and again individual members of the Body are being addressed, and although this provides no guarantee that the majority will listen, the patience and persistence of God in the address surely makes it likely that they will. At times the initial impetus seems to come more from outside the Church than within, as we see in the recent examples of the status of women and environmental issues. All this shows the freedom of the Spirit to blow where it wills, a dynamic freedom that blows pre-eminently within the Church and whose very dynamism in both individual and community we ignore at our peril.

Chapter 6
The Spirit and power

In the preceding chapter we concentrated on the inner life of the Church and on the work of the Spirit in relation to the sacraments; in the course of that chapter some use was made of dynamic images in our discussion of the Spirit's influence. As this new chapter's title suggests, we shall now take up these dynamic images, develop some of the ideas relating to them and consider some of the problems to which the association of power with the Spirit gives rise. These problems affect variously our own individual lives as Christians, the Church as an institution, and the structures of the secular world. The normal evocations of power (and perhaps some of the instinctive expectations with regard to it) as control, dominance, conquest, manipulation and dismissal of weakness will be challenged. We shall be taken once again to the nerve-centre of Christian faith, namely to the death and passion of Christ, for the cross is the paradigm of the way in which Jesus exercises power. Power does not necessarily consist in ability to effect control. There is a power of love which transforms and liberates; it was this power which, to the eye of faith, was evident, active and triumphant on the cross.

God's power, Jesus and the spirit

In the scriptures there are many references to God's power, both in creation and towards the people of Israel. In the story of the exodus we read a most outstanding sign of God's power in delivering Israel from Egypt. The whole narrative is studded with accounts of miraculous power: miracles before Pharaoh, the crossing of the Red Sea, the pillar of cloud, the manna in the desert, the water from the rock. In their song to God, Moses and the people of Israel ask, 'Who is like thee, majestic in holiness, terrible in glorious deeds, doing wonders?' (Exod. 15.11).

Yet we must face the fact that some of the instances in the scriptures in which God's power is believed to be at work strike us as arbitrary and cause many people in today's culture to feel ill at ease. For instance, chastisement with blindness is a divine judgement in the Old Testament and the New (2 Kgs 6.18; Acts 13.11); striking with leprosy is found in 2 Kings 5.27 and making dumb in Luke 1.20. Further, immunity to poisonous snake bites was provided by divine power when Moses lifted up the brazen serpent in the wilderness and when Paul shook into the fire the snake which had fastened upon him (Num. 21.9; Acts 28.3ff.). The Johannine Jesus refers to this apparent arbitrariness in an enigmatic passage in which he explicitly associates the Spirit with this feature, 'The wind blows where it wills, and you hear the sound of it, but you do not know whence it comes or whither it goes; so it is with every one who is born of the Spirit' (John 3.8).

Some of the passages on which we have just drawn come from the Acts of the Apostles, in which the Spirit is depicted as being powerfully at work in the young Church. In the Acts it is made quite clear that power in the Spirit is always the free gift of God, and never the result either of merit to be rewarded or of consensus choice or of the assuaging of demand. The narrative concerning Simon Magus (Acts 8.9–24) is particularly revealing in this connection. The account distinguishes between the (legitimate) demand that a hunger for God be satisfied, and a desire to take to oneself this particular and unique power. When the power of the Spirit is described as given, in response to the prayer of Peter and John for the believers 'through the laying on of the apostles' hands' (v.18), its effects are such that they go beyond the 'signs and great miracles' (v.13b) which had previously amazed Simon Magus. He had clearly regarded the ability to invoke the gift of the Holy Spirit as a power, and therefore as a commodity, which surpassed any acts or wonders practised or seen by him. His request to purchase this power (v. 19) is sharply rejected by Peter, 'Your silver perish with you, because you thought you could obtain the gift of God with money' (v. 20). The force of the story is less about sin and more about the nature of the Spirit's power, which is to be invoked only as a gift of God. The emphasis lies on the given nature of the Spirit's empowering; this is not to be won or earned or bought. Turning to the letters of Paul we find precisely the same emphasis. When he was faced with questions about his personal apostolic authority, he insisted that the source of this authority lay in the gift of God; his apostleship was 'not from men nor through man, but through Jesus Christ and God the Father' (Gal. 1.1); his call was 'by the will of God' (1 Cor. 1.1); and his preaching is 'in demonstration of the Spirit and power' (1 Cor. 2.4b). His power in the Spirit came as divine gift, as did also his converts' life in the Spirit, 'It is God who establishes us with you in Christ, and has commissioned us; he has put his seal upon us and given us his Spirit in our hearts as a guarantee' (2 Cor. 1.21f.).

Further, Paul clearly believed his gospel, to be 'in power and in the Holy Spirit' (1 Thess. 1.5). We may thus properly speak of the power of the gospel. This phrase expresses both the quality of power which the Spirit gives and also the means by which it is given. At the heart of this power of the gospel lies the experience of being empowered by the Spirit.

Jesus himself was empowered by the Spirit at his baptism. The Spirit immediately drove him out into the wilderness (Mark 1.12) and no doubt sustained him in his temptations here. It was 'in the power of the Spirit' that he returned to Galilee (Luke 4.14). His sermon in the synagogue at Nazareth gives us to understand that his preaching and mighty works were done in the power of the Spirit (Luke 4.16ff.). Among his mighty works was the casting out of demons; the first three evangelists see the overcoming of occult evil powers as one of the most significant elements in Jesus' ministry and as one which reveals Jesus' unique authority. Already, in Jesus' public ministry we can see two sharply contrasted tendencies: on the one hand there is the exercise of authority, evidence of his being in control, the successful performance of his mission, his work understood in terms of defeat for Satan, who was seen falling from heaven; on the other hand there is also the experience of human weakness, on occasions of failure (e.g. in his home country), in the refusal either to perform cures to order or to coerce acceptance of his message, or in his preference (on occasions) for hidden anonymity. These two contrasted tendencies, of authority and of self-chosen limitation, have to be held together and understood to be contained within the power of Spirit who equipped Jesus for his work and ministry. When we turn to the Lord's passion, the tension between these two contrasted tendencies becomes more acute. On the one hand there is the note, particularly to be found in John's gospel, that the death of Jesus is to be understood in terms of achievement (John 19.30) and triumph (John 16.33), and in all the gospels the tone of authority is to be heard unmistakeably at the Last Supper, at Jesus' arrest and at his trial. On the other hand there is weakness, failure, shame and dereliction, in the passion narratives in all four gospels. The use of glory in John's gospel holds these two emphases together: the glory of God (and that includes the power and self-revelation of God) is to be found at its most powerful and clearest in the shame and failure of the cross. In the light of the resurrection, or through the lens of the resurrection, we see Gethsemane and Calvary to be at one and the same time both the most absolute self-giving, self-emptying beyond human conceiving and also the most absolute vindication, victoriously effecting new life of a kind beyond human conceiving.

Jesus and his passion represent for us the touchstone of the power of which we speak, the means by which it is given, its effects when poured out, and its confrontation with other concepts of power abroad in the world. Christ's action on the cross involved both submission and surrender, two quite distinct categories. He submitted to his Father, and, as a consequence, he surrendered to mortality and humiliation. By contrast, the resurrection involved empowering and being justified. This resurrection power is consequential upon, not accidental to, the act of

Christ on the cross. The submission to the will of the Father, which involves for the Son free acceptance of vulnerability to both shame and mortality, is in organic spiritual relationship to the victorious power of the resurrection in the triumphant overcoming of corruptible flesh and in the glorious vindication of the one shamed.

The scandal of the cross, and power in Christian lives

It has to be said that, in some passages within the New Testament and also not infrequently in subsequent Christian thinking and hymnody, starkly triumphalist language has been used with regard to the earthly ministry of Jesus, to his death and resurrection. In the final chapter of the previous report (*We Believe in God*, pp. 116ff.) we tried to do justice both to Christ's weakness and vulnerability and also to his sovereignty and victory, all of which belong to God. It is a veritable scandal, an offence or stumbling block, that both these emphases are so deeply rooted in Christian faith.

At the heart of this Christian faith stands the cross of Christ. Thus we should expect the means by which the Spirit works to be distinguishable from the source and effect of other kinds of power. Particularly in Paul's epistles we find the cross of Christ (1 Cor. 1.23ff.), the vocation of Christians (1 Cor. 1.26ff.), the Christian life itself (1 Cor. 4.8ff. and 2 Cor. 12.1ff.) all presented in starkly paradoxical language about power and weakness. He insists that the Spirit's power is to be discovered and demonstrated in the context of human weakness freely accepted and offered to God. Indeed, it would be no exaggeration to say that in the first four chapters of his first letter to the Corinthians Paul is revaluing the nature of power. One of his most daring assertions occurs in this passage: 'I decided to know nothing among you except Jesus Christ and him crucified. And I was with you in weakness and in much fear and trembling; and my speech and my message were not in plausible words of wisdom, but in demonstration of the Spirit and power, that your faith might not rest in the wisdom of men but in the power of God' (1 Cor. 2.2ff.). In these verses he makes explicit the connection between, on the one hand, the power of the Spirit and the Christian's acceptance of human vulnerability and, on the other hand, the power which flows from Christ's own acceptance of human vulnerability and its overcoming in his resurrection. Christ's raising from the dead is of the same order as the transformation of the disciples, through the Spirit, from a defeated rabble into a dynamic and centrally bonded group of witnesses speaking with authority. Acknowledgement of, even willing surrender to, the reality of human weakness is the only condition for our receiving the power of the Spirit, provided that this acknowledgement and this surrender are accompanied by a total commitment of faith to the God and Father of our Lord Jesus Christ.

Already this treatment of power and weakness in the ministry of Jesus, in his death and resurrection and in the earliest Christians' experience of the Spirit has led us to wider consideration about the nature of the Christian life. We have already remarked that in the early chapters of 1 Corinthians Paul is re-evaluating the nature of power; in so doing, he is laying the foundation for his treatment of the corporate life of the Church in chapters 12 to 14. Elsewhere in this study we have referred to particular elements in this treatment (e.g. pp. 168ff.). Here we note that the Church's experience of the Spirit's power goes hand in hand not with the search for ascendancy, but with submission to God, even the acceptance of the reality of the cross as its way of being.

In the middle of the passage from Paul's first letter to the Corinthians, to which we have just referred, we find the anatomy of charity in chapter 13. Once again we find a markedly Christocentric reference. That chapter with its picture of suffering, gentle, indestructible love reminds irresistibly of the figure of the gospels and must surely have been shaped by Paul's reflection on the traditions which he had received concerning 'the Son of God, who loved me and gave himself for me' (Gal. 2.20). 'Love is patient and kind; love is not jealous or boastful; it is not arrogant or rude. Love does not insist on its own way; it is not irritable or resentful; it does not rejoice at wrong, but rejoices in the right. Love bears all things, believes all things, hopes all things, endures all things' (1 Cor. 13. 4ff.).

In this picture there is no space for self-aggrandizement, or for self-assertion at the expense of others. The fruit of the Spirit in its various elements, 'love, joy, peace, patience, kindness, goodness, faithfulness, gentleness, self-control' (Gal. 5.22f.), exhibits the power which flows from submission to God in Christ and from self-abnegation. This fruit is contrasted with the various works of the flesh (Gal. 5.19ff.; see also Col. 3.5,8) which all are evidence of self-assertion and of a distorted use of power. The Christocentric element remains: life in the Spirit and in the body of Christ is progressively shaped by conformity, through obedience and suffering, to the image and likeness of Jesus Christ. Wherever they are found, the various elements in the fruit of the Spirit are to be attributed to God's creative generosity, for when the Church's members are true to their calling, this fruit is particularly capable of being evoked, nurtured, sustained, made concrete, shaped and given identity by the Spirit of Christ within the body of the Church.

Empowering by the spirit

We have already perceived that acknowledged weakness is a continuing condition of the Spirit's empowering. Now we identify some of the means by which this power is communicated. First in importance among the means by which the power of the Spirit is received is the experience of God's forgiveness. Forgiveness and restoration to fellowship with God are conditional on repentance. On the day of Pentecost Peter preached to the crowd, 'Repent and be baptized every one of you in the name of Jesus Christ for the forgiveness of your sins; and you shall receive the gift of the Holy Spirit' (Acts 2.38). Peter's message was in direct continuity with the preaching of Jesus during his earthly ministry, 'Repent, and believe in the gospel' (Mark 1.15) and with his ministry of forgiveness and restoration to physical and spiritual wholeness: 'My son, your sins are forgiven . . . Rise . . . and walk' (Mk. 2.5,9). This forgiveness is closely linked with the climax of Jesus' ministry, on the cross. Through the crucified and risen Lord God dispenses the Spirit and empowers the disciples to exercise, through this gift of the Holy Spirit, that same ministry of God's forgiveness which they had received from Jesus himself (John 20.19ff.). This forgiveness, which is inseparably associated with Jesus' death, is repeatedly to be made available afresh within the fellowship of the Eucharist (Matt. 26.28). Further, Paul in his preaching and teaching insists that God's forgiveness through Christ is something given, the acceptance of which opens the channel of empowering for new life (e.g. Acts 13.39; 26.18; Rom. 4.7; Col. 1.14).

The verse from Peter's speech on the day of Pentecost to which we have just referred links baptism with repentance as one of the primary means by which the reality of forgiveness is reinforced by the gift of the Spirit. In the preceding chapter we discussed the significance of baptism in this regard. For the present we note that baptism marks for Christian believers a radical shift from destructive self-centredness and isolation into a belonging to the Christian fellowship which is no mere coming together of like-minded individuals, but is a condition of the new life itself. 'By one Spirit we were all baptized into one body . . . and all were made to drink of one Spirit' (1 Cor. 12.13). The power of the Spirit effects in the believer incorporation into a living body, the living body of Christ. Integration into the saving events of the cross and resurrection and integration into the body of Christ, the living fellowship of the Spirit, are one and the same act.

Within the New Testament we find other means whereby the power of the Spirit is given and received. Important among them is preaching; this is discussed as a means by which the Spirit acts in power. Moreover the power of the Holy Spirit may be invoked in various ways; particular examples are the laying on of hands, the handkerchief of Paul, even the shadow of Peter. Common to all these means, to forgiveness and baptism as well, is a category which is the prior channel of the Spirit's power and which is at the centre of the New Testament's account of power: namely, that of believing. All four gospels mark Jesus' own insistence on believing as the only condition within which his works of power can take place, and even Jesus was restricted in his ministry by lack of faith in his hearers (Mark 6.5f.). The importance attached by the early Church to believing as a condition of receiving the Spirit and as an authoritative channel of the power of the Spirit can be gauged from the narrative in Acts 10 and 11, which records Peter's extension of baptism to the Gentiles. This extension is accredited by the initially sceptical church at Jerusalem on the grounds that the Spirit had been given through their believing. Peter preaches to the Gentile Cornelius, ' "To him (Jesus Christ) all the prophets bear witness that every one who believes in him receives forgiveness of sins through his name." While Peter was still saying this, the Holy Spirit fell on all who heard the word' (Acts 10. 43f.). 'If then', Peter later demanded of the church at Jerusalem, 'God gave the same gift to them as he gave to us when we believed in the Lord Jesus Christ, who was I that I could withstand God?' (Acts 11.17).

Believing is indeed a condition of receiving the Spirit: yet at the same time the New Testament asserts, and we are bound to assert, that believing is itself the gift of God and the effect of the Spirit's work in us. Within believing we include both trust in the object of belief and also faith understood as the capacity to receive and to appropriate God's gifts. In both respects this believing is the gift of God to us; 'No one can say "Jesus is Lord" except by the Holy Spirit' (1 Cor. 12.3); 'By grace you have been saved through faith; and this is not your own doing, it is the gift of God' (Eph. 2.8).

Here we meet one of the major difficulties in speaking about the Spirit and power, that of distinguishing cause from effect. The problem could be stated in terms of the need to distinguish both what the power of the Spirit has effected in the lives of the Christian fellowship, and the means by which that power has been received. Both the New Testament and also the tradition and experience of the Church indicate that believing gives openness to or recovery of the power of the Holy Spirit; yet it is the power of the Holy Spirit which enables people to believe. Further reflection makes us aware that these distinctions are, in a sense, unreal: insofar as the power of God at work in the world through the Spirit is that power which was at work both on the cross and in the Easter garden, cause and effect are one; obverse and reverse of the same unimaginable action.

We have already touched on the ethical consequences of life in the Spirit, both for the individual believer and for the Christian community. In Paul's epistle to the Galatians we find an emphasis on the Spirit both as the gift of God, empowering disciples to realize their sonship, and also as God's summons to a totally Christlike obedience. 'God sent forth his Son . . . so that we might receive adoption as sons. And because you are sons, God has sent the Spirit of his Son into our hearts, crying, "Abba! Father!" ' (Gal. 4. 4ff.). That gift of the Spirit does not relieve us of the responsibility of living the life of faith which is the consequence of our sonship. Thus the Spirit is also that power by which believers are summoned to regulate their lives. 'If we live by the Spirit, let us also walk by the Spirit' (Gal. 5.25).

If as believers we find our new life in Christ who for us was crucified and raised again, then we also live in the Spirit who reveals that same Christ to us and empowers us with his salvation. The Spirit works within us both in creating our faith and also in requiring substance to our life as Christians. By substance we mean a certain quality of being and behaviour, which is recognizably Christlike. If the kind of power attributable to the Spirit is to be recognizable as power in any sense at all in which the word has common currency, then in some form or other it must have discernible effect. Thus the distinctive quality of 'power' in the Christian life is found in identification with Christ's way of self-emptying, self-sacrifice, suffering in solidarity with all victims of human hurt or natural affliction, and self-oblation to the will of the Father. For out of that will come the self-evidencing authority of righteousness, truth and love. Ultimately, the power that the Spirit gives is the power of love. It was as they beheld his wounds that the risen Christ breathed his Spirit upon his disciples (John 20.20ff.).

All of this may seem a far cry from the actual behaviour of most Christians, in Church history and today. Christians are not always conspicuously remarkable for discernible growth in Christlike qualities. Moreover, the Church as an institution has only too frequently exercised power in ways fundamentally at variance with the insights on which we have been concentrating. This uncomfortable fact does not diminish the strength and urgency of the New Testament's exhortation to us 'to become what we are' in Christ. It does, however, set a humbling paradox, between our potential and what is apparent, at the centre of anything we say about the power of the Spirit in Church. One aspect of this same humbling paradox is the fact that the Church lives both in the present and in a condition of eschatological hope. (We shall return to this theme in our final chapter.) We have the assurance that, both individually and corporately, 'We all . . . are being changed into his (Christ's) likeness from one degree of glory to another', and Paul adds, 'This comes from the Lord who is the Spirit' (2 Cor. 3.18).

There is another anomalous element which we note with regard to our new life in the Spirit: from New Testament times the consequences of corporate living by this power of the Spirit have been found both in extraordinary manifestations and the life of the commonplace, the prosaic and the everyday. The pastoral epistles stress the latter (e.g. 2 Tim. 1.7; Tit. 3.1ff.). In his first letter to the Corinthians Paul makes a distinction between gifts such as miracles, healings, tongues and interpretations, on the one hand, and the undramatic, mundane, humdrum gifts such as helping and administering, on the other (1 Cor. 12.28ff.). This point may be seen even more clearly in that other early discussion of spiritual gifts, in Romans 12; here Paul lists prophecy, service, teaching, exhorting, contributing, giving aid, performing acts of mercy (Rom. 12.6ff.). It seems as if Paul is casting his eye around the Christian community and making sure that no one's contribution is overlooked. Moreover, it is 'the same Spirit . . . the same Lord . . . the same God' (1 Cor. 12.4ff.) who inspires all these gifts in every member of the body. Paul is no doubt attempting to forestall any suggestion that the Spirit may be given in greater measure to some who have certain gifts, and in lesser measure to others with certain other gifts. He emphasizes that the weaker and humbler members, whose gifts may seem nothing to boast about, are all the more essential to the effective working of the body of Christ, just as the 'unpresentable' parts of the human body are modestly concealed, even though they have a particular vital part to play in the healthy function of the whole body (1 Cor. 12.14ff.).

Nevertheless the tradition of 'signs and wonders' following the Spirit in the life of the Christian community is a continuous one, the strength of which is of very great importance not least in the life of today's Church, which has discovered afresh these phenomena of power in the Spirit. We touched on them in Chapter 3 of this study, and it is to a consideration of these phenomena that we now return.

Signs and wonders: good and evil power

The charismatic movement as a whole has given prominence to what might be called the ecstatic gifts (tongues, interpretation, prophecy) in worship. Certain strains within the movement, however, have emphasized the more dynamic phenomena of healing, exorcism and miraculous words of knowledge in evangelism. Many people find these subjects puzzling and problematical; in our treatment of them we have borne in mind a number of general considerations: for instance, paranormal phenomena of various sorts are found in many cultures in most periods of history; they are by no means exclusive to the Bible, to the history of the Christian Church, or to the modern charismatic movement.

Moreover, there is no consensus among Christian people today about the existence of demons and therefore none about the meaning of possession and exorcism. This fact is bound to affect any evaluation of some of the biblical narratives and of some modern claims, but critical attention and assessment is not to be identified with faithlessness or with a claim to superior insight. We sit under scripture in order to discern the word of God, and we attend to modern claims in order to do proper justice to them.

Against this background we consider the claim to engage in 'power evangelism'. This claim presumably echoes Paul's boast in the epistle to the Romans that Christ had worked through him to win obedience from the Gentiles 'by word and deed, by the power of signs and wonders, by the power of the Holy Spirit' (Rom. 15.18f.). These phenomena are said to be very widespread today. Many Christian people join with religious sceptics in frank disbelief of such claims. For some, indeed, in a post-Hume era, belief in the miraculous is neither necessary nor fitting. However, this *a priori* rejection of the miraculous is by no means the general view in the Church; therefore, those who do not share it, but rather believe in the God and Father of our Lord Jesus Christ as the God of miracle, are called carefully to evaluate claims made in this area. Running through Christian history is evidence both that signs and wonders do occur, and also that seeking a sign is not an imperative of the gospel. In fact many passages in the gospels actively discourage believers from making such a demand (e.g. Matt. 16.1ff.; John 4.48). We properly enquire about biblical attitudes to these phenomena and about the way in which these attitudes bear upon our understanding of the Spirit as power.

As we noted near the beginning of this chapter, God gave a most outstanding sign of power in delivering Israel from Egypt; the exodus itself was, we read, preceded by many remarkable signs and wonders. In the New Testament Jesus is understood as effecting a new exodus. Nearly a third of the gospels is occupied with miracles, from Jesus' miraculous conception to his miraculous resurrection. He was indeed, as Peter affirmed at Pentecost, 'a man attested to you by God with mighty works and wonders and signs which God did through him in your midst' (Acts 2.22). The prophecy of Joel was fulfilled, and at Pentecost the Spirit was poured out on the followers of Jesus.

The sequel, according to the Acts of the Apostles, was a remarkable collection of signs and wonders, given not for show but for furtherance of the gospel. In the New Testament there is both confidence and reticence with regard to signs and wonders, which were perceived to accompany the ministry of Jesus and the early life of the Church. There is no doubt that God gave signs, and there is a sense of wonder at God's self-disclosure. Though references to signs are frequent in the New Testament, only a few of these references present signs and wonders as authenticating evangelism (e.g. Rom. 15.19, to which we have already referred; Heb. 2.4; and, from the longer ending of Mark – Mark 16.20). Only infrequently are these signs brought before the readers as palpable marks that the Lord is with his disciples. They are indications of his presence and power; the New Testament is clear about that, and so is much contemporary experience, but that is not the principal emphasis in the New Testament.

In this study we have frequently mentioned our Christocentric framework of reference. Precisely this point needs to be made with regard to the miracles done by Jesus. They are mighty acts performed by Jesus primarily in order to show who he is. The fourth gospel is specifically designed to show this; the miracles there are not included to make the reader feel good, nor to amaze the unbelievers, nor even to meet human need. Their function is to glorify God and to bear witness to the Son. In all the signs in John's gospel the act and the interpretation combine to bring the spotlight on Jesus; they indicate who he is and what he can do for humanity. Despite John 14.12 they are not primarily models for his disciples to follow.

Further, signs and wonders do not necessarily come from God. They did not in the case of those worked by Pharaoh's magicians; nor in that of those worked by Jewish wonder-workers who performed exorcisms in the days of Jesus (see Matt. 12.24ff.); nor in that of Simon Magus (as we noted earlier), who backed his amazing claims with amazing cures (Acts 8.11). Within the New Testament there are warnings to disciples and believers not to be carried away by signs; we note particularly, 'False Christs and false prophets will arise and show signs and wonders, to lead astray, if possible, the elect. But take heed; I have told you all things beforehand' (Mark 13.22f.), and 'The coming of the lawless one by the activity of Satan will be with all power and with pretended signs and wonders' (2 Thess. 2.9). Thus it is not surprising that we are not encouraged to place our faith in signs. The supreme sign presented to us is not God's power in miracle, but God's weakness on a cross.

In any case, signs and wonders do not necessarily produce faith. The account of the early part of Jesus' ministry contained in Matthew's gospel includes many miracles. We read that some of the Scribes and Pharisees asked him, 'Teacher, we wish to see a sign from you' (Matt. 12.38). Jesus condemned their attitude, using language about an evil and adulterous generation. No sign can compel faith, and once again the cross and resurrection of Jesus ('the sign of Jonah') is the supreme sign.

Concentration on signs and wonders can cause people to look in the wrong direction and even to value God's gifts more than God.

There is, however, another, deeper reason why signs and wonders by themselves can be misleading. This reason will cause no surprise to the reader who has followed the reasoning of this chapter: Christians must expect the way of the cross as well as the power of the resurrection. During this earthly life Christians are citizens of two countries. We remain 'in Adam', subject to weakness, fallenness, sin, suffering and death. 'In Christ', however, we are open to the power of God's future, that is to justification, deliverance from wrath, the power and gifts of the Holy Spirit; we have even 'tasted . . . the powers of the age to come' (Heb. 6.5). Thus triumphalism is illegitimate, for we have not yet arrived. Equally defeatism is inappropriate, for we are not where we were; God who has already begun a good work in us 'will bring it to completion at the day of Jesus Christ' (Phil. 1.6). Much mainline Christianity has concentrated exclusively on the power of the resurrection and the present realization of the age to come. Authentic Christianity tries to hold fast to both, taking its cue from Paul who, writing, 'The signs of a true apostle were performed among you in all patience, with signs and wonders and mighty works' (2 Cor. 12.12), had but a few lines earlier written about his thorn in the flesh which he had three times asked the Lord to remove, but in vain.

Our conclusion about signs and wonders, therefore, is that, like so much which we have considered in this chapter, they should be understood as power in weakness. If Jesus Christ suffered on a cross and is our head, there is no way in which the several members of his body will escape hardship and suffering. Equally, there is no way in which the risen Lord will begrudge to his believing followers here in this mortal life some of the powers of the age to come, for the Spirit is the first instalment of heaven.

The power of the spirit and power in the world

We now consider a rather different set of problems to which the Christian claim to power in the Spirit gives rise. What is the relation between this power in the Spirit and power as generally understood in the world? Power in the world always has an element of ascendancy of material, political or personal force. Authority in the world, to be recognized, must have the substance to make good its claim to direct the community. That substance we call power, and its qualitative nature is that of dominance. When an opposing force rises with greater ability it makes its claims good, then with the passing of dominance it seems that the reality of power as effective in the world also passes, and its authority becomes suspect. We immediately find ourselves faced by the dilemma that the Church, the body of Christ, is also an institution in the world. Yet in the life of the Spirit, power, whether individual or corporate, will be characterized not by dominance but by self-giving. That power which is authoritative and commands acknowledgement shows itself in a way of living. In Christ the way of living appropriate for the Christian community is wholly shaped by individual and corporate self-giving and self-emptying. The community which lives in the Spirit will embody that power in its acceptance of vulnerability and humbleness, serving and lowliness, and in the transformation of these qualities. This fellowship is baptized both with the shame of Christ's death and with the glory of his resurrection. Obedience in the Spirit is both authoritative and self-emptying, glorious as well as lowly.

There is, however, nothing glorious (quite the reverse) about weakness or humiliation in themselves. Sometimes too within the Church there is heard a certain romanticizing of failure and of weakness, even an assumption that the Church should not seek or expect success. In the concluding part of the preceding section of this chapter we touched on this, and here the point needs to be made again, that Christian convictions about the death and resurrection of Christ necessarily make us reconsider the criteria for power and success which most of us instinctively share with the wider world. In the Church we cherish the vision of a will directed, through the Spirit, in Christlike obedience to the Father; such power invests all that it touches, including humiliation, with glory.

Further, Jesus' saying recorded in the fourth gospel, that he has power to lay down his life and power to take it again (John 10.18) reminds us that the power with which we are concerned may, as he did, choose vulnerability in place of dominance. There is an exercise of choice and of the will: we are not talking about resignation or passivity or that feebleness of spirit which makes no choice at all. Equally, we are not looking for a Church in which human qualities such as initiative and drive have no place. Rather, the Christian community, recognizing as authoritative for it the paradoxical character of the power in the Spirit about which we write, may discover this to be the power which binds it against fragmenting, sustains it in the deserts of the world, and moves it forward disturbingly in its freedom.

The Church, however, is human as well as divine, of mortal flesh and of Spirit. The body of Christ as found in this or that group which constitutes a local or national church needs to consider how the real 'power in the Spirit' addresses the real 'power in the world' as it shapes the 'worldly' institution, the Church. It has to face such questions in relation not only to its own institutional existence, but also to the world around it, and so too do its individual members. The Church does in fact face a particular instance of a wider problem: namely, the ambivalence of all power and of all structures wherever they are to be found. No organization can do without structure, organization and authoritative decision-making; formalized patterns of authority are essential for any body, the Church included. Some complain that the structures of the Church cramp the Spirit, others that synods are but the scenes of all too human power struggles, others that the exercise of episcopal authority as a mode of church government is inconsistent with the notes of hiddenness, anonymity and submission to which we earlier referred. All are instances in which power operates: it would do no harm frankly to recognize that power and dominance of this secular, worldly kind are part of that life in the world to which the Church is called, the responsibility for which must not be avoided. Once that is recognized and once it is perceived also that all structures, including ecclesiological ones, are under the Spirit's judgement, then it should be possible to work at imperfect structures and at the way in which power is exercised in our community. There are elements in any institutional structure which may be inimical to the life of the Spirit. Thus much depends on the way in which we operate the structures. There is, in any case, much in the Pauline epistles about the defeat of authorities and powers; they hold no ultimate authority and secure their true end in submission to Christ.

To put it simply: we are summoned by the very nature of our new life in the Spirit neither to avoid the responsibility of power in the world when God lays it on us, nor to seek it. Instead we are called to exercise it in such a way that we accept its burden (for it is heavy), remain unseduced by it, and surrender it when our time for handing it on is complete. Such a response to issues of power for the Church as an institution, and for its individual members both as they live within the Church and as they function in the secular world, raises further questions so large that we can here only sketch three lines of approach to them.

First, both the attitude with which we approach our life in an institutional Church, and also the way in which we answer ingrained patterns of social interaction, can be affected by the power in the Spirit which we have been discussing, and they must be held open to it.

Second, this power in the Spirit will be reflected in the quality of the institutional Church's common life, particularly as it is expressed in the activity of prayer and worship. Here it is that the Church, ever aware of its own weakness and imperfection, is (or should be) particularly open to receiving the power of the Spirit.

Third, the Church, the Church's authority and structures are never ends in themselves, but exist only for the service of God and in dependence on God. Given a firm grasp of this truth, the Church should actually feel itself relieved that it is of little worldly consequence, indeed should delight in and perhaps boast of that fact, that the power of Christ may rest upon it.

Moreover, Christian people who play significant roles in secular institutions and exercise authority and power in the secular sphere may be helped by reflecting on the conviction of the New Testament writers that Christ on the cross deprived secular power and authority of its dominance. This being so, it is for Christian people to remember that any power they hold is, because they are Christian, given to them only to enable them to serve God in the world; that the spirit in which it is exercised counts; and that the quality of life in any institution in which they play a role may be powerfully affected by that Spirit of power in which they have a share and of which we write. These reflections about power and the Spirit lead to our consideration of truth and the Spirit, the subject to which we devote our next chapter.

Chapter 7
The Spirit of truth

Truth and the holy spirit

What do we look for when we ask for 'truth'? In the abstract, apart from some given context of enquiry, we can speak more readily of what truth is *not*. It is not falsehood, self-deception, illusion, or unsubstantiated opinion. At first glance, this bears some relationship to Christian understandings of the work of the Holy Spirit. The Holy Spirit exposes falsehoods, dissolves the self-deception of illusions, and witnesses to the truth of God. When he writes, 'it is the Spirit himself bearing witness with our spirit that we are children of God' (Rom. 8.16), among other things Paul is implying that Christians' confidence that they are sons of God is valid, and does not derive from some illusory belief which grew solely from inside their heads.

On further reflection, however, the subject becomes more complex. In the first place, how do we distinguish the witness of the Holy Spirit from merely subjective feelings of conviction or certainty? The witness of the Spirit does not seem to offer some second, independently checkable channel of knowledge which we can identify in distinction from the conviction or belief itself. Indeed the biblical traditions acknowledge without hesitation that claims to be inspired by the Holy Spirit must be examined and critically tested (1 Thess. 5.20ff.; 1 John 4.6).

In the second place, what counts as truth may be, or seem to be, a different kind of thing depending on our context of discourse. Is the truth of a poem the same kind of thing as the truth of a newspaper report? This issue is notoriously complex when we face questions about truths of religion in relation to truths of the natural sciences. On one side, we wish to affirm the unity of the world, the unity of God, and the unity of truth. An entirely pluralist view of truth which divides reality into a series of self-contained areas seeks to solve one set of problems only by ignoring another. Yet we should not expect that truth about the nature of God or even moral truth about the self, would be of the same order, or assessed by the same criteria, as truth about the location or speed of molecules. Does the activity of the Holy Spirit relate to all, to most, to some, or to none of these areas?

In the third place, questions about truth call our attention to what has traditionally been thought of as the problem of subject and object. Truth has been defined by one writer, Bernard Lonergan as 'a relation of knowing to being' (*Insight*, p. 552). What capacities to judge or to discern does the person who is seeking to know actually possess? At this point traditional Christian language speaks of the Holy Spirit as being operative in removing human blindness and preparing a state of readiness to perceive. But, once again, does this concern all kinds of truth, or does it relate only to truth in the context of faith, salvation, or redemption? Questions about the 'object' pole in the process of knowing or understanding are no more straightforward. In principle, if human perceptions can ever be true, the structures and order which seem to be presupposed in processes of understanding are potentially given and not merely imposed arbitrarily on *the given* by the human mind. We may acknowledge, with Kant, the active part played by the mind in selecting, shaping, and ordering what is thought to count as the raw data of human observation and experience. But that the whole process is even *capable of resulting* in rational understanding of the given might be said to depend, from the standpoint of Christian belief, on the prior presence and activity of God as Creator Spirit. In the biblical traditions creation is seen as an establishing of an ordered reality. Its elements can be 'separated', and are sufficiently stable to be intelligibly articulated in language through bearing names (Gen. 1.3ff.). All this stands in contrast to what would otherwise be 'formless void' (Hebrew, *tohu wa-bohu*, Gen 1.2; cf Isa. 45.18). The empty, featureless waste exhibits nothing identifiable, let alone ordered, which might become an object of thought. With the hindsight of Christian revelation, and as a piece of speculative theology, it might be said that the very thinkableness of the universe finds its ground in the creative work of God's Spirit.

This kind of approach however, has taken us far from the centre of biblical language about the Spirit and truth. The biblical writers are more than cautious about speaking of God's Spirit as that which immanently pervades the world. Indeed Paul seems to correct the idea of an immanent cosmic spirit similar to that found in contemporary Stoic philosophy when he declares, 'No one comprehends the thoughts of God except the Spirit of God. Now we have received not the spirit of the world but the Spirit which is from (Greek, *ek*; in effect 'who proceeds from') God, that we might understand the gifts bestowed on us by God' (1 Cor. 2.11ff.). To be sure, Paul closely associates the work of the Holy Spirit with that which is rational and ordered. Prophecy inspired by the Spirit does not entail suspension of mental activity and conscious assessment (1 Cor. 14.13ff.). He regrets that the Galatians have been 'bewitched' into attitudes in which their minds have not been active (Gal. 3.1, Greek *anoētoi*). The mind (Greek, *nous*) is to be renewed (Rom. 12.2). Paul could never have agreed with his Jewish contemporary Philo, that 'the mind is evicted at the arrival of the divine Spirit, but when he departs the mind returns to its tenancy' (Philo, *Who is the Heir of Divine Things?* 53:265). Nevertheless, if the Bible speaks at all of the ground of potential rationality in the cosmos, the biblical traditions ascribe this to God's Wisdom or to God's Word, or even to the cosmic Christ, rather than to the Holy Spirit.

The Wisdom literature embodies this tradition firmly. Wisdom is portrayed as declaring: 'When he established the heavens, I was there, when he drew a circle on the face of the deep, when he made firm the skies above . . . when he assigned to the sea its limit . . . then I was beside him, like a master workman . . .' (Prov. 8.27ff.). In the gospel of John, it is the Word (Greek, *logos*) who is 'with God' in the beginning, without whom nothing created was made (1.1ff.). It is in the *Logos*, rather than in the Spirit, that 'all things hold together' in potential system or intelligible order (Col. 1.17). The meaning of the difficult verse in Ephesians containing the word sometimes translated 'unite all things' (RSV, Greek *anakephalaiō*) is probably that God purposed to bring everything 'to a coherent focus in Christ' (Eph. 1.10).

The actual phrase 'the Spirit of truth' belongs most characteristically to the writings of John in the New Testament, although it also occurs in Jewish literature of the time including the Dead Sea Scrolls. Both the First Epistle of John and the *Rule of the Community* (among the Dead Sea Scrolls) draw a contrast between 'the spirit of truth' and the 'spirit of error' (1 John 4.6; Rule [= 1QS] 3:17ff.; cf. Testament of Judah 20.1). Here the reference is broad. What is at issue in 1 John is that all claims to be 'inspired' should be submitted to examination and tested. It is not certain that 'spirit' refers to the Spirit of God, although it may well do so. The Johannine gospel clearly refers to the Spirit of God whom John also calls the 'Paraclete' in the final discourses, but the notion of truth which occurs in this context is also more specific. The direction of thought in these discussions makes it beyond doubt that the well-known promise 'The Spirit of truth . . . will guide you into all (the?) truth' (John 16.13) does not in its original context deal with the human quest for truth in general terms at all. Rather it promises trustworthy guidance to the Christian community for the task of understanding Christ and the implications of the gospel message.

Other passages in the fourth gospel confirm this impression. The first reference to 'the Spirit of truth' in these discourses underlines the role of the Holy Spirit in continuing the ministry of Christ and his disclosure of the gospel. It is said that the world cannot receive him, in the sense that the world's openness to receive this Spirit reflects its measure of openness to the message of Christ (14.16ff). The coming of the Spirit fulfils Christ's promise, 'I will come to you' (v.18). 'The Spirit of truth, who proceeds from the Father, will bear witness to me' (15.26). This truth is said elsewhere in the Gospel of John to bring freedom (8.32). But here grace also entails judgement. For whereas in other religious writings light offers general illumination of the human mind, in John light shows up everything to be what it is, in an exposure which thereby brings judgement. 'This is the judgement, that the light has come into the world, and men loved darkness rather than light . . .' (3.19). Illusion about oneself, about the world, and about Christ, John affirms, may be initially more comfortable and therefore, for many, desirable.

The healing of an unsighted person now becomes a model or symbol of Christ's concern for those who cannot (or will not) 'see'. The healing narrative (9.1ff.) is set in a context of discourse which begins with the words of Jesus 'I am the light of the world' (8.1); includes the personal testimony 'one thing I know, that though I was blind, now I see' (9.25); and concludes with the judgement: 'If you were blind you would have no guilt, but now that you say, "We see", your guilt remains' (9.41).

After Jesus has completed his earthly witness and ministry, the Spirit of truth will continue this work of exposure and disclosure. 'He will convince the world of sin and of right-eousness and of judgement' (16.8). The Spirit will press home those verdicts which will become publicly definitive only at the last judgement. Meanwhile, before that time, this work of the Spirit remains more akin to that of a therapist than a prosecutor or judge. He exposes that which needs attention, so that life can then be grounded in reality rather than in illusion, or self-deception, or other people's subjective opinion. The contrast between judgements which reflect the truth of God and the seductiveness or fickleness of 'what other people think' becomes a major theme in John's gospel: 'How can you believe, who receive approval (RSV glory) from one another, and do not seek the approval (RSV glory) that comes from the only God?' (5.44). 'They loved the praise of men more than the praise of God' (12.43). By contrast, Jesus declares, 'I am the way, and the truth, and the life . . . He who has seen me has seen the Father' (14.6,9). The Holy Spirit continues the witness after the resurrection.

It would be a mistake, however, to conclude from these initial observations that a theology of the Holy Spirit addresses only narrower questions about truth as the truth of the Christian message. As we shall shortly see, even in the New Testament conceptions of truth are neither uniform nor naive. But before we can explore these issues further, we need first to clarify more sharply what we mean by 'true' and 'truth' in the wider context of more philosophical discussion.

What is truth? some approaches and models

Perhaps the most widely assumed model of truth is that which has come to be known as the *correspondence* theory. If we ask whether some oral news or newspaper report is true, we are asking whether the statements in question *correspond* with the actual states of affairs which they portray. False statements are those which fail to correspond with what is the case. Aristotle in philosophy and Thomas Aquinas in theology advocated this approach to an understanding of truth.

In common with all the major theories of truth, this approach helps us with some problems and in some contexts, but cannot address others. It operates in everyday life where we have some means of independent access to the state of affairs behind the statements which we wish to assess. Independent witnesses may verify or disconfirm the oral news or newspaper report as true or false. But sometimes we do not have independent access of this kind. Questions about historical occurrences in the ancient world, or about ultimate issues in philosophy or theology do not easily fall into this pattern. A problem of circularity can arise. To borrow a well-known philosophical simile, it is like buying a second copy of the same newspaper to verify whether what the first copy said was true. At the level of a theory of reality, or of a belief-system, the model seems to make sense, just as it makes sense as model in everyday life. But its cash value concretely for the enquirer is more problematic. Indeed even more everyday examples are not immune from difficulty. When a cartographer seeks to portray a true picture of the world by means of a map, the correspondence between the paper and the terrain rests not only on conventions of depiction but also on value judgements about what is most important in the enterprise. For various systems of projection can be chosen to portray three-dimensional reality on two-dimensional paper. One will convey truth about surface area; another truth about latitudes; another, truth about routes and distances. Truth, even for the correspondence theory, transcends flat description alone.

In historical enquiries, where direct or independent access to events can no longer be gained, correspondence models begin to give ground to questions about coherence or consistency of witnesses and sources. When we move from the appeal to experience (the empirical tradition), to the operation of mathematics and logic (the rationalist tradition), we move to a second model of truth, namely the *coherence* theory. A mathematical proposition is 'true' if it *coheres* with other propositions within the system. Logical consistency becomes the key criterion of truth. In the history of ideas, Leibniz, Spinoza, and Hegel expounded and advocated this approach.

Like the correspondence theory, the coherence theory of truth assists us in exposing falsehoods. Tests of consistency not only sharpen thinking but dispel illusion. Its limitations begin to come to light when we ask how much can be accounted for, or even described, within the same single system. It is possible to have self-contained systems in logic, in theology, or in mathematics which do not engage with the historical realities of human life. Further, we find that as disclosure, discovery, history and experience advance, either more than one system emerges, or the system becomes flexible, open-ended, and capable of embodying novelty. In the philosophy of science, the well-worn example is that of the electron which, in some respects, is to be seen as a particle; and in other respects, is to be seen as a wave. We traced some of the implications of this for an understanding of truth in the sciences and in theology in our previous report, *We Believe in God*. It is possible to have a self-consistent system of propositions gathered round an axiom which bears no relation to the reality of the world (other than a semiotic or linguistic one). It is equally possible that reality transcends what can be expressed within a single system.

Faced by such difficulties, some philosophers have resorted to a third model of truth. Truth proves itself to be what it is only by its production of constructive consequences. In its crudest form, this is the *pragmatic* model of truth. An engineer discovers whether a calculation or assumption was true by whether it *works*. C. S. Peirce argued that truth would emerge as what it was in the long run. Truth is the eventual outcome of enquiry. William James related truth to behaviour. Recently this kind of approach has been refined to a highly sophisticated level by Richard Rorty and others who reject any notion of truth in philosophy as a kind of 'mirror' of reality. Rorty entitled his major book *Philosophy and the Mirror of Nature*. The only possible criterion of truth, he argues, is whether it 'edifies'. This is not moral or religious edification, but the ability to take the next step, in a chain of enquiry, in a direction which cannot yet be specified.

The force of this approach is considerable. Falsehood and self-deception lead us into blind alleys and bring us to a halt. Jesus told his disciples, 'You will know them by their fruits' (Matt. 7.16). Gamaliel advised the court that if Christian claims were false, they would come to nothing, but if they were true, 'you will not be able to overthrow them' (Acts 5.39). But how long do we have to wait before we can see whether progress is permanent? More sharply, what counts as progress or success? Have not illusions captured the minds of thousands, if not millions, and led them on (in both senses of the phrase) towards what they perceived as success? Once again, this model makes its own contribution to the subject but it becomes seductive and anti-self-critical if it is regarded as a comprehensive theory of truth.

Another group of philosophers is quick to point out that in everyday life we utter the words 'It is true' more often, as an exclamation than as a statement. What does it add to the statement 'Smith is a good dentist' to say 'It is true that Smith is a good dentist'? The words often serve as a commentary on the stance of the speaker, or a commentary on the statement itself. A. Tarski, stressing the latter, offered a *semantic* theory of truth. P. F. Strawson, stressing the former, called attention to the self-involving character of truth claims for the speaker. His model represents a *performative* theory of truth, and develops the work of Austin. To say 'It is true that Smith is a good dentist' is both to make a statement about Smith and to add a personal recommendation, probably on the basis of first-hand experience.

These models, too, like the others, make a contribution to our understanding of truth. Certainly the performative model accords with research in New Testament studies into the nature of early Christian credal confessions. To confess Christ as Lord in the New Testament community was both to make a truth claim about the exaltation and vindication of Christ, *and* to nail one's own colours to the mast as one who belonged to Christ as his servant or his slave. True confession at this level is prompted by the Holy Spirit. 'No one can say "Jesus is Lord" except by the Holy Spirit' (1 Cor. 12.3). Apprehending truth and having a personal stake in it are both involved.

We cannot attempt to offer an exhaustive list of possible models of truth. The four or five approaches which we have examined represent the main ones. Our next step is to note that in the biblical writings and in Christian tradition all these models have some part to play. We may then consider further questions about the role of the Holy Spirit.

Truth in thought, word, deed and life

From between the end of the nineteenth century until after the middle of the twentieth, it was customary, almost conventional, for many biblical scholars to make sweeping claims about the difference between 'Hebrew' and 'Greek' views of truth. In an over-simple scheme of dialectic, it was alleged that the 'Hebraic' notion of truth was fundamentally practical; the Greek view generally theoretical; and the New Testament a synthesis which combined elements from each. Supposedly the Hebrews, largely on the ground that the Hebrew word for 'truth' (*'emeth*) could also mean faithfulness, tended to equate truth with reliability. The Greeks, by contrast, were thought to have adopted a more theoretical approach. Plato held something very like both correspondence and coherence theories of truth; Protagoras and the

Sophists held a more relativist view; the Sceptics maintained in theory a suspense of judgement; and all together were somehow perceived as representing 'Greek' thought.

Such a portrait of this part of the ancient world, however, is little better than a caricature. Many Greeks were not philosophers at all, and some Hebrews, as well as many Jews in later Judaism, reflected on issues more ultimate than the next practical matter. What mainly gave rise to this simplistic portrait was not only a semantic accident in the case of 'emeth, but also the fact that the *contexts in which* Hebrew utterances about truth happen to be recorded are most frequently practical religious ones, while the *contexts in which* the word alētheia, truth, occurs most frequently in Greek literature happen to be philosophical ones. But there are instances of a plurality of understandings of truth within the Old Testament, within Greek literature, in Paul, in John, and in the rest of the New Testament. This should not surprise us: any *one* model of truth remains appropriate only to certain contexts of life and thought.

In the New Testament and in later Christian tradition, truth concerns thought, word, deed, life, and character. It relates to witness, to revelation, and to being anchored in reality. Paul and John certainly presuppose what we should nowadays call a correspondence model of truth when they are addressing questions about truth in speech. Paul disowns attempts to use guile, or to present false claims; his intention is to communicate truth in a straightforward way (2. Cor. 4.2; 6.7; 7.14). The ethics of truthful speech is enjoined in Ephesians (4.25). In John, the Samaritan woman tells the truth about her marital status (4.18), and the Baptist speaks truth about Jesus (10.41). But at a fundamental level, reality can be masked. Paul shares with the preachers of the Jewish synagogues the Jewish-Christian convention that pagan religion and morals lead to suppression of the truth (Rom. 1.18 ff.; cf. Wisd. 13.1ff., 14.8ff.). Truth, for Paul, becomes sharply focused as the content of the gospel message (Gal. 2.5; cf. 2 Thess. 2.13).

John takes up the contrast, by implication, between appearance and reality. Israel has been chosen as God's vine, but Israel's history proved this to be more apparent than real. By contrast, Jesus Christ is 'the real vine' (15.1). Some set great store on Moses' giving manna to Israel, and this coloured their expectations of the Messiah. But Christ's own flesh, which he gives, is a 'real' food indeed (6.55). Worship is sometimes only a show arising from human religiosity and aspiration. But worship prompted by the Spirit is 'real' (4.23.f.). John has a special interest in witness. Human witnesses like the Baptist and the Samaritan woman testify to Jesus, and God's own witness is said to be added. 'True' witness is reliable, and dependable witnesses speak truth as they see it (8.13ff.). But truth, in John, always touches life as well as thought or word. Hence, probably against the background of Exodus 34, Jesus Christ as the Word-made-flesh reveals in his enfleshed person the actuality of God, 'full of grace and truth' (1.14).

What is the role of the Holy Spirit in all this? First, if Christ definitively discloses the heart of God in his enfleshed person, the Holy Spirit is said to continue this work of disclosure. The process of revelation which takes place during the ministry of Jesus both continues what was begun in the Old Testament and looks forward to clearer future disclosure. In the present there is a dimension of hiddenness. This is acknowledged. When he dons the servant's apron, Jesus tells Peter: 'What I am doing you do not know now, but afterward you will understand' (John 13.7). 'The Spirit of truth, who proceeds from the Father, will bear witness to me' (15.26). The First Epistle of John develops the same theme. After speaking of the Christian confession of Jesus as God's authentic self-disclosure, the writer continues: 'And the Spirit is the witness, because the Spirit is the truth' (1 John 5.7). It is important for the writer that this witness transcends mere human conviction or opinion (5.8ff.). As in Paul, 'it is the Spirit himself bearing witness with our spirit that we are children of God' (Rom. 8.16; cf. Gal. 4.6). Even in Hebrews, where reference to the Holy Spirit is rare, the Holy Spirit 'bears witness to us' (Heb. 10.15). In the Revelation of John, the message is a prophecy, a disclosure, and a testimony (Rev. 1.1ff.; 22.6f., 16). But here an invitation to personal experience and appropriation is offered to all who sigh for what is so far beyond their grasp; 'the Spirit and the Bride say "Come" . . . Let him who is thirsty, come . . .' (Rev. 22.17).

The truth disclosed through the presence and work of the Spirit, therefore, concerns what we earlier described as the two poles of the subject and object. Kierkegaard argued that truth cannot be reduced to what can be blandly packaged and accepted on a plate. Without genuine subjective appropriation, without perhaps conflict and struggle, certainly without change and transformation, certain kinds of truth cannot be perceived. Without such appropriation and change 'truth becomes untruth in this or that person's mouth', we turn Christian truth into 'what is its exact opposite', and then 'thank God for the great and inestimable privilege of being a Christian' (S. Kierkegaard, *Attack on 'Christendom'*, p. 150).

Kierkegaard echoes the words of Jesus in John that the truth is inseparable from the way and the life (John 14.6). 'Everyone who has a result merely as such does not possess it, for he has not the *way*' (Kierkegaard, *The Concept of Irony*, p. 340). Truth, in this context, is not merely subjective; but it does involve human subjectivity. The New Testament writers did not possess this particular terminological tool. But they could declare: 'God's love has been poured into our hearts through the Holy Spirit which has been given to us' (Rom.5.5).

The dimension which is entirely missing from Kierkegaard's otherwise helpful emphasis is the corporate one. Truth emerges not only in the conflicts and struggles of the individual, but also in the conflicts and struggles of the believing community. This is what we should expect not only when we reflect on the Church's history, but also when we recall the point made elsewhere in this volume that the Holy Spirit is given corporately to the community of God's people as 'shareholders' in the common gift (Greek *koinōnia* of the Spirit; fellowship of the Spirit in the sense of that which we share, 2 Cor. 13.14). The performative model of truth remains a contributory element: the community consists of those who are making a stand, who have a personal stake in the commonality which they share. But they are also a corroborative community. Each affirms and confirms the witness of the other to the reality of God and to the truth of the gospel. Each may also interact with others in comparing and contrasting different partial understandings which arise from the fragmentary perceptions of individuals.

This is the way in which the Spirit of truth guides the community 'into all the truth' (John 16.13). On the analogy of Paul's assertions about the sharing of the Spirit's gifts among the community, it would be unlikely that any single individual would have a monopoly of this truth. Believers and seekers need one another. 'Iron sharpens iron, and one man sharpens another' (Prov. 27.17). The conflicts at Corinth between the weak and the strong, or between the better off and the poor, sharpened understandings of the relation between knowledge, freedom, and love, and led to a formulation of a theology of the Lord's Supper in 1 Corinthians. Clashes between what amounted to cliques at Corinth led to deeper reflection about the nature of the ministry and of the relation between 'wisdom' and the cross. Struggles with Judaizing influences, or perhaps with the respective status of Jewish and Gentile Christians, led to Paul's more sharply articulating the truth of justification by grace alone through faith. Marcion's rejection of the Old Testament helped the second-century Church to appreciate its value as part of the one revelation of the one God.

All this bears some relation to the *pragmatic* model of truth. The people of God learn as they walk. Discipleship is a journey and a pilgrimage in which we never cease to be learners. All knowledge is subject to correction as we proceed. In the report *We Believe in God* we acknowledged this, and we argued that this did not make existing knowledge unreliable or inadequate for the task. The disclosures of the ever-present Spirit are for the practical purpose of 'building up' a community into Christian maturity over a process, not a single event, of growth (1 Cor. 12.7; 14.3,5; cf. Eph. 4.11ff.). The measure of 'maturity' is 'the stature of the fulness of Christ' (Eph.4.13). It is also, as we have seen, a matter of personally taking a stand; of being a witness and a partaker (1 Pet.5.1). To declare, with Luther, 'Here I stand', is part of what is meant by Christian confession of faith. When they are put on trial before hostile accusers or courts of enquiry, Christians must be prepared to give an account of their faith (1 Pet.3.15). But Jesus tells his disciples not to be anxious about what they are to say: 'For it is not you who speak, but the Holy Spirit' (Mark 13.11; cf Matt.10.20). Putting oneself personally on the line belongs, once again, to the performative conception of truth. Yet none of this, we noted, is thought to arise merely through personal decision. We examined a number of those passages in Paul and especially in John which ground statements about Christ (or about the self and the world) in a reality which is neither illusory nor merely apparent, even if public verification of this will not emerge fully until the end of history. Paul himself acknowledges the provisional nature of all human judgements: 'Do not pronounce judgement before the time, before the Lord comes, who will bring to light the things now hidden' (1 Cor.4.5). 'Now I know in part; then I shall understand fully' (1 Cor.13.12).

Coherence, inspiration and ultimacy

In spite of the importance and relevance of the performance and pragmatic models of truth, Christian claims about truth disclosed in and by the work of the Holy Spirit clearly go beyond these areas. Truth is not simply autobiography, or autobiographical testimony about what seems to 'work'. Philosophers have called attention to the intellectual vulnerability of the kind of perception which can be traced from C. S. Peirce and John Dewey to Richard Rorty, as well as the kind of standpoint reflected in Jacques Derrida's post-structuralism where truth has been reduced, in effect, to 'how it is with me'. In a pragmatic and pluralistic culture the Christian Church may also be tempted to lose its intellectual or rational nerve and to retreat into performative or functional attitudes towards truth, in which biography or autobiography, corporate or individual, becomes the order of the day. The renewal movement has encouraged a new emphasis on narrative testimony, and this carries with it some particular strengths and weaknesses. Biography and autobiography, whether on the part of individuals or groups, can be warm and living, and it is a fundamental part of performative Christian testimony, as we earlier observed. But pragmatic and performative models need to be supplemented and tested through other ways of assessment, if the claims of Christians about reality and ultimacy are to be taken seriously. There can be multiple explanations for what 'works': a *variety* of causes may give rise to a sense of liberation from anxiety or from guilt; to an experience of change and transformation; to the enjoyment of worship; to an enhanced vitality, power, or ability to cope. The Holy Spirit may well be at work here, but not necessarily in every case.

Josephine Bax calls our attention in this context of renewal to the importance of the challenge of crisis being 'strong enough to bring about a change of direction, but not so strong as to reduce us to despair' (*The Good Wine: Spiritual Renewal in the Church of England*, p.33). But, as Karl Jaspers the philosopher emphasized in these boundary situations or limit situations, what is perceived as the truth may take a variety of forms. It is truth *for the person concerned*. In keeping with his own existentialist horizons, Jaspers refused to identify this existential truth with anything given, and certainly not with the message of the gospel of Christ. Indeed his definition of truth is turned virtually the other way round: it is 'whatever I find' when the masks have been removed. But Jaspers also acknowledged that different people find different things when this cannot happen. It remains, at best, an existentialist view of truth.

Christian truth claims certainly embody and embrace this performative or existential dimension of narrative testimony, but they can never be entirely reduced to it. For *ultimacy* cannot be defined in terms of human need and experience. The Holy Spirit is not simply a mythological projection of the human spirit, but a ground beneath and beyond it. We must look further at other models of truth.

The coherence model has so far received less attention than others in the present discussion. Yet in some respects it is the most suggestive of all the models in the context of claims about ultimate truth. The most serious problem about this model, we noted, arose from the incompleteness of any system when truth viewed from within that system was related to human life, or to God. In the biblical writings, however, symbols and images of ultimacy are more usually temporal rather than spiritual. We observed Paul's contrast, for example, between the hiddenness and ambiguity of the 'now' and definitive public knowledge which God will disclose 'then'. The logical grammar of the 'last judgement' is that it is understood to represent a definitive pronouncement, at the close of history, which cannot be revised. It will publicly corroborate, or in some cases disconfirm provisional knowledge, values, or truth claims which hitherto could only be assumed or grasped in faith. In the present, in Paul's words, 'we walk by faith, not by sight' (2 Cor. 5.7). But, he continues, there will come a decisive moment when all will be made clear (5.10). John Hick takes up this principle in the context of logical positivism and calls it the principle of 'eschatological verification'. In the context of a different philosophical tradition, Wolfhart Pannenberg develops the idea in relation to Hegel's claim that truth emerges definitively or absolutely only in the context of the whole.

If we can entertain this approach seriously, even at least as an intelligible hypothesis which deserves attention, this has implications for a theology of the Holy Spirit and the work of the Spirit in the present and the future. In his book *Christ and Time* Oscar Cullmann, drawing on insights from the New Testament, particularly from Paul's epistles, describes the Holy Spirit as 'the anticipation of the end in the present' (p.72). Verdicts and disclosures, which are capable of public access and confirmation only in the future, are now already brought home convincingly to the believing heart or to the open mind. This is the thrust of the material about the Paraclete in John which we have already noted. The Spirit, as it were, anticipates disclosures which in principle belong to the last judgement (John 16.7ff.). Because history is not yet complete, our perceptions and judgements remain hidden. We see edges of God's ways, but we still await the sifting through of ambiguities and the full revelation of God's glory. Nevertheless, the axiom around which the whole growing system revolves has already been disclosed in advance: 'He who has seen me has seen the Father' (John 14.9). 'God . . . has spoken by a Son . . . he . . . bears the very stamp of his nature' (Heb.1.2f.). 'When the Spirit of truth comes . . . he will declare to you the things that are to come. He will glorify me, for he will take what is mine and declare it to you' (John 16.13f.).

This perspective holds together a number of beliefs which most Christians will wish simultaneously to affirm. It holds together the unity of truth as that which concerns all reality with the particularity of the definitive disclosure of God in Christ. It holds together an acknowledgement that the present is marked by ambiguities in which God sometimes remains hidden, with a confidence that faith, in the context of this hiddenness, will be vindicated and confirmed. It holds together the recognition that while the performative and pragmatic dimensions of truth remain important, truth claims also concern, for the Christian, matters of ultimate reality.

Two more areas invite consideration before we conclude. The first concerns the Christian tradition that the Holy Spirit has uniquely inspired the revelation of God in scripture; the second concerns the relation between continuity and novelty in the Holy Spirit's work of disclosing truth.

One of the fundamental beliefs expressed in the historic creeds is that the Holy Spirit 'has spoken through the prophets'. The phrase echoes the language of 2 Peter, where the prophets are said to have spoken as they were 'carried along' (Greek *pheromenoi*, Vulgate *inspirati*) by the Holy Spirit (2 Pet.1.21). Similarly in 2 Timothy the Greek phrase 'inspired by God' (*theopneustos*) is rendered *divinitus inspirata* in the Latin versions (2 Tim. 3.16).

In the early centuries, indeed up to relatively modern times, the Church seemed to speak with one voice about the Holy Spirit's inspiration of the Bible. In response to Marcion's attempt to drive a wedge between the Old and the New Testaments, the Church of the second and third centuries affirmed that the same Holy Spirit inspired both sets of writings. Nicene Catholics re-affirmed the principle in the fourth century. Cyril of Jerusalem asserts, 'There is one Holy Spirit who preached Christ through the prophets . . . let no one therefore divide the Old Testament from the New; let no one say that the Spirit in the Old Testament is one, and the Spirit in the New Testament is another' (*Catecheses* 16.4). In general, the Church Fathers regarded the biblical writings as the writings of the Holy Spirit. The biblical authors were, in effect, the Spirit's tool and mouthpiece. The Church had taken over the view of biblical inspiration which could be found in rabbinic Judaism and included the New Testament as well as the Old within this framework.

In modern times however, a more complex account of the nature of biblical inspiration is called for. As J. T. Burtchaell comments by way of summary of modern discussion, 'The real issue here is what confounds scholars in so many areas: the manner in which individual human events are jointly caused by both God and man' (*Catholic Theories of Biblical Inspiration Since 1910*, p.279). There are both intellectual reasons and theological reasons to do with religious devotion why we should be reluctant either to devalue or to overrate what is involved in 'inspiration'. If we minimise the part played by human agency and personality, we run the risk of idolatry, by elevating human words to the status of the wholly divine. On the other hand, if we underestimate the agency of the Holy Spirit, we risk losing sight of the givenness of the biblical writings as that which addresses us from beyond ourselves with a saving and authentic word. As James Smart has observed, while it was a genuine achievement of modern biblical scholarship to establish the human character of the biblical writings, this emphasis should not become so obsessional that it eclipses their status or function as genuinely expressing a message from

God. The Roman Catholic writer Bruce Vawter attempts to hold the two dimensions together. He writes, 'Often enough they (the prophets) insisted that the thoughts to which they gave words were not of their own devising, that they spoke them in obedience to a superior moral will . . . that at times they would even have preferred to leave them unsaid . . . It is equally obvious that these thoughts had also passed through the prophets' own minds' (*Biblical Inspiration*, p. 17).

Such comments take us forward, but they also leave difficulties. It is at this point that it may be helpful to return to an earlier consideration about the Holy Spirit and truth. For narrower questions about the Spirit and 'inspiration' (especially the inspiration of the Bible) need to be placed in a broader theological context. Four principles emerge. First, the Holy Spirit comes as one who is beyond, and yet also within. There is therefore a givenness about the Spirit's disclosure of truth which goes beyond purely human explanation or purely human discovery. Second, the Spirit does not operate independently of God's words and deeds in Christ, or in the history of Israel. There is continuity of identity in this work or witness which enables John to assert that the Spirit witnesses to Christ; that he is sent by God 'in Christ's name', or that he will 'bring to your remembrance' the words of Christ (John 14.26; cf.16.7ff.). Similarly Paul understands the disclosure and transformation that comes through the Holy Spirit as 'having the mind of Christ' (1 Cor.2.12ff.). Third, the work of the Holy Spirit makes it possible not only to perceive truth but also to appropriate truth and to live it out. While the witness of the Spirit may point to words spoken or to deeds done in the past, the focus of the witness concerns present attitudes, assessments, and actions. Through the witness of the Spirit, even the past comes alive for the present. Fourth, all these factors operate in relation to given purposes. The truth disclosed through the Spirit serves goals of human change and growth, of transformation of life and obedient service of God and of others. Bezalel's gift of craftsmanship, for example, or the Judges' gifts of administration, served particular purposes for the communities which they served.

When Christians sometimes speak, therefore, of the Spirit's witnessing to the truth or to the reality of the Christian message of the cross, what is at issue is not simply or primarily the possession of a set of facts about the crucifixion of Jesus of Nazareth, but an understanding and appropriation of Christ's death and resurrection as somehow being also my death and my resurrection in the present. The Holy Spirit is said, for example, to apply the objective truth that in Christ human persons may become children of God at the level of a subjective awareness and experience: 'Because you are sons, God has sent the Spirit of his Son into our hearts crying "Abba! Father!" ' (Gal.4.6).

In the same way, discussions about the nature of 'inspiration' usually operate on at least two different levels. One level concerns continuity, or internal coherence, between the givenness of a past which includes the founding events of the Christian faith, and lived experience in the present. In this respect James Barr has pointed out that involvement with the Bible is integral too in being a Christian; 'It is believing in a particular God, the God who has manifested himself in a way that has some sort of unique and specific expression in the Bible' (*Explorations in Theology* 7, p.52). On the other hand at a different level claims about 'Inspiration' are also located firmly in the present. Following the tradition of the Reformers, Norman Snaith observes, 'The authority of the Bible . . . for me . . . rests in the inner witness of the Holy Spirit' (*The Inspiration and Authority of the Bible*, p.45). Through the testimony of the Spirit, John Calvin writes, the scriptures ring true 'by God's own witness' (*Institutes* 1.7.5).

Questions about the inspiration of the Holy Spirit, then, especially in relation to the Bible, can best be approached within the framework of broader concerns about the Spirit and truth. The focus of such questions is such that they involve the present no less than the past; action, no less than knowledge; transformation, no less than the acquisition of understanding. To ask 'truth, for what?' is not necessarily to compartmentalize theories of truth into different areas such as truths of science and truths of religion. It is simply to recognize that the truth which is disclosed through the Holy Spirit concerns more than knowledge about certain states of affairs. It entails the gift of an angle of vision, or the apprehension of a frame of reference, which affects not only what is perceived but also the one who perceives. The emergence of the canon of scripture in the life of the early Church calls to mind the performative and semantic models of truth. The Church said, in effect 'This is where we stand. *This is* where we hear the witness of the Spirit'.

Finally, the coherence model of truth underlines an implication for questions about continuity and novelty. It is understandable that in the renewal movement attention should be paid to the element of change, transformation, newness, novelty, or even surprise which accompanies what is perceived as the work of the Holy Spirit. This is not contrary to the nature of the Spirit. For the Spirit remains sovereign creator, transcendent and holy, who bursts through all human systems of thought and practice. We cannot manipulate the Spirit's presence and blessing, for the Spirit can be like the wind, which 'blows where it wills' (John 3.8). All the same, the Holy Spirit does not undermine the Spirit's own work. What is disclosed by the Spirit of truth coheres with the revelation of the word of Christ and the apostolic witness to the gospel of the cross. The criterion of coherence is implicitly built into the New Testament injunctions about testing (1 John 4.2f.; 5.1ff.). Even if systems are expanded and transcended by the Spirit's disclosures, later revelation will not contradict earlier witness, and it will cohere with what remains in principle the central axiom of Christ and the cross.

Chapter 8
The Spirit and creation

The discussion of the Spirit of Truth in the preceding chapter leads easily and naturally to a consideration of some of the scientific truth into which we have been led. We start from the realization that any account of human existence which recognizes its meaning and purpose will have to take account (in Kant's convenient phrase) both of the 'moral law within' and of the 'starry heavens above'. The interior and exterior aspects of our experience are not two separate and disparate enterprises, disjoined from each other by a division running between a public world of fact and a private world of value. There is but one world in which the Spirit is at work, inspiring and energising. An existentialist theology, concerned only with the human psyche, is too narrowly confined. It fails to take account of the fact that that psyche emerged within the evolving process of the world. What God made together we separate at our peril.

In consequence, an inquiry into the nature and working of the Holy Spirit will have to include an inquiry into the nature and working of the physical world. We are what we are because of our past and the consideration of that past takes us back not simply to our birth and childhood, nor to the first stirrings of our culture, nor even just to the origin of biological life, but to the very beginning of all things in the origin of the universe itself. When we lift our eyes from ourselves to take in the significance of the cosmos, our discernment of the Holy Spirit will be not only through an aesthetic appreciation of the wonders of the world, but also through an intellectual understanding of that world, gained through the natural sciences.

Both science and religion spring from the same roots of puzzlement, wonder and the desire to understand. Science, it is often said, tends to ask 'how' questions whilst religion asks 'why' questions. One seeks mechanism (understood as whatever physical way things come to be, not simply the mechanical); the other seeks meaning. Quite so sharp a separation is too crude a characterization, for mechanism must be understood if meanings are rightly to be discerned. Theology must take natural science into account; the theologians need to do their scientific homework. Neglect of it may have contributed to modern feelings of the irrelevance of religion.

We welcome science's discoveries about the world. To the extent that scientists are searching for the truth (and that is the motivation of all fundamental scientific inquiry), we are glad to make common cause with them. For us today, the promise that the Spirit leads us into all truth must certainly be understood to include the truth of science. Our purpose is to argue for the widest possible context in which to do theology. Religious doctrine must take account of the history of the physical world as the setting for the history of humanity and also as the story of God's universal creative activity. Needless to say, the latter is understood as the continuous sustaining of an evolving process and not, in a deistic way, as merely an instant of initiation.

The Bible begins with creation stories expressed in terms of the cosmologies of their day. It must surely be our purpose to make similar use of the vastly better informed cosmology, now available to us. Other sources of creation theology in the Old Testament include Second Isaiah (perhaps influenced by contact with the astronomically quite sophisticated culture of Babylon) and the Wisdom writers (who in their cool appraisal of the world around them represent the nearest that ancient Israel got to a 'scientific' tradition). The prologue of John's Gospel relates the creation of all things to the action of the *Logos*. One of the concepts constellated around the Word is that of rational order. There is, therefore, encouragement from 'the book of scripture' to attempt to read 'the book of nature' with all due seriousness.

Science has an impressive story to tell about cosmic history. In brief we may say that just as man emerged through biological evolution, so the earth emerged from the ashes of dead stars, which in their turn emerged from the hydrogen and helium formed in the first three minutes of the universe's history, a history which in the shortest instants following on the fiery explosion of the Big Bang (if we are to believe the boldest speculations of the cosmologists) had already seen a sequence of remarkable transformations in the nature of cosmic actuality. Cosmologists are able to attempt to speak of the universe when it was only a fraction of a second old because it was then so simple and undifferentiated in its structure – at one stage an almost uniform energetic soup of elementary particles, for instance. Yet, over a fifteen-billion-year history, that initial simplicity has evolved systems as complex and interesting as ourselves. Out of stardust has come humankind, beings capable of selfconsciousness and spiritual awareness. To speak thus is by no means to embrace a reductionist account. The history of cosmic evolution appears continuous. Scientific inspection reveals no need to postulate the injection of a new ingredient before humankind could come to be, but that history is open to an interpretation emphasizing the need to consider entities in their totality, within which humanity can be recognized as novel and unique. 'Mere matter' (as it might have seemed) has proved to be endowed with an astonishing degree of fruitfulness. That from the processes of the universe have emerged creatures capable of understanding the cosmos is a profound and moving mystery.

It is time to be more specific. We are seeking in this book to speak not of God in general, but more especially of the work of the Holy Spirit. And the subject of this chapter is the Spirit in relation to creation. The Spirit did not first take to the world stage at Pentecost. Nor is the Spirit's activity confined simply to those who lay claim to the Spirit. Everywhere and at all times the Spirit has been at work. How are we to think of this creative activity?

Though we are mindful of the theological tradition which asserts that the Holy Trinity operates externally (*ad extra*) as a divine unity, it seems appropriate nevertheless to seek some characterization of what might be considered the particular mode of the work of the Spirit in creation. We recognize the Father as the fount of being, the eternal origin of all temporal existence, the ground and guarantor of the universe. The Word speaks to us of those rational principles with which the cosmos is endowed, since we have noted that such a notion of cosmic order is one of the concepts associated with the Greek *Logos*, used by John in the prologue to his gospel. There is a profound sense of wonder among those who study physical science at the rational transparency of the world – the way that realms of experience far removed from the everyday yet prove to be open in their pattern and structure to our inquiry – and the remarkable rational beauty so revealed, which exhibits itself most strikingly in the economy and elegance of the mathematical statements of fundamental physical law. The Old Testament picture of Wisdom acting as God's delighting consort in creation (to which we referred in the preceding chapter) is taken up into the New Testament's understanding of the Cosmic Christ. For the working of the Spirit we look to a meaning to be found in *paraklētos* (cf. John 14.16), namely the one alongside. What we have said about the Father and the Word has been concerned with the law and circumstances of the universe which are the given basis for cosmic process. If we are to speak of the work of the Spirit in creation, we should need to understand this work to be within that process, and the Spirit to be in relation to the evolving universe.

Immediately one senses a danger. Is the Spirit, then, to become a sophisticated version of that pseudo-deity, the God of the gaps, inserted wherever apologists could find room, as the 'explanation' of the currently inexplicable, and continually being moved on by the advance of knowledge? One must confess that not all recent Christian writing about the Spirit seems to have avoided that trap. A correction to such a tendency is provided by Bishop John V. Taylor in his book on the Spirit, *The Go-Between God* (p. 28):

> If we think of a Creator at all, we are to find him on the inside of creation. And if God is really on the inside, we must find him in the processes, not in the gaps. We know now that there are no gaps, no points at which a special intervention is conceivable. From first to last the process has been continuous. Nature is all of a piece, a seamless robe. There is no evidence of a break, as we once imagined, between inorganic matter and the emergence of the first living organisms; nor between man's animal precursors and the emergence of man himself. If the hand of God is to be recognised in this continuous creation, it must be found not in isolated intrusions, not in any gaps, but in the very process itself.

Our brief comments on the role of the Father and the Word in creation indicate that there is more to be said of the Creator-God (in transcendent relation to the ground of all process) than Bishop Taylor explicitly acknowledges in this passage, but we may take to heart his words as far as the role of the Spirit is concerned. The Spirit's work is certainly nothing so occasional as the word 'intervention' might seem to imply. In fact, how could God be related to creation in so fitful a way as that would suggest? There must be a continuing consistency in all that God does. It will be our contention that the process of the world is not just the inexorable unwinding of a gigantic piece of cosmic clockwork, but rather there is some flexibility to it so that a genuine becoming takes place, yielding actual novelty. In that case the possibility of some interaction between creation and the Creator-Spirit seems an appropriate expectation. We shall see in due course how the modern scientific understanding of the nature of the physical world is by no means inhospitable to this view.

One consequence of a 'God really on the inside' is that we should expect this activity to be hidden, cloaked from view by its immersion within what is going on. The Spirit's action will be subtle rather than manifest, perceptible by faith but not demonstrable by experiment. The image in Genesis 1 of 'the Spirit hovering over the waters' (if that is the correct translation) is consistent with that relationship. The hiddenness of the Spirit's activity in creation also accords with the way some Orthodox think about the nature of the divine Persons. Vladimir Lossky writes, 'The third Hypostasis of the Trinity is the only one not having His image in another Person. The Holy Spirit, as Person, remains unmanifested, hidden, concealing Himself in His very appearing.' Lossky goes on to quote St Symeon the New Theologian addressing the Spirit '. . . Come, hidden mystery; come, treasure without name; come, unutterable thing; . . . '(*The Mystical Theology of the Eastern Church*, p. 160).

Can one whose appearance is so masked truly be spoken of as a Person? As we have noted elsewhere (p. 158), it took the Church some centuries to arrive at accepting fully the divinity and personhood of the Spirit, and Christians have often subsequently found it a struggle to rise above speaking of the Spirit in terms more appropriate to an impersonal energy or influence. For many, it must be confessed, Pentecost is distinctly the least of the great festivals and it has been a benefit of the charismatic movement that it has helped to redress that balance. It is not easy to specify what personhood implies, but using 'the Christological lens' we may surely say that it must involve capacities both for action and for passion (without this exhausting the definition of personhood). W. H. Vanstone (in *The Stature of Waiting*) has drawn our attention to the way in which the verbs in the gospels relating to Christ are initially in the active but then, as the story of his earthly life draws to its close, they become predominantly passive. An account of the Spirit written only in the active voice would indeed be in danger of making the Spirit into a cosmic force, an impersonal resource of power. An account written in the passive voice alone would be the story of an impotent spectator of the world's process, a 'cosmic sponge' simply soaking up the suffering of the world. Only in a dialectic between action and passion do we discern a being whose nature calls for fitting description in personal terms. In the New Testament the Spirit is not only the source of power (e.g. Rom. 15.19) but also can be grieved (Eph. 4.30). We have to go on to ask the extent to which our experience and understanding of the physical world cohere with these theological claims for the creative work of the Spirit.

First we consider the possibility of the Spirit's *action* within the evolving process of the world. Any creative activity, bringing about that which is new, requires for its possibility that there is an openness in what is going on. Otherwise the future is just a rearrangement of what was already existing in the past, with no intrinsic novelty. In a purely mechanical universe there is no true development. Pierre Simon Laplace, the greatest of Newton's successors, conceived of a demon calculator who, knowing the present positions and velocities of all the atoms in a Newtonian world, could immediately predict the whole future and retrodict the whole past. In such a universe there would be no becoming. Time would be just an index of where one is along the tramline, not a measure of how such a universe has evolved.

There is something fishy about Laplace's picture, particularly when applied to himself. We should take with the utmost seriousness our intuition that we enjoy some room for manoeuvre within the flux of what is going on. It is a basic human experience that our futures are to some degree open. In the science of the twentieth century we have come to see that the physical world is indeed different from the way that Laplace thought about it. Partly this is due to quantum theory's abolition of precise determinism, though that is almost always only of significance for small-scale events at the atomic level or below. Much more significant for our present purpose is the fact that the theory of dynamical instabilities (the theory of chaos, as it is called) has made it plain that even Newtonian systems are far from being generally susceptible to tight prediction and control. This is due to the exquisite sensitivity that these systems display in relation to the minutest variation in their circumstance. (In a crude way this will be familiar to any snooker player!) In terms of a metaphor of Karl Popper, the universe proves to be composed of (unpredictable) clouds with only a few (predictable) clocks among them.

Laplace had supposed that his demon possessed exact knowledge of everything that is happening. It would have seemed reasonable to suppose that if that knowledge were not quite exact, then the predicted consequences would also not be quite exact, but to a degree that was contained within tolerable limits. A key discovery has been that in general this is not true. Instead, for complex dynamical systems, initial circumstances which differ from each other by only infinitesimal amounts lead to subsequent motions which diverge from each other to arbitrary degrees. One of the earliest discoveries in this area arose from the study of computer models of the weather. This is 'only half-jokingly known as the Butterfly Effect – the notion that a butterfly stirring the air today in Peking can transform storm systems next month in New York' (J. Gleick, *Chaos* p. 8). When we are concerned with systems of such delicate sensitivity, the smallest fluctuations can trigger substantial consequences.

Intrinsic unpredictability is concerned with what we can know, but it gives us unforced encouragement to go on to an option about what we believe to be the case, taking a more supple view of reality than that provided by the Laplacian straitjacket. At last a picture of the physical world is available in which there seems some degree of consonance in thinking of ourselves as among the inhabitants of that world. Its unpredictable flexibility is congruent with our experience of openness. That flexibility is not confined to living beings; the process of the universe is shot through with it. Thus there seems also the possibility for the working of the Spirit within the whole cosmic process.

It is important to be clear about what is being said. We are not claiming anything so extravagant as that the age-old problems of divine and human action are solved in detail. We simply record the death of a merely mechanical view and the birthpangs of a physics able to speak of both being *and* becoming. The openness that characterizes the modern theory of dynamical systems is due to those systems having, in their temporal development, to thread their way through a labyrinth of proliferating bifurcating possibilities. One can get some feel for what is involved by thinking of the very simplest model of a single bifurcation. Consider a bead threading a perfectly smooth wire in the shape of an inverted U. The bead rests at the top of the wire. The tiniest 'nudge' will displace it to one

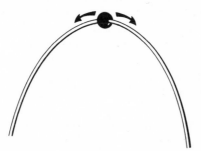

side or the other, and according to which way it is displaced the bead will fall either to right or to left. Thus infinitesimal triggers produce widely contrasting outcomes (way over to the right or way over to the left), in which no transaction of energy is required (the smallest displacement will do the trick if the wire is perfectly smooth).

Of course, we are concerned, not with beads on wires, but with the abstract structure of possibility illustrated by this simple system. It turns out that complex dynamical systems evolve through endless bifurcations, the negotiation of which involve zero-energy exchange but which result in non-zero difference in consequent behaviour (the bead falls to the right or to the left). This crude and simple parable may help us to consider the feasibility of the Spirit's action within the almost infinite variety and open flexibility of cosmic process. The picture is not of energetic causation (the Spirit is not an agent among other physical agencies) nor of arbitrary intervention in gaps (there is no suspension of the operation of those physical laws whose regularities the theist will see as reflections of divine faithfulness) but of a guiding within the *inherent* openness of the flux of becoming. Necessarily the Spirit's action is hidden within the cloudiness of the intrinsically unpredictable. There is, of course, no interference with those occurrences (such as the succession of the seasons) which do enjoy a clock-work regularity. We believe that modern physical theory is entirely consonant with theological discourse of the Spirit at work 'really on the inside'.

We do not attempt to breach the hiddenness by attempting to spell out any detailed conjectures of how the Spirit has been working. A modern scientific writer has said about the universe, 'There exists alongside the entropy arrow (the direction of decay) another arrow of time, equally fundamental, and no less subtle in nature . . . I refer to the fact that the universe is *progressing* – through the steady growth of structure, organisation and complexity – to ever more developed and elaborate states of matter and energy'. The writer goes on to refer to this increase in organisation as 'an objective fact' (P. Davies, *The Cosmic Blueprint*, p. 20). Teilhard de Chardin called this fact complexification. The universe started extremely simple and uniform. It has become remarkably differentiated, with highly structured subsystems (such as ourselves). There is no reason to suppose that this process is not susceptible to discussion in scientific terms – indeed the quotation above is taken from a book which is about such topics as the theory of complex dynamical systems. But since science is discerning processes intrinsically open in their character, there is no reason to deny to theology the right to its own point of view, as it seeks to understand the evolving fruitfulness of the universe in terms of the patient and subtle operation of the Spirit on the inside of physical process.

The Spirit's *passion* in the creative process of the world may be most clearly discerned in relation to the suffering found within it. This thought leads us from the generalities of physics to the greater particularities of biology and ecology. The costliness and blind alleys of evolution, and the precarious environmental balances necessary for life, are part of the story of creation. The processes and organisation of human societies are indissolubly bound up with a wider economy involving other organisms and non-living components. All in the end is subject to decay. Humanity is the only member of this world known to us which is able to give voice to its continuing groans and travails as part of the waiting expectation of the ultimate glory willed by God. One of the roles of the Spirit is as the articulator of hope in the midst of passion. Because of its condemnation to futility, nature only makes ultimate sense as a creation if it is oriented towards something beyond itself. It is the Spirit who enables us to be incorporated fully into the freedom of God's redemptive act in Christ and so to know our destiny in him. United in impatient straining with the rest of the created order, we are nevertheless made by the Spirit into an earnest of that hope for liberation for which all await in eager expectation (Rom. 8.18ff.). In the Spirit we are bound to the natural world in a solidarity of pain and longing, yet we are given also in the Spirit a pledge (2 Cor.5.5.) of the final glory when we shall be incorporated, together with the whole created realm, into the life of God.

Our participation in creation is a painful thing in which the Spirit shares. Understanding the process of creation is a sacrificial task in which we share in the birthpangs of nature from suffering into hope. In our exploration of the physical world we are moved by more than just a quizzical curiosity about a work already completed. Rather, we are participating in a continuing process of which our own longings are an integral part.

This understanding gives us a renewed perception of the yearning which we believe God has had from the beginning for the completion of creation, for the Spirit lets us feel God's ceaseless love for God's own creation. This hidden action and passion together are the measure of God's generosity and steadfast love, as God freely creates the other. The Spirit's presence 'really on the inside' signifies the extent of God's renunciation and sacrifice, from whose self-giving nothing is held back. In these terms we may understand in what way the Spirit is at work 'on the inside'.

Yet the Spirit is also *at work*. This work is a continuing expression of God's tactful and steadfast relationship of gift and response to all that is, and the order and resourcefulness of creation is perceived as a corresponding response to that. Each of God's creatures is called to be faithful according to its nature, even when that means, for example, that for elements of the earth's crust their nature results in earthquakes. Hard though that saying is, it is by this acceptance of individual creaturely character that the creation glorifies its Creator (cf.Ps.148). Thus we are able to see the physical world, not only as the arena of suffering, but also as a movement of praise, that is, as a reflection back to God of God's glory, a point already suggested on p. 185. The *Benedicite* expresses this view, and many Christian saints and poets have so understood the natural order.

To see the world as manifestation and celebration imposes a particular attitude to it. We are led to respect and trust nature, to explore it in the confidence that what we find can be part of our apprenticeship of praise. We learn to affirm the diversity and gratuitous abundance of creation in its own right. Like the writer of the Book of Job, we can see God's glory even in the remote and (humanly) irrelevant aspects of the universe. The grand sweep of evolutionary process is part of this vision: out of cosmic history emerged beings capable of praising God through lives of conscious freedom, acknowledged dependence and respectful authority. In humanity the praises of creation find an articulate voice.

Such an understanding provides both a test and an affirmation for the work of science and technology. We ask how well they glorify God through the enlightenment of our imaginations and the enablement of our activity. A similar affirmation and challenge is presented to the artist. The key is the belief that God's fundamental act is the sharing of the divine life, diffused and reflected throughout creation. For human beings that reflection is expressed in the generosity of love, that love demonstrated and set free in the cross and resurrection of Christ.

Our theology must look beyond the narrowly Christian or the narrowly human whilst retaining its Christ-centred vision. Because the nature of God's intended new humanity is revealed in liberation from self-assertion, a Christian theology of art and nature can furnish a critique of a distorted anthropocentrism. A prophetic word is to be spoken against fantasies of absolute control and unlimited exploitation. Humanity is not empowered to exercise a ruthless domination, cutting down rain forests for short-term gain, but it is called to a careful stewardship, preserving the integrity of the earth's environment. We must seek a technology that is genuinely oriented towards living in and with creation, working with the grain of nature and taking seriously its ecological balance. There can be no absolutizing of immediate human wants, and we must struggle against a technocracy which fails to have a sense of our belonging to this whole planet.

Yet we also acknowledge that we have every scientific reason to suppose that eventually the sun will explode, killing all life on earth and that, even more remotely, the whole universe will collapse or decay. While these predictions lie billions of years in the future, they serve to warn us against any facile utopianism within the course of present physical process. In the end, even the universe's fruitfulness will prove to have been a transient episode. We need not be dismayed, for in the end the only source of lasting hope is God. 'The whole creation has been groaning in travail together until now; and not only the creation, but we ourselves, who have the first fruits of the Spirit, groan inwardly as we wait for adoption as sons, the redemption of our bodies . . . If we hope for what we do not see, we wait for it with patience' (Rom.8.22ff.). The patient working of the Spirit within physical process will find its final completion in the transcendent act of bringing about a redeemed new creation, beyond present physical process, a point which will be developed in our concluding chapter. However, before we consider the consummation of all things, we devote a chapter to a point on which in this chapter we have touched but briefly, namely artistic and intellectual creativity, and we seek there also to discern the Spirit's work.

Chapter 9
The Spirit and creativity

The subject of our last chapter, divine creation, would seem to lead naturally into reflection on the theme of human creativity. Indeed, that very opening chapter of the Bible which tells us of the divine creation also speaks of our being in the divine image (Gen. 1.26f.); thus some sort of analogy between divine making and human making, however remote, must be implied, and it goes without saying that the divine making is qualitatively unique. Both in creation and salvation it has the power to make the wholly new, what in the language of later theology came to be described as *creatio ex nihilo*. Though in the Old Testament this may be only implicit, nonetheless the qualitative difference is just as much stressed through the use of a different word for divine, as distinct from human creativity (the Hebrew *bara*). Yet even with this qualitative difference fully acknowledged, the analogy remains. Sometimes this has meant that the term creativity has itself beeen used to express the character of the relation, but more commonly some more particular feature of human making has been highlighted. Two of the most common aspects associated with the divine image in human creativity are the rationality of human activity and its free character, both of which set us apart from the animal world. They have also been used to underpin two very different approaches to the arts. They will therefore form a recurring but contrasting theme in what follows. First we must set these two models against a wider biblical background.

The opening chapter of John's gospel has a richness of meaning which defies easy translation into other thought forms. Even so the reader who knows only English must at the very least take away from the passage the astonishing claim that Jesus is the expression (the 'Word') for what God is like. The opening verse with its deliberate parallel to the opening verse of Genesis ('In the beginning . . .') shows that even more is at stake, something which becomes much more obvious when we realise that the Greek word *Logos* means not just 'word' or 'expression' but 'explanation' or 'intelligibility'. Moreover it is not too hard to understand how the one word may be used to convey what may initially seem to us very different ideas, for any attempt to make something intelligible involves trying to express it in words. However that may be, the point of the comparison is that, just as the divine *fiat*, the divine word, brought intelligibility and order to the earth which 'was without form and void' (Gen. 1.2), so now we know Jesus to be the key to the intelligibility of our own lives and indeed the life of the world as a whole, for 'all things were made through him' (John 1.3).

In John's gospel it is the Spirit who will teach all things (John 14.26) and will bear witness (John 15.26) to the Son who is this Word. So we may legitimately infer that it is the Spirit who makes possible our perceiving of Jesus as the clue to the world's intelligibility. The Old Testament of course makes no such attributions to specific persons of the Trinity. What we do find is the insistence that the discovery of a rational order to the world is a divine gift and that perception of this is equally the gift of God. The whole of what we now call the Wisdom literature stands in testimony to this. To many of us today much of this literature, such as the Book of Proverbs or Ecclesiastes, may seem all too worldly advice, but there is no doubt that for the Bible such perceptivity into the way things are was taken as indicative of closeness to God, as in the magnificent description of Wisdom 'playing' before God in Proverbs 8.30f. or in the lyrical equation of Law and Wisdom in Ecclesiasticus 24. Occasionally also the fact of this 'spirit of wisdom' being a divine gift is highlighted by its being portrayed as conveyed through a rite of laying on of hands (cf. e.g. Deut. 34.9). Thus there is firm biblical precedent for understanding the divine image in us as, among other things, that rational perception of the world's order given to us by participation in the divine Spirit.

On the other hand another very different understanding of the image is also available. It need not be seen as in conflict with the model described above, but as a matter of fact it often has been. It finds its natural point in doubts whether the rationality of the world and God's purposes for it are as readily accessible as the other tradition often seems to maintain. Might it not be the case that human creativity, so far from being a matter of perceiving what is already there for all to see, is really a question of transcending the way a fallen world is, of breaking out, of discovering through God's grace a new order of existence, one to be achieved by us as we live under a new order of freedom, which is very different from the free choices which have embroiled us in the world of sin? From such a picture it is not hard to derive the idea of reason and religion being opposed, and thus also the creativity of the spiritual world being in opposition to the world of reason. That is a shallow view, but it is important to be aware of the way in which the Bible can be used to generate such an account, as it has played an influential role in one of the two approaches to the arts which we shall consider later. In fact it is possible to derive from both Old and New Testaments the view that creativity is essentially a matter of our being caught up by the Spirit into a new order of existence and thus of our sharing in the creative work of God. Thus, while a passage like Exodus 35.30ff. portrays the Spirit as enabling the ordered work of craftsmanship, there are plenty of other passages to suggest that the Spirit operates more like an invasive power which transcends our natural faculties. Think for instance of the way in which Israel's Judges seem suddenly to acquire their powers without any obvious reference to natural leadership (e.g. Judges 3.10; 6.34; 14.6), or the manner in which prophets are portrayed as acting under an ecstatic trance (e.g. 1 Sam. 10.6; 19.23f.). Again in the New Testament it is tempting to read Paul's frequent contrast between the freedom of the Christian in the Spirit and the slavery of the Law as implying the superiority of the Christian to all rules. One might also recall that probably the best-known verse in the New Testament about the nature of spirit speaks of it blowing 'where it wills' (John 3.8).

A spontaneous freedom and a constrictive rationality are thereby contrasted instead of their both being seen as integral to any approach which attempts to do justice to the richness of the biblical narrative. That any deeper penetration of the biblical perspective requires their integration would seem obvious. Paul's speech on the Areopagus Hill (Acts 17. esp. vv. 23,28) insists that pagan perception has not gone far enough, not that it contained no truth. In his own writings Paul seems prepared to admit that our freedom as Christians is exercised within the context of the endowments which God has given us by nature, and that the Spirit operates through and develops these natural endowments. Elsewhere in the Bible we find this principle at work: for instance, Peter, who had a certain rock-like quality, became through the Spirit a more reliable rock.

We have mentioned these two models for understanding the way in which human making reflects the divine, not primarily so as to discuss the biblical approach in its own right but in order to provide a framework which will enable us to think better and more deeply about an issue of vital importance for our own times, this question of creativity. So concerned have Christians been with the divine paradigm that we have failed to give adequate attention to two major concerns of our own society: first, the crisis about the meaning of human labour, and secondly, the role of the arts in human self-understanding. The biblical world was one in which there was little or no choice about the sort of work one pursued and one in which many of the art forms which are now so prominent in our lives formed no part (e.g. novels, painting, cinema, television). That does not mean that the Bible can have nothing to say to us on the matter, but it does mean that we must think deeply in order to perceive the connection.

In the case of work, the Bible unhesitatingly declares this good and ordained by God: man is put into the Garden of Eden 'to till it and keep it' (Gen. 2.15). Such stewardship of the divine creation had already inherent within it an intrinsic intelligibility and order. Whether one pursued a nomadic or an agricultural form of life, this stewardship meant maintaining the order that God had already given to nature, either through activities like feeding the flocks and lambing or through attention to the cycle of the seasons and the rotation of the crops. It is this order that we find reflected in the Old Testament feasts (Passover with its unleavened bread marking the beginning of the barley harvest, Pentecost the end of the wheat harvest, and Tabernacles the autumn fruit harvest). All that changed with the Industrial Revolution and with the micro-chip revolution which has succeeded it. Many people are now much more free about the choice of job they pursue, but there has also come with that a crisis of meaning: whether in our making there is after all any intelligibility to be discovered in what we do (apart from the obvious fact of the necessity of making money to earn our keep). Through the centuries much toil has been experienced as tedious, not merely because the work is routine, but precisely because the worker fails to perceive himself as a true part of the process that gives order and intelligibility to what he is making; the final product appears to bear no intrinsic relationship to his own role. More recently the same problem has expressed itself in new ways. Think how once skilled jobs like an engine driver or print worker have with the new technology become quickly learnt, and how this has led to a crisis of meaning for the worker who continues to pursue the same occupation. He has ceased to be a maker, an imposer of intelligibility on his world; instead he has become a mere operator, someone who sets the process in motion but who cannot really take the credit for the way it turns out.

Thus it would seem that for many of us the modern world of work is pulling in two opposed directions so far as the divine image is concerned. On the one hand, there is far more freedom about what we do than there ever has been in the history of the world, but, on the other, with this has gone a decline in the need for the exercise of our own imposition of intelligibility upon the world. The machine is already there, providing it. This is an issue which industrial psychologists take with increasing seriousness, but reflection upon it within Christianity, unfortunately, still remains in its infancy. Yet, if this imposition of order is an essential part of what it is to be truly human and of what it is to be in the divine image, then we have clear justification for Christian involvement in issues of the workplace: for instance in ways whereby work can be given greater meaning by worker participation in the process as a whole, or in the refusal to reduce human labour to a role purely subordinate to that of the machine. Such reflections remind us that the problem of unemployment is much deeper than the loss of earnings, devastating though that always is. The loss of one's job is also the loss of a chance to impose meaning on the way the world is, and thus to gain recognition from others that one's contribution is worthwhile.

The sharp distinction between artisan and artist with which we are all so familiar dates back only to the fifteenth century. As a symbol of changing attitudes one may note that it is only with the Renaissance that the framing of pictures began; their framing deliberately set them apart. It is also at this time that one begins to get the stress on development and originality that was to become such a marked feature of the Romantic Movement in the late eighteenth and early nineteenth century. This stress is a marked feature of Vasari's *Lives of the Artists* which was published in 1550.

Intellectual history is seldom simple, but as a rough characterization we may say that at the Renaissance one understanding of the arts began to give place to another, though the victory for the latter was decisively won only with the Romantic Movement. For simplicity's sake we may therefore call the earlier view the classical view of the arts, and the later the romantic, though the reader should recall that both these terms have often been used in a variety of other ways. That change of perception can also be said to correspond to a change from one model to another among the two ways of understanding the divine image which we outlined above. The earlier, classical conception of the artist saw him helping us to identify more closely the order already inherent in the divine creation, and indeed he also saw himself doing this within the context of an existing tradition. By contrast the Renaissance began to stress the free role of the individual, a view further accentuated by the Romantic Movement. The free, innovative, unpredictable character of art then became the norm, and the concern was not with the discernment of a rational order in things but with the evocation of feeling and one's response to it.

Temperamentally people are often much more attracted to one form of artistic expression than another. In music, for instance, for some Bach and Mozart are taken as the norm, while for others music only really begins with Beethoven's Third Symphony and the Romantic composition to which that gave birth. But we must be on our guard against making our theories correspond to our prejudices. The later Romantic understanding of the artist was motivated just as much by religious concerns as was the earlier model. It is perhaps initially easier to understand why a concern with order should be seen in essentially religious terms and so why Barth could write of Mozart that 'hearing creation unresentfully and impartially, he did not produce merely his own music but that of creation'. Equally we find that great theorist of the Romantic Movement, Samuel Taylor Coleridge, declaring the imagination to be 'a repetition in the finite mind of the eternal act of creation'. What had happened is that religion (and indeed society in general) had lost its trust in the power of human beings to break through to a perception of the rational, and so, if another world was to be known at all, it had to be known through another medium, through the response of the imagination and emotions to the inspired prophet. The change of attitude is well illustrated by Goya's etching in the Prado in Madrid, *The Dream of Reason Produces Monsters*, or, if a more religious painter is preferred, we recall William Blake's portrayal of Newton with his eyes firmly fixed on the ground and his comment that 'he who sees the Ratio sees only himself'. Inevitably in such a major cultural movement it would be misleading to suggest that only one position was adopted towards reason. Probably more common than Goya's stress on the distorting power of reason would have been the suggestion that the power of reason is strictly limited and should take second place to such notions as insight, feeling, imagination and intuition. Perhaps the difference is best illustrated by William Blake's portrayal of the Trinity. In it a massive, hovering bird, the inspiring Spirit, is given central place, and the crucified Christ is seen with body curved and arms outstretched being drawn by the Father in imaginative flight towards that same Spirit. Readers will no doubt already have spotted some parallel between, on the one hand, the romantic and the classical and, on the other, the work of the Holy Spirit, for it is possible to discern the work of the Spirit in bringing both invention and order. Yet, just as in the explicitly religious case it is difficult to determine the proper balance between free innovation and ordered rationality, so is the problem, if anything, more acute in the artistic case. Here all we can do is to provide a few pointers to enable readers to reflect more deeply on the issue for themselves. We shall take each of the two major approaches in turn, and note a few of the points, both positive and negative, which can be made in respect of each.

To describe, as in the classical model, the artist's role as one of enabling us to see the order and intelligibility in the world, may seem to make the artist redundant. Can we not already perceive it easily enough for ourselves? But the fact that we have eyes to see does not mean that we use them to see. The artist can thus help us to perceive what might otherwise pass us by unnoticed. Think for instance of symbolic connections made in medieval stained glass between the various decisive events in the biblical story, or the links made between the life, death and resurrection of the incarnate Lord and the people and events of the artists' own day. Stanley Spencer's portrayal of the involvement in the crucifixion of his fellow villagers in Cookham in Berkshire ensures that we cannot artificially divorce Pilate, Caiaphas and the crowd from the England of our own day.

Nor should we suppose that such perceptivity is confined to explicitly religious art. Indeed art critics have often drawn attention to the way in which what appears to be a purely secular subject can have a profoundly religious character. This would seem particularly so of the landscape painting of sixteenth- and seventeenth-century Holland. It is not that the artists were retreating into secular themes, in what remained after all still a deeply religious nation. Rather, it is that the Calvinist ethos now perceived God within the perfect balance of landscape; there was no need to point to another world in order to establish symmetry and balance, especially as in any case this would have involved the dangerous use of 'images'. Again, the scientist's work is not explicitly religious, but it remains true that many practising scientists have experienced something bordering upon religious awe and wonder at the nature of the order in the universe which they have made known to us. This certainly includes the most famous physicist of our century, Albert Einstein whose attitude was one of wonder and submission to the way things are. Indeed one of his most famous remarks ('God does not play dice') was a response to Heisenberg's uncertainty principle, and indicates his reluctance to allow that there could be an element of unpredictability and so an element of 'disorder' in the universe. Likewise theoretical physicists like Paul Dirac have used the search for mathematical beauty as a powerful guiding principle in their research. Towards the end of this chapter we shall suggest ways in which the creative work of the scientist may be understood in terms of the activity of the Holy Spirit.

Yet at the same time we should be on our guard against supposing that perception of structure and order necessarily leads to a religious response. Indeed even in the case of great painting the structure and religion may be fundamentally opposed. The Cubism of Picasso's *Les Demoiselles d'Avignon* may well be a case in point. Does not Picasso in this painting reduce the unfortunate prostitutes of Avignon Street in Barcelona to mere impersonal structures, mere things? Yet at other times even when there is no explicit connection with our faith, the Christian cannot but be grateful to the artist for opening his eyes to the way things are. Solzhenitsyn made the point thus in his Nobel Prize speech: 'Art and literature can perform the miracle of overcoming man's characteristic weakness of learning only by his own experience, so that the experience of others passes him by . . . Art recreates in the flesh all experience lived by other men, so that each man can make this his own.' Almost all of us have had that experience in reading a novel and seeing the plight of others in a new light for the first time; we feel ourselves chastened for lack of insight into ourselves and for lack of compassion towards others.

In an influential book on Christian aesthetics the French philosopher Jacques Maritain defined beauty as 'intellect delighting in matter intelligibly arranged'. This well reflects this particular tradition in art. Aquinas for instance insisted upon three criteria for beauty: proportion, integrity and clarity. By proportion he meant essentially order or balance: by integrity fitting shape or size (small people on his view cannot be beautiful); and by clarity luminosity, the right balance of colour and light so that an object stands out appropriately. His view and that of his contemporaries that there is a right measure for everything may well seem to most of us today as absurdly over-confident. Indeed there is a whole genre of theological reasoning based on such criteria that has now vanished and which seems strangely foreign to us. How often for instance will one ever hear a sermon today on the way in which the Cross as the tree of life was deliberately intended by God as a balance to the tree that brought death in the Garden of Eden? Even the circle no longer carries the same immediate symbolic resonances as it would once have done. For those firmly entrenched in the classical tradition it was the most beautiful of geometrical figures because the most perfectly proportioned (the circumference always equidistant from the centre), and it is for this reason that it was deemed legitimate to use the symbolism even of God. In Rublev's icon of the Trinity it is somewhat hidden, but one does find on inspection that the external outline of the three angels employed to represent the Trinity when joined together do constitute a perfect circle. The intention is to indicate not just perfection, but also indissolubility, since the circle, unlike lined figures, has no obvious parts. However, perhaps a better example than the Rublev icon, and certainly one more pertinent to our theme of the Spirit, is a mosaic from the Baptistery in Albenga in northern Italy, dating from the fifth century. Here the Holy Spirit is represented as a perfect circle of doves encompassing Christ's monogram. In other words, in striking contrast to the Blake drawing to which we referred earlier, the Holy Spirit, so far from being seen as the key to imaginative flight, is viewed as the source of access to perfect order and proportion.

Another feature of this tradition which has all but vanished from our thinking is the ascription to God of beauty itself, not just in the weak sense that God is its source but in the strong sense that God's very being is beautiful. We are still prepared today to speak of God being Goodness itself or Truth itself, but what we need to recall is that for our ancestors in the faith it was once just as natural to speak of God's being Beauty itself. So for example in a famous passage in his *Confessions* Augustine does not hesitate to write of God: 'Late have I loved thee, O Beauty.' The use of such language exudes confidence in a wholly integrated world. The creation as perfect balance and proportion is for all its beauty but a pale reflection of the creator, who is perfect beauty. One reason, perhaps the principal reason, for this attribution was the conviction that what made a proportion beautiful was its intrinsic simplicity, and that therefore simplicity itself must be beautiful. But, if that is so, the argument goes, then God is the most beautiful of all beings because God is the most simple, in the sense that one has only to think of one of the divine attributes and immediately the others are seen to be implied. For instance, it was commonly argued that one who knows all thereby also knows the good and thus is goodness itself. Also, one who is truly good would be inhibited from the perfect exercise of goodness unless possessing complete power to bring this goodness to fruition.

Today we no longer share the same confidence in such arguments. It is, however, worth drawing attention to the way in which one major theologian of the twentieth century has attempted to revive this tradition for us, but in a way which takes seriously the fact that we live in a post-romantic world, namely, Hans Urs von Balthasar (d.1988), whose major work *The Glory of the Lord: A Theological Aesthetics* is currently being translated into English. Though a Roman Catholic, he has been heavily influenced by two major Protestant theologians, Kierkegaard and Barth; and this is reflected in the way in which he looks through the lens of revelation at the numerous writers whom he examines and evaluates. In effect revelation has become his measuring rod; it is this which secures beyond doubt that his work is no mere attempt simply to return to the past, but rather a serious engagement of the classical tradition with the romantic challenge. Perhaps the difference between von Balthasar's approach and earlier classical accounts could be described by saying that whereas the latter took account of the presence of the creative Word in all things, he refers everything more explicitly to the Word made flesh. In effect what has happened is that notions like *kenōsis* and crucifixion now play a central role, whereas for the earlier classical tradition these were incidental or secondary to a stress on the intelligibility and rationality of creation, as implied in the notion of *Logos*. Of course all Christians would be agreed that the crucified Lord is indispensable to a total understanding of reality; where they differ is whether this means that no part of reality is intelligible without such reference. Perhaps the difference can best be brought out by contrasting the recurring reference to the crucifixion in von Balthasar with the irrepressible optimism, despite his own ill-health, of the poet Alexander Pope. For instance in his *Essay on Man* of 1734 we find him writing:

> All nature is but art unknown to thee;
> All chance, direction which thou canst not see;
> All discord, harmony not understood
> All partial evil, universal good.

There we have the earlier classical tradition's ineradicable confidence in the uncomplicated goodness of the world. By contrast, for someone later in the classical tradition, like von Balthasar, the beauty of an integrated world is hard won, and then only thanks to the gift of revelation. A twentieth-century poet in the classical tradition like T. S. Eliot takes a similar view: 'The life of the soul does not consist in the contemplation of one consistent world, but in the painful task of unifying . . . joining incompatible ones, and passing when possible, from two or more discordant viewpoints to a higher which shall somehow include and transmute them'. Some artists have indeed seen and experienced a kind of crucifixion in their creativity; in God's creative activity there is, as it were, simultaneity of cost and joy.

Though von Balthasar and Eliot insist on the pain and difficulty in producing an integrated vision, they remain within the classical tradition because they think it possible. By contrast, it is because of the romantic tradition's lack of confidence in the power of reason that even its religious exponents remain doubtful whether such a reconciliation can become accessible to us. Instead, the role of the artist becomes a much more limited one, namely to evoke within us an imaginative response to the possibility of different worlds and different realities. The difference may perhaps be seen at its starkest in the approach to evil. Whereas for the classical tradition evil has always been to some degree an embarrassment, because it represents something resistant to proportion and elegance, for romantic writers it is often the harshness of reality (including suffering and moral evil), which is seen as the primary vehicle through which God acts; thus part of the artist's role has become to help us to see God through the apparent darkness, in which there is no tidy balance and proportion. So for instance in Evelyn Waugh's *Brideshead Revisited* the narrator Charles Ryder is made to come to faith despite all the odds, and, in so far as it is a response to other human beings in the story, it seems to be precisely because his friend Sebastian remains loyal to his faith despite the fact of its preventing him from being a 'happy and healthy man'; likewise his mistress, Sebastian's sister Julia, leaves him so that she may fulfil a commitment which seems to bear no relation to human happiness. Again, in the novels of Graham Greene it is by plunging his characters into impossible dilemmas and a morass of human suffering that he evokes from them the response of faith. As a yet more extreme example one might consider the case of Flannery O'Connor, a Catholic novelist from Georgia in the United States. Were readers unaware of her own personal suffering and the very moving character of her letters, we might well be forgiven for thinking that the intention of her stories was simply to create some awful piece of black humour rather than to open our eyes to the terrible consequence of our own prejudices and to the redemptive character of suffering. Again, if one turns to the world of painting, Georges Rouault is one of the great Christian painters of the century, but his attitude to the world's ugliness is romantic, not classical. It is only by bringing us face to face with all the nastiness of life that he believes it is possible to evoke from us the response of faith; hence his series of etchings called *Miserere* and his pictures of prostitutes.

The issues are too complex to be resolved quickly here. Readers must be left to themselves to decide whether the response of feeling to the world's agonies better represents a Christian approach to art as the romantic might well say, or whether the classical emphasis on the divine goodness inherent in the world is more accurate. It would be good if we could solve the dilemma by simply saying that we need both. That is already to compromise and weaken both positions. So probably in the end we must decide that one or other more accurately reflects the way in which God has placed us in the world.

Fortunately with another of the romantic challenges to the classical position, the claim that we are more than a mere reasoning faculty, it is much easier to weigh the rights and wrongs of the argument. We shall look first at the ways in which the romantic insistence on feeling and imagination can be seen justly to earn their place; then we shall consider how the argument can be carried too far in valuing any and every sort of expressiveness for its own sake.

The Church can justly be proud of its patronage of the arts both in the past and to some extent still today. But it is as well to recall that such recognition has often been hard won, and that this resistance was more often than not due to the suspicion that feeling and imagination could only detract from, rather than enhance, a true faith. Part of the worry was no doubt the Old Testament's prohibition of images, and the conviction expressed by it that the nature of God is beyond all human attempts either to conceptualize or even to imagine. Another concern was almost certainly associated with the truth that God is unembodied; access to God must, therefore, be through that part of our being which most resembles God, namely our reasoning faculties, rather than through the emotions which seem essentially bound up with our nature as physical beings. Both worries are fundamentally misconceived. Nowadays some Christians assume that such worries about the distorting and distracting power of art were products of the Reformation, but in fact they long antedate the sixteenth century. One need only recall the iconoclastic controversy of the eighth century and Emperor Leo III's attempts to prohibit all icons, or the attacks of Bernard of Clairvaux in the twelfth century on the distracting intricacies of Romanesque art, or Aquinas's reluctance in the thirteenth to have any other than unaccompanied singing in church. Nevertheless, while we take seriously the possibility of distortion, our basic attitude on this matter can never be that of the Old Testament, for the simple reason that God who is beyond our imagining has taken a concrete icon or image in the person of

Jesus Christ. So it is hard to see how one could condemn artistic representation without condemning the divine artist's self-portrayal. Artists take up pen or brush, and in doing so they do something analogous to God's activity (in which the Spirit had a full share) both in creation and in the incarnation; indeed all Christians can do something similar when through the Spirit they seek to model their lives after the pattern of Christ. As for the other worry of distraction, there are two ways in which art might distract from bringing us into closer relation with God, and both seem mistaken worries, though for rather different reasons. First, it might draw us away from the exercise of our reason. That is true, but why should this always be viewed negatively? We are more than disembodied spirits, and this is presumably taken into account in the range of ways in which God chooses to communicate with us. Secondly, if the point rather is that the seductive power of art is such that it makes us contemplate the work itself as distinct from using it purely as a vehicle towards God, this is a false contrast, for it is precisely because we value things in and for themselves that we are often led on to God. It is because we value other human beings in their own right that we are led to see them as an image of God; precisely because we value truth for itself, we come to see in God the source of all truth, and so on; in short, precisely because we value other things unconditionally, we come to see meaning in God as pre-eminently the unconditioned.

The artist David Jones in an influential essay has spoken of the 'gratuitous' character of all art. In so doing he intended to draw a contrast with a purely utilitarian approach, and he insists that even in ordinary human work this is what raises it above the merely animal, that here is a free expressiveness over and above any further ends. Another way of putting this might be to say that, though unlike the divine creation it does not proceed 'from nothing', art properly speaking is nonetheless 'for nothing'. Inherent in human creative activity is a joy which is not necessarily utilitarian. Eliot indeed refers to the sense of joy in artistic achievement as exhaustion, appeasement, absolution. Further, it needs to be said that we should value such expressiveness simply for its own sake, especially as much of it can be bought at great personal cost. There is something deeply sacrificial in artistic creation, an element of self-negation, not unlike God's own creative work, itself rooted in self-giving. For some artists pain becomes an inescapable element in their struggle to express and give of themselves to others. In such cases it is not unfitting to remark that the artist has come to share something of the life of our Lord himself, he who was the very incarnation of pain and self-giving inextricably intertwined. One instance of the painful cost of creativity may be seen in 'the weeping, walking, breaking his pens, repeating and altering a bar a hundred times' which Georges Sand tells us was composition for Chopin.

Such an approach has its dangers, and such valuing always needs to be set in some wider context. In a world in which gratuitous violence and sex are a routine part of the artistic medium it is salutary to recall the world of little more than a century ago, when a novel as apparently innocuous as *Madame Bovary* was put on trial. What so shocked the Paris of 1857 was merely the portrayal of adultery (not the sexual acts) without accompanying moral comment. There was no attempt to set the presentation in a wider frame of reference, and ever since mere expression has often been taken as sufficient justification of artistic creation. Is this not one case where the classical approach has the edge over the romantic? Though expression definitely has its value (and we are not arguing for censorship), it remains of only limited worth except in so far as it can be integrated into a larger whole. It is for this reason that morality and aesthetics cannot be totally prised apart.

It must, however, be conceded that Christians have frequently taken all too easy a route to such integration. For instance the Cambridge Camden Society which played such a large part in the revival of Gothic architecture in the nineteenth century took the view that only the good and religious man could effectively produce the right kind of architecture (Decorated Gothic), while only a little later we find the hymn writer, F. W. Faber, declaring in his correspondence that Lord Byron could not have been a great poet because he was not a good man. Life is more complicated than that. Certainly there is no guarantee that great art will necessarily affect the moral quality of people's lives; the officers at Auschwitz saw no incongruity in relaxing to Schubert's music after their dreadful deeds. Equally the equation does not hold the other way round: moral goodness is not a *sine qua non* for great art, (recall, for instance, the scandalous character of Caravaggio's life), nor is it even the case that religious belief is necessary for the production of great religious art. Agnostics like Verdi with his *Requiem* or Mahler with his *Resurrection Symphony*, and not just undoubtedly devout composers like Bruckner, have the power to move us religiously.

Christians remain divided on the question whether the Holy Spirit is active outside the Church as the community of the redeemed, though we have stated our own view on this subject in our introductory chapter (p. 41). Certainly Schleiermacher's readiness to describe a non-Christian philosopher like Spinoza as 'full of the Holy Spirit' would have shocked many a Father of the Church. Even those who wish to say that response to the Spirit is confined within the Church must agree that the Spirit can and does use the work of non-Christians to deepen the response of faith in those who already believe. In other words the Spirit may work through unbelief in much the same way as Second Isaiah once saw God acting through the pagan monarch Cyrus (Isa. 45.1), though it would be wrong to say that there was any direct response from Cyrus himself (v.4). The obvious objection to this account remains, that it suggests too manipulative a view of the Spirit's operation in the world. Yet, even if we say that the Spirit always operates in terms of personal response even among non-believers, it will still need to be conceded that the production of artistic genius is often heavily dependent on non-personal factors. Arguably Rembrandt is the greatest religious painter of all time. Yet he learned his use of light and dark contrasts from Caravaggio. Had the latter's style not been condemned by the Roman Catholic Church of the time, the Protestant Rembrandt would probably not have been able to adopt an approach to painting first advocated by this violent and licentious Catholic.

While Christians can thus rightly be criticized in their turn for too often taking too easy a route towards an integrated vision, their criticism of unqualified romantic exaltations of expression for its own sake remains justified. The excessive cult of newness and novelty which seems so often to mar some later developments of this romantic approach may also be justly criticized. We can acknowledge the fact that this romantic cult may well have helped generate the explosion of art forms which the twentieth century has witnessed. Public reaction to these has often been hostile, but Christians too have reason to be grateful for some of the possibilities that have now been realised. For instance Kandinsky and Chagall explored new possibilities for conveying 'the spiritual' by means of colour, Kandinsky even writing a book entitled 'Concerning the Spiritual in Art'; indeed they both did not hesitate to see their art in essentially religious terms. Chagall for instance has commented that, 'Art, painting is religious by nature – like everything creative'. If an explicitly Christian example is preferred, one might think of the way in which one of the great composers of our century, Olivier Messiaen, has pioneered the use of bird song as a way of conveying the presence of the divine to his fellow-believers. Nevertheless we must resist the conclusion that great art has to be innovative to be truly creative. Even the completely unoriginal can be great art. So for example when one steps into one of our great medieval cathedrals, one wonders at its grandeur and beauty, even if every feature of the building finds an exact parallel elsewhere.

The literary critic Helen Gardner has suggested that it is enough if the artist 'makes more vivid to us what we already know and feel'. No doubt this is often so. To make this the norm would however, be to err just as much in the opposite direction. Though the romantic errs who claims that art must offer something wholly new, there nonetheless remains a sense in which most art is after all striving after something new – not new in the sense of totally new to the world, but new in the sense of new perceptions for the artist or for his audience. In the ability of the artist through his work to bring new perceptions to other people, we may see some parallel with the work of the Holy Spirit; they both have a relational element. It is the Holy Spirit who establishes and perfects our relationship with Christ; it is often thanks to art or literature that we are enabled to relate to the world around us in a new way. But, just as the Holy Spirit brings what is only to us wholly new (that same relationship is already a reality for others), so can much the same be said of the role of the artistic medium. It is also often this more limited sense of newness of which artists themselves are speaking, as Aaron Copland has remarked of his composition, 'Each added work brings with it an element of self-discovery . . . a part answer to the question "Who am I?" '. We may also use it to explain how our own mundane work or hobbies can be experienced as creatively new. There are of course hundreds of others who have solved exactly the same sort of management problem or created exactly the same sort of herbaceous border, but it is the first time for us, and that is what makes it feel so creatively exciting and rewarding. The same principle applies not only to problem solving in business and to creativity in gardening: it is capable of wide application, for example to the solving of problems in personal relations and to inventiveness and creativity exhibited, say, by a child making clay models or by a student writing an essay.

Such examples, like our earlier discussion of work, remind us that human creativity is much wider than the arts, important though these are. That is why it would be wrong to conclude this discussion without a brief consideration of the natural sciences within the sphere of human creativity. It is one of the great and dangerous myths of our time that there are two cultures, one nurtured by the creative arts, the other by objective science. This false dichotomy, manifested in the division between the so-called Arts and Sciences in education, has been nurtured, among other things, by a powerful but fallacious philosophy of science – that of positivism. Accordingly science is perceived to be a purely empirical enterprise based on the twin pillars of observation and inductive verification. There is little or no room in this scheme for the creative, imaginative, conjectural faculties and consequently science is reckoned to be a cold, dispassionate, objective enterprise in which the human imagination and emotions have no part. Although this philosophy of science has long been discredited it still exercises a grip on the minds of many, including those working scientists and theologians who adopt it unquestioningly. It accounts for a great deal of the disillusionment with science and rationality which is so widespread in our age.

Sir Karl Popper, above all, has devoted his life's work to combating this fallacy and to developing an alternative interpretation which embraces the whole range of human endeavour – the arts, the sciences, and the political institutions within which they function. Bryan Magee in his book on Popper succinctly comments:

> If Popper is right, there are not two cultures – one scientific and the other aesthetic . . . but one. The scientist and the artist, far from being engaged in opposed or incompatible activities, are both trying to extend our understanding of experience by the use of creative imagination subjected to critical control.

A passing knowledge of the history of ideas reveals the great scientist not as an impersonal, detached, systematic observer of the world, but rather as a passionate enquirer, displaying the whole range of human faculties and emotions. One can cite the heartrending struggles in the move from the Ptolemaic to the Copernican Solar System; the epoch-making conjecture of Darwin regarding Natural Selection; Einstein's profound imaginative grasp of the structure of space and time that led to the formulation of his relativity theories; the challenging development of quantum theory in the early decades of this century; the fascinating story of the unravelling of the DNA molecule in the early 1950s; and most recently the daring theories of contemporary cosmologists stretching the mind's power of abstract thought to the limit.

This reminds us of a further parallel between the arts and the sciences with regard to problem-solving and the importance of history and tradition. Although we have referred to divine creativity as making wholly new, human creativity must work with existing material. We can never make an entirely new start, either in the arts or in the sciences. That distinguished historian and philosopher of art, Sir Ernst Gombrich, in his book *Art and Illusion* accounts for creativity in the visual arts as Popper accounts for it in the sciences, in terms of the gradual modification of a tradition under the pressure of novel demands. The history of art, like the history of science, is more like a running argument than a series of cataclysmic upheavals.

The creative, imaginative probings of the scientist help to provide a unifying picture of the world and of our part in it. He shares this vision with the religious enquirer for whom the picture cannot be complete unless it is set within the context of divine creativity which is manifested to us as the work of the Holy Spirit of God.

Though such a role for imagination as well as reason in scientific creativity is now very widely acknowledged, it would be misleading to end this chapter on that note of happy balance. Whereas in the sciences the relationship between the two is clear, with imagination providing clues and reason arbitrating, there is no such easy truce in the arts between the classical and romantic traditions. That is why in the course of this chapter we have felt it necessary to leave some issues between them unresolved. However, let us end on a positive note about both. The romantic tradition must be right in insisting that our response to God is about our whole being responding and not just our reason; thus the emotions and the imagination too must play their part, as equally the creation of God. On the other hand, in taking this into account we must not lose sight of the classical tradition's insistence on an integrated vision. Even if the romantic is right that most of it must remain hidden in this life, it still remains true that ultimately this is where the Spirit is calling us. It is to that integrated vision of a new order, the final destiny to which all the world is called, to the vision of our future in the Spirit that we next turn.

Chapter 10
The Holy Spirit and the future

Every chapter of this report implies a decisive connection between the Holy Spirit and the future. We have spoken of the experience of the Holy Spirit. This present experience comes as an anticipation of what is destined to be enjoyed more fully in the future. We have spoken of the Spirit and Christ. Experience of the Spirit is bound up with our being in Christ because we share in advance his resurrection life and resurrection mode of existence, even if this is hidden before the general resurrection of the dead (Col.3. 1ff.). The power of the Spirit, of which we have also spoken, represents an anticipation of the future, releasing us from bondage to the past. Nevertheless, as we have seen, this power is shaped by the pattern of the cross. For the present it remains power-in-weakness, for Pentecost lies on the yonder side of Calvary, but also comes as a gift reserved for the 'last days' (Acts 2.16 ff.).

Other chapters have introduced further themes which belong to the future. The Church is the community of the Holy Spirit, the members of which will share in the final victory when all shall be well. But meanwhile the Church yearns for a freedom and fulfilment which is only in process of being brought about. The present work of the Spirit in the Church represents the first fruits of what is to come: 'We ourselves, who have the first fruits of the Spirit, groan inwardly as we wait for adoption as sons, the redemption of our bodies' (Rom.8.23). The sacraments offer pledges of God's covenant faithfulness to his promises 'until he comes' (1 Cor.11.26), and all is publicly fulfilled. Truth is disclosed through the Spirit definitively in Christ; but our grasp of this truth remains partial and imperfect until everything can be seen in the light of the whole. We shall see more clearly the truth of the world and of history, in a sense, only when the whole is complete. But in advance of this context every judgement remains open to revision in the light of such truth. The truth of the Holy Spirit is therefore closely connected with the notion of a definitive revelation of the whole, traditionally represented through language about the Last Judgement. The Paraclete in the fourth gospel is the one who comes alongside to help and defend; but the Spirit also places men and women at the bar of such judgement in advance of its occurrences. The Spirit 'convicts' or 'exposes' to the human heart what will be publicly and openly demonstrable only at the last day (John 14.16ff; 16.7ff.).

Our discussions of the Spirit and the world, and of creativity, pointed to the reality of the Holy Spirit as the one beyond and yet within. The Spirit comes as God in transcendence and as God in God's immanence. In early Christian faith it seemed natural to use spatial imagery to express this 'beyond': God and divine activity were conceived as being 'above' the world. The divine Spirit transcended the realm of human comprehension, whether of conceptual thought or imagination. But biblical formulations did not rely exclusively on spatial imagery to express this transcendence or beyondness. For the writer to the Hebrews, faith is 'the assurance of things hoped for' (Heb.11.1). Faith is directed towards the invisible not only in the sense of that which lies beyond the material world, but also in the sense of its being directed towards God's promises and power to bring about that which is unseen because it has not yet become reality. In this sense, the Holy Spirit brings forward a reality which is grounded in divine promise rather than in human thought or achievement. Even though in processes of creativity the Spirit of God works through the instrumentality of natural processes and through the agency of human thought and imagination, we can never reduce the reality of the Spirit in such a way as to equate it with these processes exhaustively and without remainder.

Without some reference to 'the last things' of Christian faith it is difficult to determine what movements are to count as constructive from some intermediate vantage point in history. The old debates between those who saw creative meaning in terms of supernatural purpose and those who saw it in terms of natural or emergent processes cannot be settled simply by invoking some principle of immanent purposive process, such as we find in classical forms of Marxism. As we saw in the chapter on creation, modern scientific theories explore the interplay of order and disorder, of structure and flux, in ways which help us to discard an outmoded picture of a closed universe predetermined by a tight chain of cause and effect. They help us to see how novelty and creativity can emerge without recourse to hypotheses about interruptions of natural processes. Nevertheless, these do not take us beyond an account of the processes themselves. They offer models which facilitate our understanding of the creative processes through which the Spirit operates, but they do not plumb the depths of the ultimate reality which is the ground of their possibility and the End which gives them definitive meaning.

How the new and innovative is related to the future is seen more clearly in the realm of redemption. In the New Testament the experience of the Holy Spirit is an experience of release and freedom. In Paul, this stands in contrast to bondage to the law. But law, in this context, means more than obligation to obey divine commandments, for these laws continue to have relevance within the new creation, and the Spirit calls us to the obedience of sonship. Neither is bondage to the law simply a matter of pressure to conform with the particular traditions of Judaism. The issue is wider than this. Human beings remain under the law as long as the determining principles of their lives emerge out of their own past decisions and actions, and out of past choices and values reflected in human cultures and societies. Men and women are bound by the limited range of options which emerge from their own past. Theologically, the most serious of these is the circle of negative processes set up by being caught in a net of sin, guilt, weakness, and the law.

Into this network of bondage enters the liberating power of the Holy Spirit. In place of guilt and estrangement, we read of 'the Spirit . . . bearing witness with our spirit that we are children of God' (Rom. 8.16), that 'the Spirit helps us in our weakness' (Rom. 8.26), and that 'the law (i.e. cause-effect processes) of the Spirit of life in Christ Jesus has set me free from the law of sin and death' (Rom. 8.2). All this is seen in the New Testament as a breaking in of the future. I am determined by the future God has promised rather than by the past I have made. The gift of the Holy Spirit in the present is only the beginning of the harvest proper, of which it is a foretaste (Rom. 8.23). This experience of the Spirit is that of sonship, whereby we share Jesus' intimacy with God as 'Abba', 'dear Father' (Rom. 8.14ff.). This is described as a right to inheritance: to be a son is to be an heir (Rom. 8.17). Christians will receive what Christ has received, and they look forward to a future glory (Rom. 8.18). They 'wait with eager longing' for the redemption of the body; for God to fulfil in their whole person what God has promised (Rom. 8.19ff.).

Sonship, redemption, and freedom all have future aspects, yet to be fulfilled. But because the Spirit has already been given as the first-fruits of a harvest to come, the future is guaranteed. The future is anticipated, as it were, in advance. The Spirit is the 'earnest of the inheritance' or 'guarantee' of this future (2 Cor.1.22; 5.5). What is guaranteed is the fulfilment of God's promises, the inheritance of redemption, and a resurrection mode of existence characterised by the Spirit. In the power of the Holy Spirit human persons can begin to be what they are to become. The first three gospels use language about the kingdom of God which is also both present and future. There is a parallel between our standing between the kingdom inaugurated and the kingdom accomplished and our standing between the gift of the Spirit as first-fruits and the Spirit's coming in fullness.

On several occasions in the course of this study we have touched on the work of the Holy Spirit in connection with healing (e.g. in Chapters 3 and 6). It is appropriate in this chapter entitled 'The Holy Spirit and the Future' to refer once again to the work of the Holy Spirit in this connection. We have noted the elements both present and future in the sonship, redemption and freedom brought by the Spirit; in these respects Christian people have been given through the Spirit a real, though partial, anticipation of that which they may confidently expect to be fulfilled hereafter. We have also observed how this is congruent with the material in Jesus' teaching contained in the first three gospels, in which the kingdom of God is understood to be both present and future. In this material there are links between the Spirit, the kingdom of God and healing, for instance in the version of Jesus' saying to be found in Matthew's gospel, in connection with his exorcism of a blind and dumb man (Matt.12.28). In the version of Jesus' sermon in the synagogue at Nazareth in Luke's gospel (Luke 4.16ff.) we find the Spirit particularly associated with his work of healing; in this passage the idea of the kingdom of God is not far distant. Readers of the Acts of the Apostles are given to understand that the Spirit who rested upon Jesus is now active in the Christian Church and thus that the healings done by Peter and Paul are done through the Spirit present and active in the Church.

We need to apply the same principle with regard to healing, as with sonship, redemption and freedom. The healing done through the Spirit by Jesus, by the apostles in the early Church, and subsequently in Christ's name within the Church's history is real and effective, though of necessity only partial and temporary in the present life. Already the first-fruits of the Spirit are a real, true and present possession given to Christian people; through these first-fruits we are given future hope and grounds of confident expectation that fulfilment, understood in this context in terms of healing complete and enduring, will be given us through the Spirit hereafter. This healing may be outward, physical and visible; certainly it will be secret and hidden, deep in the centre of the human person. This latter activity is generally beyond the conscious awareness of people, for the Spirit touches and teaches the heart. Thus the Spirit's healing and transforming influence works outwards, gradually correcting humans' thinking, feeling and spontaneous reactions, gradually bringing forth the fruit of the Spirit, which will be harvested in its fullness hereafter.

Meanwhile, however, the present experience of the Holy Spirit cannot be isolated from the ambiguities which characterize the present. Even within the New Testament period the difficulty of trying to offer watertight or unambiguous criteria of the Spirit's operation and presence is acknowledged as we have already recognized in Chapter 3. In 1 Corinthians, members of the community make great play of their status as 'spiritual people'. Yet where there is jealousy and strife, Paul cannot address them as people controlled by the Spirit (1 Cor. 3.1–3). He redefines true 'spirituality' in the light of the cross, and within a framework of what builds up the whole community in love. Nevertheless, love remains a quality which belongs to the new order of the future. The poem on love which forms the centrepiece of Paul's discussion of spiritual gifts (1 Cor. 12–14) makes it clear that the Corinthian community has not yet reached full maturity in this respect. Many are still boastful, jealous, arrogant, and at times insistent on their own way (cf. 1 Cor. 13.5). Love will relativize the other gifts, because love alone will never become obsolete through changing circumstances and conditions: 'love never ends; as for prophecy, it will pass away; as for tongues, they will cease; as for knowledge, it will pass away' (1 Cor. 13.8). Until it can reflect that quality of love which still lies in the future, the Church's claims to speak with the voice of the Holy Spirit must remain qualified by a persistent ambiguity, which invites careful discernment.

In the period from the New Testament to modern times, the history of the Christian Church underlines the fact of this ambiguity. No movement of the Church's life, whether of spiritual revival, or of spiritual renewal, or of its institutional developments, has ever been free from ambiguities which reflect human failures or exaggerations alongside the work of the Spirit. Neither the voice of the Church nor that of its critics can be identified absolutely and unambiguously with the voice of the Spirit before the consummation of its deliverance from weakness and sin. Paul Tillich insisted that this was an implication of what he called 'the Protestant principle'. He writes: 'The paradox of the churches is the fact that they participate, on the one hand, in the ambiguities of life in general and of the religious life in particular, and on the other hand, in the unambiguous life of the Spiritual Community' (*Systematic Theology* vol. 3, p. 176). This has been expressed, he adds, in the traditional distinction between the Church invisible and visible. The Church is holy, one, and universal, in as far as the Holy Spirit has in principle made the Church what God destines it to become in the Spirit's grace and power. But the Creator-Spirit's work is not yet complete. There may even be fallibility and self-interest, manipulation and desire for power where there are movements in the Church which may otherwise represent movements of the Holy Spirit. Only when the future destiny of the Church becomes manifest, and the work of the Spirit is complete within it, will this ambiguity dissolve, to give place to an unmixed manifestation of the Spirit's creative and renewing work.

This should make us hesitate to judge the nature of the future in the light of the present, or to equate what we see of the Spirit's work now with that which is yet to be. No responsible critic will judge an artist's work while it is still in the making. 'Do not pronounce judgement before the time' (1 Cor. 4.5). To change the metaphor into those of the Matthean parables, only at harvest time can the weeds be finally separated from the wheat, or only in the boat or on the shore can the good fish be separated from the bad ones (Matt. 13.24ff.; 47ff.). 'Now I know in part; then I shall understand fully' (1 Cor. 13.12). Even given an awareness of what it is to experience the Holy Spirit, it is still possible, ahead of future growth and maturity, to speak, to think, and to reason 'like a child'. The indirect and sometimes enigmatic reflections perceived in a bronze mirror are not to be confused with the reality which we wait to see face to face (1 Cor. 13.12).

At the same time, we should not make the opposite mistake. Because the Holy Spirit determines this future, it is not entirely adequate to say that such a future is in principle *totally* beyond all potential human experience or completely beyond the range of crude or provisional human understanding. For the Holy Spirit, as the first-fruits of our inheritance, also represents a foretaste of a reality of which more is to come. The yearnings and longings, as well as the joys and promises, which the Spirit of God places in the human heart do not stand in sharp discontinuity with the promised future. Newness of life stands both in contrast to, and in continuity with, the old. For Christians, new life in the Spirit has already begun. This does not mean that each new movement and renewal of the Spirit takes a wholly predictable course. Like the wind, the Spirit cannot be controlled or readily predicted (John 3.8). Nevertheless, as we have already noted in connection with the Spirit's revelation of truth, the Spirit's work remains coherent and self-consistent, and does not undermine or contradict what the Spirit has already achieved. While the future disclosed by the Spirit therefore outstrips all present conceiving or imagining, this future will not be at variance with those 'first instalments' of the Spirit which in Christ we have already received. ' "What no eye has seen, nor ear heard, nor the heart of man conceived, what God has prepared for those who love him", God has revealed to us through the Spirit. For the Spirit searches everything, even the depths of God' (1 Cor.2.9f.).

The image of the first fruits of the Spirit (Rom.8.23) conveys the truth that the present experience of the Holy Spirit is only the beginning, but nevertheless a real beginning, of the harvest proper which will come to ripened fruition in the future age. Until the harvest comes, the whole creation 'groans in travail' as it waits for this with eager longing. Paul feels the need to re-affirm his point that much of the centre of gravity still lies in the future: 'Now hope that is seen is not hope. For who hopes for what he sees? . . . We wait for it with patience' (Rom.8.24f.). But he also underlines the aspect of continuity and promise. The first fruits of the Spirit come as a partial bestowal in the present which guarantees a complete bestowal in the future. This notion of guarantee is even more explicit where Paul speaks of the Spirit as the assured pledge that what

God has destined will be fulfilled: 'He who has prepared for us this very thing is God, who has given us the Spirit as a guarantee' (2 Cor. 5.5). In a later epistle the idea of guarantee is combined with that of a protective seal of authenticity and safety: 'You . . . were sealed with the promised Holy Spirit, which is the guarantee of our inheritance until we acquire possession of it' (Eph. 1.13f.). The same two ideas are combined by Paul with reference to God's faithfulness to his promise and commission to service. The Spirit here is given as down-payment on what God has promised (2 Cor. 1.22). The metaphor is that of a financial deposit which guarantees the completion of the larger transaction. As God's own seal, the Spirit marks out and protects a reality and identity which would otherwise be only hidden or subject to ambiguity. The Spirit pledges the completion of a process which the Spirit has decisively set in motion.

Earlier in this chapter we concentrated on our future hope, of which our present experience of the Spirit is both foretaste and guarantee. Here we are seeking to explore more fully this present experience. There is indeed both continuity and contrast between the present and the future, as can be seen in other respects with regard to the Holy Spirit's work. The Spirit prompts within us Jesus' own cry of trust and intimacy: 'Abba, Father' (Rom. 8.15; Gal. 4.6). Nevertheless sonship reaches fullness in the future, for it carries with it, as we have noted, a right to 'inheritance'. In Paul's language, 'It is the Spirit himself bearing witness with our spirit that we are children of God, and if children, then heirs, heirs of God and fellow heirs with Christ' (Rom. 8.16f.). Because even heirs wait for that which they inherit, the sufferings of Christ have still to be shared, equally as a mark of the Spirit, and we 'who have the first fruits of the Spirit groan inwardly as we wait for adoption as sons' (Rom. 8.23). The emphasis here lies equally on the reality of the present and on the greater fullness of the future: 'He who sows to the Spirit will from the Spirit reap eternal life' (Gal. 6.8). Pentecost has already come, because God's love has already been 'poured into our hearts through the Holy Spirit' (Rom. 5.5). But 'we rejoice in our hope of sharing the glory of God', and even 'rejoice in our sufferings' (Rom. 5. 2f.), which now fall short of this future glory. With the whole of creation, we eagerly await our fuller freedom from bondage to decay, and fuller freedom of the children of God (Rom. 8.21). This yearning and longing is articulated within us by the Spirit 'with sighs too deep for words' (Rom. 8.26).

Can more be said, even indirectly through the use of symbols and imagery, about this future for which creation sighs? In the New Testament the 'last things' comprise the Parousia (or appearance of Christ in glory), the final judgement, and the general resurrection of the dead. These are cosmic or public events, rather than those which primarily concern the perceptions or hopes of the individual as such. In his book *In the End God* . . . John Robinson rightly draws a contrast between the western individualism which focuses hope on the hour of death and the expectation of immortality, and the wider cosmic perspective of the New Testament which focuses hope on the day of the Parousia, the reality of the last judgement, and the event of the general resurrection. Creation longs for the coming of Christ in public vindication and glory. It longs for the dead to be raised, transformed and incorruptible, and yearns for the hidden ways of the Judge of all the earth to be made public and to be seen to set all wrongs to right. Judgement means the end of illusion and ambiguity; resurrection means the end of weakness and decay.

The New Testament attributes the resurrection of the dead directly to the agency of the Holy Spirit. Paul writes: 'If the Spirit of him who raised Jesus from the dead dwells in you, he who raised Christ Jesus from the dead will give life to your mortal bodies also through his Spirit which dwells in you' (Rom. 8.11). If Christ himself is called the first fruits or firstborn of the resurrection order, the agency of the Spirit which raised Christ will raise those in Christ to share his resurrection mode of existence. The resurrection life of Christ and the future resurrection of Christians belong to a single process, initiated and sustained by the Holy Spirit. That the Spirit of God sustains the resurrection life was already anticipated figuratively in the Old Testament (Ezek.37). In Paul's great chapter on the resurrection (1 Cor. 15) the mode of existence demanded by the resurrection is itself 'spiritual' (1 Cor. 15.44), which is best interpreted to mean 'of the Holy Spirit'.

The immediate context of this verse confirms that 'spiritual' refers to that which is of the Holy Spirit. When he tells his readers that 'flesh and blood cannot inherit the kingdom of God' (1 Cor. 15.50), Paul is not addressing the Greek or western problem whether a physical entity can achieve a non-material, non-spatial, mode of existence. He is addressing the Hebrew-Christian problem whether an untransformed humanity, characterized by failure and sinfulness, can enter the immediate presence of God who is holy. Transformation through sharing in the resurrection of Christ is the key to hope. The Spirit has begun this process already, but the process culminates in a final decisive event. The whole person is raised imperishable. 'It is sown in dishonour, it is raised in glory. It is sown in weakness, it is raised in power' (1 Cor. 15.43). The *Revised Standard Version*, which we have followed elsewhere, misses the point of the contrast by translating the next verse 'It is sown a physical (Greek *psychikon*) body, it is raised a spiritual (Greek *pneumatikon*) body' (v.44). Paul uses the Greek word *psychikos* elsewhere in this epistle to denote the 'ordinary' or 'unspiritual' person in contrast to the person who is controlled or led by the Holy Spirit (1 Cor. 2.14). Hence it is more accurate to translate the word to mean 'ordinary'. The *New English Bible* translates this as 'animal' body. But our fully functional and fully operational mode of existence (equivalent for the biblical writers to 'body') will be characterized by the sustaining power of the Holy Spirit. Paul is not arguing here about the composition of the 'body', as if it were composed of (human) spirit; he is spelling out how the Holy Spirit transforms the Christian's mode of existence.

We should expect that a mode of existence animated and sustained by the Spirit of the living God would be conceived of in dynamic rather than in static terms. This is also implied by these verses. The process of decay or 'corruption' is reversed. Fine questions are raised about semantic contrasts here. It is likely that the opposite of decay is not simply lack of decay, but the very reversal of decay which we associate with rejuvenation, for the Spirit throughout the biblical writings is associated with strength and vitality. Paul consciously connects this with the completion of the process whereby the Christian is freed from the weakening and debilitating effects of sin, guilt and 'dishonour'. Behind the Greek word for decay stand the Hebrew words for what is marred and spoiled, and what is vain or fruitless. The spiritual mode of existence will not be like this: it will be fruitful, glorious and go on from strength to strength. The notion of a 'glorious body' is thus that of a fully operational and effective mode of existence, freed from weakening associations with sin, to enjoy an ongoing and progressive experience of life in the Spirit according to God's glory.

Nevertheless, neither resurrection nor judgement should be conceived of in over-individualistic terms. To be sure, the resurrection of the body affirms the value of the individual, in that it implies a future continuity of personal identity rather than a mere absorption of individuality into some all-encompassing whole. Judgement likewise underlines individual accountability and therefore individual identity. The Creator Spirit is the God of variety in creation, not of dull uniformity. However, the resurrection constitutes a cosmic event of renewal, for which all creation waits in travail. Is it merely speculative to suggest that this might be conceived by analogy with the transformation by which the human body is transposed into some transfigured mode of being? At very least, elsewhere in the New Testament the Seer beholds 'a new heaven and a new earth; for the first heaven and the first earth had passed away' (Rev. 21.1). He conveys a vision that when history as we know it has reached its end, a new arena or context of existence will be revealed. Into this new arena of existence are absorbed qualities of the present creation, albeit in transformed or transfigured modes. The new Jerusalem is prepared as a bride beautifully dressed for her wedding. A great voice said that God would dwell with his people; it went on, ' "He will wipe away every tear from their eyes, and death shall be no more, neither shall there be mourning nor crying nor pain any more, for the former things have passed away." And he who sat upon the throne said, "Behold, I make all things new" ' (Rev. 21. 4f.). This is the cosmic, public, and climactic fulfilment of the process already begun by the Spirit: 'We all, with unveiled face, beholding the glory of the Lord, are being changed into his likeness from one degree of glory to another; for this comes from the Lord who is the Spirit' (2 Cor. 3.18). This is the glory which even now fills 'the whole earth' (Isa. 6.3).

The event of the resurrection, then, is a corporate event as well as one which involves us as individuals. The metaphor of the last trumpet conveys the idea of a sleeping army jumping to its feet when the signal is given. Judgement, equally, is both individual and cosmic. Creation yearns for that moment when the ways of God will receive visible and unequivocal vindication. Judgement means the end of ambiguity and illusion. God will be seen to be all in all.

The Holy Spirit begins this process of removing illusion now in the present. We have seen already that part of the Spirit's work as Paraclete is to convict us of sin and to expose those things which need forgiveness, transformation and healing (John 16. 8ff.). The Spirit brings the whole Church to judgement in advance by bringing home where we need the Spirit's defending and supporting help, and where there are failures that need to be corrected. The Spirit achieves this work in a variety of ways, including prayer, preaching, prophecy, theology and the witness of particular groups and persons. All this in principle brings forward aspects of divine judgement which will be revealed without ambiguity only at the last day. Meanwhile, it is because of this work of the Spirit at the individual level that we say to our Saviour Christ in a hymn, 'They who fain would serve thee best are conscious most of wrong within'.

We cannot yet conceive of the more detailed nature of this last judgement. We know that evil will be destroyed, but will human persons be caught up in destructive aspects of this decree? That evil attitudes on the part of persons will be destroyed is clear. The biblical and liturgical images of the Holy Spirit's activity as wind, as fire, and as water help us to see the two-sided nature of this work. Wind cools and refreshes, but it also blasts and destroys. Fire illuminates and warms, but it also burns. Water cleanses and purifies, but it may also submerge and drown. The new order will be a pure, untarnished realm. By definition, because it is pure and holy 'nothing unclean shall enter it' (Rev. 21.27). Those spiritual writers who, like Thomas à Kempis, Julian of Norwich, or Richard Baxter, speak most warmly of God's love also speak of the need to fear

God's judgement. When this judgement is pronounced, all stand exposed in their final awareness of what they truly have been and are. Yet by the same token the plea for acceptance lies in nothing else than the grace and generosity of God's mercy as it is given and received through Christ. In Baxter's words, 'O terrible, O joyful, day!'

It is a different question whether God allows any human being or other creature finally to say 'no' to this generosity. Different traditions of Christian thought have answered this question in different ways. Some see the irresistible nature of grace in Pauline language about the reconciliation of all things: 'through him (Christ) to reconcile to himself all things, whether on earth or in heaven, making peace by the blood of his cross' (Col. 1.20). Others view this as expressing, rather, universal acceptance of the divine decree, whether of judgement or of mercy. Some see a reference to universal salvation in New Testament language about uniting 'all things in him (Christ), things in heaven and things on earth' (Eph.1.10). Others underline the wide range of possible meanings covered by the Greek word translated 'to unite' in the RSV (*anakephalaiō*). At least one writer interprets this verse to mean that all things achieve a focus of meaning in Christ. Perhaps the biblical writers refrain from offering a neatly-packaged map of these last events because they function more strictly as an assurance of mercy to the humble and the seeking, and as a warning to the presumptuous, than as a piece of general information derived from some practical context.

In this sense, language about the last judgement is like the notoriously difficult verse about blasphemy against the Holy Spirit. Mark recounts the charge of some of the teachers of the law that Jesus was driving out demons by the prince of demons. Jesus replies that by its very nature and definition his work stands in conflict with that of Satan, and Mark attributes to him the saying: 'All sins will be forgiven the sons of men, and whatever blasphemies they utter; but whoever blasphemes against the Holy Spirit never has forgiveness, but is guilty of eternal sin' (Mark 3.28f.). The saying stands as a warning against a wilful and deliberate manipulation of good and evil, by which evil is called 'good' and good is called 'evil' (cf. Isa. 5.20). If a person were to manipulate all moral value and truth with such wilful cynicism, there is no way out of the vicious circle which has been erected. But Jesus does not mean a serious but hypothetical warning to be understood primarily as a general statement which is divorced from all context or questions of subjective concern. In everyday life, where people are concerned or deeply anxious about the possible applicability of this passage to their own lives, this very anxiety is itself full evidence that they do not share the callous cynicism and indifference to truth which this particular text addresses.

The same distinction between practical concern and general statement applies to language about the last judgement. Writers as strikingly different as Karl Barth and Julian of Norwich see the day of judgement as characterized equally by certainty and by hiddenness. Barth reminds us that God's grace and generosity is not limited by justice. Nevertheless, the person who persistently tries to change the truth into untruth 'cannot count on' God's eternal patience (K. Barth, *Church Dogmatics*, IV.3:1, p. 477). In the late fourteenth and early fifteenth century Julian of Norwich wrote in a parallel way of the hiddenness and certainty of that day, and of how its nature and form would be determined by the goodness and love of God. She writes: 'What the deed will be and how it will be performed is unknown to every creature who is inferior to Christ, and it will be until the deed is done. The goodness and love of our Lord God want us to know that this will be, and his power and his wisdom, through the same love, want to conceal it and hide it from us, what it will be, and how it will be done . . . through which deed he will make all things well' (Julian of Norwich, *Showings, Longer Text* ch. 32).

If we turn from the spiritual writings to philosophies of history, we may note that it is often said that the final significance of the events of our individual lives can be measured only in the hour of death. We must extend this principle corporately and trans-historically: only at the end of history will the full significance of historical moments be seen. The Holy Spirit, within the framework of faith, brings anticipation of this trans-historical perspective forwards to us in provisional forms (which are admittedly open to further elucidation and expansion). The Spirit does this for example in witnessing to our freedom from condemnation through Christ. The Holy Spirit also provides a witness that the individual is not alone in God's world, but is loved and valued along with all God's creation in heaven and on earth. This is a very different perspective from that of the secular futurologist who speculates about the future on the basis of extrapolations from the present. This more secular perspective fails to take account of the discontinuities and potential reversals which are implied by the notion of a last judgement. It represents a fragmented viewpoint which is caught up in a process of relativization, seeking to assess the future in the light of the present, rather than the present in the light of the future. The Holy Spirit has already revealed to faith enough of the 'last things' and of the Spirit's own part in them, to give us grounds for confident hope.

This hope for the future which is inspired by the Spirit moves beyond narrow concerns of self-interest and hopes of self-centred vindication. Creation yearns for an end to the power of all that is destructive. Love is the one quality which always abides and can never be left behind. In the present this is anticipated by a desire for change now, which begins with the transformation of the self in holiness and love, and shows itself in wider concerns for the world and society. Here the Spirit makes use of natural and scientific processes, but cannot be reduced to them exhaustively. For example, biology and medicine have increased life expectancy, but have thereby produced fresh problems of world population and scarcity of resources. Struggles to increase food supplies by chemical processes raise further difficulties about the control of bacteria and of related by-products. Yet amidst pain and suffering, the yearning of the Holy Spirit, as a divine discontent within, expresses itself in deeds of love, and longs for the future which God alone can bring. The final verse of Charles Wesley's hymn 'Love divine' sums up this longing:

> Finish then thy new creation, pure and spotless let us be;
> Let us see thy great salvation perfectly restored in thee.
> Changed from glory into glory, till in heaven we take our place,
> Till we cast our crowns before thee, lost in wonder, love, and praise.

The Mystery of Salvation

Preface

This Report, like its two predecessors, is published under the authority of the House of Bishops and is commended by the House to the Church for study.

On behalf of the House of Bishops
+GEORGE CANTUAR:
Chairman

Foreword

This report by the Doctrine Commission of the General Synod of the Church of England on the subject of salvation is the third in a series. *We Believe in God* was published in 1987, and in 1991 it was followed by *We Believe in the Holy Spirit*. These three reports have several common features. They all treat major themes which lie at the heart of the Christian religion. They seek to do so in a way which, it is to be hoped, will make the Christian faith more readily comprehensible and more easily accessible to a non-specialist and enquiring public, which may include regular worshippers as well as enquirers and seekers who stand on the margin of the Church's life. This report, like the others, has been prepared by a group of theological teachers and thinkers who have been appointed to the Commission by the Archbishops of Canterbury and York, and who represent a wide spread of professional expertise and of theological standpoint. We have tried to write in a non-technical way, though it has not always proved possible to avoid the use of technical terms. Our aim has been to express the Church's faith as received by us from Scripture and from the Church's subsequent understanding of its inheritance, in such a way that we are true to the tradition received and give fresh expression to it; we take account of the present context and of modern difficulties, and we indicate ways in which understanding of our subject may appropriatcly be expressed and set forward in our day. Thus we modestly hope that our work may be of service to parish study groups, to theological students, to other provinces of the Anglican Communion, and, indeed, to the wider Church.

Each of these reports has taken several years to compose, and all have been the fruit of corporate writing. This exercise has proved to be both time-consuming and worthwhile. At the first stage, papers on various topics associated with our central theme were prepared by members of the Commission and by others on whose services we were able to draw. After a while a pattern for the report emerged, and various members of the Commission undertook to write the first draft of entire chapters or of parts of chapters. These drafts were discussed, rewritten, amended, refined, until at last a form of words was achieved with which everyone who was a member of the Commission at the time of final drafting could concur. Thus this report, like its predecessors, comes with the unanimous support of the entire Commission, composed, as it is, of members who represent a diversity of viewpoint and background. We can all live with, endorse and happily commend the agreed text. We have been careful to phrase our report in such a way that we do not exclude some other expressions of Christian truth which have an honoured place in the Anglican tradition. Christian truth as a whole, and Christian teaching on this particular topic of salvation, are so rich and complex that one statement does not necessarily exclude all others. Our unanimity over such a wide field of issues associated with the topic, which surely is the nerve-centre of Christian faith, needs to be underlined, as also does our readiness to leave room for some other views and to leave some questions open; equally, on occasion we do not hesitate to express opinions critical of various points of view which we consider inadequate.

In this report, as in the two previous reports, we have been trying to weave together in a coherent and systematic way the biblical faith as understood and transmitted by the Church, while bearing in mind the intellectual climate and the practical concerns of our time. We have not set out to write a history of the doctrine of salvation, though we draw frequently on some of the numerous ways in which salvation has been understood through the Christian centuries, and in chapter 5 we provide some modern versions of traditional themes. Equally, we have not attempted a full examination of the complex biblical threads which combine to form this theme of salvation. We have, however, drawn extensively on the Scriptures throughout our report, particularly near the centre of our work in chapter 4, in which we concentrate on the witness of the New Testament. That chapter is immediately preceded by a chapter in which is examined the nature of the historical content and context of Christian faith, and in the first two chapters of the report an attempt is made to set the Christian doctrine of salvation within the context of today's world and of the Christian faith as a whole. Readers of the two earlier reports will notice a certain measure of continuity between the earlier reports and some parts of these two chapters. Common to all three reports has been the concern to root the subject under discussion within the world and the Church in our time. Common too has been the trinitarian nature of Christian faith which in all three reports has been treated with full seriousness. Linked with the basic trinitarian structure of Christian belief is our repeated reference, in all three reports, to Romans 8, to the Lord's cry of 'Abba, Father', and to the eventual remaking and transformation of the entire created order.

In our survey of the context in which this report is being prepared we have identified several features which require particular attention. To one of these features, the rise of feminist consciousness, we return on several occasions in the course of our report, as we touch on some of the ways in which it affects our subject and in which it affects the understanding and expression of Christian faith as a whole. For two other features of our context we reserve treatment near the end of our work in chapters 7 and

8, in which we address respectively the ways in which Christian understanding of salvation bears upon other faiths, and the future of the universe, in particular of individuals after death. When we were commissioned by the Archbishops to undertake this work, we were asked to give close attention to these two issues. Not surprisingly they have been the subjects at which we have had to work the hardest. In our consideration of other faiths we have been immensely helped by experts in this field, principally by the Revd Andrew Wingate, Principal of the College of the Ascension, Selly Oak, who was recruited to this Commission as a consultant for the preparation of this report. We have sought to identify the positive points which are being made by each of the three most frequently trodden approaches to this particular topic, and to advance understanding of it by combining these positive insights in such a way that we set discussion of the subject a step further forward. With regard to the future of the universe and to the life of human beings after death, we have sought to balance the bearing of the doctrine of salvation on this present age with its bearing on what the Nicene Creed calls 'the life of the world to come'. Here we encountered particular difficulty because the dualist assumptions about human beings (body and soul), which underlie much traditional Christian thinking on these subjects, are not commonly held nowadays; in any case, life after death is hedged about by mystery more than most other subjects, and it would be unwise to write with precision of detail about our future expectations. We have, therefore, treated it in a way which we consider takes account of the Church's understanding of the Scriptures, of the intellectual climate of our time, and of the mysteriousness which necessarily attends this element of Christian faith in particular.

In the central chapters we set out some of the principal features of the understanding of salvation in the New Testament, and we also provide some modern restatements of classical Christian ways of understanding salvation. These chapters are followed by one in which we include a treatment of some of the more important ideas which have been associated with our subject, among them forgiveness, suffering, sacrifice and sacrament. We are conscious of the impossibility of doing justice to such grand themes in so limited a compass, but they are all so closely linked with our general theme that our report would be the poorer without some reference to them and to the bearing of our subject upon them. Christian liturgies all reflect the Church's understanding of these truths, and as we are the Doctrine Commission of the Church of England we have provided an appended note on understandings of salvation to be found in the Book of Common Prayer and in the Alternative Service Book.

In our last two reports we quoted the Bible from the Revised Standard Version. In this report, however, we generally use the New Revised

Standard Version. On this occasion, as on previous occasions, we have been fortunate enough to be able to draw on the advice and help of scholars who are not members of the Commission nor formally appointed as consultants to it. We wish particularly to express our appreciation to Dr Gavin D'Costa, now of Bristol University, and Dr Grace Davie, of Exeter University, both of whom prepared papers for us and attended a residential session of the Commission. Dr D'Costa enriched our understanding of the relationship between Christianity and other faiths, and Dr Davie helped us to understand better the sociological factors which bear upon our subject. We also owe a debt of gratitude to those who have been of assistance to us in various ways, among them: Dr S. Alsford, Dr D. J. Davies, Dr L. J. Francis, Dr K. S. Harmon, Dr D. Hewlett, Dr C. Lamb, Dr B. Martin, Dr J. A. Williams, Dr M. Winter.

In the first book of his treatise *Of the Laws of Ecclesiastical Polity* Richard Hooker sums up a long discussion in these words: 'There resteth therefore either no way unto salvation, or if any, then surely a way which is supernatural, a way which could never have entered into the heart of man as much as once to conceive or imagine, if God himself had not revealed it extraordinarily. For which cause we term it the Mystery or Secret way of salvation.' In the following paragraph he continues in a similar vein; 'Behold how the wisdom of God hath revealed a way mystical and supernatural . . . This supernatural way had God in himself prepared before all worlds' (I.xi.5,6). It is our hope that our discussion of this mystery of faith will help our readers 'to comprehend, with all the saints, what is the breadth and length and height and depth, and to know the love of Christ that surpasses knowledge' (Eph. 3.18f); our work is offered to the Church at large and to a wider readership with that intention.

Chapter 1
Posing the problem

To the drowning passengers of a sinking ship salvation does not need to be explained, only offered – and quickly. Discussion in such circumstances is as unnecessary as it is dangerous. Those trapped on the top storey of a blazing building require a different remedy for the danger that faces them, but they too are clear what salvation means in their situation. Their need is for a fireman's ladder, not a learned discussion.

Such illustrations may seem altogether too ordinary and material to furnish insight about the nature of salvation. For is not salvation a word from the technical language of theology, bearing centuries of confession on the part of Christians that Jesus Christ came down from heaven for us 'and for our salvation'? Are we not speaking here of the situation facing the whole of humanity rather than the specific needs of those facing the waves of the ocean or the flames of a burning house?

Yet the examples of danger from drowning or fire do illuminate the ease with which it is possible to speak of being saved when the nature of the peril is clear, and, by contrast, suggest a much greater difficulty when the danger being faced is either not clear or is the subject of controversy. What if the smoke alarm has a fault, or the smell is just that of bread overcooked? What if the water seeping across the cabin floor is not a fatal leak but simply the spilling of a drink or the appearance of condensation? Then the rescue called for, in either case most probably a mass evacuation, is unnecessary.

So if we are to speak of salvation in a Christian sense we have also to seek more clarity about the peril in which the world is believed to stand. To know the danger is to be more than half way to understanding what is required to deal with it. If God is said to be acting towards the world in order to save it, from what is it being saved? There are, of course, other questions too: how did this danger in which the world stands come about? And for what continuing purpose is humanity being saved in any case? But these further questions arise when we have understood what the human situation is, what is the danger in which we stood until God chose to act as saviour through the life and self-offering of Jesus Christ.

Most religious traditions, and certainly the Christian tradition, have a name for this peril, a diagnosis. In Christian terms, the peril from which humanity has to be, and has been, saved is the power of sin and its consequence, death. Yet this naming of the human peril arose in the context of a culture in which religious language was widely used and understood; controversy there certainly was, but there could be conversation that assumed that humankind had to reckon with a common destiny, and that such a destiny was determined by the power of a divine world towards which human beings had to turn if their lives were to have meaning and shape.

That world was one in which human beings were understood to have to reckon with a realm other than this, with a power beyond human powers, and with a reality beyond human imagining, let alone control; it was also a world where the human situation could be understood as a shared one. If all human beings have to reckon with a transcendent reality, then all human beings share the same fundamental peril and the same ultimate opportunity. In such a world it came naturally to speak of a universal saviour, for in such a world there was a universal peril with which humanity had to contend, a common disaster which men and women faced and from which they needed to be saved. Not only that: God's concern for the whole person is more naturally expressed in a culture which has not polarised our 'inner' and 'outer' worlds as modern culture does.

Is that the thought-world which we still inhabit and in terms of which it is still possible to speak of one who died for our salvation, the salvation not of believers only but of all who have been and are yet to be born? And if, as has been widely stated by those who have observed western culture, such a world has passed from us irrevocably (so far as we can tell), how can we continue to speak of salvation? Does our witness require that we first of all restore for ourselves and our fellow human beings a shared diagnosis of the peril in which we stand, and of the transcendent reality which human beings must face?

A concern, therefore, to address the question of salvation draws us inevitably into the discussion of how far our society is secularised, and of the extent to which that is a development which cannot be resisted, and so has to be accepted as the context within which the message of salvation has to be proclaimed. Secularisation is a hotly debated concept among sociologists, both as to what it is and whether it is a dominant feature of our culture. Similarly theologians have by no means been of one mind in their discussion of whether such a secularised world is to be accepted and valued, or opposed as inimical to the practice and proclamation of the Christian gospel.

Even in a secularised society, however, it is not to be assumed that 'salvation' has no meaning. Quite the contrary: much of modern literature, not to mention many of the television 'soaps', are about salvation (though they seldom use that word), trying out various versions of it and often rejecting them as inadequate.

The recently revived 1955 classic document of western secular society (written by an Irishman in French and translated into English), Beckett's *Waiting for Godot*, offers perhaps the most precise and profound exploration in twentieth-century secular literature, even using salvation language. It is a drama about waiting for salvation: but from what, to what, by what means – none of these are clear. The mysteriously salvific figure, Godot, is never defined. As the play ends, one of its two main characters says to the other:

> We'll hang ourselves tomorrow. Unless Godot comes.
> And if he comes?
> We'll be saved.

(Samuel Beckett, *Waiting for Godot* (Faber edn. 1961), Act 2, p. 94)

The play reflects the sense of many that 'salvation' means release from the sufferings and painlessness and accidie of human existence, though into what better kind of life is not clear. A more precisely religious dimension to this is not lacking in writers throughout the century, up to our own time, such as Peter Ackroyd, Muriel Spark and Margaret Drabble. Even in *Waiting for Godot* there are frequent references to Christ:

> One of the thieves was saved.
> It's a reasonable percentage. (Act 1, p. 11)

And the crazed philosopher, Lucky, speaks for the religious confusion and anguish of this century:

> Given the existence . . . of a personal God . . . with white beard . . .
> outside the time without extension who from the heights of divine
> apathia . . . loves us dearly with some exceptions for reasons
> unknown but time will tell and suffers . . . with those who . . .
> are plunged in torment . . . and what is more that as a result
> of the labours left unfinished . . . it is established beyond all
> doubt . . . what many deny that man is seen to waste and pine
> to shrink and dwindle . . . I resume for reasons unknown . . . the
> facts are there . . . the labour's abandoned, left unfinished. (Act 1,
> pp. 42–4)

This focuses a secularised society's problem with the very concept of salvation: 'The facts are there' – that humanity continues to suffer.

Salvation, therefore, must lie somewhere in the unknown territory between that human suffering and the paradoxes of belief: 'divine apathia', God's 'dear love' of us and allowed torment of us. The conclusion bleakly reached by the large mass of those who think about it at all is that 'the labour's abandoned, left unfinished'. But by whom? By God? By humanity?

The sufferings of the present time, therefore, remain a common denominator between Christianity and the secularised world. But their theological meaning (if any) is wholly in dispute. What of the world to come? Would most of the secularised West, like Macbeth, 'jump the life to come' were all well in this one?

Here the language of poets and novelists and mass media is even more ambiguous. Inspector Morse, in one of the last episodes screened, said of a drug dealer who had destroyed several teenagers and then been killed in a car chase, 'I don't believe in hell, but when I meet people like him, I wish I did.' Beckett's tramps were not sure if they believed in hell – for them it was almost synonymous with death. Indeed, salvation from death preoccupies much of the western world, but the state beyond death remains a troubled question mark.

William Golding, Nobel prize novelist of the evil and the holy, spoke in *The Paper Men* for those for whom the latent sense of divine judgement remains a reality. His fugitive novelist fleeing from that symbolic Recording Angel, the literary biographer, comes face to face in his flight with a statue of Christ in a church, which he sees as the epitome of divine judgement, 'the universal intolerance'. He is delivered from the anguish of this sense of imminent divine wrath by an extraordinary revelation of God's mercy, expressed in golden light, and harmony of music and form and movement; death becomes

> Narrow steps to a door with a drumhead . . . I think that there was a dark calm sea beyond it, since I have nothing to speak with but metaphor. Also there were creatures in the sea that sang. For the singing and the song I have no words at all.
> (William Golding, *The Paper Men* (Faber 1984), p. 161)

But this God-bestowed peace in the face of divine judgement is rare in twentieth-century writing, though perhaps it is not without significance that it is described by a novelist recognised as one of the greatest of this century. But for most of the western secularised world, what emerges most clearly is the sense of loss attendant on the conviction that there is no 'God up there' weighing and assessing and evaluating us, caring about us enough for it to matter how we go on.

When you're young you prove how brave you are, or smart; then, what a good lover; then, a good father; finally, how wise or powerful or what the hell ever . . . But underlying it all, I see now, there was a presumption. That I was moving on an upward path towards some elevation, where . . . God knows what . . . I would be justified or even condemned – a verdict, anyway. I think now my disaster really began when I looked up one day – and the bench was empty: not a judge in sight. And all that remained was the endless argument with oneself – this pointless litigation of existence before an empty bench.
(Arthur Miller, *After the Fall* (Penguin Plays 1968), Act 1)

Many serious writers have charted how the loss of a sense of ultimate accountability has meant losing the shape and meaning to life.

Against such loss have been the stratagems of existentialism, hedonism and the other 'isms' of our age. The language of despair and hope are so intertwined and reversed as to become inextricable. What is clear, as the century moves to its close, is that for many people in our culture there are not only no more divine certainties, but no 'divine'. And equally clear is the perplexed sense that the language of computers is an inadequate exchange for the language of the seer.

> . . . What anthems have our computers
> to insert into the vacuum caused
> by the break in transmission
> of the song upon Patmos?

(R. S. Thomas in 'Reply', *Experimenting with an Amen* (Macmillan 1993))

So in attempting a contemporary understanding of the nature of salvation, we must reckon with the fact that our prevailing culture has little room for the sacred, or with a transcendent world on which this one depends. However, while some cultural trends seem hostile to faith, we have to take seriously the significant phenomenon of 'folk' or 'common' religion. This can comprise seasonal church attendance, use of the 'rites of passage' provided by the Church (baptisms, marriages, funerals), inherited beliefs which are largely Christian (about God as creator, about Jesus as Son of God, about the efficacy of prayer or meditation) and adherence to basically Christian moral values. Such 'folk' religion bears witness to the continuing quest for God. There is a religious component in many public observances; and there are on occasion less orthodox (from a Christian standpoint) manifestations of a transcendent world-view including new spiritualities, and even the more disturbing phenomena of witchcraft and Satanism. But for many people in modern western societies life is carried on without reference to a divine dimension, and all religious institutions reflect attempts to respond to that change in social attitudes.

If society as a whole does not assent to a transcendent dimension to life, such assent becomes a matter not of public doctrine but of individual choice. Alternatively, society fragments into smaller groupings each with its own frame of reference and religious outlook, and the individual chooses to which, if any, to belong. All religion therefore, even religion which claims universal truth or the capacity to offer universal salvation, comes to be seen in the society at large as a matter of personal choice, and therefore it becomes harder to treat universal truth claims as such. Such is the effect of the privatisation of values, a process by which the publicly accepted order of society is replaced by an order chosen by the individual and not subject to contradiction by the community at large.

Such a social situation, one in which there is no agreed human peril from which to be saved, easily also generates a wide range of more or less exotic pursuits by which individuals and groups seek to give shape to their lives, in a world in which no common peril is acknowledged and no generally accepted transcendent dimension is accepted. These are the privately chosen roads to salvation, the cults and movements of those who are forced to invent for themselves means of salvation to fill the vacuum left by the departure of a religious frame of reference.

Those movements are not to be criticised just because they are privately chosen: they may contain much that is good, and many of the insights which traditional religious belief has either promoted or neglected. For example, many of the movements and disciplines that promote a holistic view of the human situation and therefore promote ideals of human wholeness are affirmed by many Christians. On the other hand, some adherents of traditional religions, Christianity in particular, may see grounds for resisting some of the movements and cults of modern times: but they have to take seriously the extent to which they too, no less than those who have ceased to practise traditional religion, are part of a world where their own language and ritual, whatever the claims to truth they may make, are seen as personal choices of a way of salvation in a world where no generally necessary road to salvation is readily accepted.

A further effect of modern culture on religious belief and attitudes is the increased tendency to make ways of salvation available only within sects of the saved. As the way of salvation is not generally accepted in society, the need to belong to the community of the saved can only be fulfilled by the creation of units of intense belonging. Salvation is then seen as a crucial feature of identity, and to belong is to be joined to the community of the saved. Many Christian groups show such signs of exclusivity in belief and practice, and indeed such groups show many of the signs of institutional success. There is, however, an inevitable contradiction between the message of universal salvation in Jesus Christ and the proclaiming of that message by a group which holds that salvation tightly to itself. What cannot be avoided is the harsh question of how that message can be conveyed and lived out in a world in which transcendence no longer functions as part of the common currency, where there is no sense, therefore, of shared human peril and therefore no common quest for salvation.

We have also to accept the significance of the fact that this report makes its appearance at a particular time in our society's political history. 'Privatisation', of which we spoke earlier, is also a word in the language of politics and economics, spheres in which notions of individual responsibility have come to take on powerful significance in a country which in recent years has moved sharply away from a much stronger view of the role of the State in welfare provision and in the direction of the economy. What has the gospel of salvation to say to those who have gained materially from these far-reaching political changes? And what to those who have lost by them? Release from debt is a strong biblical image of salvation, and an image grounded in experience; how is such language to be used and heard in a society where public debt has come to be regarded as economically dangerous, while private debt, seen as a crucial part of the engine of the economy and strongly promoted by the advertising of financial institutions, has increased by leaps and bounds? If a primary aspect of the gospel of salvation is that it is good news for the poor, when the Church speaks about salvation it has to bear in mind who the poor are in our time, how they come to be the poor, and what their experience of poverty is: their identity and their experience may indeed be a reflection of a common feature of all times and societies, but it also has a quality and a character particular to this time, and their salvation and ours has to be within history, our history.

So in considering the context in which the Christian understanding of salvation has to be understood and communicated, we take as examples three of the most pressing challenges of our particular time:

1. the impact of scientific cosmology on our human self-understanding;

2. the challenge of the social context, of which the issues raised by feminism have come to the fore and call for particular attention; and

3. the greatly increased awareness, in the world generally and in western societies in particular, of the variety of religious belief and the existence and antiquity of faith traditions as central to the development of other civilizations as Christianity has been to our own.

These three vital aspects of our context will now briefly be described in turn.

The context of contemporary science

In the twentieth century, science has learnt that the cosmos itself has a history. It has not always looked the same. A fraction of a second after the Big Bang, the whole universe was simply an expanding ball of energy. Such initial simplicity has given rise, after fifteen billion years of cosmic history, to a rich, evolved, complexity, of which we ourselves are far and away the most striking examples known to us. Four billion years ago, the Earth was lifeless, though its chemically rich shallow waters held the promise of the eventual development of replicating molecules and living beings. Humankind is a very late event in this story, our own variety of hominid, *Homo sapiens*, having only appeared within the last fifty thousand years. Many details of the evolutionary history of the universe are still unknown to us, but its general sweep appears well established and there are no pointers to a radical discontinuity of development setting humanity apart from the physical world which gave it birth. The universe is not just there to be the backdrop for the human drama; we are actors who have emerged from the scenery.

Within this apparently continuous story of human origin, the coming-to-be of consciousness is the most profoundly novel development in the course of cosmic history. A world which was once just a hot quark soup has become the home of beings endowed with self-awareness and the ability to understand that physical world of which they are a part. The unriven unity of evolutionary history encourages a view of men and women as being psychosomatic unities, integrated beings, and the most impressive example of the fruitful potency of matter-in-organisation, rather than their being soul-body hybrids, in whom a divinely provided spiritual component is housed within an evolutionarily constructed physical shell. Our ignorance of the true nature of humanity is so great that it is impossible to be dogmatic, but a dualism of soul and body, such as is associated with the philosopher René Descartes, has become an increasingly difficult position to hold in the twentieth century. It always suffered from an inability to give a convincing account of how the two contrasting substances, extended matter and thinking mind, could interact with each other. We now know, from studies of brain function, brain damage, and the effect of drugs, how intimately these two aspects of our nature influence each other. A plausible theory of the material and the mental must be capable of accommodating this interaction, and of acknowledging our emergence historically from the world of animals and, initially, inanimate matter.

The Christian may not find great difficulty in being pressed to move in the direction of a psychosomatic understanding of human nature. The concept of humankind as animated bodies rather than incarnated souls is generally characteristic of Hebrew thought. It is true that a dualist as well as a unitary view of human nature can be supported from Scripture, though the latter predominates. While Platonic notions have often influenced Christian theology, they should not be taken to be determinative of it.

Even if this picture of human psychosomatic unity is correct, there is no adequately worked out articulation of it available to us at present. A contemporary philosopher, Thomas Nagel, has spoken of our being able to indulge only in 'pre-Socratic flailings around'. The implied comparison is instructive: six centuries BC, the Greeks began to speculate that the variety of objects in the world might be but the manifestations of a single underlying stuff. Guesses at air or water as the basic substance were hopelessly awry, but the germinal idea has come to flower in our own time as physicists seek a unified theory of matter. Similarly, we may be centuries away from a psychosomatic theory of human nature, but it may still be the most hopeful direction in which to wave our arms. For our present purpose it would be imprudent to pin our thoughts on any particular contemporary speculation, but nevertheless it will be valuable to consider how a doctrine of salvation can be framed in psychosomatic terms. It would not be possible to speak of salvation in terms of the destiny of souls after death, if the soul is thought of as the detachable spiritual part of ourselves. If the essential human being is an embodied whole, our ultimate destiny must be the resurrection and transformation of our entire being.

To speak thus is not to abandon talk of the soul, but to seek its redefinition. When we speak of salvation in terms of the destiny of souls we must be using the word to represent the essential nature which constitutes us in our individual particularities. That essence of humanity is certainly not merely the matter of the body, for that is continuously changing through wear and tear, eating and drinking. What provides continuity and unity through that flux of change is not material but (in a vague but suggestive phrase) the vastly complex information-bearing pattern in which that material is organised. That 'pattern' can surely be considered as the carrier of memories and of personality. We are close to the Aristotelian notion of the soul as the 'form' of the body, found also in Aquinas. Language is here being stretched to a limit, but to think of the soul in this fashion is by no means to embrace a reductionist concept of human nature. 'Pattern' is a word with deliberately holistic overtones, for its essence is the web of relationships in which the parts are organised. Eventually, an understanding of 'pattern' will have to be adequate to accommodate what has traditionally been spoken of in terms of the mind and heart and will.

'Information' is not to be construed in a narrow computer-model sense; there are good reasons for rejecting the strong programme of artificial intelligence, equating thought with computation, and for believing that thought transcends the mere execution of algorithms, however complex. Human beings are very much more than 'computers made of meat'. At present our understanding of that 'much more' is insufficient to provide us with a vocabulary precise enough to express a psychosomatic picture of humankind, and we have to be content with language which is evocative rather than adequate. In this respect, the view of human nature that we are presently pursuing does not differ from its reductionist or dualist competitors. We are all groping in the dark. Yet Christian discourse on salvation which can lay claim to serious attention in the context of a contemporary understanding of humankind will have to be prepared to speak in terms which are not exclusively those of a soul-body dualism.

There is a second scientific problem which such discourse must also address. It arises from the perception that present physical process is condemned to eventual futility. Cosmologists not only discuss the very early universe. They can also peer into its future. They tell us that it will end badly, either in a collapse back into the cosmic melting pot of the big crunch, or in the low-grade radiation of a cooling, ever-expanding universe. These prognostications are to be taken with the utmost seriousness. One way or the other, the ultimate prospects are bleak. Of course, the futility of this fate is not just around the corner. Tens of billions of years are expected to elapse before these things come to pass. But it is as certain as it can be that within the unfolding history of the present universe, humanity will ultimately prove to have been a transient episode.

It is possible to speculate that intelligence will nevertheless continue. It will have to engineer for itself new forms of embodiment, 'computers' taking more and more bizarre forms as the circumstances of the universe change. In the dying phase of an endlessly expanding universe, one might suppose that 'thinking' entities would come into being which were extended systems capable of processing information ever more slowly as energy runs out. In the hectic final stage of a collapsing universe, the whole cosmos might become an ever faster racing computer. Ingenious as these speculations of a 'physical eschatology' may be, they are subject to a variety of objections. They are framed in reductionist terms which equate fulfilment with unlimited processing of information. They suppose a persistent purpose for survival to be present in intelligent being, despite the possibility for self-destructiveness perceptible in human sinfulness. They do not meet the hope of individual destiny and fulfilment which belief in the God of Abraham, Isaac and Jacob encourages (Mark 12.24–7).

The final futility of the universe puts in question any ultimate recourse to evolutionary optimism. The unfolding of the present process will end either in collapse or decay, so that those who trust in a true and everlasting hope will have to look elsewhere for its ground and guarantee. Only God could release the universe from its 'bondage to decay' (Rom. 8.21).

On a much shorter time-scale, scientific knowledge already poses problems in relation to human significance and destiny. Culture's power to transmit information from one generation to another has profoundly modified evolutionary history, which previously had relied for such transmission on the limited resource of DNA. In the past the average life of a species was of the order of a few million years. It is not clear whether *Homo sapiens* may be expected to give way to an evolutionary successor in the same way that earlier hominids gave way to us, but claims of an ultimacy for humanity are problematic from a scientific point of view.

We are gaining the possibility of interfering with life by manipulating human genetic material. This ambiguous gift not only raises hopes of curing genetic disease but also the spectre of a eugenic programme reminiscent of Aldous Huxley's *Brave New World*. The more we are successful at biochemical manipulation, the greater will be the temptation to think of human beings as complicated biochemical machines. At the same time, the advance of technology increases the divorce between humanity and nature and, by the provision of greater leisure time, poses the question of what are the activities which truly enhance human value. These developments affect human self-perception and so impinge upon how the need and nature of salvation may be conceived. Scientific advance of itself is neutral; it simply extends the range of human choice for either good or ill. Yet its great success encourages the expectation that every problem will have its prompt and full solution, produced by a suitable research programme. Even in medicine this hope is illusory (the elixir of life will always elude us) and the pursuit of the good life requires much more than technological facility. Science is too external to our deepest nature ever to present the ground of a salvific programme. To suppose the contrary would be the grossest scientism, making the processes of the natural order as science has disclosed it the basis of religious belief.

Feminist challenges

If our intellectual environment has been changed out of all recognition by the advances in scientific knowledge, the social environment in which faith is professed and lived out has changed just as dramatically.

While there is, of course, much political debate about how egalitarian society should seek to become, there is no question that previous generations were ready to assume a far more hierarchical ordering of the life of the community than would be at all acceptable today. The rise of the welfare state, our enhanced sensitivity to all forms of discrimination, and the widespread emphasis on human rights all affect at a deep level the way in which we now see the world. A particular example of such a change of consciousness, and one which has affected Christians most strongly in recent years, has been the widely dispersed awareness that the relations between the sexes have changed to an enormous degree.

The aspiration to change the relationship between women and men in a direction that remedies the political, social and economic disadvantage which has been suffered by women presses upon us in nearly every part of our lives. The action that is increasingly being taken to secure equality of opportunity in the workplace is probably where most people experience the pressure for change; the economic and political power of women and the possibilities which that power gives for influencing political and social structures is something which is recognised not only by women themselves, but by those who seek their money or their votes.

It is no exaggeration to say that all movements which seek political or economic justice, whether or not they seem initially to concern the relationship of women and men, have at some point, and now increasingly early in their development, to address the contribution of women to their programme, their ambitions and their strategy. It has not always been expected that women would play such a key role in determining the course and the outcome of campaigns for racial justice or industrial disputes; now that is largely taken for granted, and male protesters, campaigners, politicians and social activists find that they ignore the role of women at their peril.

Such a change of consciousness is not confined to women who see themselves, or are seen, as 'oppressed' though its form may vary according to the particular situations of particular communities. There is no single set of policies or ideas called 'feminism'; hence we speak of 'feminist challenges' rather than speaking in the singular. The implications of this change of consciousness cannot be avoided by simply noticing (quite accurately) that there is no single 'women's movement' or pointing out (equally accurately) that there are many women in positions of power and prestige. Neither of these observations takes away the force of an immensely important change of moral, social and political consciousness that belongs particularly to this century.

In such a context, it is hardly surprising that the contribution of women to the prayer, life and thought of the churches is far nearer the surface of Christians' awareness than has been the case in the past. The decades of debate about the place of women within the ordained ministry were in that sense inevitable, even though many denominations made a much more rapid adjustment. One result of that debate has been that most Christians, not least in the Church of England, can be expected to have formed an opinion on the matter, and those supporting and those opposing the admission of women to the priesthood find it equally necessary to demonstrate that in coming to the view which they hold they have taken seriously the social context of women's liberation.

That these social and ecclesiastical developments were bound to affect the conduct of all sorts of theological discussions was to be expected. All the major branches of theology evolved in a context in which the dominant role of men passed for the most part unquestioned and indeed unnoticed. The question therefore was bound to be raised, how the major theological disciplines should develop at a time when the influence of patriarchal assumptions is increasingly being suspected and a wide range of proposals is being canvassed for countering those assumptions in the present day. These proposals in their turn constantly raise the question how far and in which ways the authority of biblical and doctrinal statements can be questioned in the changed climate brought about by the rise of feminist thinking.

In considering the effect of feminist challenges within the life of the Church two particular points need also to be borne in mind: first, as in the case of secular thinking, theologians who regard themselves as speaking from a feminist perspective are engaged in vigorous debate among themselves about the scope and nature of feminist challenges to traditional theological thinking. There is a burgeoning literature expressing varied points of view and covering different aspects of Christian witness, much though not all of it concerned with very fundamental issues. Secondly, while theologians may differ on the detail and in their response, there would be widespread agreement that much of the Bible and of the later tradition of the Church contains material which assumes male supremacy, and that therefore any attempt to take feminist issues seriously is bound to involve discovering criteria for discriminating among different parts of the tradition.

While the emergence of feminist critiques of traditional expressions of Christian faith is a general issue in Christian doctrine, it has some very particular points of contact with the Church's witness to God's salvation of the world. It is important to note that we speak here of 'critiques' in the plural; for not surprisingly in the case of new and developing thinking, the arena is one of considerable debate. But the two main points which have to be addressed in a climate of which feminism is so important a part are the description of the human situation – the nature of the human peril as we have denoted it – and the divine response.

If sin is that from which humankind is to be saved, to what extent has the definition of sin been affected by the male-dominated cultures in which the doctrinal tradition has developed? There has been much debate about the core of human sin, so often represented as overweening pride, and also about the role of male domination in the development of the story of Adam's and Eve's disobedience in the Garden of Eden. From the earliest days of feminist theology, there has been a questioning of whether the character of human sin was traditionally understood as pride because men had seen it that way. If women had been allowed to play a fuller part in the development of the concept of sin, might they not have wished to place a greater emphasis on sin as the failure to assert and take responsibility for oneself? If that is so, then while it might be very appropriate to exalt the virtues of gentleness and sacrificial vulnerability when you have a male audience in mind, to describe sin in that way to women might simply compound their negative self-image and encourage them to collude in a position of abiding weakness.

The tendency of traditional understandings of sin – and therefore of the human peril – to be drawn from 'a man's world' is very pervasive. Among the Ten Commandments are some clearly aimed at discouraging the people of Israel from adopting some of the oppressive features of the slave-owning culture from which they had emerged; even so women appear in the tenth commandment simply as adjuncts of the male audience to which the words are predominantly addressed. This will not pass unnoticed in our day; for to continue to speak in the same way about sin, without a good deal of interpretation and even, some would say, adaptation is bound to compound the situation of women: it conveys the message, whether intentionally or not, that for women rescue from the human peril consists in their accepting a highly negative self-image. In a society seeking to be sensitive to the place of women we have to take seriously the use to which concepts of sin have been put in the past and might be put in the present.

If the understanding of the human peril we can hold is affected by changes in male and female consciousness and the relationship between the sexes, so equally will be our understanding of how God has responded to human need. The statement that God in Christ responded to human violence, to hatred and the abuse of power, by absorbing on the cross the worst that humanity could do raises this question in an acute form. Was Christ responding to, and absorbing, primarily the sins of men? And was God's saving response of willing and meek self-sacrifice not simply an acting out of the role in which women have tended to find themselves, though in their case not willingly but as the result of the coercion and socialisation to which they have been subject? And if the self-sacrifice of a man is indeed a healing and saving response to the sins of men, what would be the response of a saving God to sins of collusion and of failure to act with an appropriate self-assertiveness and responsibility?

These questions go uncomfortably near to the heart of the gospel. For the doctrine of sacrifice has, as will necessarily appear throughout this report, been a central theme of the Church's preaching of salvation; and many statements about sacrifice within the Christian tradition are quite distant in their assumptions from modern understandings of what it is to make sacrifices or to display self-sacrifice. Such modern understandings are bound to affect the way in which Christian witness is heard in our time. That being so, the Church's witness to a God who saves by sacrifice is open to being suspected of being an attempt to exalt an alleged virtue which women have been obliged to practise in order to show that they knew their place. Such a witness is hardly likely to be experienced as saving, and whether a version of the doctrine of sacrifice can be expressed in terms which meet this objection is a matter to which we shall have cause to return.

The changing consciousness of women and men about their relationship goes to the heart of the doctrine of salvation in another way also. For the question is now bound to be asked whether a male saviour can save women. As has been evident in many of the debates about the ordination of women, this may be the sharpest form human beings have encountered yet of the paradox of Christ as both particular human being and universal saviour. It is true that the maleness of Christ has not been given much emphasis in traditional teaching about the incarnation; but recent debates have made clear that God's incarnation as a man is held by some to be a crucial dimension of our salvation.

That raises the issue of equality and difference which is so central to the quest for justice between women and men in a central matter of Christian belief. On the one hand equal treatment for women is being expected (for example in the workplace) and on the other proper consideration is demanded for differences of biological function, and whatever social and psychological differences they are thought to entail, if any.

Thus the rise of feminist consciousness is a very important part of the context of whatever we say about salvation. In any church or community there may be debate about this or that item of the feminist agenda; but such disagreements are dwarfed by the immense gap that separates our generation from those that have gone before; what makes us different is that for us these questions, whatever we think about them, are unavoidable. In the realm of Christian faith, that is particularly true when we consider how it is that we shall continue to say that God has saved the world through the cross.

Other faiths

The other major world faiths present a further challenge in any Christian reflection about salvation. Hinduism, Buddhism and Judaism predated Christianity; Islam and Sikhism have coexisted with the Christian faith for hundreds of years. Countless generations of believers have lived their lives within these religious frameworks, and passed on their faith. They have largely resisted the appeal of the Christian gospel, and found seemingly satisfactory answers to life's questions where they are. What is the place of these religions in a Christian understanding of salvation? Is their inclusion ruled out a priori? Or can they be salvific, in any sense of that word? And if we consider they can be, within a Christian understanding of the content of salvation, then are we imposing our content on something that these religions would define in various different ways? What is their doctrine of salvation, if they have one at all? Whom would they include within this, and under what criteria?

These questions now seem imperative to us, because of the presence of large numbers of adherents of other faiths in Britain, a development largely in the last thirty years, except in the case of Jews. This context is elaborated later in chapter 7.

However, the theological issue of the relation between other faiths and the Christian understanding of salvation is there, regardless of whether a single Sikh or Muslim actually lives in Britain. The fact that Christianity was born out of Judaism presented this issue from the beginning, as is highlighted in Romans 9–11. Questions have always been there for those in the so-called mission field. The difference now is that the challenge presents itself much nearer to home.

The Second Vatican Council's constitution on the relationship of the Church to non-Christian religions (*Nostra Aetate*) lists questions it considers always to have stirred the human heart:

> What is a human being? What is the meaning and purpose of our life? What is goodness and what is sin? What gives rise to our sorrows and to what intent? Where lies the path to true happiness?

What is the truth about death, judgement and retribution beyond the grave? What, finally, is that ultimate and unutterable mystery which engulfs our being, and whence we take our rise, and whither our journey leads?

It then takes a revolutionary way for a Church which had affirmed for so long that outside the Church, by this meaning the Roman Catholic Church, there was no salvation: it speaks of salvific possibilities in other religions, as they try to answer in their own way these fundamental questions.

Even if the questions are the same, the answers they give vary greatly. This applies to what we need to be saved from, to what we are to be saved for, and to the means by which we are saved. They may not even use the world 'salvation'.

As we look at the self-understanding of various faiths, we can distinguish between the religions of the Book, Judaism, Islam and Christianity, on the one hand, and eastern religions on the other: these last are concerned primarily with how to be saved from the negativity of this world; in the former, on the other hand, this world is important for its own sake; history is where the events of the salvation story are determined, both within this world and in the 'not yet' of what is beyond history. In what follows we are inevitably summarising, both for lack of space and because within each religion, as indeed within Christianity, understandings vary greatly.

For classical Hinduism, salvation is a central concept; Hindus use the word *moksha* or *mukti*, which can be translated 'liberation'. This is the liberation of the soul from *karma*, from the chains of previous deeds, and from *samsara*, the endless cycle of birth and rebirth. The soul is liberated by being absorbed into God, or entering into total communion with God. This liberation may be by deeds, by devotion or by knowledge. Grace plays a varying part in different traditions. In general, the source of wrongdoing is seen to lie predominantly in ignorance, *avidya*; hence the well-known prayer from the Upanishads: 'From the unreal, lead me to the real, from darkness lead me to light, from death lead me to immortality.' On such a view there might be various ways to truth; and the Christian way may be one of them. Buddhism began as a protest movement within Hindu Brahminism; it largely shares the Hindu world-view. The central concept to describe salvation is *nirvana*. This is not annihilation in a metaphysical sense, but elimination of desire and clinging to self. It centres on liberation from attachment, from aversion and from ignorance about our true nature. It is clinging that causes suffering; the aim of the teaching of the Buddha is to be saved, not from suffering itself, which is universal, but from the mastery of suffering over us. Salvation is not brought by God – even if God exists; rather it is the responsibility of each to gain it for ourselves, with the help of teaching and meditation. We are responsible, too, for the salvation of the whole of creation; hence the centrality of compassion in Buddhist practice. There is no exclusivity here.

Sikhism also has an inclusive understanding of salvation. We are all dependent on the grace of God. Guru Nanak wrote:

> If a man goes one step towards him, the Lord comes a thousand steps towards man.

> Good actions may procure a good life, but liberation comes only from his grace.

Salvation can be described as union with God, and from this flow deeds of service to others. Heaven can be now, where God's praise is sung.

In Islamic understanding, Allah accepts whom He wills and condemns whom He wills: 'Allah leaves in error whom He will and guides whom He pleases' (Qur'an, 14.4). We can only throw ourselves on His mercy and do our best to do His will. It matters what we and our community do now, within history. We will be judged after death: 'To us they shall return, and we will bring them to account' (88.26). Heaven will be the reward for the faithful, which is graphically described in the Qur'an; this is what Muslims believe is going to be the reality, and includes being in the closer presence of God. Punishment is being cut off from Him. The best insurance for the moment is to do our religious duties, and those include our social duties, including caring for the poor. As regards those from outside the Muslim community, the Qur'an may not appear fully clear, but peoples of the Book at least, Jews and Christians, seem to have a chance of salvation too: 'Believers, Jews, Christians, and Sabaeans – whoever believes in Allah and the Last Day and does what is right – shall be rewarded by their Lord; they have nothing to fear or regret' (2.62).

Judaism generally prefers the word redemption to salvation. Repentance and returning to God are centrally linked. At times concentration is on individual repentance, at times on the corporate. In some traditions, the emphasis is on spiritual redemption, in others on the concrete experience of a return to the promised land and Jerusalem; at times, it is in the hands of the individual or the people of Israel, at other times it depends largely on the intervention of God from beyond history. The whole world must now be mended, because the whole world has been implicated. In general, Judaism is concerned with redemption within Jewish tradition;

it respects the integrity of other faiths, and tends towards universalist possibilities, resting this on obedience to the convenant with Noah, which is available to all.

In dialogues about salvation, clearly it will matter greatly which faiths we are involved with. With a Hindu or a Buddhist, the nature of humanity will be central: what is it to be saved? For a Hindu, Jesus as the incarnation of God will not be a problem, but Jesus as the only incarnate one will be. For what does that make of Rama and Krishna and other incarnations? Jesus on the cross as a moral example will not be a problem; exclusive salvation through the cross will be. Most Buddhists will be able to affirm the example of Jesus enduring suffering in compassion for the whole world; but this can only be an example; we are accountable for our response to this example, or that of any other teacher. Sikhism will respond to Jesus as the Guru, teacher of a salvific way; Sikhs cannot see him as the only way. The Muslim and the Jew will be able to affirm much of our world-view; but not the place of Jesus, nor, above all, the cross. What is central is the almightiness of God, and total dependence on him; and for them Jesus is not God.

In general, it is the person of Christ, and the cross, which remain stumbling-blocks. The more these are central to our understanding of salvation, the harder it will be to find common ground. If we concentrate on concepts such as the kingdom of God, and the liberation, righteousness and peace that lie at the centre of the kingdom, if we look at the central teachings of the Sermon on the Mount, and if we are content to see the cross as primarily an example of the ultimate sacrifice of selfless love, then dialogue about salvation becomes much easier. But given that we profess that God became incarnate for us and 'for our salvation', there can be no escape from the way in which the life, death and resurrection of Jesus Christ are seen as decisive for human history and the fulfilment of God's purposes. There is no alternative, therefore, to the facing of these matters as they arise in dialogue between the faith communities.

These are the theological issues. In practical, day-to-day questions, people of all religious faiths may feel they have more in common than that which divides them, within an increasingly secular Britain which does not see any religious response as relevant. Is what we have in common a concern with similar questions, as the Vatican II declaration suggests? There will be many issues of individual and social concern, not least concern for the poor and weak within our competitive society, that may unite us. This is related to questions of healing and wholeness on which different communities of faith can work together now. Should this not be of central concern in any study of salvation?

By living and working with people of other faiths, and by recognising their integrity and faithfulness as well as, in many cases, their goodness and love, questions of salvation arise. Can the God of love, revealed in Christ, reject such people whom we admire? They follow a way of life based upon religious discipline, prayer and reading of Scriptures. Can the quality of their lives be separated from their religious belief? If not, how can we find an adequate way of speaking of salvation, one that both affirms the significance of the biblical witness to Christ and at the same time can take account of what we see before us? We return to these questions later in chapter 7.

Conclusion

We have sought to do no more in this opening chapter than sketch an agenda which indicates why witnessing to the salvation God offers in Christ is both vitally important and especially challenging: we are brought face to face with some of the most pressing questions of our age. Whatever the Church says in proclaiming the gospel will be judged by the extent to which we show awareness of the profound challenge which our culture presents to us. The Church is called to witness from its own experience and on the basis of the charge which the Scriptures lay upon it, to the truth that God is one who saves.

Yet to speak of the challenges of our 'culture' runs the risk of suggesting a range of somewhat abstract issues, matters which concern the particularly thoughtful or literate. This would be a quite inappropriate message for a discussion of salvation, a theme which has to embrace the whole range of human concerns and be offered to all, particularly to those to whom life appears to offer little, who are excluded from the adequate meeting of their material needs as well as participation in the range of human culture.

It is of the essence of all human communication, and has been a central feature of witness to the gospel of salvation, that as much attention is given to the message that is heard as to the message that is spoken. To speak of God saving humankind from the peril in which it stands, requires that we take seriously our context in a society in which there is no clarity, let alone agreement, about the peril in which we stand, and in which religious language has no natural and agreed reference point among our contemporaries. That is not to say, and the evidence of our quotations from contemporary literature supports this, that there are not seekers after salvation outside the churches: there are, and discerning the nature of the predicament they describe is an essential first step to sharing the Christian message of salvation.

We live also in a time when the universe has expanded dramatically through what modern science has revealed. That means that some of the language of Christian witness, even language that has appeared to stand the test of time, can well appear naive and even obscurantist if we speak as if only human history were the arena of salvation, and as though hope were a self-evident response to what we see around us in the material world. Profound questions about the nature of persons and the universe they inhabit present themselves to us.

As well as the new perspective presented by scientific cosmology, we have sketched two other major concerns of our time: the changed consciousness of women and men about what justice between the sexes requires, and which images of God and accounts of the work of Christ would be truly liberating for both; and the issues raised for the preaching of the gospel by the dialogue with members of other world faith communities, now much closer at hand in a smaller world and a nation of many peoples.

It is against such a background that what we have written will be read, and by its response to our contemporary situation that its truthfulness and not just its effectiveness will be judged. We are convinced that the gospel of Christ contains the resources we need when it comes to facing such questions, and the following chapters seek to present those resources. We do so while keeping in mind the questions contained in this chapter; they are not just those of our hearers and readers: they are ours also.

Chapter 2
The giver and the gift

Salvation: a flexible concept?

The previous chapter explored the context to which the Christian message of salvation today must speak. But in order to clarify what that message is in our contemporary context, we need to explore the notion of salvation itself. What do we Christians mean by salvation? A sampling either of the history of Christian thought or of Christian opinions today could easily suggest that the term is an extremely slippery one, by which Christians in different times and places have meant a wide variety of different things. Is salvation going to heaven when we die or something experienced here and now? Is it deliverance from guilt and the threat of divine punishment or from the transience and mortality of earthly life or from demonic forces which tyrannise over human life or from oppressive political and economic conditions? Is it a matter of knowing God or of living a better life? Is it the salvation of individual souls from a corrupt world or the creation of an alternative society in contrast to the world or a means of transforming society into the kingdom of God? Does it make people divine or truly human? Differing answers to such questions about what salvation is relate very closely to differences on other important issues, such as whether what Christians mean by salvation is also available through other religions or to those who have no religious faith.

One response to the questions could be that many of the alternatives posed are false alternatives. Salvation need not be this *or* that; it can be *both* this *and* that. For example, salvation may be both something enjoyed in this life and also a destiny beyond death. Probably most Christians have thought so. But although not all of the alternatives need be exclusive alternatives, they do represent wide variations of emphasis in Christian understandings of salvation. Moreover it looks as though such differences of emphasis have a lot to do with the different social and cultural contexts in which the Christian message is presented and believed: the different ways in which people identify what is wrong with the human condition and the correspondingly different aspirations for deliverance or improvement.

For example, in the second and third centuries there was a widespread sense of human mortality and a corresponding aspiration to escape this mortal life and to share the immortal life of the gods. There was also a fatalistic sense of the domination of human life by demonic forces. The

300

Christian gospel therefore appealed in part because it promised immortal life beyond death, which was often called deification: God's gift to humans of participation in God's own divine, immortal life, of which there can be a foretaste in the present. The fearlessness of the Christian martyrs in the face of death testified to Christ's conquest of death. Similarly, his conquest of the demons, demonstrated by exorcisms in the name of Christ, offered a kind of liberation for which many people were looking. By contrast, in the twentieth-century West, across the whole spectrum of types of Christianity, there seems to be a fairly consistent emphasis on salvation here and now rather than after death, which must be partly related to increased life expectancy and to the way modern western society has tended to push death to the margins of its consciousness. Humanisation rather than deification is naturally the theme in a society whose general sense of the divine is weak. Only a minority now sees present salvation as liberation from the demonic, though in the different cultural circumstances of some parts of Africa this theme does come into its own. In the affluent West, the typical existential ills of modern urban culture – lack of meaning and purpose in life, loneliness and quiet desperation, satiation with a materialistic lifestyle – have often been the plight from which Christ delivers, although pursuit of the kingdom of God through overcoming social deprivation has also had a place. But an emphasis on salvation as liberation from political and economic oppression is more characteristic of some types of Christianity in the Third World (more accurately called the Two-Thirds World). It is no accident that other agencies or movements beside the Church – such as psychotherapy or the New Age movement in the West, political liberation movements in the Two-Thirds World – often parallel both the diagnosis of the need of salvation and to some extent the kind of salvation offered by the Church in particular contexts.

We need not be too disturbed by these contextually varying interpretations of Christian salvation. Certainly the Church should be in the business of criticising and correcting the way people perceive the human situation, but it must also make connections with its cultural context. Varying emphases may be justifiable so long as it is not the case that just any concept of salvation will do. Other examples can show that this is in fact not the case. To return to the second and third centuries, one way in which the culture of that period differed so radically from ours was in its sense, not only that mortality was an evil, but that the physical and material world is a place in which the human spirit does not belong. Liberation from the body and the physical world into a purely spiritual existence was therefore the most culturally appropriate form for salvation to take, and it was the form offered by the Gnostics. But the Church rejected this Gnostic understanding of salvation because of its conviction that the material world and the human body are God's good creation. Salvation is not liberation from them, but redemption of them. Thus one way of viewing the human plight and salvation from it, highly appealing in its cultural context, was found not to be an adequately Christian understanding of salvation.

So it is not the case that anything goes, but emphases do vary, and, up to a point, rightly so. But in that case, two issues arise. First, is there anything that provides continuity within the varying emphases? Second, does Christian salvation really differ from other claims to remedy human ills? In a pluralistic society like our own (which, in this respect, it is worth noting resembles the Roman world of the first three centuries AD) one cannot avoid asking whether the Church's understanding of salvation simply puts Christian packaging on a product essentially the same as that offered by others too.

The argument of this chapter will be that answers to both these questions can be found by thinking about the relationship of salvation to God. Salvation is not *only* the various good things that God gives us – forgiveness or eternal life or liberation from oppression or healing of relationships or finding our true identity. It is all these things – almost as many of these things as Christians have ever supposed it to be. Because it is all these things, emphases may vary, as the human situation and people's perception of it vary. Because it is all these things, what Christians experience as salvation always overlaps with experiences of liberation and greater fulfilment and enhancement of life that others experience in all kinds of ways. But what we mean by salvation is not only all these things. It is receiving these things from God in an experienced relationship with God as the source and the goal of them all. In Christian talk of salvation there is always an absolutely necessary reference to God. Moreover, this God who is both our saviour and our salvation is the triune God. In the next section we shall see why, as Christians, we cannot talk about salvation without talking about God. In the following section we shall see why, when talking of salvation, Christians find they need to talk not simply of God, but of the trinitarian God. The doctrine of the Trinity, we shall see, stands in the closest possible relationship to what we Christians mean by salvation.

God and salvation

Christians cannot talk about salvation without talking about God. For us in contemporary Britain this means talking about God and salvation in the kind of society described in the previous chapter – a pluralist society which, even to the extent that it is religious, is by no means exclusively Christian. In this chapter we leave aside the question of salvation in other faiths, and how this may relate to the Christian understanding of salvation. Another chapter is devoted to that question. For the moment we shall focus on the fact that ours is a society in which many people live their lives without reference to God. This will enable us to pose the question: what is it that distinguishes the Christian understanding of salvation from parallel notions of human fulfilment which make no reference to God?

The point is not at all to show that there is nothing in common between the two. The point is rather that, given that there may be a great deal in common, we are seeking what distinguishes the Christian understanding of salvation from notions of human fulfilment which make no reference to God. We shall use the term 'fulfilment' to describe what secular people seek when they aim (as all people do in some way or another) at some form of greater human well-being, but seek this without reference to God. The very use of this term shows that what they seek is in many ways comparable with what those of us who are Christians call salvation. The word 'fulfilment' could very appropriately be used to describe the experience of Christian salvation, and some theologians have so used it. Christians believe that true and complete human fulfilment can be found only in relation to God. The word 'fulfilment' puts the emphasis on what we, from our side, attain, while the word 'salvation' puts the emphasis on what God, from his side, gives. But this is no antithesis. The human search for fulfilment and the divine gift of salvation could appropriately be seen as two sides of the same coin. So it is only for convenience in the present context that we shall use 'fulfilment' to refer to the secular quest for fulfilment *without* God, and 'salvation' to refer to the religious concept to which God is essential. Because we wish to focus on the presence or absence of reference to God, 'fulfilment' is the more appropriate term for non-religious aspirations.

In our contemporary society it is increasingly the case that secular people seek *autonomous* forms of self-fulfilment envisaged in *individualistic* terms. We shall speak here of this dominant cultural trend, which can easily be observed in such indices of dominant culture as soap operas and advertisements. Of course, there are many people without religious faith whose understanding of their lives is quite different from this dominant culture's. There are many, for example, who hold to the highest ideals of a humanist vision of the world, strongly committed to moral norms. Nor are we here in the least concerned to pass judgement on people. It is not the moral or spiritual quality of people's lives that is at issue, but the kind of understanding of human fulfilment which is most characteristic of our secular culture at present. Various sectors of society may be more or less influenced by it. Reactions against it may even be gaining ground. But we shall certainly all be living with its influence for some time to come.

This dominant cultural trend is part of the transition, in which our society is currently caught up, from a modern to a postmodern culture. The term 'postmodern' is a useful means of signalling the idea that contemporary western culture is undergoing a major shift from the culture of modernity, which dates from the eighteenth-century Enlightenment, into a new phase. Postmodernity is more easily characterised negatively, as marked by the discrediting and disintegration of the major features of the culture of modernity, than it is positively. But autonomous individualism, which we have suggested is a keynote of contemporary aspirations to self-fulfilment, is certainly a significant feature of postmodernity. The emergence of this radically individualistic concept of self-fulfilment has accompanied the demise of the idea of human progress, which was so characteristic of the modern period and still retained some vitality until quite recently. This nineteenth-century idea of progress envisaged the progress of the whole of society towards goals which were perceived in moral and spiritual as well as material terms. It depended on some sense of normative values and ideals which defined the greater good of all people. But the only remnant of this notion which survives in any strength is the still widespread belief in the importance of technological advance, with which is closely associated the absolute imperative of economic growth. Ecological considerations have not yet significantly qualified the latter. Everincreasing affluence is the only form of progress in which as a society we still believe, clinging to it with almost desperate devotion. It is widely assumed to be the essential prerequisite for most possibilities of self-fulfilment, but it scarcely constitutes in itself a form of self-fulfilment.

In our postmodern culture self-fulfilment has become a matter of individually self-chosen goals. Freedom – in the sense of the absolute autonomy of the individual – has become the single, overarching ideal to which all other goals are subordinated. I must be free to be whoever I choose to be and to pursue whatever good I define for myself. There must be no normative goals, models or ideals for which I *should* aim. The point is not simply that there *are* no such normative goals, but that there *must* be none, if I am to be truly free to be myself – to be the self I choose to make myself. Needless to say this contentless freedom is much more of an ideology than a reality. Most of us in fact seek fulfilment in goals presented enticingly to us by society, not least by commerical interests, as those normally thought desirable – especially in sexual relationships, work and an affluent lifestyle. But these are ideologically packaged as means to a freely chosen, non-normative path of self-creation. This ideological packaging is seductive. It leads people to set great value on, for example, freedom to buy things (consumer choice) and freedom from long-term commitments in relationships – understanding these things as important to their self-fulfilment. Such notions of self-fulfilment have all the potent allure of the ideal of freedom. They also have their victims: people impoverished by debt and children thrown out of a parental home to live on the streets are just some of the more obvious of these.

The roots of this particular ideology of self-fulfilment lie in the rejection of God, and it requires the rejection of God. This is because it envisages freedom as absolute autonomy. The freedom it desires is not freedom to discover and to embrace truth and goodness for oneself, but freedom to create one's own truth and goodness for oneself. 'God' is only conceivable as a kind of function of one's freedom, and in some debased forms of contemporary religion 'God' becomes a mere means to the religious person's self-fulfilment – a genie in their lamp. In a culture which has lost the sense of what it could mean really to believe in God, this is not surprising. But it illustrates how carefully Christians need to distinguish the Christian understanding of salvation from the culturally dominant notions of self-fulfilment.

Fulfilment as the pursuit of absolute autonomy has freedom from God as its presupposition. By contrast, salvation – in the Christian sense – is what people seek when they know that God is the reality to be reckoned with from first to last. For people who seek salvation, whatever else they may think they can know about God, it is self-evident that God is the source and goal of all things, never a means to an end. God is the source and the goal of my freedom, never its function. I do not know what Christians mean by salvation until I realise I can be fully myself only in receiving myself from God and in giving myself utterly to God. Salvation is to experience as the source and the goal of my own being and living the one who is the source and the goal of all things.

The point of drawing so sharply the contrast between postmodern secular self-fulfilment and Christian salvation is not at all to deny that many of the particular things in which people seek self-fulfilment – self-integration, healing of relationships, finding a purpose in life, and so on – are also aspects of Christian salvation. The point is that, beyond all such correspondences between secular fulfilment and Christian salvation, God makes all the difference. Fulfilment is sought axiomatically without God, whereas salvation is nothing at all without God. From one point of view the various aspects of salvation which can be sought and even attained by secular people without reference to God are good things. Their value should certainly not be denigrated. Christians themselves are constantly, rightly, engaged in pointing people to them and helping people find them. But nevertheless from the point of view of the Christian desire to see human life attain its fullest meaning and destiny, consciously integrated into its ultimate source and goal, these good things, had without reference to God, lack the one thing necessary. They are Hamlet without the Prince. From this point of view, we can see what Augustine of Hippo meant when he said that 'whatever God promises is worth nothing without God himself'.

In insisting on salvation's essential reference to God, we are not just saying that salvation comes from God. If salvation were just the various gifts which God gives us, then to have the gifts without recognising the giver, without even recognising them as gifts which come from a giver, would not be to miss anything essential. If this were the case, then we might well be able to say that, from a Christian point of view, the human attainment of a chosen self-fulfilment is in fact the divine gift of salvation, though not recognized as such. This is more or less how every twentieth-century Christian attempt to disguise the loss of God by putting a Christian gloss on secular experience sees it. There is a real element of truth in this perspective, for various human goods – all that genuinely contributes to healing and wholeness and life-enhancement – are recognisably aspects of what Christians call salvation. But still they are not salvation itself, because salvation itself is not only gifts from God, but God's gift of God's own self to us in his gifts and as himself.

This point can be easily understood by analogy with gifts in human life and relationships. Suppose I receive something valuable, gratuitously but not as a gift from someone who meant me to have it. It may fall off the back of a lorry or I may win it in a competition. It is worth having; I shall be pleased with it; it will be useful to me or enhance my life. But this experience is quite different from receiving the same object as a gift from someone who loves me. In this case the object has not only the same value in itself as it would have if I had won it in a raffle; it also mediates a relationship between myself and the person who has given me it as a gift. It will have the added value of an expression of the giver's love, and the more my relationship with the giver matters to me the more this value will surpass the value of the gift in itself. Valuable or useful as the object is in itself, the greater difference to my life is made by the discovery or assurance that someone loves me. Because the gift expresses the giver's love, the giver, in giving the gift, also gives herself or himself to me. In receiving the gift as a gift, I receive at the same time the giver's gift of himself or herself. In the same way, God gives himself to us in all his gifts of salvation. If we have any of them without recognising them as gifts of God, we have something valuable. But to experience them as gifts, to recognise the giver in the gifts, is to know God. This is what Christians call salvation.

The point is always implicit and frequently explicit in the biblical account of salvation. In the Old Testament salvation is experienced in a wide variety of concrete human goods: deliverance from political oppression, economic want and threatened death, healing of disease, protection from war, wild animals and natural disaster. But the heart of these is always Israel's relationship with Yahweh, repeatedly expressed in the covenant formula: 'You shall be my people and I shall be your God.' Psalm 85, for example, beautifully illustrates how inseparable for Old Testament thought are, on the one hand, the identification of salvation with the political and economic well-being of the nation, and, on the other hand, the experience of God, known in God's steadfast love, God's faithfulness, God's righteousness and God's peace precisely in this very tangible gift of salvation. This experience of God in God's gift of salvation is the depth-dimension of the gift itself, without which it would not truly be salvation.

Similarly, in the gospels, the salvation Jesus initiates in his ministry takes many concrete forms in relation to a variety of human needs, but comprehensively it is the kingdom of God – the inclusion of all human life in the fully realised purpose of God – and at its heart it is the experience of God as Father. The terminology of salvation is used most frequently with reference to Jesus' acts of healing, but the regular association of these healings with faith on the part of the recipients shows that salvation is more than bodily health. For faith – which is not simply the will to live but the entrusting of oneself to God the source of life – the gift is inseparable from its giver. This is especially clear in Luke's story of the healing of the ten Samaritan lepers (Luke 17.12–19). Only to the one leper who returns, praising God, to give thanks for his cleansing does Jesus say, 'Your faith has made you well (saved you).' The point is not that God, like some patronising benefactor of the poor, requires us to be grateful. The point is that gratitude is a response to personal love. The thankful leper has experienced not only something, as the other nine have, but also someone. His thankfulness shows that for him his healing has been a new experience of God the giver in God's gift.

This essential relationship of faith to salvation receives its fullest exposition in Paul. Its significance needs to be appropriated in different ways in different periods. In the sixteenth century, the Reformers thought it important to stress that salvation is received from God as gift, against the misunderstanding that it could be merited as reward from God. Emphasis on faith made this point because faith is the appropriate attitude to what is received from God as gift. In our context, in which the issue of salvation must be subordinate to the issue of God, the New Testament's correlation of faith and salvation as gift makes an additional point. For those who receive the gift of salvation in faith, the fundamental human act is not the reception of the gift but the entrusting of themselves to God the giver of the gift. Where the Reformation emphasis was on the correlation between faith and the gift of God the giver, ours must be on the correlation between faith and God the giver of the gift. Where the Reformers insisted that salvation, by its nature, can only be received as gift, we need to insist that salvation, by its nature, can only be received as the gift of the God who gives himself in his gift.

The New Testament never dissociates salvation from the variety of specific ways in which God heals and enhances human life now and brings it to ultimate fulfilment beyond this mortal life. These are often comprehensively expressed by the term 'life', in its fullest sense of life in eternal union with God as the source of life. But alongside this positive emphasis on the gift of God fulfilling human aspirations, there is also a demand for self-denial and self-renunciation. The two are paradoxically combined in Jesus' teasing aphorism: 'Those who try to make their life secure will lose it, but those who lose their life will keep it' (Luke 17.33; cf. Mark 8.35 and other parallels).[1] It is important to address this paradox, because the secular quest for self-fulfilment can today so easily become self-seeking individualism, and a claimed duty to be oneself and to fulfil oneself can be used to justify disregarding one's responsibilities for others. The gospel demand for self-renunciation can sound quite contradictory to the quest for self-fulfilment. Of course, Jesus' aphorism deliberately exploits this contradiction, but affirms instead the paradox that self-renunciation and self-fulfilment are not in contradiction. The possibility of this paradox lies once again in our fundamental distinction between autonomous self-fulfilment without God, and the salvation which is sought in relation to God through faith. As we have seen, even when salvation means receiving concrete benefits from God here and now, its human heart is the entrusting of oneself to God as the source and goal of one's life. Because salvation is found in God, who gives us himself and can be trusted to give us all things in himself, there is no need for anxious preoccupation with the task of fulfilling oneself. One is free to give oneself for others and for God – even in death, which the aphorism certainly envisages. While self-renunciation seems to contradict autonomous self-fulfilment, it is consistent with God's fulfilment of one's self.

Throughout the history of Christian thought about God and salvation run two themes, which are all too easily set against each other. The first is the thought that all aspects of human wholeness and well-being, all that heals, enhances and fulfils human life, is included in the experience of God which is salvation. To know God and, indeed, to live God as the source and goal of one's self, as of all things, emphatically affirms, while also surpassing, all other aspects of human fulfilment. False oppositions between the spiritual and the material, the individual and the communal, the this-worldly and the other-worldly have no place in this vision of the all-encompassing good encompassed only by God. But the second thought, from which the ascetic impulse in Christian spirituality springs, is that for the sake of finding God, in whom alone is salvation, everything else can and may have to be given up. In its authentically Christian form, this thought also has nothing to do with the false opposition between the spiritual and the material (although this Gnostic opposition has in fact had an unfortunate influence on Christian asceticism). In the dark night of the soul even spiritual goods have to be renounced for the sake of God himself. The point is not to distinguish among God's gifts, but to distinguish the giver from the gifts. And the aim is not to lose the gifts, but to find the giver who is infinitely more than the gifts. The two themes are not in the end logically incompatible, but their reconciliation in life is only found existentially and contextually.

In this section we have seen that Christian salvation encompasses all that heals and enhances human life. This gives it its continuity with much that takes place in human life outside an explicitly religious context. We have also seen that at the heart of the Christian understanding of salvation is a transforming relationship with God. This both distinguishes it from secular aspirations to human fulfilment and provides the common thread by which all the varying ways in which Christians have talked about salvation are united. But in speaking of God we have not yet considered God as Trinity, God as Christians know God through Jesus Christ is the trinitarian God: the Father, the Son and the Holy Spirit. So we have not understood salvation in fully Christian terms until we have understood its relationship to the trinitarian being of God. In the next section, we shall see how the approach to salvation we have outlined so far can be spelt out more fully in trinitarian terms.

The Trinity and salvation

Just as Christians cannot talk about salvation without talking about God, so they cannot talk adequately about salvation in Christian terms without talking about God as Trinity. The God to whom salvation is necessarily related is the God of Jesus Christ: God the Father, God the Son and God the Holy Spirit.[2] We can see this at once if we put in trinitarian terms the main point we have been making about salvation: that God does not just give us various gifts such as forgiveness or immortality, but gives us, in and with these gifts, the gift of himself. This point is most emphatically made in the New Testament when it is said that God gave his Son (e.g. John 3.16; Rom. 8.32) and gives his Spirit (e.g. John 14.16; Acts 11.17; Rom. 5.5). These phrases mean, of course, that God gives himself to us in self-giving love. In the incarnation and death of Jesus the Son, God *gave* himself *for us* in the once-for-all historical event which constitutes our salvation, and as the indwelling presence of the Spirit in our lives God continually *gives* himself *to us* in our present experience of salvation. To use the fully trinitarian terms, the Father gave his Son for us (e.g. John 3.16; Rom. 8.32; Eph. 1.22), the Son gave himself for us (e.g. Mark 10.45; John 6.51; Gal. 1.4; 2.20; Eph. 5.25; Tit. 2.14), the Father has given us the Spirit (e.g. Acts 5.32; 1 Thess. 4.8; 1 John 3.24), and the Son has given us the Spirit (cf. Acts 2.33). With this divine self-giving all other specific aspects of salvation can be taken for granted: 'He who did not withhold his own Son, but gave him up for all of us, will he not with him also give us everything else?' (Rom. 8.32).

The formulation of the doctrine of the Trinity in its classical form as a result of the debates of the patristic period took place in close continuity with this New Testament emphasis. The doctrine insisted that all three trinitarian persons are truly and equally God, because it is as these three that God gives himself to us in salvation. If the incarnate Son Jesus were less than truly God or if the indwelling Spirit were less than truly God, salvation would be jeopardised. It would not be God's gift of himself. The gift of the Son would be a gift of something less than God himself, and the gift of the Spirit would be a gift of something less than God himself. The divine activity in salvation – the gift of the Son and the gift of the Spirit – would not be the activity of divine *self*-giving that the New Testament witness sees in it. Salvation would be only the receiving of certain good things from God – forgiveness, immortality, and so on – not the experience of the self-giving love of God. This argument from the nature of salvation was the really decisive argument for Nicene orthodoxy against all of the more or less Arian positions in the fourth-century controversies.

The doctrine of the Trinity, which states that the one God exists as three truly divine persons, Father, Son and Holy Spirit, is a statement of who God is, both essentially in himself and historically in God's self-giving for our salvation. It is vital to recognise that this statement of the divine being was never intended to *replace* the story of what God has done and is doing for our salvation in history. This is why the terms it uses (the Father, the Son and the Holy Spirit) are those which the New Testament uses, not in trinitarian statements of God's being as such, but in trinitarian *narratives* of God's self-involvement in human history. The New Testament statements of God's self-giving which we have quoted – God gave his own Son, the Son gave himself for us, God has given us the Spirit – are examples of brief trinitarian narrative summaries. They summarise the much more diffuse and extended narratives of the gospels and Acts, which themselves are the climactic continuation of all the Old Testament narratives of God's activity in the world and in the history of God's people Israel. In fact, the gospels and Acts are also trinitarian in the way that they speak of the acts and involvement of God in the human historical story they tell; they too speak of God as Father, Son and Holy Spirit, and narrate the relations between these three in God's activity in history for our salvation. But the summaries, by crystallising the theological essence of the stories, also succeed in bringing their trinitarian shape into particularly sharp relief.

The summaries are still narratives of divine action and passion. The doctrine of the Trinity takes a further step away from the primary narratives. It derives from the narratives a statement, not in narrative form, of who the God is who acts and suffers in this story. If we ask whether it is legitimate to derive such a statement about the divine being from the story of God's activity, the answer is that it is legitimate precisely because the story narrates God's *self-giving* in history. If God really gives himself, then who God is in the story of God's self-giving is who God really is. In God's own eternity God is none other than who he is for us in the story of our salvation. In this way, the doctrine of the Trinity is an understanding of God's being derived from the narrative, while at the same time it serves to safeguard the theological reality of the narrative as the story of God's self-giving. Because God is Father, Son and Holy Spirit, because the Son and the Spirit are as truly God as the Father is, therefore the self-giving which the story narrates is a real giving of God's own self for us and to us. The doctrine of the Trinity assures us that what happens in the biblical story of salvation really is salvation in the fully biblical sense. It is not that we can ever do without the narrative. The doctrine of the Trinity does not replace the narrative, but it crystallises an insight conveyed by the narrative itself in order to help us read the narrative aright. We can see how appropriate it is that both of the creeds we regularly use – the Apostles' and the Nicene – tell the story of salvation within the framework of a *trinitarian* confession.

The doctrine of the Trinity, properly understood, is not a speculative prying into the eternal mystery of God. But it does affirm that God in his own divine self really is such that God *can share himself* with his creation. God is not only the utterly other, who infinitely transcends creation; God can also be deeply and intimately present within creation, as the Spirit, and God can also be one of us, a genuinely human person, as Jesus Christ the Son. Therefore God can and does open his own life for his creation to share. Moreover, because God is Trinity God can share his life even with those created beings, ourselves, who are alienated from God and opposed to God. As incarnate Son and indwelling Spirit, God enters our situation of evil, suffering and mortality, shares with us the pain of our alienation, bears for us the pain of overcoming our enmity and healing our estrangement, sustains us in the struggle to be truly human, redirects our lives towards the Father as the source and goal of our being. The New Testament summary narratives of trinitarian self-giving imply all this. It is as Father, Son and Holy Spirit that God can and does save us.

The intimate connection between the trinitarian being of God and the nature of Christian salvation can be explored a little further by way of comment on two major themes in the biblical and Christian understanding of salvation: life and love. In the biblical tradition that which, more than anything else, characterises God in distinction from creation is God's essential and eternal livingness. Only God has life inalienably as his nature. All other life is received as God's gift. It is God's Spirit, the breath of life from God, which animates all living things and without which they cannot live. To be alienated from God, the source of all life, is to die. To be saved from mortality is possible only through permanent union with the undying source of all life.

This essential and eternal divine livingness is trinitarian life. It is the common life of the Father, the Son and the Holy Spirit. This is why it can be shared with mortal creatures. As the Fourth Gospel puts it, the Father communicates to his Son the intrinsic divine livingness ('life in himself') so that the Son – meaning the divine Son become human as Jesus Christ – may give life to other human beings (John 5.21, 26). But this is not a straightforward mediation of eternal life from God to mortals. The incarnate Son participates in the eternal divine life in an extraordinary form: the form of a mortal life taken through death into eternal life. Because of his uniquely unbreakable union with his Father, Jesus received life from God even in death. Death is the loss of that life which comes from God, but in Jesus' case not even death could put an end to his eternal participation in the common life of the Trinity. Thus by entering our experience of death his divine life overcame death. In the book of Revelation, therefore, the risen Christ can claim the uniquely divine titles of eternal livingness: 'I am the first and the last, and the living one' (Rev. 1.17–18). But he claims them in his own way, not in the way the Father claims them. He claims them as the one who participates *through death* in the indestructible divine life: 'I was dead, and behold, I am alive forever and ever; and I have the keys of Death and Hades' (Rev. 1.18). This then makes a difference also to the way the Spirit communicates life to created beings. The Spirit of life is now the Spirit of the risen Christ and is therefore now the Spirit of life-from-the-dead, the Spirit of resurrection life for the dead (e.g. Rom. 8.11).

Thus God does not give us eternal life as something other than and separable from himself. God gives us life by giving us himself: by giving us God's Son to share our mortality and thereby to transcend it, and by giving us God's Spirit to unite us with the Son and to share his resurrection life with us. To have eternal life is to know God as Trinity: to experience the Spirit of Jesus Christ who unites us with Jesus Christ the Son of the Father. It is to share, through the Spirit, that unbreakable union of Jesus Christ with the Father which has broken the power of death. It is to experience the trinitarian life as our own life, within and beyond the conditions of this mortal life.

When the New Testament and later Christian tradition use 'life' as a term for salvation, the term is an appropriately comprehensive one. Life is a word which stretches from a minimal to a maximal sense. In the minimal sense life is that without which human persons do not exist. Even though we nowadays find it difficult to define the minimum (is it breathing or brain activity?), it remains an essential distinction between inanimate things, which exist without life, and human persons which can exist only by living. However, life in the maximal sense is much more than mere existence: it is real life, all that it is to be fully alive, all that makes for a life worth living. In this maximal sense, life is an open-ended concept. The maximum of life transcends description and imagination. Thus life as a term for salvation is, on the one hand, rooted in our creaturely dependence on God for sheer existence, which in salvation God gives back to us, out of death, but on the other hand it also extends to the prospect of unlimited abundance of life which eternal union with God opens up for us.

Because life as a term for salvation means much more than mere existence, we can also complement it with other terms, of which perhaps the most important is love. For human persons life and love are inseparable. Real life is living with others, for others, through others, from others, in others. It is the reciprocal giving and receiving of life in love. But it is this for us because it is in the first place this for God. God's eternal livingness is no merely abstract existence, but consists in the loving communion of the Trinity. It is the life which exists in the reciprocity of the Father, the Son and the Holy Spirit. Therefore the sharing of the divine life with us, which is possible for God because God is Trinity, is equally a sharing of the divine love with us, possible because God is trinitarian loving communion. This does not mean only that we are objects of God's love, but that we are drawn into and included in the divine life of love. The Father's love reaches us in the Son who identifies with us in love. Drawn out of lovelessness by God's love, we experience the Spirit as our own power to love God and others.

One of the most revealingly trinitarian statements in the New Testament is Paul's claim that 'God has sent the Spirit of his Son into our hearts, crying, "Abba! Father!" ' (Gal. 4.6). If we ask how it is that we may know God as Father, the answer is twofold. In the first place, it is because there is already in God's eternal being the loving reciprocity of Father and Son, and from eternity the Spirit is God's openness to sharing that reciprocity. In the second place, it is because the eternal communion of the Father and the Son has been actually incarnated as human possibility in Jesus of

Nazareth and actually opened by the Spirit who indwells us to enable us to share it. Therefore the Christian relationship to God is defined by the characteristic, first-century Aramaic term used by Jesus of Nazareth – Abba! – while at the same time it is included in the open circle of the divine love. Finding ourselves within the story of salvation, we find ourselves also within the love that God eternally is.

God, language and gender

One way in which the feminist challenges, discussed in chapter 1, have impinged on Christian theology has been in relation to traditional language about God. Traditionally Christians have used, almost exclusively, masculine pronouns for God (he, him, his, himself), along with a variety of masculine images such as Lord and King. Trinitarian language about God has used two masculine images – Father and Son – as the normative terms for the 'first' and 'second' persons of the Trinity, though the normative term for the 'third' person – the Holy Spirit – is not inherently masculine. Occasionally feminine language has been used for the Spirit,[3] and striking examples of feminine imagery for God as such and even for Jesus the incarnate Word can be found in the Bible and the tradition. But these have been no more than variations from the standard pattern of masculine language. Such language has come into serious question only in recent years, when the reasons for questioning it have been broadly two. In the first place there is the strictly theological consideration that God is beyond gender. Christian theology has never supposed that God actually is male. Moreover, it is not only male human beings who are created in the image of God. This is equally true of women (Gen. 1.27). It is therefore difficult to see how, when our language refers to God in terms otherwise used for human persons, these should be exclusively or even predominantly masculine. Such language can be felt to exclude women from participation in the image of God. But secondly, feminist critics point out that this is a far from narrowly theological issue. The use of masculine language for God has functioned to legitimate male dominance and the oppression of women. The masculine God is the heavenly counterpart of patriarchy on earth. Even if, in a society where there was no discrimination on grounds of gender, the use of masculine language for God might be treated as an arbitrary linguistic convention, this is not how it has actually functioned and feminists cannot be expected to see it as harmless.

The reason for addressing this issue briefly at this point is that readers sensitive to it will have had ample opportunity to observe our own linguistic practice in the earlier sections of this chapter. Some may have concluded by now that we are not taking the issue seriously, because we continue to use some masculine language for God.

The practice we have adopted is no more than a provisional solution to the problem of language about God at a time when the issue is only beginning to be widely appreciated in the churches in Britain, and is no more than a practice we have thought appropriate for our present purpose in writing this report. Addressing first the issue of the use of pronouns with reference to the noun 'God', the problem, of course, is that English lacks common-gender third-person singular pronouns (which some languages have). There are therefore currently three practices. There is the traditional practice which treats 'God' as a masculine noun and uses masculine pronouns. There is a new practice of alternating the use of masculine and feminine pronouns, implying that 'she' and 'he' are equally appropriate with reference to God. Finally, another new practice which is gaining ground in theological writing is that which avoids pronouns altogether. The word 'God' itself is repeated where traditional language used 'he' and 'him', 'God's' is used in place of 'his', and 'Godself' substituted for 'himself'. This practice has the advantage that for much of the time it is unobtrusive, and so can avoid offence to those who feel deeply either that exclusively masculine language should not be used or that traditional usage should not be changed. However, at times, especially when God is the subject of discussion, as in this chapter, this practice inevitably does become obtrusive, and those whose ears have not become attuned to it find the repetition of 'God' and the use of the neologism 'Godself' awkward. Some also hear it as a retreat from personal language, though this is far from the intention of those who use it. The practice which we have adopted is a compromise. We recognise that the constant use of masculine pronouns can give a misleading impression of divine maleness. We have therefore avoided pronouns wherever this can be done without linguistic awkwardness, but have retained the occasional masculine pronoun where natural English necessitates a pronoun. In other words, we have greatly reduced, but not eliminated the use of masculine pronouns.

With the question of masculine images for the persons of the Trinity, we are in deeper theological water. In this chapter we have deliberately continued to use the terms Father and Son for the 'first' and 'second' persons of the Trinity, despite the criticism of this usage by some feminist theologians. There are important reasons for retaining these terms, while also ensuring that they are understood neither as attributing gender to God nor as in any sense privileging the male over the female. In the first place, the terms Father and Son, as terms of reciprocal relationship, point to a loving reciprocity already within God which is the source of God's relationship with us. Proposed alternative series of terms, such as Source, Word and Spirit, are not adequate substitutes for Father, Son and Spirit, because they do not indicate the relationship within God. As ways of indicating how God as Trinity relates to us, such terms can certainly be helpful enrichments of the classic trinitarian terminology, but they cannot replace it. The use of Creator, Redeemer and Sanctifier, on the other hand, may well be misleading, if it is understood as dividing the work of creation and salvation between the trinitarian persons.

The substitution of the terms Parent and Child for Father and Son would indicate reciprocal relationship in non-gendered terms. But the second reason for retaining the terms Father and Son becomes relevant here. These terms not only refer to an eternal reciprocity within God, but refer to it in the terms in which Jesus of Nazareth perceived and expressed his own relationship with God. They keep us aware that the way we glimpse the loving reciprocity within God is by seeing its human historical form in the life of Jesus. They make it clear that the Trinity is not an abstract definition of God, but a summary of how God is known in the biblical story of salvation which climaxes in the history of Jesus. And so perhaps the most important means of ensuring that the doctrine of the Trinity does not exclude or subordinate women is to tell the trinitarian story of salvation in such a way that those disciples of Jesus whom he calls his sisters and mothers (Mark 3.35) are no less prominent than those he calls his brothers. But in addition it needs to be said that, while the trinitarian terms Father and Son cannot be replaced by others, they can certainly be supplemented by others. They do not say all that Christians want to say about the 'first' and 'second' persons of the Trinity, and they have never been the only terms used. The Book of Revelation, for example, develops a rich trinitarian doctrine of God with only occasional, though significant, use of Father and Son. Where terminology is misunderstood and misused, it can often be rescued by the use of other terminology alongside it, which prevents misunderstanding. Patriarchal misunderstandings of the terms Father and Son can be corrected by the use of both other traditional images and appropriate new ones, such as mother and child, lover and beloved, friend and friend, but the terms Father and Son remain theologically normative in Christian trinitarian discourse.

Creation and salvation

So far in this chapter we have been concerned with God as saviour. But God is also creator. In the context of a global crisis due to disastrous distortions of the human relationship to the rest of God's creation on this planet, it hardly needs to be said that a renewed sense of God as creator is urgently needed. It is needed for its own sake. But it is also needed for the sake of putting the Christian understanding of salvation in its proper relation to the doctrine of creation. Some recent critics have charged the Christian tradition with emphasising the need for salvation in such as way as to denigrate creation, leading to the neglect and abuse of the created world. The Christian tradition is alleged to have encouraged people to think of themselves as essentially distinct from the rest of creation and metaphysically superior to it. Preoccupation with the material world is a temptation and a distraction because our true destiny is to be saved from this world. The creation is no more than a transient environment for spiritual beings like ourselves, and its only valid function is to serve our needs. This kind of caricature of the Christian tradition warrants, for some contemporary thinkers, the charge that Christianity itself is the ideological source of the ecological crisis.

The charge does rest on a caricature, but we should recognise the elements of truth in it. We can confine ourselves at this point to the medieval and early modern periods, which are the most relevant to current debate about the intellectual origins of the modern project of technological domination and exploitation of nature. In these periods we can identify two relevant ways in which the Christian tradition was not entirely faithful to its biblical roots and its fundamental insights. Firstly, some forms of medieval Christian spirituality inherited, and continued to be influenced by, a kind of matter-spirit dualism which is Greek in origin and encouraged people to think of salvation as the liberation of the human spirit, which is akin of God, from the material world, which is the source of temptation. This kind of thinking has had a considerable legacy in western Christianity. However, it is an aberration which the Christian tradition, in the medieval period as in others, has continually corrected from its biblical and traditional resources. The authentic Christian view of the world has a strong sense of the essential goodness of God's creation, which is nowhere more emphatically expressed than in the creation narrative of Genesis 1. As far as human destiny is concerned, the insistence on bodily resurrection throughout the Christian tradition makes clear that salvation is not the salvation of the spiritual from the material, but the redemption of human nature in its essential solidarity with the rest of God's material creation. But, secondly, the interpretation of the passage in Genesis (1.26, 28) which gives humanity dominion over other living creatures has been problematic. In the medieval period this belief in a special role for humanity within creation was usually balanced by the sense that human beings are themselves creatures who belong within creation. Even when misinterpreted to mean that other creatures exist for the sake of human beings, it coexisted with the strong sense that all creatures, human and non-human, exist for the glory of God. It was in the Renaissance that the sense of human creatureliness began to be lost. The Genesis dominion then took the form of a view of humanity's relation to creation which set human beings intrinsically above creation, exercising godlike power and creativity on it. It was this development which coincided with the modern development of science and technology. It therefore fed into that modern ideology which conceived of science and technology as the means of remaking the world to our own design and to serve our own needs. In effect, this was a secularisation of the Genesis text which disastrously removed the idea of dominion from its context in a doctrine of creation.

It may be debatable how far aberrations in the Christian tradition are implicated in the roots of the ecological crisis. This is a difficult issue of historical interpretation. More relevant now is the fact that in the modern period the Church's message has tended to take creation for granted, concentrating on the plight from which people need to be rescued. This coincided with the way that people in modern western society lost that sense of createdness (of being creatures of God, part of a created world, and as creatures dependent on God) which was much more common in pre-industrial society. Living in a world which could easily appear to be mostly a human creation, alienated from natural relationships with the rest of creation, understanding their relationship to the world in terms of mastery and exploitation rather than reciprocity and appreciation, modern urban people have generally lost an existential sense of creation and of God as creator. They can and do experience it, but not with the easy availability of pre-modern people. To the extent that the Church has responded to this situation by accepting it and focusing its message exclusively on God as saviour, it has made a serious mistake, since it is dubious whether belief in God as saviour can long retain its existential reality where belief in God as creator is weak.

If creation has been neglected in favour of salvation, the remedy is not to neglect salvation in favour of creation, but to explore the essential connection between salvation and creation. Salvation is not the rejection or replacement of creation, but its renewal and completion. Indeed, it is helpful to realise that there are ways of talking of God's relationship with the world which do not obviously require the distinction between God's creative and God's saving activity. We could say, for example, that the God from whom all things derive is continuously active, enabling all things to reach their goal of perfection and fulfilment in God. Is the distinction we habitually make between creation and salvation therefore perhaps a case of misleadingly dualistic thinking?

The distinction between creation and salvation should not be absolutised. It makes a distinction within a continuity. But it does serve two important purposes. In the first place, it acknowledges that God's good creation has been disrupted by evil, which is not inherent in the nature of creation. Damage has been done which needs to be repaired. Because this point has often been misunderstood in recent criticism of the traditional Christian emphasis on salvation, it needs to be said very clearly that this emphasis, so far from contradicting the fundamental goodness of creation, including human nature, actually entails it. Only a fundamentally good creation could be redeemed. Not even God could redeem a creation fundamentally corrupted by evil; such a creation God could only replace. The doctrine of salvation itself means that human beings are not trash, to be thrown away, but the good creation of God which God can and does rescue from evil. The doctrine of salvation does not contradict, but presupposes the doctrine that God created human beings in God's own image.

Belief in a fundamentally good creation which God rescues from evil requires a doctrine of the fall. Essentially this means that human beings, originating as morally innocent creatures, chose evil. The story in Genesis 3 is a picture of this, not a literal account of how it happened. At one level of interpretation, the story of Adam and Eve represents the choice which confronts all human beings, and the disobedience to God into which all of us fall. However, when we repeat the disobedience of Adam and Eve, we do so in a context in which sin is already endemic and from which innocence has already vanished. The story in Genesis 2–3 depicts a state of human innocence which existed before any human sin. Given that this primal innocence is represented for us imaginatively, not literally, in Genesis 2–3, there is no conflict with our modern awareness of evolution and pre-history. Traditional elaborations of Genesis 2–3 are much more problematic, for they have depicted a state of paradisal perfection before the incursion of evil. This is not required by a doctrine of the fall as such. Such a doctrine entails only that our first genuinely human ancestors, when moral awareness first dawned in their experience, faced moral choices, not with an inclination to evil, but in innocence. They might have chosen only good, but in fact chose evil. The mystery of this primal choice belongs to the insoluble mystery of evil itself, but it was a real choice, not determined by the created nature of human beings themselves or of their natural environment.

Traditional doctrines of the fall sometimes claimed that physical death and all other forms of what we call physical evil resulted from – and so only appeared in the world subsequently to – the sin of our first human ancestors. What we now know of the physical and biological world and its history makes this impossible. Since death occurred in the animal world for hundreds of millions of years before human beings appeared, death cannot be the wages of sin in the sense that physical death would not have happened apart from human sin. But we can still maintain that death as sinful human beings experience it, as the fate of the godless and the godforsaken, is given its fatal and fateful character by the fact that human beings have turned away from God the source of life. Similarly, the evils that come upon us purely as a result of the physical nature of our world – earthquakes, floods, some forms of disease, and so on – cannot as such result from the fall. But we can say not only that the experience of them in a world of moral innocence would have been different, but also that their destructiveness is in fact greatly increased by human negligence and malice. So the distinction between physical evil (disasters which happen to us) and moral evil (evil we choose to do) is vital. To some degree the former are inevitable in a physical creation like that of which we are a part, though we cannot fully tell how they would have affected us had we not turned from God. Moral evil, on the other hand, is not inherent in the nature of the created world. It is a corruption from which we can be healed.

Of course, the inherent goodness of our created nature was marred but not eradicated by the fall. It is true that some parts of the Christian tradition, especially the Augustinian and Reformed theological traditions, have placed much emphasis on the corruption of human nature. But this emphasis was polemically directed against Pelagianism. It was intended to make the point that human beings are not able to achieve their own salvation without saving grace. When these same theological traditions have been faced with Manichaean dualism, which treats the material world as the source of moral evil and irredeemable, they have made the opposite polemical point: that the material world, including human bodies, is God's good creation and remains so. Such emphases – either on the inherent goodness of creation, despite the fall, or on the plight of creation, subject to the ravages and corruption of evil because of the fall – are relative. They are always contextual and often polemical. The important point is that all Christian traditions have held both that evil is serious and that creation is redeemable. Without a distinction between creation and salvation it is difficult to maintain both.

One possible result of eliminating this distinction is that moral evil is reduced to a necessary stage in the development of creation. Creation develops from the less good to the better; it does not need redemption from evil. But then the nature of evil as what is not merely less good but radically opposed to good cannot be recognised. Alternatively, the seriousness of evil can be recognised but treated as integral to the nature of creation. Evil is how creation had to be. But in that case it is hard to see how evil can be overcome without the abolition of creation. Avoiding either of these unsatisfactory conclusions, the distinction between creation and salvation takes evil seriously without attributing it to creation.

The second important function of the distinction between creation and salvation is that it makes it possible to see the future of creation, in the purpose of God, as more than the realisation of potential already inherent in creation. Salvation is often portrayed in the Bible as new creation. Raising the dead, to take a key example, is not literally the same as creation out of nothing, but it is comparable, because resurrection is not a possibility the dead have within their created nature. It is a new possibility given them out of the creative transcendence of God. It is not surprising that a theological tendency to collapse salvation into creation often results in confining the scope of Christian hope within the limits of this mortal existence. Again we must guard against a current misunderstanding. What we are suggesting has nothing to do with the picture of salvation as God's intervention from 'outside' in a creation he had previously left to manage itself. Language of divine intervention, like all such language of divine action in the world, is metaphorical, and has usually been used, not to imply that God was not present and active apart from his intervention, but that at this point he did something different and distinctive. Miracles were called divine interventions, not because God was thought to be usually inactive in the world, but simply because God does not usually work miracles. Much modern theological polemic against an interventionist God has misunderstood a relatively useful metaphor and attacked an Aunt Sally. However, the more important point is that God is, of course, unceasingly involved in God's creation. But God is involved as the transcendent God of infinite possibility, who in the work of healing and perfecting the world transcends not only its negative corruption by evil, but also its positive potential. In particular, God promises to take creation beyond transience and mortality into permanent union with God's own everlasting aliveness.

Alongside the essential distinction between creation and salvation, the Christian tradition has frequently emphasised also the continuity. For example, our Anglican tradition has often emphasised the connection between creation and the incarnation, in a way that has precedents in the Fathers and in Duns Scotus and his school in the late medieval period. It is the same divine Word who was active in the work of creation who then becomes incarnate within creation. The incarnation thereby brings to perfection the relationship of creation to God. The Scotist view was that incarnation would for this reason have been necessary even apart from sin and evil. Those who have detected a danger that this emphasis plays down the reality of sin and evil have often countered an emphasis on incarnation as such with an emphasis on the cross. The latter connects with our first reason why the distinction between creation and salvation is important. The Son of God did not come into a good world simply to make it better. As incarnate in this fallen world, he bore the full brunt of its sin and evil in order to rescue it from that sin and evil. It would also be possible to counter an emphasis on incarnation as such with an emphasis on the resurrection. This would connect with our second reason why the distinction between creation and salvation is important. The Son of God did not simply fulfil the inherent potentiality of this creation. When God raised him from the dead, God gave creation a new possibility of life beyond its otherwise natural end in death. But these various emphases are precisely a matter of emphasis. Both the continuity of creation and salvation, which an emphasis on incarnation highlights, and the discontinuity, which is emphasised by attention to the cross and the resurrection, are important. The Christian view of the world makes sense only if neither is absolutised.

Thus the essential distinction between creation and salvation needs to be held within a broader sense of the one God's consistent purpose for the same created world to which God remains faithful to eternity. This means that to know God as saviour is necessarily to know God also as creator. Those who experience the gift of God's self in Christian salvation – God's Son given for them in the incarnation, death and resurrection of Christ, God's Spirit given to them in indwelling power to live for God and for others – also discover or rediscover the gift of God's self in creation and all its blessings. And they know these not as two gifts but as one: the self-giving of the same God giving himself to us and giving himself back to us in all things. Those who find God in word and sacrament are often those who love God's creation most and find God, differently but equally, in their fellow-creatures, human and non-human. For salvation, as we said in the second section of this chapter, is experiencing the one who is the source and goal of all things as the source and goal of our own being and living.

Chapter 3
Saving history

Introduction

We have now argued that 'salvation' is the work of the one true, triune God. This inescapably points us to the question of salvation within history. The triune God who saves is known as such supremely in Jesus Christ. It is thus a direct implication of the doctrine of the Trinity that this salvation is somehow planned, effected, and offered within history.

But how? What is the relation between 'salvation' and history? This question lies near the heart of a good many issues that have troubled Christian people throughout the history of the Church. It has many facets and dimensions. This chapter cannot address all of them; it offers some guidelines as to how they may be approached.

To begin with, some comments about the two key terms 'salvation' and 'history', and how they are used here.

The word 'salvation' is a shorthand way of referring to quite an elaborate set of ideas. When we say 'the Christian doctrine of salvation', we call quickly to mind a set of stories about the plight of the world and the action of its creator to rescue it from this plight. Within non-Christian systems of thought, the word can evoke quite different stories. They may, for instance, speak of the solution to the plight of the world, and of humans, as coming from the humans themselves, unaided, or from some other force already within the world, rather than from a transcendent god. Thus Marxism (for instance) would see the solution to the world's problems as lying within the range of this-worldly possibilities. Or it may speak of salvation coming from a force outside and beyond the world entirely – that is, a force other than the God revealed, precisely within the world and history, in Jesus and the Holy Spirit. They may offer different diagnoses of the ills of the world, and prescribe different solutions. Part of the task of exploring the meaning of the word 'salvation' is therefore to unpack and examine the implicit stories which the word evokes. The role of the present chapter, within this larger task, is to see just what sort of stories make sense, within Christian understanding, of the relation between salvation and history.

Most people who think of 'salvation' today, be they Christian or not, think in one of two apparently watertight worlds. Many Christians think of 'salvation' in exclusively 'religious' or 'other-worldly' terms, assuming that the word 'salvation' itself, not least when it occurs in the Bible, refers to a state of bliss outside our present space and time. Many non-Christians, however, are happy to use the language of 'salvation' to denote political and social events or processes. We shall need to keep in mind the question of how the 'religious' and 'secular' salvations relate to each other. Are we justified in separating them out so neatly? Does 'salvation' in the Christian sense have anything to do with actual history? If so, what? Is 'salvation' (and its opposite) to be found within socio-political processes, or outside them altogether? Or is there a more complex relationship between them, and if so what can be said about it?

A further level of questioning has to do with where salvation may be found. Does it have one point of origin, or is it available and findable in many places? The Judaeo-Christian tradition speaks of the one God acting decisively within history; it is therefore bound to stress the uniqueness, particularity, or specialness of this action. In consequence, it has seen itself (in various ways) as having a responsibility to share what it has with the rest of the world, who, by implication, do not have it. 'Salvation is from the Jews', as Jesus in John's Gospel said to the woman at the well (John 4.22). Others, including some Christians, find it simply incredible that one small tradition within world history should be the carrier of salvation for all the other vast tracts of human and cosmic history. All, or at least most, must find their own way. This has the effect, of course, of moving 'salvation' away from direct correlation with specific events. Between these two extreme positions there are, predictably, many others which seek to combine in some way the specialness of Judaism and Christianity and the availability of salvation in and through other traditions.

The second term in our puzzle is 'history'. There are four ways in which this word may be used, and it is important to distinguish them from the start.

First, 'history' can refer to 'events taking place in sequence'. History here is simply the events themselves. When we say 'Did that really happen in history?' we are not asking whether somebody wrote about it, but whether the event in question simply took place. 'History' can then come to mean simply the sum total of all the events which have in fact taken place. In principle at least, this ought of course to include the entire history of the cosmos; in practice, it usually refers to the history of *Homo sapiens*. Earlier events are sometimes, understandably though perhaps somewhat illogically, referred to as 'prehistoric'.

Second, 'history' can often mean 'human writing about things which took place'. Indeed, many would say that it is a vital part of being human that we tell the story of what has taken place, interpreting it and commenting upon it (inevitably and rightly) as we do so. It is perhaps because of this second meaning that the phrase 'pre-history' regularly refers to human events prior to the writing of history.

Third, there is a more abstract meaning. This is 'history' as the *fact of* events occurring in sequence within the space-time world. To say 'God is at work in history' does not necessarily mean 'God is at work, always and equally, in all events that have ever taken place' (meaning 1); nor does it mean 'God is at work in the writing and reading of history books' (meaning 2) (though that might be true as well). It means 'God is at work *within* the connected sequence of events in the world'. 'History' here denotes the process, the *fact* of a connected series of space-time events, rather than the events themselves.

Closely connected with this, there is a fourth meaning of 'history' which draws attention to the *space-time location* of events as opposed to their occurrence within the world of thought and ideas. To say 'God is at work in history' in this sense stresses that God is at work within the space-time world, rather than simply within some 'religious' world which only intersects with the space-time world at a tangent.

How then, within Christianity, might 'salvation' and 'history' be related to one another?

Obviously, all will depend on which meanings of the two words we are choosing. Fortunately, we do not have to labour the point, since the reason for talking about salvation and history in the first place within the Christian tradition grows out of the central Christian emphasis that in Jesus Christ the one true and living God has revealed himself fully, finally and above all savingly within history. This means that we are talking about 'history' more specifically in senses 3 and 4: (3) God has acted savingly in Christ at a specific point within the ongoing sequence of events; (4) God has acted savingly in Christ within the world of space and time, not merely in an abstract, non-historical, non-physical way. And this in turn means that we are claiming that 'salvation', within Christianity, cannot belong purely in a 'religious' world, removed entirely from space and time, from the flow and flux of historical causation.

This conclusion would be acceptable to most Christians. But it does not, of itself, answer the questions we raised a moment ago. These questions are vital; according to the answers we give to them, the entire character of our perception and practice of Christianity will differ quite radically.

This has been so from quite early on in the history of the Church. Professor Henry Chadwick, in his well-known book *The Early Church*, described the great divide at the start of the Middle Ages as the cleavage between those who wanted to rule the world and those who wanted to renounce it: in other words, the papacy and the monastic movement. But it is not only popes and monks who have taken these routes. They are well travelled highways, and most Christians live somewhere near one or the other.

In order to understand these routes, and to make (perhaps) some intelligent choices in relation to them, what we need is of course a map. That is what this chapter seeks to provide. As with all maps, much is hidden and much distorted, in order that key elements of information may be highlighted. (Consider how accurate, and yet how inaccurate, is the map of the London Underground.) We cannot hope, in a single chapter, to indicate and name every stream of thought, every contour of opinion. What we can offer is a description of the two broad highways of theological thought, each of which takes its own route through the landscape of theological questions. We shall then be in a position to stand back and see what the strengths and weaknesses of each position may be, and to ask the further question: can we learn from these two routes? Is it possible to find a route in which the good points of both are retained, and the weaknesses and dangers eliminated?

In each case, there is of course a further spectrum of opinion. Among the distortions of the mapping process is an inevitable element of caricature; not all popes actually wanted to rule the world, not all monks sought to renounce it. Not all theologians who seem to be travelling along the first route, or the second, take exactly the same turns and twists as one another. The description will be broad-brush, risking caricature for the sake of clarity of line. Numerous possible variations within each position will be quietly ignored. This makes it all the more important that we distinguish, within each position, two alternatives: in each case, (a) a more extreme and (b) a more nuanced and subtle version of the route in question. And, just as theologians, and ordinary Christians, may well combine in themselves some aspects of the two main routes, so some may exhibit now the more extreme, now the more nuanced, version. We are, after all, not the first people to see the shape of the problem and to attempt to find ways through it. Others have laboured; and, though our solutions may not resemble theirs in all particulars, we are attempting to enter in a fresh way into their labour.

The two main routes, then, are ways of putting together the great concepts of salvation and history. To caricature by way of introduction: The first route ('ruling the world'), seeks to affirm the world, the created order, and history, and to find salvation through working with, and within, history. The second route ('renouncing the world') seeks to escape history, as it seeks to escape the created order. If we are to do justice to the whole history of Christian tradition (that is, the history of what Christians have said and done as they have read Scripture and thought seriously about it), we must be sure that the strong points of the rulers and the renouncers are contained in any fresh suggestion that we may make.

One final comment by way of introduction. The question of salvation and history has sometimes been marginalised in theological discussion. The approach taken in this chapter demonstrates that the question is in fact intricately interwoven with the many other great questions that the word 'salvation' generates. 'Salvation-history' is not a category that can be shunted to one side, dealt with as a curious oddity or aberration, and then forgotten. Whatever we say about salvation is bound to include a position of some sort on the question of history.

Route 1: Salvation within history

The first Route through the landscape of Christian theology recognises from the beginning that the world is God's world. Creation is his handiwork; history (the flow of events within the world) was his idea. God reveals himself through both; and he saves through both.

For this Route, the historical process is a story which will all come right in the end. It is the means through which salvation will be accomplished. The role of grace is to complete nature. Sometimes, in this view, it may even look as though grace simply *is* what-is-going-on-in-nature. On the broadest canvas, some have suggested that the entire cosmos is evolving towards its Omega point, spiritually as well as physically. Process theologians have attempted to discover God, not just directing this process, but actually within it. This might be classified as 'salvation within *cosmic* history'.

A second version of this Route shares the same outline, but with a much more political slant. This is seen in certain forms of liberation theology, which offer a salvation *for* the world, *within* its history, with the Church (ideally) as the agent of this salvation through its prayer and action. God is at work in movements of liberation; the Church must not be shy of recognising this and putting its shoulder to the wheel. As in the Marxist theory with which this is sometimes allied, it is by no means clear whether the process of liberation is driven by some inner determinism (in which case it might be better to let it go on its way without interference), or whether it can only come by human aid (in which case the argument that it is predetermined looks very shaky). At any rate, at least some liberation theology clearly follows this Route: it stresses the saving nature of the divine acts in the Old Testament, especially the Exodus, and asserts the continuity between such acts of God within socio-political history and the saving acts of liberation which God desires to effect in the present and future, still within space and time.

On a smaller scale, thirdly, the story of Israel in the Old Testament, and of the Church in the age after Pentecost, is often seen as a progressive unfolding of salvation, in which, within history itself, God's purpose is steadily accomplished:

> God is working his purpose out,
> as year succeeds to year . . .
>
> Nearer and nearer draws the time,
> the time that shall surely be,
> when the earth shall be filled with the glory of God
> as the waters cover the sea.

This view – 'salvation within *ecclesial* history' – has had a solid foothold in the sub- or semi-conscious mind of British culture ever since Handel's *Messiah*, and is further reinforced by the traditional Christmas service of Nine Lessons and Carols. In the former, the Church preaches the gospel to every creature ('Their sound is gone out into all lands') after the resurrection of Jesus, and at the end of this mission there comes the Hallelujah Chorus, celebrating the fact that 'the kingdom of this world is become the kingdom of our God, and of his Christ'. It is only *after* this that the final resurrection of the dead takes place. In the traditional Carol Service, the sequence of carefully chosen prophetic readings gives an impression of smooth historical process, of prophecy steadily working towards fulfilment. If we were to examine the whole books from which the passages are selected we might well find this idea called into question.

Sundry varieties of salvation-within-ecclesial-history may be found within some Catholic thought, in a view of the Church as simply marching forward through time towards its historical salvation. This, of course, is quite compatible with a negative view of non-ecclesial history; though, as debates in former days between missionaries would indicate, the 'Protestant' missions tended to be deeply suspicious of all 'non-Christian' culture, while the 'Catholic' missions, though sure that salvation was to be had within the fold of the Church, tended, true to Route 1, to affirm all that they possibly could within a local culture. Again, the Protestant rejection of Catholic salvation-within-*ecclesial-*

history has, in our own century, gone hand in hand with a more general rejection of Route 1 as a whole. This happens, for instance, in the rejection (by Barth and others) of 'natural theology', the attempt to see the creation as a revelation of the true God, and of its political equivalent, the attempt to see what God is doing within history and then simply join in. At this point, and at many others in the discussion, one might want to enquire whether there are other factors involved: whether, for instance, some people incline, for psychological reasons, towards a form of self-hatred which inclines them towards Route 2, and whether others incline towards a form of self-assertion which inclines them towards Route 1. The basic, unadorned, version of Route 1 underestimates the seriousness of sin. Sin, in fact, may well be seen merely as human consciousness of problems within God's good, albeit developing, world. In the same way, there will not be much need for a strong theology of the cross; it may sometimes be seen simply as the preliminary to the resurrection, the birth of renewed creation. This means that followers of Route 1 are unlikely to have a strong critique of human sinfulness; they are more likely to seek things to affirm wherever they can. In particular, they are very likely to affirm the goodness and perhaps the saving power of religions other than Christianity.

There are, of course, more nuanced versions of Route 1. Many Christians whose basic stance has been world-affirming have nevertheless been conscious of evil as a real and potent force, and have seen the need to show how God deals with it. They have emphasised the presence of salvation within history, while allowing at least some weight to the serious problem of evil. This version of the Route would be eager to affirm the presence of salvation in various places where Route 2, as we shall see, would be unlikely to recognise it at all: in various forms of social, political or psychological change, for instance, and in various religious beliefs and experiences with no connection to the Judaeo-Christian tradition. The excesses of the naive Route 1 can be avoided: 'salvation' does not come about simply by some immanent process in which the world is automatically moving towards its goal. Evil is a reality: in particular, evil is found in 'exclusive' systems (including various forms of fundamentalism) which oppress, judge and condemn other forms of religion and experience. A nuanced version of Route I might thus affirm 'history' in the sense of 'the fact of events taking place in the world', while being deeply critical of 'history' in the sense of 'the *actual* events that are taking place'. Salvation comes about by the activity of God, and also by the activity of human beings, working to rescue people and situations from the evil into which they have fallen. Salvation is thus at work within history, even though not identical with the historical process itself. It is much wider than the Christian tradition, though the Christian tradition also bears witness to it. Salvation, in other words, is very much a this-worldly matter, but without the naive optimism of the more basic type of Route 1.

The great strength of all forms of Route 1 is that they take creation very seriously indeed. They refuse to see evil as an equal and opposite force to the creator God and his providential working. They refuse, likewise, to write off the social and political dimensions of human existence as irrelevant to the processes of salvation, and try to include them within its overall theological compass. The Route 1 theologian takes the story of Israel in the Old Testament seriously as part of the saving work of God, which is arguably (in those general terms at least) something which the New Testament also stresses; and tries in various ways to understand the whole of church history under the rubric of the continuing saving work of God. To these extents this Route is clearly crossing some terrain which must be included within any fully Christian proposal.

The weaknesses of all forms of Route 1 have to do with a refusal to take seriously two features which are central to biblical and mainstream Christian theology. First, this Route blurs the *ontological* distinction between the creator and the cosmos: pantheism and process theology are the most obvious culprits, but the tendency is, perhaps, present in other forms as well. Second, it is always in danger of losing sight of the moral distinction between good and evil. For Route 1, particularly in its more naive form, Evil is, if anything, simply not quite as good as Good. It is not a radical, dark power, threatening the world and humans. Over the whole of Route 1 stands the charge of Anselm: you have not yet considered the seriousness of sin.

As a result, the work of God and the processes of the world are not as clearly distinguished as they should be. The radical newness of salvation, bursting upon the world with the force of an apocalyptic revelation, is lost sight of behind a smooth, steadily developing historical process. If the cross does very much towards the achieving of salvation, it is held within this steady process, rather than being the abrupt, shocking scandal and folly of which Paul speaks. Though the more nuanced versions of Route 1 do their best to avoid these weaknesses, all sorts of questions remain. That, in part, accounts for the popularity of Route 2, to which we now turn.

Route 2: Salvation *from* history

The second Route to be mapped here is perhaps the more familiar. In some well-known varieties of Christian theology, world history is regarded as simply the strange and somewhat alien environment where human souls are prepared for a non-historical 'eternity'. Attaining to this non-historical goal is what is meant by 'salvation'.

Examples of this viewpoint can be found all over the history of Christian thought. A modern, popular one is provided at one point by John Betjeman (though in other ways he belongs in Route 1; poets, like theologians, are allowed to be inconsistent), according to whom Jesus taught that

> This world is just an ante-chamber where
> We for His Father's house prepare.

The only value of history, in this scheme, is that it is the place where the all-important decisions of faith and morals have to be made, according to which the non-historical salvation will either be granted or denied. History is seen as one aspect of the world of sin, corruption, decay and death; salvation consists in humans being rescued from history, set free from its endless cycles of futility, and liberated into a non-historical world. This, broadly, has been the belief of millions of Christians, for whom phrases such as 'eternal life' have meant, basically, non-historical life, a dimension of 'eternity' in which time as we know it, part of the present created order, will be no more. Several other religions, too, would agree that a 'salvation' of this sort is the ultimate goal; disagreement between them would then focus, not on the meaning of 'salvation', but on the route by which one might attain it. Many, too, who do not profess any religion understand the term 'salvation' in this way. That is part of what they disbelieve in when they disbelieve in Christianity, or other religions which teach it.

Route 2 has had a strong influence on certain aspects of biblical scholarship, especially when it comes to interpreting St Paul. It has often been thought that Paul was expounding just such a view of salvation when he set forth his doctrine of justification. Rudolf Bultmann, alluding to Romans 10.4, wrote that 'Christ is the end of history as he is the end of the law'. The second-century heretic Marcion, who believed that the God of Jesus Christ was different from the God of Israel, claimed to be expounding Paul. He has had many followers.

The history of theology suggests that this Route can branch off quite easily into various forms of Gnosticism. For the serious Gnostic, the world of space, time and matter, and hence of history, is simply evil; salvation consists of rescue from the world, history, time and space altogether. There are, of course, various half-way stages on the route to this extreme position. Most serious Christian theologians would reject the full-blown Gnostic position on sight. Yet, as we have seen, the view persists, not least at a popular level, that salvation and history simply do not belong together. History, including our own history, is a chaotic muddle; God's answer is to save us from it.

Within the naive versions of Route 2, all history, including the history of Israel before the coming of Jesus Christ, is seen in a very negative light. It is, at best, the dark backcloth for the bright jewel of the gospel. Jesus is the one who comes from the non-historical world, to rescue those trapped in history and free them for a non-historical salvation. So, too, the life of the Church is compromised as soon as, and to the extent that, it becomes an 'institution' within history, whether in its own life or as an agent of social and political change. Tinkering with society, i.e. acting to affect the course of history, is simply a distraction. The Church's task is to present to humans the timeless call to decision, to conversion, which is ultimately aimed at snatching people out of history and into eternity.

When it comes to other religions, Route 2 takes a very negative line. (This is actually a little odd, since the escape from history is something it seems to share with Hinduism and Buddhism [see p. 295].) Christians who travel by Route 2 will probably regard all other religions, and indeed many other versions of Christianity (especially Route 1 in all its variations), as delusory and dangerous. They are human attempts to find a salvation which is, in fact, uniquely offered in Jesus Christ. The scandal of particularity becomes, on this view, the scandal of divine action which judges the entire world, including all human religion.

There are, of course, several far more nuanced versions of Route 2. The main and most interesting one, which does its best to build into Route 2 some of the strengths of Route 1, allows that, though salvation is ultimately *from* history, salvation may nevertheless be reflected, or foreshadowed, *within* history.

In this more nuanced version of the Route, it is recognised that there is, within history, something that can properly be called 'salvation'. At the same time, one must insist that the full meaning of that term be reserved for something which lies beyond history altogether. The Exodus, the Return from Exile, and the acts of healing in Jesus' ministry are in some sense 'salvation', but they are not the thing in itself; rather, they are reflections, examples of the saving action of God, designed to lead the eye up to the reality of spiritual salvation. In terms of the map, this nuanced Route attempts to retain the direct line of Route 2 while wanting at least some of the view one might get from Route 1. In theological terms, 'salvation' remains beyond history; but God is the Lord of History, and God effects within history events which share something of the character of that non-historical salvation. In terms of grace and nature, grace works in parallel to God's actions in nature, and is reflected there, but remains ultimately in a different sphere altogether. This way of travelling across the terrain allows for foreshadowings of salvation: it gives rise, in particular, to allegory (seeing hidden meanings about eternal issues within the space-time events) and to typology (seeing an earlier saving event as a foreshadowing of a later one).

In both cases, one might debate whether it really matters that the original event actually happened. This is actually a significant and recurring question whenever Christians discuss salvation and history: how important is it that, for instance, the Exodus actually took place? Logically, one might expect those travelling on Route 1 to insist that the saving events must have taken place, and those travelling by Route 2 to sit light to such a necessity. In fact, however (this is another example of the way in which these categories are more simplistic than most real theologians), many Route 2 thinkers come from a very conservative background, and many Route 1 thinkers from a more radical background; so that Route 2 often finds itself asserting the importance of the historical events, if only to 'prove the Bible true', while Route 1 often asserts their unimportance, even if only to show that salvation is found far more widely within history than in a few selected and unprovable occurrences in the past.

This more nuanced version of Route 2 encourages a particular form of the promise-fulfilment scheme. This consists of isolated texts in the Old Testament, taken out of context, and supposedly fulfilled piecemeal by Jesus and/or the early Church. This attempt to discover 'fulfilment' in the atomistic accomplishment of contextless prophecies has often given the whole idea a bad name. Those who have tried to 'love' the truth of Christianity through listing such supposed fulfilments, as though their apparently miraculous nature provided sufficient evidence of divine intervention, have courted their own nemesis in the retort (made often enough in the last two centuries) that the early Church made up 'events' in the life of Jesus to show such fulfilment. Since this is what many people at once think of when 'promise and fulfilment' is mentioned, we should not be surprised that the concept is often rejected.

What would this more nuanced version of Route 2 say about other religions? The 'biblical theology' movement which exemplified the more nuanced version of Route 2 a few decades ago was not particularly sympathetic to non-Christian religions, with the important exception of Judaism (since it shares the biblical salvation-history). Route 2 would not normally regard events in other religions' histories as examples of 'salvation', despite texts such as Amos 9.7, which speak of saving events within the history of nations other than Israel.

The main strength of Route 2 is the seriousness with which it takes the fallenness of the world and the sinfulness of sin. It feeds on the observable dangers of its mirror opposite (Route 1), which insists on the goodness of the historical process. It claims support from Paul, though arguably at the cost of some central Pauline emphases (such as the renewal of creation of Romans 8). It recognises, in classic Protestant fashion, that any self-congratulation on the part of the Church is hollow and pretentious. It sees very clearly that historical process by itself, and even historical process somehow invisibly steered along by providence, will never bring salvation in all its fullness. The symbol of this strength is of course the cross, which stands as the great God-given 'No' across all attempts to find a straightforward equation between salvation and history. Indeed, this view often stresses the cross as a decisively new event, bringing divine judgement on the old world as well as the promise of salvation. In all these ways Route 2 strikes what may be thought a necessary note.

A second strength of this Route, related to the first, is the fact that it allows fully for the transitoriness of the present world. Evening and morning, built into the present creation, witness to its impermanence. This is not simply a matter of the fallenness of humankind or the world. The creation was made, it seems, to point beyond itself. Birth, growth, decay and death all indicate that, even apart from sin, the present creation was not intended to be the creator's last word. How much more, then, when it has been corrupted by sin? Salvation must then be more than simply a matter of historical process. God, we are told, will make new heavens and a new earth; Route 2 emphasises the word *new*, and focuses on heaven rather than earth.

The weaknesses of this Route are as easy to point out as its strengths. First, despite the impression given at first glance, it is unbiblical. As we shall see, the New Testament writers regularly link the 'mighty acts of God', in saving his people in the pre-Christian era, to the events of Jesus' death and resurrection in a far more organic and interlocking way than this view can possibly allow. The notion of time fulfilled, which Jesus preached and Paul echoed, indicates a positive attitude towards that time.

Second, it is dualistic. Creation may be transitory, but it was and remains good – and that includes its history. The view we have been expounding has at best a shaky grip on the first article of the creed, and hence on the presupposition of all biblical thought. As the orthodox writers of the second century saw, and as some even within the Bultmannian tradition have come to see, the line of thought that runs from Genesis through the Psalms and Isaiah to Jesus, Paul and the author of Revelation envisages a good creation, and hence a salvation which will involve, not the abandonment of creation to its corruption and decay, but the elimination of that corruption and hence the renewal of creation itself. This finds classic expression in Romans 8.18–30.

Route 2, in fact, can only be sustained in practice by operating a 'canon within the canon'. Obvious examples are the treatment of Romans and Revelation. The first eight chapters of Romans are much beloved by adherents of a strong version of Route 2, since they are read as setting out the eternal message of salvation; chapters 9–11 are regularly marginalised. Equally, within chapter 8 itself, verses 1–11 are favoured, as speaking (apparently) of an individual and 'spiritual' salvation, along with verses 28–30 and 31–9; but the vital passage, 8.18–27, is often played down, since its message – a salvation which offers the Exodus hope to the whole cosmos – cannot so easily be fitted into the scheme.

The book of Revelation, where it is not treated simply as a rag-bag of proof-texts, is normally regarded as a book 'about heaven', conceived as non-spatio-temporal. But this, in fact, represents a thorough misreading of the apocalyptic genre on the one hand, which certainly intends a reference to this-worldly events, and a marginalising on the other hand of the vital and climactic chapter 21, in which heaven and earth are not separated, but are finally married. This seems clearly to indicate a salvation that consists in the total transformation of the space-time world. We are therefore driven forwards in the quest of a more satisfactory solution.

The salvation *of* history?

We began our consideration of the two main types of Christian approach to salvation and history by quoting Chadwick's dictum about those who would rule the world and those who would renounce it. But is there not a middle position? Might not salvation be God's means of redeeming history? Might there not be a way of combining the strengths of both Routes and eliminating at least some of their weaknesses?

This possibility, like the two Routes just outlined, can itself only be outlined here. In any case, it would be silly to suppose that we can solve, in one chapter or even in one report, a problem which has taxed the greatest minds of Christianity for two thousand years. Equally, we should not imagine that we are breaking completely new ground in moving cautiously forward towards a position which does more justice to the data than either of the basic Routes have done. One of the main characteristics of all truly great Christian theologians is that they have seen beyond the confines of the basic structure of thought within which they were working. For us, then, hindsight has certain advantages. It is at least possible to note certain boundary-markers, certain points which must be included in any eventual solution and certain other points which must be avoided. Within the framework that this offers, there may be further things that can be said, pointing forward to other parts of this report where some of the details are followed up more fully.

The category of 'redeeming' (as opposed to 'ruling' and 'renouncing') has this great virtue: that it takes with full and equal seriousness both the God-givenness of the whole created order and the reality and awfulness of sin. There is no hint of Route 2's incipient dualism, or of Route 1's glossing over of the problem of evil. The notion of redemption, on the contrary, implies a threefold story about the world, and hence about history: (a) that it is basically good, (b) that it is in deep and serious trouble, and (c) that the aim is neither to jettison it, nor to offer a less radical diagnosis, but to deal with the problem at the root and so to reclaim and restore the created order. This, it seems, is what the more nuanced versions of both Routes have been struggling, not always successfully, to say.

What might a Route look like which took seriously the strengths of both those we have examined? For a start, it would have to say that the world, and history, are the good creation of the good God, though not in themselves complete. They are made for the further purposes of the creator, and he will one day be 'all in all' in relation to them. The analysis of evil, within such a Route, would stress that the plight of the world, and of humans, is that they are dislocated from their intended order, in relation to the creator, to themselves and to each other. Sin and death, as they now appear, do not represent the creator's best and final intention, and both will at the last be done away.

The story of the salvation, or redemption, of history would have to give a large place to the story of Israel. The history of Israel, and the Old Testament as it both records that history and interprets it as the story of the creator God with his covenant people, would be seen as the God-given narrative of how the creator set in motion his plan to deal with the plight of the world, and of humans. It is, strictly in its own terms (i.e. not merely with Christian hindsight), a story in search of an ending. As things stood in the first century BC, no Jew would have retold the story of Israel in such a way as to claim that this story had reached its complete fulfilment; all retellings at that time pointed forward to a great act yet to come within history. This act, which would liberate Israel from her enemies, would also be the time when God's justice, and hence salvation, would in some sense or other spread to the rest of the world.

If the story had come to a stop at that point, it would have been a tragedy. That is, it would have spoken of a remarkable plan for the world, which ran out of steam because of Israel's failure and exile, and her bondage to the very pagan nations to whom she was supposed to be shining with God's true light. However, Christian hindsight from the very beginning saw Israel's ambiguous and recalcitrant character as itself a part of the divine purpose. The line of covenant history was not, and was not intended to be, a smooth unfolding path to glory. The prophets had seen this already. The covenant history reached its goal, not in the smooth triumph of Israel over paganism, but in the crucified and risen Jewish Messiah who was to redeem the world. That was, from the beginning, the point of Israel's vocation.

This is where a very different scheme of 'promise and fulfilment' may be found to that which formed part of Route 2 above, and which, as we saw, has come in for a good deal of justified criticism. The Old Testament as a whole moves towards a great climactic act of redemption, with '*all* the Scriptures' – not merely a collection of obvious 'proof-texts' – leading towards the great Return from Exile, the Coming of the Kingdom. It is important to recognise that the events of Jesus' life, death and resurrection were manifestly not what Jews in the first century were expecting. Further, the way in which scriptural prophecies were used in the early Church was not to 'prove' the truth of Christianity, but to demonstrate to Jews who already believed in the Old Testament as a story in search of an ending that this ending, this climax, had in fact, however surprisingly, been reached in the events of Jesus and the Spirit. These events were, to the eye of Christian faith, the real 'return from exile', the coming of the kingdom.

How might we tell the story of Jesus, within a Route that was attempting to do justice to the best of the two standard ones? It might, perhaps, follow this fourfold outline, in which this history (Israel's history, as the focal point of the world's history) comes to its intended fulfilment. We may here anticipate, and perhaps set in context, some features of what will be said in chapter 4 below.

(a) The *incarnation* was not a tangential intrusion of the creator into his world, an invasion from outside followed by a return to the beyond. It was the completion of the long divine plan, which, with hindsight, Christians see to have been all along a plan devised for God's own use. It is *completion*, not merely fulfilment: that is, it brings the continuous (and highly ambiguous and potentially tragic) story of Israel and the world to its critical and climactic point, rather than merely 'fulfilling' various predictions and types scattered at random in earlier sayings and events.

At the same time, it brings a decisively new element into the story, namely the living presence of Israel's God, the creator. According to some texts (e.g. Isa. 40–55; Zech. 2), Israel longed for her God to return to her in person, to liberate her from her sins and their effects. The early Christians were unanimous that this had happened in Jesus of Nazareth. The story of Israel, *and* the story of Israel's God, both reached their fulfilment in Jesus; but in both cases there is a vital element of subversion as well as of completion. In neither case does the story exhibit a smooth, simple line. The story of Jesus offers itself both as the climax of what went before and as something decisively new. The stone which cannot be fitted in to the regular building now turns out to be ideal as the head of the corner. History is the sphere in which fresh divine action takes place.

(b) Jesus' *proclamation of the kingdom* was the prophetic announcement to Israel that her story was reaching its long-awaited crucial moment, and that this story possessed, like many good stories, a vital twist in its tail. Jesus, in the prophetic tradition, announces that divine judgement must fall on Israel herself, and that only those who join his renewal movement will constitute the new people of God who will be the beneficiaries, and thus the agents, of the kingdom. Jesus' announcement puts himself, as the announcer, fair and square at the centre of the kingdom's in-breaking presence, with the totally unexpected corollary that he will be, in himself, the place where Israel's judgement is borne and Israel's new life comes into being. As the bearer of salvation, he himself belongs firmly within the history of salvation. He is not simply announcing a message about something else. He is, in his own actions, words and personal story, the focal point of his message.

(c) The *cross*, from this point of view, was not the mere negation of history, nor simply the fulfilment of types, shadows and predictions. Nor was it simply the tangentially historical outworking of an abstract 'spiritual' or 'theological' theory or mechanism of atonement. It was the completion of Israel's covenant history, that is, the story of the creator, the world and the covenant people. In going to the cross, Jesus acted out his own version of the total story, according to which Israel, represented by himself, must be the people in and through whom the creator God would deal with the evil of the world and of humankind. The cross, as the execution of Israel's Messiah outside Jerusalem at the hands of the pagans, was thus the great summation of Israel's exile, which was itself the fulfilment and completion of the ambiguous and tragic story of Israel as a whole. At the same time, the cross was the supreme achievement of Israel's God, returning to Zion as he had promised (e.g. Isa. 52.7–12; Zech. 14.5; Mal. 3.1; etc.; picked up by e.g. Luke 19.11–48) to deal with his people's sins and their consequences. This view seeks to take evil totally seriously, while the goodness of creation – and of Israel as the covenant people – is at the same time reaffirmed.

(d) The *resurrection*, from this point of view, was not (of course) the mere resuscitation of Jesus, as though history were simply continuing without change. Nor, however, was it merely the coming to faith of the first disciples, as though it were not itself an event within history. Rather, it was the event (presupposing incarnation, kingdom and cross) through which history itself was and is redeemed; through which, that is, the return from exile finally takes place, and the story of Israel comes to its fruition in the birth of the new cosmic order. The story of Jesus thus takes on its full colouring as the climactic moment in the story of Israel, which offers itself as the focal, and redeeming, point of the story of the world.

Proceeding to think through the story of the salvation, or redemption, of history, we come to Pentecost. The Holy Spirit was not given merely to provide humans with a new sort of religious experience, as though their happy subjectivity were the aim of the whole business. Rather, it was the creation of a community of renewed human beings, still subject to sin and death, but with the sure hope of sharing the resurrection of Jesus Christ. They are not required to repeat the story of Israel over and over again in an endless cycle. Rather, they are to live at its new leading edge, as history moves forward into uncharted territory. Tragedy has been turned to victory, and the returned-from-exile Israel goes on its way, charged at last with its proper mission of bringing God's justice and salvation to the world. If Christ is the goal/end of the covenant history that had begun with Abraham, this can only result in his being also the start, the launching-pad, for the movement – still within history! – whereby the creator now completes the purpose for which Abraham was called in the first place.

The story of the Church is therefore neither a sorry tale of mistake, and of declining away from a true vision, nor a triumphant story of marching from glory to glory. Church history matters; that is, it matters that the story of the creator and the creation has not come to a full stop with the Christ-event. But the post-Pentecost chapter of this story must be told both as the story of what the creator has done and is doing by way of inaugurating his kingdom and as the story of human distortion of vocation – *and*, further, as the story of how even that distortion is taken up into the continuing divine purposes.

In this light, the task of the Church cannot be conceived simply as the summoning of men and women to a non-historical salvation. The Church is to be the agent of a salvation that transforms history; and it can only be this as it implements the work of Calvary, by living and praying at the place of pain in the world, so that the apparently automatic entail of sin, violence and degradation may be stopped in its tracks and replaced, however partially and fitfully, with actual historical forgiveness and reconciliation. The movement which flows from the Messiah, to implement the salvation for the world which he accomplished, is thus itself ambiguous, involving the call of sinful human beings to become disciples, followers, preachers and teachers. Yet this ambiguity is not simply identical with the ambiguity which characterised the people of God between Abraham and Christ. It would be misleading, not to say ironic, if, under the blanket rubric of 'salvation history', we were to lump together the people of God BC and AD as if they were but two manifestations of the same non-historical phenomenon – 'salvation history'! Rather, we must allow fully for two different modes of historical life, contained within the one complete divine plan.

The place of 'other religions' within this combination of Routes 1 and 2 raises one of the largest questions of all. How can it be that the salvation of the world should hinge on one incident within one small historical strand within one tiny segment (the history of the earth) of total cosmic history? Despite Route 1's coyness about it, this scandal of particularity is a non-negotiable part of Christian tradition. The whole point of the Judaeo-Christian world-view is that the creator of the whole cosmos is in covenant with Israel; this always was ridiculous, seen in terms of the scale of near eastern empires, let alone in terms of the aeons of cosmic history. It always was something visible only to the eye of faith. But to abandon it because it makes such an extraordinary claim is tantamount to abandoning the equally extraordinary claim that a first-century Jewish man executed by the pagan authorities is the Lord of the entire cosmos. One cannot abandon the essential oddness of the particularity of God's choice of Israel – and of Jesus – without dismantling the very centre of Christianity.

At the same time, precisely because in this rethought Route history itself is redeemed, it would be wrong to assume that the exclusiveness which characterises most versions of Route 2 will necessarily be retained. On the contrary, we might come to insist that salvation, precisely as the redemption of history, can never remain merely God's gift to the Church, but must also be, at least, God's gift *through* the Church; and not necessarily 'through' in the sense of conscious mission. If it is true that there now exists a body of men and women indwelt by the Spirit of the crucified and risen Jesus, their very existence, irrespective of their activity, might be supposed to make a difference. Down some such path, perhaps, we may wish to say more of a positive nature about those who have stood, and who still stand, outside the Christian tradition. How might this be done?

We need to take a step backwards to get our bearings. According to the controlling Jewish story which the New Testament writers saw as having been fulfilled in Christ, Israel was to be saved *in order that*, through that event, salvation might come to the Gentiles. To elevate Israel's separation from the Gentiles into an absolute principle for all time was therefore to nullify the purpose for which that separation had been commanded in the first place. This, more or less, is what Paul argues in Galatians 3. But, according to John 20, Acts 1 and the whole letter to the Romans, the purpose for which the Church has itself been saved is that, through the Church, the sovereign and saving rule of Israel's God might reach to the ends of the world. Within this controlling story, the salvation of those who have faith cannot be the end of the matter.

The New Testament's retelling of the Jewish story, after all, looks back to the divine purpose in creation, where humankind was created to bear the divine image before the whole created world. For the Church, as the redeemed humanity, to clutch at salvation as a private possession, or (in traditionalist terms) to clutch at the private spiritual salvation of one's own soul as of the essence of the gospel, might just be to make the same mistake that Paul and Luke saw the Pharisees making. By speaking of the redemption of history, we might perhaps point towards new ways of articulating an alternative to the exclusivity of Route 2 or the casual inclusivity of Route 1. We will have more to say on this matter in chapter 6 below.

The hope for the future, within this rethought Route, is for a history which will be fulfilled in God's new creation. Just as Jesus was both the culmination of the history of Israel and the world, and yet marked a decisively and qualitatively different stage in both those stories, so the final kingdom will be the true culmination of the story of salvation from Abraham onwards, and yet will remain the fresh gift of God, the stone that will go nowhere else in the building yet will finally take its place at the top of the corner. The New Testament holds out the pictures of birth (Romans 8) and marriage (Rev. 21) as major images of the coming new age. Both speak of continuity with the past and yet also of a decisive moment in which all things become new. When God liberates the whole cosmos from its bondage to decay, consequent upon the resurrection of his people; when heaven and earth are joined together in God's new order, the fulfilment of his purpose from the beginning; then *of course* the story will reach its ultimate goal in Christ himself. Whether the *phrase* 'second coming' does justice to this reality may be doubted; that there is a reality to which that phrase attempts to point seems an essential part of the entire narrative.

How much strength does this middle way possess? We have aimed to take with full seriousness both the fact of sin and wickedness and the God-givenness of creation and history. We have tried, that is, to do justice to the central insights of the two main Routes, while not falling victim to their inadequacies. Within such a reading of salvation in history, history itself is redeemed and transformed. Transformation does not mean abandonment. If we were to allow for a moment the Route 2 assertion that 'Christ is the end of history as he is the end of the law', we would have to assert equally strongly that, in the resurrection, Christ is the rebirth of history, a redeemed history, just as in Pauline language those who are 'not under the law' are nevertheless under 'the law of Christ' (1 Cor. 9.21). The world of space and time, along with the material world, are reclaimed in the resurrection of Jesus, and are to be fulfilled in the resurrection of Jesus' people and the consequent transformation of the whole cosmos (Rom. 8.18–27). *The one saving plan always was cruciform*; that is the point that ties together the continuity and discontinuity, the affirmation and the negation, the emphases of Routes 1 and 2.

From this perspective, it is not sufficient to see the Old Testament as merely a book of types and shadows. That cannot be the full story of how salvation and history work together. Types and shadows there are in plenty, of course; but the Old Testament is far more. It is the story of the people of God, chosen by the creator to be the bearers of his salvation for the cosmos, the world of space, time, matter and hence of history. Equally, it will not do to see the New Testament as a book which merely offers 'individual salvation'. To be sure, there can be no corporate or cosmic salvation that does not call each human person, as a responsible being, to the obedience of faith. But the New Testament is the charter document for a people, living still within history, chosen by the same creator to be his agents in putting that salvation into effect. The more nuanced readings of Routes 1 and 2 do not go far enough. What is required, if we are to do justice to the biblical record – that is, to the overarching story of creator, cosmos, covenant and Christ – is a scheme of thought that catches up the other two Routes and holds them in a new creative scheme.

Conclusion

What then may we say about salvation and history, about the questions with which we began?

The relation of 'sacred' to 'secular' turns out to be more complex by far than has been supposed by the would-be 'secular' thought, and for that matter the would-be 'religious' thought, of the last three centuries. From the Christian point of view, nothing is 'secular' in the sense of being outside the order of things created, and claimed in love, by the one creator God. The question of the this-worldly 'salvation' of people, nations and races cannot therefore be either highlighted (by secularists) or marginalised (by Route 2 Christians) as though it had no 'religious' (or, better, 'God-oriented') dimension. If we are to take seriously the possibility of a more integrated soteriology such as the nuanced versions of the two main Routes are striving towards, Christian missiology must address the task, which faces the whole world in this post-Cold War and post-Apartheid period, of grasping the full dimensions of that salvation for which the world cries out, and of finding ways to bring it to birth.

But that raises all the more acutely the second question. By what right does any nation, any group, any person suppose that he or she has the answer, or an answer, to someone else's problem? 'Secular' analogies are ready to hand. Western aid in the Two-Thirds World, it is sometimes alleged, has made things worse, not least because it has been self-serving. Might the same be true of Christian mission? Is it not better to let all peoples find their own way to salvation?

The Christian remains committed to the belief that Jesus Christ is the Lord of the whole cosmos. This belief is non-negotiable; it looks the charge of particularity in the face, and answers it by speaking first and foremost of the cross and resurrection, which rule out arrogance or triumphalism by highlighting the vocation of the suffering servant on the one hand, and the renewal of creation on the other. It is the events to do with Jesus, at the heart of the whole matter, which claim the undivided allegiance of the Christian. Either they are the unique, definitive self-disclosure of the one God of all the world, or Christianity from first to last is a horrible mistake.

At the same time, those very events warn Christians against being arrogant, patronising or self-serving in their mission. The scandal of particularity is meant to generate the vocation of service. If history is to be redeemed, that must mean that the course of events in the present world can be changed; can be changed by God; can be changed by God acting in various ways, including action through human agents. This, indeed, is part of the Church's own agenda and vocation. One crucial part of the Church's service to the world is that it should be the agent of healing and salvation within history itself. The sorrows and pains of the world will not be healed finally, to be sure, until the creation of the new heavens and the new earth. But the cross and resurrection indicate that healing and salvation can and do begin in the here and now; that is, within history itself. To work for this is to work for the coming of God's kingdom in earth as it is in heaven; in other words, for salvation and history ultimately to meet and merge. That, after all, is at the heart of the prayer that Jesus taught his followers to pray.

Chapter 4
The story of the saviour

We shall now look more closely at what the New Testament says about salvation, both how it continues Old Testament emphases on the physical reality and corporate dimension of salvation; and also how it introduces a new note of completedness and finality – of salvation achieved through the atoning work of Christ. And we shall explore some of the ways the rich imagery of atonement in Scripture has been reflected upon and developed in Christian tradition.

Continuity with the Old Testament

The various words in the Hebrew and Greek Bible which we translate 'save' and 'salvation', along with related terms like redeem, restore and deliver, have an originally material connotation: they refer to rescue from dangers, both those that afflict individuals like sickness and private feuds, and those that involve the whole of society like war, famine and plague. To be saved is to escape from anything that threatens to damage or destroy life, and conversely to enjoy health, peace, prosperity and blessing. The religious connotations of the English noun 'salvation' and the verb 'save' when used with persons as its object, are much less material; to be saved and to attain salvation, is to be assured of sins forgiven, to escape eternal punishment, to go to heaven and glorify God for ever. In English one can be saved in the religious sense at the same time as remaining unsaved in the physical sense without any hint of contradiction or even tension. In the Bible, religious and material salvation are much more closely related; and when one is claimed in the absence of the other, there is always an element of tension and paradox involved.

The vocabulary of salvation cannot be considered in isolation from the basic biblical paradigms for salvation from which it takes its distinctive colouring. For Israel this was the Exodus; for the Church the death and resurrection of Jesus Christ. The Exodus, with its themes of election and covenant takes precedence even over the creation stories, both as a matter of historical reconstruction of the development of Israel's faith and in terms of its literary presentation in the final form of the Pentateuch. The early chapters of Genesis function as an introduction to the history of salvation, and anticipate many of its major themes: election, rebellion, wrath and redemption. While later Christian systematics has tended to move from creation to salvation, Old Testament theology develops backwards from salvation to creation. For the New Testament also there is a movement backwards from the death and resurrection of Jesus 'according to the Scriptures', from the saving event to a reinterpretation of the history of salvation, beginning with creation in which Christ is already active as the agent of God (John 1.2; Col. 1.15). The parallel with the Exodus is sometimes made even more explicit: Jesus' death is compared to the offering of the Passover Lamb (1 Cor. 5.7) which protected Israel from divine retribution on its enemies; Jesus is to accomplish a new Exodus (Luke 9.31) bringing victory and release from slavery. One effect of this common biblical pattern of movement back from salvation to creation, from history to cosmology, is to make the Fall less pivotal for biblical theology as a whole than it was to become in later Christian thought. It is not contemplation of the human plight as such which gives rise to soteriology, but particular historical experiences of the saving power of God.

The Law of Moses sealed the Covenant with the elect People and provided a juridical and cultic system of atonement for sins committed against that covenant. The People experienced God's judgement and mercy, not only within the pattern of salvation history, but also through the outworkings of the Law and the offering of sacrifice. In the latter we can glimpse a more mysterious insight into the enduring effect of human sin and disobedience – a glimpse into the sphere beyond time where relationship with the eternal God is, as it were, suspended in the timelessness of liturgy. In this context, we encounter those images of sin offering, unblemished victim, and the cleansing, life-giving power of blood, which will be taken up so powerfully in Christian reflection on the meaning of Christ's death.

These two approaches to atonement, the historical and the cultic, already begin to converge in the prophets of the Exile. If the cult were to become a purely ritual way of dealing with sin, it would imply a mechanical, external operation, and an evasion of the human responsibility to live with the consequences of our actions; but conversely, a purely historical concept of judgement, that failure to keep the Covenant is punished by historical disaster, would have great difficulty explaining the problem of innocent suffering. The great prophets of the Exile, Second Isaiah, Jeremiah and Ezekiel, saw their role and that of faithful Israelites as bearing the consequences of the sins of others and purging the guilt of their disloyalty to God by means of suffering. This theme is then reapplied in later crises of Israel's history, notably in the Maccabean period (see 2 Macc. 7.14). The cultic idea of sacrifice is thus merged with a moral notion of self-offering and this forms the essential background as we shall see for the understanding of the death of Christ. He both fulfils the vocation of the prophets to innocent, vicarious suffering and is also offered as the one unblemished substitute and sacrifice for sin.

For most of the Old Testament period, Israel had no concept of personal survival after death: the body returned to the dust of the earth or continued a shadowy existence in Sheol (the underworld) and the life force returned to God who gave it; only the People lived on. But in order to defend belief in the justice of God in the face of the experience of injustice, torture and martyrdom in the second century BC, and partly also under the influence of neighbouring religious systems founded on beliefs concerning life after death, this concept began to enter Israel's tradition. However, its introduction did not, surprisingly perhaps, displace the older view of salvation as having a primarily this-worldly reference. There was no radical restructuring of traditional soteriology; the new belief was simply placed alongside it. God would save his People, both in this world, by political and even military means, and in the world to come, mysteriously by resurrection. The two were seen as complementary moments of salvation; belief in the latter was not a compensation for loss of belief in the former. The book of Daniel combines an immediate, earthly hope of freedom and human victory, with a longer vision of ultimate and universal divine victory. This apocalyptic vision represents not the breakdown of traditional Israelite historical theodicy, but its reaffirmation and extension.

In the New Testament period there was still in Judaism a variety of beliefs about the after-life, ranging from the outright rejection of the doctrine by the Sadducees to a rather individualist and spiritualised hope of survival after death in Hellenised varieties of Judaism, but the form which was to become orthodoxy was the Pharisaic/Rabbinic doctrine of the final judgement and resurrection of the dead, which retained the corporate and physical emphases of the older soteriology. Early Christian belief in the resurrection of Jesus must be interpreted against this eschatological horizon. It was not the resuscitation of one individual to continued earthly existence, but the anticipation in one special instance of the future hope for the general resurrection of all God's People. Belief in Jesus' resurrection was the partial realisation of a future hope; it allowed early Christians to see salvation, in continuity with Old Testament tradition, not just as something to be hoped for at the end of time, but as something to be experienced here and now insofar as they were incorporated into the body of the Risen Christ, the Church. In other words, the Church was enabled to resist the possible disintegration and divergence of the different ideas of salvation that existed alongside each other in inter-testamental Judaism. The death and resurrection of Jesus became the new centre around which the various strands to which we have referred, the Exodus and Covenant, sacrifice and atonement, the Exile and Return, prophetic suffering, and vindication beyond death, could be integrated into a consistent and comprehensive soteriology.

Salvation in the ministry of Jesus

An examination of the use of the word 'save' in the gospel accounts of
the ministry of Jesus confirms the observation already made that there is
a strong continuity between the testaments in their physical and
corporate understanding of salvation. The themes of Jewish apocalyptic,
deliverance from famine, pestilence and earthquake, civil war, betrayal
and persecution are reproduced in the Synoptic apocalypse (Mark 13 and
parallels in other Gospels) with its typical mixing of this-worldly
political concern and hope for the ultimate victory of God. Jesus' words
here assume that such threats are real and pressing; they have not
therefore receded with the appearance of the Pax Romana and the
Emperor as 'saviour of the world'. On the contrary the rhetoric of the
self-divinising State and its false claim to have ushered in the age of
universal peace constitute a blasphemy, which recalls that ancient
prophecy in Daniel of 'the desolating sacrilege' (Mark 13.14). Jesus
expects salvation to come not from armed rebellion but through the
perseverance under present oppression of the politically helpless and by
the imminently future and dramatic intervention of God: 'The one who
endures to the end will be saved' (Mark 13.13); and 'If the Lord had not
cut short those days, no one would be saved' (Mark 13.20).

Along with the meaning of 'to save' as rescue from the turbulence of the
end time, we find the meaning to heal, to regain health. Almost half of
the references in the ministry of Jesus to salvation are of this therapeutic
kind. The opposite of being saved in this sense is not to be judged or
condemned eternally, but to be maimed or die. To take just two
examples: the ruler of the synagogue asks Jesus to heal his daughter,
'that she may be saved and live' (Mark 5.23), and the woman with the
haemorrhage is commended for her persistence and will to live, with the
words, 'Daughter, your faith has saved you' (Mark 5.34). It is no doubt
true that this formula 'saved by faith' was retained in the tradition
because it echoed the post-Easter doctrinal principle of salvation by faith
developed in the Church's controversy with Pharisaic Judaism. What the
Church ultimately came to mean by the phrase was that we receive
ultimate 'religious' salvation from sin and eternal death through the cross
and resurrection; but in the original context of Jesus' ministry it would
have had a broader, simpler, more material meaning.

Even references to the future hope of resurrection and entry to life
beyond death are expressed with physical analogies in the New
Testament and in continuity with the materialist understanding of
salvation. This may be illustrated by Jesus' humorous warning against
the rich: 'It is easier for a camel to go through the eye of a needle than for
someone who is rich to enter the Kingdom of God' (Mark 10.25). The

disciples' astonished reply is 'Then who can be saved?' And their logic seems to be: 'If not the rich, then what chance is there for the poor? The rich are blessed, their wealth allows them to give alms and not cheat their neighbours!' In his reply, Jesus does not dispute this line of reasoning; what he says, rather, is that entry into the kingdom is hard but not impossible, for nothing is impossible with God.

As if to reinforce this reluctance to retreat into a private, spiritual realm of salvation, the key term in Jesus' preaching, the kingdom of God, holds together at least three ideas. As we have just seen, the kingdom may be synonymous with eternal life, entered at death by any individual (Luke 23.42–3) or experienced by all at the moment of resurrection (Luke 20.34–6). But equally, the kingdom of God is a reality present wherever healing and freedom from the forces of evil are attained (Matt. 12.28). And again, the coming of the kingdom is that universal, public vindication of the elect poor, for which the disciples are to pray as a future earthly hope (Luke 11.20; cf. Luke 6.20). The kingdom image is remarkably varied and combines all these facets together.

In stark contrast to the life-affirming attitude to salvation in the references we have looked at so far, there is in the teaching of Jesus what appears to be a life-denying ascetic strand. The best example is the saying in Mark 8.35: 'Those who want to save their life will lose it, and those who lose their life for my sake, and for the sake of the gospel, will save it.' This saying puts a question mark against the natural human instinct for survival, health and prosperity, and recommends instead the path of self-sacrifice and martyrdom. While elsewhere in the Gospels to be saved means not to die, here it means willingly to die. The saying has often been interpreted in a non-literal sense, referring to inward detachment from worldly concerns or self-denying service to others. Such interpretations depend on a sudden denying service to others. Such interpretations depend on a sudden switch in mid-sentence in the meaning of either 'life' or 'save'; but we ought to hesitate to collapse a sparkling paradox into a linguistic ambiguity, in this way. At Mark 8.35, the first clause is a common-place: 'Those who save their life will lose it', i.e. those who are preoccupied with their own safety are the ones most at risk of accident. But such traditional wisdom, if so, is immediately confronted by the challenge of the antithetic parallel: 'If you lose your life, you will save it.' So, the first and primary meaning of 'save', even in this saying, is the physical, life-affirming sense outlined earlier. It is then confronted sharply with the opposite sense, as a deliberate paradox designed to jolt the listener.

This discussion of paradoxical references to salvation in the gospel tradition leads us naturally into a consideration of Jesus' attitude towards his own death. This topic is a very controversial one in New Testament study; the authenticity and interpretation of the relevant material is hotly disputed. It may be as well, therefore, simply to list the main data and outline some of the options. Jesus predicts his own passion in a series of references to the necessary suffering of the Son of Man (Mark 8.31; 9.31; 10.33, 45 etc. with parallels in other Gospels). Depending on one's interpretation of the Son of Man designation, the necessity referred to here could be that of the human race generally born to suffer, with the case of the speaker as its immediate instance, or the pattern of prophetic suffering, or the end-time suffering of the faithful remnant, or the unique and vicarious suffering of the Servant of the Lord of Isaiah combined with the Danielic image of future vindication as an alternative Messianic title to Son of David. What we may safely say is that the necessity ('The Son of Man must suffer') is scriptural, even though the precise textual background may be elusive. A scriptural pattern of suffering also lies just beneath the surface of the Parable of the Wicked Tenants (Mark 12.1–9 and parallels). The servants represent the prophets, and the death of the son represents the rejection of the vineyard owner's final appeal. The result of that rejection is unmitigated tragedy and loss. No hint is given of any positive meaning in the son's death; his father's patience, so sorely tried, is now exhausted. The parable is, therefore, not explanatory but exhortatory. Jesus' parable itself functions as God's final exhortation to repentance.

In the passion narrative there are three other sayings directly relevant which probably go back in essence to the historical Jesus, for they display a similar understanding of his death. The words at the Last Supper (Mark 14.22–5) acted out in the breaking of bread and pouring of wine, imply at the very least acceptance of imminent death as within God's purposes of salvation for many. The more explicit interpretative details which appear in Matthew's version, 'for the forgiveness of sins' and 'the new covenant' (Matt. 26.28), may be his own additions. Without them, the Last Supper scene is consistent with the prayer of anguished self-dedication in Gethsemane (Mark 14.36). Jesus does not presume to know the reasons behind the death he sees rapidly approaching, but he accepts it in obedience to the Father's will. The cry from the cross in Matthew (27.46) and Mark (15.34), quoting Psalm 22, again offers no theoretical explanation of atonement, but rather conforms to the scriptural pattern of obedient submission to the will of God.

Thus, even staying within the strict limits of what can be said with some historical certainty about Jesus, and resisting the imaginative speculations offered by popular apologists or hostile critics, we are nevertheless in a position to claim that the atonement has its basis and ground in what Jesus actually said and did. But this conclusion also means that it is legitimate, and indeed necessary, to go beyond the evidence of Jesus' ministry, and in the light of Easter and Christian experience to begin to offer explanations of how atonement through Christ was achieved. The New Testament after all contains many examples of this, to some of which we shall return later. It is important for Christian doctrine to be able to trace the fact and work of atonement to Jesus himself; but elaborate theories of the atonement are secondary, necessarily diverse and all to some extent inadequate to the reality of their subject and to the profundity of its meaning. The Apostles' Creed seems to sense this in its remarkably plain statement: 'He suffered under Pontius Pilate, was crucified, dead and buried.' And that plain, hard realism is preserved for Christians in the gospel passion narratives, as they are read in devotion, recalled at every Eucharist and recited dramatically in the liturgy of Holy Week. It is to these that we now turn.

Narratives of the passion

The origin of the passion narratives is to be found in the forms of earliest preaching. The first Christians preached a scandalous message of the crucifixion of Israel's Messiah. They did not hide the scandal but paraded it. The way of salvation through Christ was preached, both within the community (1 Cor. 11.26) and for those outside it (1 Cor. 1.23 and Gal. 3.1), in the form of a rehearsal of the story of his Passion. The one constant element of theological interpretation was the connection by quotation and allusion of the events with the predictions of Scripture. This layer of interpretation did not interfere with the dynamic of the story or distract the hearers' attention from its often brutal actuality. This is why the passion narratives in the Gospels remain the best examples from ancient literature of utterly realistic narrative.

The passion narratives all tell recognisably the same story. This may be due in part to their literary interdependence, but it is also because they arise from similar settings in communal life and are in touch with the same basic facts of history. There are, however, several discrepancies between them in detail: the chronology of events, the nature of the Jewish trial, the motivation and fate of Judas, the words from the cross, the number of visitors to the empty tomb and so forth. These have long been noticed as a problem and explained away by different means: allegory, harmonisation and (in modern critical study) by tradition-history. The differences between the accounts not only pose a problem, they also provide insights into the intentions of the different evangelists. The method of gospel study known as Redaction Criticism has been developed to illuminate, by comparison of the accounts, the distinctive theological stance and purpose of the individual gospel writers and the peculiar situation of their communities. So, for example, it is possible to detect in Matthew's Gospel a series of small but significant changes in wording which build up into an emphasis on Jewish culpability for the death of the Messiah and its dreadful consequences (e.g. 22.7; 27.25), and then to explain this anti-Judaic tendency by reference to the memories and present experiences of the Matthean Church.

Using Form and Redaction Criticism, scholars of the previous generation attempted to divide gospel material sharply into what was tradition and what was Evangelist's interpretation. But these methods have in recent times been called into question. They are sometimes too blunt and uncertain to deliver the precision their analysis requires. The processes of oral tradition are not easily reduced to laws of transmission. Wildly varying explanations are offered for the distinctive features of a particular Gospel, which depend on speculative reconstructions of its date, setting and purpose. And further, to emphasise redaction at the expense of those features of the story which all the narratives have in common is to distort the reading of the text, so that what is distinctive, in comparison with others, is taken to be disproportionately significant.

For these reasons, New Testament scholars have begun to adopt what is known as a 'holistic', or 'narrative-critical' reading of the Gospels, where every part of the narrative is treated seriously within the overall literary dynamic. Clearly it is impossible here to do more than illustrate the approach. The last words of Jesus may serve as an example. In Matthew and Mark they are the cry of dereliction which we have already discussed. By contrast in Luke's Gospel, Jesus utters three sayings: forgiving his persecutors, reassuring a fellow sufferer and delivering his spirit into the hands of his Father. In John, he makes provision for his mother to be taken to the home of the Beloved Disciple, fulfils Scripture by crying out 'I am thirsty' and dies with the words 'It is finished'. Abstracted like this from their surrounding narratives, these divergences have seemed to constitute a major historical problem, and to call for explanation in terms of the different and even contradictory theologies of the Evangelists. Thus, for example, Mark's view of the atonement could be seen as substitutionary, with the sinless one becoming sin and experiencing alienation from God for our sake. Luke on the other hand appears to portray Jesus as an inspiring example of forgiveness and quiet serenity; while John's doctrine of incarnation and his high Christology have, it is claimed, all but eclipsed Jesus' human suffering. But seen in the context of their respective narratives, these explanations become much less convincing. Mark quotes Psalm 22.1 in Aramaic before giving its translation and he is more concerned with the crowd's mishearing of it as an appeal to Elijah than with its theological content. It is typical of Mark, especially in this part of the passion, to emphasise irony and misunderstanding. The second loud cry which tears through the veil of the Temple and convinces the Gentile centurion that Jesus is truly the Son of God may tell us more about Mark's own particular view of the atoning death of Christ. In Luke's account there is no agony in the words from the cross; but this is because he has already covered the theme in the special material of his Gethsemane story (22.44), in which Jesus also confronts the powers of darkness (22.53). Nor should we forget that his final self-commendation into the hands of God is not quiet resignation; even in Luke, it is accompanied by a loud cry (23.46). Similarly, in John's narrative taken as a whole, the reality of the human suffering of Jesus cannot be in any doubt. Peculiarly the Evangelist emphasises that Pilate brought Jesus humiliated out in front of the crowd wearing the crown of thorns and purple robe, and presented him with the words: 'Here is the man' (19.5).

The deficiency of narrative criticism, as currently practised, is its tendency to dismiss those questions of history and tradition that the older methods were designed to address; but its great value is that it has restated an obvious truth which scholarship had managed somehow to ignore, namely that the gospel narratives are story. Although they are rich in theological meaning, they cannot be replaced by a series of abstract propositions or by conjectural historical reconstructions. And as story they are appropriated in the first instance by the listener through sympathetic imagination, in the manner of tragic drama. The desertion, betrayal, denial, mockery, scourging and execution move the audience to pity and to that sympathy which searches the memory for parallels in their own experience. The story carries the reader beyond the crucifixion to the denouement of the resurrection, with the implication that Jesus' claim to bring the kingdom of God was here vindicated. As a consequence Jesus is able to grant to his disciples access here and now to the banquet of the kingdom, uniting in a fellowship of forgiveness and new life all who follow him in simplicity of heart.

Images of the atonement

The resurrection is the presupposition in the light of which faith in Jesus was preached and the documents of the New Testament written. The resurrection implies that in Jesus God has already acted to open the kingdom to all. Many who might have expected to have been excluded, or to have had great difficulty in qualifying themselves for participation, will be included. The judgement will reverse expectations. Those proud of their righteousness, like the Pharisees, will make way for publicans, the humble in heart, the poor and the outcast. Even those who fulfil their religious obligations will need to say: 'We are worthless slaves' (Luke 17.10).

Traditions such as these drove Paul to formulate the view that Christ died for us while we were helpless, and still in our sins (Rom. 5.8). God's action in sending Jesus is pure grace, not the result of what we have deserved or merited. So our being put right with God (our 'justification') is an act beginning with God's grace, to which we can only respond with the full commitment of faith. This God-given faith brings us out of a life of sin and death in which we are trapped, into the new life of resurrection, a life of love in the Spirit of Christ. Thus justification by grace alone to be received by faith alone is the fundamental resurrection message. Jesus Christ was betrayed to his death for our sins and was raised for our justification (Rom. 4.25). Those who have by faith participated in Christ's death and resurrection are now joined inseparably to his love (Rom. 8.39).

Yet this message, which lies at the heart of the gospel, raises numerous consequential questions. The most obvious of these is why the death of Christ should have this astonishing result. In the New Testament writings a great variety of scriptural images is called upon to illuminate some facet or other of the central mystery of the faith. They are pressed only as far as they are helpful and then the believing imagination moves on to feed elsewhere, with no sense of obligation to restrict the interpretation to one standard form. In the Fourth Gospel, for example, Jesus is the Lamb of God who takes away the sin of the world (1.29); he dies at the same time as the Passover sacrifices (19.31f); he is silent (19.9), like a sheep dumb before the shearer; but at the same time he is the Good Shepherd who lays his life down of his own accord (10.11), whose own recognise his voice (10.4) and who silences his enemies (18.6).

Christian tradition taken as a whole has seemed intuitively to recognise this fact of the diversity of images for atonement in the New Testament and has not tried to impose one particular theory as an agreed dogma. Some interpretations bear very centrally upon valued understandings of the sacraments and ministry, for example the death of Christ as perfect sacrifice for sin. It may even be possible to speak of a consistent teaching in the New Testament on the 'sacrifice' of Christ, as long as it is recognised that, when the term is used in this way, it is being refined and redefined by the atoning work of Christ. But sacrificial imagery in the stricter, cultic sense, is only one among many images that are used. When New Testament writers refer to Christ dying for us, or for our sins, or to Christ's blood, they do not necessarily imply that they have this image of sacrifice in mind; they could be referring more generally to the benefits of his passion and the violent manner of his death.

We should remember that, before the disappearance of the Temple cultus with the destruction of the Temple in AD 70, the word sacrifice would normally have had straightforward, literal reference, usually to the offering of a ritually slaughtered animal. After this time, of course, both in Christianity and in Judaism, non-literal understandings of sacrifice become the norm. But to appreciate its earliest uses in the New Testament, we need to recall this literal sense, in order to see just how daring, and indeed subversive, it is to describe an event like the crucifixion as a sacrifice. Paul may be alluding to this imagery in several places, but the clearest instance is Romans 3.25. Nowhere else does Paul use the term he uses here, variously translated as 'expiation', 'propitiation', or 'mercy seat'; his Gentile readers may not have been so concerned with the technicalities of Jewish sacrifices. In the context, Paul wants to emphasise the importance of faith and the present justifying activity of God, but Paul was probably borrowing the language of sacrifice from a lively tradition in Jewish Christianity.

The Epistle to the Hebrews, more than any other document in the New Testament, sets out to explore the richness and depth of the cultic image of sacrifice. It is used as the key to understanding not only the death of Christ, but also his person as high priest and mediator, and the whole of his work, his earthly testing and consecration as well as his final ascension and continuing role as intercessor. From the vividness of its references to the actual circumstances of Jesus' crucifixion, it is clear that Hebrews is fully aware of the metaphorical character of the language of sacrifice. The horrific and intrinsically defiling public execution of a condemned criminal is very far from being the serene self-offering of the perfect priest and unblemished victim. But when the two images come together, they interpret each other. The sordid realism of a crucifixion becomes the occasion for discovering the forgiveness and reconciling power of God.

The sacrificial metaphor is therefore a deliberate paradox. Although it has been developed and extended into an overarching motif in the Epistle to the Hebrews, there is no doctrinal statement anywhere of how precisely the death of Christ atones for sin. Many different types of Old Testament sacrifice – the Day of Atonement, covenant, purificatory rites, communion offerings and so forth – are all conflated into one composite idea, the principal purpose of which is to assist a moment of disclosure concerning the meaning of Jesus' historic death: that it was not merely what it appeared to be – tragic, coerced, shameful and unholy – but was in truth the freely chosen path of obedience and access into God's presence, effecting atonement and sanctification.

The sacrificial metaphor is prominent in Hebrews, and appears explicitly at other points in the New Testament. But it is by no means the only metaphor used in the New Testament to spell out the belief that 'Christ died for our sins'. Similar uses of striking images, deliberately superimposed over the story of Jesus' death, can be found. As we have seen, the Exodus was for Israel the classic saving event; and Exodus typology, the Passover Lamb, the testing in the wilderness, and the hope for freedom and deliverance, are used to illuminate aspects of Christian experience and relate it to the work of Christ. The Book of Revelation in particular exploits these images; and constructs its vision of heaven around the throne of God and the Lamb slain (5.6). In Colossians 2.11–15 are details from the institution of slavery, and the image of slave release is held up to reflect the event of the passion. The nails that fixed Christ to the cross in fact pinned up the notice of our liberation from slavery or 'manumission' in the technical sense. It was our old nature that was stripped and exposed to humiliation. It was the powers of this age that were led in public spectacle. When we recall that crucifixion in the Roman Empire was the punishment particularly reserved for runaway slaves and captured rebels, the full irony of this use of imagery comes home.

When in Paul's Epistles the death of Jesus is referred to as an act of acquittal or justification, the image again paradoxically reverses the remembered facts of Jesus' trials: as in the narrative presentations in the Gospels, those who presume to judge are themselves judged by their encounter with Jesus. It has often been claimed that, in his arguments in Galatians and Romans with some who wanted to impose the marks of Jewish identity on his Gentile converts, Paul interprets the condemnation of Jesus under the Law as the condemnation of the Law and the acquittal of those who live by faith. This metaphor works, like the others, only as long as the paradoxical tension between the language which it uses and the event to which it refers is constantly borne in mind.

One of the most significant images used by Paul to convey the meaning of the cross is that of reconciliation. This would have had a particular appropriateness to Gentile converts who formerly, viewed from the Jewish standpoint, had been enemies of God and idolaters, but who had now found peace and forgiveness. The image of peace negotiations and diplomacy, like that of the law court, slave-release and the sacrificial cultus, is surprisingly and daringly inverted. If a public execution is needed to keep the peace, that implies that all human diplomacy and humanly constructed peace have failed. God's diplomacy and peace are, however, revealed in the cross.

The common feature of all these uses is the way positive metaphorical images are held in conscious tension with the negativity of the remembered facts of the crucifixion. Realism and the imagination interact. The passion narratives in the Gospels are very stark; the story is allowed to speak for itself without gloss or technical explanation. And yet in the New Testament also, the imaginative creativity of early Christian reflection on the death of Christ is everywhere apparent. It seems that these opposing poles, realism and imagination, were deliberately kept apart in order to retain the full power of their mutual attraction. The writers of the New Testament have in common also the need to testify that in Christ they have encountered a salvific experience of freedom and transforming new life. So vivid is this conviction that they are driven to employ a variety of metaphors in order to try to articulate what has happened to them. It is like a new creation (2 Cor. 5.17) or new birth (John 3.3–8); a new covenant (Heb. 9.15) or life from the dead (Rom. 6.5–11). Salvation for them is not a theological concept but a present reality.

In this chapter we have looked at some of the New Testament evidence on salvation and the atoning work of Christ, and we have emphasised above all the primacy of the event of the passion with the cross as its central symbol. Story and symbol come first. They are worked out in images and metaphors, sometimes striking often paradoxical. Eventually doctrines of the atonement emerge, which are attempts to devise as coherent answers as possible to the questions raised by the narrative; and these doctrines have been many and varied in the history of Christian thought. To try to reduce this variety to a single agreed statement on the doctrine of the atonement would be untrue both to the New Testament and to our Anglican heritage. Far better, and more consistent with our rich Christian tradition, to provide a series of angles of vision, or reference points, to sketch the great mystery of the atonement. These are complementary insights and are not in competition with each other; they are facets of the central jewel of Christian faith, that in the cross and resurrection of Jesus God has won our salvation. In the next chapter, entitled 'Retelling the story', we provide modern restatements of some of the principal ways in which Christian people have understood that mystery of salvation, which is the subject of this report.

Chapter 5
Retelling the story

Christ in our place

In its deepest dimensions what is wrong with human life is the lack of God. We could offer a threefold diagnosis. First, there is sin, that deeply rooted tendency to selfishness which in all of us taints even our best intentions and implicates us all in the web of human evil. In sin we turn our backs on God and find ourselves on the well-frequented highway that leads us ever further from God. In our consciousness of sin we know that God, the absolute good, must oppose and condemn our evil. As sinners we are the godless – in the real sense of that word: alienated from God. Second, there is the meaningless tragedy of life. This is not the evil for which we know we are responsible, but the incomprehensible suffering that comes upon us and may overwhelm us. In pointless suffering we feel that it is God who has turned his back on us. We are the godforsaken – for it seems that God has left us to suffer. Finally, there is death. Death may be seen as the end to which our culpable failure in life must lead. The fate of the godless is to perish. Death may also be seen as the final surd which threatens everything else in life with meaninglessness. Godforsakenness is to be left to die.

In all three experiences human beings sink to the depths and find the deepest horror of those depths to be the absence of God. In evil and tragedy and death – when we manage to face up to each without illusions – what we miss is the love at the heart of reality. This is why, in such extremities of life, the word 'God' comes to the lips even of those who have rarely used it seriously before. They cry out for God or they cry out against God. They recognise that in its deepest dimension the human plight is alienation from God.

The depth of our alienation is such that God is not to be found by us unless God enters that alienation and finds us there. This God did in the crucified Jesus. Jesus lived a life of loving identification with others, in all sorts and conditions of human life. In other words, he practised the kind of love which is not mere benevolence, wishing people well from a distance, but that love which enters people's situations and makes their plight sympathetically its own. Jesus identified especially with those who experienced the depths: healing the very sick and the destitute beggars, restoring the dying to life, touching the lepers, befriending the outcasts, freeing the demented from the demons of oppression and isolation, attracting the notorious sinners with his freely forgiving love. Finally, he ended up where any of these people could have ended up: a failure, condemned as a criminal, in agonising pain, deserted by his friends, forsaken by his God. He died the kind of death which symbolised God's verdict on sinful humanity: condemned to perish. He died expressing the tragic meaninglessness of the human fate: 'Why have you forsaken me?' As Jesus died he entered those depths where godless and godforsaken human beings can only cry out to God or for God or against God. But he did not enter them on his own account. He did so in consequence of the loving choice of identifying with others which he made in his life and sustained in his death. He died our death, sharing our failure, condemnation, despair and godforsakenness. So throughout Christian history the guilty and afflicted have recognised their own plight in his.

In doing so they have found God in their alienation from God. For the crucified Jesus was not just one more godless, godforsaken human being, dying as all of us must. He was the man who chose to identify himself in love with the godless and the godforsaken. It was his mission from God to do this. As the one who came from God, the incarnate Son of God, it was God's love he expressed and enacted in his identification with the godless and the godforsaken. Therefore the crucified Jesus brings the love of God into the depths where God's absence is known. Because he suffers that absence of God, no one else need do so.

For the guilty this is forgiveness. Because he bore their condemnation, they can face up to its truth without the hopeless alienation from God it otherwise creates. On the contrary, in the crucified Jesus God's love reaches them where they are, with forgiveness, enabling them to put sin behind them, initiating a life lived out of God's love instead of in flight from God's demands. For the godforsaken, who suffer life's meaningless tragedy, the cross does not, of course, remove the suffering, but it heals the heartless depth of that suffering: the lack of God. Even when incomprehensible tragedy overwhelms, the suffering may find God's love incomprehensibly greater. Because Jesus suffered their abandonment, in their affliction they are not abandoned.

Only because he died our death can his resurrection also be ours. We participate in his resurrection through the transformation of life which begins now, as God's love penetrates the depths of our human plight, and which culminates in the future in God's new creation of all things. Though this new creation also includes all rightings of wrongs and healings of hurts, it does so because it overcomes the last enemy: death. Because Jesus died our death, identified with us in death, God's love reaches even the dead and raises them to new life. Because Jesus died our death, death need not be the fate it otherwise is. The light of Jesus' resurrection dispels the shadow death casts over life.

Christ the friend betrayed

Anyone belonging to a political party knows well how much more acrimonious are the quarrels one has with one's friends than those with one's enemies. With friends and allies any disagreement quickly brings the sense of betrayal, and betrayal is one of the most difficult things ever to forgive. We hear it in the angry shouts directed at those who work during a strike, see it in the headlines that appear whenever a spy is discovered in high places, and can practically touch it in the atmosphere when a spouse feels the marriage covenant has been violated. It takes a miracle to find a way back into relationship when betrayal is in the air. Of all wars, civil war is the most devastating, as we have seen daily on our television screens in recent times; and it leaves wounds that are the hardest to heal.

So 'on the night of his betrayal' cannot just be another way of giving the date. It links every Eucharist with the most scaring aspect of what the passion of Christ represents, and in a way which, if words do not simply become a habit to us, speak of something most of us know about at quite a deep level. We know, too, that it is not simply a matter of something Judas is supposed to have done: the story of God's dealings with humankind is a story of repeated betrayal, and Jesus is the climax and symbol of all those times when God comes to, and is rejected by, God's own.

So the God who is to be known as the one who saves from all that ruptures our relationships with one another has in particular to be known as the one who can even transform betrayal into a source of hope, so that the worst that has happened is transformed into the best that can happen. The mention of the 'night when he was betrayed' presents us with the character of God's constancy that can even confront and transcend betrayal. When we are in contact with human constancy that goes far beyond what could be expected we are most especially aware of seeing the character of God at work: when people stand by those who let them down badly, when parental love stands firm against every attempt of a child to bring about rejection, or when children retain their capacity for affection towards adults who betray their trust, when Muslim befriends Serb or when a community refuses to cast out those who let it down, then we are presented with the most powerful picture of what salvation is, and of the way in which God deals with humanity.

The gospel is about how the most death-dealing aspects of our life were and are transformed into what is most life-giving, through the fact of

God's unwavering constancy. Through that constancy the one who was handed over becomes the life that is handed on, and through the retelling of the story of the passion we are made aware again and again of that holding on through rejection which is the way God saves us and the way we are to be with each other. That holding on is what could transform a meal in the presence of treachery into the first taste of the kingdom banquet.

Christ who justifies

Broken promises are amongst the most disappointing features of relationships: we hate letting someone else down, and feel even worse when our hopes are not fulfilled. Christ keeps the promises of God to us and for us so that God neither lets us down nor finds us lacking in keeping our promises. The whole framework in which to understand this is the covenant promises of God to Abraham that by him 'all the families of the earth shall be blessed' (Gen. 12.3). God makes repeated agreements or covenants with his people, and they are repeatedly aborted by the people's failure to keep their side of the bargain. God's intention to bless everyone through Abraham is thwarted. Human failure frustrates the purposes of God, in a way like a man's broken promise to marry his fiancée, makes it impossible for his fiancée to keep her promises to the man she loves. When human beings refuse to keep the covenant which God has made with them, they prevent the full relationship with God which had been his intention for them, and through them to others. God does not stop loving and caring any more than the fiancée does: we read about what that feels like in the story of Hosea which compares God to a husband whose wife has betrayed him; who knows that the 'sensible' thing to do is to divorce her, but whose love is so strong that he finds himself compelled to take her back and restore the relationship.

In Jesus Christ, God begins the relationship again with human beings on a new, but parallel, basis to the one offered in the old covenant. At the Last Supper, Jesus makes clear that the death, which he is about to die, initiates a new covenant between God and his people. This covenant is one which cannot be broken since God in Christ has kept both his part and ours. Because Jesus Christ is fully divine and fully human he is able, in his own person, to keep God's side of the agreement but what is new is that he keeps the other side too – he is able to keep our side, in perfect obedience to God, such as God asked of his people of old. We participate in this covenant in the same way as we could have participated in the old one, but there is a radical change as well. We participate by trusting God, as Abraham did, but we accept Christ's obedience on our behalf; so salvation is by grace and faith in a radically new way. Our obedience becomes an expression of our gratitude to the God who in Christ has done everything on our behalf and who calls us to welcome the blessing offered to all the families of the earth through this descendant of Abraham by whom God has kept his original promise.

There is no exact parallel to this unique event, but it is something like a parent who is playing chess with a child; they begin the game expectantly, each concentrating earnestly on the task, but the child gets into major difficulty and clearly cannot think of an appropriate strategy; body language signals that he is on the point of giving up, which will destroy the game for both of them. At that moment, mother walks round the table and gives careful thought to how it looks from the other side. She makes a splendid move, which neutralises the faults, and not only makes it possible for the contest to continue but makes it clear how the child's future strategy might develop. She resumes her place and the game progresses, since the child accepts this gracious act on his behalf. Mother's promise that she will play a game of chess with her son is fulfilled because the relationship does not end with the son's error; it continues because of the mother's adoption of his place and side.

This is called justification because it shows that God is just or right to keep his side of the covenant or agreement even though we have not kept our side, since God does not ignore human failure, but puts it right in Jesus Christ. The result of this is our justification or right-eousness, since we are now in a right relationship with God again because of what Jesus Christ has done. This means that the only question which is left for us to decide is whether we will receive what God in Christ has done on our behalf, for us, and in our place so that we accept the proffered relationship of blessing. 'We do not presume to come to this your table, merciful Lord, trusting in our own right-eousness, but in your manifold and great mercies' is our proper response to this new covenant of which we are reminded every time we come to the Lord's Supper.

Christ who makes amends

All of us feel at some time in our lives the need to give concrete expression to our feelings of regret for what we have done. A mere verbal apology seems inadequate: so we offer as well a bottle of wine or a bunch of flowers, or perhaps breakfast in bed! It is all part of our embodiedness, a fact upon which this report has laid much stress. To achieve reconciliation, we need not only to say something, but to express that penitence and desire for a renewed relationship also in the language of our bodies. This was something of which medieval society was acutely aware, and from this arose a system of 'satisfactions', embodied ways of making amends: sometimes token, sometimes substantial – depending on the nature of the offence – but always symbolic of a desire for restored fellowship and mutual inter-dependency.

It is from this background that at the end of the eleventh century St Anselm, Archbishop of Canterbury from 1093 to 1109, developed the so-called Latin theory of the atonement, traces of which can still be found in the Prayer Book, as also in some of the imagery of the Reformers. Anselm was the greatest philosopher of his age, and so it is important when considering his position not to confuse the dryness of his argument in *Cur Deus Homo* with its intended religious implications, which can be more clearly ascertained in his prayers, or in his much briefer *Meditation on Human Redemption*.

The latter work ends with the plea: 'O Lord, draw my whole self into your love . . . let your love seize my whole being; let it possess me completely.' This, Anselm holds, is the only possible response once we understand what God has done in Christ. For, had we properly understood our situation before his intervention in our world, we should have seen how desperate our situation really was. To give a modern parallel, it was rather like those who have done some dreadful deed from which they know no release. In anguish they cry: 'I shall never be able to forgive myself!' and search endlessly for forms of reparation, none of which seems quite to do the trick. Similarly, we owe everything to God as our creator, and so the more conscious we become of that debt, the more anything we offer as amends seems hopelessly inadequate to match the mess we have made of things. Such gifts are in any case only returning to God what we have already received from his own bountiful generosity towards us.

So how is the process of amends to begin? What if God himself became human and helped us to achieve reconciliation? To give a modern analogy, it is as though a group of vandals having ruined a pensioner's home – and unable to afford the tools and equipment and lacking the know-how to right the situation – are joined by the pensioner working alongside them. Instead of youths resentful at an externally imposed community service order, the pensioner has become the catalyst for a radically new situation: one in which by his 'mucking in' the guilty youths are transformed from those who feel themselves merely to have 'done their time' into human beings who both desire and know themselves to be forgiven.

What we have here thus is not some purely legal exchange nor the simple following of a moral example, but God taking with the maximum seriousness our embodied condition. Our longing to say 'sorry' becomes increasingly incapable of realisation, the more we understand how far we have departed from the plan God intended for our world. But with that realisation can also come not only the cry 'How can I ever be forgiven?' but also the certainty of forgiveness in the conviction that God the Son became one of us and stood in solidarity with the mess that is the human condition. Through his embodiedness he was able to offer a life of perfect obedience and thus make perfect amends, a life which can now empower our own feeble efforts at amends as they are transformed through his ever-present life in us as the head of his continuing embodiedness, the Church.

Christ our representative

Among the various models of the atonement to be found in Scripture and the Christian tradition, that of Christ as our representative has particularly commended itself to modern Anglican theologians. This model of the atonement links up with the insights of Peter Abelard in the early twelfth century. The Abelardian interpretation is also known as the 'exemplarist' view – not because it takes Jesus Christ as a mere example to Christians but because the death of Christ is held to set forth or exemplify in an unparalleled way the love of God for estranged humanity, and at the same time to set forth or exemplify uniquely the authentic response of humanity to God – the response of penitence, faith, gratitude and love.

This tradition of reflection on the atonement sees Jesus Christ not as a mere individual, a solitary saviour who on the cross accomplished a remote transaction with God from which we can benefit by a legal fiction, but as a representative or corporate figure in whom the whole of humanity is really embodied and involved by virtue of the incarnation.

Scriptural support for this interpretation rests on the Gospels and the Epistles. The Gospels present the representative character of Jesus Christ in three ways. First, as the Son of Man (the truly human one and plenipotentiary of God: cf. Dan. 7.14; Luke 22.69). Second, as the Suffering Servant – the embodiment of Israel for the fulfilment of God's purpose (Mark 10.45; cf. Isa. 52–53). And, third, as the True Vine – the remnant of Israel, God's husbandry (John 15; cf. Isa. 5.1–7). Paul portrays Jesus Christ as the Last Adam (Rom. 5.12–21; 1 Cor. 15.20–8) and other Pauline letters speak of the new humanity in Christ (Col. 3.10; Eph. 4.24). The Epistle to the Hebrews depicts Jesus as one who shared our human lot to the full, was tested to the uttermost yet did not fail. He was qualified by his sufferings to offer himself to God and thereby to lead his people, as their forerunner or pioneer, into the presence of God (Heb. 2.10, 14–18; 4.14–16; 5.7–10; 12.2).

As the mediator between God and humanity, Jesus Christ represents in his person, and especially in his death on the cross, both God's gracious approach to lost humanity and the appropriate human response. On the one hand, he perfectly displays the compassionate love of God for estranged humanity. On the other hand, his outpoured love on the cross awakens in us a corresponding penitence, faith, love and obedience.

The representative perspective enables us to do justice to the redemptive significance of the broader context of the death of Christ – above all the incarnation, followed by Christ's ministry, active obedience, solidarity with sinners and outcasts, compassion, confrontation with evil and judgement on corrupt ecclesiastical structures – together with the resurrection, the ascension and the heavenly intercession of the risen Christ. Clearly it is vital to be able to integrate the events of Jesus' life before the passion into his saving work.

The western Christian tradition has tended to concentrate in a one-sided manner on the death of Christ at the expense of the incarnation and his 'active obedience'. This emphasis is reflected in the Book of Common Prayer. But in modern Anglican theology the balance has been redressed. The incarnational strand of Anglican Catholic theology, which was deeply influenced by the Greek Fathers (notably in Charles Gore), converged with developments in biblical scholarship that brought out the true humanity of the figure of Jesus of Nazareth in the Gospels. This influential conjunction of incarnational theology and biblical criticism tended to eclipse the atonement in the narrow sense (regarded as a decisive act accomplished at Calvary) by the incarnation, 'the cross by the crib', so to speak. In one phase of modern Anglican theology (represented by the contributors to *Lux Mundi* in 1889, and Archbishop William Temple) this emphasis on the representative humanity of Jesus Christ culminated in a 'Christocentric metaphysic' that attempted to 'explain' the world, rather than a redemptive gospel that radically changed the world. This concern with rational explanation went too far, as even Temple recognised. But the emphasis on the incarnation and the real humanity of Jesus enabled theologians to affirm the salvific significance of the whole person and action of Jesus Christ. As Benjamin Jowett put it in the mid-nineteenth century: 'Christ died for us in no other sense than he lived or rose again for us.' The report of the 1922 Doctrine Commission, *Doctrine in the Church of England* (1938) rightly insisted that 'the cross is not to be separated from the person of him who died upon it or from the content of his whole life. It is the consummation of the earthly life of Jesus' (p. 92). We need to hold together the life and death, the incarnation and crucifixion, the person and work of Christ our representative before God.

Salvation and a suffering God

The twentieth century has seen a radical shift in our understanding of the nature of God. Classical Christian theology presupposed a God whose bliss could not be touched by the pain of God's creation. God was invulnerable or 'impassible'. It followed from this presupposition that Christ could only suffer in his human nature, not in his divine nature. This assumption, which owes more to Greek philosophy than to the biblical presentation of the God of Israel and the Father of our Lord Jesus Christ, has undergone widespread collapse in the face of our intensified awareness, in the present century, of the scale and depth of human suffering. The traditional theology has been challenged by Protestant theologians such as Bonhoeffer and Moltmann, and Roman Catholic theologians such as Schillebeeckx and Küng. This perception of a God who freely makes himself vulnerable to the suffering of his creation has converged with the strand of atonement theory stemming from Abelard to create a new emerging consensus that has as its central conviction the solidarity of God in Christ with our sin and suffering.

It seems that the interpretation of the atonement which sees Christ as the embodiment of God's solidarity with human suffering best reflects our (admittedly selective) contemporary moral sensitivities. The theology of a reconciliation of humanity to God through God's bearing of human pain (as well as of human sin) has emerged from the massive human experience of affliction in the twentieth century – from the trenches of the First World War to the extermination camps of Nazi Europe, and from our deeper awareness of the darkness of mental illness to our growing realisation of the innumerable ways in which women have been exploited and oppressed. The gathering conviction that 'only the suffering God can help' (as Bonhoeffer wrote from prison) has led to widespread questioning of the traditional assumption that the divine nature cannot enter into or share human experience, especially suffering (the traditional doctrine of divine impassibility). A strong connection has thus been forged between the doctrine of the atonement and the acute theological problem of theodicy – of reconciling the course of the world with the nature of God. The only ultimately satisfactory response to the problem of unmerited or disproportionate suffering is to believe that our creator, through a wonderful act – at once of self-limitation and of self-expression, is present in the darkest affliction, shares our pain, bears our sorrows, and sustains us through it all, creating good in spite of evil, so revealing the true nature of divine power as showing mercy and pity.

These insights have hardly penetrated the official liturgies of the churches. But there is little doubt that the traditional patriarchal images of God as king, lord, judge, warrior, etc. that belong to the traditional vocabulary of atonement with its central themes of law, wrath, guilt, punishment and acquittal, leave many Christians cold and signally fail to move many people, young and old, who wish to take steps towards faith. These images do not correspond to the spiritual search of many people today and therefore hamper the Church's mission. In responding, through liturgical revision, to contemporary aspirations of spirituality, we might take our cue from W. H. Vanstone's reflections on the cross of Christ as revealing the heart of a fellow-suffering God (*Love's Endeavour, Love's Expense*)

These receive eloquent expression in his hymn which bears the title 'A Hymn to the Creator' and which may be found on the final two pages of his study *Love's Endeavour, Love's Expense*. We quote the last three verses of this hymn:

> Drained is love in making full;
> Bound in setting others free;
> Poor in making many rich;
> Weak in giving power to be.
>
> Therefore He Who Thee reveals
> Hangs, O Father, on that Tree
> Helpless; and the nails and thorns
> Tell of what Thy love must be.
>
> Thou art God; no monarch Thou
> Thron'd in easy state to reign;
> Thou art God, Whose arms of love
> Aching, spent, the world sustain.

Christ our sacrifice

Of all the biblical and traditional images of the atonement, that of Christ's death as a sacrifice to God is particularly problematic today. It is felt by many to be peculiarly open to abuse. A number of modern theologians have alerted us to the danger of sacrificial language being invoked to exploit and oppress the vulnerable. Feminist theologians have protested that exhortations to sacrifice, appealing to the sufferings of Christ, have hardly been distributed evenly between men and women in the history of the Christian Church. The example of Christ's sacrifice has been invoked to legitimate the burden of pain, drudgery, personal humiliation and social inferiority borne by women in a tradition that is overwhelmingly patriarchal, sexist and androcentric. The German theologian Jürgen Moltmann, who served on the Eastern Front in the

Second World War, suggests that the rhetoric of totalitarian militarism has rendered the language of sacrifice debased and unusable. Moltmann therefore declines to employ traditional terms like 'atoning sacrifice' to interpret the death of Christ. He does not believe that sacrifice can be understood in a humane and personalist way. Similarly, Hans Küng believes that sacrifice can only be used in connection with the death of Christ if it is detached from its Old Testament connection and pagan cultic background and used in an ethical and metaphorical sense for self-dedication in the face of suffering.

How should we respond to this veto on sacrificial imagery? To put a moratorium on all sacrificial language would be to cut ourselves off from one of the primary biblical images of salvation. A vital dimension of biblical revelation would be lost. Sacrifice is one of the most prominent images for the death of Christ in the New Testament. It is explicit in Ephesians 5.2 where Christ is described as 'an offering and a sacrifice to God'. There is a rich vocabulary of offering and sacrifice in Hebrews. The sacrificial motif is marked in the Johannine literature: the Lamb of God – probably the Passover lamb – (John 1.29, 36); the 'eucharistic' discourse in John 6; the 'High Priestly prayer' in John 17. Indeed, wherever in the New Testament we find the language of blood, covenant, expiation, cleansing, sanctifying, offering, eating and drinking, the sacrificial theme may not be far away.

So if we are to think in line with the Scriptures about the death of Christ, sacrifice must remain a normative model. However, we need constantly to be vigilant and sensitive to the unacceptable connotations and threatening reverberations that sacrificial language has for many thoughtful Christians today. Some of the difficulties and objections mentioned above can be defused if we bear in mind a number of points about the meaning of sacrifice.

To begin with, sacrifice is a fundamental sacred metaphor with a wide range of meanings and is not confined to cultic practice, to literal blood sacrifice. Etymologically it means to make holy. There is no 'orthodox' or received interpretation of sacrifice, either in Judaism or Christianity, to which we are bound. For Christians the sacrifice of Christ becomes definitive of all sacrifice and the criterion by which all invocations of 'sacrifice' are measured.

Sacrifice is not intrinsically violent. Even in the Old Testament sacrificial cultus, the death of the victim and any concomitant suffering was not a necessary aspect of sacrifice. Libations and cereal offerings were also sacrifices. Sacrifice is not necessarily propitiatory. Not all sacrifices in the Old Testament were of an atoning nature, intended to effect reconciliation between the people and their God. There were thanksgiving sacrifices and communion sacrifices as well as sin-offerings and guilt offerings. Old Testament sacrifice was far from dominated by expiation. Aquinas's view that 'a sacrifice, properly so called, is something done for that honour which is properly due to God, in order to appease him' is a one-sided restrictive interpretation of sacrifice.

Sacrifice is essentially about communion with God. While sacrifice is an image that is used in a variety of ways in the Bible and in Christian worship and theology, its central meaning is communication with God through an intermediate object that is both offered and received. Consistent with this is Augustine's classic definition that 'sacrifice is offered in every act which is designed to unite us with God in a holy fellowship'. Sacrifice seems to involve a transaction or exchange and this is taken up in the familiar New Testament equation 'the just for the unjust' (1 Pet. 3.18; cf. Rom. 5.6–21; 8.3f; 2 Cor. 5.21; Gal. 3.13 – all of which arguably imply a broadly sacrificial framework), sacrifice involves 'a pattern of interchange'.

Sacrifice is set within a gracious, God-given relationship. Sacrifice is given its effectiveness as communication with God through its setting in a covenant relationship – that mutual commitment and spiritual marriage graciously initiated by God and accepted by God's people – both in the Old Testament and in the New. Hence the trouble taken by the four Evangelists to link Christ's passion to the Passover season, when God's redemptive, covenant-giving act in the Exodus was celebrated. This connection becomes explicit in Paul's affirmation: 'Christ our Passover is sacrificed for us' (1 Cor. 5.7)

Finally, this interpretation of sacrifice is grounded in the Old Testament as well as in the New. There is already a critique of cultic sacrifice within the Old Testament: for example in the Psalms (Ps. 50.13f: 'Do I eat the flesh of bulls, or drink the blood of goats? Offer to God a sacrifice of thanksgiving, and pay your vows to the Most High') and in the prophets (Hos. 6.6: 'I desire steadfast love and not sacrifice, the knowledge of God rather than burnt offerings'). This prophetic interpretation of sacrifice points to the fundamental ethical and devotional meaning of the concept of sacrifice. In Hebrews, Christ's sacrificial death is interpreted in terms of his ethical obedience to the will of God. Christian sacrifice is primarily the dedication of our lives to the service of God in gratitude for all that we have received in Christ (Rom. 12.1) Rightly understood, it is subversive of all attempts by one group to exploit, abuse and oppress another.

Christ the victor

Although the biblical tradition repudiates any ultimate dualism, in a fallen and sinful world the forces of evil are powerful, dominating and deceiving. The God who creates the world and sees that it is very good is the righteous God who judges and condemns evil, working to liberate his children from the idolatry of false gods, enslavement to the principalities and powers of this world, and the ultimate denial of meaning in death. The powers of evil that dominate and destroy are seen as both the tyrannies of the political order in this world and superhuman forces. In the apocalyptic writings a cosmic battle between good and evil, the angelic hosts of heaven and the demonic forces which enslave humanity, provides a dramatic context for the ultimate triumph of God in the day of salvation, when God's will is perfectly done and God's Kingdom comes.

The New Testament writers see the redemption achieved by Jesus as the definitive victory of God over the power of sin and evil. In Jesus the rule of God is present and God's Kingdom comes. In the power of the Spirit Jesus casts out demons and heals the sick. One of the prominent themes of St John's Gospel is the understanding of Jesus' ministry as a conflict between light and darkness. In going to Jerusalem he engages in the last battle; he is judged by religious and political leaders, but in reality he is the Truth which judges them. In the end, nailed to the cross like a criminal, he nonetheless reigns as king. As the darkness over the land engulfs the one who claimed to be the Light of the World, Jesus dies, and death seems victorious, the powers of evil have triumphed. But although he enters the domain of death and darkness, sharing to the full our human mortal destiny, death is not the end. From death he is raised in triumph. New life is born in the grave, the powers of death and evil are defeated, the Day of the Lord comes, and, as the first-fruits of God's new creation, Christ is raised to new and endless life, and he bestows this Easter life as the eternal life he shares with his people in baptism.

In the icons of eastern Christendom the resurrection is portrayed as the 'harrowing of hell' (a theme dramatised in the apocryphal Gospel of Nicodemus and powerfully portrayed in medieval miracle plays). Christ defeats the powers of evil, Satan and his minions are bound, the imprisoning gates of hell are broken open, and Christ grasps the hands of Adam and Eve, the representative figures of all humanity, to lead them from death to life. Our Easter hymns echo this ancient understanding:

> From hell's devouring jaws the prey
> Alone our Leader bore.
> Earth's ransomed hosts pursue their way
> Where he hath gone before.

The cross is seen as the place where:

> Death and Life have contended
> In a conflict all stupendous;
> The Prince of Life who died
> Lives and reigns immortal.

In the Orthodox Liturgy, as Christ's resurrection is proclaimed, words from an Easter sermon of St John Chrysostom ring out: 'Christ is risen and the demons are fallen! Christ is risen and hell has lost its prey! Christ is risen and Life reigns!'

This vivid pictorial language has had a particular influence on liturgy, particularly the liturgy of Holy Week and Easter, where it is well adapted to depict the drama of salvation. Theologically it reflects the deeply rooted sense of the Christian Passover, which holds together Good Friday and Easter, the passion and the resurrection, a resurrection fulfilled in the ascension in which the principalities and powers are seen being led captive by the ascending Christ (Eph. 4.8; Col. 2.15) Of all the images of the atonement, the theme of the victory of Christ over sin, evil and death is the only one to hold the cross and resurrection closely together. The cosmic Christ, who fills all things, has destroyed all that imprisons. The liberation he offers is good news to the poor, and the hope of eternal life in the face of death. 'Death has been swallowed up in victory. Where, O death, is your victory? Where, O death, is your sting?' (I Cor. 15.54f) In the victory of love won through sacrifice, the kingdoms of this world have indeed become the kingdom of our God and of his Christ (Rev. 11.15)

Christ's victory overcomes the world, and Christians are those who are called to live in the power of that victory. This Easter faith gives strength to the martyrs of this and every age, and underlies the Christian protest against tyranny and oppression. The reality of evil which engulfs and enslaves nations and peoples, known in this century in the Holocaust, the killing fields of Cambodia, and the tribal genocide of Rwanda, is countered by the victory of the love of God who in Christ freely chose to plumb the depths of hell and the darkness of death. The gospel of the resurrection gives to us a hope, that 'neither death, nor life, nor angels, nor rulers, nor things present, nor things to come, nor powers, nor height, nor depth, nor anything else in all creation, will be able to separate us from the love of God in Christ Jesus our Lord' (Rom. 8.38f).

Chapter 6
Receiving the gift

A treasury of images

In previous chapters we have observed how both in the Bible and in the subsequent history of the Church writers ransacked, as it were, the treasure-house of metaphor in order to convey the full impact of our Lord upon their lives. Thus within the New Testament the image now is of ransom from slavery, now of victory over supernatural powers, now of sacrificial victim, here of deliverance from bondage in Egypt, there of restored health from blindness or some other debilitating infirmity, now of reconciliation with enemies, now of bringing to birth new life, and so the list might continue. It is a pattern which is then repeated in later centuries. For, though at times one image may seem to dominate, further investigation discloses others just bubbling beneath the surface. So, for instance, though the image of victory was most dominant in Christianity's first millennium and then seemed to decline, not only did it find a major place in Luther's theology, it continues to be reflected in some of the hymns we sing today (e.g. 'Sing my tongue the glorious battle'; 'The royal banners forward go'). Again, penal imagery, though it only becomes dominant at the Reformation, has clear antecedents as early as Athanasius in the fourth century. This is an argument which can be repeated for almost all the principal metaphors, and so, as we noted in the previous chapter in introducing the various 'angles of vision' with which that chapter ends, it would seem a mistake to search for a single 'theory' of the atonement and its appropriation. Instead, we should, so far as possible, draw on the whole range of this rich imagery, while fully acknowledging that now one, now another may have been proved more fruitful either in the wide range of historical circumstances with which the Church has been confronted in its mission, or for particular Christians in their practice of discipleship even within the same historical period.

One key factor affecting choice of imagery concerns where the stress is put, on salvation as escape from something unpleasant or as the realisation of some good. It is a tension which one finds reflected in both the Greek and the Latin words for salvation, which depending on context can mean either being brought to safety from a position of peril, or a making whole and healthy, or both. Unfortunately in English the term is all but confined to theology, but the two senses are well illustrated by the French use of the ordinary word for safety (*salut*) and the German resort to a word (*Heil*) whose normal resonances are those of health. Other religions of course exhibit a similar tension, sometimes speaking of release from such things as ignorance, sin, death, punishment or suffering and at others more of an ultimate goal in fullness of being, though where this is held to involve loss of personal identity (as in some eastern religions) it clearly stands at a considerable remove from Christian understandings of what could be meant by such fullness of being. In what follows we shall seek to give due weight to both these aspects, but given the prominence of the former in the New Testament, it is appropriate that we should begin with the question of what it is from which we are saved.

Salvation as our deliverance: sin and forgiveness

In what is perhaps salvation's most familiar sense, Matthew opens his Gospel by explaining Jesus' very name in these terms: 'you are to name him Jesus, for he will save his people from their sins' (Matt. 1.21). A similar present stress is not uncommon elsewhere in the New Testament (e.g. Luke 1.77; John 1.29; Eph. 2.5). But also frequent (and perhaps predominant in Paul) is reference to a future rescue, from the forthcoming divine wrath. Jesus is the one 'who delivers us from the wrath to come' (1 Thess. 1.10) and that is why we can talk of 'the hope of our salvation' (5.8). Such a stress was almost certainly conditioned in part by expectation of the imminence of the world's end ('salvation is nearer to us now than when we became believers', Rom. 13.11). This may explain why the theme is less prominent in later strands of the New Testament. But, whether or not there is such a change of perspective, this should not blind us to the permanent validity of the underlying issue, that as Christians we need not only to be delivered from the sins of our past but also from our continuing sins, including those that will remain clinging to us on the Day of Judgement. Such language thus highlights the Christian hope that not only now but on that day also forgiveness will be ours in Christ. So, though elsewhere in the report much consideration has already been given both to the work of Jesus on the cross and to his future role, here we ought not to omit how these two aspects impinge upon the present reality of our lives as Christians.

> Bearing shame and scoffing rude,
> In my place condemned he stood,
> Sealed my pardon with his blood.

So runs one verse of the familiar hymn 'Man of Sorrows', and dating from the nineteenth century its use of penal imagery is almost as predictable as was the battle metaphor we quote earlier from two sixth-century hymns. For many Christians today the notion of God offering himself as a substitute to be punished for our sins is deeply repellent. Morally they recoil from such a narrowly retributive conception of human justice, far less divine. But from that we should not infer that the image has lost all appropriateness, as we consider the impact of Christ's death upon ourselves. Far from it. Indeed, arguably in a world which has lost any deep consciousness of sin there remains a version which can speak very powerfully to our own day.

There is of course the characteristic New Testament imagery of cost, as in Paul's phrase 'bought with a price' (1 Cor. 6.20), that underlines the costliness to God of our salvation; behind it lies implicitly the recognition of how great our value is to God. One may also observe that even someone hostile to penal imagery might still find singing 'There was no other good enough to pay the price of sin' a powerful reminder of the way in which sin always has its innocent victims. They might also recall the way in which it is so often the case that it is the innocent who must take the costly initiative in correcting the consequences of others' sin, as with the bomb-disposal expert who risks life and limb to immobilise the device which threatens many lives. But among modern theologians it is perhaps Karl Barth who comes closest to giving a generally acceptable sense to penal imagery. Though excluding any necessity for punishment, he uses the metaphor to show how consciousness of judgement and forgiveness might be effected in the one and the same act. In his short work *Dogmatics in Outline* he writes that 'in the strict sense there is no consciousness of sin except in the light of Christ's Cross' (p. 119). Though, if taken literally, this must be an exaggeration (as the Old Testament's consciousness of sin amply illustrates), nonetheless there is an important sense in which reflection on the events surrounding Jesus' death can heighten our sense both of sin and of the forgiveness that comes with it. As we read the story of Jesus, what we discover is the wickedness and weakness in ourselves, the Judas who betrays his friend, the Caiaphas not open to new possibilities, the Pilate wanting the easy way out, the faltering Peter, and so on. This innocent man sent to his death was not sent there by the scum of humanity but by the humanity in each and every one of us that is all too capable of acting as scum, even ordinary English villagers as in Stanley Spencer's powerfully evocative paintings of the passion based on Cookham in Berkshire. Yet that same discovery of the depths of human wickedness also reveals its cure. For this innocent man was also God incarnate and yet that, so far from merely intensifying the crime, also provides its resolution as he offers forgiveness from the cross. We have discovered the worst that we are capable of doing both to our fellow human beings and to God; yet God forgives.

But what are we to understand by such forgiveness? Here it is important to be clear about the sense in which it is and the sense in which it is not a blotting out of the past. Sin is constituted by all the wrong deeds and thoughts which make us fail to hit the mark of the kind of people God intended us to be, all the badness in us that alienates us from his goodness and holiness. To suggest that at one fell swoop all that disappeared would be to reduce our faith to an implausible fairytale. Rather, what happens is that God assures us of a new status as we throw ourselves on his mercy, upon that offer of forgiveness from the cross. Not only does he make explicit the worth he has already assigned to us in creating us, he declares that worth to be absolute in his eyes, despite all the evidence we have created to the contrary. Thereby we are freed for a new future, one in which we can now be confident of our own worth, that value that has been accorded us by God, and so there ceases to be any need for self-justification, for in any sense proving to others or to God that we are indeed of some worth or importance. The result is not only a new status for us vis-à-vis God as accepted and forgiven in Christ but also a new status in respect of our relationships with fellow human beings. Indeed, these relationships are now profoundly altered. For one of the major occasions for sin is self-assertion, nagging doubts about our own worth leading us aggressively to prove it by gaining advantage over others. At a stroke, such a motivation is slain, and the Christian acquires a freedom and confidence unknown to unredeemed humanity.

But that this much can be instantaneous should not be allowed to conceal from us the more gradual character of much else. Anyone who has ever been faced with the possibility of forgiving a burglar knows how much more complicated the issue can be. In that case not only are there wider social issues – reporting the crime to the police, social expectations of punishment and so forth – there is the obvious practical point that ostentatiously to forgive would be to invite a spate of further burglaries! But the point is certainly of wider application. All of our actions carry with them consequences which may not admit of easy or immediate remedy. So it no more follows that the penitent burglar of today can escape all the consequences of his actions than could the penitent thief who continued to hang on his cross despite Jesus' gift of forgiveness.

This is a point which needs much stressing as there is a natural human desire for a totally new start, which is fine if it is possible, but so often it is achieved only at the cost of concealing from ourselves the continuing consequences in the present of our past bad actions. Take, for instance, the modern habit of declaring that no one is to blame for the breakup of a marriage. No doubt this is sometimes true, but one suspects that more commonly the explanation constitutes an unwillingness on the part of both partners to face the truth, to acknowledge the flaws in themselves. And is not the presence of these defects highlighted by the fact that second marriages are even more likely to end in divorce than first? Or take another common, but equally problematic declaration: 'I don't want just your acceptance, I want your approval.' Loving acceptance is declared not to be enough. What the person wants is a declaration they are just as good as the next person. In one sense this is of course true: we all stand in need of the mercy of God. But what it ignores is the obvious ways in which it is not true: not all of us are liars, adulterers or whatever. One illustration of this attitude is the way in which prisoners commonly place their own crimes on the right side of some imaginary divide: 'Everyone engages in a financial fiddle somewhere, even if it is just their income tax form'; 'She was asking for it anyway'; and so on, with only child molesters in the end left beyond the pale. Clearly such attitudes make reform of the prisoner difficult, but much the same could be said of those of us who may never see the inside of a prison cell but are equally indulgent of our own particular failings. It is almost as though what is desired is an easy society of mutual endorsement, whereas what the Bible calls us to is realistic repentance and a gradual appropriation under God of the full implications of what is meant by the indwelling of the Holy Spirit: 'God's temple is holy, and that temple you are' (1 Cor. 3.16–17).

It is interesting in this connection to contrast such attitudes with an allegedly more corrupt world, that of the Middle Ages. Corruptions there no doubt were, but at least there was full recognition of the arduous path before us. This can be seen even at the heart of its corruptions, in its penitential system, which had its origin in the severity of the Celtic penitential rules, but even if we look only to preaching, a similar seriousness is to be observed. For drawing on authorities such as Augustine and Gregory the Great, the raising of Lazarus (John 11.38–44) became the favoured text for explaining our need for continued repentance and re-formation throughout our Christian lives. Sin, it was argued, was as bad as the death of Lazarus, with the stone against the tomb a symbol of our hard-heartedness, and burial 'the load of sinful habit pressing down upon us', our only possible release being Christ's summons out of the grave and the Church's help in loosening our bandages (v. 44). Those who took their faith seriously were thus left in no doubt (nor should we be) of the fact that, despite being forgiven, throughout a Christian's life there will continue to be the need to die afresh to sin, so that through God's grace we may live once more. To quote the exhortation to godparents with which the Prayer Book Service of Baptism ends: we are 'to follow the example of our Saviour Christ, and be made like unto him; that as he died and rose again for us, so should we who are baptized, die from sin and rise again unto righteousness, *continually* mortifying all our evil and corrupt affections, and *daily* proceeding in all virtue and godliness of living'.

Then in due course will come that other aspect of salvation as deliverance which we said we would discuss, escape from the divine wrath in the judgement that is to come. It would be unfortunate if, bewitched by the metaphor, we failed to take the notion of divine wrath seriously. We should not of course think of God seething with temper and resentment, ready to 'zap' us with his thunderbolt in due course, should we not obey him. The intention of the image is to tell us that God is utterly opposed to selfishness, social injustice and ruthless exploitation of resources. It tells us of the seriousness with which God regards human sin, that, though psychology and sociology may help explain the conditions which lead to the act, they do not exonerate: human wickedness remains a reality which precludes enjoyment of the vision of perfect goodness which is God.

What allows us to escape that judgement is not that we have necessarily passed beyond the point of wickedness. It is a commonplace to observe that it is usually the greatest saints who are most acutely aware of their own sin, but – more insidious and more problematic – it is not unknown for an otherwise saintly individual to have (unacknowledged by him or her) a character which is fundamentally flawed, for instance through pride or lack of self-perception. So it is certainly not passing beyond sin which makes the difference; rather, it is a matter of remembering that inseparable from the divine judgement is the Father running to embrace the prodigal son (Luke 15.20) and the outstretched arms on the cross which welcomed the penitent theif (Luke 23.34).

Suffering

If our discussion thus far has been along essentially the right lines, one interesting correction needs to be made to one of the most common contrasts drawn between Christianity's understanding of salvation and related concepts in other religions. For it is often said that western and eastern Christendom differ precisely in this, in what they see as the source of the problem: that whereas western Christians identify factors such as sin and death, eastern Christians locate this in ignorance. However, if the analysis given above is correct, then the twentieth-century decline in consciousness of sin has in fact brought us closer to the eastern understanding. For, as we argued above, forgiveness is always accompanied by, and perhaps only properly comes through, a simultaneous discovery of the depths of one's own depravity.

But, if that is now a point of analogy, a major contrast remains in attitudes to suffering. For, whereas Hinduism and Buddhism both see salvation as requiring detachment from suffering, central to the Christian claim is its potentially, redemptive quality. The aim is not so much escape from it, as a willingness to give it a new significance, a fresh dimension. However, this is not to say that the Christian should invite suffering; only that, should it befall, then it has the capacity to bear a redemptive quality, just as Christ's suffering also worked for the good. Moreover, Christians committed not only to praying for God's kingdom to come, but to working for it, may well find that commitment leads beyond hungering and thirsting for right into suffering for it, as in the long tradition of Christian martyrdom that began with Stephen and has continued in our own day with the many who risk torture or death for their faith. We need to remember that 'martyrdom' literally means 'witness', and thus that someone like Sheila Cassidy, tortured in Chile for treating wounded revolutionaries, was no less a martyr than Oscar Romero, assassinated for attempting to relieve the conditions of the poor in El Salvador.

But before considering further this question of suffering's potential role, the issue must first be set in its wider context. In ordering the world, God chose to give human beings freedom in such a way that it became possible for them to choose to rebel against him; in short, God valued that choice more than the production of mere automata who always obeyed the divine will. A tragic dimension therefore entered into the divine decision to create a world of the kind in which we live. God might have created one without suffering in which automata who looked like us always did what was right, but instead, because he wanted us freely to choose to love him, he risked a world from which the Lover must stand at a distance from the beloved, waiting and longing to be invited, yet at the same time knowing all the suffering which we as human beings are capable of imposing upon one another. The atheist declares the result not worth the candle, but before the Christian engages in oversimplistic debate, what needs to be recognised is that what is at stake has nothing to do with differing estimates of how much suffering there is in the world. Rather, it is all a matter of two entirely different, clashing value systems, with opposing estimates of the worth of that freedom and the resultant life which it makes possible. The Christian insists that God has personally encountered and disarmed human rebellion by taking the full force of it upon himself; not only did God by entering into our suffering on the cross endorse human protest against unjust suffering by identifying with that protest in his own cry of agony, he exhibited human freedom in accepting the cross, he honoured that same freedom in allowing himself to be nailed to it, and granted real freedom to us by opening up to us possibilities for new life. Moreover, no human suffering need be unmitigated; compassion is called forth by people needing help; courage flourishes in situations of fear, and so forth. This is not to say that the good result justifies the occurrence of some particular suffering or evil, but it can go some way to ameliorate it, and even to redeem it.

One further tragic dimension needs to be mentioned. Much, though not all, suffering that occurs is essentially arbitrary, and part of the reason that it is felt to be evil is precisely because it is inexplicable and undeserved. (We do not think to blame God for things which we have brought upon ourselves, though we may protest at such suffering.) It is for this reason that there is a thread of Old Testament witness which simply will not allow the easy connection found in other parts between rightness before God and prosperity. Such questioning as to why the wicked flourish is to be seen in some of the psalms, while the obverse side of the coin, the righteous suffering, is explored at length in the Book of Job. The New Testament is equally emphatic against any simple equation of suffering with deserts, or even attempts to lay blame (cf. Luke 13.4; John 9.2–3), even though it is also clear that none is guiltless before God.

In creating the world, God's plan involved the regular operation of laws for the natural order. Generally they are beneficial and proportionate; for instance, pain has at its root a fundamentally beneficial purpose, in warning us to take action, but sadly sometimes such action may well be beyond our present powers. On other occasions, generally beneficial laws can turn evil for all sorts of reasons, some beyond our present knowledge. Of course, God knew that suffering was a consequence of his creation, but it does not follow from this that he wills individual suffering. To suggest that all suffering arises for a person as a result of the divine plan, as if earthquake, cancer and so forth were deliberately intended to strike one individual rather than another, would make God sound like a moral monster. But we must also admit that occasionally Christians believe themselves to be called to suffer for their faith, and in freedom are able to respond. Equally, in suffering, they, and others are free to accept it, fight it, or overcome it, depending on what is the most appropriate response to the kind of suffering that it is. Later, finding God's grace in the midst of it, they can sometimes talk about it almost *as if* God caused it for this good effect, seeing parallels between their own suffering and the cross of Christ.

It is against such a background that the Christian's more positive understanding of suffering should be set. It is not that tragedy is absent from the world. The inevitability of it is at the very heart of God's decision to create, as Revelation reminds us, with its talk of 'the book of life of the Lamb slain from the foundation of the world' (Rev. 13.8 av). Nor is it that God willed the pain of any particular individual: its essentially arbitrary quality should not be denied. Rather, the point is that through divine grace the possibility is there for its creative transformation, certainly in the response of others to the person experiencing the pain as their love and compassion are deepened, but also often in the people who are themselves experiencing the pain.

Of course one should not underestimate the debilitating power of much suffering, whether physical or otherwise. Yet it is true that, at least for the northern hemisphere, there never has been a period in history in which it has been so easily subject to human control. Think for instance of life before the invention of modern anaesthetics! But it is not for us to judge how others face pain. Human beings have very different psychological capacities. In response to the same physiological intensity of pain it may take little effort for one individual to continue working normally, while for another not only is early retirement and constant care necessary but it takes a supreme effort for that individual not to slip back into self-pity and resentment against all those better off. The point rather is that God offers each of us the necessary help or grace to respond positively in our situation, to the degree to which our psychology and antecedent experience permit. In other words, what is possible will vary enormously from individual to individual, and it certainly does not mean that the Christian must be able to accept his suffering without any inner conflict: some of the psalms and lives of the saints give ample endorsement to the need to work through towards acceptance, in the meantime giving full vent to one's natural resentment against God.

But more than psalter and saint one can appeal pre-eminently to the crucified one himself. Certainly the crucifixion's redemptive quality is seen most obviously in the fact that it was through such dreadful suffering that the supreme benefit for humanity came, the guarantee of divine forgiveness. But it is not just the possibility of external benefit to others to which it bears witness. Because our Lord fully entered into our humanity, it also demonstrates how such a transformation can be effected internally. For whether we compare the last words from the cross in Mark and Matthew with Luke and John or simply take Mark in isolation, the evidence suggests that Jesus' initial reaction to his suffering was that of all of us – fear, depression and uncertainty. But through prayer he moved beyond that to confident assurance in the ultimate loving purposes of his heavenly Father – a confidence which we can find detected in either the conclusion of the psalm from which he quotes the initial verse in Mark and Matthew or in the last words attributed to him in Luke and John. He is there then alongside us in our suffering as one who understands in the deepest sense of that term.

Salvation as our transformation: transforming grace and human freedom

Our discussion of suffering has already taken us beyond the more negative aspects of salvation as release to its more positive side, of how it can also effect our transformation. Though more prominent in later strands, this notion also finds its appropriate echo in Scripture. Particularly fine is the image used in 1 Peter: 'Like newborn infants, long for the pure, spiritual milk, so that by it you may grow into salvation' (1 Pet. 2.2). But occasionally Paul also talks of us 'being saved' (e.g. 1 Cor. 1.18), and indeed on one occasion even stresses its provisional character, as depending upon our response: 'Now I would remind you, brothers and sisters, of the good news that I proclaimed to you, . . . through which also you are being saved, if you hold firmly to the message that I proclaimed to you' (1 Cor. 15.1–2).

At this point it would be all too easy to allow traditional Reformation disputes to raise once more their divisive head, and to set grace and freedom, faith and works firmly in opposition to one another. But now through the welcome efforts of ecumenists in the churches it is possible for us frankly to acknowledge faults on both sides. So afraid has the Protestant tradition been of admitting anything whatsoever which might appear to detract from the absolute priority of grace that it has tended to ignore the key role assigned by Paul to works – passages which, if pulled out of context, might easily be mistaken for extracts from the Epistle of James! Romans 3.28 ('We hold that a person is justified by faith apart from works prescribed by the law') and James 2.24 ('You see that a person is justified by works and not by faith alone') may seem irreconcilably opposed, but in fact for Paul as much as for James good conduct is an indispensable element in our relation with God – 'faith working through love', as Galatians (5.6) puts it. One further difficulty with traditional Protestant approaches has been the way in which in their overspecification of the content of faith they themselves had been in constant danger of introducing a new system of merit, one based this time on intellectual belief rather than practical works. None of this is of course to deny the equally serious faults on the Catholic side, particularly in the degenerate scholasticism which treated 'created grace' as though once granted it then operated as a power at the individual's disposal, able to act quite independently of God, instead of as the medium of a continuing and personal relationship between creator and creature.

Against that we must emphatically assert the absolute priority of grace, that the initiative at every stage is always God's, not ours. But this is entirely compatible with acknowledging a key human contribution, that God carries us no further than our wills assent; hence the appropriateness of T. S. Eliot's repeated prayer in the Four Quartets, 'make perfect our will', or the Prayer Book request to 'make us to love that which thou dost command' (Collect for Trinity 14). How else are we to explain that sadly all too common phenomenon of otherwise outstanding Christian souls who have nonetheless totally blocked God from some aspect of their lives? The pride or self-deceit are all too obvious to the rest of us, but God chooses not to act, because he values something more, our free human response. At the same time we need to acknowledge that the free response need not always be fully conscious. For instance, as a way of making the terrible reality tolerable a woman who has been sexually abused as a child may throw all the blame upon herself. Yet there is also a deeper level at which she knows the truth, and, through response to which, God can eventually draw her into a starker, yet fuller and healthier reality.

One suspects that a major factor in generating Reformation and Counter-Reformation positions was their cultural background in Renaissance individualism, a stress which has of course continued to accelerate until our own day. For, so long as one thinks in purely personal terms of one individual (me) confronting another (Christ), it is all too easy to suppose that some sort of conscious transaction must take place, with our decision of faith or good action in turn generating a divine decision (justification) or action (gift of created grace). But that of which both Bible and early Church speak is of something much more intimate, of our personal identities transcended in such a way that all that we do, including faith, is not really ours at all but God's work in us – 'yet not I but Christ in me', as Paul puts it at one point (Gal. 2.20). Certainly the major Reformers as also the Counter-Reformation Council of Trent sought to avoid the worst of these faults, but the way in which the modern inheritors of the Reformation can so easily slip into talk of 'our decision of faith', a phrase Luther or Calvin would never have used, illustrates how easily the individualism which has been growing since at least the Renaissance can trap us into an inadequate grasp of the process of salvation. For the primary stress should be neither on our own faith nor on our own works, but on the gracious initiative of God, working at all levels and not just that of our conscious selves, and indeed working not just directly upon us but also indirectly through those with whom we live and work, as well as in the prayers of others, whether known to us or otherwise.

Our new identity in Christ

In the Old Testament the social assumptions implicit in this way of viewing things were given expression in a corporate understanding of the nation or its remnant. Such an idea continues into the New, with our interdependence upon one another within the Church continually stressed. But there is also something new, and wonderfully profound. For the divine presence is no longer externalised but seen as constitutive of the very identity of the Church, particularly in Paul's image of her as the Body of Christ and John's of the vine and its branches. It was a position which was then reinforced when the Church extended its mission into the

Greek world. For a basic assumption of Platonism is that something only has reality in so far as it imitates or participates in the perfect exemplar of its kind (the theory of forms), and so through much of the Fathers' writings runs this subtext, that we are only really truly human in so far as we participate in the perfect human being, Jesus our Lord. It is also this same subtext which explains the recurring patristic theme of salvation as deliverance from death. It is not that Christ's resurrection offers hope for our own. Something much deeper is at stake: because Christ's humanity is infused with the power of divinity, we too can hope to share in divinity's characteristic attribute, eternal life, in so far as we become part of that humanity through participation.

The modern reader may find such mystical language obfuscating, but it is worth wrestling with, as it is as much biblical as patristic. How else are we to interpret verses such as 'as all die in Adam, so will all be made alive in Christ' (1 Cor. 15.22)? Paul is comparing the two human natures by which our identity may be given: one which rebelled and the other which embodied a life of perfect obedience. As 'Adam' is the Hebrew for man, it was possible to think more easily in inclusive terms, so that 'Adam' could come to stand for all human beings, both male and female, under the old order, just as Christ would include all under the new. Such an understanding is also a recurrent theme in the writings of the Church Fathers as they seek to explicate what they understand by the Nicene Creed's phrase, 'he became man': the Greek verb cognate with *anthropos* is taken to mean not that he became a male person (though of course he was that), but that he was inclusive in the widest sense. He was not only a human being, not only definitive of what it is to be a human being (though again he was of course all of that), he was also the human being whose presence within us can save and transform all humankind. This does not mean the destruction of our individual personalities, but it does imply that we do not only exist as individuals; as part of Christ's Body, the Church, we are part of something much larger than ourselves, as Christ's humanity suffuses our own in ways not always accessible to our conscious selves. Unfortunately, English, unlike Greek or Latin, has hitherto used only one term, 'man', for both 'male' and 'male and/or female', whereas other modern languages are able to translate less ambiguously as in German's *ist Mensch geworden* (not *Mann*). But the English 'man' did at least have one merit in terms of this tradition of understanding: it could be used generically of humanity as a whole as well as referring to a specific individual. Such language of incorporation into the perfect humanity that is Christ's finds its natural application in the sacraments.

In Romans 5–6 Paul develops his baptismal theology through a contrast between Adam and Christ which seems to assume the historicity of

Adam ('sin came into the world through one man and death through sin'). Even if we now read Genesis 3 rather differently, as the story of each and every one of us, Paul's basic point surely stands. In baptism we are symbolically moved out of the sphere of influence of 'fallen humanity', all those social influences around us that incline towards sin and which are prior to any conscious choices of our own. Then instead of being subject to such 'original' sin, all the sin that is prior to any reflection on our part, we are granted the presence of the Holy Spirit in our lives, there to conform us to the image of Christ, the definitive human being, will we but let him. Yet what is offered is more than mere conformity. We become one with him, a true part of his Body as the humanity God intended us to be. To extend the Pauline image, we have become his hands and his feet. For, as St Teresa of Avila once put it, 'Christ has now no body on earth but yours, no hands but yours; yours are the eyes through which to look with Christ's compassion at the world, yours are the feet, with which he is to go about doing good.' Through baptism Christ can thus become the primary social force working in and through us, gradually replacing the wider society in which we are set and to whose less healthy influences we can so easily fall prey without even being aware that this has happened.

Baptism, like Eucharist, is an essentially social activity. One cannot baptise oneself, and that very fact points us to the reality that being a member of Christ can never be only about the individual and Jesus, but about joining the company of all the faithful, in this life and the next. Being baptised, and continuing to enjoy in the Eucharist all the benefits of Christ's passion, commits us to one another and the whole creation for which Christ died. Baptism projects us into the ecumenical enterprise, for we all belong together in Christ; and, more widely, it projects us into the ministry of reconciliation, for God was in Christ reconciling the *world* to himself.

Such a life of increasing identification with Christ is also conveyed sacramentally in the Eucharist. By eating his Body and drinking his Blood and by feeding on him by faith we strengthen our identification with him, and thus continue one with him, part of his Body as the humanity God intended us to be. Therein lies the justification for those who insist that the Nicene Creed should continue to speak of Christ becoming 'man' (in some wider or more inclusive sense of the kind already outlined) and not only 'a man'. For the Fathers were right that what we identify with is a humanity valid for all ages, not the various idiosyncrasies of first-century Palestine which scholarship may happen to discover. That is why he comes to us in the Eucharist not as a stranger from a remote age but as the Lord of every age.

At this point it would be very easy to get side-tracked into a discussion of the sense in which he 'comes'. Paul speaks of some dying as a result of profaning the Body and Blood of the Lord (1 Cor. 11.27), and ever since most Christians have sensed that the Eucharist is an awesome mystery in which they are participating, one in which they are privileged to share in Christ's presence in a distinctive way. At times this has led to a crude and distorting literalism. However, more precise definitions of that presence have more often than not hindered rather than helped the building up of the Christian community. Elizabeth I wisely foreshortened controversy by declaring:

> Christ was the word who spake it,
> Christ took the bread and brake it,
> And what his word doth make it
> That I believe and take it.

Much more important than reviving old disputes is to identify that to which the symbolism points. As Cranmer put it, God the Father 'does assure us thereby . . . that we are very members incorporate in the mystical body of his Son'. What that means is the transformation of our lives both personally and socially through divine grace.

Our sacrifice in his

In the past, our personal transformation has often been understood in excessively passive terms, with the traditional theology of the Eucharist, whether Protestant or Catholic, unfortunately merely reinforcing such passivity. Thus the characteristic Protestant stress on thankfulness, ascribing all to God, has not always escaped degeneration into quietism and dismissal of the necessity of action on our part. Similarly, the traditional Catholic stress on a providentially ordered, hierarchical world has at times produced its own tragic consequences in the unnecessary acceptance of suffering, as the poor find their only relief in their identification with the suffering Christ of whom the liturgy speaks. One place that this has been most evident is in Latin America, and against such a backdrop present-day liberation theology surely represents a very understandable and natural revolt.

Christian endorsement of such passivity, whether Protestant or Catholic, has often found expression in the notion of 'sacrifice'. But the word 'sacrifice' literally means being made dedicated or consecrated to God, and so should more properly suggest not a giving up of something but some positive offering. Certainly, quiet acceptance, even resignation, can be on occasion the appropriate response, but in general we should see ourselves as summoned to action. This is not to suggest as an alternative endless activity. There remains a vital role for receptivity and response both in relation to God and to our fellow human beings. But such a capacity to listen and to react still remains essentially different from pure passivity, with us then like wet sponges merely absorbing whatever befalls us. Instead, we should see ourselves as called to let Christ's Spirit invade us, so that all we do, whether by action or response, is made sacred, made holy.

In this sense, we offer our whole lives as a positive sacrifice of joy and thanksgiving, as well as being willing to suffer birthpangs to bring new life to birth. Certainly not all that Paul lists under 'the fruit of the Spirit' could be described as passive – 'love, joy, peace, patience, kindness, generosity, faithfulness, gentleness, and self-control' (Gal. 5.22–3). Inner assurance is combined with a warm outreach towards others, and it is this pattern which we find confirmed in the life of our Lord himself. It is difficult not to read even some of his hard sayings as tinged with humour (for example, 'a camel through the eye of a needle'!), and of course it is of Jesus that it is remarked: 'Behold a glutton, and a drunkard' (Matt. 11.19). Leading graced lives, having thankful hearts will of course mean willingness to face sacrifice in the narrow sense, should that be required, but it must surely also be taken to include sheer enjoyment of the beauty and wonder of God's creation and all the blessings of human fellowship which it can bring.

Elsewhere in the book we have suggested that, despite some potential pitfalls, the idea of sacrifice can perform a valuable and important role in furthering our understanding of salvation. In the history of the Church the idea of sacrifice has often been at its most contentious in its application to the Eucharist. But, if difficulties can be overcome elsewhere, it is surely worth making the effort here also.

Though Protestant objections are much more common and familiar, it is a notion which has raised worries across the spectrum of Christian belief. To some of Catholic persuasion the doctrine has at times appeared to be presented with such stress on the efficacy of the divine action that any sense of personal responsibility on the part of the individual believer is either undermined or lost altogether. On the other hand, among Protestant objectors a major critique has been that any use of the concept leaves the principal role to the priest, who in consequence is almost taken to control what happens when he 'offers Christ in the mass'. Both protests have their legitimacy. The 'Catholic' realises that not all can be the result of divine action; the 'Protestant' that not all can be a matter of what we do. However difficult it may prove, we need an account of both Christ's sacrifice and Christian sacrifice in general that places an appropriate emphasis on both the divine and human contribution. The divine and the human were alike involved in the sacrifice of Christ on the cross, and in an analogous way it is the divine Spirit that makes possible a cruciform pattern to any life of Christian sacrifice today.

Some medieval writers wrote as though not only was the mass all that counted, its gifts were entirely at the disposal of the priest who celebrated the rite. But, however consistent such an account may seem with some liturgical practices as well as a popular tradition of piety, it is grossly unfair to most of what passed as official teaching or as theology. Chapter 5 has already alluded to 'the timelessness of liturgy', the belief that the eucharistic liturgy participates in the timeless worship of heaven, and this is certainly an important factor which needs to be taken into account. For often, when theologians or church formularies spoke of Christ being re-offered or represented what they had in mind is not that blood flows once more as on the cross, but rather that what Christ once did can be appropriated at any time or in any place. What is thus at stake is the eternal availability of the cross, rather than its repetition.

It is a point about the permanent relevance of what Christ has done on the cross; and, lest we become too narrowly confined within our twentieth-century perspective, it is worth adding that there is here an obvious parallel with the modern, Protestant stress on the continuing suffering love of the crucified God for his creation (an emphasis present, of course, also elsewhere in this book). For, not only are both concepts ways of mediating the permanent concern of Christ for our world, they also raise similar problems. Thus, just as the permanent availability of Christ our sacrifice needs expansion to be intelligible and defensible, so too does the parallel notion of a suffering God. For to make sense of the notion in both cases we must surely speak of a suffering that is of a differing order and significance from that experienced upon the cross; otherwise precisely the same objections that were once made to the agony of Christ being renewed in Catholic theology, must also now be raised against much Protestant theology. In respect of the issue which concerns us here, the difference in kind between cross and Eucharist may be expressed in terms of the double role of Christ as victim and priest. On the cross, unrepeatably, Christ suffered and died on our behalf, as the sacrificial victim; in the Eucharist, again and again, as we recall and celebrate that unique sacrifice, we are joined with, and participate in, Christ's continuing action in heaven, where, as our great High Priest, he offers himself, and indeed the whole world which he has redeemed, to the Father.

But if the divine element in the idea of eucharistic sacrifice needs careful explication and qualification, so too does the notion that the human role is preeminent. The priest as a wielder of power over Christ is deeply ·

troubling; but so too, it must be added, is the idea of any Christian, whether priest or worshipper, as purely passive. It matters what we do; to say that we need to respond and accept that initial sacrifice of Christ implies a summons to action, not passivity. It has been a repeated theme of this book that the notion of sacrifice has been wrongly applied – as demanding passivity of those whose lives are already wrongly made too passive – the obvious, but by no means exclusive, instance among Christians (as chapter I emphasised) being that of women. Instead, we must think of us all as called to identify with Christ's sacrifice – whether we be priest or people – in active outreach to the world. This means that 'taking up our cross' (Mark 8.34) is a matter not only of 'completing what is lacking in Christ's afflictions' (Col. 1.24) but also of 'rejoicing in the Lord always' (Phil. 4.4), as we learn in obedience to our Lord 'both to be full and to be hungry, both to abound and to suffer need' (Phil. 4.12 AV).

It is this sense of active participation in Christ's original sacrifice that modern ecumenical documents (such as BEM, Lima, 1982 and ARCIC, Final Report, 1982) stress, and which we would also wish to endorse. Nothing that we can do can add to the perfection of Christ's sacrifice of complete obedience upon the cross, but what we can do is identify with that sacrifice in both word and deed, as its effects are made available to us once more in the drama of the liturgy. In seeing ourselves as drawn thus into the movement of Christ's self-offering, we approach more nearly the biblical notion of sacrifice which was never intended as a matter of something we do, but as something in which we are privileged to participate, most obviously perhaps in the notion of the shelem or communion sacrifice (Lev. 3); significantly, its celebration carried with it a summons to 'rejoice in the presence of the Lord' (Deut. 12.18).

The complexities of Christian history mean that inevitably not only great care ought to be taken in determining the appropriate expression of such a notion in the Church's liturgy, but that great care will in fact be taken! Nonetheless, such care will have been worthwhile; for without its expression something very valuable is lost. Cranmer in so sharply separating off as a post-communion response the offering of 'ourselves, our souls and our bodies' as 'a reasonable, holy, and lively sacrifice unto thee' intended something rather more than mere Reformation polemic. Not only were the corruptions of medieval notions of eucharistic sacrifice thus firmly circumvented, a very laudable stress on the manner and necessity of our response was appropriately highlighted. But, moving though the words undoubtedly are in their context, for many something significant and important was lost, which the restoration of the eucharistic prayer to a single unity in modern liturgies more effectively conveys. This is the fact that cross, Eucharist and response are all part of a single act: the gracious initiative of the Son who not only made – 'once offered' – a 'perfect and sufficient sacrifice . . . for the sins of the whole world', but also enables thereby whatever sacrificial response we are now able to make on our part. It is only in and through him that we can offer ourselves to the one Father whom by our adoption we and he both share. It is the desire to stress the single character of this act which explains why some also find it helpful to think at this point of the Passover prayers over the bread and wine – 'work of human hands' – which in all probability Christ used at the Last Supper. Their use at the Eucharist may be interpreted as a sign of all creation being offered in and through Christ back to the Father.

What such sacrifice in detail will mean we have already sought to elucidate in earlier paragraphs: that it must firmly be seen as having a positive, joyful aspect, as well as involving a summons to self-denial. It is within that wider context that the traditional play on holiness as wholeness can find its natural setting. In this life the process of bringing our natures and their potentialities to their proper and integrated completion has already begun. We are being healed of our wounds. In understanding how such wholeness may be brought about, modern psychology has many useful insights to offer, and these should be gladly welcomed. At the same time two cautions need to be issued, even in respect of psychologists whom many Christians have found sympathetic such as C. G. Jung and Carl Rogers. Wholeness remains essentially only an ideal, for seldom will human brokenness and fragility ever be fully resolved this side of the grave. Secondly, and more importantly, such wholeness must never be pursued simply for its own sake; we are freed in order to serve others. There is much reason to suppose that such holiness and wholeness cannot be found outside of community. Even Christian hermits, if they are to flourish, need not only the prayers of the community but also to be in some form of continuing relationship. If we take seriously our baptism as making us fellow members of the Body of Christ, then it is not something to be pursued alone, but something to be received through mutual ministry, encouragement, fellowship and love.

That social dimension is a repeated biblical theme, which is well encapsulated by the Hebrew word *shalom*. We are most familiar with the translation 'peace', but it means so much more than the mere absence of conflict. Its field of meaning includes wholeness or well-being, but it means wholeness realised in the context of a society as a whole, with no aspect of human need neglected, which is why we find it sometimes translated as 'prosperity'. A famous verse of Jeremiah urges the Jewish exiles in Babylon to the realisation that in the 'welfare' of their enemy is their own 'peace' to be found (29.7). Modern New Testament scholarship has helped us to recover the sense in which the Eucharist as messianic banquet was intended to symbolise a new social order, but full recovery of that social sense will be delayed for so long as the Church continues to be corrupted by secular individualism. We are all one in Christ and 'just as you did it to one of the least of these who are members of my family, you did it to me' (Matt. 25.40).

In other words, the Church is intended as the model of community, as the Body of him who will draw all people unto himself (John 12.32). Of course, individuality transcended can be narrow and jingoistic, as with Nazism or, at a more mundane level, with some football crowds. But it can also be what makes a community flourish. Christ is so much more than substitute or representative, more than just one individual relating to another (ourselves). For it is he who gives us the grace to see things from others' perspective, he it is who builds us up into a common whole, he who creates that peace of complete integration of ourselves and one another that will be finally ours beyond the shadow of death.

Augustine defines 'the sacrifice of Christians' as 'the many being one Body in Christ' (*City of God*, 10.6). Whether it be at the Eucharist or elsewhere, he argues, it is as individuals and as a society being made whole through him that the 'head' offers up its 'members'. But can such language be applied to those who seek after God in ways other than our own, in the pluralistic world of which we are all increasingly conscious? It is to that issue that we turn next.

Chapter 7
Christ and world faiths

This report of the Doctrine Commission is the first to include a full chapter where Christian understanding of a key theological concept is considered in relationship to other faiths. This is appropriate because the inter-faith issue has in recent times become a kind of touchstone in some quarters in connection with the doctrine of salvation. It is also a subject on which theologians within the Church of England hold a variety of approaches. In view of the fact that some readers may not be familiar with the nature of the subject-matter, this chapter makes a number of references to recent literature. Details are given in notes at the end of the book for those who wish to follow them up.

In our introductory chapter, we considered some ways in which people of other faiths view the nearest equivalent concept in their faith to that of salvation in the Christian faith, and we do not intend to go over the same ground again. If a group of Buddhists were to write a doctrine report, they would be asking in a chapter like this how Buddhists see faithful Christians or Muslims in relationship to the Buddhist doctrine of *nirvana*. Here we are considering some Christian understandings of salvation and asking where they leave the faithful Hindu or Buddhist, not in Buddhist or Hindu terms, but in Christian terms. We are not pretending Christian salvation is '*moksha*' or '*nirvana*'.

We note that the status of adherents of other religions is only one aspect, if a very important one, of a general problem, the particularity of the Christian claims about salvation on which we have touched in chapter 3. There seems to be a paradox between, on the one hand, a 'universal' vision of Christian faith and the open generosity of God, and, on the other hand, the social situation of the early Christian churches; these communities included small groups of Jewish Christians who were living increasingly uneasily with other Jewish people, and of Gentile Christians who were trying to assert their identity within the powerful culture of the Greeks and the Roman Empire; in both types of community emerged a seemingly 'exclusive' position. The paradox received expression in the report of the Lambeth Conference of 1988: 'Anything that is "exclusively" true of the incarnate Lord, is true of one who is precisely the most "inclusive" reality, the divine life rejoicing in itself and seeking to share itself. All of creation is caught up in this moment, for all of creation has been called into existence by this moment of divine love.'[1]

This chapter is in three sections. In the first section, we outline some theological responses to experiences of living in multi-faith contexts, both in Britain and in other parts of the world. Then we consider the interpretation of some biblical passages and themes which may relate to other faiths. Finally we identify key elements in a theology of religions that can provide an appropriate framework for Christian understanding of salvation and other faiths. These sections will, incidentally, also enable us to reflect on the subject within the well-known Anglican appeal to Scripture, tradition and reason.

The context of experience

Experience should not be isolated from the Bible or from reason, for experience can be misleadingly subjective, particularly if not checked out with the experience of contemporaries and with that of the past expressed in Scripture and in the teaching of the Church. It can be ambiguous in itself, and be read differently by different people. People's experience, for example, of a religion like Islam varies enormously, depending on whom they have met, and in which contexts. At a recent weekend course for Christians on Islam and Muslims in Britain, participants found their views moving in many directions as they met the great variety amongst Muslims, and heard Muslim exponents of the theology and practice of their faith make their presentations. Equally, theology without experience is also in danger of great inadequacy, particularly in respect of other faiths, on which too many people have pronounced without having met people of other faiths at all.

The context of contemporary Britain

Only since the considerable immigration from the Indian sub-continent in the 1960s have members of the Church of England met people of other faiths on any large scale. Until perhaps the mid-1970s, apart from the long-established but comparatively small Jewish community, their presence was low key. They were seen largely as 'immigrants' whom we were concerned about 'integrating' into society, rather than as people of various faiths whom we had somehow to integrate into our theological thinking, whether negatively, neutrally or positively. Since then, the profile of Muslims, Hindus and Sikhs in particular has been much raised, at a time when Christian churches have been in decline, both absolutely and relatively to these other communities. It is reckoned there are about 400,000 Sikhs in Britain, 300,000 Jews, 300,000 Hindus, 25,000 Buddhists, and between 1,000,000 and 1,400,000 Muslims. It is hard to estimate the number who attend synagogues, temples and mosques regularly, but those involved with these communities are all clear that the number attending is a much higher proportion than that of those who are nominally Christian.

This higher profile is not merely numerical; it is the result of what Muslims, Hindus and others have done for themselves, as they have ceased to meet behind closed doors, and have converted or built places of worship and community centres throughout our major cities. In Birmingham, for example, there are now more than seventy mosques of various kinds, including several large purpose-built ones. The City Council has recently produced a religious map of the city on which Christian buildings are portrayed alongside mosques, synagogues, temples and gurdwaras, as the diversity of religious life is displayed and, indeed, celebrated. In the centre of Leicester, there is a Jain temple converted from a URC building, with not only richly artistic pillars and statues inside, but also a public facade of ornate carvings of high quality, carved by sculptors from India. Even Buddhism has been raising its profile, with much publicised four year retreats in rural Scotland, undertaken largely by European converts.

In addition, they have been fighting for various rights which are religious in origin. The Sikhs have demanded the right to wear their turbans on construction sites, the Muslims to have single-sex girls' schools, and now their own State-funded schools, the Hindus to build temples in suburban areas.

It is partly because of issues prominent in the media that Muslims have a higher profile: for example, the Salman Rushdie affair, the Gulf War and the various hostage crises. And some within the media seem to wish to build up Islam as 'the enemy', to replace 'communism'. So, also, to a lesser degree with Hindus and Sikhs and Buddhists, with the conflicts in India and Sri Lanka, and the repercussions amongst their British relatives here.

As a consequence of the widening spread of people of other faiths more Christians are meeting them on a day-to-day basis, and are forming attitudes, not just to them as people, but also to their religions. How are we to view them, how does God see them, can they be saved? Three 'positions' about salvation were set out ten years ago for British readers by Alan Race,[2] and then became established surprisingly quickly as broad categories; there are exclusivist, inclusivist and pluralist approaches to people of other faiths, or to those faiths themselves. We return to these later, but in brief, and generalising, the exclusivist sees salvation exclusively through explicit faith in Christ, or through the Church; the inclusivist sees salvation as being ultimately through Christ, but inclusive of all, or of particular people who follow other faiths, and indeed of those faiths themselves; and the pluralist sees there being as many paths to salvation as there are religions. This theological use of 'pluralism' needs to be distinguished from the descriptive use of 'plurality' as one popular way of describing British society, and the educational sector in particular. 'Pluralism' is also used in connection with the school curriculum in general and to assemblies and religious education in particular.

The General Synod document *Towards a Theology of Inter-faith Dialogue,* and the consequent debate leading to the commendation of the report in 1984, and the report on Multi-Faith Worship, with the debate in July 1992, mark points where the Church of England has begun to grapple seriously both with the practical realities and with the theological issues involved. In between came the Lambeth Conference Report of 1988, where a commitment was made by the Anglican bishops, to 'affirm all they can affirm in the faith of Muslims and Jews, especially when it resonates with the Gospel', and the report writes of the common hope for the kingdom, felt by both Jews and Christians, and 'the deep Islamic reliance on the grace and mercy of God'. 'Although often misunderstood and misrepresented by Christian theologians as teaching salvation by works, all schools of Islamic thought are marked by a deep sense of the gratuitous mercy of God.'[3] Such appreciation leads to the way of dialogue, understanding and sharing, which is commended to the Communion.

The world-wide context of mission

Mission is clearly an imperative everywhere, including Britain, but much can be learnt from the practice of mission in multi-faith contexts elsewhere, both at the present time and in the twenty centuries of Christian history. All we can give are a few glimpses from that history.

As the Christian gospel encountered the Gentile world questions inevitably arose about the relationship between the Christian faith and other religious traditions. In the writings of the Greek apologists, most notably Justin Martyr, there is a willingness to recognise the religious philosophy of Platonism in particular, as providing a preparation for the gospel. Just as the Jewish prophets pointed forward to Christ, so a preparation for the gospel can be traced in Greek philosophy. Just as the revelation of God to Moses at the burning bush was interpreted as the appearance of the divine Logos, so that same Logos was seen as present in the 'seeds' of the word in the truth witnessed to by pagan philosophers. Christ is therefore the fulfiller of other religious yearnings as he is of the Jewish prophets.

Not all early Christian theologians were willing to follow this line. Others, most notably perhaps Tertullian, drew a sharp line between

Greek philosophy and the Jewish/Christian revelation, asking 'What has Athens to do with Jerusalem?' There were many who characterised pagan religion as 'demonic'. And even those like Justin who had a positive attitude towards pagan philosophy, tended to combine this with a clear condemnation of pagan worship.

After the rise of Islam, large numbers of Christians (and Jews) continued to live in what came to be the 'Islamic world'. They were certainly restricted in many ways in their life and witness and often there were tensions between the communities. They made, nevertheless, a considerable contribution to the emergence of 'Islamic' civilisation, especially in the areas of philosophy, medicine and government. Already in the seventh and eighth centuries, St John of Damascus represented the Christian community in the court of the *Umayyad* caliph. He had a number of discussions with Muslims on religious matters and two of his 'dialogues' with Muslims survive to this day. His theological method, which became so influential in the Christian world, also greatly influenced the emergence of formal theology, or *Kalam*, in the Muslim world. The 'Nestorian' Patriarch Timothy also maintained a presence in the court of the great *Abbasid* caliphs and accounts have survived of his discussions with them and prayers for them.

These two examples of the oriental Christian encounter with Islam differ markedly in tone from the polemics of both Byzantium and the West. There Christian–Muslim relations were often polarised, from both sides, as is graphically illustrated in the sad story of the Crusades and of the struggle to dominate Spain. But even in the West a more respectful note can, on occasions, be heard. For instance, we read in a letter from Pope Gregory VII to the Muslim ruler of Bijaya (modern Algeria) in 1076: 'Almighty God approves nothing in us so much as that, after loving God, one should love his fellow man. You and we owe this charity to ourselves, because we believe in, and confess, one God, admittedly in a different way.' There was the celebrated meeting between St Francis and the Sultan, Melek-El-Kamil, around 1220, which is portrayed as a deep dialogue about truth, in which each was led to respect the other, even if they could not convince each other; St Francis' heart was moved to prayer out of deep compassion for the brother for whom also Christ died, and the Sultan out of great respect for the simplicity and humour of Francis and his companion, Illuminato.

Two further medieval pioneers of dialogue with Islam were Ramon Lull and Cardinal Nicholas of Cusa. Lull endeavoured to search out common principles of Christianity, Judaism and Islam, while Nicholas was provoked by the fall of Constantinople to the Muslim Ottomans in 1453 to write *De Pace Fidei*, in which he argued as one deeply engaged in the dialogue with Islam that there was only one religion but in a diversity of rites.

We note that many of the oriental Christian traditions have long missionary histories: the Copts in North East Africa, the Church of the East (or 'Nestorians') in India and China, and the West Syrians in India. The Sigan-Fu stone (set up in the eighth century) bears witness to the seriousness of the 'Nestorian' missionaries in expressing the Christian faith in Chinese terms. Similarly, the ancient churches in India had reached an accommodation with Hinduism well before the arrival of European missionaries. In the late seventeenth century, the Italian, Matteo Ricci, who spent over a quarter of a century in China, endeavoured to express Christianity in terms acceptable to the Chinese, and to make use of indigenous Chinese ceremonies in Christian worship, in much the same way as, so many centuries before, Augustine of Canterbury had been urged by Pope Gregory the Great to baptise as many customs as possible of the Anglo-Saxons.

Such experiences have long been those of both British missionaries and British people serving overseas, and also with local Christians, with whom they worked, and all have learned by interaction with adherents of other faiths among whom they lived. This has been particularly so in the Indian subcontinent which we give as our main example. Christians in Kerala have been posed with practical and theological questions related to their Hindu or Muslim neighbours for at least seventeen hundred years. If we consider missionaries from the Church of England, they came out in increasing numbers from the early nineteenth century. They came largely following what they saw was Christ's call to rescue the lost, typically expressed in the words of Sankey's hymn:

> Go forth, and rescue those that perish,
> Where sin and darkness reign;
> Go, lend a helping hand to save them,
> And break the tempter's chain.

This was the time when Mohammed was frequently condemned as 'that imposter', and where Hindu practices such as *suttee* (widow burning) or the self-immolation of worshippers before the Hindu deity on the juggernaut were highlighted vividly. The missionaries were bringing the possibility of salvation to the Hindu, Sikh or Muslim, and their view of those religions was completely or largely negative.

But experience gradually changed the attitudes of many of these missionaries. They began to experience the kindness of character of many people of other faiths, people who did not convert to Christianity, but responded to them personally; far from opposing Christian mission, they gave space for it and trusted its schools and hospitals. The missionaries began to read the scriptures of other faiths and to see there a depth that had to be considered seriously. Also, for all the efforts of the missionaries, these religions did not collapse.

Such pioneers were faced with the critical question, what was the ongoing status in God's eyes, both of people who followed these faiths sincerely, appearing to gain a framework for their lives in doing so, and also of the faiths themselves? Did God have a purpose in these religions, even a saving purpose? And what of someone like Mahatma Gandhi, who responded to the person of Jesus Christ, and read the Sermon on the Mount regularly as well as the Gita, and appeared to put the teaching of Jesus into practice much more faithfully than most Christians? Could he be saved, who wrote, 'Today, supposing I was to be deprived of the Gita and forget all its contents but had a copy of the Sermon on the Mount, I should derive the same joy from it as I do from the Gita', and, 'The Cross is an eternal event in this stormy life . . . Living Christ means a living Cross, without it life is a living death.'? (We should note at the same time that such admiration was not related to the necessity of the historical Jesus, for Gandhi. He also wrote, 'I should not care if it was proved by someone that the man called Jesus never lived, and that what was narrated in the Gospels was a figment of the writer's imagination. For the Sermon on the Mount would still be true for me.') And what of the many ordinary Hindus, who admired and responded to Christ in various ways but did not wish to become part of a western colonial church, or would have faced ostracism if they had? Could they be saved?

Experiences such as these can be seen in relationship to various theological positions. Theologians such as Schleiermacher, in the nineteenth century, or Otto, in the early twentieth century, saw a common essence within religious experience. Karl Barth said that anyone who has not felt the compelling power of Schleiermacher has no right to criticise him. But, having said this, Barth regarded all religion, including the Christian religion, as man-made, and needing to be reformed by being centred on the singular revelation of God as seen in Jesus Christ.

But, in the 'mission field', and in India in particular, theologies of salvation were based on much deeper meeting. In 1913, J. Farquhar wrote his famous book *The Crown of Hinduism*. Here, he recognised and evaluated positively the achievements of Hinduism, the sincere aspirations of Hindus, and the good that many of them showed in their lives. But, in the end, 'Jesus, the Son of God, who died for our sins on Calvary, produces a religion which satisfies the modern mind, and which also proves to be the fulfilment and goal of all the religions of the world, the crudest as well as the loftiest.'

The first World Missionary Conference at Edinburgh in 1910 had shown great wisdom in its balance. It is a striking example of how creativity in theological reflection comes directly out of a concern for mission, rather than, as so often, doctrine and mission being held in separate compartments. It was unashamedly evangelical in that it called for the evangelisation of the whole world in one generation. But also, in its Commission 4 on inter-action with other faiths (thought essential more than eighty years before this Doctrine Commission is considering the issues), it began by drawing on evidence submitted from all parts of the world. There were no less than sixty-one extensive reports related to experience with Hinduism, with a range of opinion. Wesley Ariarajah analysed these replies and concludes: 'Almost all the replies received emphasised that Christians should possess and not merely assume a sympathetic attitude towards Hinduism. Such sympathy should be based on knowledge and not be the child of emotion or imagination.'[4] The Commission concluded: 'More harm has been done in India than in any other country by missionaries who have lacked the wisdom to appreciate the nobler side of the religion which they have laboured so indefatigably to supplant.' They studied also Hindu concepts of incarnation (*avatar*), devotion (*bhakti*), and salvation (*moksha*). Of the latter, the comment was made 'Though the idea of salvation (i.e. *moksha*) is always associated with the conception of rebirth, yet there is also connected with it an earnest longing and passionate desire for union with God.'

In contrast to both Farquhar and the searchings of Edinburgh, the conference at Tambaram, Madras, in 1938, affirmed a revitalised exclusivism. Hendrik Kraemer represented an approach to mission characterised by Dialectical Theology. He dominated the conference, as did his book *The Christian Message in a Non-Christian World*. Here he wrote: 'If we are ever to know what true and divinely willed religion is, we can only do this through God's revelation in Jesus Christ, and through nothing else', and, 'In this light and in regard to their deepest and most essential purport, other religions are all in error.' He therefore urged on converts a radical discontinuity from their former faith as they entered the Church of Christ.

This is still a powerful view, not least in India, and leads to a powerful missionary imperative. Salvation, in whatever form, is available only through Jesus Christ and explicit confession of him. It is the predominant voice that has led most Asian converts in Britain to deny any continuity with their past, and, indeed, this has been almost required of them by the zeal of those responsible for their conversion. It is experience-based, since

Kraemer was a long-term missionary and represented a widely held view. Often such a radical discontinuity is demanded by the convert; otherwise why suffer what he/she often does? It is because in the new faith salvation is assured.

Since the Second World War, two other broad theological approaches have come alongside those of Farquhar and Kraemer. Both arise from the experience of mission as Christian presence with people of other faiths: (i) being alongside in presence, service and witness, and seeing where the Spirit leads (associated with the name of Max Warren); (ii) the dialogue movement, in its various forms – dialogue in daily life, dialogue in common social action and nation-building, theological dialogue, dialogue in depth (in spirituality).

C. Murray Rogers wrote of the last: 'I long for the only dialogue which will help me to realise more deeply the mystery of the Spirit in me.' It requires an acknowledgment that one does not know everything. Dr Gangadaran, one of the two Hindu observers at the WCC Assembly in Canberra, speaks of the basis of such dialogue: 'Only a person with the highest knowledge can understand their own ignorance. When they have understood their scriptures, such a person will leave a space. Only so can God find place to come in.' This reveals an essential willingness to learn. The same Hindu comments: 'If I do not understand now, this does not mean I may not understand later. I can never know that something is not going to be of significance for me in my search for truth.' Remarkably, he then quotes the story of the thief who hung beside Jesus on the cross, how he was given the promise of salvation, because at the end of his life he realised the significance of the one hanging next to him. The Roman Catholics, Abishiktananda and Bede Griffiths, are amongst those who have gone furthest in this identification with another faith while remaining committed to Christ.

Some theological responses to experience of other faiths

Amongst those mentioned above, some would call themselves, or be called by others, pluralists. Some may be described as inclusivists and others as exclusivists. Most pluralists in no way deny the centrality of Christ for the Christian tradition of which they are a part (though some who disagree with them have a suspicion that they have a tendency to diminish Christ in the interest of inter-faith harmony). But they see different world-views in other faiths which also seem to work for people of those faiths, enabling them to lead integrated and holy lives. Pluralists like John Hick have been deeply influenced by experience with certain people of other faiths. Like Schleiermacher and Otto mentioned above (p. 396), he has an experiential concept of religion. Instead of a christological centre, for Hick, there is now God at the centre (or more recently, 'the real'). In his now famous 'Copernican revolution' in religion, he writes: 'And we have to realize that the universe of faiths centres upon God, and not upon Christianity or any other religion. He is the sun, the originative source of light and life, and whom all the religions reflect in their own different ways.'[5] There are different ways to salvation, however that is understood, different paths to the top of the mountain. Some would claim there was still one mountain top, one ultimate reality, which is seen in different ways. Others, that the idea of one mountain is beyond reach, we are on different mountains, and this does not matter, provided that we reach the clear air at the top of our mountain. This allows each faith to keep its own integrity, but little motivation for mission, in the sense of a call for conversion, which is merely a distraction. Mission is about working for the kingdom, with our neighbours of all faiths and none. This has been described by a Hindu scholar as 'mutual dynamic mission in which God wants us to be partners'.

Stanley Samartha, in a recent book, puts it like this:

> When alternative ways of salvation have provided meaning and purpose for millions of persons in other cultures for more than two or three thousand years, to claim that the Judaeo-Christian-Western tradition has the only answer to all problems in all places and for all persons in the world is presumptuous, if not incredible. This is not to deny the validity of the Christian experience of salvation in Jesus Christ, but it is to question the exclusive claims made for it by Christians, claims that are unsupported by any evidence in history, or in the institutional life of the church, or in the lives of many Christians who make such claims. If salvation comes from God – and for Christians it cannot be otherwise – then possibilities should be left open to recognise the validity of other experiences of salvation.[6]

To this challenge this entire report seeks to respond.

Others are often grouped together as 'inclusivists', and they are a very broad category. But, basically, again from experience, their contact with people of various faiths has led them in two directions, which may seem contradictory, but which they wish to hold together. On the one hand, they have come to respect not only the persons of the other faith, but also that faith itself, very deeply, not just for the good works that may flow from its adherents, but also for the spirituality that evidently lies behind it. On the other hand, through encounter, they have become more, not less, committed to the place of Jesus Christ in questions of salvation, and of what he reveals uniquely, as they see it, of the nature of God. Holding these two together, they wish to see Christ at the centre, and that means his cross and resurrection, as well as his teaching and incarnation, and, at the same time, to include within God's saving grace the possibility of salvation in every respect for people of other faiths. Some would say they are saved as people, outside their religion; others would include elements given to them in their faith. We would prefer to use the term 'inclusivist' for the second group. As a criterion for what can be included, they would tend to use what conforms to the ethos and teaching of the New Testament, or what they estimate Christ would accept. And they would use such criteria for what is acceptable in the Church.

Anglicans from the Church of England historically have made a significant contribution to the development of these various theologies. F. D. Maurice and Bishop Westcott can be seen to be amongst those who before their time struggled to some extent with these questions. In his book *The Religions of the World, and Their Relations to Christianity* (1847), Maurice sets out a positive view of the religious aspirations of humanity combined with a need for the Christian to prevent such religious aspirations becoming idolatrous and superstitious. Maurice saw Christianity not as the destroyer, but the preserver of what is strongest and most permanent in Hindu life and character, a kind of fulfilment theology sixty years before J. Farquhar. Recognising how Hinduism reveals a desire and longing for converse with the unseen world, Maurice writes: 'I contend that he who is able to give the answers to the Hindoo's deepest questions is not a destroyer, but a preserver: that he will have a right to boast of having upholden all that was strongest and most permanent in the Hindoo life and character.'[7] C. F. Andrews, Verrier Elwin and Jack Winslow were three Anglicans who allowed experience with the people of India to transform their theology; Henry Martyn and Temple Gairdner became pioneers in mission and dialogue with Islam. In the modern period, we can think of bishops such as Kenneth Cragg, Stephen Neill, George Appleton, John Robinson, John V. Taylor, David Brown, Lakshman Wickremasinghe (of Sri Lanka) and Michael Nazir-Ali, all of whom contributed diverse and significant writings, as have Max Warren, Roger Hooker, Christopher Lamb and others. Common to all these is a link between mission, experience and theology.

In what has sometimes been recognised as a growing trend of Anglican theology of inter-faith encounter,[8] Max Warren speaks of 'the unknown Christ' who saves even when 'unrecognised as the Saviour'. Through his method of Christian presence, Kenneth Cragg seeks to 'unveil the hidden Christ, that is the elements that are already "in Christ" within the other religions'. John Taylor points out that every religion has its 'jealousies', its tenets that carry a 'universal significance and finality' for all humankind. For Christians this jealousy is the assertion 'that Jesus is central to God's purpose for mankind . . . that from the beginning the world was held in existence by the Redeemer who was to die'. This Christ is 'the invisible magnetic pole that draws all peoples in their quest for the Ultimate.' All three views, exclusivism, inclusivism (of both a wide, and the more specific sense which we are using) and pluralism, are present today within the Church of England, and also increasingly related to experience within Britain. But the difference may be that those in the 'exclusivist' area are less willing to be influenced by experience, positive or negative. They may be just as friendly and accepting of people of other faiths at a human level, 'loving your neighbour as yourself'. But theological presuppositions will determine attitudes finally. This is illustrated by the much quoted story of the conversation between D. T. Niles, the Sri Lankan ecumenical theologian, and Karl Barth. D. T. Niles asked Barth how he could know that Hinduism was unbelief if, as he had admitted, he had never met a Hindu. Barth's reply was 'I know that *a priori*'. (On the other hand, Barth can be said to be extremely inclusive in the sense that he sees all people, though not of course their religions, already included in the crucified and risen Christ. This would make him inclusivist in the wide sense, but not in the specific sense we are using the term.)

Wesley Ariarajah's book mentioned above suggests that the non-Roman Catholic churches are still dominated by the Tambaram spirit, even if it is subtly expressed. Dialogue is enshrined in the WCC structures, but has not brought a decisive move away from exclusivism at any of the major resolution-making conferences. Edinburgh 1910 is shown as all the more radical in the light of the decades since.

As we have seen in chapter 1, during these same years, the Roman Catholic Church has moved from the position that there is no salvation outside the Roman Catholic Church. Vatican II represented a sharp shift. In *Nostra Aetate* it is affirmed that 'the Catholic Church rejects nothing that is true and holy in these religions', and that they 'often reflect a ray of that truth which enlightens all men'. But Christ remains the way, the truth and the life. 'It is in him, in whom God reconciled all things to himself (2 Cor. 5.18–19), men find the fullness of their religious life.' Writing of Christ's redeeming sacrifice, Vatican II teaches:

> All this holds true not only for Christians but for all men of good will in whose hearts grace works in an unseen way. For since Christ

died for all men, and since the ultimate vocation of man is in fact one and divine, we ought to believe that the Holy Spirit in a manner known only to God offers to every man the possibility of being associated with this paschal mystery.[9]

In similar vein, Karl Rahner made two clear points in relationship to salvation. He said that people of other faiths are saved *through*, and not *despite* their religion and faith. And there followed the phrase for ever associated with him, 'anonymous Christians' – they are saved because they are inspired by Christ, though they do not know it; this phrase has been much criticised, but it is a consequence of Rahner's desire to honour the positive experiences of many, while being true to his conviction about the centrality of Christ. Hans Küng added the distinction between other religions as 'ordinary' ways to salvation, and Christianity as the 'extraordinary' or special way. The present Pope, John Paul II, in his encyclical *Redemptor Hominis*, embraces what has gone before: 'The human person – every person without exception – has been redeemed by Christ; because Christ is in a way united to the human person – every person without exception – even if the individual may not realise this fact.'[10]

Pluralism can mean there are no absolutes, and each finds their own way, and even creates their own reality. It fits also with a Christianity which has lost its confidence. We can leave others to follow their own way, while we do our best to be faithful Christians. It avoids the necessity for the rather uncomfortable task of evangelism and witness. More positively, it takes seriously the cultural diversity experienced in modern Britain, and shows genuine respect for the various faiths around, without either threatening them or suggesting their adherents need to be converted. It also fits well with the obvious fact that good and devout people are to be found in all our religious communities. But, even with this open approach, there still remain the key questions of criteria and limits. In the face of cults and sects, or the loosely defined New Age movement, most pluralists would draw the line at some point. If we return to the image of the paths up a mountain, is anything a path? Are there not paths that fade out like sheep tracks, or even end at the top of precipices half way up the mountain? Is it possible to find salvation through something that is not true, even if it seems to satisfy its adherents? There is a question to be addressed by pluralists as to whether they take seriously the necessary exclusivity of truth.

The witness of converts

Finally, in terms of experience, it is vital to hear the witness of converts, who of all people have actually lived on the margin between different faiths, and have often suffered in consequence. While pluralism admits of the possibility of conversion, there is little point in it, as salvation is already available within each faith, in terms which satisfy within that faith. Yet there is hardly a convert who is a pluralist, unless perhaps converted for convenience or marriage. The genuine religious converts, whether to Christianity or to any other faith, certainly believe that their conversion makes a difference, and that is why they face whatever befalls them. Such converts usually either deny any continuity with what came before, and see salvation coming only through the new, or they accept the past with thanks, seeing their relatives in the old faith as preparing the way.

For example, a Christian convert from Sikhism writes of his Sikh family:

> They know how important they, and my Sikh upbringing, are to me. Over the years they have developed respect for me, as a Christian, just as I respect them. I wear the Sikh bracelet as a sign of my pride for my roots, and as a sign of my commitment to stand for God's truth and justice that it demands.

Such a person has suffered for his conversion, for his commitment to the calling to be a disciple of Jesus Christ, experienced as read in John 15.16: 'You did not choose me but, I chose you.' But he is convinced that the same Jesus Christ reveals a God who will include his relatives as well as himself. He echoes the approach of his great fellow Sikh, Sadhu Sundar Singh. The well-known story is told of him that when someone said that his mother, a saintly Sikh woman, would go to hell if she did not become a Christian, he replied: 'Then I will ask God to send me down to hell so that I may be with her there.'

A Hindu convert in Britain became a Christian as he observed the way a particular fellow Christian student lived his life, and moved with people. He hardly knew him, but observing was enough. As he had been brought up, he had been deeply influenced by the holiness of a particular older Hindu, who died after the conversion of the student. He comments:

> I cannot believe my old Hindu will not be accepted by the love of God. 'The fruits' were so evident in him. From my limited understanding of missionaries throughout the ages, the attitude has often been one of the missionary offering their knowledge of God to others. Often it appears to me that people are not led to understand Christ as the fulfilment of the quest, but that their quest itself is demolished.

A convert from Islam in Britain put it like this:

> I was already seeking for God as a Muslim. Muslims have the same
> hopes and fears. I know that it is the same God who has created us
> all, Christians and Muslims. Both as a Muslim and as a Christian,
> I worshipped that same God. But I have come into a new and
> personal relationship with God through Christ. Before I was in awe
> of God, and felt every small evil I did would be weighed against my
> good works. Now I feel the love of God.

From a very different context, Bishop Clement of the Diocese of Central
Zambia, tells how when the missionaries first came to Zambia, as it
became, the people recognised the God the missionaries spoke of as
the God they already knew who was creator of the great plains and
mountains and forests of Africa.

But other converts do not see this type of continuity of experience of
God, or acknowledge common experience of worship, or possibility of
salvation in their previous faith. Another convert from Islam spoke of
how she felt the continuous need of prayer for protection since she had
experienced so much suffering and real persecution leading to the break
up of her family life, due to her conversion. She saw things in terms of
spiritual warfare. The assurance of salvation is felt by her to be radically
discontinuous with anything understood before.

Such individual responses often depend on the overall context. How
Muslims and Christians see each other and relate to each other is a very
different question in Britain as compared with certain Middle Eastern
countries, and how they relate in one part of Africa is very different from
another. Hence the need to look at these questions both in general, and
within the specific context for which this report is written.

The Bible

Faced with this wide-ranging and complex set of questions, we naturally
turn to the Bible. Both Old and New Testaments are confessional
documents, written out of faith, to encourage faith. They are written out
of particular cultures, to encourage loyalty, commitment and conversion
within particular traditions. The major faiths of the world today were
either unknown to the writers because they did not exist, or were beyond
their geographical experience. So we are not able to read off easy biblical
answers, even if we wished to. We look for insights which may illuminate
our doctrinal task from several sources: from the ways in which the
Jewish people reflected on their relationship with Canaanite and other
religions among which they lived, from the way the Church reflected on

the parting of the ways between Judaism and Christianity, and from the way the Church expanded into the world of Greek culture and Roman imperial rule.

In doing this, we recognise a dynamic relationship between Scripture, tradition and reason. We need to interpret Scripture in the light of the experience of the centuries in between; thus this section should not be abstracted from the first part of this chapter. Nor must we neglect reason, as we reflect on what has been handed down to us. Nevertheless, we hold by the Anglican understanding, as in Article 20 of the Thirty-Nine Articles, that 'It is not lawful for the Church to ordain any thing that is contrary to God's Word written. . . .' We should be wary of a doctrine of salvation in relationship to people of other faiths that was not consonant with Scripture in its main thrust.

Old Testament

In the Old Testament there is no doubt that the God who revealed himself to Israel as Yahweh is the God of the whole world and of all the nations. The early chapters of Genesis set a universal context for the rest of the Old Testament story. From Adam and Eve to the Tower of Babel the story concerns the common origins of all the nations. It tells not only of rebellion against God, but also of people, such as Abel, Enosh, Enoch and Noah, who knew God in primeval times. It is only after this universal context has been set that the story narrows to Abraham and Sarah, the man and the woman through whose descendants, Israel, all the nations of the world are eventually to be blessed.

Once the Old Testament story becomes that of Abraham and Sarah and their descendants, the religions of the other nations Israel knew are usually represented in wholly negative terms, as idolatrous. But there are four ways in which the Old Testament portrays Gentiles (non-Israelites) in a positive relationship to the one true God. In the first place, God acts for and through other nations without their acknowledging him. He calls Cyrus to be his servant (Isa. 45.1) and leads Gentile nations in exodus events of their own (Amos 9.7).

Secondly, Israel's knowledge of the God revealed to them can be and is shared with non-Israelites who also come to worship Yahweh. The Old Testament never suggests that it is necessary to be a born Israelite in order to know and to serve Yahweh. In some cases, such as Rahab (Josh. 2.1–21; 6.25) and Ruth, members of other nations not only turn to Yahweh but also join his people. In other cases, such as Naaman (2 Kgs 5) and Nebuchadnezzar (Dan. 2–4), they acknowledge the God of Israel as the true God without becoming Israelites. Jonah is a reluctant missionary to the people of Nineveh because he knows that they can be saved by repentance and faith in the true God. The message of the book of Jonah is that God desires the Gentiles, even Israel's bitterest enemies, to turn to him.

Thirdly, the prophets, especially of the exilic and post-exilic periods, predict the time when no longer will there be merely a few Gentile converts to the God of Israel, but the nations in general will turn to God. Egypt and Assyria will worship Yahweh and, like Israel, will be his peoples (Isa. 19.24–5, cf Zech. 2.11). God's word will go out from Zion, and the nations will be drawn to the light of the restored and glorified Jerusalem (Isa. 2.2–3; 61.1–3). All people will worship Yahweh in Jerusalem (Isa. 66.23; Zech. 14.16–19).

In the second and especially the third of these categories, we see the development of the kind of universalism which is the most characteristic of the biblical tradition. It is a movement from the particular to the universal. Yahweh chooses one people so that he may become known to all peoples. God reveals himself to Israel so that this revelation may be shared with others (cf Isa. 49.6). These are the roots in the Old Testament of the Church's mission in the New Testament to preach the gospel to all nations. This kind of universalism need not imply that there is any true knowledge of God in other religious traditions.

However, there is a fourth theme in the Old Testament's portrayal of Gentiles, which is not so often noticed, but which may have implications for a positive Christian evaluation of faiths other than those which derive from the Israelite-Jewish-Christian tradition. There are a few Gentiles in the Old Testament narratives who know and worship the true God quite independently of Israel. Their knowledge of God does not derive from his revelation of himself to Israel, but is nevertheless acknowledged as valid by the biblical authors. For example, Melchizedek is priest of God Most High (Gen. 14.18–20), who is identified with Abraham's God (14.22). Jethro, Moses' father-in-law, the priest of Midian, seems already to worship the same God as Moses, before recognising this God's activity in saving Israel from Egypt (Exod. 18.8–12). Balaam, the prophet, is commissioned and inspired to prophesy by the true God, even though he tries to disobey this commission out of a reluctance which is the Gentile counterpart of Jonah's (Num. 22–24). Job and his friends are also Gentiles (Job 1.1; 2.11; 32.2) whom the book of Job does not place in any relationship to the Old Testament salvation-history. We are told that God says about Job that 'there is no one like him on the earth, a blameless and upright man who fears God' (Job 1.8). Though no doubt they are fictional characters, they show that an Old Testament wisdom writer could easily imagine devout worshippers of the true God unrelated to the Israelite context.

More generally, the wisdom literature, in both the Hebrew Scriptures and the Apocrypha, sometimes displays a notable openness to the thought and language of Gentile cultures. In incorporating elements from other cultures and sages, these books provide some basis for a broad understanding of God's activity in the world and human society. In this literature an extensive role is played by the increasingly personified figure of Wisdom, emanating from God, pre-existing creation and active throughout it. Her activities (according to Prov. 8, Wisd. 7, Ecclus 24) seem to be without boundary: 'The first man never managed to grasp her entirely, nor has the most recent one fully comprehended her' (Ecclus 24.28).

In Jewish Wisdom literature, however, wisdom is also firmly linked to the tradition of Israel. Thus Wisdom is firmly identified with the Torah in Ecclesiasticus 24, and dwells in Israel: 'All this is no other than the book of the covenant of the Most High God, the law that Moses enjoined on us' (v. 23). (At the same time, a book like Ecclesiasticus also centres firmly on a Messianic hope for Israel (ch. 36), and on the story of the illustrious who stood by the covenants (chs 44–50). Wisdom (chs 10–19) concentrates on the Exodus and on salvation history, and it has extremely strong strictures against idol worship.) Some of the teaching in Proverbs emerges later as the background to some of the teaching of Jesus. And Paul often incorporates general wise teaching as current in popular Hellenistic philosophy in the lists found in some of the Epistles. Wisdom 7 and Proverbs 8 prefigure Colossians 1, where the language is now applied to Christ. Such borrowing is also seen in early Christian art, in the way helpful models from pagan mythology can be found in the painting of the catacombs.

In general, in the Old Testament, the focus of attention is not on the question of salvation or otherwise for non-Jewish people, either as communities or for the good amongst them. They had their own ways to salvation or otherwise (though it should be noted that righteous Gentiles mentioned in the Old Testament are normally monotheists).

New Testament

While the Old Testament is primarily concerned with the present and future destiny of the Jewish people and is only tentatively missionary, Christianity developed in its early stages a strong sense of commitment to a universal mission, since God 'desires everyone to be saved and to come to the knowledge of the truth' (1 Tim. 2.4). A confidently missionary religion is unlikely to be positive towards other faiths whose adherents it is seeking to convert; it is likely to look either for a complete break from those faiths, or for bridges from them, which will then be left behind after conversion.

With very limited exceptions, the books of the New Testament direct attention to the death and resurrection of Jesus Christ. Salvation is deeply related to those events, and the assumption through and through is that they are decisive; they are decisive both because of the Person who was on the cross and in the tomb, and because of the subsequent effect. A doctrine of salvation which is in any real sense biblical must focus significantly on this fact. Jesus in no way can be seen biblically as one among many examples. The God to whom he points is a very specific one, the God of Abraham, Isaac and Jacob, the God whom he calls Abba and with whom new possibilities of relationship are established through his ministry. Though it is true that much of the ethics of Jesus can be found elsewhere, his cross and resurrection, both as events and in the interpretation given to them, stand in a class apart. No book could be more cross-centred than the Epistle to the Hebrews, where the sacrifice of Christ is seen as abolishing the sacrifices of the Old Covenant, and being something once and for all.

As has been seen in the chapters on the meaning of salvation in the Old and New Testaments, there is a general sense of being enabled to escape from what destroys life on this earth, and produces health, peace, prosperity and blessing. As well as most of the Old Testament references, many of the New Testament references lie in this area. As we consider the world around us, and the effect of different faiths within their various contexts, corporately and individually, we may be led to recognise diversity in the understanding of salvation in practice. We do, in fact, find that the major faiths bring salvation in this sense to their followers in varying, but significant degrees. If we wish to use a term from the Jewish-Christian tradition, we seem to see signs of the kingdom of God. The pluralist would say that such are there in their own right. The inclusivist would say that they are there because of the Spirit of God, revealed in Christ, whether recognised as such or not. The exclusivist would say that these are signs, good in themselves, but ultimately not significant in terms of final salvation.

Another important strand in the meaning of salvation in the Bible is about forgiveness, escape from eternal punishment, and citizenship of the renewed heaven and earth. There is no question that, in the New Testament, this normally becomes inextricably linked to the death and resurrection of Christ. The assurance of such forgiveness is possible only because of the length to which God has gone, in Christ, in order to reconcile the world to himself. It is not mere wishful thinking that God is love and will forgive. Since that is so, there is no way that the cross can be by-passed, in order to include people of other faiths. They must in some way be included through the cross and resurrection, as Christians are, because there is no other way. In the Fourth Gospel, it is in the hours before he goes to the cross that Jesus says 'I am the way, the truth and the life'. In John 14.6 he continues: 'No one comes to the Father except through me.' Such passages are accepted by many exclusivists as expressing Jesus' definitive self-understanding; inclusivists tend to point out that they need to be interpreted in terms of the logos Christology of the Prologue that pervades the Gospel as a whole, while pluralists tend to assume that the logos Christology was a mistaken development. But 'the way' can be seen as the way of the cross, and that is why this way of salvation is a scandal. And the initiative remains with God: 'No one can come to me unless drawn by the Father who sent me' (John 6.44).

Clearly there are parts of the New Testament which can be read as strongly exclusivist. A much quoted verse, for example, is Acts 4.12: 'There is salvation in no one else, for there is no other name under heaven given among mortals by which we must be saved.' But we must see this statement of Peter, speaking to the Jewish rulers and elders, in the context of the healing miracle that has just happened at the Beautiful Gate. He is answering the question in interrogation, 'By what power or by what name did you do this?' It is a question of power in healing primarily, not of ultimate salvation in an inter-faith context. Of course, physical healing and salvation are linked, not least in Luke's use of the same Greek word. But even then, Acts 4.12 clearly centres on Jesus and is compatible with an inclusive theology, of either of the kinds mentioned above (pp. 399–400), as well as forms of exclusivism.

There are also elements which can be read in an inclusivist way in terms of the meaning of ultimate salvation. The parable like that of the sheep and the goats (Matt. 25.31ff) has been argued as indicating a way whereby those of other faiths can be included, who do works of mercy for their own sake, not seeking a reward, and find themselves, to their surprise, welcomed into heaven. The occasions when Jesus commends the faith of a Gentile, such as the centurion or the Canaanite woman, can be argued as being a commendation, not of their faith as such, but their faith in his authority and healing power. Yet on these occasions Jesus commends in striking terms deep stirrings in the hearts of these people who come from such diverse backgrounds. Some passages would seem to go further. For instance in the parable of the Pharisee and Publican (Luke 18.9ff.) the despised tax-collector not only is commended, but goes away 'justified', and this because of his willingness to acknowledge his utter dependence on the forgiveness of God: 'God be merciful to me, a sinner.' Also it is the behaviour of a good Samaritan who, astonishingly, is chosen as the example of what we are to do to enter eternal life (Luke 10.25ff.). Whatever our exegesis be of any particular verses, however, we should not hang our whole theology on isolated texts or on one or two verses, rather than on the overall picture we get from Scripture. In general terms, it is by fruits that we can recognise authenticity of faith. And if we consider the Beatitudes (Matt. 5.1–12), we find that appropriate reward is given to surprising groups of people – the poor in spirit, the gentle, those who mourn, those who hunger and thirst for right, the merciful, the pure in heart, peacemakers, and those who are persecuted in the cause of right. Romans 1.18ff. would suggest that in principle not only knowledge of God but also appropriate response to God is possible outside the Jewish tradition. Romans 2.15 speaks of conscience as providing a guide for those who do not have the Law. Admittedly Paul mentions these things only to support his argument, that therefore everyone is without excuse since, in practice, no one can respond appropriately and so all are equally dependent on the action of God in Christ and the Spirit.

This openness to the affirmation of the righteousness of some outside the believing community does not normally extend to an affirmation of their religious quest. Paul is as uncompromisingly hostile to Gentile idolatry as any prophet in the Old Testament. Only in Acts 17 is there a suggestion that people of all nations may 'feel after and find' the unknown God, and only there poets quoted as giving them already an understanding of God as creator. The altar to the 'unknown God' may represent only a kind of insurance, but nevertheless this is something that Paul feels he can build on. Yet Paul faces the problem that the majority of Israel has rejected Christ, and he finds himself unable to judge them lost. In the end 'all Israel will be saved' (Rom. 9–11). This is a matter of eschatological hope, grounded in the unfathomable providence of God; one aspect, maybe, of the hope for the redemption of all humanity in the Last Adam (1 Cor. 15.45; cf. Rom. 5.12ff.).

The New Testament concentration on Christ is often seen as a stumbling-block to more open inter-faith theology, because it encapsulates 'the scandal of particularity', that it is only through Christ and his cross that God's salvation is mediated, and that is through a Christ who lived at one time, in one province of the Roman Empire. This is what was such a scandal for Mahatma Gandhi, attracted as he was by the figure and teaching of Christ. But it could be argued that for Paul and the Pauline tradition Christ represents a universalisation of God's dealing with humanity, not a contracting of it. Christ's death and resurrection releases the love and salvation of God for the whole world, and indeed for the whole of creation. It challenges all human pretensions ('religion' in Barth's terms), and also affirms the possibilities of universal redemption. We see this in Romans 8.18ff., where it is the whole of creation that groans for release. We can see this also in the first chapter of the Epistle to the Ephesians, in particular in verse 9: 'He has made known to us the mystery of his will, according to his good pleasure that he set forth in Christ, as a plan for the fullness of time, to gather up all things in him, things in heaven and things on earth.'

Theological perspectives

Christian theology seeks to be loyal to biblical and church tradition, and also open to the experience that encounter and mission have brought, not only in the present, but from biblical times. It is also concerned with reason, and in particular it poses the question, 'What is God's purpose for those who came before Jesus and his cross and resurrection, and those who have come after but followed faithfully other traditions?'

We believe that the terms exclusivism, inclusivism and pluralism have performed a useful function in laying out a map of some possible ways of describing where people are in terms of our subject. But, at their best, they remain ambiguous, and are places on a spectrum rather than separate options. At worst they can label people, often in a judgemental way. Pluralists can see exclusivists as bigoted, and inclusivists as lacking the courage of their convictions, trying to have it both ways, and being 'the same old exclusivists' in disguise. Exclusivists can see pluralists as betraying the mission of Christ, and easily slipping into mere relativism. To some extent they may agree with pluralists in the way they see inclusivists. Exclusivists and pluralists may also agree in seeing real differences between faiths, for example, between Buddhism and Christianity. Where they will differ is in assessing the significance of these differences in terms of salvation. Inclusivists can see exclusivists as being dogmatic and hard-hearted, while pluralists have lost the centrality of Christ, and so they can feel superior to both, though their position can lack the clarity of the other two.

Both as individuals and as a Commission, we find ourselves moving beyond any one of these three positions; indeed, it may be that our statements can be found to give support to all three at various points.

It has been suggested that the big divide is between pluralism on the one hand, and the other two positions on the other, both of which centre in some implicit or explicit way on the work of Christ as being critical for all humanity.[11] With this understanding, readers might see in what follows a position that could be labelled 'an open and generous exclusivism' or 'a Christocentric inclusivism', or 'trinitarian pluralism', and all may be right. Another view would be that it is pluralism and exclusivism that have a clear commonality, in that they both take seriously the difference between religions, while inclusivism blurs that distinction, as in the name of Christ all religions are claimed for Christianity.

The common assertions we are able to make are based upon our understanding of God's Love, Spirit and Word, and their pivotal expression in the cross and resurrection of Jesus Christ. God's Love is unconditional, beyond restriction, for all, not only for some. The guarantee that God is love is shown by the ministry of Jesus. As women and men experienced this ministry and linked it with the person of Jesus, this conclusion about the nature of God was confirmed. That love cannot be narrower than a love which includes tax-gatherers and sinners, penitent thieves and quarrelling disciples. These are the very people whom 'religion' excluded. Is it to include these, but not the good Hindu or Muslim? – or indeed the bad Hindu or Muslim, who throw themselves on the mercy of God, as they experience it? Such a love is not so restricted that it cannot reach out across religious barriers.

It is also love related to justice and holiness. God does not save despite his justice and his holiness (1 John 1.5: 'God is light, and in him there is no darkness at all'). Such love and justice are at the very heart of the concept of the kingdom of God which is also inextricably linked to salvation through the proclamation of Jesus. Those reflecting theologically on experience outside Europe have shown us how salvation, unrelated to liberation and participation in a just society, as God intended, means little to the struggling majority of the world who live in grinding poverty. Every religion needs to take this into account, whenever it drifts towards spiritualising the centres of its faith. Such spiritualising has left many Hindus as outcasts, untouchables, now Dalits (the oppressed and crushed ones) by their own naming, despite the subtle philosophy in the Hindu tradition. Another terrible example is the acceptance of slavery for so long within the Christian tradition.

Secondly, there is the concept of the Spirit. There is an essential continuity between the Spirit moving over the waters at creation, experienced by prophets and rulers in the Old Testament, and then publicly displayed in the person of Jesus Christ, through his baptism and then through his Church. Some may say the Spirit moved more widely before Christ's time and that afterwards the Spirit is confined to the Church. We do not say that. Certainly, the character of the Spirit is now revealed by Christ. St Paul writes of the Spirit of Christ, the Holy Spirit, the Spirit, the Spirit of God, but he appears to mean the same personal reality. The last Doctrine Commission report on the Spirit clearly argues for the view that the Spirit is not confined to the Church, however named or described:

> The Spirit, though particularly at work in the Christian Church by covenant and promise, is also at work outside it, in the lives and characters of people of other faiths and none . . . Naturally the touchstone of the quality of the Spirit's activity in the life of any person, whether Christian or not, is the evidence of a Christ-like spirit. Wherever that spirit is to be found, it must surely be attributed to the unseen, inward working of the Holy Spirit. (p. 141)

The Spirit's fruit is described in Galatians 5 as love, joy, peace, patience, kindness, goodness, trustfulness, gentleness and self-control. This fruit of the Spirit is to be seen in the life of Christ, who brings us to a realisation of the character of the Spirit. As such, he is the criterion for judging whether the Spirit is present in any context or situation or person. Thus our judging that the Spirit may be found outside the Church is not an arbitrary one, nor does it mean that the work of the Spirit can be identified everywhere. Those of other faiths and indeed of none who display such fruit are we believe amongst those who have responded to the Spirit of God; there is evidence that God is savingly at work in them, and he will bring his work to fulfilment. 'The doctrine of the Holy Spirit allows us theologically to relate the particularity of the Christ event to the entire history of humankind.'[12]

It is timely to listen once more to the witness of those who have lived closely with those of other faiths over a long period:

> The simplicity of life of a South Indian Hindu woman who has the sense of detachment that enables her to give a clear message to those around her: 'Whether I live or die, I am the Lord's.' Within that ultimate security, she gives out so much love to others. The row upon row of Muslim men, prostrate in prayer, each morning and evening in so many mosques in the midst of a Westernised secular city. The witness of a young Western Buddhist about to go on a four-year retreat as a novice monk, and who testifies to how he has been saved from a hopeless life of drug addiction through this new faith. The witness of peace of Buddhists as they walk in procession . . . The unshakable faith in God displayed by the Jewish community, even in the deepest darkness of the Warsaw Ghetto, as they recited the psalms daily, and sang a song they had learnt from the Vilna Ghetto:
>
>> Never say that you have reached the very end,
>> though leaden skies a bitter future may portend,

and the hour for which we've yearned will yet arrive,
and our marching step will thunder, 'We'll survive.'
From green palm trees to the land of the bitter snow,
we are here with our sorrow, our woe,
and whenever our blood was shed in pain,
our fighting spirits will now resurrect again.[13]

Other examples can be added like that of the Sikh lay person who leads
evening worship every day, for more than two hours, in a local Sikh
gurdwara, and where about two hundred are present each time, of all
ages, as he expounds the Scriptures on which the Sikh faith is based,
and truly ministers to the community in the spirit of love that flows
from his faith. His openness is such that if a Christian minister is
present whom he knows, he will often invite him up to share a word. The
writer adds 'Such is the trust of this remarkable leader that I feel free to
witness to Jesus Christ, reading and commenting directly from the New
Testament, in the heart of this community.' Or the Hindu who, staying
in a Christian college for three months attended the Eucharist daily,
receiving a blessing, and, in the quiet, listening and absorbing all that was
going on.

We would affirm that such people live as they do through the grace of
God and through his Spirit. However, as we look around our world we
can give many contrary examples from people of all faiths and none,
who show that they do not live by that Spirit, whatever they profess with
their lips. We need not rehearse such: for example, the list of places of
religious conflict is endless at any one time. Mahatma Gandhi rightly
said that it is those who want to save religion who so often destroy it.
Again our judgement is not arbitrary, it is by the Spirit of Christ.

Thirdly, there is the concept of the Logos, the Word of God, the cosmic
Christ, without whom was not anything made that was made. The
possibility of life, meaning eternal life, is there within all human beings,
through the Logos. This cosmic Christology is reflected in John 1,
Colossians 1 and Hebrews 1, the opening chapters of three major works
in the New Testament. To have a Christ-centred understanding of
salvation does not mean that we need to be confined to what happened
to Jesus of Nazareth in the first century AD. This is the conviction of
Raymond Pannikar, with his understanding of Christ transcending time,
being incarnate in Jesus of Nazareth but not confined to him:

> The ultimate reason for this universal idea of Christianity, an idea
> which makes possible the catholic embrace of every people and
> religion, lies in the Christian concept of Christ: he is not *only* the
> historical redeemer, but *also* the unique Son of God, the Second

Person of the Trinity, the only ontological – temporal and eternal – link between God and the world.

Whatever God does *ad extra* happens through Christ.[14]

God is creator of all through his Word and Spirit. God wills all to be saved that he has created. This can only happen through that same Word and Spirit. The Word is made flesh in Christ, and so we are given a criterion for the presence of that same Word elsewhere. It is the poor, the lost, the little ones who are given as examples. The Spirit can be seen specifically in the Church, both corporately and through its members. But the Spirit also blows where the Spirit wills. The Church extraordinarily is to include, not just Jews and Greeks, but those beyond the pale, barbarians and Scythians. God is surely not confined after the birth of Christ and after Pentecost, any more than he was before. The Spirit is the one who points to the future, as he leads us to all truth, beyond what we can bear now. That will not be contrary to the teachings of Christ (John 16.12–15), but it will build on them. Maybe people of other faiths, and indeed of no religious faith, will teach us more than we yet know ourselves, as we interact with them and discover new things together.

Fourthly, there is the distinctive understanding of God as Trinity, which should be at the centre of any inter-faith reflection. As Gavin D'Costa puts it:

Without Jesus, we cannot speak of God, but that speaking is never completely exhausted in history, for the Spirit constantly and in surprising ways calls us into a deeper understanding of God in Christ. In this way, the Trinity anchors God's self-revelation in the particularities of history, principally focused in Jesus Christ, without limiting God to this particularity through the universality of the Spirit.[15]

He writes of a 'Trinitarian Christology', which reconciles the exclusivist emphasis on the particularity of Christ and the pluralist emphasis on God's universal activity in history. The instruction to love our neighbour opens us to people of the world religions.

The recent book by Clark H. Pinnock, written to persuade his fellow-evangelicals to hold open attitudes towards questions of salvation, concentrates interestingly on the Logos, the Spirit and Trinity. He writes of the Logos as connecting Jesus of Nazareth to the whole world and guarding the incarnation from becoming a limiting principle, and of the Spirit as the overflow of God's love, 'active in human cultures and even within the religions of humanity'. Referring to the breadth of this activity of the Spirit, he returns to the Trinity: 'The doctrine of the Trinity means that God, far from being difficult to locate in the world, can be encountered everywhere in it. One needs to take pains and be very adept at hiding not to encounter God.'[16]

He ends by quoting the well-known hymn by Frederick Faber:

> There's a wideness in God's mercy
> Like the wideness of the sea;
> There's a kindness in his justice
> Which is more than liberty.
>
> For the love of God is broader
> Than the measures of man's mind;
> And the heart of the Eternal
> Is most wonderfully kind.
>
> But we make his love too narrow
> By false limits of our own;
> And we magnify his strictness
> With a zeal he will not own.

Where then does the cross and resurrection come into the picture? Here the challenge is different in connection with people of other faiths only in one particular way. Even with regard to Christians, we are required to say how this apparently obscure event in the past is connected with our salvation today. We refer the reader to our discussion in chapters 4 and 5. The particular difficulty with people of other faiths is that they do not express a particular faith in Christ or that they may explicitly deny the central and saving importance of the cross. We have to explain how our belief that 'Christ died for all' relates to them.

What saves is not the cross itself, but God. We have elaborated this in considerable detail in earlier chapters, and here we can give but the briefest outline. In essence, God alone saves, and that is his mission. God saves as Trinity, Father, Son and Spirit; all save, and none saves without the others. He wills to save all people, as he created them all. All fall short of his will for them, and so all need his forgiveness and acceptance. Salvation is not something that can ultimately be earned, but comes as sheer gift, as happened to those surprised people in Matthew 25. The cross and resurrection are God's gift to us. They both reveal and save. They reveal the love of God because of the nature of him who is on the cross. And they change human history because here we believe is uniquely revealed the depth of God's love for us. Here also, however it may be expressed, something occurs which makes a decisive difference to human destiny, indeed to the whole of creation. Salvation is opened up to the whole world by the cross. For some, this leads to a direct response to that love, as they become witnesses to it as members of the Body of Christ, the Church. But the death and resurrection remain objectively the ultimate victory of good over evil; in sacrificial language, they show the seriousness of human sin and the degree to which God will go to show a way beyond it. He does something once and for all, on the cross. What is revealed is not the narrowness of God's action, but the sheer breadth of it. And that breadth, with all the suffering involved can be effective beyond the limits we try to put upon it. The Lamb of God who takes away the sins of the world gives his life as a ransom for many and is the passover sacrificed for us. We see 'the world', 'many' and 'us', as inclusive and not exclusive categories.

In the past, much of the discussion about salvation has rested on the cross alone. But as we focus our attention on eschatology, we focus our attention also on the resurrection of Christ and its relationship to our future destiny. Inter-faith dialogue brings out sharply the differences between the Christian understanding here and that of other faiths. The resurrection of Christ is not an optional addition to any discussion about salvation; it is at the core of Christian understanding, and that is why Paul says that if it did not happen, then we are of all people the most to be pitied. Is it to be an exclusive rising, though it was an inclusive creation and fall in Adam? And what are to be the criteria for judgement? They are about attitude, whether there has been an awareness of grace, and a sense of unworthiness and need for forgiveness; and along with this our lives can be judged by what has flowed from that response to grace.

The question of salvation is not only about whether we have responded to the Christian message, if we have been lucky enough to be born into it, or to have heard it clearly as we grew up or in later life. For there is forgiveness at the heart of God, which is the very centre of the Christian message, and that is most specifically proclaimed on the cross, in Christ's words in St Luke: 'Father, forgive them, for they know not what they do.' The prayer is that those who crucified Christ should be forgiven; are not the humble and good followers of another faith to be the recipients of the same prayer? Christian assurance about salvation can go along with a deep hope that others may be included in God's saving purpose both now and finally. We can never say that someone is not saved.

Two Hindus, both prisoners in an Indian jail, witness to this centre of Christian revelation in the God of forgiveness. The first was a life prisoner, who had also been operated on for a brain tumour and had continually to wear a bandage round the scar on his head. He remained a Hindu, but attended the weekly Christian worship service. In Holy Week, he asked to give a testimony. He said, pointing to his bandage, 'Only someone who is guilty of killing a man, and who has suffered a disease like mine, can understand how much Jesus and his cross can mean.' As a Hindu, he felt included in the saving power of the cross and indicated with sure conviction where that power lay.

The second had killed a relative in a family fight. He was also a Hindu. He attended the Eucharist month by month, at first out of curiosity. But then he began to receive unconsecrated host which was given to Hindus, as is done for catechumens in the Orthodox Church. One day he asked if he could join the Christians and share the cup. When asked why he wanted this so much, he said that since coming to the service, he had realised for the first time that he was guilty of sin, not just that he had made a mistake. He longed now for forgiveness and acceptance by God. He was told that he received this by the absolution pronounced each time. He said: 'That is not enough. Unless I can kneel shoulder to shoulder with the priest, and receive from the same cup, I may know with my head that I am forgiven by God, but I cannot feel it!' As a Hindu, again, he had seen where the centre of the Eucharist lies.

An example has even come to our attention of a Muslim who, contrary to all doctrinal orthodoxy, as a young student in Palestine and reflecting on the suffering following the Gulf War, wrote: 'Every day they crucify him, every day they hang him.' People under persecution so often seem to identify with the crucified Christ, of whatever faith they are. One of the Indian newspaper headlines, reporting the news that Gandhi had been assassinated, wrote 'Gandhi meets his Calvary'. A Jewish example in similar vein comes in the novel *My Name is Asher Lev*, by Chaim Potok. The novel turns on the quest of an Orthodox Jew who is an artist to express the pain of being a Jew in the modern world. To the horror of his community, he chooses to paint crucifixion scenes.

All finally focuses on what flows from our doctrine of God. As we have seen, it is God alone who saves, and God saves only according to, and not against, his nature. At the centre of our Christian faith is the belief that God is love. This is revealed through Christ's birth, his teaching, his ministry, his death and his resurrection. That love is expressed memorably in a parable like the Prodigal Son, where the father goes out in love to receive back the child who has wilfully wasted the inheritance which he had demanded.

Conclusion

It is incompatible with the essential Christian affirmation that God is love to say that God brings millions into the world to damn them. The God of Love also longs for all to come into relationship with him, and this is his purpose in creation. When he chooses certain peoples, such as Israel, or certain persons such as the prophets or Apostles, he chooses them not for exclusive privilege or salvation, but for a purpose in the expression of God's self-revelation and showing of his saving love for all.

In practice, all religions are open to grave distortion, as Barth rightly asserts. The history of religions, including the Christian religion, reveals this graphically, as does the present map of conflict in our world. This is so corporately, between individuals and within persons. It is by the criterion of Christ, his life, teaching, cross and resurrection, that all faiths, including Christianity, are judged and/or affirmed. It is by the criterion of Christ that we in practice discriminate provisionally between different religions as we consider how to relate to them.

As a fact there are conflicting truth claims made by religions. As Christians, we cannot agree with Muslims, for example, in saying Christ did not die on the cross, or with Hindus, in accepting reincarnation.

In terms of ultimate salvation the decision is entirely God's. As Christians we cast ourselves on the mercy of God as revealed in Christ, assured that God will receive those who respond to him in faith. Trusting in his just and merciful treatment of ourselves, so we are able to trust that God will act in the same just and loving way towards all his children, including those of other faiths. Ultimately, we believe, and this is why we are Christians, that it is through Jesus Christ that God will reconcile all things to himself. How that will come about, we can only be agnostic about, whether it is through some real but unconscious response to the Christ within them now, or whether it is in response to some eschatological revelation, or by some other means.

Meanwhile, we live in a world of many faiths, and it is our very Christian calling that leads us to feel humility and respect before the transparent goodness of many within other religious traditions (and indeed, many of no overt religious faith). We do assert that God can and does work in people of other religions, and indeed within other religions, and that this is by his Spirit. Such is an essential basis for genuine dialogue with them. We do assert that God has not only worked through the peoples of the Middle East, but that he did intend, for example, some significant experience of his presence in the Indian subcontinent in the centuries before Christ, and indeed amongst many of those who follow the so-called 'primal religions'. This is to be expected, since God created the potential for a religious sense in all human beings, and this is indicated in the diverse and widespread phenomena of the religions of humanity.

We can see empirically that people are enabled to live better lives through loyally following other faiths, and this must mean that God is at work in these faiths, even if it cannot determine the question whether those faiths have value for ultimate salvation or not. God can and does encounter people graciously outside the Christian religion, making it possible for them to come into relationship with himself and to receive his gifts. Several of us would also affirm from personal experience their authenticity as we would judge it by the above criteria already mentioned: the lives and also the spirituality of particular people coming from other faith traditions. We can be ready to affirm this without prejudging the issue of salvation: 'People sometimes fear that to affirm the presence of any encounter with God outside Christianity is to imply that any truth to be found there may in its own right be "saving truth". We wish to affirm that the only "truth" which has saving power is God.'[17]

We would also sensitively and firmly assert that fullness of relationship with God is possible only in Jesus Christ, who is the definitive revelation of God. For many this may happen only in an eschatological dimension (cf. 1 Cor. 15.22–8). But it is from this assertion that comes the imperative, expressed throughout the New Testament of the universal mission of the Church, to proclaim the gospel to all nations.

A Pakistani Christian woman working in London, reflecting on what she sees as the reticence of people in Britain about witnessing to people of other faiths, and comparing it with the difficult context in which she lives, reflects: 'If we love our neighbours, it is our duty, out of that love, to tell them about the sacrifice Christ has made for them. Otherwise we are keeping them in the dark, forgetting our mission of love and the sharing of good news. And that love will make us work at finding the language that will be understandable by them.' An Indian Christian woman, working in a British city amongst people of various faiths, echoes this: 'Our mission is to show people life in its fullness as experienced in Christ. Standing by our Muslim brothers and sisters, as they fight for a better deal in education, health and recreation, standing by them when they face racism, that is part of the Christian mission of love.'

Hence, we read in the report of the Lambeth Conference of 1988:

> We are called to proclaim God's love and forgiveness by word and deed. We must use every means available to spread the message of

salvation. Our proclamation must be sensitive to the culture and beliefs of others. Nevertheless Christ calls all people to turn from evil and all that hurts or enslaves, and to receive the fullness of life that he alone can give.[18]

Unfortunately, as we well know, the Church often gets in the way of such a proclamation: 'Christ is not the property of us Christians, and if we rejoice when the Holy Spirit opens men's eyes to His glory, we must at that moment remember how often the church has blinded them, and pray that we may be not once more a stumbling block.'[19] But, as John Taylor also points out, the Holy Spirit, who has been at work in all ages and cultures, often breaks through, not by evolution, but revolution, with the experiences of awakening and disclosure that the Spirit gives in encounters between Christians and people of other living faith.

Lakshman Wikremasinghe, the former Bishop of Kurunagula, Sri Lanka, died prematurely, as on his troubled island he struggled in his ministry to hold together people of different races and faiths. In the Lambeth Inter-Faith Lecture of 1979, in similar vein to the quotations above, he said:

> Now we see the goal of dialogue but darkly. In the realised realm of truth and righteousness, recorded in the last chapters of the Book of Revelation, we shall see face to face. The servants of God shall see him, who is the Source, Guide and Goal of all that is, and adore. The riches of other streams of salvation will be drawn into that realm by the Divine Light that illumines and attracts. What is now hidden will be revealed. Until then, we follow the path open to us in this era, and seek to have foretaste of what mankind in its fullness can be. Then togetherness will enrich uniqueness, and uniqueness will illuminate togetherness. To that final dawn may the Father of all lead us.

So there is a plurality of ways by which people are being made whole in the here and now; these are ways the Spirit of God is working. And there is an expectation in the future, that, while people may have the freedom to reject the salvation that is available to all, through God as Trinity, God will save ultimately those who are willing to be saved, by their penitence and acceptance of the love which stretches out to them, in the way that it meets them in their lives and within their traditions. There is only one way, but that way is one that is without barbed wire or boundary fences, so that all may join this way. If we think of salvation in the broadest sense as encompassing all that heals and enhances human life, then clearly aspects of salvation are available in many ways, not only explicitly through Jesus Christ. In the ultimate sense, salvation is defined by having Jesus Christ as its source and goal. To use the terms we deliberately put aside earlier, this pluralism and this exclusivism are reconciled, not in some form of inclusivism (in the usual sense) but eschatologically, in the final purposes of God. To recognise the life, death and resurrection of Jesus as 'constitutive' of salvation as well as revelatory, as Christians do, is to anticipate that he will prove to be the definitive focus of salvation in its fully comprehensive meaning. It may be, too, that our understanding of Christ will itself be enhanced when people of other faiths are gathered in.

Because this ultimate salvation is found in Christ, mission remains the central task of the Christian Church. The task is to proclaim by word and to display in action that God has created a world that is good, and that we are responsible for that creation; that the Kingdom of God, a kingdom of justice and peace, has already begun in Christ, and that we can be assured of its future consummation through him; that the gift and assurance of salvation and eternal life is available now, and the mark of this life is love. We deny the fullness of that love if we deny the truth and goodness which Christ, as Logos, and God by the Spirit, can also inspire in those of other faiths and of none. We believe that God has chosen to provide the fullest revelation of himself in Christ, and the fullest revelation of his love for all humanity in the cross and resurrection. Hence we naturally pray that God will bring all people, including those of other faiths, to explicit faith in Christ and membership of his Church. This is not because we believe that the God revealed in Christ is unable to save them without this, but because Christ is the truest and fullest expression of his love, and we long for them to share it. In the Lord's words in St John's Gospel, 'I came that they may have life, and have it abundantly' (John 10.10).

Chapter 8
Ending the story

Towards the end of the preceding chapter we referred to the final purposes of God and to the eventual consummation of God's kingdom. Christian people live in this hope, a hope which springs from Easter faith and from the knowledge of the love of God in Christ from which 'neither death, nor life . . . nor things present, nor things to come . . . nor anything else in all creation' will be able to separate us (Rom. 8.39). We live by this hope in a world of injustice, flawed by sin, and marked by an ultimate futility, for, as we have already commented in chapter 1, the universe as we know it will sooner or later die. Our hope is therefore of a new creation, new heavens and a new earth. It is a resurrection hope of cosmic dimension. But because it is a hope grounded in the victory of the love of God who loves each one of us so uniquely that even the very hairs of our head are numbered, it is a personal hope for us in the face of the darkness of death. So in the Nicene Creed we confess that we 'look for' – that is to say we 'wait with longing expectation for' – 'the resurrection of the dead and the life of the world to come'. It is a hope that is corporate, cosmic and personal.

The character of Christian hope

Christian eschatology, or the endeavour to understand the 'last' or 'ultimate' things, covers a wide and complex area, and in Christian history has been expressed in different ways. But there is a consistent theme in the hope of believing people that their incomplete present experience of God will be resolved and their present thirst for God fulfilled. Christians have looked for a final vindication of the good and definitive revelation of the consistency and purpose of God in his provident action in history. It is a hope that has taken many forms in the history of the Church. In times of oppression and persecution a sense of crisis and imminent expectation of the end has prevailed. Apocalyptic images of final judgement and catastrophe, a cosmic violence that destroys the world and its sinful institutions to let God begin again, have been the predominant note. At other times there has been a more muted note – of the world 'growing old' and running out of resources, coming to an end, but an end which will be God's new beginning. Faced with the world's evil, Christians have prayed in longing, even anguished, hope for the coming of God's kingdom.

> When comes the promised time,
> When war shall be no more,
> Oppression, lust and crime,
> Shall flee thy face before?

Eschatological hope has also meant a different emphasis: an ordered doctrine of the last things, personal expectation of final justice and retribution and a personal longing for rest and satisfaction in a new life that will begin at death. In the Christian mystical tradition, union with God in knowledge and love, already known in part in this life, will be consummated in that final transfiguring union when the understanding of the thinker and the contemplation of the lover are made one. But Christian hope is not only personal, it is cosmic. The whole universe itself is condemned to eventual collapse or decay, so that if it is really a cosmos, making ultimate sense of its history, it too must have a destiny beyond its death. God must surely care for all of his creation. Matter matters to him and it will not be abandoned to futility. A credible eschatology must be one of cosmic scope.

The Christian waits with expectation for a 'new heaven and a new earth' (Rev. 21.1), and lives in and by the Easter faith that in Christ God has defeated death and overcome the power of the grave. In baptism the believer shares sacramentally in the death and resurrection of Christ. In the Eucharist Christians are fed with the bread of heaven, the bread of the Day of the Lord, the banquet of heaven. In the Lord's Prayer we not only pray that God's kingdom may come and his will be done; but we also pray that we may be sustained, both by our earthly food and by that true and living bread which is Christ's own life. In being so fed we have a foretaste of the life of the world to come.

The language in which Christian hope has been expressed is necessarily imaginative and pictorial. It has also been shaped by different philosophical outlooks and understandings of the world. An uncritical literalism has contributed to the sense that Christian eschatology is largely attenuated to a life beyond death, and even then, as the Rural Church Project found, for instance, among churchgoing people only 69 per cent believed in a destiny beyond death, whilst for the general public that proportion was reduced to 42 per cent. There can be no doubt that Christians need to articulate in a coherent way a doctrine of the 'Last Things'.

In the strictest sense, of course, it is God who is the one 'Last Thing' of creation. The creator, who is Alpha, the source and origin of all that is, is no less Omega, the final horizon of history and the ultimate reality existing at the end of time. In his self-giving, God brings the created order into being. It is sustained by and dependent upon his will and purpose, but that will and purpose sustain it in its own freedom. The present universe is a creation *ex nihilo*, 'out of nothing', and, in so bringing it into being, God has 'made way' for it as an entity other than himself. Its evolutionary history is understood as the divine gift of 'freedom' by which creation is allowed to make itself, exploring and realising the fruitful potentiality with which it is endowed.

Within the complex patterning of creation, life and personality have emerged, and that which we might characterise as the realm of spirit. That realm of spirit may well include orders of being beyond human personal being. In the creed God is confessed as the creator of 'all things visible and invisible', and the worship of heaven in the Scriptures and Christian liturgies is portrayed not only as the worship of redeemed humanity, but of angels and archangels.

In the Scriptures the description of human nature as made 'in the image and likeness of God' (Gen. 1.27) is at the heart of the Christian understanding of our human existence as persons. Human nature is only understood rightly when it is seen as having an openness towards, and a capacity for, communion with God. The potentiality of human personhood finds its consummation in that relationship, and that 'capacity for God' is the ground likewise of our being as persons in relationship with each other. It is no accident that the two great commandments are the love of God with all our heart, and soul, and mind, and strength, and the love of our neighbour as ourselves. From those made in his image God calls a people to be his own, and enters into a covenant relationship with them. God promises a future to his people and to each unique human person he has created, whose uniqueness is fulfilled in communion with Christ. Those made in God's image are called to grow into his likeness and receive the gift of God's eternal life. Already Christians receive the gift of the Spirit and so are united to Christ. Their ultimate salvation is *theosis*, participation in the life of God himself. We are to be 'participants of the divine nature' (2 Pet. 1.4) and, 'seeing the glory of the Lord as though reflected in a mirror, are being transformed into the same image from one degree of glory to another' (2 Cor. 3.18).

Death and resurrection

Human hopes, human aspirations, and human achievements, the thirst for eternity and immortality, are mocked by death. It cuts across all human hopes. It denies and breaks relationships, it sunders the love which is at the heart of our personhood. Although in earlier and in less developed societies the ravages of disease and natural disaster meant that death struck very often in the prime of life, in our generation and in western culture many live into frail old age with severe diminishment of their mental and physical faculties. That pre-death diminishment places the same question marks against life and hope. Humanity born to die makes life a 'tale told by an idiot, full of sound and fury, signifying nothing'.

As we have already seen in chapter 4, for the faith of Israel, death is the taking away of breath, perceived as the gift of God which makes human beings truly alive. As the Psalmist writes: 'when you take away their breath, they die and return to their dust' (Ps. 104.29). In the Old Testament the wraith-like existence of *Sheol*, the place of the departed under the earth, is a place of non-being, far removed from the gift and fulfilment of eternal life. Such non-being is the triumph of death, often envisaged as an engulfing power opposed to God. Such a destiny provokes sharp questions. Is this non-being the destiny of those made in God's image and likeness? Are the holy ones of God to see corruption? Is the end of the righteous to be one with that of the wicked? Is there to be no ultimate redressing of the moral balance? No, the answer came. God *will* vindicate his people. He will deliver them not only from sin but also from death, and death was seen as the consequence of disobedience (Rom. 5.12) and as 'the wages of sin'. Salvation, liberation, deliverance will come on the Day of the Lord, when his righteous judgement will triumph, his will at last will be done, and the dead will be raised to life. The hope of the righteous, of the people of God, is resurrection. The wicked also will be raised to judgement. The Day of the Lord, the day of messianic hope, is the day of resurrection.

The predominant theme of first Jewish and then Christian hope in the face of death is that of the resurrection of the body. Language about the immortality of the soul is also found in the inter-testamental period. The passage from Wisdom 3.1, 'The souls of the righteous are in the hands of God, and no torment will ever touch them', has been used in the later Christian centuries to support a dualist view of death as being the release of an immortal soul from a mortal body, a view which came to predominate, though still combined with a doctrine of the resurrection of the body. The modern inclination to understand human nature in terms of a psychosomatic unity (chapter 1) makes this form of expression of the Christian hope highly problematic. Even before this modern questioning, the relation between the destiny of the world and the destiny of the human person, between 'corporate' and 'individual' eschatology, was often strained. The fate of souls after death, and their judgement at that point, were uneasily integrated with the apocalyptic drama of the final judgement and the resurrection at the Last Day. If today we are to continue to use language about the soul we may perhaps best understand it as the 'information-bearing pattern' of the body, as we have suggested in chapter 1. Death dissolves the embodiment of that pattern, but the person whose that pattern is, is 'remembered' by God, who in love holds that unique being in his care. The strong sense of the worship of the Church being set within the communion of saints, witnesses to the life to come as a present reality as well as a future expectation. When Jesus rebukes the Sadducees, who denied there was a resurrection, he quotes the words of God to Moses at the burning bush. God is the God of Abraham, Isaac and Jacob, who are not simply figures of the past. 'God is not God of the dead, but of the living; in his sight all are alive' (Luke 20.38). Moses and Elijah appear on the mountain of the transfiguration. Even though there is still a final transformation to which we look forward at the resurrection at the Last Day, already there is a sharing in the life of heaven. For some this will be adequately characterised as the holding in the mind of God of the information-bearing pattern that is the meaning of the soul. Such a state is less than fully human (since it is disembodied), but it is certainly not unreal (since it is in the mind and heart of God). Nor need it be purely static, for it would be open to the possibility of some degree of pattern-changing activity. For others, if we are to take the sense of ourselves as a psychosomatic unity with full seriousness, this needs to be envisaged in terms of an appropriate bodiliness. But, however conceived, all will agree that there remains a fuller realisation of God's purpose for us all at the end.

If we speak of the resurrection of the body it is not to be supposed that the material of the resurrected body is the same as that of the old. Indeed, it is essential that it should not be, for otherwise the new creation would simply be a re-run of the old creation, and presumably it would recapitulate the latter's transience and death. St Paul warned that 'flesh and blood cannot inherit the kingdom of God, nor does the perishable inherit the imperishable' (1 Cor. 15.50). In that context, Paul speaks of a 'spiritual body' (*soma pneumatikon*), a phrase which does not mean 'a body consisting of spirit' but 'a body animated by the Holy Spirit'. The only clue we have to this bodily reality is the glorified body of the Risen Lord, for the resurrection of Jesus is the seminal event of the new creation. In his victory over death, the Last Day has arrived. The resurrection of Jesus is the beginning within history of a process whose fulfilment lies beyond history, in which the destiny of humanity and the destiny of the universe are together to find their fulfilment in a liberation from decay and futility (cf. Rom. 8.18–25).

'Christ has died, Christ is risen, Christ will come again'

In Jesus the kingdom of God comes, the Day of the Lord is here. He 'empties himself' in the self-giving of love to live and die in solidarity with humanity. He refers to himself as 'Son of Man', which, in one interpretation, is 'mortal man', 'man born to die'. Yet, so living, he embodies no less God's eternal life, so that in his presence the kingdom comes, and with it the judgement of God. In his being judged by Pilate, the representative of the political authorities of this world, the judgement of the world takes place. '*Now* is the judgement of this world; *now* the ruler of this world will be driven out' (John 12.31).

In Jesus the divine gracious freedom coincided with our human obedient freedom to the point of death itself. The Apostles' Creed confesses that he descended into the place of the departed. That is the meaning of the term 'hell' in that particular clause of the creed, though there is also Christian truth in the understanding that God in Christ freely chose to go to the point of utter estrangement from the Father, so that, we might say paradoxically, for the sake of the love which is his nature, God chose to know the darkness of the utter absence of love. In this understanding, the cry of dereliction from the cross, 'My God, my God, why hast thou forsaken me?' signals the 'descent into hell' in which the love of God plumbs the farthest depths of alienation and apartness from God. Not only the cry of dereliction, but also the silence of Holy Saturday express the cost of Christ's saving work. Love's redemption encompasses the dead and contends victoriously with the powers of evil.

The Easter hope in the victory of Christ, 'who has overcome death and opened the gate of everlasting life' is known not only in the mythical drama of the harrowing of hell, but in contemporary theologies of liberation, which find in that victory salvation from political and social oppression, from the principalities and powers of the secular world. An essential part of Christian hope is the anticipatory realisation of God's new creation, in the bringing into being of a foretaste of that new order, 'when God will wipe away all tears from their eyes, and there will be no more death, and no more mourning or sadness' (Rev. 21.4).

In the creed, we confess our hope that Christ 'will come again in glory to judge the living and the dead'. Our human destiny, and that of the world, is centred on Christ himself. When God remakes the whole world, as he has promised, Jesus Christ will be personally present as the living heart and focus of all.

The New Testament uses a variety of quite different images to express this vital belief. 'He is coming with the clouds; every eye will see him' (Rev. 1.7). 'This Jesus, who has been taken up from you into heaven, will come in the same way as you saw him go into heaven' (Acts 1.11). 'The manifestation [the Greek word is literally "epiphany"] of the glory of our great God and Saviour, Jesus Christ' (Tit. 2.13). 'Your life is hidden with Christ in God; when Christ, who is your life, is revealed, then you also will be revealed with him in glory' (Col. 3.3f). All these ways of saying essentially the same thing draw on the rich symbolic language of the Old Testament, not least the book of Daniel. They are not intended to provide literal depictions of the event, as though Jesus were (for instance) a space traveller returning to earth. They refer, in the far more profound language of biblical imagery, to the manifestation in this world of that which is already true of Jesus Christ in heaven, that is, that dimension of reality which is immediate to God. In that dimension, Jesus is already victorious over all evil, ruling over all things, mediating the Father's love for the world and embodying the true response of humankind to that love. When God creates the 'new heavens and new earth', this same Jesus will be manifest as the victor, the Lord, the mediator and the high priest of all creation.

These are among the things which in the present we know 'only in part'. But, as John insists, we know that 'when he is revealed, we will be like him, for we will see him as he is' (1 John 3.2). In this faith and hope we live as Christians, not towards the horizon of death and futility, but towards the horizon where 'the Sun of righteousness shall rise, with healing in his wings' (Mal. 4.2 AV).

A new creation

Our Christian hope is also that at the End and in the End God's new creation will mean the vindication of the oppressed, and the establishment of that kingdom, for which we pray every time we say the Lord's Prayer – the kingdom in which the righteous will of God will be done, 'when justice will be throned in might, and every hurt be healed'. Then 'the kingdoms of this world will indeed become the Kingdom of our God and of his Christ', and of that Kingdom there shall be no end.

The present creation is characterised by disease and disaster, with mortal transience as the necessary cost of new life. An evolutionary universe, allowed by its creator to explore and realise its God-given potentiality, cannot be otherwise. The same processes of cellular variation which produce new forms of life will also produce the possibility of malignancy. If the new creation is to be free from physical evil and mortality (Rev. 21.4) then the laws which govern its 'matter' will have to be radically different from those with which we are familiar. If this is the case, the question immediately arises, why the first creation was not made by its creator so that it would not be subjected to suffering. A clue to answering the problem of physical suffering may lie in the direction of the old creation being a world allowed to exist as something 'other', given by God the freedom to be itself. The new creation will be a world freely reconciled to God in Christ (Col. 1.20), a transfigured universe completely suffused with the divine presence. The 'matter' of such a world can coherently be supposed to possess new properties not seen in our present experience, so that the new creation is not a second attempt at creation out of nothing, but it is the eschatological transformation of the old creation. It will be a *cosmos pneumatikos* – a universe animated by God's Spirit, in the most intimate connection with its creator.

It is an old accusation that Christians have so stressed a future salvation beyond death that they have neglected to realise that '*now* is the acceptable time, *now* is the day of salvation' (2 Cor. 6.2), and have failed to live as those who are already in Christ part of the new creation. But there is, in reality, no essential opposition between a concern to live as citizens of the kingdom of God in this world, and a longing for that final consummation which must include victory over death. In fact they belong together, and the hope of the coming of God's kingdom is a living hope, which already breaks into a realisation in the present in Christian worship participating in the life of heaven, and Christian service, participating in the life of the world. The value of the old creation is implied by its redemptive transformation being the raw material of the new creation.

Christian dying and the communion of saints

The present gift of life in which Christians share does not mean they do not die, but that their death, as their life, is now *en Christo*, 'in Christ'. They die as sharers in the common life of the Body of Christ. Their life is 'hidden with Christ in God' (Col. 3.3). So Christians die in hope – a hope that is depicted both as resurrection at the Last Day and life already with Christ.

Living by the Spirit and in Christ we are brought home to the Father, and to that eternal life which is Christ's gift and promise. Heaven is the name we give to that reality. The Book of Revelation portrays it in vivid symbols as the life of the new Jerusalem, the heavenly city, which has as its centre, the Lamb both slain and victorious, the triumphant sign of sacrificial love. As Austin Farrer said, heaven is 'the pattern of perfect relations . . . an endless beginning, a ceaseless wonder, perpetual resurrection in the unexhausted power of him who makes all things new'. In heaven God will be manifest in his works 'but his works will there be like music in the hands of the master, the mere utterances of his mind.'[1]

Participating by grace in the communion of God's love, here and now we have a foretaste of that union, and the Christian life of prayer opens us up to that reality. The great Christian teachers of prayer remind us that Christian mysticism speaks of union, not absorption, for God is love, and love unites and does not overwhelm. In heaven we shall know as we are known, perfectly ourselves and perfectly related one to another. It is because heaven is such a participation in the communion of God's love that it is right to believe that we shall see and know those whom we have loved, but we shall see and know them in God. In heaven, 'Christ is himself through taking us all into his heart, and we shall be ourselves by taking him to ours'.[2] All whom we love will be loved in Christ the source of love.

Human destiny in heaven will not be the attainment of an eternal and static perfection, but rather an everlasting participation in the exploration of the inexhaustible riches of the divine nature. Because the 'time' of the new creation is a new time, it need bear no simple or sequential relationship to the time we presently experience. Though we die at different times, we may all enter into our destiny together.

Since heaven is participation in the life of God, only those fitted to share that life may fully enter into it. Heaven is a communion of saints, a communion of those made holy by the work of the Spirit in the response of faith. Sanctification, growth in holiness, is the condition of heaven. And there is no holiness without God's grace because only God can make holy. Yet such holiness requires our human response; it is not the product of a mechanistic determinism, but a fruit of our love freely given, won from us by God's transforming love for us. Those Christians who have wanted to speak of 'purgatory' have by this language wanted to stress that God's love and mercy reaches out to fit for heaven those who still at their dying need to grow in that holiness which is the very condition of communion with God. Those who have resisted the language of purgatory have done so because they believe that God uses death itself as the instrument to complete the necessary task of dealing with that sin which, up to that point, still distorts the life of all Christians. This view claims support from such texts as Romans 6.7: 'Whoever has died is freed from sin.'

We confess our belief in the Communion of Saints, and Christian prayer is one expression of that communion. It is therefore appropriate to mention the Christian dead in Christian prayer, in thanksgiving for their lives and as an affirmation that they are in the hands of God who works in them the good purpose of his perfect will. This kind of prayerful remembrance of the faithful departed is prayer in Christ, and an expression of love for them. In the Spirit, through Christ, we are made free to remember and love the faithful departed, in a trusting love which overcomes the barrier of death.

Furthermore, because Scripture makes it clear that God created, loves and sustains all humanity, and that Christ died for the sins of the whole world, to pray in the name of Christ for God's will to be done may appropriately include a prayer of commendation 'for those whose faith is known to God alone', as is included in the ASB litany. It is for this reason that the Doctrine Commission of 1971 commented: 'We do not know the ways of God with those who have died outside the faith of Christ, but we do know his saving will for all, and we recognize the pastoral urgency from which the need for this prayer arises.'[3]

When death occurs and we bid farewell, we rightly seek to commend the soul of the departed into the hands of God, and in this context language about the soul indicates that living centre of human personality, which is no longer present in the dead body before us. A commendation into the hands of God is a commendation into a deeper participation in the communion of love which is God's being, and so into the communion of saints. The earliest funeral prayers were rich in images of refreshment after a journey (green pastures and springs of water), fellowship with the saints (the Old Testament patriarchs and the martyrs), and rest after struggles and conflicts. Liturgical prayers for resurrection at the Last Day, the final consummation when God will be all in all, co-exist with prayers which emphasise that the heavenly places are a present reality, for each Eucharist is offered 'with angels and archangels and with all the company of heaven'. Here and now in our worship we anticipate the life of the new creation, and share in the life of the world to come. We wait in expectation for that Last Day, when God will complete his purposes in creation by making all things new.

In the Communion of Saints, heaven and earth are united in a common worship, and it is in this context that the prayers of the Christian dead should be seen. Christians pray for one another on earth; this of course does not take away from the centrality of Christ as the one High Priest who intercedes for us. We join our praises with those of the saints, and that praise is always the praise of God's holy, loving and righteous will; praise and prayer are united in the longing that God's will may be done. In the end it is Christ, the true once and future King, who is the Lord of both the old and the new creation, and it is in him that the mystery of the prayerful relations between the living and the departed must find its true expression.

Final judgement

No one can be compulsorily installed in heaven, whose characteristic is the communion of love. God whose being is love preserves our human freedom, for freedom is the condition of love. Although God's love goes, and has gone, to the uttermost, plumbing the depths of hell, the possibility remains for each human being of a final rejection of God, and so of eternal life. As John Burnaby has written:

> Dogmatic universalism contradicts the very nature of love, by claiming for it the kind of omnipotence which it refuses. Love cannot, because it will not, compel the surrender of a single heart that holds out against it . . . Love never forces, and therefore there can be no certainty that it will overcome. But there may, and there must, be an unconquerable hope.[4]

Final judgement therefore remains a reality. Moral and spiritual choices are ultimate and serious choices. In the past the imagery of hell-fire and eternal torment and punishment, often sadistically expressed, has been used to frighten men and women into believing. Christians have professed appalling theologies which made God into a sadistic monster and left searing psychological scars on many. Over the last two centuries the decline in the churches of the western world of a belief in everlasting punishment has been one of the most notable transformations of Christian belief. There are many reasons for this change, but amongst them has been the moral protest from both within and without the Christian faith against a religion of fear, and a growing sense that the picture of a God who consigned millions to eternal torment was far removed from the revelation of God's love in Christ. Nevertheless it is our conviction that the reality of hell (and indeed of heaven) is the ultimate affirmation of the reality of human freedom. Hell is not eternal torment, but it is the final and irrevocable choosing of that which is opposed to God so completely and so absolutely that the only end is total non-being. Dante placed at the bottom of hell three figures frozen in ice – Judas, Brutus and Cassius. They were the betrayers of their friends, and through that they had ceased to have the capacity for love and so for heaven. Annihilation might be a truer picture of damnation than any of the traditional images of the hell of eternal torment. If God has created us with the freedom to choose, then those who make such a final choice choose against the only source of life, and they have their reward. Whether there be any who do so choose, only God knows.

The God of hope

The images of Christian eschatology are rich and complex. They developed historically in ways that do not enable them to be fitted into a single coherent and systematic picture. In particular the integration of talk about the end of the world, time and history, is uneasily related to what we want to say about the death of those we love, or about our own future dying. Nevertheless, as we have seen, there are important Christian affirmations to be made.

St Paul reminded the Christians of Corinth that, if the hope of Christians was for this life only, then we were of all people the most to be pitied (1 Cor. 15.19). Death remains a deep challenge to belief in a God of love. And yet it is only a God of love who can overcome death and make of it 'the gate of life immortal'. It is such a God who in Christ entered our human living and dying, and gave us at Easter the sure hope of eternal life. St John of the Cross said that 'at the end he will examine thee in love', for love is both judgement and salvation. The One God in Trinity, whose being is communion in love, is the true Last Thing of every creature: 'gained He is heaven; lost He is hell; purifying He is purgatory; encountered He is judgement'.[5] In Christ his gift to us is the Easter life of the new creation, which sweeps us into that heaven where we shall praise, and we shall love, and we shall adore, because we shall be made like Christ and know him as he is, 'changed into his likeness from one degree of glory to another'. And that praise will flow out of the life of the new creation, when the kingdom of justice, and love and peace, will be established, and all will be gathered into the city, whose light and glory is sacrificial love, 'for behold, I make all things new'.

Conclusion: That nothing be lost

In these words Jesus asks his followers to gather up the surplus pieces of bread after the feeding of the multitude: 'that nothing be lost'. They are words that leap off the page of the Gospels as a statement of God's limitless ambition to save. They tell of the depth of God's longing, the expansiveness of God's design and the unwavering care with which God continues to pursue the completion and perfection of the whole of creation. The words tell, in short, of the breadth and length and depth and height of a love that passes knowledge. That is the gospel of salvation.

To speak in this way, however, might seem to confine the scope of that gospel within the limits of our perception. It might suggest a God of limitless ambition waiting to be fulfilled and undying love waiting to be requited; that is just a part of the story. For the bread was gathered up, and what might have been lost has again and again been saved. In the God who saves we have to do not with mere dreams and hopes, with what might be and one day, we hope, will be; we testify to a gift already received and signs already enacted of that gathering up which is God's will for all things. Already God's realm is inhabited by those who have known God's grace and lived lives empowered by it; already many who were plagued by oppression or sickness of body and mind have experienced release. If it is the case that we are part of a world where pain and alienation still abound and where therefore anything that might reasonably be called salvation is still far off – and such is the world we inhabit – it is nevertheless also and equally true that God's salvation has already drawn near.

It is the vast scope of God's design for salvation that requires the breadth and complexity of the topics over which this report has ranged. At the outset we sought to point to some critical aspects of the particular context in which we find ourselves. We observed the plurality of our society, our sense of individuals and communities going their own way. We reflected on the absence of any generally accepted diagnosis of the needs of humanity, let alone a commonly agreed religious framework for meeting them. Our world presents what can appear as an entirely hostile environment, one which the gospel of salvation has therefore simply to confront. But even when features of our contemporary world seem hostile to Christian faith and the values it seeks to promote, is it open to the community of faith to write them off as wholly negative?

What would that say about a God who is determined that nothing be lost? So we have found ourselves required in this report to consider how God's gift of salvation can be discerned and received within human history; we seek in our generation, as all the generations of faith have done, for the wisdom to discern God's saving action even within experiences of suffering and at times when there seems to be no sign of the fulfilment of God's promise.

Similarly, we felt compelled to face at the outset the enormous scale of the universe in space, its duration in time and above all its inevitable mortality, even if its final decay is billions of years away. We noted the huge question mark which all that places against the weight Christians have traditionally given to the history of the human species, let alone that apparently minute piece of human history that is covered by the Christian Scriptures. It can sound immensely bland to continue using the language of the 'scandal of particularity'; how much more scandalous has that particularity become in the light of what we now know. Yet the infinite range of God's concern to save all that has been created has still to be declared, though in the face of that vastness of scale and inescapable dissolution which cosmologists now take for granted. At the same time our message must not lose the particularity of God's love, imaged by Christ as a love that numbers the hairs on our heads and lets no sparrow fall to the ground unnoticed.

The salvation God offers to the world has always engaged particularly with the needs of the poor in each generation, those who have been victims of deprivation, discrimination and oppression. Theirs is the history that is often unread and even untold. Yet the God who is concerned that nothing be lost has a particular care for those whom the world counts lost, or who find themselves to be so. We could not write this book unaware that this century has generated overpowering examples of the human capacity for cruelty and injustice: it has seen the Holocaust as well as other less chronicled instances of national and racial persecution and wars of enormous scale and violence; it closes with unprecedented numbers of starving and displaced persons. The conviction we share with Christians world-wide is that the gospel of salvation has to be declared in the face of those realities and in a way that both responds to them and inspires and enables us to engage with them.

Among the forms of injustice of which the awareness is so much stronger in our generation than has previously been the case, and which we constantly kept in mind, are the disparities of power and resources available to women and to men: to those disparities the God who saves invites us to respond. Yet in doing so we have needed to face the fact that this particular issue of justice, that between women and men, has come to involve as one of its aspects a sensitivity to the way in which language reflects, and in turn affects, our apprehension of the Christian tradition. For the language of faith, not least in the way it has spoken of salvation, has presented, for centuries unconsciously, what now appears as an unmistakably 'male' perspective. We have sought to address this very current issue, aware that our observations and suggestions are made in a situation where forms of speech are in a state of constant and rapid change.

If the relations between the sexes have been topical in the life of the Church, and therefore have needed to be addressed in a statement of our belief about salvation, so has that other issue of our time to which we referred in our opening chapter: that is, the Christian understanding of whether, and how, God saves the adherents of the world's other faith traditions. It might seem easy enough to say that the God who desires that nothing be lost continues to offer the gift of salvation to all, from whatever culture they come. But we have had to reflect further on this matter: for is there not a question how the God who desires that nothing be lost regards the history, culture and achievement of the world's various faith communities? The God who sent his Son as saviour of all ensures also, we believe, that the richness of other faith-traditions, the fruits of prayerfulness and compassion they have borne, are also not to be lost. In what we have said about this vitally important issue, therefore, we have maintained three essential points: the centrality for Christian faith of the person and work of Jesus Christ, the universal range of the salvation God bestows through him and the real gifts bestowed upon humanity through the world's great communities of faith.

These issues are raised for us not simply because we are people of this time; they are raised also because we are part of the Church, ourselves beneficiaries of the gift of salvation as Scripture and the life and witness of God's people down the ages testify. This double imperative, deriving from our being people of this time and from our being people of this faith, has driven us afresh to the resources of faith and tradition in the search, if not for conclusive answers to the needs of our time, at least for means of living creatively and faithfully in it. In that encounter we have been aware both of the need for new ways of expressing the faith, and at the same time of some central themes which, however problematic, are constant features of the Christian message of salvation at any time.

Principal among these is the conviction that there has been no salvation without sacrifice. No other word suffices to describe the character of what Christ offered; if nothing is to be lost – and that is Christians' undying hope – then it required, and requires, paradoxically, the expenditure of everything. That desire and gift of God are presented to

the world on the cross, claimed by the Church in the experience of
worship and prayer, baptism and Eucharist, and called for in the life
of disciples at all times. Such sacrifice is not to be understood as a
requirement that human beings degrade themselves, or allow themselves
to be degraded, a demand which not least those who experience the
oppressive yoke of injustice would reject for good reason; rather it
consists in God's willingness to risk all to save all, and to reveal the glory
of humanity supremely in losing all. We are called to follow in that way,
and the Christian testimony is that those whom the world considers of no
account can claim their true dignity in this way as in no other.

Throughout our reflections we have seen the need to hold on to the sheer
scope of God's design, recognising that God's promise is for this life
and not only for this life; it is for persons one by one, and no less for the
communities and nations of the world. It is for humanity, and no less for
the enormous variety of creatures with which we share our planet; it is
for our world, and no less for the vastness of the universe. All things are
'returning to their perfection through him from whom they took their
origin'; our calling is to act faithfully in all the situations which cry out
for that salvation to be revealed in this life, sustained by the hope that
ultimately God will be all in all.

Appendix: Salvation and the Anglican heritage

As Anglicans, we shall want to ask whether the historic formularies of the Church of England, especially the Book of Common Prayer and the Thirty-Nine Articles, contain any particular version of atonement doctrine. We may also find it instructive to compare these historic formularies, which still have canonical authority, with the *Alternative Service Book 1980* and more recent supplementary liturgical material in respect of the doctrine of the atonement.

But before turning to the liturgies and Articles, we are bound to take note of the fact that these are by no means fully representative of Anglican piety in practice. For example, the theology of Richard Hooker, the sermons of Lancelot Andrewes, the poems of George Herbert, the hymns of Charles Wesley and the spiritual writings of Edward Pusey all serve to remind us that the tradition of Anglican spirituality draws on deep resources of catholicity that transcend those particular notions of salvation and the atonement that dominate our historic formularies. In particular, the doctrine of union with God, participation in God, and transformation by the power of God into the likeness of Christ is strongly present in these authors and stems from the Greek Fathers of the Church with their concept of theosis. This motif is not absent from the Book of Common Prayer – the Prayer of Humble Access includes the words 'that we may evermore dwell in him and he in us' and in the post-communion prayer communicants thank God that 'we are very members incorporate in the mystical body of thy Son' – but it is hardly conspicuous. These themes have recently come to enrich our ecumenical theology of communion (*koinōnia*).

Classical doctrines

The Thirty-Nine Articles were promulgated in 1563, though they drew heavily on earlier formularies, and received their final form in 1571. It is probable that they did not intend to define positively a particular doctrine of the atonement. The Articles were not intended to serve as a summary of Christian belief, a potted systematic theology. They deal with points of contention in the sixteenth century, over against the Church of Rome, the Anabaptists and rigorous Calvinists. The atonement as such was not in dispute and the Articles allude to it merely incidentally. Their aim was to be inclusive not exclusive. They gave theological liberty within the bounds of legal conformity. The laity in general have never been required to subscribe to the Articles. The clergy are now required to make only a general assent that the historic formularies 'bear witness to Christian truth' as set forth in the Scriptures and creeds, and to affirm their belief in 'the doctrine of the Christian faith as the Church of England has received it' (ASB Ordinal). (See further on the nature of the Articles: the Doctrine Commission report *Believing in the Church* (1981), pp. 109–41). Nevertheless, a particular tradition of the interpretation of the atonement can be clearly discerned in the Articles. Let us now look at some of the evidence.

Article 2, in stressing the true deity and true humanity of Jesus Christ against alternative Christologies advanced by some strands of the radical Reformation, affirms that he 'truly suffered, was crucified, dead and buried, to reconcile his Father to us, and to be a sacrifice, not only for original guilt, but also for all actual sins of men'. Read in the light of Article 9 ('Of Original or Birth-sin'), this statement makes it clear that the framers of the Article believed, in accordance with the traditional doctrine that stemmed from St Augustine, that Christ's death removed our guilt before God in three respects: the guilt believed to have been imputed by God's decree to all humanity on account of the first disobedience of their putative progenitor Adam; the guilt incurred by the present depraved condition of our human nature; and the guilt incurred by individual sinful acts.

Article 31, which was directed against the propitiatory conception of the Roman mass, stresses that the death of Christ on the cross constituted a 'perfect redemption, propitiation, and satisfaction, for the sins of the whole world, both original and actual'. These words echo the wording of the Prayer of Consecration in the service of Holy Communion as found in both Prayer Books of Edward VI (1549 and 1552) and the Book of Common Prayer (1662): 'Almighty God, our heavenly Father, who of thy tender mercy didst give thine only Son Jesus Christ to suffer death upon the cross for our redemption; who made there (by his one oblation of himself once offered) a full, perfect and sufficient sacrifice, oblation, and satisfaction, for the sins of the whole world . . .'.

The Litany (which predates the Edwardine Prayer Books, having been composed by Cranmer in 1544, drawing on Roman, Eastern and Lutheran sources) invokes the active as well as the passive obedience of Christ (to use a traditional theological distinction) and rehearses the history of salvation from the incarnation to the sending of the Holy Spirit upon the Church in words that had been used in England since the Anglo-Saxon church: 'By the mystery of thy holy Incarnation; by thy holy Nativity and Circumcision; by thy Baptism, Fasting and Temptation, *Good Lord, deliver us*. By thine Agony and bloody Sweat; by thy Cross and Passion; by thy precious Death and Burial; by thy glorious Resurrection and Ascension; and by the coming of the Holy Ghost, *Good Lord, deliver us*.' It thus sets the cross at the centre of an unfolding drama of redemption, emphasises Christ's sufferings as truly human, and balances the victory of Easter with the solidarity of Christ with our needy human condition.

The collects of the Book of Common Prayer contain a wealth of profound theological reflection. Do they also teach, explicitly or implicitly, a particular doctrine of the atonement? Sometimes they merely echo the phrase of the creeds 'for us': '. . . circumcised and obedient to the law for man' (The Circumcision); 'who for our sake didst fast forty days' (Lent 1). The Easter collects state that Christ 'overcame death and opened unto us the gate of everlasting life' (Easter Day); that he died for our sins and rose for our justification (Easter 1); and that he is given to us 'both as a sacrifice for sin and also an ensample of godly life' (Easter 2). But they do not appear to bind us to any particular theory of how Christ overcame death, died for our sins or became a sacrifice for sins. The collect for Palm Sunday contains an exemplarist doctrine of the atonement (in the weak sense of exemplarist – setting us an example – rather than showing forth or exemplifying the reconciling love of God) when it affirms that God, of his tender love towards mankind, sent his Son 'to take upon him our flesh, and to suffer death upon the cross, that all mankind should follow the example of his great humility'.

The Proper Preface for Easter in the BCP is rich in atonement imagery. The crucified and risen Christ is seen as 'the very Paschal Lamb, which was offered for us, and hath taken away the sin of the world; who by his death hath destroyed death and by his rising to life again hath restored to us everlasting life'. The Paschal or Passover Lamb is a sacrificial image; to take away the sin of the world is an expiatory motif; and the Christus Victor theme is sounded in the destruction of death and the bringing of life. Here certainly we have the raw material of atonement theology, but no actual explanatory theory of why sacrifice, expiation and victory were achieved by the death and resurrection of Jesus Christ.

This summary of the teaching of the historic authoritative documents of Anglicanism suggests several reflections.

These sources clearly depict Christ's atoning work in terms of sacrifice – both explicitly and in the implicitly sacrificial language of oblation and offering. But within the broad sacrificial framework of the doctrine of the atonement that is present in the BCP there are a number of important distinctions to be discerned.

Personal and impersonal

The tradition in which the Anglican formularies stand is often labelled 'objective' in discussions of the atonement because it looks for a transaction 'out there' between God the Father and God the Son, independent of the response made by the beneficiaries of that transaction ('something accomplished, something done'). The alternative tradition, associated with Peter Abelard (1079–1142), is often dubbed 'subjective' because it focuses on the human response to the sacrificial love of God, and 'exemplarist', not, as is sometimes assumed, merely because it proposes Christ as the perfect model or example of the human response to God in obedience and love, but because his faithfulness unto death on the cross for our sake shows forth or exemplifies the love God has for us in a way that nothing else could. Clearly this Abelardian concept of the atonement is just as 'objective' in that it postulates an objective act of divine revelation intended to awaken human response. Moreover, the juridical models of the atonement obviously have their subjective aspect in the human appropriation of Christ's atoning work through repentance, faith and the sacraments of the Church. Evidently the terms 'objective' and 'subjective' are of limited value and ought to be employed with caution, if at all.

The model of atonement presupposed by the Thirty-Nine Articles belongs to the so-called 'juridical' tradition: the model employed is provided by legal concepts and has primary reference to the law court. The juridical tradition is associated particularly with Anselm of Canterbury (1033–1109) and John Calvin (1509–64). Anselm interpreted the atonement in terms of the principle of feudal obligation that gave cohesion to early medieval European society. Sinful humanity owed a debt of honour to its creator – a debt that could only be repaid by someone who belonged to Adam's erring race yet was able to offer a virtually infinite compensation to God: the sinless God-man Jesus Christ. This is presumably one source of the term 'satisfaction' that appears in the Articles and the Prayer of Thanksgiving. Calvin, influenced not by feudal law but by the recently revived Roman criminal law, thought of Christ's death as dealing with the punishment required by God's justice rather than as making reparation to his honour. This is the significance of the term 'propitiation' in the Articles (in the liturgy 'propitiation' is used only in the recitation of the Comfortable Words, from 1 John 2.1–2; it is not used in the Prayer of Consecration).

Since the dominant model of atonement in the Articles and Prayer Book is juridical, it is constructed in terms of the impersonal considerations of law and justice rather than the personal categories of relationship and response. To say that is not by any means to disparage the notions of law and justice, for without them what hope would there be for the oppressed, the victims of cruelty and exploitation? But while justice must have the first word, it cannot be allowed to have the last (cf. Jas 2.13). Justice must give place to mercy, even while mercy presupposes justice. The claims of retributive justice equate to the seriousness of wrongdoing or sin and therefore must be heard, but retributive justice alone can never effect reconciliation. Only mercy inspired by love that reaches out to the wrongdoer and absorbs the barrier of hostility, hatred and fear can reconcile. This is precisely the emphasis of exemplarist theories of the atonement – they are framed in personalist concepts. Juridical theories of the atonement have often pictured God's law, God's wrath, and human sin and guilt not as aspects of the relation between God and humanity, but as though they were actual objects or things that had somehow to be dealt with. That is to say, these concepts were 'reified' – as though they were objectively existing entities which curtailed the freedom of divine action so that God could not forgive sins if God wanted to without some equally reified compensation or satisfaction being offered to the supposedly implacable attributes of God. The alternative Abelardian or exemplarist tradition in its most radical form sees no barrier to God forgiving sins except the barrier of our own hardness of heart, while in a more moderate form it regards the death of Christ as an acknowledgement of the dire consequences of sin and therefore of the price paid by God to reconcile humanity to God.

Moral issues

Strong moral objections have often been made to juridical theories of the atonement. Juridical concepts include moral factors and so enable the atonement to be interpreted in moral terms. But juridical theories of the atonement tend to make legal considerations primary and moral ones secondary. Ultimately, they seem to confuse moral and legal categories. In the realm of law a debt must always be paid and a penalty must always be enforced. But in the moral sphere there is no such necessity. Loving parents will often waive a debt owed to them by their own child and they will do all they can to spare the child the self-destructive effects of its own wrongdoing. Again, in the legal sphere one person can sometimes pay the debt owed by another (though they cannot undergo their punishment), but in the moral sphere each person must be responsible for their own obligations. Moral responsibility is ultimately incommunicable. The great weakness of juridical theories or models of the atonement is that they appear to eclipse moral considerations by legal ones. This runs counter to our best theological instincts which suggest that personal analogies are the most appropraite ones for the character of God as revealed in Christ.

The view of the atonement reflected in the Thirty-Nine Articles is *substitutionary* in that Christ acts in our place and stead. In Anselm, Christ as substitute pays our debt; in Calvin, Christ as substitute bears our punishment. Thus Calvin's is a *penal* substitutionary theory while Anselm's is not.

In addition to the moral difficulties of the notion of substitution, there is also the question how we are involved in Christ's atonement and how we benefit from it. There is certainly a vital truth enshrined in the notion of substitution: Christ does indeed act 'in our place' and does for us what we cannot do for ourselves. But the danger of using substitutionary langauge in isolation is that it can appear to make the work of Christ external (or extrinsic) to us; in itself it cannot show how we have a saving interest in our redeemer. The term 'vicarious', however, which has the dominant sense of an action performed by one person on behalf of another, while preserving the intention of the Reformers, is not open to this objection. Our unity with our redeemer may be effected retrospectively, so to speak, by faith, the sacraments and the indwelling of the Holy Spirit.

Propitiation?

Finally, the Articles employ the term 'propitiation' (Article 31) and state that Christ 'reconciled his Father to us' (Article 2). When combined with the penal substitutionary interpretation of the atonement, this terminology seems bound to suggest that Christ's death was a divinely inflicted punishment which appeased the wrath of God against sinful humanity and enabled God to change God's attitude towards us, from one of rejection to one of acceptance. This interpretation is consistent with the translation in the Authorised Version of *hilasterion* (mercy-seat) and its cognates by 'propitiation', etc. (Rom. 3.25; 1 John 2.2; 4.10), where the AV is guided by the literal meaning of the Greek (to propitiate) rather than by the Hebrew meanings lying behind the text (*kipper*: to cover, wipe away).

The 1938 report of the Doctrine Commission was clear that 'The notion of propitiation as the placating by man of an angry God is definitely unchristian' (p. 146). It is significant that modern biblical translations render *hilasterion*, etc., not as 'propitiation', but as 'sacrifice of atonement', 'atoning sacrifice', 'expiation' or 'means of expiating sin'.

In this they are influenced, as were the Reformers themselves, by the fundamental biblical principle that God is primarily the subject of the atoning action. Thus in the key text, Romans 3.25, we read that God *put forth Christ* as a *hilasterion* to bring redemption through his sacrificial death. Whereas the object of the propitiation is God, the object of expiation is sin. To propitiate means to assuage wrath or displeasure. To expiate means to remove the sin that is the cause of separation, and to offer an atoning sacrifice means to reconcile two parties who have become estranged. It is nevertheless true that in Paul's thought the effect of expiation is the same as that of propitiation – to neutralise the sin that is the cause of God's displeasure and so to avert God's wrath (however that should be understood).

The nineteenth-century Anglican theologian Frederick Denison Maurice insisted that the mercy-seat of the Old Testament does not represent the propitiation of divine wrath against the sinner, but rather reveals that 'he who had established the mercy-seat was the Lord God of that earth from which the foulest steam of human sacrifices was ascending to the Baals and Molochs. He was testifying there that from him came freely down the blessings which they were hoping to buy of their gods; that he blotted out the transgressions of which the worshippers were seeking, by the cruellest oblations, to escape the penalty' (*Doctrine of Sacrifice*, p. 150). Christ's work is rightly understood as God's way of reconciling the world to God (2 Cor. 5.19) through a perfect sacrifice which we make our own in penitence and faith. It is in this sense that the Church sings (in the words of William Bright):

> Look, Father, look on his anointed face,
> And only look on us as found in him;
> Look not on our misusings of thy grace,
> Our prayer so languid and our faith so dim:
> For lo! between our sins and their reward
> We set the passion of thy Son our Lord.

God is the sole author of atonement. The expression 'propitiation' may obscure the truth that Christ's saving work originates with God, that it is the expression of God's infinite love for God's human creatures that no sin can ever destroy ('God so loved the world that he gave his only Son . . .' – John 3.16), and that Christ's will was entirely one with that of his Father, not pitted against it in order to wrest forgiveness from a reluctant and hostile God, as the cruder, popular expressions of penal substitution tend to suggest.

Some interpreters have attempted to avoid the unacceptable consequences of a doctrine of propitiation (i.e. that God's attitude to sinners is capable of being changed or that God's love and God's justice are at loggerheads) by entertaining the paradox that God propitiates himself. Athanasius spoke of God's act of self-reconciliation. Augustine confessed: 'In a manner wondrous and divine he loved even when he hated us.' Calvin employed the strongest language of propitiation (Christ 'procured the favour of God for us', 'appeased the wrath of God' and 'rendered the Father favourable and propitious towards us') and penal substitution (our sins were 'transferred to him by imputation' and by his death 'the justice of God was satisfied'). But Calvin acknowledged that this doctrine presents us with an irreconcilable paradox: 'How could he have given us in his only begotten Son a singular pledge of his love, if he had not previously embraced us with free favour?' Calvin appealed to the words of Augustine already quoted.

It can never be right to speak of God hating God's human creatures. The Prayer Book collect for Ash Wednesday (here echoing Wisdom 11.24) supplicates God 'who hatest nothing that thou hast made'. We should surely say, God always loved us even though God condemned us as sinners. It is precisely because God is already and eternally gracious to us and lovingly disposed towards us that God has, in Christ, demolished the barrier of alienation and bridged the gulf of separation so that his children might be restored to full and free communion with God.

The Alternative Service Book

The *Alternative Service Book 1980* contains a rather different emphasis in its implied doctrine of the atonement and draws on other aspects of the varied range of images to be found in the New Testament.

In Rite A, the First and Second Eucharistic Prayers are content simply to state that God gave his Son 'to be born as man and to die upon the cross' in order to free us from the slavery of sin and make us a Spirit-endowed people for God's possession.

The Third Eucharistic Prayer is more eloquent. It recalls that Jesus Christ was sent by God in his great goodness to be our saviour. He 'took flesh', 'was seen on earth' and 'went about among us' (perhaps an attempt to express the thought in John 1.14 of the Logos dwelling or 'tabernacling' among us – this passage reads like a poetic paraphrase of that key verse). The reference to the cross is evocative: 'He opened wide his arms for us on the cross; he put an end to death by dying for us' (note the repeated biblical and credal 'for us'). He 'revealed the resurrection' (which sounds like 'showed that it was there hidden all along', rather than constituting it and making it a reality).

The Fourth Eucharistic Prayer broadly follows the lines of the alternative order of the Communion in the 1928 Prayer Book (as does Rite B), except that where 1928 retains the 1662 Prayer Book's '. . . to suffer death upon the cross for our redemption; who made there (by his one oblation of himself once offered) a full, perfect, and sufficient sacrifice, oblation and satisfaction for the sins of the whole world', the ASB omits the language of oblation and satisfaction. It has instead: '. . . to suffer death upon the cross for our redemption; he made there a full atonement for the sins of the whole world, offering once for all his one sacrifice of himself'.

The language of penal substitution and propitiation is avoided in the ASB. The theme of *sacrifice* that runs through the BCP is usually retained in the ASB and the vicarious nature of that sacrifice is affirmed ('his offering of himself made once for all upon the cross': First Eucharistic Prayer). However, the theme of Christ's sacrifice is strangely absent from the Second Eucharistic Prayer, though this prayer refers to the transformation of the communicants into the likeness of Christ, a theme on which we touched at the beginning of this note.

Some of the most evocative language of the ASB is found in the Proper Prefaces. The Rite A Proper Preface for Easter retains the substance of the BCP Preface which refers to the Paschal Lamb who has taken away sins, destroyed death and restored everlasting (now 'eternal') life. An alternative Preface invokes victory and healing: 'in his victory over the grave a new age has dawned, the long reign of sin is ended, a broken world is being renewed, and man is once again made whole.'

A richer, more evocative liturgical language is also found in the recent supplementary material published with the authority of the House of Bishops: *The Promise of His Glory* and *Lent, Holy Week and Easter*. It is naturally the latter which provides, especially in the 'Prayers on the Passion', references to the atonement. Through the cross, we are reminded, Christ blotted out our sins, bore our sins, unlocked the gates of paradise, perfectly revealed the loving nature of the Father, won a complete victory over evil, and made a perfect and eternal sacrifice to God.

Notes

Foreword

1. *We Believe in God*, Church House Publishing, 1987; *We Believe in the Holy Spirit*, Church House Publishing, 1991; *The Mystery of Salvation*, Church House Publishing, 1995.
2. A list of members of each Commission is presented on pp. ix-xiii.
3. See pp. xxxii–xxxiv.
4. A celebrated, unexplained reference to 'the questionably orthodox early fifth-century Macarian homilies' comes to mind. See *We Believe in the Holy Spirit*, p. 155.
5. Elsewhere I have disputed this. See, 'Anglicanism and the Anglican Doctrine of the Church', in S.W. Sykes, *Unashamed Anglicanism*, Darton, Longman & Todd, 1995, pp. 101–21.
6. *Doctrine in the Church of England*, SPCK, 1938.
7. *Being Human*, Church House Publishing, 2003.
8. Briefly referred to in *We Believe in God*, pp. 18–20, along with Ayer's subsequent admission that nearly all of logical positivism was false.
9. The first report of this Commission was on *Subscription and Assent to the 39 Articles*, and was published in 1968. This was followed by *Prayer and the Departed*, SPCK, 1971, and a document on the consecration of additional bread and wine at Communion. See D. L. Edwards, *Ian Ramsey, Bishop of Durham*, Oxford University Press, 1973, pp. 86–91.
10. *Christian Believing*, ch. 3, pp. 14–20. See chapter 2 of his *Religious Language* (1st ed.), SCM Press, 1957; reprinted 1967; also the posthumously published *Christian Empiricism*, Sheldon Press, 1974, Part 2, 'The Meaning of God Talk'. After Ramsey's death, another Oxford philosopher, Basil Mitchell, was to play an influential role on the Commission.
11. English translations of the *Church Dogmatics* began in 1936 with Part I of Vol. I. This was reissued after the Second World War in 1949, followed by Part II in 1956. From then to 1969, 10 volumes appeared at regular intervals. The series remained unfinished.
12. In this connection the positive but not uncritical response to Barth of the Anglican New Testament scholar, Sir Edwyn Hoskyns (1884–1937) who taught in Cambridge, is particularly noteworthy. Hoskyns translated Barth's *Romans* (6th ed.) in 1933, and contributed 'A Letter from England' to the 1936 Festschrift for Barth

(English in *Cambridge Sermons*, SPCK, 1938, pp. 218–21). See also Anne-Katherine Finke, *Karl Barth in Grossbritannien*, Rezeption und Wirkungsgeschichte, Neukirchener Verlag, 1995, for a comprehensive survey.

13. *We Believe in God*, p. 122.
14. MacKinnon's Cambridge tenure of the Norris-Hulse Professorship of Divinity lasted from 1960 until his retirement in 1978. See the bibliography of his publication, compiled by Paul Wignall in B. Hebblethwaite and S. Sutherland (eds), *The Philosophical Frontiers of Christian Theology*, Cambridge University Press, 1982, p. 19.
15. See P. G. Wignall, 'D. M. MacKinnon: An Introduction to his Early Theological Writings', in *New Studies in Theology*, I, Duckworth, 1980, pp. 75–94.
16. G. K. A. Bell, *Randall Davidson, Archbishop of Canterbury*, Oxford University Press, 1935; 3rd edn, 1952, ch. LXXII.
17. *Doctrine in the Church of England*, p. 19.
18. See, on the method adopted by the Anglican Roman Catholic International Commission, Henry Chadwick, 'Unfinished Business (1992)', in C. Hill & E. Yarnold (eds), *Anglicans and Roman Catholics: The Search for Unity*, SPCK/CTS, 1994, pp. 12–13, 211–21.
19. *Doctrine in the Church of England*, p. 23
20. *Doctrine in the Church of England*, pp. 24–5. See *The Mystery of Salvation*; 'all three reports treat their subject matter in a way which, it is to be hoped, will make the Christian faith more readily comprehensible and more easily accessible to a non-specialist and enquiring public, which may include regular worshippers as well as enquirers and seekers who stand on the margin of the Church's life' (p. 275).
21. See J. Hartin and J. Knight, 'Catechism', in S. Sykes, J. Booty and J. Knight (eds), *The Study of Anglicanism*, rev. edn, SPCK, 1998, pp. 165–76.
22. Trevor A. Hart, Review Article, The Mystery of Salvation, *Anvil*, Vol. 13, No. 3, 1996, pp. 260–66, see p. 260.
23. Paul M. van Buren, *The Secular Meaning of the Gospel*, based on an analysis of its language, SCM, 1963.
24. *Secular Meaning*, p. 161 The word 'really' is placed in inverted commas by van Buren.
25. J. A. T. Robinson and D. L. Edwards (eds), *The Honest to God Debate*, SCM Press, 1963, pp. 13–44.
26. John Hick (ed.), *The Myth of God Incarnate*, SCM Press, 1977. See also M. Goulder (ed.), *Incarnation and Myth: The Debate Continued*, SCM Press, 1979.
27. M. F. Wiles had already produced some carefully argued studies

advocating the possibility of a radical re-appraisal of Trinitarian theology, notably *The Making of Christian Doctrine*, Cambridge University Press, 1967; *The Remaking of Christian Doctrine*, SCM Press, 1974; *Working Papers in Doctrine*, SCM Press, 1976, including essays from the 1950s and 60s; and *Exploration in Theology*, SCM Press, 1979.

28. G. W. H. Lampe, *God as Spirit*, Oxford University Press, 1977.
29. Don Cupitt, *Taking Leave of God*, SCM Press, 1980, p. 36.
30. Cupitt, *Taking* Leave, p. 14.
31. Cupitt, *Taking Leave*, p. xiii.
32. Don Cupitt, *The Sea of Faith*, BBC, 1984, p. 269.
33. Cupitt, *Sea of Faith*, p. 20.
34. Notably, K. Ward, *Holding Fast to God, A reply to Don Cupitt*, SPCK, 1982 and B. Hebblethwaite, *The Ocean of Truth, A defence of objective theism*, Cambridge University Press, 1988. See also Stephen Ross White, *Don Cupitt and the Future of Christian Doctrine*, SCM Press, 1994.
35. All these complaints were advanced by Maurice Wiles in his review of *The Sea of Faith* in *Theology* 88 (1985), pp. 232f.
36. 'Carried about by Every Wind: The Development of Doctrine', pp. 262–85, *Believing in the Church*; see p. 278.
37. See Rowan Williams, 'Religious Realism: On Not Quite Agreeing with Don Cupitt', *Modern Theology* 1:1, 1984, pp. 3–24.
38. *We Believe in God*, p. 89.
39. *The Mystery of Salvation*, p. 309.
40. *The Mystery of Salvation*, p. 312.
41. *The Mystery of Salvation*, p. 312.
42. *The Mystery of Salvation*, p. 313.
43. *The Mystery of Salvation*, p. 314.
44. *The Mystery of Salvation*, p. 49 Compare the passage in *We Believe in God* where the approach to the Trinity through prayer is held to justify the need to balance so-called masculine with feminine characteristics of God, for example, patience, compassion, endurance, forgiveness, warmth, and sustenance, pp. 95–6.
45. David Ford, *Theology, A very short introduction*, Oxford University Press, 1999, p. 40. See the list of writing on the Trinity in *The Forgotten Trinity*, BCC, 1989.
46. See *We Believe in the Holy Spirit*, pp. 185, 241.
47. See 'The Impact of Other Faiths' in *We Believe in God*, pp. 15f, 24–5; *We Believe in the Holy Spirit*, p. 287f, and esp. the chapter 'Christian World Faiths' in *The Mystery of Salvation*, ch. 7.
48. See *The Mystery of Salvation*, p. 176. The report cites two authors as evidence for the positive value of Trinitarian theology, Gavin D'Costa, *Christian Uniqueness Reconsidered*, Orbis, 1990, pp. 18f and Clark H. Pinnock, *A Wideness in God's Mercies*, Zondervan,

1992, p. 104. Dr D'Costa had attended and advised the Commission. See also the substantial work of the Church of England's Inter Faith Relations Adviser, Michael Ipgrave, *Trinity and Inter Faith Dialogue*, Peter Lang, 2003.

49. J. K. Mozley, *The Impassibility of God*, Cambridge University Press, 1926. Though this is mainly an historical work, Mozley makes very clear the kinds of questions which those abandoning impassibility need to confront. Not all of these are faced in the reports.

50. *Doctrine in the Church of England*, p. 56.

51. *The Mystery of Salvation*, p. 366. The works of two past Chairmen, Bishops John V. Taylor, and John Baker, contain similar emphases.

52. 'The Suffering God', *The Hibbert Journal* 47, April 1914, pp. 603–11. These references remarkably enough derive from the treatment of the passion of God by the German Protestant theologian, Jürgen Moltmann in *The Trinity and the Kingdom of God* (German 1980; English 1981) pp. 30–36. Moltmann regards as characteristically Anglican the holding together of the eucharistic sacrifice, the cross on Golgotha and the heart of the triune God in a single perspective.

53. G. A. Studdert Kennedy, 'The Suffering God', *The Unutterable Beauty*, Hodder & Stoughton, 1968, pp. 11–14.

54. *We Believe in God*, pp. 69–70, 72–3, 73–4, 78–9.

55. Here *The Mystery of Salvation* pp. 365–6 implicitly refers to the terms of the Collect for the 11th Sunday after Trinity, cited explicitly in *Being Human* p. 47.

56. *The Mystery of Salvation* p. 293.

57. *The Mystery of Salvation*, pp. 384–9.

58. *We Believe in God*, pp. 87–8. See also pp. 101–2.

59. *We Believe in the Holy Spirit*. See pp. 153–6. The Commission believes it detects a 'lurking dualism' of positive and negative impulses, 'as in the questionably orthodox early fifth century Macarian homilies'(p. 155)!

60. The reference is to Hans Urs von Balthasar, *The Way of the Cross*, London, 1969, anticipated in this regard by a sketch by William Blake (1757–1827), reproduced as Plate 3 in the original edition, though not reproduced in this edition.

61. *Doctrine in the Church of England*, p. 28.

62. *Doctrine in the Church of England*, p. 33.

63. *Christian Believing*, SPCK, 1976, p. 29.

64. *Christian Believing*, p. 31.

65. Compare D. H. Kesley, *The Uses of Scripture in Recent Theology*, SCM Press, 1975, speaks of making an 'imaginative *discrimen*' about the central point or message of Scripture.

66. Anthony Harvey, 'Attending to Scripture', in *Christian Believing*, p. 32. See *We Believe in God*, pp. 2, 21.

67. *We Believe in God*, p. 7.

Notes

68. *We Believe in God*, p. 8.
69. *We Believe in God*, p. 47.
70. See in particular, Hans W. Frei, *The Eclipse of Biblical Narrative: a Study in Eighteenth and Nineteenth Century Hermeneutics*, Yale University Press, 1974 and Dietrich Ritschl, *'Story' als Rohmaterial der Theologie* (mit H. Jones) (ThExh 192), Chr. Kaiser, München, 1976, 75 S.
71. *Believing in the Church*, SPCK, 1981, p. 99.
72. *We Believe in God*, p. 49.
73. *We Believe in God*, pp. 50–52; *The Mystery of Salvation*, ch.3 'Saving History'; ch. 8 'Ending the Story' (eschatology). *We Believe in God*, pp. 52–4.
74. H. R. Niebuhr, *Christ and Culture*, Harper & Row, 1951.
75. *We Believe in the Holy Spirit*, p. 176.
76. *We Believe in the Holy Spirit*, p. 190.
77. *We Believe in God*, p. 66.
78. *The Mystery of Salvation*, pp. 351–2.
79. *We Believe in God*, pp. 24–6.
80. *Being Human*, Church House Publishing, 2003, ch.2 'Listening to Scripture', esp. p. 12.
81. Maurice Wiles, 'Marching in Step', *Theology* 90 (1987), pp. 461f.
82. *We Believe in God*, p. iv. *Believing in the Church* had been warmly commended for serious study in the Church, by the Archbishop of Canterbury, Robert Runcie.
83. Article XX, and Questions to the Bishop-Elect in the 'Form of Consecrating a Bishop'. It should also be noted that the choice of the Chairman and members of the Commission are in the hands of the Archbishops.
84. *We Believe in God*, p. 17.

We Believe in God

4. The God of the Bible

1. *Believing in the Church*, SPCK, 1981, pp. 30ff.
2. *Believing in the Church*, pp. 34–36.
3. Cf. *The Motherhood of God*, Church of Scotland, 1984.

The Mystery of Salvation

2. The Giver and the Gift

1. On this saying, see also the discussion in chapter 4 below.
2. This section takes further the discussions of the Trinity in the two

earlier Doctrine Commission reports: see *We Believe in God*, especially chapter 7; *We Believe in the Holy Spirit*, especially chapter 4.
3. See *We Believe in the Holy Spirit*, above, pp. 135–6.

7. Christ and world faiths

1. *The Truth shall make you free*, Church House Publishing, 1988, p. 83.
2. Alan Race, *Christians and Religious Pluralism*, SCM Press, 1983.
3. *The Truth shall make you free*, p. 304–5.
4. Wesley Ariarajah, *Hindus and Christians*, Eerdmans, 1991.
5. John Hick, *God Has Many Names*, Macmillan, 1980, p. 52.
6. Stanley Samartha, *One Christ, Many Religions*, Orbis, 1991, p. 97.
7. F. D. Maurice, *The Religions of the World* (6th edn, 1886), p. 56.
8. For example, these quotations are taken from the Roman Catholic writer, Paul Knitter, in his section on Anglican views in *No Other Name?*, SCM Press, 1985, p. 135.
9. *Pastoral Constitution on the Church*, para 22.
10. *Redemptor Hominis*, 14.
11. As suggested by Michael Barnes in *Religions in Conversation*, SPCK, 1989.
12. So writes Gavin D'Costa in his essay 'Christ, the Trinity and Religious Plurality', published in the volume he co-edited, *Christian Uniqueness Reconsidered*, Orbis, 1990, p. 19.
13. Andrew Wingate, *Encounter in the Spirit*, WCC, 2nd edn, 1991, p. 82.
14. Raymond Pannikar, *The Unknown Christ of Hinduism*, Danton, Longman & Todd, 1964, pp. 82, 83 and 167.
15. Gavin D'Costa, *Christian Uniqueness Reconsidered*, Orbis, 1990, pp. 18–19.
16. Clark H. Pinnock, *A Wideness in God's Mercy*, Zondervan, 1992, p. 104.
17. *The Truth shall make you free*, p. 95.
18. *The Truth shall make you free*, p. 30.
19. J. V. Taylor, *The Go Between God*, SCM Press, 1972, p. 196.

8. Ending the story

1. Austin Farrer, *Saving Belief*, Hodder & Stoughton, 1964, p. 143; *The Brink of Mystery*, SPCK, 1976, p. 51.
2. Austin Farrer. *A Celebration of Faith*, Hodder & Stoughton, 1970, p. 90.
3. Doctrine Commission, *Prayer and the Departed* (1971), p. 55.
4. John Burnaby, *Amor Dei*, Hodder & Stoughton, 1938, p. 318.
5. Hans Urs von Balthasar, *Word and Redemption*, Herder & Herder, 1965, p. 147.

Index of biblical references

10.10 422
10.11 353
10.18 213
10.30 75, 78
10.33 82
10.41 223
11.38–44 375
12.23 79
12.31 428
12.32 389
12.43 219
13–17 178
13.3 80
13.7 224
14 164
14–16 81
14.6 219, 224, 409
14.9 78, 219, 228
14.12 164, 211
14.16ff. 219, 260
14.16–17 81
14.16 181, 235, 309
14.18 219
14.23 75, 80, 195
14.26 81, 181, 230, 244
15 363
15.1 223
15.16 403
15.26 134, 181, 219, 224, 244
16.3 218
16.7ff. 228, 230, 260
16.8ff. 269
16.8 219
16.12–15 415
16.13–14 228
16.13 225
16.28 78
16.33 203
17 367
17.4 79
17.5 78
17.20–21 75
17.21 80
18.6 353
19.5 352
19.9 353
19.30 138, 203
19.31–2 353
19.34 138
20 341
20.19 206
20.20ff. 208
20.22–23 81
20.22 138

Acts
1 341
1.11 428
2 161
2.4 160

2.16ff. 260
2.16 160
2.17 80, 185
2.22 210
2.33 310
2.38 161, 206
4.12 341
4.29–30 164
4.32–3 164
5.32 310
5.39 221
5.41 164
6.3 160
8 161, 166
8.9–24 202
8.11 211
10–11 207
10 161
10.43–4 207
11.15–16 165–6
11.17 207, 309
11.24 160
13.11 201
13.39 206
15.8 166
17 410
17.23 245
17.28 245
19 166
19.2 134, 160
19.6 134
21.4 160
26.18 206
28.3ff. 202

Romans
1–8 335
1.4 75,137
1.5 75
1.18ff. 223, 410
2.15 410
3.25 354, 444–5
3.28 380
4.7 206
4.25 353
5–6 383–4
5.1 80
5.2–3 266
5.5 225, 266, 309
5.6–21 368
5.8 353
5.12–21 363, 410
5.12 426
6 189
6.5–11 356
6.5 178
6.7 431
8 74, 92, 140, 276, 334, 341
8.1–11 335
8.2 262

General index